SIMPSON

IMPRINT IN HUMANITIES

The humanities endowment
by Sharon Hanley Simpson and
Barclay Simpson honors
MURIEL CARTER HANLEY
whose intellect and sensitivity
have enriched the many lives
that she has touched.

The publisher gratefully acknowledges the generous support of the Simpson Humanities Endowment Fund of the University of California Press Foundation, which was established by a major gift from Barclay and Sharon Simpson.

The publisher also gratefully acknowledges the support of the Leslie Scalapino Memorial Fund for Poetry, which was established by generous contributions to the UC Press Foundation by Thomas J. White and the Leslie Scalapino–O Books Fund.

The publisher also gratefully acknowledges the generous support of the Humanities Endowment Fund of the University of California Press Foundation.

The Selected Letters
of Robert Creeley

Group, 1963: "Jerry Heiserman (later Sufi 'Hassan'), the car whose? Dan McCloud (later editor of Georgia Straight underground paper), Allen Ginsberg, Bobbie Louise Hawkins Creeley, Professor Warren Tallman our host, Robert Creeley above big Charles Olson. Seated below left, Thomas Jackrell (student poet who wrote about Campbell soup cans), Philip Whalen poet, and postmodern poetics editor Don Allen—in front of Tallman's house—he'd sent me ticket to return round world after year-and-half in India for Vancouver B.C. Canada university poetry conference, last days of July 1963" (Allen Ginsberg). Photo by Allen Ginsberg. © Allen Ginsberg Estate.

The Selected Letters of Robert Creeley

Edited by

Rod Smith

Peter Baker

Kaplan Harris

UNIVERSITY OF CALIFORNIA PRESS

University of California Press, one of the most distinguished university presses in the United States, enriches lives around the world by advancing scholarship in the humanities, social sciences, and natural sciences. Its activities are supported by the UC Press Foundation and by philanthropic contributions from individuals and institutions. For more information, visit www.ucpress.edu.

University of California Press
Oakland, California

For acknowledgments of permissions, please see page 459.

First Paperback Printing 2020

Library of Congress Cataloging-in-Publication Data

Creeley, Robert, 1926–2005.
  [Correspondence. Selections]
  The selected letters of Robert Creeley / edited by Rod Smith, Peter Baker, and Kaplan Harris.

      pages   cm.
Includes bibliographical references and index.
ISBN 978-0-520-24160-2 (cloth : alk. paper);
978-0-520-32483-1 (pbk. : alk. paper)
1. Creeley, Robert, 1926–2005—Correspondence.   2. Poets,
American—20th century—Correspondence.   I. Smith,
Rod, 1962—editor of compilation.   II. Baker, Peter, 1955—
editor of compilation.   III. Harris, Kaplan, 1975—editor of
compilation.   IV. Title.
  PS3505.R43Z48   2014
  811'.54—dc23   2013026610

Manufactured in the United States of America

23   22   21   20
10   9   8   7   6   5   4   3   2   1

The paper used in this publication meets the minimum requirements of ANSI/NISO Z39.48–1992 (R 2002) (*Permanence of Paper*).

What you do is how you get along.
What you did is all it ever means.

—ROBERT CREELEY, "PLACE TO BE"

CONTENTS

PART TWO. BLACK MOUNTAIN REVIEW, 1953–1956:
MALLORCA, BLACK MOUNTAIN, SAN FRANCISCO

ILLUSTRATIONS

ACKNOWLEDGMENTS

This project would not have been possible without the generous support of Penelope Creeley. She has responded to our every question with detail and encouragement. We wish to thank our press editors Rachel Berchten, Laura Cerruti, Mary Francis, and Kim Hogeland for seeing the manuscript through the production process. Forrest Gander assisted with electronic files from the very end of Creeley's life. Charles Bernstein, Benjamin Friedlander, Peter Gizzi, Bobbie Louise Hawkins, and Tom Raworth were among those closest to Creeley who deserve our thanks.

Michael Davidson deserves our gratitude for detailed feedback from the beginning to the end of our work on the manuscript. We wish to thank colleagues and staff at Bridge Street Books, Towson University, and St. Bonaventure University. Thanks go to the Honors College at Towson University and its dean at the time, Maria Fracasso, for providing material support for reproduction of archival materials. Thanks also go to Danielle Frownfelter for research assistance at St. Bonaventure University.

We wish to acknowledge the following curators and librarians who assisted in the search for letters and who fielded our many inquiries both big and small. They offered expertise and unfailing generosity often in the face of severe budget cuts and staffing shortages during the period of our research: Michael Basinski, curator; James Maynard, assistant curator; and staff members at the Poetry Collection, the University at Buffalo; Lynda Corey Claassen, director, Mandeville Special Collections Library, University of California, San Diego; Melissa Watterworth, curator of library, Natural History and Rare Book Collection, for assistance with archival materials from the Charles Olson Research Collection, Archives & Special

Collections at the Thomas J. Dodd Research Center, University of Connecticut Libraries; William McPheron, the William Saroyan Curator for British and American Literature at Stanford University Libraries; Polly Armstrong, public services manager; and Margaret Kimball, university archivist, Department of Special Collections, Stanford University Libraries, Stanford; Nancy Kuhl, curator of poetry, Yale Collection of American Literature, the Beinecke Rare Book and Manuscript Library, Yale University; Tony Power, Contemporary Literature Collection, Special Collections & Rare Books Division, Bennett Library, Simon Fraser University; John Hodge, curator, Modern Literature Collection/Manuscripts, Olin Library, Washington University; Molly Schwartzburg, Cline Curator of British and American Literature; and Richard Workman, research librarian, Harry Ransom Center, the University of Texas at Austin; Nicolette A. Dobrowolski, reference and access services librarian, Special Collections Research Center, Syracuse University Library; Marvin J. Taylor, director, Fales Library and Special Collections, New York University; Isaac Gewirtz, curator, and Anne Garner, librarian, Berg Collection, the New York Public Library; Becky Cape, head of reference and public services, the Lilly Library, Indiana University; Carrie Hintz, processing archivist, Rare Book & Manuscript Library, Butler Library, Columbia University; Holly Snyder, North American History librarian and university archivist, John Hay Library, Brown University; Russell Maylone, curator, McCormick Library of Special Collections, Northwestern University Library; David M. Hays, archivist, University of Colorado at Boulder Libraries; Genie Guerard, manuscripts librarian, UCLA Library, Department of Special Collections; James M. Smith, assistant curator, Rare Books and Manuscripts Library, the Ohio State University Libraries; and the late Aggie Stillman, director of Sage Archives, Sage College.

Many friends and colleagues offered advice that helped shape the present volume. This company includes Rachel Blau DuPlessis, Anselm Berrigan, Michael Gizzi, Anne Waldman, Elizabeth Willis, Bill Morgan, Leslie Scalapino, Anselm Hollo, Philip Levy, Keith and Rosmarie Waldrop, Terry Cooney, Michael Kelleher, Libbie Rifkin, Lisa Jarnot, Kevin Killian, Lee Ann Brown, Tony Torn, Susan Howe, Steve Clay, Carolyn Forché, Harry Mattison, Marcella Durand, Jerome Rothenberg, Robert Grenier, Barrett Watten, Stephen Fredman, Michael Ruby, Cathy Eisenhower, Mark Wallace, Lorraine Graham, Tom Orange, Al Filreis, Bruce Jackson, Diane Christian, Jessica Smith, John Roche, Ed Sanders, Jen Bervin, Catherine Wagner, Michael Boughn, Cass Clarke, Victor Coleman, Albert Glover, David Landrey, Donald Wellman, Marilyn Brakhage, Phil Solomon, Fred Wah, Lauren Matz, Nancy Kuhl, and Richard Deming. Gary Lovesky, Genevieve Vidanes, and Martin Reddy opened their homes during travel research; Martin also rescued correspondence files that were corrupted by computer viruses. Mel Nichols, Deborah Lesko Baker, and Maggie Harris patiently endured the ballad of despairing editors, and we send them our gratitude.

CHRONOLOGY

1926	Robert White Creeley born in Arlington, Massachusetts, May 21, to Oscar Slate and Genevieve Jules Creeley.
1928	Left eye injured in accident.
1930	Father died. Family moves to West Acton.
1940	Entered Holderness School.
1943	Entered Harvard College.
1944–45	Served in the American Field Service in India and Burma.
1945	Returned to Harvard.
1946	Published first poem. Married Ann MacKinnon.
1947	Left Harvard without a degree. Son David born.
1948–51	Lived in Littleton, NH, where he bred pigeons.
1950	Son Thomas born. Began correspondence with Charles Olson. Became American editor for Rainer Gerhardt's *Fragmente*.
1951	Lived outside Aix-en-Provence, France.
1952	Daughter Charlotte born. Published *Le Fou,* his first book of poems. Moved to Majorca to establish Divers Press.
1953	Published *The Kind of Act of* (poems) and *The Immoral Proposition* (poems).
1954	Published *The Gold Diggers* (short stories). Taught at Black Mountain College. First issue of *Black Mountain Review,* edited by Creeley, published in March.

1955	Divorced from Ann MacKinnon. Published *All That Is Lovely in Men* (poems).
1956	Left Black Mountain College. Published *If You* (poems). Visited San Francisco. Moved to Albuquerque. Received BA from Black Mountain College.
1957	Married Bobbie Hall. Published *The Whip* (poems). Daughter Sarah born.
1959	Daughter Katherine Williams born. Moved to Guatemala. Published *A Form of Women* (poems).
1960	Received MA from University of New Mexico. Received Levinson Prize. Included in *The New American Poetry: 1945–1960*.
1961	Instructor at University of New Mexico.
1962	Published *For Love: Poems 1950–1960*. Instructor at University of British Columbia.
1963	Moved to Placitas, NM. Participated in Vancouver Poetry Festival. Published *The Island* (novel).
1964	Received Guggenheim Fellowship. Received Oscar Blumenthal Prize.
1965	Participated in Berkeley Poetry Conference. Published *The Gold Diggers and Other Stories* (short stories). Edited, with Donald Allen, *New American Story*. Published *Words* (poems). Received Rockefeller Grant.
1966	Featured in National Educational Television Film, *Poetry: Robert Creeley*.
1966–70	Visiting professor at State University of New York, Buffalo.
1967	Published *Words* (poems). Edited with Donald Allen *The New Writing in the USA*. Collaborated with R. B. Kitaj on *A Sight*. Recorded *Robert Creeley Reads* (reading).
1967–2003	Named Professor of English at SUNY, Buffalo.
1968	Taught at University of New Mexico. Published *The Finger* (poems). Published *Numbers* (poems).
1969	Published *Pieces* (poems). Published *The Charm* (poems).
1970	Moved to Bolinas, CA. Taught at San Francisco State University. Published *A Quick Graph : Collected Notes & Essays* (criticism).
1972	Published *A Day Book* (journal and poems). Published *Listen* (radio play).

1973	Edited *Whitman: Selected Poems*. Moved to Buffalo, NY. Published *His Idea* (poems).
1974	Published *Thirty Things* (poems).
1976	Published: *Presences: A Text for Marisol* (prose); *Away* (poems); and *Selected Poems*. Divorced Bobbie Hall Creeley.
1977	Married Penelope Highton.
1978	Published *Hello: A Journal* (poems). *Boundary 2* published a double issue titled *Robert Creeley: A Gathering*.
1979	Published *Later* (poems).
1980	First volume of *Charles Olson and Robert Creeley: The Complete Correspondence* published by Black Sparrow Press.
1981	Son William born. Awarded Shelley Memorial Award from the Poetry Society of America.
1982	Received NEA Grant. Published *The Collected Poems of Robert Creeley: 1945–1975*.
1983	Daughter Hannah born. Published *Mirrors* (poems). Received DAAD Fellowship in Berlin.
1984	Appointed David Gray Professor of Poetry and Letters, SUNY Buffalo.
1985	Awarded Leone d'Oro Premio Speziale, Venice.
1987	Received second DAAD Fellowship in Berlin. Awarded Frost Medal by Poetry Society of America.
1988	*Robert Creeley's Life and Work* published. Received Distinguished Fulbright Award as Bicentennial Chair in American Studies, Helsinki University.
1989–91	Named New York State Poet.
1990	Named Capen Professor of Poetry and Humanities, SUNY Buffalo.
1991	Published *Autobiography* (essay).
1993	Tom Clark's *Robert Creeley and the Genius of the American Common Place* published. Received Horst Bienek Lyrikpreis from Bavarian Academy of Fine Arts. Published *Tales Out of School: Selected Interviews*.
1994	Published *Echoes* (poems).
1995	Published *Loops: Ten Poems*.

1998   Published *Life and Death* (poems).

1999   Elected a chancellor of the Academy of American Poets. Received the Bollingen Prize.

2001   Received the Lannan Lifetime Achievement Award.

2002   Published *If I Were Writing This* (poems).

2003   Named Distinguished Professor in the Graduate Program in Literary Arts at Brown University. Moved to Providence, RI.

2005   Died at sunrise on March 30, 2005, in Odessa, Texas, from complications from pneumonia.

2006   *On Earth: Last Poems and an Essay* published. *The Collected Poems of Robert Creeley 1975–2005* published.

One thinks of Robert Creeley, foremost and primarily, as a writer. That being the case, it must be said a large part of that writing, even the largest part—the *volume* of it—was correspondence. Simply the list of names of correspondents, available at the Stanford Special Collections website, runs to well over one hundred pages; there are in addition substantial collections of his correspondence at Washington University (St. Louis), the University of Connecticut at Storrs, as well as numerous other archives and private collections around the world. We have sifted through this correspondence with three aims in mind: (1) as he requested of us, "to tell a story," that is, what he did; (2) to track his thinking, his poetics, philosophy, and politics, across the six decades this selection represents—in other words, what he thought; and (3) to tell the larger story, through the prism of his engagements, of the individuals and societies he encountered. This last, of course, is necessarily the most contingent aspect of the project, yet it seems fair to say this volume represents not simply a history of Robert Creeley but also a version of recent history, literary and otherwise, of and within the post–Second World War world.

   We begin this selection the same year as the first volume of Creeley's *Collected Poems*, 1945, which finds him on his way to Burma to serve as an ambulance driver. There follow a few lengthy letters to fellow writer and editorial collaborator Jacob Leed; these reflect the humble situation of the young New Hampshire chicken farmer with the voracious intellect that would shortly engage Ezra Pound and William Carlos Williams and inaugurate an intense dialogue with Charles Olson that would quickly and irreversibly change, quite literally, the concept of poetry for our time. With his friend Leed, Creeley had hatched a scheme to start a literary magazine to be called the *Lititz Review* (after the small town in

Pennsylvania where they planned to print it). In contacting Pound, Williams, and others, Creeley was soliciting both writing and advice from the previous generation.

Creeley was twenty-four when he began writing to William Carlos Williams, then sixty-seven, initiating his connection with a poet who was and remained for him a guiding poetic sensibility. The Williams correspondence proves remarkable, not only for its invaluable contribution to the poetics of our time, but also as autobiographical document. Creeley wrote regularly, but by no means weekly or even monthly, to Williams (as he often did with other correspondents, particularly Charles Olson). As a result the letters are often a summation of recent developments—writings, moves, romances, literary politics. It was through Williams that Creeley came into contact with Charles Olson.

The celebrated Olson-Creeley correspondence, edited primarily by George Butterick and published by Black Sparrow Press in ten volumes between 1980 and 1996, covers only the period of their letters between April 1950 and July 1952. As Butterick notes in his introduction to the first volume, "There are roughly one thousand surviving pieces of correspondence in all, with Creeley outwriting Olson at a rate of three to one." The approximately three thousand pages of Creeley's letters to Olson housed at the Olson archive at the University of Connecticut, Storrs, make up about a fifth of the fifteen thousand or so typed or handwritten letters, cards, and faxes we have collected or reviewed, along with a practically uncountable number of e-mails. Creeley early on recognized the potential literary value of the exchange with Olson, publishing as *The Mayan Letters* a selection of Olson's letters from the Yucatán (1951–52) on his own Divers Press in Majorca in 1954 and reprinting them in his edition of Olson's *Selected Writings* for New Directions in 1966. The letters by Creeley to Olson after 1952 appear here in print for the first time and only hint at the dimensions of Butterick's unfinished project to print all of the letters by the two poets to each other. Lasting and influential connections also made in the early fifties are documented in the correspondences with Cid Corman, Larry Eigner, and Denise Levertov. With each of these poets Creeley played by turns mentor, mentee, publisher, and friend.

From Littleton, New Hampshire, Creeley moved his young family in 1951 to the south of France, first to Fontrousse and then Lambesc, both in the environs of Aix-en-Provence. Mitchell Goodman and Denise Levertov had convinced Creeley that the cheaper cost of living in postwar France would allow them to live on his wife's small trust fund (about two hundred dollars a month), thus freeing him to devote time to writing. In the decade of the fifties alone, Creeley lived in New Hampshire, in the south of France, on the island of Majorca, at Black Mountain College in North Carolina, briefly in both New York City and the San

Littleton, N.H.

April 24, 1950

Dear Olsen,

Have your poems at hand. These are too much — unlike what I had seen; forgive, etc. But the others didn't make it for me, and, perhaps, useless to go into that here. Except to say that you have my vote on the matters of language, etc. It was, in those, that I couldn't come to it, etc., but as you will.

So will print MORNING NEWS in this first issue; and will keep, if you will, the others to look at for a subsequent one. I w'd say that MOVE OVER w'd be it, for something later; but will write you on this, when I can come to it.

Good that the Dr. took the trouble to say those things, etc. This means much. I.e., more than goodwill, some help. Very few can make this. Anyhow, I'll make use of his 'program' and also, by way of emphasis, a reprint of his article on Eliot in the Feb '48 issue of 4Pages. Do you know this? Expect you w'd. At the moment, have a rather tenuous relation with same, via so many, that I can only shout, etc. But for one: T.D. Horton has been of great help in these matters; through him, some fine things by Paquette, which will also make use of in this first is-sue. But you will see. It comes, at times, to making peace among these various, but granted the will, perhaps (dare we hope) the way, etc. So much for that.

I saw ASYMPTOTES, and have to say I'm happy with what I've got. Again, forgive, etc. You will know how we are about these things. To each his own, etc.

Very grateful for the copy of Y&X; the first thing very,

Page one of Creeley's first letter to Charles Olson, April 24, 1950. Courtesy of the Archives & Special Collections at the Thomas J. Dodd Research Center, University of Connecticut Libraries.

Robert Creeley, Black Mountain, North Carolina, 1955. Photograph by Jonathan Williams.

Francisco Bay area, then on to New Mexico, and finally, ending the decade in Guatemala. Having deliberately sought isolation in remote, inexpensive living situations, Creeley compensated for his lack of face-to-face contact with his peers through his prolific letter writing. The fifties alone account for about 40 percent of the present volume.

Creeley's spirited rejection of the dominant poetry climate was spurred by letters from Pound and Williams, and although his esteem for Pound the poet and editor remained, Creeley recognized fairly quickly that his advice was seriously hampered by both his monomania (to use a relatively neutral term) and his sycophantic, not to mention racist, retinue. Williams, however, proved an invaluable collaborator in the push toward new forms, and their correspondence never diminished despite Williams's failing health in his later years.

The *Lititz Review,* perhaps predictably, never materialized; however, Creeley exercised considerable influence on the editorial direction of Cid Corman's journal *Origin,* the first issue of which prominently featured Charles Olson. Creeley began his own Divers Press in 1953. The following is from a handbill advertising the Divers debut, featuring new titles by Paul Blackburn, Olson, Eigner, and Creeley:

> Printing is cheap in Mallorca, and for a small press like our own it means freedom
> from commercial pressures. It means, too, that we can design our books in a way
> that we want, since they are handset and made with an almost forgotten sense of
> craft. Above all, it is our own chance to print what we actually like and believe in.

Creeley also, at Olson's behest, served as editor of the *Black Mountain Review,* the first number appearing in the spring of 1954 and running through seven issues, to the fall of 1957. This editorship proved one of the crucial contexts for a generation of writers associated not only with Black Mountain but also for Beat and New York School poetries. It also plunged him into some bruising literary feuds, notably with Kenneth Rexroth and even for a brief time with Robert Duncan. His friendship with Duncan recovered and flourished; his association with Rexroth did not. Meanwhile, his brief time spent at Black Mountain College (spring 1954 and autumn 1955) allowed him to form lasting relationships not just with Olson but also with Ed Dorn, Fielding Dawson, and others, and gave rise to the name of the "movement" or "school" with which he is most often associated.

If Creeley's letters from this time are deeply inflected by the literary politics of the period, they are even more concerned with how an alternative poetics might be constituted. A letter might include a vignette of seeing Picasso in a café in Aix or a long description of a trip to Spain, or a car crash at Black Mountain, before delving extensively into his own practice of poetry, or offering in-depth critiques of poems by his friends, or overviews of exciting tendencies among the San Francisco group. Some of this poetic theory shares Williams's concerns with the American idiom. Some of it relates to Creeley's shared passion with Olson for their differing articulations of a Projective Verse poetics, though this is but one aspect of the prodigious range of their discourse. He strongly differs with Williams on the question of measure: "We don't need a 'measure' so much as we *do* need, desperately, some sense of our materials, the elements if you will from which the poem forms" (January 26, 1955). The jazz idiom of Bop, and Charlie

Parker in particular, is an important source for this approach. This to Olson, April 8, 1953:

> I am more influenced by Charley Parker, in my acts, than by any other man, living or dead. IF you will listen to five records, say, you will see how the whole biz ties in—i.e., how, say, the whole sense of a loop, for a story, came in, and how, too, these senses of rhythm in a poem (or a story too, for that matter) got in. Well, I am not at all joking, etc. Bird makes Ez look like a school-boy, in point of rhythms. And his <u>sense</u>, of how one rhythm can activate the premise for, another. Viz, how a can lead to b, in all that multiplicity of the possible. It is a fact, for one thing, that Bird, in his early records, damn rarely ever comes in on the so-called beat. And, as well, that what point he does come in on, is not at all 'gratuitous', but is, in fact, involved in a figure of rhythm which is as dominant in what it leaves out, as what it leaves in.

Creeley headed to New York from Black Mountain in late 1955 to see to the details of his divorce from Ann MacKinnon. There he also spent time with Williams and Louis Zukofsky and became for a brief time a regular at the famous Cedar Bar, fraternizing with the likes of Franz Kline and Jackson Pollock, among others. He was then on to San Francisco in early 1956, where his association with Ginsberg and Kerouac began. After a few months marked by an intense, ultimately unhappy affair with Marthe Rexroth, Creeley landed in Albuquerque, New Mexico, securing a job as a French teacher at a boys' high school. After a spell he met and soon married Bobbie Louise Hawkins (then Bobbie Hall), with whom he had two daughters, Sarah and Katherine.

The Creeleys moved, in the fall of 1959, to Guatemala. He had secured a job tutoring the children of the owner of a *finca*. The hope had been to have time to write and also to live cheaply and save up some money. Clearly, only the former transpired. Creeley grouses regularly about the cost of living in Guatemala in his formidably prolific correspondence of this period and is deeply critical of his employers and the economic injustice of the Guatemalan situation generally, not just his own. Nevertheless it is in this period that he begins to see a way to "make it," as he often said. This was largely a result of the reception of his ninth book, *A Form of Women* (1959), of his inclusion in Donald Allen's high-profile anthology *The New American Poetry* (1960), and of the news, received while in Guatemala, that Scribner's had accepted his early collected poems for publication as *For Love* (1962). After living a somewhat marginalized, slightly vagabond existence through the fifties, Robert Creeley, in the sixties, would soon become one of the most celebrated poets of his time.

Though his affiliation with the University of British Columbia in Vancouver was relatively brief (one academic year, 1962–63), it did allow him, with the help of Warren Tallman, to stage the famous Vancouver Poetry Conference in the summer of 1963. As letters to key figures reveal, Creeley clearly felt the large part of the "work" of the conference would get done not at the official events but in relatively private settings with good friends. By the time he began his first real, long-term teaching position at the University of Buffalo in 1966, Creeley was the poetic equivalent of a rock star, his letters increasingly devoted to the schedules of cross-country and international reading trips and the consequent demands on his time. His poetry also was changing. In this period he writes to Olson, and others, that the poems in *For Love* already seem to have been written by a different person. In the books *Words* (1967) and *Pieces* (1968), he breaks out of the model of the single poem as crafted artifact toward a serial practice influenced in part by the works of Zukofsky—a move that became crucially important to a younger group of writers that would come to be known as the Language poets. These changes in Creeley's verse were not a break with his practice of the fifties. An unpublished poem sent to Olson (May 28, 1956) can be seen as of a piece with *For Love* as well as a clear foreshadowing of the work of the sixties and seventies:

HOW ABOUT THAT
It must be horrible
when you are dead
to know you planned just a little
too far ahead.

While Creeley's success as a poet was increasingly secured by the late sixties, his personal life became more chaotic during the extended period of his breakup and eventual divorce from his second wife, Bobbie Louise Hawkins. His letters to her in Bolinas, where they had acquired a house in 1970, are often troubled and conflicted but also loving and filled with the quotidian concerns of a long-term intimacy. Adding to the emotion of the time were the untimely deaths of two of his dearest friends and collaborators: Charles Olson in 1970, at age sixty, and Paul Blackburn in 1971, at age forty-four. This period of personal dislocation eventually resolved with Creeley's marriage in 1976 to his third wife, Penelope Highton, and the births of their two children, Will and Hannah, in the early eighties. Creeley had met Penelope on an epic reading tour of the Pacific Basin, which became the primary subject of his first book for New Directions, *Hello: A Journal, February 29—May 3, 1976*. One aspect of Creeley's personal life that becomes apparent when viewing the overall body of letters is that for almost his entire adult life, his home life, often with small children, dominated his concerns.

Although he had taught in various contexts since the mid-fifties, Creeley only settled into full-time teaching in Buffalo in 1973. Clearly, he was a one-of-a-kind professor, as this from Peter Middleton's account of studying with him, "Scenes of Instruction: Creeley's Reflexive Poetics," demonstrates:

Robert Creeley was usually the last to arrive for the seminar. He liked to stand sideways in the door for a few moments, his good eye looking us over and his blind eye safely out in the corridor, his army surplus hat still on as if he might decide not to enter once he had assessed his classroom, whatever the timetable said, because this was to be an act of choice. What mattered was the quality of the encounter and there would always be part of him that would be reflecting with an inner eye on its implications. He came in, put down his shoulder bag on the desk, placed his hat ritually on the table in front of him, began to talk as he sat down, and then talked on solidly for the entire class, only occasionally interpolating a question or appeal for responses, rarely waiting for a rejoinder. (*Form, Power, and Person in Robert Creeley's Life and Work,* ed. Fredman and McCaffery, University of Iowa Press, 2010, 159)

Starting earlier, but particularly in the seventies, Creeley, in addition to teaching, increasingly authored essays, engaged in interviews, and collaborated with visual artists; thus, although his correspondence does not reveal a lack of concern with poetics, his venues for that conversation multiplied radically compared with those of the fifties. A multigenerational poet, he sought to keep up with the formal and compositional developments of avant-garde writing, having up-and-down—sometimes heated—relationships with correspondents whose writing practices he came to view as dated or reactionary. At other times he spoke well of W. S. Merwin, whom he had once dismissed, and had friendships with relatively conservative poets such as Robert Bly and James Dickey.

Creeley was an early adopter of fax machines, word processing, and e-mail, and his epistolary habits evolved with each new technology. What this record shows is that in the last decade or more of his life, Creeley was as generous to a newer generation of poets as he had been solicitous of his precursors when he was getting his start. Simply for reasons of space, much of this book might be thought of as representative of, rather than encompassing, Creeley's letter-writing practice. We have represented, as far as possible, the *kinds* of letters he wrote; to "tell the story," but also to provide as useful a document as possible. The letters compiled here are "representative" not only of Creeley but also of what it was like to be a poet in his time, albeit an unusually successful one. Letters reflecting the work of poetics with friends, critics, and editors; family concerns; communications with students; dealings with his many publishers; the responsibilities of coordinating reading series; institutional politics—all have been offered here as examples of which there are many more. Our only wish is that we could have been even more inclusive.

This is not the first volume dedicated to Creeley's correspondence. The ambitious Olson-Creeley correspondence published by Black Sparrow has already been mentioned, but we would do well also to mention two other, quite different

Robert Creeley (*right*) and Tom Raworth, Maryland Institute College of Art, 1999. Photograph by Rod Smith.

publications: one with an important contemporary, *Irving Layton and Robert Creeley: The Complete Correspondence, 1953–1978*, edited by Ekbert Faas and Sabrina Reed (McGill-Queen's University Press, 1990), and the other, *Day Book of a Virtual Poet* (Spuyten Duyvil Press, 1999), which collects e-mail correspondence to high school students participating in an online honors poetry course. For an excellent overview of the development of Creeley's poetry as well as greater biographical detail, we would suggest Benjamin Friedlander's introduction to Creeley's *Selected Poems, 1945–2005* (University of California Press, 2008), as well as Tom Clark's *Robert Creeley and the Genius of the American Common Place* (New Directions, 1993), which includes Creeley's own ten-thousand-word "Autobiography." An excellent bibliography as well as a generous selection of Creeley's writing may be found at the Electronic Poetry Center (http://epc.buffalo .edu/authors/creeley/). A wealth of audio and video recordings of his readings, lectures, and interviews are available at PennSound (http://writing.upenn.edu/ pennsound/x/Creeley.php).

In 2003, at the age of seventy-six, Creeley left Buffalo for a new teaching position at Brown University, in Providence, Rhode Island, an appointment that lasted only a few years. Robert Creeley died at sunrise on March 30, 2005, in Odessa, Texas, of complications from pneumonia. He had been in residency with the Lannan Foundation in Marfa, Texas, for the spring, after a brief teaching

Robert Creeley, Ligura Study Center, Bogliasco, Italy, 2002.
Photograph by Penelope Creeley.

stint at the University of North Carolina, Wilmington, during the winter. He
had given his final reading at the University of Virginia just days before he died.

We were fortunate to benefit from Creeley's advice on the shape of this volume
while he was still with us (see, for example, his e-mail to Rod Smith 7/17/03). He
definitely wanted letters to family included and saw no reason to impose an
artificial distinction between typewritten letters and their electronic equivalent.
While all of the individuals and university archives listed in our acknowledg-
ments have helped make this volume possible, it is finally, and of course, Robert
Creeley's extraordinary energy and acumen that give this book its inherent value.

A NOTE ON THE TEXT

Our editorial policy for the presentation of these letters has all along been to
maintain a minimum of editorial interference in the body of the text and to
present letters only in their entirety. There are no excerpted letters, also no edito-
rial headnotes to sections, and no editorializing about which letters stand out

for whatever reason. We have kept Creeley's famous dictum that "form is never more than an extension of content" in front of us while making decisions on the presentation of these letters and have allowed this to guide us at the micro- as well as the macrolevel.

Creeley, like Charles Olson, wrote many letters that reflect a projective verse or field poetics in his approach to use of the space on the page. These letters date almost exclusively from the early fifties, though aspects of this style remain visible throughout his life as a correspondent. We have endeavored to reproduce these field poetics letters in their original appearance, including not only nonstandard indentation but also blocked paragraphs separated by space. The spacing of the original letters is presented through the entirety of parts 1 and 2. At the request of the press we've allowed unindented paragraphs separated by a space in later letters, parts 3 through 6, to be presented as standard paragraphs. Nonstandard indentations, regardless of date, have been preserved.

With a few exceptions, our notes to individual letters are located at the end of the text, with notes keyed to the correspondent and date of the letter. Within the text itself all of our contributions are in square brackets and in plain type. The bracketed material typically identifies an addition to the text made after the original typescript, for example, "[note in left margin: *Creeley addition*]." When these additions are handwritten, they are presented in italics. We have employed the caret symbol, "^," to signal marginal or intertextual insertions indicated by Creeley in the document. When an entire letter was handwritten we have presented it in roman type to avoid large passages in italics. We do present postcards, when handwritten, in italics. Much of Creeley's marginalia, sometimes typed, sometimes handwritten, is simply the continuation of a letter after signing off, at times signaled by a "P.S.," just as often not. In many instances additions above the salutation are clearly intended to be the first thing the recipient read. Whether jokes, commentary on writing or music, news of friends or family, and so forth, these have often been presented in their original location in the typescript. Notes above the salutation of lesser import have been presented at the end of the letter, with their position indicated in brackets.

Influenced by Olson and Pound, Creeley's style as a letter writer included a number of nonnormative usages of punctuation. Slashes, hyphens, em-dashes, commas, periods, colons (including a space preceding them), and open parentheses are variously employed in nonstandard ways as rhythmic devices. We have attempted to preserve all of these characteristics of the original documents. In the interest of conveying the changing technological contexts Creeley as a correspondent negotiated, we have also chosen to include aspects specific to the various technologies he used. These include transcriptions of university or other letterhead, postcard descriptions, exact transcriptions of telegrams, and typical fax and e-mail headers. Occasionally basic information such as subject and e-mail address did not survive in the electronic files. In those instances we present only what has survived.

Creeley was a skilled and fast two-fingered typist. He also clearly proofread his letters once completed and corrected what few typos there might be. Our commitment has been to respect the original text, though on occasion we have silently corrected clearly unintended mistakes. We are appending a short biographical and bibliographical chronology for the reader's reference.

Rod Smith, Peter Baker, Kaplan Harris
October 2012

PART ONE

The Charm, 1945–1952

Burma, New Hampshire, Aix-en-Provence

Jan.20.'45

Dear Mother and Helen,

We soon will land, and after that I suppose everything will become something over which I shall have little or no control. I am actually looking forward to that time, though I should never have thought I would. But then many of the things that have occurred in the past year I could never have predicted, and they are the very things which will make me think as I do. It will be quite pleasant to carry out someone's orders, to do what one is told. Yet, should I find myself on my own at anytime, I have enough strength, enough intelligence to rescue me. I do not worry about that, and it would be little help if I did. Anyhow, I am ready, as much as I can be ready, for what is coming.

Being at sea for a month, away from all past influences, did a great deal for me in many ways. On ship, having only one companion and he so different in his tastes, I found all the time I could possibly need for thinking and reading. It was rather like waking from a nightmare with the realization that the nightmare had only been oneself. All I have done, and so much it was, to ruin myself, to hurt those who love and trust me, to cloud my eyes to everything while it was so very important for me to see, all of this I saw and realized. I thought about it over and over again, until at last the mistakes were clear, were obvious, and I could know them as mistakes myself; and to call an action a mistake has nothing to do with knowing one is. The little good that was left I have kept, and on that I must begin to build my whole new structure, nothing more or nothing less. I have a great deal of work to do.

I wrote quite a bit, and very little of it is good, or I think is good, yet that will do for now. I can't alter my wish to write. That remains, and I can only adjust to it. I do believe that I shall be able to someday; I will not admit ever that it is only a dream or something which I can never realize.

I think of a number of quotations, all of them admirable, which I might now use for my own life. The very obvious one is in Polonius' speech to Laertes in Act I, Sc. III of <u>Hamlet</u> "This above all, to thine own self be true, and it must follow as the night the day, thou canst not then be false to any man". Oh, that would help, I think, but not answer. So much more is necessary. I think of Walpole's <u>Fortitude</u>,[1] and I remember reading it when I was quite young and almost wishing someone would beat me, so that I could be as brave as Peter Westcott. That book begins with this: "Tisn't life that matters; 'tis the courage you bring to it". And that's much more than true, and still not nearly enough.

3

No quotation is enough. How could it be? Nothing outside oneself can ever be enough. I cannot be told, and I cannot be shown how I should live. I can only find out for myself. But I sincerely wish to hear how others have done it, to have them tell me what they have learned, for they may lead me to my own answer, though they can't actually give it to me. Enough of this. I will learn, because I must.

Remembering letters I wrote in prep school, even when at Harvard, I am afraid that you will think I am insincere, verbose, because of what has preceded this. Believe me, I am not; this is not a time for that, and it was then. If I appear to take myself too seriously now, it is because for the next year and a half I shall hardly be a "self" at all. And think of the last year where I took myself seriously in such an unserious manner. I love you both much, more than I can tell you, and it will always be so. Take care of yourselves, *Bob.*

[RC's note, upper left margin] *¹The ship's library happened to have and I reread, enjoying it as much as I once did.*

. . .

LETTER TO GENEVIEVE AND HELEN CREELEY

> 2012 Volunteer Robert Creeley
> A Platoon Section 1
> S.E.A.C.
> April 13, 1945

Dear Mother and Helen,

Cooler this morning, God be praised, and letter-writing becomes an actual-ity instead of a hope. We're having the preliminaries to the monsoon at pres-ent—rain which comes in the later part of the day and clears about night-fall, though I'm by no means happy to see the advent of the monsoon, the respite from the heat is undeniably welcome.

Working at last. I'm attached to ▉▉▉▉ and have begun to do the work I wanted to do five months ago. To give you some picture of what it consists, the following is more or less typical. About six the I.O.R.s (Indian Other Ranks) begin to chatter and make sleep for anyone within hearing range impossible. So I get up, grab the canvas bucket which someone considered a curio, get some water, and wash—the latter action is for the most part futile, because in an hour I'll be sweaty and consequently dirtier than before. Then I sit around waiting for breakfast, which, if we're in luck, means eggs, bacon or sausages perhaps, and tea, but, if we're not, it is something quite indescribable. After breakfast I try to find something to do—sweep out the ambulance, straighten out my kit, talk with anyone who will, or do what I'm doing now, anything, you see, to fill up the time between breakfast and the arrival of casualties. These come in at about nine thirty. They're treated as quickly as possible, loaded into an ambulance (we'll say mine), and taken back to the C.C.S. (Casualty Clearance Something). Now the last sentence involves a half day's work where I am at present. From our A.D.S. to the main road, which is very fortunately tarmacked, there's some four miles of bumpy, dirt road, and it's difficult to drive more than five miles an hour without making the patients very uncomfortable. And in the case of bad stomach wounds or something similar it's impossible to go that fast. Once on the tarmack I can go much faster, and in a relatively short time I've arrived at the C.C.S. some twenty miles distant (in this case).

I drive up in front of "Reception", get out, and, forcing all the authority summonable into my voice, shout "stretcher bearer!" Sometimes they come, sometimes they don't. Should they not come, I go ferret them out from wherever they're sleeping and prod them into taking out my patients. Once the ambulance is clear, I simply turn around and come back to my A.D.S. and spend the rest of the day doing whatever I can find to do until it's time to sleep.

The joke about waiting being the greater part of military action, as you may have gathered, is no joke out here. Luckily I've a few books and my own writing to fill out some of the blanks. (Books, understandably, make the ideal package from home.) Nevertheless, many times I think I'd have had it, had nothing happened within a few minutes later.

It's literally impossible to tell you what is happening here, the atmosphere is always changing, first grotesque, then absurdly funny, now poignantly sad, and then quite pointlessly ugly. One's system of values shifts from day to day. Last night, for example, six feet from where I was sleeping, an I.O.R. was lying with his side shot away, still living after a day and a half; they could do nothing for him. Just before I fell asleep, he died and, as I was dozing off, I could hear his death rattle. But I was too tired to think about it. I suppose normally one sees very few people die, and their death means shock and great sadness. Here there is only a minute for the shake of a hand, a comment rather bitterly appropriate, and then it has passed; all of it, until the next. And who's to say even that much is not wasted?

War, as well as Elizabethan drama, is a good exponent of comic relief. For me there have been infinite numbers of instances. I remember one time when I was still driving a water truck for H.Q. we could find no water point with a pump. So I with two I.O.R.s began an extremely ineffectual bucket brigade. Well, the sun was hot as I think it can ever be, and I was streaming with sweat, and the damn tank seemed bottomless. Yet I was laughing and thoroughly enjoying the situation, all because the pants of the I.O.R. in the middle fell down every time he passed the bucket up to me on the truck. Thank God for British issue butts!

Please keep your letters coming—especially, Helen, ones like the last long one from you. They help so very much. And if you can find time for photographs, they'd also be appreciated. You can rely on my writing as often as it's possible.—In the meantime take care of yourselves and Sandy.

> *All my love,*
> *Bob*

P.S. I have a photograph enclosed in this letter. Hope it comes through alright.

Volunteer Robert W. Creeley

[The black square indicates censored content.]

. . .

LETTER TO GENEVIEVE AND HELEN CREELEY

Vol. R. W. Creeley

May 10, 1945
Am. Field Service
A.P.O. 465, c/o P.M. NY NY

Dear Mother and Helen,

Your letters are coming in regularly, and I am more than thankful that they are. Mail is the most effective morale-builder there is out here; an oft repeated fact, but one well worth repeating.

At the present there is a temporary lull in activity. Consequently, I'm getting a rest which I can't say I'm glad to get, but which, I suppose, is good for me. Since I haven't reached a point where I'd be glad to be back and take things easy, I'd much rather be working. Anything is better than inactivity I've found; the latter makes me extremely restless and moody, gives me too much time to think.

All this serves to introduce the subject of reading material. I can never have too much of it. To date I've received no copies of the "New Yorker" nor any of the "New Directions" publications which I thought might be most convenient for you to send me. If you can pick up any copies of the "Partisan Review," "Poetry" or "Furiosa" (I'm not sure that the last is still being published), I should enjoy having them. Please do not consider this in any way a reprimand for what I might think a lack of cooperation. The blame, if any can be justifiably placed, might well be put on postal facilities. They are certainly not all one might wish for. So I think that that is where those various things I have asked for are— somewhere between you and me. They'll probably arrive some day.

I'm looking forward to the monsoons with a great deal of curiosity and uneasiness. I've heard some very incredible tales about them, and they've come at one time or another from fairly reliable people. Naturally the more imaginative will tell me tales of how the rain comes down to within six feet of the ground at which point it changes to steam. The effect of this on the average person seems obvious—driving conditions, I am told, are impossible. Sometimes vehicles are mired down for days waiting for someone who can't move himself to come and tow them out. The whole procedure becomes a symbol of gullibility—the monsoons, consequently, must be pretty God awful, and the fact that they last for two or three months makes them hardly more attractive.

It's unfortunate that the people involved in the field work part of a war can't know where and when they will be wanted. But that, I suppose, would terminate the war a bit too quickly to suit the ambitions behind it. Moreover, if it weren't for the suspense and the frustration, which constant waiting creates, the people involved might forget their negations, surely the type of thought produced by unavoidable and unending ~~expectation~~ repression, and come forth with some constructive thought. And who knows what that might lead to?—I will always feel pity for those who are forced to wait for something they actually see no reason to wait for, caught in a situation they can neither correct nor understand. What can they do but gripe?

I have written to Arthur. I wish in a way that he were not overseas—my reason for that is apparent. Yet, since I know he shared the curiosity I had, I'm glad that he will be satisfied. The experience he is having can intensify or blunt appreciation of the things most elemental in our lives; it can make or break a person as sensitive as Arthur, and I think his comparatively sound sense of logic and reasoning will cause it to have the former effect.

Your descriptions of Sandy and his explorations into what makes things work make me wish that I were back with you to see it for myself. I spend a great deal of time thinking of the various things I should like to do with him, picnics and all the rest, and if Arthur can spare him long enough, I'll see those hopes come true. It is something for me to look forward to.

Thanks for sending the camera. It hasn't arrived yet—no packages, other than the almonds, have, for that matter. It's a very slow process I've found from the experiences of my friends. But God willing they do get here eventually. I would like some films for it, if you can get them—rather difficult to get out here.

Please take care of yourselves. And keep writing as often as you can. Give my love to Sandy and tell him that I'll bring him back lots of presents.

All my love,
Bob

· · ·

LETTER TO GENEVIEVE CREELEY

Mrs. O. S. Creeley	Vol. R. Creeley
65 Sparks St	Am. Field Service
Cambridge, Mass.	A.P.O. 465, c/o P.M. NY NY
U.S.A.	May 15, 1945

Dear Mother,

I've sent you a package containing the artificial eye which I got in Calcutta. It was cracked a few days ago quite mysteriously. Rather annoying, since I had it in a tin packed in cotton. Anyhow, see if you can get me another of similar measurements. You might have them use one of my old eyes for determining the placement of the pupil. Please try to obtain one and send it to me as quickly as possible, for the mails are very, very slow, and it would take almost four months, were you to send it immediately. Do what you can, anyhow.

All my best,
Bob

. . .

LETTER TO BOB LEED

June 21, 1948

Dear Bob,

This will be, I should think, the last letter before I see you. Little more than a week to go. I wonder what Cambridge will look like (all of it); the same, without a doubt. It used to bewilder me to go back there when we were living on the Cape because no matter how long it had been since the last visit, I could go into Jim's place, sit down, and finish the sentence that had been left hanging in the air when I'd been forced to leave suddenly two months before. To some that might seem even pleasant, but for me it was unbelievably horrible. It confirmed my suspicion that I never talked to anyone but myself.

Speaking of Proust (which we have) recalls a particularly good comment by William Empson (Seven Types of Ambiguity which I figured out once he wrote when he was little more than twenty) on Proust to the effect that Remembrance of Things Past read like the paraphrase or better, the verbal recollection, of a great novel that had unfortunately been lost. I forget which of the 7 types this was supposed to illustrate (if any) but I do remember that it came somewhere in the next to the last chapter. I'd get it and quote it if the book weren't buried somewhere under all the rest. Last night I came on another comment on Proust in Otto Rank's Art and Artist, i.e., 'in contrast to Homer's spatial metaphor Proust's is temporal; that is, it attempts, by the temporal association of the present with the past, to restore the latter to life, just as Homer puts it in living form before us by means of plastic presentation. (All this is pretty obvious.) The two

kinds of metaphor are, however, distinct from each other in the same way that space and time are conceptually and factually distinct. Space is a concrete idea, time an abstract, and thus Homer's metaphor is plastic, Proust's intellectualist. (Now it gets a little better but for my money still a gross over-simplification so damned common to the psychologist and his use of any material beyond what is potentially his own by way of jargon.) In fact, the temporal quality of Proust's metaphor is typical not only of his famous similes but of his whole work which one might take as a single gigantic metaphor (le temps retrouve). (Of course that has been stretched to include all of the life function, i.e., 'life is but a dream' or a metaphor which in this case depends on a very slim basis of actual objective fact. I do him an injustice, however.) But in Proust the intellectualist outlook— which is almost a self-evident necessity in the modern poet—proves that at the bottom it is a matter of ideas of death and the fear of death, of will to maintain the actual life-process in himself, rather than of a will to reconquer the past, which could only come out as a neurotic expression thereof.' He goes on to conceive of Shakespeare's metaphor as <u>dynamic</u>, i.e., an incorporate jumble of both past and present, use of myth, present, and so on, personified metaphor— 'Shylock inhumanly avaricious <u>like</u> the devil of gold himself'. Well, I started the book, bought it, to find out something more about the psychologist personality and this is perhaps the best evidence (not the quote) of it that I've yet seen.
It is strange to consider, for example, strange for me at any rate, that Rank is propounding what must eventually get back to something not very far removed from the spiritual and just about as lucid. His rejection of Freud's idea of the artist as thwarted neurotic whose basis of creativity depends on the sexual I like and think it well-grounded in fact (the recitation of which would take too long to include here). But since I have never subscribed to the idea of man as animal or at least sufficiently well explained in these terms, I may be merely applauding the reiteration of my own beliefs. I can't tell you how many fights (actual) I've had with Ann on this score since she is a thorough-going Freudian, at least in so far as she is concerned with explaining the actions of anyone who may interest her. For example, I recently read Sorokin's <u>Reconstruction of Humanity</u> whose theory of conflicting loyalties on the 'socio-cultural' (i.e., the women's club, business, boy scouts level, group affiliations almost) level as the basis of the most neuroses impressed me as comparatively sensible and whose quite violent attack on Freud at least warmed me. I was nasty enough to read a number of the comments to her and we had a rather rough time of it for a while. But as she says, 'I don't like poetry', so sooner or later I'm bound to be confounded. I was annoyed, for instance, by her absorbed reading of Richard Wilbur's book, i.e., these things hurt. However, be that as it may, Freud is a thorn in both our sides. I recall at this point Paul Goodman's essay, 'The Father of The Psychoanalytic Movement', (Kenyon Review, yours), i.e., 'We must think of Freud as methodi-

cally eyeing himself for half a century, as a doctor does, and seeing that he had become old, ill, and tired. Or as a parent keeps an eye on a child who has a tendency to masturbate; what can the child do but get out?' or 'Freud was the first of the psychoanalysts and therefore had to analyze himself.

'Resisting the analysis, he had no one to vent his hate on but himself.

'Therefore Freud said, 'The heavy burden of psychoanalysis.'[1]

'[1]This excellent reason was suggested to me by Dr. Erich Kraft' Who turns out to be our landlord in Truro.

Now supposing that this, all this, were not enough, you could try as I have reading several other books at the same time, all conflicting, all confusing. Each night I usually have the chance to read for an hour or so and since all of the following books arrived at the same time I somehow am reading them all at the same time, i.e., Philosophy in a New Key, Susan Langer or something, Art And Artist, Sartre's The Psychology of the Imagination (now he denies the unconscious completely but doesn't go into 'why'.), William's Paterson 2, which I finished and thought very good, Wilbur's The Beautiful Changes which is also terrific, T. S. Eliot, A selected critique, which god knows is stimulating but makes your head spin. Ransom, D. S. Savage are the best so far. Also Schwartz who is for, the other two aren't. Van Wyck Brooks and Winters, the lowest, utterly stupid. Then in a corner staring at me is Gide's 2nd Journals which I haven't the energy to start for the time being and anyhow Ann's reading it and tells me it's very good which of course makes me want to start it but I'm running out of book marks. I write nothing.

What you tell me about Greenberg is interesting but now it doesn't matter very much since the place was too 'rough'. He came with his son who was quite a little character and who, I'm inclined to think was responsible for their not taking the barn, Example: Mr. G. had to use the toilet which was in the house and left his son in the barn while I was making coffee in the kitchen. In the mean time a lot of men were up on the roof, shingling it. Then I hear the cry, father, father where are you, and so help me god it was as close to unearthly as I've yet come. The little joker was dashing about in the yard giving out with this plaintive shriek and the men on the roof were almost falling off with laughter. I don't think his father heard him. Anyhow, I've been amusing myself this morning with the idea of Zoe as his mother. He's eleven, excuse me, thirteen.

For the last few days I've been spending most of my time in the garden, hoeing and trying to shoot chipmunks who have eaten quite a number of the potatoes and beans as well as other things. Sort of a new phase of activity for me, the latter, not so much from the 'can you hit it' (usually) idea as from the 'do you want to' which I certainly don't. When I was younger I wasn't allowed to have a .22 and my relation to animals (wild) was confined to watching them whenever I got the chance. I can remember well enough spending a great deal of time in the woods trying to catch sight of a pheasant or even a squirrel and to see one was something big for me. The circumstances of the chipmunk-hunting are much the same as that was except that now when I see one, I'm obliged (notice the attempt to make it an imperative act) to shoot them. Perhaps because I do sit in the garden with the effects of their work quite visible, chewed potatoes and torn up roots, when I do shoot one I have only to look around to see what it probably would have gone on doing if I hadn't but then there is the fact of the quiet, then the apprehension of the sounds of the field, birds, the wind making the brush rustle, then perhaps a distinct crackling noise which comes nearer, a little at a time, and then I can see the brown of the chipmunk moving through the leaves. I raise the rifle and shoot. Once I shot and there was the most horrible sound of thrashing together with a chirping cry and I ran over and shot again to end it. Usually, thank god, I either kill them immediately or miss completely. Anyhow it isn't pleasant. Related to this is the problem of porcupines which gnaw everything they can find. For example, there is a sizable hole in the barn door which is the result of their work. So they have to be hunted as well and the other night I treed one and then had the task of shooting it down with a .22. You see, even a larger caliber gun is usually not enough to kill them first shot especially at night with them 20 feet or so up in a tree. It's a matter of shot after shot until slowly you see them begin to slip and then again until at last they let go and come down, crashing, to the ground. And then you have to walk over and perhaps fire again until you're convinced that they're dead. What this does is a strange and unpleasant thing. Of course, make it a matter of necessity and much of the problem (you'd at least like to think) is gone because they have to be killed. But it does very little to the dead, cold feeling you have standing there, shooting at that desperate, dark form some 20 feet over your head with its claws biting into the limb, as desperate, determined, as life can ever be. To make it worse the one I shot was a female, pregnant. I've felt like a murderer several times this last week.

The ideology of the country as opposed to the city contains that aspect of passive brutality which, however, it is usually impossible to attack or even for the most part to define. No one, at least no one I know, performs any act comparable to that of some Irish policeman in the 3rd precinct, Boston, (I am thinking of a specific occasion) who without the slightest appearance of anger can beat a negro or white to unconsciousness as part of an incredible routine (it is). But this complete understanding of woods, of land in a primal sense (I am thinking of some neighbors who are lumbermen), finds itself coupled to the practice of killing which it would be difficult to characterize. Perhaps 'passive brutality' is a poor phrase but what I intend it to mean is the act minus the intention which one would normally ascribe to it. A man beats his wife because he is angry with her.[2] Active brutality. A man shoots a woodchuck when miles from his home doing something, say cutting wood (in this case) which has no reference to the woodchuck because he does or does not like the woodchuck? It could be one or the other. Because he thinks the woodchuck is doing damage? Again it could be one or the other. It doesn't really matter to him because all that he seems to care about is shooting the woodchuck and strangely enough it often isn't even that. There is no logic. Sometimes he might chase the woodchuck, beating it out of brushpiles, for several miles in order to eventually shoot it. Or let it go. And he might have five cords of wood to go or might be finished or he might not even bother to pick up his gun. I call it passive brutality because it doesn't have the logic of the active variety. But no matter how I characterize it and I'm sure that I've done it wrongly, it is the problem that I am interested in and it also is one representative of most of the country people. It isn't that they function without logic but that they are willing to let it go at any time. You know, perhaps I'm right here, that in general the city seems to be made up of people like this; they all care about something and to say they don't care about something is almost to say that they care about something else instead. But there is to be found a logic of 'caring', a reality of action behind most of their activities. Well, in the country with the slowing down of activity in general (I don't mean that a farmer plows a furrow any slower or faster than anyone else could plow it) the reactions to logic seem to slow down too so that a man can, say, get off the train, do something and get back on again without suffering a shakeup. And to discover the reality of the action performed when the man is off the train would tax anyone's perception. Sometimes it is, sometimes it isn't—which doesn't mean for a minute that I don't care which. That's about it.

That would come under the heading of pure and simple musing, why the grass is green without reference to a chemistry book. We know why it is but, really, why is it even if it is and should be. Is that the end of it. Say A hits B and B crys. Can we eventually say that it can all be explained because if we do, then we also know that the explanation can be explained and so on, so far as anyone wants to go on with it. Cause and effect. What often seems to me like a priori classification. That is to say, each assumes the other and both exist after the fact, so what has been proved is the one fact that a single aspect of reality often causes an instance of 'cause and effect'.

[note in left margin] [2]*In the case of the police man, you might ascribe the "active" to his relatively simple 'enjoyment'. This is not the case with the man I am thinking of. He doesn't consider, or doesn't seem to, the animal as more or less than himself—apart and still part of, and there is no enjoyment to be derived from this aspect. Of course there are cases of it where it would be similar to that of the policeman.*

. . .

LETTER TO BOB LEED

Friday [ca. August 1948]

Dear Bob,

To begin with, I hope that Edith is feeling much better and that you will both be here before very long. Your telegram depressed me very much (selfishly enough) and it wasn't till your letter came today that I felt again as I should feel in a place like this.

Several years ago when I was a brief, subversive member of the Advocate I used to take the books that were sent to it for reviews. Among them was that New Directions selection of Melville's poems and to tell the truth it's the only thing of Melville's I've ever read. At the same time I remember being contemptuous, safely enough, of the crude phrasing, etc. and in consequence I never got much more than an impression of 'fatal' strength out of them, i.e., there was that connection with Hardy that you mentioned but it wasn't a very satisfactory one. Since that time I haven't looked at the poems and for some reason have never had the chance to read either Moby Dick or any of his other novels despite the fact that next to James his name was very often heard. 'the noble acts of violence. Premeditated and done with righteousness. He laments that the people and institutions do not understand and condemn it.' 'Primitive strengths.' Last night I unfortunately heard over the radio an instructive program about a juvenile delinquent who was 'made' so by the fact that his mother did not respect his father and so on. His acts of violence were not 'noble' but they were premeditated and they did lament by their very accomplishment the fact that the people did not understand and condemn them, i.e. that would have been necessary for their full accomplishment. I do not believe that the word 'noble' means very much. It has been too often used in varied connections. For example, even the Latin offers several implications. Right off it occurs to me that a Roman would hardly apply it to a poor man, or better a slave, or better an individual 'self-detached' from the state. Or if they should it would be because he might have been an asset to the state. Nobility in all of its forms recommends the 'common, i.e., available' to all virtue. So that when a man is considered 'noble' or his acts are thought of as 'noble', my own immediate impression is that the man or his acts in some way have contributed to an ideal held by one or several groups. 'Noble' has no meaning other than that of a well-meaning abstraction. Contrast, for example, with the familiar 'good man'. Try to think of a noble act, a noble man. Does a simply grasped idea occur to you? I strongly doubt it. So 'a noble act of violence' becomes 'an act of violence' which in some way after its accomplishment contributes some sort of apparent reality to someone's sense of the ideal. For myself, to go on with it, the word, 'noble', has the connection with 'regal', lordly, which I cannot overlook in my own consideration of its use. The obvious connection is with a noble, nobles, barons, kings, knights and so on. To get back we have the idea of a noble act of violence / can it be. To propose a noble act of violence or a noble act of any sort is to me an impossibility. It cannot be done. When someone attempts it, it occurs to me that he is trying to justify a course of action already decided upon which is doubtful enough to need the approbation of a sentiment supposed to be 'common' but, what is more, important above the ordinary realm of criticism. One can, for example, question the actuality of a good act. 'He thought he was doing them a good turn but what he really did was insult them.' A noble act, on the other hand, is one agreed upon and cannot be divided against itself. One can say he's a good man but he didn't know what he was doing when he insulted them unintentionally. There is little question that the motive was 'good'. But a 'noble' motive (which I believe only is considered after or in strict relation to the act itself) has to produce a noble act. When you say that a man thought he was doing a 'noble' act when he killed John Smith but that he actually wasn't, you do not suppose that his motive was 'noble', i.e. 'it couldn't have really been that'. Consequently, the concept of nobility is linked with a priori reasoning, in fact, depends on it for its meaning. Getting back to Melville, I would say on the very scant basis that I have that he was more interested in the act of violence than in the noble act of violence. The horror of the concentration camps was and is that there is no attempt made to make the acts noble or for that matter to justify them in any way. On the other hand, self-sacrifice, suffering, all manner of socially beneficial (individually so) acts have nothing whatsoever to do with the noble. They cannot be considered in relation to this word. I would personally think that much the same thing could be said of 'righteousness' and its intended concept although here the implications are even more involved. Oedipus was actually less noble, for many reasons, than was Creon and he was also less righteous. What he was eventually was something a great deal more human, more understandable than either the idea of nobility or righteousness, i.e. humble. Here I think of Achilles and I try to understand him as a noble man but that is not what I think of. It is of course, via Jaeger, 'areté' and that in itself is a great deal more than noble.

But another idea comes with that of the 'just crime'. The paradox suggested by the words themselves is not the least interesting feature. Right off I get the idea of justice versus crime and I see that it must be either one or the other. The just crime of course depends on an ironic interpretation of 'crime', i.e., it is not a crime, they only think so. The act itself as realized by the person who performs it has nothing to do with what he believes to be crime. It is rigidly opposed to it and hence he states it as an ironic paradox, a just crime. Taken literally, a just crime does not exist. Taken figuratively, you come across it every day. To take Melville at his word, of course when the 'tyrant' (injustice) rules, 'the good

heart (which I oppose to the rigmarole of the tyrant which he uses intellectu-
ally to justify himself in opposition to the wisdom of the heart) whose patriot
(he is of course thinking of his people, the real country) fire leaps to a deed of
startling note (see Fourth of July), do it, then flinch?' Of course not. Because
what the good heart proposes is not a crime but an act of the most basic justice,
i.e., a democratic act intended to bring good to the many not the one as would
an act which conformed with the tyrant's idea of justice.) What has this to do
with crime? I mean the kind of crime I visualize when I read a report of it in
the newspapers? Nothing. The just crime then begins with the idea of itself as
the very opposite of crime and its success depends on its being considered by
a sufficiently large number of people (sufficient for the 'actor', that is) as a 'just
crime'. The 'evil grit' has also another purpose which is not that of the good
'grit's.' I do not believe for a moment that Melville would like to consider a basic
comparison between the 'grit' of a homicidal maniac or even a pick-pocket and
the 'grit' of an intended self-styled patriot, Booth, for example. The two are
distinctly separate. As for the dictators of our own country, noble men would
not assassinate them and I doubt that even good men would. I recently read
an article on the concentration camps by Hannah Arendt which spoke of the
necessity of destroying the 'juridical' sense in man as a means of rendering him
fit for totalitarian society. What prevents action of this sort is of course that very
same sense coupled with a moral one. So that to kill a dictator is to kill the idea
of justice itself. 'The mills of the gods grind slowly but they grind exceedingly
small' or something. The idea that justice since it is thought of as an absolute by
many will eventually exert itself prevents one from using injustice (the tak-
ing of a man's life whoever he is) to aid it. During the war and in many other
instances it was necessary to destroy the idea of the Germans or the Japanese
as human beings in order to facilitate their destruction. I could not kill a man
(flesh and blood and heart) but I could kill a Nazi. An idea also demonstrated
in that article that human nature can be changed and man destroyed before he
is actually dead makes the just crime seem remote since it removes the sphere
of justice and injustice from its place as an absolute governing realm to that of
a parlor game. For example, the prisoners in the german concentration camps
represented roughly three layers or better four. Criminals, politicals, Jews
and people. In the case of the first two and even the third there was in part a
knowledge of something done by the prisoner that had caused him to be placed
in a concentration camp. The politicals, although their 'crimes' were certainly
not so easily grasped by themselves, could at least use their beliefs as a means to
understanding the reason for their being there. And the Jews had also at least
a part of this understanding, they were Jews, hence . . . But the people who had
none of these classifications had the problem with no possible solution. So long

as a man has done something, he can understand or at least fabricate a reason for his being subjected to all manner of horror. The juridical sense in him will grasp his action as a means of explanation. But when there has been no such action the juridical sense is blocked and can be destroyed. The fact that the Nazis used vague and shifting classifications for the inmates of their concentration camps is evidence of their appreciation of the necessity to avoid giving the prisoners a means of orienting themselves in a juridical sense. Also, the people were at the bottom and usually the criminals were at the top of the prisoner society and for a while at least Communists were given the rule but primarily (according to Arendt) because the criminals were utterly useless as leaders. To go on, the mass executions fall into the pattern as a way of producing evidence of the fact that justice and man and reasons are equally superfluous. Remember that at that time the bestial element had gone and that the men in charge of the operations, executions, were for all intents and purposes as sane and as normal as you or I. We could not understand their actions in terms of pathology. I would strongly suggest that you read this article (Last PR) because I have only paraphrased a brief part of it which I thought came in here. Consider then, the idea of no crime, no justice, only the violent act. Melville's idea of it becomes the expression of a strong individual in an age where he sees what he believes to be social evils, etc. There would be little 'crime' connected to their righting. As for the 'taboo murder', etc., that is something else again which relates to the symbolic strength of justice and depends on reference to an abstract force. Because the people have a diverted (through 'priests', etc.) relation to it, they are not in a position to consider it as right or wrong provided that they have an implicit, unshakeable belief in its machinery. If they should happen to distrust the 'priest' as a representative, I don't think the sacrifices would be so easily performed because they wouldn't be 'right'. But the dissatisfaction would still be with the priest and not with the sacrifice. As for 'he who lives by the sword shall die be the sword'; usually, but again an assumption which can hardly be justified as anything abruptly actual. Certainly the converse doesn't make much sense.

I suppose I have purposely avoided what you intended by the quotations, etc. It's due not so much to the fact that I dislike Melville's poetry (which I do) but more particularly to my own attempt to posit my sincerely believed 'fact' that we can no longer consider a concept so inextricably romantic as that of the 'just crime'. Notice that you assign its implications to the pathological and noble men. Do either exist for you? I understand personally neither the feelings or implicit motivations of the pathological nor of the noble man. To be noble has come for me to mean to do something which is considered for arbitrary reasons noble and it has nothing specifically to do with causes. The romantic is not to be discarded in toto but the almost pseudo-religious intentions which the generally romantic can have is what I myself have come to dislike. I have read that Lawrence was one of the most religious men of our time and if I divorce my attention from a consideration of his style I would consider him what is generally called a 'romantic'. But what is different is Lawrence's self-destructive attempt to deal <u>specifically</u> with the problem which is of course what no romantic can ever do. Yet what I admire in Lawrence is particularly the intense sincerity and ceaseless warfare against the general classification and his attempt to make actual what was at best a poorly apprehended generalization, i.e., love. Lawrence's characterization of love between men and women is certainly one (taken as a concept, though unattached to Lawrence's particular recasting of it) which has served the romantics better than any other. What I intend here is to produce the problem of the specific, the actual, versus its abstraction to a realm where it can be dealt with at leisure. The existentialists speak of a world in which man alone is responsible; the world of choice. But what makes them sound often impotent is for me at least the fact that they have intellectualized an immediate and forceful way of life. When for example Heidegger (via Sartre) says that nothingness is the constitutive structure of the existent my understanding of his words produces an activity that is desperate in the extreme. For if I can posit the idea of a world I can also negate it which is of course to produce the eventual statement that nothingness, and so forth. To believe this is to believe that the action has to be continual and constantly performed or nothingness will be constant. I do A, I reflect on A, I achieve the ability to posit A in a relation to myself and my world, I can then negate A. So the process has to be continued. But all this I know absolutely nothing about and can say nothing about. I read elsewhere that Malraux (of whom I have read nothing except a dialogue between him and Burnham having to do with the 'THIRD FORCE') 'was the first to introduce French contemporary culture to the themes that have come to be popularized under the label of 'existentialism'. Apparently he is of the opinion that if one chooses to involve oneself in an action, one cannot withdraw. Now consider a world which if not ours is at least close enough to cause apprehension where forlornness, anguish and so on are our fate because of our existential nature, i.e., because we are to define ourselves through what we choose to act. The positing of a 'to be or not to be' in terms of a noble act of violence becomes at once a treachery and a devastatingly unreal question. I know what are perhaps my immediate needs and I understand something of their nature. But they do not constitute my reality because my reality is that which I am able to project into meaning. On the other hand, the meaning must be actual in relation to these needs which I deny to be my reality. I cannot sell bathtubs to savages nor accept one if I have no plumbing. So although the problem is not that of putting 'real toads into imaginary gardens', it is not to write a 'sex' poem about a political comment. Cf. Yeats in last poems,

the one prompted by a speech of Thomas Mann's. It is the paradox of posit-
ing the imaginary as real in connection with the real as a possible imaginary
fact. Sartre commits the beautiful to the imaginary and pronounces the 'real'
world as one which produces nausea and disgust after it is returned to from the
imaginary. But the problem is not particularly to create an imaginary world like
that of a schizophrenic but to contain the imaginary in relation to the real. To
sing in the bathtub if you like but to include the bathtub in the singing. What
confused me this winter was the realization that Communism is effective both
in achieving its own ends and more particularly in offering immediate solu-
tions. But if you'll read Sorokin on any of these current political institutions,
United Nations included, it will I think convince you of the absolute fallacy of
the 'right' government. To be an altruist is my hope, both naive and sincere.
And to constitute my reality in relation to it is what I hope to do as a writer.
Violence is productive of violence and I deny it absolutely. You must read this as
what I began writing a little while ago and what I never thought would end up
as this. I see that I can't begin to include a description of my own beliefs or even
the idea of what my intentions are and yet both are necessary for an adequate
discussion of the problem brought up by the 'just crime'. Which I see has a suf-
ficient effect on me as an 'understandable' concept to get me excited. You should
have stopped several pages ago.

I'm afraid that I won't be able to meet you in Boston as planned but the train
does come to Littleton after many stops so if you could tell us when we'd
arrange to meet you there. Give us some idea and we'll meet you without fail.

All our best,
Bob

. . .

LETTER TO WILLIAM CARLOS WILLIAMS

Littleton, N.H.
February 11, 1950

Dear Dr. Williams,

This letter will be in some sense an intrusion, since it will assume that you
will have time to read it and to give some thought to the request which it will
make. Its only excuse is the fact of your own work and interest in poetry.

To be brief, I'd like to ask you for your help with respect to a magazine I'd
like to get going some time this summer. The magazine will attempt these
things: (1) to provide an outlet for prose, poetry & critical work and to present
it in a way that will avoid undue emphasis on the writers' present position in
the literary hierarchy; (2) to present criticism which reinforces understanding

of the poetry & prose used and to have the latter serve as a demonstration of the attitudes implicit in the critical work; (3) to have the magazine's entity as a critical attitude be coherent and recognizable to its readers. I don't know if this is enough, or too much, for a magazine's 'general program' but it's the only one which occurs to me as being of any practical use. I know I have little liking for magazines that don't use such a program and since I find myself about to edit one, no other policy falls to hand.

In any event, whatever you yourself might be able to contribute, prose or poetry, would be very gratefully received. To be frank, I've put myself to school with your work, can think of very few others who've written verse comparable to your own, and would be honored to have you represented in the magazine. The only thing I don't like is the need to couple that appreciation with a request for a contribution.

Yours sincerely,
Robert Creeley
Robert Creeley

. . .

LETTER TO WILLIAM CARLOS WILLIAMS

February 27, 1950

Dear Dr. Williams,

Very, very glad to have your letter, i.e., it helps. At this point it gets to be a question of material, what I can get hold of, and being here, away from the centers, real or imagined, it's a problem. I don't know how much of it one can do with letters but at least those I've sent have brought answers of varying sorts. And it's to the point to mention that people like yourself and Wallace Stevens are freer with their reputations than those who are still worried about being printed in Harper's, etc. Anyhow, things move a little.

The idea, or better, what I take as the idea of any of this, has much to do with the flabbiness of PR and magazines like PR. And on that score, it's a question of having a magazine that has the nucleus I mentioned in the last letter, that much anyhow, which will have to depend on demonstration to get around the sounding generalities involved in talking about it. I'm acquainted with some of the West Coast magazines where I'm told 'poetic activity is humming, etc.' and would agree that this, simply this, isn't much to the point, if at all to the point. The kind of outlet which they maintain, which they maintain they maintain, is of the kind that comes up, usually, when A or B can't get printed, etc., and so print themselves, this leading to an eventual distortion of their own position, the old dead end. Anyhow, not that.

To begin with, I spent some time the last week, looking over what little mags

I have here, in an attempt to work something out of them, to learn, one way or the other, what was good or bad about any of them or all of them. Briefly, it comes to this; that magazines like WAKE, etc., come to little because of no center, no point, if you will, beyond a collection of 'available' material, printed without much of an eye as to why A should come after B, and so on. And this leads to embarrassment all around. An instance, or so it seemed to me: the kind of eclecticism that prompts the HUDSON REVIEW to print Valery, Stanislaus Joyce, & some comment on Ezra Pound all in one issue. Here missing, that Valery may be grouped verbally with Joyce et alii, but suffers in being printed even with an indirect representation of this other next to him. It comes to the kind of logic that would delight in a big fat book, Dostoyevsky, Mann, Shakespeare, etc. etc., all under one cover. Or like the college intelligence that points with some pride to a course on Proust, Mann, & Joyce with, by way of an introduction, Eliot's Wasteland. I can remember with some pleasure Prof. Levin's progress through this particular instance. Anyhow, this is an indication of what poor editing can amount to, what incongruities can be found.

So, on the other hand, I would find in magazines like KENYON, etc., at least a very shrewd & usually able, at least for their own purposes, editorial hand. Here everything blends, if you will, and alien & conflicting criticism is never less at home, nor more crude, than when allowed in, by way of a 'fair' represen-tation of both sides of the question. In any event, this kind of worldliness is to the point, that being, to have some apprehension of what you have got on your hands and what you can do with it. And is a means of survival, this kind of editing, preserving its bridges, as it does, establishing attitudes.

To get back to my own problems, and about money, means in general: this thing began by way of a suggestion to a friend of mine who had just got himself a printing press in Pa., that he, having the means, use them to print a magazine. For the past five or so years, this had been an idea we'd both had, and beyond the usual college friendships, etc., I would say he and one or two others would be those I still have and not by way of the usual college friendships, etc. This beside the point, but to suggest some knowledge of each other, etc., and what we might be up to. Anyhow, this much of his letter would be to the point here: ' . . . an immediate limited objective to start with, though 'no point of view', no attitude to start with. For the prose and poetry—selected by taste and if anything real was being talked about in the critical selection. The p & p could not help but have some relevance & connection to it—or rather vice versa . . . ' This being the idea of demonstrating rather than beginning with a problematic manifesto that will limit any kind of development that comes from the act of editing, the act of selection. It doesn't imply a literal lack of attitude, since the act of selection is a demonstration of attitude, like it or not.

So far as qualifications go, he worked with printers for some time, both of us have had stints on college magazines (the Harvard Wake, mine being at the laying away of E. E. Cummings), both of us are now busy with work other than literary and if this last isn't a necessary qualification, it helps. He's doing butchering, etc., for a locker plant, deep-freezing, and I am a poultry man of sorts when not writing, etc. I don't know if this is to the point, any of it, but I mention it by way of getting to, again, the source of my own discontent with current little mags, and the reasons, again, why I'd undertake to introduce another. Many things annoy me in the former, that is, the insular criticism, the literary tone, the 'littleness' of much that they print. Since I have my own concerns with poetry, I don't read with much pleasure the many instances of impacted imagery, for lack of a better name, I hit; all the images, all the words. Little or no force, little or no reason. Not simply to disparage, but to suggest, to insist that this level of verse isn't an end, to be aimed at, to be 'representative'. And the implications of a 'return to form', being in that sense a 'going back', and not, as it must be, a development, invention, new use. And language, or a dichotomy of language as it now is, split & emasculated. Where criticism is a kind of witty implication of value, that may, or may not, exist. What is all this, anyhow, that being about it. And at least that much for impetus.

So you say 'how in the hell can you do it'. What else is there to do? Giving up this isn't simple, although waited, like they say, long enough. And also like they say, now is the time, etc.

So for now, it's the problem of getting material, getting enough to be able to work it into a first issue, to be able to demonstrate some of that assumed taste, etc. To make it an evidence. There are, as there would be, one or two, I can get work from, which I'd want to print. But to make it into something that can be noticed in point of size is a little more difficult. I don't want it unwieldy, but 60 or so pages or a little less, would give room for everything and not be too big or too little. Something you could pick up. Summer is still the time we'd like to publish a first issue. I think we can make it. Anyhow, your own interest goes for something here. And your advice.

Forgive me for taking so long with this. I suspect that you are busier than you say, having had doctors and nurses in the family. They are busy people. So again thank you for taking the time to write; should welcome a letter whenever you can find time for it. And should add that either poetry or prose will be very welcome.

Yours sincerely,
Robert Creeley

· · ·

Monday [ca. February 1950]

Dear Larry,

Your letter at hand, and much obliged. I'll try to go into some of this, while there's time. To begin with, 'logic' has this sense for me, applied to poetry, or most anything for that matter, this sense beyond its philosophic and/or academic, though the meanings overlap: Logic is the demonstration by a poem of its meaning. It is, in other words, simply the means by which a poem makes known its sense as opposed to its rhythm or its use of vowels or its visual aspect, if you will. But this is, at least for the most part, sophistry. And logic can be put as the direction of thought in a poem. So that a poem concerned with having the reader consider the plight of the bumblebee would in all probability run counter to its own logic, if bumblebees weren't mentioned. It's an arbitrary use of judgement to speak of a poem's logic as though we had the right to determine it; better, it will be ours to appraise if we will, as we find it in the poem. It goes back to <u>logos</u> which would imply both <u>word</u> & <u>reason</u>, this from the dictionary.

About writing verse or anything else for that matter, I would say that you can find about any approach you might use condoned, encouraged, or as you will, somewhere. That is, a few years ago now Horace Gregory advised me, on the basis of a few minutes conversation, to set myself the work of writing in the strictest verse forms I could find, without making an attempt to express profundities, etc. I can't say that I did that, but at least, I've worked in a variety of forms from time to time, with the logic that it would be to the point to have a technique capable enough to write in any form I might need for what I wanted to write; this to avoid being contained by a form, rather than having the form contain one's thought, as an instrument of expression. On the other hand, the development of one's thought and by this I mean no more than an apprehension of what is around us, how it relates, what one has to deal with, here, that seems no less important. And a too-ready grip of form allows for a kind of technical virtuosity that must always embarrass sincerity. Here, it is difficult to say what I mean by such a use of form without seeming to encourage slack or incompetent poetry, that suffers from lack of form, or from a lack of familiarity with verse forms and technique generally. It's just that a preoccupation with form, a preoccupation that excludes the building of the form with the building of an idea's expression in the mind, that makes the form dominate the sense (simply), isn't good. Like virtuosity in general, it results in shallowness. I think this would be the best way of putting it, in terms of analogy; with virtuosity in any field.

About rhyming: the mention of 'Clementine' with 'time', etc. This in spite of what the school may have told you is as good a rhyme as any, since it has its uses, like any, and they can be well used or misused. You will see what you've done is to depend on your vowel sounds for your sense of rhyme. The 'i' sound in each, and as is the case here, the consonants modify this sound. This is what's called <u>assonance</u>. And is often used to avoid heaviness, a banging, sometimes got by an overuse of strict rhyme. For example, in Yeats:

> One had a lovely face,
> And two or three had charm.
> But charm and face were in vain
> Because the mountain grass
> Cannot but keep the form
> Where the mountain hare has lain.

Here, you see, assonance is used to keep off the 'end' of the poem, before it occurs, and so he saves the pure rhyme for his final one, i.e. lain & vain. And in this poem, for example, since it is a kind of questioning, and that sense of movement, query, it has its justification, for shifting, a little, as it goes. And the use of assonance has its effect. But in the case of a different intention, as would be almost all of Pope, for example, assonance would destroy the completeness of the couplets, and would in turn weaken the intended patness of the statements. For example, a little learning, etc., would not be an epigram in the sense that it is, a kind of circle, complete unto itself, if we found anything but <u>spring</u> or a word like it, in sound, rhyming with <u>thing</u>. So you see that assonance has its uses, but can also have its misuses. The latter often occur in relation to assonance <u>in</u> the line itself, that being, when a word in the line is made to rhyme in terms of vowel sounds with the end word, or a word in the following line, and so on. Often a poet, caught by the sound of a word he is using for a rhyme will use it unconsciously, its sound, that is, in a word following it, and unless it is conscious and deliberate and used with an apprehensible purpose it will irritate the reader's ear. As usual, it will be the use which determines whether or not it is 'right', schools notwithstanding.

About Basic: it's to the point to memorize the list. That is, you'll do it anyhow if you use it. I don't think one should let it be a <u>limit</u> in the sense that one should exclude other words from one's speech, at least, not for a general rule. What Basic can serve is the purpose of breaking down into unavoidably clear words what may confuse in the state of the language in which we find it; for example, Richards' translations of Aristotle into Basic read with a wonderful clarity and openness of thought that all of Aristotle's translators garbled. So where we can put Basic to work is in those cases where we are concerned with understanding the exact meaning of each word & phrase as we come to it. Now this, paradoxically enough, is not always the case in poetry, for example, nor in prose. Hart Crane can't be read word for word. Meaning there depends on the color or, better, the sound of the words as much as it does on their denotative sense. And in poetry generally, we'd destroy the connotative sense by translating into Basic. And to this, would be to destroy much of the poem's intention. Anyhow, as a critical instrument, Basic has its uses, but like anything else, it needs care.

Would like very much to see you whenever you can get up. The farm, or as much of a farm as it is, at this point, doesn't take much of my time. Just enough to keep me busy when I give up on the writing, etc. We are building up a breeding flock of several varieties of poultry, or Barred Rocks, Rhode Island Reds, Buff Leghorns, and Partridge Wyandottes in the big birds and then in the bantams, Partridge Wyandottes again, and the Reds, then Silkies. Also have geese and pigeons, and these last are Pigmy Pouters & Pensom Rollers. When I read on Cid's program, my business in Boston was, simply, the Boston Poultry Show. The idea here is to build a good stock flock of birds for exhibition. And that's what we're doing. Here, the winters are too cold for commercial poultry to do very well, that is, eggs & broilers, etc. And the soil is about as bad in its own way as the winters, a kind of gravel. We have a fair-sized garden, but just for our own needs. And at the moment we're negotiating for a milking goat, not having the capital for a cow at this point. As usual, it's a question of survival. The poultry sells for good prices, anywhere up to $100, they tell me, for a good show bird, and about $25 and up for good Pigmies. And about $15 a pair for the Rollers, and a goose will get you $15 for meat, much less for show. So it's one way of doing things. And it's a lot of fun.

By way of other things, I'm 23 and have a wife and son, aged 2 and some, and here we all are, like they say. And would like to see you anytime.

And is 'Wallace Stevens literally America's greatest poet'? I don't know, that is, these final judgements on my part would be irony. Not thinking much of that kind of criticism. But Stevens I like very much indeed. And Williams. And a few others. It's hard to say.

So that would be it for now. And will hope to hear from you when you have the time. All best,

    Bob

P.S. By way of the little magazines and WAKE, in particular. WAKE began in Harvard some years ago, now, and then about 2 years ago was taken out, at first to be subsidized by NEW DIRECTIONS, the publishing house, but that fell through, so it published a few sporadic issues, and has now settled down to publishing once or twice a year, depending when its editors, Villa, and Lawrence, are there to see to it. It prints a number of good things, this I'm obliged to say, by way of acknowledgement of their kindness to me, but there is no center, that is, everything thrown in altogether with no coherent editorial policy. And by way of contradicting Cid, though I haven't seen a recent issue, POETRY is a kind of sloppy magazine in itself. That is, there is an awful lot of slop in it. By this I mean not much more than an antipathy to verse, removed only by a very little from the 'moon'-'June' school. Cid tells me that Karl Shapiro is about or is editing it, and this to my mind, is the kiss of death. Cid and I, incidentally, disagree violently on this one issue. And I think you'd find better poetry in almost any other magazine, this for a general level, if you will, and not to deny that POETRY may print some very good work. But watch their minor poets, so-called, because that's where they begin to smell. This, too, not to suggest they can't make mistakes and print something very good. But it's no rule. And having my own interest in these things, would say KENYON, for both prose & poetry, and then in a letter from William Carlos Williams about the magazine he says: 'There are several new magazines, new little magazines on—not the market because they don't sell—but circulating in the mails. Look up IMAGI especially and POETRY: NEW YORK, etc. etc.' So perhaps you could try those.

. . .

LETTER TO EZRA POUND

Littleton, N.H.
April 14, 1950

Dear Mr. Pound,
    Very grateful for your letter.
    A few random comments: I'm very interested in your thought, E. P.'s, as to what this quarterly might come to, get at. I.e., these concerns, intentions, a demonstration of both, <u>can't</u> be found anywhere that I can think of, certainly <u>not</u> where they should be. I had yesterday a letter from Mr. Horton about this same thing, and have written him to this same purpose, i.e., I am interested but, simply, confusion coming from the fact that I <u>don't know</u>, as what 'member' of my recent 'school' does, i.e., Harvard, etc., what's this to them. Hence: a confusion about <u>Del Mar</u>, since this was the only thing Mr. Horton gave me to go on. Your letter makes what I had thought seem correct, but it's a favor you could do me, ~~(wait a minute—this name comes back—1800's—forgive this random method, but I'm trying to get to this anyhow;~~ help me with this; I'd be grateful. You see, what it comes to, here, in any event. To get on, I have written Dr. Williams about permission to reprint his note on Eliot which I found in FOUR PAGES; this to serve as another evidence of his good sense and an occasion for making a point of FOUR PAGES on the fact of its revival and, too, to serve as example for what can be found there. This seems to the point. If he's willing, I'll write Simpson, etc. The size of the magazine will be about 40–50 pages. That is, more is not to the point both for your reason and by reason of the work involved

in setting type, etc. For that space, then, I intend the following: space for current poetry & prose, that finds a place in my own taste, etc. That is, I w'd agree that a magazine like IMAGI, though by no means like HUDSON, as Horton suggests, can carry a lot of the weight here. In the matter of prose very damn little is or has been done. Then, too, the matter of an adequate representation of the people involved, i.e., the matter of longer poems which seem to be an anathema for most now current. There is not enough 'room'—that is, it's to the point to make 'room' for those who merit it. I take the consequences of my own taste, etc., here. I ask no one to share this. But, this leaves a good deal of room for critical prose, for reprints that are needed, for a concern with what you want to see in it. Then: a first issue is planned for midsummer, possibly before. The job of setting and printing taking the time it does, material has to be in in a fairly short time. Then: what use can I be to you, for this issue now. Have you anything there or do you know of anything that I could make use of for this first issue. I see no reason why current poetry and prose should not be printed in the company you suggest. I.e., a direct and deliberate representation of those concerns will make a way for getting at what these 'examples' imply, this current work. The mind that can get at the one can get to the other. Does this seem reasonable. I have no wish for the critical material to run beyond or counter to what the other work shows, but if this latter fails there, it comes to finding what doesn't. That can be done. Anyhow, I'd be very grateful to hear more. Let me say, too, that the 'tradition' by way of Eliot, I could never get to; by way of Pound, it came to the only way. Williams, as well as Pound, has shown what's of use. Williams would make it <u>now</u>, the insistence on this that's here; I can't betray my belief in that. Then: what can be a demonstration of both these concerns. I don't think one need belie the other, etc. I can't see how an actual concern with one doesn't come to a concern with the other. But this may be my own way of thinking. <u>Two</u> things seem of importance, (1) the getting back to what we've lost by way of the universities & 'Winchell's employers'; (2) the maintenance of outlets for what is now worth print. We can't expect anyone to find what <u>they</u> want in any of this, i.e., 'many years of reading have not made you wise' or how could they, that alone, etc. But to give (1) the basis for the concern by explanation, example, and demonstration; (2) to make evidences of what is and has been of import there for one to get at (by reprints, etc.); (3) by the fact of that belief coming to more than words and more words—this to point to what now groans as concern (verbiage, etc., obfuscation, etc.); (4) to mean to make sense as Pound, Williams, have for the past 40 years, etc., to give room, always to that speed: what would this come to. More than much that I now see. The keynote, or what you will, the 'reason' for FOUR PAGES making elemental sense for anyone, like it or not, <u>is</u> the fact of its method coupled with its concern. So many ways of saying anything; and damn few saying it.

So, please write about anything that can now be of use, for this first issue. That seems the first step, etc. Thanks again for the help.

Best—

Robert Creeley

. . .

LETTER TO WILLIAM CARLOS WILLIAMS

Littleton, N.H.

April 15, 1950

Dear Dr. Williams,

I'm very grateful for your letter, the permission, etc., but much more for this evidence of your faith. I hope that I can make it. It's hard, now, even useless, to go into all the reasons that come into the one for why I attempt any of this. Perhaps, not much more than a vanity or even pride. That I could help, etc. That I could be of use. Here, it's a very lonely place; the few people we live with, that we see, are farmers and lumbermen. For the last few years it's been what we've been concerned with. I grew up on a farm, so this comes to hand. There's no language lacking. And, of course, with the chickens, etc., going around to the shows, and once in a while, helping with the birds, I get to a sense of what language can be, what, even, it must be. I couldn't live here if my own language wasn't whole. They'd shoot me. So 'attacks'—they couldn't come to anything that would matter. Because these people, these others, have lost that sense, altogether, of what makes language whole, the reason, the sense.

Then, to be attacked, granted, 'we who have nothing to lose', can only come to at least some thinking about what is being attacked. Even that would make a dent. Would make the beginning of a 'point'.

During the last few weeks the correspondence with Ezra Pound and D. Pound, etc., has come to this: his concern with what makes false history. 'You would very considerably revive him if he thought you would align your quarterly in the fight against the smother, and against the pollution of the whole of U.S. thought by Luce and the 'lesser Lice . . . the REAL american culture . . . ' I come back to your own comment in Letter To An Australian Editor in a past issue of BRIARCLIFFE QUARTERLY, i.e., beyond, perhaps, a simple aping of your thought, the thought to be found in the above makes the tragedy, that forgets the nature of the reality which we now face, that thinks these single men in the past hold all that is of use to us now. But that this kind of intensity is needed, god knows, seems much more than reasonable. Reading this past week, (1) The Serious Artist, (2) Meditations, and then (3) A Retrospect. 'Mr. Yeats has once and for all stripped English poetry of its perdamnable rhetoric . . . ' . But it grows fast, no matter how often its dug up. But there it would be; the immense use, the overwhelming intensity. Who could match it. It may be useless to expect now something like that. For what, I expect, would be a good question. If one could only shift that attention to full center—to get it to bear on what is here, now, I'll bet they'd run for cover. And yet, it comes to how much do the younger of us expect a right to from a tired man; it comes time for us to make some sense. Beyond the watering down of methods, the borrowings, etc. To come into our own intensity. Then, it comes to not being able to stop any of this. The friend who wrote the letter I make use of in the 'Comment' writes as well: why be concerned with 'clearing the air' when you should be concerned with giving 'a new substance'. And yet to stretch that, the air comes first. But better than they should come together. What my own writing can come to now is, perhaps, a method, a means. Nothing final, certainly, nothing ever final in their dried sense if I can help. Conclusions have their own betrayal. Anyhow, this now seems the point, what can be done.

The connection with Simpson can be something, I think, provided I keep my head, as it were. Their kind of insistence, granted, certainly, its point, is apt to include a smothering of my own. But that I have a good deal of respect for the past issues, and the effort, etc., they make, is true enough; so I think that reason enough for them to make use of me and I of them. I think perhaps the fact that Pound is the intermediary will keep both of us in line.

Anyhow, take it that right now I do get scared, and can suffer little beyond that, the pressures of selecting material, trying to find it, trying to make the whole thing come to sense. A little viciousness would be, even, a relief from the rather honest pain I've given some of the contributors, when I have sent back their work, trying to say something, etc., about it. The nightmare of trying to make my own sense; it couldn't get worse, and if I'm wrong, I'm wrong now, not when they tell me. And if not, then to hell with what they say.

Thanks again for your help.

All best to you,
Robert Creeley

· · ·

LETTER TO CID CORMAN

Sunday [April 23, 1950]

Dear Cid,

Your letters, and the CRISIS & GRYPHON, and the other letters, yesterday. And many thanks for all of these. The past few days had brought a few discouragements, or perhaps not much more than the to be expected 'doubts', etc. In any event, these got me back to it.

Anyhow, let me try to get a little sense here. I have your own intent to get to a clear appraisal of these things. Perhaps, first of all, to get to the 'they' to whom Williams was referring. You will know of Williams' belief in the need to make use of the currents, of language, of method, that are closest to hand, this in the sense of 'environment', what we live with, closest to. What we are, beyond what general pattern of belief, etc., might get us to by way of possibilities. And you will know, too, of Williams' insistence on <u>new</u> forms, new progressions, in terms of what is now around us. To this point: general language. But perhaps I can get beyond it by coming to the question of enemies, and why he, or I, would take them to be such. For example, you say these 'enemies' or, here, the little magazines like PR, even KENYON, are those who back the people which either Williams or I, might back. What, then, is the difference sufficient to make us enemies? It comes to the question of <u>use</u>, the use to which this 'interest' is put. For what purpose. So far, so good, i.e., to see these people in print is certainly a point. But, now we come to the 'interests'. Does this seem well-grounded to you? A poem, story, etc., will have, certainly, its individual effect, no matter where it appears, i.e., Stevens in Vogue, etc., has, certainly, his effect as Stevens, etc. But, now, what <u>is</u> this effect in relation to the magazine, etc., the purposes, etc., to which this magazine is committed? I take it as naiveté, to believe that Vogue, etc., is committed to a policy which makes clear their own attempt to publish <u>good</u> verse. I w'd have my own thought, that much more is involved than this, i.e., an attempt to maintain a 'tone', to 'satisfy' certain conditions of what is necessary to maintain this tone of 'tolerant intellectualism' mixed with a taste for good, expensive dress. So then, taking the idea that to publish someone's work, at best, can indicate a belief in the method, the concerns, implicit in it—we come to the reverse, which would be—to publish in a magazine, <u>for the usual reader</u>, means to agree with the editorial policy implicit in that magazine's behavior. Now this may seem even idiotic to you, or I, who know the difficulties of getting into any magazine, but I think we can both see that for someone not interested in these difficulties, etc., that such an assumption w'd be possible. And, for example, when the poetry, etc., doesn't come to any explicit statement to the contrary, what else could be supposed. The use to which much of Auden's work has been put in these past two years, and Stevens, etc., will show you some of what I mean. I.e., there has been an attempt, often as blundering as any attempt to make use of things without having a concern or an understanding of them may be, still there has been an attempt to include good art, or instances of it, in a deliberately maintained level of <u>false</u> art, art <u>calculated</u> to deal with a specific demand, related, directly, to commercial standards. Now, to go into the matter of PR, & KENYON, I think you'll know enough of each of these magazines, certainly the first, to find my thought not too far-fetched, i.e., that each of these magazines has a very coherent editorial policy, one which can be got to by reading half a dozen issues of either. Now take, first, the case of PR, and why I take them to be very actual enemies. Politically, PR is dedicated to the usual disillusion of the usual Marxist, after the facts of the past 10 years, and the developments of certain aspects of the Marxist tenets, to a point which makes them capable of individual existence, i.e., witness the many rifts, etc., among the current Marxists, and the very bitter chasm between the Stalinists & the 'Marxists' now bitterly opposed to this use of the original tenets. Now, to bring this attitude into a system of evaluation, into a basis for critical observation, etc., is, perhaps, not immediately recognizable as the destructive force it, in all actuality, is. But where we can first get to it is in the method, the way the language is put to use—there it betrays itself, and all the emotional bitterness, vindictiveness, etc., comes to bear. Then, too, the attitude, given its original orientation, is one which must have definite, prescribed limits; it cannot come to the work in hand without having, already, plotted the extent to which that work can possibly effect it. Now this may seem like a mild form of insanity on my part; but I commit myself to it, nonetheless. I do not think we can ignore, ever, the nature of the criticism a magazine prints, since that will be, always, the explicit demonstration of the magazine's way of getting to value in any given instance of art. Now, does it seem that the intelligences which put such vindictive limits on criticism in any issue of PR can differ from the ones, which in the same magazine, give us, now and then, examples of art worth our time & trouble? I can't think this, nor can I think, even less, that these intelligences relapse into acquiescence when they come to judge work for any given issue; I believe that work printed by PR is printed no less deliberately than the criticism; I believe that this work is intended to maintain the precepts of the criticism, even in such unlikely instances as Williams' poetry. Such a magazine must recognize that people like Williams, etc., are too much of a force to be ignored; but, if by including them, they can seem to be concerned with the values these men represent, they are free of the battle of fighting overtly against these values, and can 'by-pass' and so get to their own concerns, without running too much of a risk. Because one book review of Williams' poetry, or of Stevens', can undo the very slight foothold these men can get by an occasional appearance. Remember: [William] Phillips & [Philip] Rahv, etc., are there all the time; the others very rarely.

In all of this: I don't think we should lose sight of the grip criticism now has on all creative work. I think it of supreme importance to bring again into focus Pound's idea of the critic to be found in Date Line in MAKE IT NEW. That is, the literary hierarchy is just as powerful as it ever was. Certain instances of supposed tolerance shouldn't be mistaken for the rule. They are not. Witness the fact of the 'new' writers PR usually prints. That will get you to the 'facts' in my assumption. KENYON is no less to be suspected, though, I grant you, lacking the very strong political overtones of PR, their method doesn't seem as bitter.

But: witness, if you can get hold of it, Ransom's <u>method</u> in the Winter 1945 issue, in relation to Savage, etc., whom I certainly don't commend, etc., but <u>see</u> how it is done. That is what keeps me awake nights. That's what makes me distrust KENYON, i.e., they aren't interested in the development of individual artists, or in the development of any group. They are interested in the maintenance of a deliberate and perfectly coherent critical method, confined, as it must be, by the ideas of Ransom on everything imaginable, to be put together, eventually, with the more rash, and consequently, more overtly stupid, pronunciamentos of Tate. Don't watch a man when he's judging something 100 years dead, in time; because he may fool you, having the benefit of the 'tradition.' Watch what he says on what's at hand; if he can't come to sense there, or if his method reveals itself as definitely limited for purposes having nothing to do with its subject, then, dammit, shoot.

So, as you might suspect, we come, at last, to Thomas Sterns Eliot, etc. What's wrong with T. S. I'll tell you one thing that's damn wrong, and that's his values as they exist now, and as he attempts to apply them. I know, certainly, that Eliot's work, in the past, is of immense value for anyone who wants to take the time to go into it. I certainly have. <u>But</u> when a man who <u>up to this point</u> has driven the car very nicely begins to go all over the road, we do not let him keep his seat. We kick him to hell out before we <u>all</u> crash. We don't let him go on, in the case of Eliot, representing us, <u>since</u> he was once able to. Hence: Eliot, insofar as his methods concern us <u>now</u>, as he <u>now</u> attempts to have them concern us, hasn't the slightest reason for being spared anything, short of actual murder. He should be revealed, completely, for what he is; he should be stripped publicly; he should be made to account for every one of his subsequent moves. I know, I know, I know, the danger this has for his past work—this certainly seems to me great, i.e., the fact that any attack, now, may confuse the values to be found in the past criticism & poetry. But we cannot allow this man to go on as he is going, without making a substantial attack on his method. This is what Williams was commending in my own COMMENT—this is not, perhaps, the substantial attack I have in mind. I would rather see that effected by <u>counter</u> demonstration; that would seem much more to the point. But since Williams' criticism is that <u>counter</u> demonstration, I'll certainly make use of it, when I can.

So we come to the younger. That is where I look. The fact that the 'tradition' has shut up all but a very few like [Richard] Emerson, I take as having some fact in it. There is no counter method, now, coherent enough, strong enough, articulate enough, to fight it. But it must be found. It can only be found in the younger men, the men, who have & will have a stake in what comes of it. The difference between the magazine I hope to have and PR, etc., is this: I am committed to finding a way for poetry, etc., to assert the concerns implicit in it, to, simply, make room where it can assert its own value—PR is committed to finding examples of poetry, etc., which will serve as implied illustrations of its critical concerns. On the face of it, this seems, only, like two ways of saying the same thing. But to expand each, perhaps absurdly, we can get to it, i.e., I am committed to that best of all possible worlds where art needs <u>no</u> criticism; and PR to that where all art serves, only, as a means to criticism's ends.

I am impressed with CRISIS; but like yourself, I hold somewhat to be lamented, the great coloring the method relies on. But, the times are hard ones. Little else will serve better, though, eventually (and why not now), it must come to a less flavored way. But certainly, he has my vote. I like the format, everything about GRYPHON, <u>except</u> the pleasant statement of the editorial 'position' to be found at the front. That makes it all a little meaningless, or so it seems to me. That is, each time these chances are put down, in place of pleasantries, each time, we agree to let PR, etc., be the articulators of critical concerns & method. That is the 'destruction' we face. That the 'destruction' is real,—take what passes for good work in PR, POETRY, etc, etc. If these people are not <u>dented</u>, and soon, we won't be talking about poetry, as we now are, but, whatever happened to it.

Your own poem there I liked. And, very much, Emerson's, and Ferrini's, though a little slight. The rest, all pleasant, though some a little mediocre, etc., but not much else to stir. But don't take this as my lack of faith in what might come out of these things, i.e., the little magazines. I agree that would be the place, perhaps the only place, to look.

Will write again soon, to get to more of this.

All best,
Bob

Will return the CRISIS etc. the middle of the week.

• • •

LETTER TO WILLIAM CARLOS WILLIAMS

[Littleton, NH]
April 24, 1950

Dear Dr. Williams,

Thanks for the push with Olson. I had seen some of his work, but nothing like what I have on hand, or what I find in the copy of X&Y (the first poem there being what we have to get to). Anyhow, have now on hand by him a very fine thing for use in this first issue. Then some results from T. D. Horton—some poems sent by him, Donald Paquette—these too what's needed. Albeit the inevitable amount of deadwood, picked up when things looked tough, and I'm now hung with, I think she'll float. Also, good word from the one who'll print it, i.e., he wants smaller issues more often; and I think I can work better with that—to make these things 'come up' as often as possible. I hope that the issues to come can get deeper into what this first one suggests, perhaps, or can't get into altogether certainly. But for this first, I thought it best to let what articulate criticism I could get my hands on do its work, and not try to pack that end of things with stuff that couldn't make it. Then, too, poetry like Olson's & Paquette's will serve me here; certainly better than ever would the 'professorial' tone.

Have no exact date for when it will be ready. This end is apt to be slow, since it's all hand work. But sooner or later. And will have a few copies for you, when they come. Anyhow, thanks again.

All best to you,
Robert Creeley

· · ·

LETTER TO CHARLES OLSON

Littleton, N.H.
April 24, 1950

Dear Olsen,

Have your poems at hand. These are too much—unlike what I had seen; forgive, etc. But the others didn't make it for me, and, perhaps, useless to go into that here. Except to say that you have my vote on the matters of language, etc. It was, in those, that I couldn't come to it, etc., but as you will.

So will print MORNING NEWS in this first issue; and will keep, if you will, the others to look at for a subsequent one. I w'd say that MOVE OVER w'd be it, for something later; but will write you on this, when I can come to it.

Good that the Dr. took the trouble to say those things, etc. This means much. I.e., more than goodwill, some help. Very few can make this. Anyhow, I'll make use of his 'program' and also, by way of emphasis, a reprint of his article on Eliot in the Feb '48 issue of 4 Pages. Do you know this? Expect you w'd. At the moment, have a rather tenuous relation with same, via so many, that I can only shout, etc. But for one: T. D. Horton has been of great help in these matters; through him, some fine things by Paquette, which will also make use of in this first issue. But you will see. It comes, at times, to making peace among these various, but granted the will, perhaps (dare we hope) the way, etc. So much for that.

I saw ASYMPTOTES, and have to say I'm happy with what I've got. Again, forgive, etc. You will know how we are about these things. To each his own, etc.

Very grateful for the copy of Y&X; the first thing very, very good. You'll have to take it, that lacking this kind of substance, or better, not knowing about it, the first poems I saw suffered, accordingly. Not to back down on that matter— NEVER. But this much to say how much I like what I find here.

Anyhow, send some more of these fine things, whenever you have them to spare. Also: when you want to come to these matters in prose, send that too. Always room, or will make it, for these things.

Best to you,

Robert Creeley

Nota: I am still laughing, like they say. I hope people can pick up on this thing (MORNING NEWS). I think, with horror, of those who are not amused, etc. This, in any event, saves me a lot of wind, etc. Thanks.

· · ·

LETTER TO CHARLES OLSON

[Littleton, NH]

Will plan to print the 2 other
poems here in the next issue.   Apr/28/50
Plans shift at the moment; I had
a note from the one who'll print
this he wants something to run 8–16pp to appear every two weeks.
Myself, double that length, once a month. But we get to it.

Dear Olson,

    This is redundant, etc. But these past few days, have been looking at the poems in the little book, staring. Very, very good of you to have sent it. When loot, etc., allows, will ask for a few copies to send to those who are still looking for something like this. What can I say: I take you to put down here movement beyond what the Dr., Stevens, etc., have made for us. Wonderful things.

    Have taken the liberty of making a short note on these things for the magazine; together with one on Crews who is dead, somewhat, in the head, but no matter. It's yourself I'm concerned with. Because of space, etc., not much chance to say more than LOOK AT THIS, but that's part of it. For the note: quote some of La Preface & The Green Man. Now, I wd take parts of The Moebius Strip to be it, but again I take La Preface to show something the deadheads never thought of, and/or, the 'simple' condensations of WHAT'S HAPPENED. And/or 'not only "comment" but container.' The compression, without DISTORTION, in this thing: too much. And through all of this, you make your own rhythms, language, always the POEM. With all the deadwood around, & all the would-be 'form', etc., I take these things as coming headon.

    Thinking of Stevens, who slipped into PR, with this: 'Poetic form in its proper sense is a question of what appears within the poem itself . . . By appearance within the poem itself one means the things created and existing there . . .' Basic. Yet they won't see it, that it cannot be a box or a bag or what you will.

Like Eliot: the imposition of tradition, etc., etc. Both senses to apply. You <u>cannot</u> put 1 tradition on top of another, without losing what APPLIES in each . . . Like these idiots who will not take what <u>is</u> of use, but insist on 'returns' &tc.

Anyhow—sick at the heart.

So, then, must count on yourself to help me at times with this, by way of poetry, & criticism. A suggestion. We plan an open forum on American Universities, etc. To be, in point of fact, on <u>methods</u> of blocking what few IDEAS this country possesses, etc. False representation: beginning with when the prof said, no, that is not so, etc., etc. You must SEE it THUS, etc., etc. A matter of life <u>in</u> death, if you will. So, then, what you could bring to bear on these matters wd help. A suggestion: what we can get on this will at times be from 'names' which the 'public' takes as red, etc., so better, perhaps, to print these things anonymously, and explain: this is to avoid these preconceptions & to get to what's being discussed. The ideas, etc. But when you will. Always good to hear, so when you can. Let me know how people take the little book. Those who have eyes, etc.

> Best to you,
> *Robert Creeley*

. . .

LETTER TO CHARLES OLSON

[Littleton, NH]
Monday/june 5 [1950]

Dear O,

Blood from a stone and all that sort of thing/ USELESS to kick against the pricks, i.e.: 'If it were at any other time of the year we could send you an advance check for the story. But the Summer issue is the last of our fiscal year, and our comptroller, the College Treasurer, has imposed it as a rigid rule that we cannot make advances for material that may appear in the following fiscal year, etc., etc. . . . '

'Consideration of your account will be appreciated. If your check has been mailed, please accept our thanks. . . . '

Well, subjectivity, etc. For my money / never was: else. I.e., take it, or not (little matter): that concurrent with the 'deliberatism' of 'science': came the supposi-tion: that a 'cool head' needed an explicit tag. A disastrous split, nonetheless; and opposition on this head: altogether useless & a waste of precious time. No such thing as 'objectivity' for the man who wants to do a good job. Or . . .

Will pick up: on this comment: since it's a center. I.e., 'a man must create him-
self . . . ' [note in lower margin: *(looking back, I see I misread you—it is: "man
must create himself—instrument—" Still, my first reading is close enough (ha!).*]
I wd say so: and more, that it is the possible variations on the center/creation:
that make up the plot of art, granted its center is: what you say. Or as they used
to say: the foci & the loci, etc. Or words to that effect. We are NOT mathemati-
cians/ or we are: and then some. Breaking down the supposition/ that prose
& poetry: depend on perhaps counter/ at least 'different' kinds of attitude &
intelligence: we can get to the agreement you take to exist: in the use of both: of
the S. I. The need. Again: what posits A as A, is the existence of B/ no MATTER:
if it 'exist' . . . It is the variation: that can accomplish its status in the sense of: A.
I see no need for MORE than ONE head: if it's a good one. Or better: I can not
see that such a head: should feel that OTHERS were essential. This is to break
down: the supposition: that we are first & foremost: a continuum.

Abt 'myth' & the Kollektif Basket: the talking ABT myth: it would seem to me:
works to destroy the essential feature/ pervasiveness MINUS exact root/ or
'in the air' like they say. Now, granted the 'use,' valid or otherwise to which it
has been put/ as a 'name' for a body of 'information'/ as an insight into past or
existing 'group' intelligence . . . [note in left margin: *blah*] It seems only: when it
can be used/ as a manifestation of its own character: that it has valid testament.
To be such: it must again become: pervasive & unidentified. Here/ of course:
myth: IS in the air/ and none to do more than MAKE USE OF it in reasoning/
in apprehension of what might be around. (This is way off the beat, etc . . . [note
in left margin: *I dont know shit abt any of this—*]

Again: abt 'instruments . . . ' ('becoz he is instrument, & uses all available
instruments only to dominate 'em, not his fellow cits . . . '): you will know of all
the blah: abt possible 'audiences' in the case of both prose & poetry/ you will
also know: absolute bull/shit. That is: the intelligence that had touted Auden as
being a technical wonder, etc. Lacking all grip on the worn & useless character
of his essence: thought. An attitude that puts weight, <u>first</u>: on form/ more than
to say: what you have above: will never get to: content. Never in god's world.
Anyhow, form has now become so useless a term/ that I blush to use it. I wd
imply a little of Stevens' use (the things created <u>in</u> a poem and existing there . . .
& too, go over into: the possible casts or methods for a way into/ a 'subject': to
make it clear: that form is never more than an <u>extension</u> of content. An enacted
or possible 'stasis' for thought. Means to.

Abt the Uni/s, etc. Leed's poets as pedants;/ to mean: the academic use of the
'particles,' etc. carried into a raison d'etre for SONG. Or, more precisely, the
analyzers, in poetry; who are NOT the analyzers in poetry, etc. You see/? Well,

put something down on that head/ using Leed anyway you want. Granted,
I can: that the Poet as Pedagogue/ is the TEACHER. That, too: you had put
down fully.

Take this for now: will try to catch up soon.

Best to you,

Creeley

I had read once with delight: de Gourmont's attack on 'romanticism' which was,
praises be: a good stand for subjectivity. . . . [Added: *he "subjected his data"*—]

Opener in PG's [Paul Goodman] The Dead of Spring: which has just come
under the hand, like they say:

> 'Friends have reached the most beautiful part of their meeting: the
> impasse from which <u>nevertheless</u> they do not get up and leave. They are resting in
> this hell . . . '
>
> Then he begins to 'chew'. . . .

[Added:] *Vol. 2—Del Mar—<u>also</u> here this 5th day of June—*

*Was thinking if, perhaps, Wasserman, et al.—had not provided the "transition"
from Dostoevsky—to the social observer—others as well (it was that 'way')*

Some more abt the poets being the only pedagogues// at this point, or at
this stage of the game: the only possible pedagogues. I take this in the sense
of/ 'science of teaching' (flat phrase) or better: those capable of demonstrat-
ing, thru USE: a method, a way: of transmitting: communicating: idea/
thought/'history,' etc.

Leed's thought: only to do with a related word/ coming only from the peda-
gogue's MISuse of his calling, etc. Pedantry/ many poets now ARE pedants,
or they have been put to the same dry work of evolving superficial, for already
assumed, often already completed: analysis, etc. Again: an insistence of having
made the way; the end. Well: do such need any kind of attention. A hard
thing to comment on; IF one is busy with one's own work (and be damned,
and rightly, to the MISuse of others . . .) A pounder/ wd know this/ as did
he: constantly reiterate the dreariness of talking ABT aht, etc. It comes to/
how far do you take the current pedantry in poetry to block: understanding &
development of same/ how great do you take the damage, if any, to be: to what
the Dr. called 'means to leap the gap . . . ' That they are: the 'nonpurveyors' . . .
one wd take that as fact. That one's work sd be concerned with their failure/
well, that's the question . . . If one can shake free, fair enough that he should:
certainly . . . But very damn hard to find room, these days . . . free of them, or
their thought, or their damned rigidity, and ugliness. Hence: the magazine:

first—the point wd be, or better: cd be: to cast light on: illumine: make avail-
able: aspects of the universities: not taken seriously, or not usually seen to be
harmful. Some months ago, re this whole thing, Bud had written: I hate to
think of you as 'clearing the air' rather than trying to give: 'a new substance . . . '
Beyond my capabilities to do either: it's the pivot round which one's actions,
in such matters: can swing, or loop. Or just damn well droop. That is, I grant
you, certainly, yr own good reasons for not seeing (I have to assume this, at
this point . . .) how effectual Leed's slant can be/ put against yr own idea of the
poets as pedagogues/ one, the first, being against, and the second, yrs, moving
at least to a: projection, a positivism: of attitude. Having thought much, like
they say, abt these matters, and the limits best set/ for a first launching, etc.: I
had to take the fact, that very damn few wd be willing to come to a demonstra-
tion of yr own statement. Obviously, the point is NOT to come to something
ABT it, but rather: to make it, actual, in the corpus of yr work. Well, the dead
wood/ and the lack of guts, and the general hate & fear: of what a poetry, a
prose: cd grip/ given the center: just, dammit, plain suspicion: having only to do
with the 'possible' pride a man might feel: IF he were capable, actually, of more
than ruminations . . . for these it must be: well, you had yr Lawrence & you had
yr Pound/ and a few others: and they cd never agree among themselves/ and all
they were: was arrogant, and, at last: we couldn't understand a damn thing they
said . . . And, if for example, either Lawrence or Pound had had: an educational
system going full steam: to back THEM up??? The point: a certain am't of clear-
ing has to be done . . . A magazine, or anything, with a reader potential: has the
chance: and I will make use of it. But not RIDE it to death, or anywhere similar.

This is obtuse/ and I hate to beg off, each time I get to where I sd be hitting the
point. Somewhere (back) it's in there, but to weed it out/ cant do it: now. Or at
this moment.

Well, hitting something, elsewhere: it is simple enough to take the law, of S.I.,
if you will: as bearing on both aspects of the word. I wd transpose one or two
words here & there, only for purposes of my own coherence: say . . . 'illumina-
tion . . . ' vs. 'expression' as you had it there. Wd become for myself: (expression)
the line running

off.

And (illumination) the line: running, IN STASIS . . . which means no more
than it: is held, in tension, the line of the intelligence as manifest by its expres-
sion: in 'words,' material, or has: more simply: posited itself as 'complete' in an
'example.'

That given: you have the basis for a distinction between good & bad prose/// the difference coming to, what is a 'circle' in prose & what is: an 'ending . . . '

I.e., a good novel, as a good poem: CANNOT: 'conclude . . . ' /// it exists/ only to be returned to.

(Obviously, here I dont give a damn with what the author cites as 'ending' [^ *rhetorical convention*] on pp. 250–255, etc.)

Sd not think that language, per se, wd have any more reality than Blake's Nature/ it is the Imagination which has Outline . . . or better, that which defines: the real. In its first aspect.

This is the bulwark of 'romanticism' they say, but that argument is fruitless.

Again: very much wish that it were possible to see you. That is, the impossible time/lag in mail, etc. Well, no ultimate bug, but a nuisance. Here/ impossible to move, or to travel anywhere. No money, and damned by inconsequent possessions of one sort and another. Well: we wait only for the best time: to heave them/ tho perhaps the waiting is itself: disaster. So, during the war, while impossible to realize anything that was going on/ tho I cd see all of it with my eyes (i.e., can there be any reality in suffering of that sort, the physical*, when it reaches a proportion you cannot, in any sense, imagine, etc.) [Marginal note: *(i.e., the consistent: pitch of actual pain: was such: that you could not believe it: anymore than you can take it as fact: that a hen 'suffers' after you've chopped the 500th head: THO it is that consciousness: of reaction: that one MUST maintain. But the continual death, & pain/ at that point: were such that they were NOT.)]: became, like an idiocy: delight in the movements possible. The greatest possible pleasure in shuttling abt.
                    I pay it back, at this point.

With great vividness: Tel Aviv, which was an end in itself: a city at that point: one cd not have designed more perfectly. Or filled with such people. After having come from Burma, etc. The Am. Field Service/ which was a group of completely divers people/ having no 'head' or nothing more than one cd think of: at the moment. Truly: Fabrizio:s/ Anyhow, spent abt 2 weeks in Tel Aviv, after the Americans had left/ Arabs & Jews were then/ holding off. But a crazy city. Well, the freedom that cd get you on a boat/ sitting down/ two days at sea: to look out at the water & possible birds, etc. That wd be it.

The point: there are parts of Burma, villages. And people: who maintain; a way of looking altogether distinct from our own. And while this is simple enough to talk abt/ say you are alone in such a place/ with the air abt you: only then IS IT FELT.

Trying to keep up, etc.

A note from Leed/ that he agrees: yr way in the prose bits/ the right one, i.e., : 'olson on projective and on g-pa [Pound] extremely what we want . . . ' He will have the stuff back to you shortly; i.e., wants to get well into it. Etc. Slow but sure/ and not so slow, at that. I.e., it has to be/ a human being talking abt what he might reasonably, as evidenced by his 'style,' be supposed to have some stake in . . . etc. We wd have no use/ for the 'casual' eye, etc. The so-called objectivist, etc. I have yet to figure: WHY in point of style, say, the heart sd be taken: as necessarily out of it: granted Kenneth Patchen aint usually: it. Still: I'd go with some of it/ seeing he can shake it up: now & again: tho I feel sad: that it sd come to so very damn little. Rather: it was Henry [Miller]: now & again: letting loose with the round-about story/ that had the right kick. Or/ 'if I call M/ Claude a whore . . . what am I going to call other women . . . ' Or: the long bit about Brooklyn/ which has always warmed me. Better than what passes for better/ god knows. Then the 'gems'/ like they say: abt the arguing with the customs official/ which documents the incongruities of this life, etc. Or that little excursus/ The Hamlet Letters/ or death IS (not) enough???

　　　　　Then Fraenkel's kick / jesus / how dull can you get . . . NOT that it cdn't have been MAKE: but he sure didn't make it . . .

　　　　There is so very damn little to warm one, these days, or, as when once a friend was staying with us/ and I was sitting in another room reading: I heard her say to him: 'He often laughs like that, when he reads . . . '

　　　　　Or somewhere not too long ago/ I read a 'seri-ous' comment abt the possible 'reason' for WHY EP had written: Papyrus . . .
　　　　　Well, GONGULA.

So it wd go.

Word To Live By: 'You know, if there weren't distribution expenses, we might come close to break even . . . '
　　　　　R. Leed
Who had also sd: 'I am engaged in that worst of all possible occupations: mak-ing money . . . '

yes: abt Francis Thompson/ had hit a bit of his in the Summer HOPKINS REVIEW// all that I cn remember. But that fair enough. Tho little to go on. What wd be the background/ or what can you tell me, old sport, re these deep things:

I suspect . . .

hmm. USE??? What use?

Just give the possible slant, & will be glad to do the
work, etc. Always on the job/ and ready to talk chickens.
yr old poultry friend.
C.

. . .

LETTER TO DOROTHY POUND

6/15/50

Dear Mrs Pound,

I'm grateful for all the periodicals, etc. This afternoon I was able to give some time to them, & well-spent. Many, many things/ to think abt. A few: (re the ballot, for example): the practice of tagging the candidate: which amts to use of the ballot for advertising. Well, nothing new/ nothing new. I have had some experience re the difficulties of getting a minority candidate on the state ballot. An almost impossible job (in Mass/ & probably even more difficult in other states). Then: the various uses of the press. At 18 I had taken a job with the Boston GLOBE/ copyboy & apprentice (everything). I expect anyone with that experience, however brief, and mine was abt 10 months thru the first landings in Italy, etc., wd have a good grounding on what to expect of the press. Impossible. The reporters/ averaged: abt 10 yrs in the head. One: a 'star': used to relax with BLACK BEAUTY, & it still haunts me/ the intense expression . . . Well, what a mess it was: just abt everyone loaded all the time: bitterness & personal ambition thruout/ due to the hierarchy system (which might have had its merit, but now makes room for partisanship, etc.: blocks who might be of use). That was: is: Catholic dominated. Again: their attitude toward matters political, usually forecast, broadcast: in the mouth of one Uncle Dudley, well good (but, jesus, rotten . . .). So, much of what you had sent, re the campaigns, were echoes. Of when the now: Secretary of Labor, used to sit around & drink with the boys in the backroom: waiting for the returns. Ole times & Mr Tobin.

Other things: again & again: these things hit me . . . Yr point re: Illiteracy is the inability to recognize the same idea in different formulations & civil infantilism is the inability to collaborate . . . That seems the whole picture. Or that main block. What cant be traced from that head.

So many: sick, and give up—want to give over, to those whom they might think have the head for it: (of all people) the gov't. What is it, socialism, but this wish: to lie down. We get NOTHING now, & so many: cant see that even LESS is. I say: we get nothing, well, something: but Americans: dream of potentials.

In a hurry. I had thought (here) of the thing in VIGIL re: only in countries in a
hurry, do the people consider the lie, immoral. But what an edge, the americans,
for a clever man/ men: given their slants. Was anyone ever sitting/ more like a
duck. Someone else: that who cd keep up with the data/ granted the blockage, &
deceit. Well, it comes to, what Lorca's brother had noted: the complete political
immaturity of the average, the American. Inconceivable (to him) that there
should be: shades: of democracy. That this cd be put to USE.

Again: yr words / cd they be seen? By 155 million, ; ; ;
what is the answer to: the gov't by the people, & how. Now, a slush, slop: of inter-
ests. Who 'elects'? Christ, NO. No one underlines elects anyone. I, you, or he: PICKS: one.
Who cares. You do not exercise yr vote/ they say, I do, but? When what I want to
know abt any one candidate/ IS not to be known. A problem. Well, so much for
that. Will write again soon,   All best to you,

Creeley

. . .

LETTER TO CHARLES OLSON

June 21—50

Dear O,

   If I keeping hitting the biz re seeing you, forgive—not to suggest an expira-
tion of hopes elsewhere, simply that it now seems important to have that chance
to get to some of the things suggested by the letters, tho impossible that they
should get the full weight there. I mean no more than: who is around these
days, somewhat in the sense you had it, in a recent letter, but more: who is
around that can come over, thru, for me, for those like Leed et al. Fighting with
the writer of the notes, the indicator of these presents/ as he had it: abt yr own
groundsense: I am crippled by no little dogma & inexperience. I know: I am
right/ but that matters little. Nor is he, less right/ for his purposes. But it is now
NOT that he is dealing with/ nor what's to be coming. In some sense/ let us
now deride the smugness of Pound's followers: I have thought that often; at the
beginning, had written such a note to H[orton]/ to forget to mail it, and then to
get into the correspondence with him, etc. Well/ out of it, it is. In many ways:
foolish that I am in this, any of it, since here I am, alone, and here I damn well
mean to stay. A yoking up with divers & sundry is an effort, hard to consider,
tho nothing to do with the big cheese possible, etc., : simply, my own nose, is
all I can follow. God forbid that it should be pinched by their fingers, etc. To
talk, then, not abt art, which is a topic not for a man with full possession of
his senses/ but better: simply, again, the drift possible, what gets to ground in
spite of itself, any afternoon, anywhere. Or should. Because/ much talk from

the others: but from yrself: the facts of the poems/ the prose on P/ & the verse.
The letters. That wd be enough, any one of them. Having eyes, etc., was able to
SEE what you can do. I dont see it being done in any sense, kind or condition/
elsewhere. Simple enough to flatter anyone: but very difficult to make plain
wherein the basis for a trust: puts itself. I wd take as the first obvious & most
'clear' step/ in making a way for oneself: to make 'there' oneself: the tempering
of a method. Or, simply, the acquisition of one. Insofar as anyone IS a derivative
of a style current, rather than its USER, he is, briefly, damned. But as before/
content being the shaper: it is, too, that looking for the content/ its root: in the
head & self: that takes the time. ('Why do I write today . . . ') Well, a time give
to that, most probably, a long time. 20 years? Or something. A long time. If
one is striking off, for oneself, free of the 'existing' forms, then the product is
presented with an apparent 'quickness' (Stein, Pound, Williams, etc.). But just
as we go thru the whole of Joyce looking for one IDEA, beyond the reiteration of
echoes, & are somewhat put down, just so: an apparent logos in method/ new/
can mean no NEW content. A man, each man, is NEW. If his method, his form,
IS the logic of his content: he cannot be but: NEW/ 'original'. But the changes,
whatever, in an existing method, by a man coming up, will most certainly, not
of necessity: mean: new content. In the sense that it must be. Lawrence was
going by the head & heart. I had wondered: what kind of an answer to a ques-
tion about his 'style' would one have got from him . . . I mean, what more than
CONTENT? what more was the point. Less obvious, since he has been tagged
so, is the 'stylist': Gide/ but why . . . That he had the strictness in his gripping of
ways & means/ that he should make, for example, the 'neat distinctions' about
conte & possible: novel. That a possible reader can 'see' surely, having been told,
but much more to the point: that he see why it was again: CONTENT, that was
pushing. Never a man worked more deliberately with his own vision/ seeing:
than Gide. I simply cannot think of any that can pass him/ & so put him up
with my own teachers: Stendhal, Do/, etc. The counterfeiters/ wd be enough
to make the point. And the other work/ taken with this slant: then points the
reason of its sometimes apparent slightness (I am thinking of the Isabel, etc.) It
is useless, altogether, to make assumptions about what can be done, until such a
method is in the head. So, whereas a 100 idiots can flash in the pan, etc., yrself,
one of the damn few concerned with a method/ that can get to the shape, be the
shape, of yr content. Just there, for that reason, is my respect. Not knowing you,
but for these letters, and they, much help tho they are, cannot make the point
altogether. Well, that is why I should like to see you/ if & when you will be in
NE. I wd confess/say/ I have to make a deliberate way of not being caught to or
by: anyone, and that is no less fatuous that it sounds. Stupid, such a comment.
No, I am here for the same reason anyone is here: to be so caught up. The sweet
afflatus, or what you had, something. The season. It is. So when you can, give me

word on when you might be around. Wd not like to be obliged by other things, and to not be, wd take some planning. So when you can.

> Best to you,
> *Creeley*

. . .

Wednesday [October 18, 1950]

Dear O/

Yr letters here (the Monday ones) on Corman, et al. You'll have my own spleen of yesterday. I wrote him a real pisser, which will set him on his heels— but what the hell. It will rock him, for the real punch, I tossed out today. I mean: you wrote him abt the possible THREE—& I wrote him five pages of close document on the WHYS. I mean, I played it straight with him, gave him the gig as clear as I cd , showed him why this advising, minus clear hand in, led only to headaches (viz: 'Creeley's ideas . . . ' & the way I blew my top), and left him very reasonable outs. Or 1/ we are editors with him, have the way you note on mss, et al; or 2/ we are contributors just like any others, who take it, he's a good outlet. In the first case, we stand responsible for the workings, the policy of the magazine, etc. In the second, we have no commitment more than what our work, in the magazine, intends. Just that he damn well can't throw the names around, any I or you, or anyone else, is 100% behind him, without giving us the exact say as to what it is, and will be, we're behind. Now that don't force him. He knows, and I say it there again, I take it a magazine is one man's work; and I figure he should be very damn sure as to who he wants in. I mean: no pressure play here—not cool. I have been putting the facts to him for 4 months now, for longer, and he knows what I cd do for him, or should. Obviously, I can't assess my use for him, nor can you, etc., of your own, etc. He's the one who has to do that. The thing, I don't figure he'll buck here, and no matter which way he goes—we'll still be in with him, without blow-ups, etc. Just that he call it. He says he's using a letter I wrote him to handle the Brandeis gig, which proves, at least, I can hit him with sense. Okay. Is he going to heave that out, & what more you would be? That's the hinge, and I put it to him, without calling it open—and/or he'll be left with, without having it yelled at him: can I make a real gig without these two, or can't I? The question, and I don't figure he'll be able to squeeze out. In any case, we'll have some clarity. (I'll stick his letter in here, the one today, after yesterday's, to show you where you stand, and it's that, for one thing, I most certainly don't want to fuck up, & see no reason why I should. We can play this straight, all open, and still be holding the right cards. This IS a fucking game—no sense in figuring it otherwise, but you can hold longest, when you have that flavor of real openness, & it's what I want to hold to.) He floats all over the place, and I do damn well feel that without us, he'll have a splurge & not much else. He just can't see BALANCE or figure what goes with what—which is editing, which is the key. He goes this way and that, tells me Kitasono is old hash, and then asks if Spender wd be good, says Michaux aint it, and then someone else gets his ear, and he's all excited abt him—he'll never get a damn thing done IF he doesn't have us there to call the plays. Just won't, no matter 'you' or 'I'—it's him who's the fuckup. All over the place, he is. Gets my ass. But there it damn well IS—40 pages, old friend, let's ride. Now the thing I wd figure, to, say, let GATE & CENTER stand as prose; to make up real strong bunch for poetry, into which, given spread, the Ez one should most certainly go—let stand at end, group of excerpts from letters, on heads like, 'long poem' which was to Emerson, etc., etc. I think such a section, the letters using excerpts, etc., can document the finished thing of the poems—can show the energy & spread in back of them, & that wd be it. Think here you should make use of spread of yr correspondence, i.e., Cid mentioned Ferrini, & there's Emerson, & myself, etc. And there must be a real range there, which can document the spread, show it, in fact, as it picks up kinds, varieties, of people. Okay. The thing: make that 40 pages he plans—a real gig, NOT the soupy 'I am sooo fond of Chas Olson, and there . . . ', with the dinky little po-ems at the very end—BUT, what a mag can have over a book—fragmentation—burst—plunge—spontaneous—THE WHOLE WORKS. Think it should be played so. Just have it in, making only the very rough divisions I note : but make it, continual, all the energy, & the commitment. Think it should go—Gate & Center; poems; letters. With, if I can work it, a two or so page note on you, on where you are, this such & such day of our lord, this country, this world—OF WHAT'S UP—to document it: OLSON—here he fucking well is. Well, tell me what you think. He don't YET see it as a, strictly, Chas Olson number. But it's going to be just that. I mean: 40 pages with a clear commitment to them pages, on part of magazine, outspoken, noted, pointed. To DEMAND attention—not sudden & unexplained 40 page growth in magazine, as wd a reader think—why this, & wonder. It occurs to me—IF you do go in as a contributing editor, and I am 3–1 against this, at bottom, as I am for myself, can't then work this so. But let's cool for the time, & see what's up. I mean: what's that going to seem—40 pages by one of the contributing editors, eh? No soap. Stay free, the real gig, be free to play it any way it comes. Very damn little is worth heaving that over, and I don't take it this magazine is it. IF you can get these 40 pages, open, giving, committed to you, free of any overt tie-in—it's worth all the damn time & trouble. I hate to see it thrown, as it will, I think, have to be, IF we take on that job of steering overtly. Well, again, something to wait for, to see. How it goes.

Emerson: he'd sent on the book. Not much there. Here & there, technique I like, turns, tricks. Don't see any head in it, or in this collection. The Gug biz—I can't take it seriously, for him or me. Just that you don't get squashed there, what matters. Very damn good of you to come out at him on the biz of the book. He & I square pretty well, but then, have not gone in deep with him, because, to be honest, I can't understand what he is talking abt (and that's not snide here, jesus, I can't honesttogod understand a lot of it, he talks abt). Well, I think we get along ok. Aint he too late now. Seems as though he is. What the fuck. To hell with it.

Coming back to life, real slow. Spent abt 3 hrs of last night's rest period, thinking of nuances of situation, I wd like to have story on. What I flopped trying to write abt a month or so ago—just before MR BLUE. I.e., those people were here this summer. Very odd. You see, was equal thing—3 of them, 3 of us—2 little boys, 2 men, 2 women. Very odd it was. You see, they came wearing clothes which were even more fitted to this place, than what we did or do. Ours being continual, what is at hand, etc. Anyhow, I had to leave the very night they came, talked only, an hour or so, and then off that next morning, early, to get back here, 4 days later, to find myself, almost, the guest arriving. Was goofy, very odd. And they fitted so strong, into this place, so complete, the 3 of them—we were displaced, as any one is, having 'guests', as beds are switched, as Dave was pushed down, etc. Well, I wanted to figure that, & the fact of the shifts in it, the heaves, et al. And the sets of figures, so thrown. Maybe something. The first time I worked it, I left too much out, figured only a switch of women, me to this new one, which was wrong—I mean, sure, me key of heaving, but must have their unit, their 3, as complete thing, to make that force for the breakage. Too much it was.

Wd like to figure story abt that time with the house. A climax, somehow. So much that night. I mean, what I hadn't put in the letter. Briefly. We had been over to visit some people, a yng couple, like they say, the man of which was at divers times drawn, like they say, to Ann, but more, he had, at root, a hate for me. I was just figure, I mean, just stood against, unwittingly, so much he held to, made, not was, that I threw him off without meaning to, and certainly not intending, etc. Anyhow, this night, Ann had gone home, leaving me there, somewhat drunk, and I decided to take off for Boston, spur of the moment. Got the dog, and then the biz with him, who tried to dissuade me, et al., much time, this horrible wet night, and he trying to talk me out of it, and at last I got into the car and just left. Several times, before I did crack up, I felt the car dragging, sober as some drunks get, and skidded badly, tho I was going slow, on some of the curves, but not OUT, as speed would pull you, but IN, the back end, pulling

IN, on these curves, sliding over against the edge of the road. And then it did come, there 80 miles away, the slide on the curve, the car going over and into this tree, right at the back end, cut in between the bumper & the fender, at the back. Not much, even, of a shakeup. Just hit, and stopped, but it had, I thought then, strangely wrecked my tire, the back inside one, or it was almost flat. And the tree had managed to whack the frame. A mess, tho to look at it, you'd think, just change the tire and knock the dent out, and you'd have it fixed. But the chassis frame was hit, so was a mess. Anyhow, then came the biz I've told you of, the house, et al, then the cops, the diner, and from then on, was getting home. After the cops left the diner, everyone started to ask questions; before that, while they were in there, dead silence. The dog got doughnuts, and one of the truck drivers offered to take her & me in the cab of his truck, etc. So we got to Hyannis. I tried to get her on a bus, it was abt 8 or so in the morning, but no soap. Had long wrangle with timer on buz biz, but no dogs. So went over to taxi-place where I sat and answered calls for them for abt 4 hrs and so got reduced rate on cab ride home. The road to our place, from the main one, too drifted to get thru, so I walked the distance left, in sneakers, & just abt made it. Real cold it was. Both of us, dog & me, just abt done when we got in. Now what came as sequel to all this, and what, later, made it more pointed, as climax, than I then saw, was that the man, this man who had tried to dissuade me, seeing he couldn't, decided to fix the car so I couldn't use it. I take it, any damn fool knows at least six ways to fix a car so a drunk can't drive it: steal keys, take wires off the spark plugs, detach lead to battery, take out rotor, detach ignition wires, etc., etc. I mean, any damn fool wd know one of them, or so I figure it. This man, be it known, was a fair mechanic, had helped me once or twice to fix the car, certainly knew HOW to fix it so I couldn't drive it. Here's the thing—what he DID do, was deflate the back tire, NOT flat, but only abt 3/4, enough so a sober man wd feel it, but never a drunken one. He let me drive out of there with that tire like that, on roads were so icy, you'd have trouble walking on them, much less driving on them. I don't know if you know that road from the end of the Cape up. From Truro to Wellfleet there are real curves. I don't yet figure how I ever made the 80 miles. Looped as I was. Anyhow, there it is. I can't figure it. I mean, did he do it cold, to make that attempt, which must have been, to finish me, figuring how a drunk normally drives, etc., or did he, somehow, keep it under, think, perhaps, what he did do, was the cool thing??? I saw him a good bit afterwards. He still writes us, i.e., a letter here a week ago now. One other time, someone confused my name, i.e., Creeley with Curley, and as you'll know, around East Cambridge, the gangs, etc., the way things can work, no matter what's thought—this night I was sitting in a bar, and a friend comes over to tell me, this man is after me, has only this name, & for me to get moving. I mean—

very weird thing. I was, then, like this other, drunk, so only kept moving from bar to bar, until abt 4 hrs later, this same guy catches up with me, to say, the mistake had been corrected. Maybe I work each too much, but there it is. This last thing: drunk, etc., cd still see it, as what might happen, i.e., wd it or wdn't it . . . because you damn well can't believe, for no reason BUT a mistake, some-one's after yr skin. And the other: I didn't know what was up until abt 4 months after it happened. Crazy things, both of them. But you see, anyhow, to take that first story—it's so damn many strings there, so much that has to be cleaned. But I take it, as you suggest, that the part first told you, sd stand as enough, and will try to do it.

Ah . . . and next week, we will bring you, etc.

Had another friend, who sat looking down thru a sky-light while these two men looked for him, this on Charles Street. He was House of David, his wife the same, and her mother: fanatic—& she hated him, and COULD so arrange to get rid of him, COULD. I mean—there they were, guns and all, right below him— where he was sitting on the roof of this place, a stone's throw from the common, right in the middle of Boston. Ah, but that's another story. To hell with it.

You see, the thing with the first gig, with the car biz—he told Ann, not then, right away, but told her, later, what he'd done. Which means??? I mean, no one thing is complete—this is endless. I take what's given, etc., or see it as no one thing alone.

Abt Race—he was a good friend when I was in Cambridge, etc. But to spot it—I had 3 friends there, Bud, Leed & Race. Race & Bud now both in Albuquerque. Race studying there. Bud plays in band, for which Race plays too: piano. He's too much. Has one of the most, most beautifully whimsical: humors—I ever met with. Very strange yng man, he is. He's the one who they told at Harvard, removing him for no other reason: that they had no place for the exceptional. He was, & is. He drove up here with me, in the truck, when we brought the things up, first, before we moved in. We'd be going along, beautiful day, and you'd see this spread of field, sky, too much, and he'd let the truck slide that way, look at me, and pull UP on the wheel. I expected us to sail right out & over it all. Very hard to tell you of these. No letters here, I cd send, etc.

I forget one, above: Joe Leach. But that's the four.

Wish I had this picture that Bud showed me, of Race him & the Prez (Missis Berlin) walking along thoroughfare in Mex City . . . like they are snapping 24 hrs per—real crazy it was.

Well, write soon. Feel I'm getting back to it, slow, but anyhow. Hate that dead-
ness, even for a day, or whatever.

Yr lad/

Bob

. . .

LETTER TO CHARLES OLSON

Wednesday [November 9, 1950];

Lieber Herr Olson:

zuerst mochte ich mich fur Ihren herzlichen brief bedanken, uber den wir uns
so gefreut haben . . .

Etc.

Anyhow: COOL. It is, and/or: yez is speaking with the NEW American repre-
sentative of the Groooopa. Fair enough, I figure. Real nice gig: he says—wd be
very happy if we cd have something thru you, for every (each & every) issue.
Well, like he sez: Machen Sie mit? Sure. In or out/ I'll take IN. Anytime. It
excites me, considerable. Anyhow, gig can be much greater, I wd figure, than
anything with Cid, etc. I mean, like: ok—he came back strong—takes me in,
writes to those I gave him names of, even offers to pay me back for postage (I'll
keep that card, thanks . . .). Anyhow, he listens. By luck, happen to hit things
he never heard of—& stirred him. He's sending me: his own gig on ars poetica.
Let me know: he takes it back wall is Perse/ front Pound: area within: area,
which I will shake him out of, eh? YOU WILL. Anyhow, as long as my german,
holds (I stagger thru this stuff, & then hit him with every idiom I can think of:
IN ENGLISH . . .)—we can make something here. Is sending little bk of new
german stuff—can then see, clearer, what's up with these boys. No, this one
sounds real straight—I mean, he's willing (1) to take chances; (2) to give free rein
or semblance of same; (3) to commit himself on 1 letter. I like that fucking way.
Contrast with Cid. Anyhow, DONT figure the Old Man to fuck this one—this
Gerhardt sounds too straight, & figure him too awed by Ez, too respectful, to
bother him with details, like Olson will be featured in 1st issue. Ha.

Don't figure the stuff sent, will make any difference. But still suggest, if possible,
get the work translated, what you put the stake on, there, & send off to him,
that, when you can. Can then explain logic to him, etc. Well, think something
cd happen here. He sounds a little tight, by that I mean, he's got it: poetry, he
wants to center on that, & don't want much that don't relate directly to sd head.
BUT, you know what you can do with such; and/or: show them. OK.

On Kitasono: hard one. Depends, exactly like you note, on what you wrote him.
Real cool, he is. I believe this: with any such, the way to excite them, is to make

it: TRANSFER—that is, why not make this point, as you certainly can—that you wonder what the fuck is up THERE (their front) & cd perhaps help to get same out, over here (Cid, et al). I mean/ that keeps them close. Well, wd only figure, come out, exact, on what yr want to know—and/or: you people dead? Which is relevant question, or seems so, looking at his letter. Yez must get very old very fast over there. Ez' hand there—wdn't care to say, like they say, because I somewhat doubt it. I wdn't care to say, because this sounds, K/ speaking, somehow: not a voice thru. Well, what else, but hit him back—push him into saying more than he does here? I dunno.

A breather. Space it so. Because, but for these heaves, have sounded the bottom, the past weeks. Jumpy, can't be touched: hate it, & want out, clear of: all; of this biz, of the handling. Language: I remember, say, first time trying to learn French, in class, listening, etc., to what I had heard of it, cd then mimic sounds, or enough to be asked, as it happened, if I was kidding, i.e., HAD I studied it, etc., from which point—I mean, learning what it was I was saying & making effort to say—got worse & worse, until I cdn't say a sound right. Self-conscious. That difference, between own tongue—& a language. No chance for the thing to come clean up, from the heels. With language. Well, with this man, say, german, it is ok, since to follow him, & I am, god knows, more painfully conscious of every damn nuance than he is—is to get from A to B. But I can't, easily, go over into poetry. To the push. Since there, what I damn well fall back to, what I hate the lack of, in Wilbur, in Hoskins : is somehow, what's up from the heels. It rocks you.

Damn ROUND of this room. Exact spacings of it. What I CAN reach—what I hate these days. Nothing comes of it.

No word from Emerson. I burn bridges fast with Cid, i.e., hit him, but what else: since if he goes flabby, it's the end, anyhow. I keep getting little cards, (well, one, from Sister, but you had been away too): saying, I have been away for a few days. That Gerhardt: the same thing, you see. I sit here all the damn time, right here—never more than a stone's throw from here.

Write soon.
                    Yr lad/
                    Creeley

[Attached is Rainer Gerhardt's letter in Creeley's translation, which begins: "First I would like to thank you for your fine letter, which we were glad to get."]

· · ·

LETTER TO PAUL BLACKBURN

[Littleton, NH]
Wednesday [November 29, 1950]

Dear Blackburn,

Very good to have yr letter, & fine news about the translations. Hope very much they use them. Thinking of that headache you note, i.e., aristocratic vocabulary, etc., vs the other, I wd figure metric wd be your way out, and/ or, placing of words, or what I am thinking of, just that tone, is got by such, tho I wonder if he intends it, etc., G. S. Fraser in opening of MANNERIST POEM, #2 Nine. Just for that, worth looking. I.e., if you keep the vocabulary relatively stripped, meaning by that, to use words not overloaded with relation (grubby, filth, incredible, gorgeous, etc.) & let yr metric maintain the bulk of yr tone: you have an out. Well, not much matter.

[Dallam] Simpson sent the poems. That preface/ shit. He wrote it, i.e., one of his many aliases. Hideous thing, it is. Blabber, about all I can make of it, & wonder what the hell he's up to with such. But he's fair enough, i.e., warm heart, etc., tho idiotic at times (viz preface). His address: P.O. Box 6974, Congress Heights Station, Washington, D.C. Which is, I'm told, just around the corner from St Liz.

I wd argue with you, re Pound's prose style, but not by that fact, certainly, say it was a question of poor imitations, as pathetically poor as Simpson's et al. But it's not to be put down, i.e., that in the prose, he stripped off a rhetoric no damn less actual than its counterpart in poetry/ 1912. No, I like it very much; find it moves with good balance, & weights. Viz translations from Kung, etc. Early essays. Beautiful writing, they are. Bunting, you'll remember, was one of those in Pound's ACTIVE ANTHOLOGY; i.e., it shows where Simpson got him, etc.

The Olson poem. I lack a copy at present. Don't agree that a lyric is a matter of length, tho, as you suggest, this instance may not hold its tensions, etc. But it sure could, etc. One thing: what is objective realisation of subjective material— had gone to war with Russell on this head, & took that fort, so willing to try same with you. 'State yr time & place. Well, fuck it,—get yr sense, but don't like this use of 'objective'; i.e., means almost nothing to me. Can't see logic of such a word with respect to the altogether subjective act of poetry. If it means, only, the cool head—fair enough.

Well, I like that poem, but can't show why, without a copy. When I get one, I will.

Am now acting as Am/ representative of a german magazine, edited by Rainer Gerhardt, & wd be very grateful if you wd keep him in mind as an outlet for yr work. An exceptional man: plans a monthly to run 32–48 pp of main text, 24 of marginalia & criticism. Also edits a series of contemporary poetry; has done some of the Cantos, etc. Apparently an excellent translator, & a good poet himself. Excellent letters from him. Well, send him anything you think he cd use—am sure you'll get a good deal from him. Rainer M. Gerhardt, Verlag der Gruppe der Fragmente, Freiburg im Breisgau, Postfach 336, Germany. Will have re Am/: unpublished Pound prose, Olson poems, perhaps Williams, Stevens, etc. Also Perse, Benn, Italian work, Jean Genet. Etc. I'll send you a prospectus when I have them. All german text.

Well, hope yr not killing yourself in the print shop. Leed, who was in on this summer's effort, worked for abt a yr in one, in Brooklyn. Cleaning presses. Not good. Hope you have a better end of it.

Well, this much for now, & write when you can get to it. Cold, bitter days. My wife expecting a baby any minute, which is hell on the nerves. However. Not the first, or the last, I expect.

All best to you,
Creeley

Did you see Olson piece in current POETRY: NY. Very much with same. Also, have you read CALL ME ISHMAEL/ on Melville: Harcourt Brace, now, I think. You cd get same from nearest library, I wd think.

. . .

LETTER TO CHARLES OLSON

Thursday [December 7, 1950]

Dear O/

Thinking of yr letter on the biz of the staying/ going, et al. And that you take me as/ direct. By no means so, in truth, i.e., Ann had read that, and snickered, i.e., am simply by no means so. Because, with this way of it, the figuring of all the ways, or making of it, each item, the possibles, very damn often: I sit where I am, etc. But no matter, here. What does, is yr notes on yr own way of, it, and the thing abt Williams, that is, what you note of his staying. I don't feel the same things there [^ *as in you, i.e., that you are similar*], to be straight; i.e., I do suspect that in him, which made it the job of staying home, that precise, work, and don't like it, and when it comes up, in the comments in a note he had written on Ez (Letter To An Australian Editor) it isn't good, i.e., it makes of this thing, a local thing, saying, finally, but how he cd know, then, how cd he, having gone away. That is, Lawrence, most certainly, had demonstrated, been, much more than Ez, the one who moved, and each place, found, deliberately the materials he needed. I wish that sometime, a precise, a warm, for that wd be it, saying of this thing in him, someone who knew of it, cd give a real sense of it, as it wd have been, in the act; well, some note it, etc., but the essays, the bits, seem still the only real sense of it. Anyhow, my thought that it is not Ez and Bill, come to the 'ways'; because I do have the feeling, those two are almost: a common ground. Think of it, quick: who is comes WITH Ez/ with Bill? Who IS the TWO? Not, then, Joyce & Pound, Lewis, Eliot, et al. IS/ always has been: Williams & Pound; and Williams' kick, the bitterness, I think, grounded on a sensing of the crowding, the space, for one, two had to stand on. Well, lucky there were those differences, i.e., Ez & his method, Williams' & his localism, gave them a distance; but cut it away, heave out the bad stories, Williams', the bits & pieces, pare it down to essentials, & yr close to the insistencies of Ez, back of the method, back of the items, the divisions, into what comes of: hard as youth these 40 yrs. Precise. Because, I do get a sense of the local in Ez; very strong, as both, all: Flaubert/Stendhal/ James—also have it, as part of them. Check me, i.e., see if that isn't something, something runs thru all 3, because here I figure beyond, much, what I have a right to. Was Ez the traveler, i.e., think of Lawrence, in Italy, starting off to the New Land, comes, via Ceylon, then Australia, and into San Francisco, down to New Mexico, into Mexico. Etc., etc., etc., old stuff, sure, but think of it—where he did go. I mean/ it goofs me, that man. Or where did Ez go, to put it that way, i.e., I have the sense of 2 main moves: England/ Italy, via France. 1/2. Finish. I also have the feel, his way of it, his tone, remains as local as the first day he must have got into London, to be looking around, & figuring it. But, jesus, take it as Lawrence had the thing; i.e., walk with him, (which sounds fatuous, but what the hell) thru south Germany, Switzerland, into Italy: i.e., FEEL. That's the kick, yr difference, that Lawrence wd be getting it; and Ez/Bill: trying to go out for it, etc., which is inexact, but HERE: precise—TOUCH/ as you note same. Bill/ in Rasles gig (which is frightening thing)—'he touched', I think he says, and, quick, I ask you to throw that, that way of the act, against EVERY DAMN TOUCH Lawrence EVER noted, and/or, sure, the triteness of it, what wd stare, did, back at one: Broadway: YOU TOUCHED ME/ NOT: (the KICK) I TOUCHED YOU. Well, too simple, I wonder, and yet it falls for me, into place; makes me, my sense of this coming & going, shows me that complex, what wd be too easily put down as 'passivity' comes to characterize the traveler, but that it is, that he is so, open; not man sitting on ground, trees abt, starts to hack, clear the circle, which is Williams for me, and Ez. Well, here, it is easy to look out, to the edge of the woods, to know of such, blend there, move there, without displacing a single THING. How to do such—Lawrence, his whole life: intent, or what is at the root of his method/ to be touched: relation. Look, again, at that biz in the Plumed Serpent. But to stay, is to sit in yr circle, to be hacking, clearing, which is, let me say, honest work; the one way of it. And the other, the moving, is the other, that insistence, to be so, moving, not displacing, but sitting, coming to rest, where, how, but somehow: some hollow, shallow of the earth/ any damn thing: makes that: place; to sit till/ again/ the shift, & to move again, on/and so on.

I mean: myself, can clear nothing, can only look for the fit, to somehow figure it, & conjecture the thing, falls to hand. I don't want a battle, fight, of it; not against, but somehow, to fall in, not step, but swing, not swing, but: as there is that moving. To have the feel, to have that riding of it.

Not to say, then, that staying is, in itself, to be anywhere, 7 yrs, or 70, inexact, or inexact, as sense of the way of it; since, say, Ira, or others, just so/ or yr Douglas, and how cd, wd, you move him; i.e., there is that fit, BUT lacking it, we cd not sit, or HOW? Well, Bill/ was he against it, was it that gig, the fighting, constant, i.e., you answer me, since you know. As with Ez: is, tho bitter, the place, now, less a place, is it, that it cd have been elsewhere, i.e., was or is there a place, he doesn't start to clear out the underbrush, knowing there were, was, such for Lawrence, that he moved so, from such, place to place to place.

To jump: wd say, that, too, is in some of it, is the prose, under, makes that the way of the man, exceptions, notable or otherwise, notwithstanding. I.e., movement, such, is common, peculiar, to those men. Well, the under, that move, in Melville, Lawrence, Dostoyevsky, the people, who move, that shift of it.

Because, what the hell, beach, the sun, the boats, down, drawn up, and let's make it—a most beautiful day, & what, what: is assured, but that we might (1) be like a bulk in it, an extraneous, or (2) fit. And what room, more, is there, to figure.

Here, I had it, or some of it, that I cd sit back, down; but myself, I know when that's done with, or how long, it can be done so, serves. So/ move. Because, it's not there, i.e., address, place, etc., matters; but that another place, should now be coming. To have the context, might come.

Well, to hell with it. Anyhow, that wd be some of it.

Myself, just as fucking nervous, to have this out, away, too.

Yr lad/

Bob

Reading this over, wake up, to see I come over, repeat, much of yr own ground, comment; well, let it go, for what anyone wd have to be making for himself, anyhow.

I.e., yr 'Cannot think of environment.. as so much out there, separate, as it is extension of, self, or, . . . it is not much use but as I am it also . . . ' What else.

I.e., one thing else, i.e., thinking of yr comment, to be where there is nothing
American, i.e., against that, wd put this: that the thing is, somehow, not so
much that as to be, in a place so much its own way, any, that it cd make you,
push you, somehow to a difference, not that change, i.e., to the 'new' personal-
ity, but to that shade, variation, cd plot you, new, the line to yr self, etc., to the
in. As such wd goof me, in Burma, as it was, happened, one time in Tel Aviv,
was sitting in this place, cafe, open, & the 7 languages, running on, then later,
was sitting in another, and this German, old, somewhat fat, with the baldhead,
him trying to play jazz, drums, and the old 1/2. 1/2, throwing him everytime,
what he threw back to, constant, and blushing, he had leaned to me, talked one
incredible moment, of it, that pull, exact, then back to the play and, later, was
girl, Arab, who was waitress, the place packed, had come over & sat to talk, was
to see her later, & it was that, sitting as she had taken me in, looking out at the:
OTHERS. The end. That kick, to somehow: get in/ each place/ each time: IN.
I mean, I was waiting for her, & fixed. And have found, oddly, always it is, to
come straight out, in, anywhere: gets you, always in. Too much.

· · ·

LETTER TO MITCH GOODMAN

Thursday/22nd [1951]

Dear Mitch,
    Very fine to have yr letter—all the information, etc. Will see what might be
done on the money; cannot bring great am't because we don't have it, but what
we can, in cash. As for after that—it's certain that the Trust Co. will probably
make it impossible to work any gig straight from them—what I mean: part of
their responsibility, is to make such funds as are coming to Ann, 'available' in
the sense, deposited to a reliable holder. Hence, they will want the name of the
bank there in Aix, & wd be grateful if you cd note it for us, in yr next letter. But
perhaps they wd be willing to deposit some of it, here, in this country, & then,
by check, we might be able to get someone here to cash same & send over, cash.
Devious, but perhaps, etc. The am't now, thanks to this war, has increased, i.e., it
was $185 a month & is now $215, from which we can probably save considerably
by living in France—or hope to. Well, time enough.

To say a bit abt
the Olson biz, etc. Yr note that the alternative, in or out, seem obvious, etc.
doesn't in my opinion, allow for this fact: that almost no prose, now being writ-
ten, falls in either category. That is, there certainly are other 'places', so to speak;
immediately, I think of the 'half-management', which he notes; being where
the writer mixes 'objectivity' with an attempt to interpret. I think any number
of examples can be got from PR, or from many of the magazines, i.e., think of

those stories, etc., where the writer posits a case, against an overt set of psycho-logical references, i.e., makes this last, by either inference or overt noting, the 'interpreter'. Such work is meddling, i.e., is neither in nor out, because it vacil-lates between these two assertions—on the one hand, figures that the 'objective fact' finds its own coherences & on the other, still believes that this coherence will be missed unless some 'referent' is given by which to 'explain' it. And there is another pattern, or way, in current prose, certainly as used (mis-used) as any ever was; i.e., the mnemonic. This makes 'recall' the major factor, i.e., intends that coherence be got by asserting a continuity, that continuity, which people believe the memory to assert, etc., along with the balance of emphases, etc., that the act of 'recall' can get to. Well, no more than a good many detective stories make use of, as well as, Proust.

Well, play that one again, then, i.e., figure that this in & out biz, is precisely what it asserts itself to be. The fictive, just so, blasted—to mean, construction, along given lines of practice (the novel & the 19th century, etc.), no longer relevant. If prose is to be 'document', in the sense that it be, the precise assertion of forces in relation, minus insofar as is possible an 'interpret-ing' ego, it is already a good deal more than 'naturalism' &, as well, a good deal more than 'record'; because, you see, this intention means full force, no thing left out, no construction, no thing but what IS pulled in by the thing focused on, etc. It's not my own way, & so that difficulty in trying to define it here, etc. But I think, even this brief note, can make clear its difference from the bulk of current writing.

Now, the other, the in, is what I myself intend; and it's best defined, by, again, harking back to what Olson has said of it—that is, if the writer make himself, the context, or the beginning, of the con-text, if, there, he allow all play of all that relates, if, without warp or interpreta-tion, he make himself force, in relation to what surrounds, is so related, again he can achieve a coherent other than the fictive & other than what now is prevalent in the writing of most prose. What happens is not 'experience recalled, etc., etc., etc.'; what happens is what happens—i.e., throw yrself on the mat, like that, & you get the exact movements, of any force so introduced to any other, or group of others. Well, you walk out on the street, etc., & who's to say what's to happen, etc. And tho this may seem I believe much too turgidly in the 'gratuitous', it isn't quite so simple—what it does mean; that I figure all force & its relations, to have relevance, & a relevance a good bit beyond the fictive (to mean, again, that which is constructed, to coincide with a given set of premises, such as, man is good, man is bad, man is not so good, man is not so bad, & all the way down the line.) And I believe, further, that, given a man, thrown so, by his own act, into this field, in the act of writing, what comes out has a coherence & a <u>present</u>

not to be found in the fictive. Well, one comment Stendhal had made, which has some relation here: "I write out the plan after having written the story . . . to make the plan first freezes me, because after that, memory is the active agent instead of the heart." The 'heart', is, even as it is, in Olson's "the HEART, by way of the BREATH, to the LINE . . . " emotion, exactly in the act, as it comes there, I mean precisely, occurring as the writing occurs, etc. Without this, you have construction, etc., & no need to speak further of that.

I don't think that "methodology" means anything more than what you yourself say, somewhat before your note of it, i.e., (where you note James' comment on Flaubert) " . . . two ways in which a novelist may go about to handle his material . . . ", that is, this 'handling' is, precisely, "methodology", well, it's what he means, & I don't think that meaning is far-fetched or so very irrelevant, etc., or even, that the word itself is so bad. Thinking of James, it's Pound who says that the Notes (appended to the Ivory Tower) are a landmark in English prose, the history of the novel, because they demonstrate a comprehension of the novel as a "form" (and I have quoted P/ beginning with 'comprehension'.) Anyhow, you must see that what James brought to the novel, was, exactly, METHOD; prior to him, there was NO method, no plan, no outline, nothing but an 'intention', etc. Now it happens, this emphasis on 'plan' that James got to, seems to me, overbalanced &, finally, crippling; but I can't deny that the emphasis was precisely what English prose needed, having run out, etc., or having degenerated into a series of poorly written tracts, etc. At least, he shook off the conception of the novel as a vehicle for moralisms, and how he did, was, exactly, by asserting that the novel, being a 'form', must have its own ends & intentions, squarely related to this character of its form. Of course, assert a form for anything and you make impossible its manipulation without strict attention to this form; which is to say, why a thing is 'present' is because it has form, & why a thing finds an 'end' (instead of being, only, means) is again, because it has form.
        Well, to get back—I wanted to note that, reading some letters of Flaubert's, he does make the point that James makes, but a little more cogently. That is, James mixes 'interest' (which is subjective, call it, impetus to the act), with the act in progress, which is this "The more he renders it, the more he <u>can</u> feel it . . . " I mean only, that I am left with too general a sense of this 'render' & this 'feel'—I don't know exactly what he means by either one—being that they can, each, be applicable to a range of intentions, etc. Anyhow, what he says of Flaubert's sense of form. Here it is in Flaubert's words: "To suppose an idea without form is impossible, and vice versa . . . " I like that, because it gives both emphases, i.e., that without form, you have no content, & without content, you have no form, etc. Very fine. And enough? I figure it is. My own emphasis is: form is never more than the exten-

sion of content, i.e., I believe it begins so, from that prime: content. But that cd be argued, etc. It's a matter of the work. Etc.

Talking of a 'methodology' makes this sense: that is, if you agree to this idea of this methodology, coming to mean, no more than the handling, I figure you'll see why, certainly, it's relevant. I don't believe 'great works' or any, fall out of the head, like apples from the tree, etc. Or I believe the job of finding articulation, of, simply, gaining some precise sense of one's own capabilities & faults & of, further, having enough grip on them & their extension into use (the actual writing) to be able to give <u>presence</u> to whatever comes to hand, is the one precise job we might have; we can't set ends for our work, prior to its writing, we can't, or I believe we can't, work assendto, & begin by holding the burning belief that man is evil, etc., because I believe the act of writing to assert its own relevancies & even, its own discoveries, & that which makes such impossible, by clamping on a 'view' prior to the act of writing, or a view, so rigid & ridiculously dogmatic, that it twists lust into virtue, hate into love, etc., is what should drop off, fall off, even as the apples, etc. Anyhow, we can't talk about 'ends' because they are precisely what, the work can assert, & only the work; but means, —certainly we will have to give some attention to them. Not, by that, to fall into, what I expect is precisely USA, AD 1951: The Engineers, etc. But to have sufficient competence, & understanding of method, as means, to be able to be, articulate, open, coherent. Well seems pretty certain, etc. [^ *Well.*]

Leed's address: 309 South Clinton Street, Iowa City, Iowa.

I don't have a copy of WHITE MULE: I'd read it sometime back, & at that time, figured there wasn't anything there, one couldn't find in the stories, & anyhow, don't figure either the bulk of the stories or these novels, to be up to: 1) IN THE AMERICAN GRAIN; 2) A DREAM OF LOVE. No matter that they are this 'history' & 'drama' respectively—well, do believe they are much better prose, & even as such pertains, or might, to the writing of a novel, have much more use. Myself, I don't think he ever wrote better than: IN THE AMERICAN GRAIN—& for the total in, i.e., the full gig, the play is a good deal better than any of the stories, because in the last, you get a certain staginess, I mean, a fixing of elements, now & again, is not too good; this doesn't have to do with the best of the stories but does have to do with some & the novels, which ramble & finally bore one stiff (tho this is snobbish, & I don't mean to make it just that, etc. It is, they are very slack writing, as opposed to these other two instances, of his prose.)

Well, about it for the moment. Snow here, even snowing at the moment; slush & a hell of a mess. Also, neighbors get tired of saying goodbye—since we had first thought we were leaving April 3rd. And no one more beat than ourselves, etc.

But soon.

I'm not quite sure which port we'll come into; I think, Cherbourg, & if not that, le Havre. The idea of going to Marseilles, is a good one, & I'd tried to find out, earlier, abt boats going there, but at this distance, & lacking addresses, etc., it's next to impossible. Just that we can't look around, etc. It's meant (being here) about 2 weeks' delay on every item we've had to get (as the passport took 4 weeks, instead of 2, etc.); well, no matter.

Hope that something comes on the house; when you know, send us the address, i.e., wd be a great help to have it before taking off from here. Cd leave it at the post-office, etc.

Also, many thanks for the note about yr friend, & the hotel, in Paris. Certain to be a help.

We go, I believe (I don't, know, anything at the moment), on the Ile de France.

Well, enough for the time. Will write soon again; and looking forward to Dennie's letter.

All our love to you,
Bob

Ann says to ask Dennie, if she wants her baby clothes back; i.e., my sister is having a baby pretty soon, & wd otherwise leave them with her, along with what we have, etc. Whatever you say.

> A drab America, with or without
> advertising is only possible
> always in this limited century
> if we stand up and take it, not lie down
> what then, why, downtown will be gloomy
> like corner lots beside the banks already
> on cold evenings many things darken
> the bright stream of jazz, our classic stuff
> also the network of river-drowning
> not daily be pronounced history
> (Sent in by Mr. L. E.
> of Swampscott, Mass.)

. . .

LETTER TO DENISE LEVERTOV AND MITCH GOODMAN

April 18th, 1951

Dear Denny & Mitch

Very fine to have your letters; a little damn breather in this other hell, etc. The thing, that we are still in the same fix,—don't yet know just what will come. There's nothing we can get for a place around here,—in fact nothing in France that we've been able to get word on. And have had, god knows, enough people looking, etc.

But not at all sure this is the country in the 1st place; Italy, from what you had said, and what, too, others say, sounds the much better place. I wrote to D. D. Paige and he says we could get something there in Rapallo; but that's very fancy, etc. Don't know how the hell that would set, and expensive, & might be simply another headache.

Otherwise, I guess to come back. Olson says we could come there to BMC; wouldn't pay anything but would mean room & board and that's the main thing, on any quick jump back. Well, it is still very unsettled. Have less than two weeks left, so should know soon what will turn out as 'it', etc. Will keep you posted.

On the poem,—just now checking back to see the copy you'd sent. I think this present comment of yours has mixed itself into two of my own, etc. I.e., first of all to get straight on which poem this one is; I figure, the one called, or beginning:

Perched on a bristly grass, a shaved steep slope, etc., etc.

If so, my comment wasn't aimed against the 'change' element, but about certain slownesses in the progression. Or I damn well think it was? If you have that letter still,—could check me. Otherwise, no matter.

(I remember I'd hit another poem on this thing of a 'central image' or what I'd thought could, or even should, be one.)

Wait a minute,—I haven't got the right poem, it is that other I take it you're talking about. The one with the door, & fire, etc.

— That one don't surface,—somewhere in all this litter, but damned if I know just where. Anyhow, what you say here makes sense—change, I get it,—I hope I got it that first time. Anyhow, you are the boss; what strikes you as it, that's it. Voila.

Let me read it in ORIGIN, eh? Ok.

I got another issue of that there WINDOW—he is an idiot but there are two poems, in this one, that are, strangely, very damn fine. A man named Martin Seymour-Smith; do you know anything about him?

Otherwise, it is such lush & loose crap. And the reviews sound like they were all wearing little lord fauntleroy suits, etc. How sweet & correct they get to be; and it could, as always, be something else,—they do have paper, type, etc. But to hell with it.

ALL DEVILS FADING

All her devils here tonight,
    Duly expected: a sour mouth,
And ache in the head, and her voice
Ceaseless in anger. In blurred sight
Angels on her wall rejoice
    At a sudden end of drouth;
But here, still this blight.

There were no easy years:
    Always, in glut, a vague hunger
At spring. "You were never divine,"
She says, "and over your affairs
The shadow will always incline,
    Closing in. It is your anger
At nature," she says, and stares.

Why then, with her slight smile,
    All devils fading, does she give
Me her hand? and close her eyes,
Thus in her sorrow to beguile
My death. It must be she too dies,
    But with no love to forgive
Me for her own betrayal.

Very goddamn fine GRACE to that poem; one can be pedantic about it. It is a fucking RARE ingredient. Second verse has rhythms ONLY Blackburn could top. And he couldn't do better, and third verse has a damn fineness of edge, of position, NO ONE beats. A wonderful fucking USE of the conjectural, there, "It must be she too dies . . . "; that is damn, damn fine. Just that beautiful damn sliding into MEANING; this guy has GOT it.

Words here & there forced by rhyme structure, but handled with grace at that. GRACE: quality which is the result of perfect bevel between the means used to suggest a meaning, and that meaning (itself) resultant.

Read that thing aloud, let it ride out; fine fine thing.

But slight? But a good poem if one figure, it's not at all easy to say anything, and the mind here used to say this, can then go on to say other things, and it is, anyhow, not at all easy to say anything about the relation outlined above (in the poem) and this man has done it sans fatuosity or pompousness. And has himself a real HEROINE, and she seems very very lovely. It is beautiful statement of CONTACT, between two human-beings; and I have not the slightest difficulty in believing either of the two exists, and they do not go blurred or dim when I look out the window, or simply think of something else.

Etc., etc. I got the 2nd issue of GOAD; same damn enthusiasm, and excites me all over again. Why not get him some stuff? Some notes even on what is NYC now,—what the feel is. Or stuff like that item of the Italians getting soaked, etc. Or do get in touch with him; I asked him to write you, hope he does. The address is now: 207 South Mayfair Avenue, San Francisco 25, California.

Have been writing a little, poetry, etc. It was good to get anything out, after the bleak winter.

> THE INNOCENCE
>
> Looking to the sea, it is a line
> of unbroken mountains.
>
> It is the sky.
> It is the ground. There
> we live, on it.
>
> It is a mist
> now tangent to another
> quiet. Here the leaves
> come, there
> is the rock in evidence
>
> or evidence.
> What I come to do
> is partial, partially kept.
> [CP I, 118]

I was reading Rexroth's damn long thing there in ND #13; I never did get thru the last part. What the hell does he think he is? Eh? This damn form beats me,—just don't make it at all. But sense impeccable in many places,—but drones on & on & on.

You relieve me about this crib, and will get down there, shortly, to see what the hell they have done. I thought someone else had a baby, etc. And so, etc. Well, good to know it is still within reach; shall try to grab it.

Did you read Pound's ABC of READING? Good book,—very clear exegesis of his main heads. Terrific school bk/ if anyone would ever consider actually USING it.

Read Kenner's damn bk/—THAT is horrible. Christly pompous style he's got: "When the widow of Ernest Fenollosa perceived that the poet of <u>Lustra</u> was ideally fitted to work into articulated forms, etc., etc., etc." Very hard to even get THRU that one—incidentally, it continues (on the book-page) for five more lines. Ending, " . . . of penetrating an utterly alien poetic method from which unworn procedures and formulations might be drawn . . . " O/ utterly!

Fuck that.

Creeley's Law: any novel you can't pick up and read the last 20 pages of and
            then go back to the beginning and read the whole of, with
            pleasure, is a bad novel.

Sequence. Novel written on premise of logical surprise: no good.

That is, sd law: all other things being equal. Men who satisfy sd criterion:

Stendhal

Lawrence

Melville

etc., etc. The emphasis is this: IS the going-on of sufficient tightness, & persistence in its own right (as in this formulation: a) detail for its own sake; b) detail in pattern of whole—to have those 2 ingredients balance tightly & cleanly) to break up that usual continuum of which the detective-story gives us such pleasant examples?

Henry Green, by the way, is also satisfactory, judged by this 'law'. A man could certainly write a very bad book which would, anyhow, satisfy this way of looking at things,—but he could not write a good one which did not satisfy this way of looking at things.
                                    It shows what a hell of a ham
Graham Greene finally is.

In short,—IS the main line straight to the sod & all? The grave, like they say? IS that the main significance. Or is it, more simply, precisely what Rimbaud was shouting,—the particular energies of any instant? What Lawrence put to such exact work.

If one writes narrative prose on this line, the line of a to b to c,—c as climax, the dying-off, etc., IF he writes on that line, then what is his emphasis? On fact all things head for the bucket, voila.

It's a dull point, actually. It is not the main one.

Sure, this is a broken way of putting it,—any way is but the demonstration. However. "Today all American novels try to be shockers. If it doesn't shock? and French writing that is looked at tries to be the same on an "elevated" (snobbish) plane : the "profound" insight. All forget that writing is simply writing FIRST. It is writing, an elemental and pleasing thing. I am sick of it. What is going to shock us? We are tired of being shocked." Wm. C. Williams, etc. It makes sense.

He said he got the chair of poetry, Library of Congress; that makes a hell of a lot of SENSE,—damn damn fine. He follows Aiken,—shows you what it had been, etc.

Ok, about it, and will keep you on. Do likewise. Things can't keep on in this present mess, etc. Should be something decided damn soon. Will tell you what, when we know.

All love to you all,

Bob

April 27th/ Just landed a place, & some damn ankle catch at that! It's in Lambesc, campagna, & ok. Six mille the month; fair enough. Plenty of room, fine grounds, etc. We even got a big GATE, just like the aristocrats! Phew. (Got to Rapallo, & that wasn't it. But driving thru Sori, saw yr bell tower, & thought of you all—that, incidentally, looked a hell of a lot better than R/—latter place simply too lush, & cheap damn lushness at that.)
PS—will get you address later this week

[note in left margin] MITCH: how abt trying REVIEW of Wms' Auto/ for New Mexico Quart/, Albuquerque, NM. Man is Lash, Kenneth Lash (remember . . .), but seems chastened & trying to do something; make it, say, 5,6 pp/s double-spaced. They pay a little. Wd get you to movies maybe! Once. (But he was saying, how great he thought it was—I mean, iron is hot, etc.)

• • •

LETTER TO DENISE LEVERTOV

[Editorial note: This letter contains superscript numerals that are part of Creeley's original typescript.]

April 22/ 51

Dear Denny,

Very pleased to have yr letter; an answer to the last just mailed, & so won't go into same biz again (i.e., the house, etc.).

Fruitless enough, to go on arguing the biz of 'frenzy'—but if only to have the last word (which I very well know, I won't), I make this logic for those other comments. Take it this way, or break it down, so: one can have (among a variety, larger) at least 2 kinds of 'essence' for any <u>thing</u>, coming to exist in his writing (& here, of course, it's poetry we are thinking of)—& by 'essence', I mean those solids, which come to make substance for the given poem, etc. Simply, materials & the presence given to them, in the work.

So, then: (for our use) 2, 2 kinds. And the first, let's make it: of the <u>instant</u>, having no 'history' beyond the given context, no attachment to an external set of actions or premises (& it should be made clear, this is not to confine the possible associations, but rather to make clear, emphases) which the reader might be given, in another instance, by either implication, or overt reference.

In other words, like this:

> "Then see it! in distressing
> details—from behind a red light
> at 53rd and 8th . . . "

That is, here, in this instance, the emphases all fall to the <u>immediate</u>, to that <u>instant</u>, of coherence, of the <u>thing</u>, just here, just in this one context, being: NOW.

Like, Williams, most of his work (the example being, also, from him) where the fact is, NOW, is of, this instant, & the 'history' is, for that time, put down. And all falls, comes to bear, on this complex, of the instant, & all 'value' gets its weight from precisely, this complex—which is to say, no 'prior value' can 'act' in this complex.

Well, 2, that is, another way for it. Think, first, of two phrases: "the aged oak . . . " & "that place, where we had been . . . " The first, by an adjective (aged) implies a history, which the context, in all probability will make use of. This is the language of, <u>recall</u>, of, then, the mnemonic, wherein (usually) a shifting thing is held, the flux being, between this present & that past. Well, you must know the usual uses, of same. The second example is abt the same thing; the phrase, "where we had been . . . ", implying again, a 'past', which again probably, will be exploited in the poem's whole.

Now, when I argue this biz, of 'frenzy', & whether or not, say, this palm tree cd be, so, itself, the act of frenzy, & by token of such, for that instant, what the act is, and/or, itself, the tree, in fact this frenzy—it's clear enough, I'm pushing off from this biz of the, <u>the</u> instant; which is to say, the palm tree, here, is & insists on being, an entity held in, this instant, held just so, there, in the immediacy, of its context. It doesn't matter, say, whether an old woman had planted it to commemorate the birth of a child, to her, at the age of 88; or if, as well, this same storm came, finally, to uproot it; or even if, by vote of the town, it was decided to move it precisely 1 mile SSW, from its present site.

And so, even the more reasonable 'history' you tell me of, that is, "most of the time . . . as calm as could be . . . ", is, as well, irrelevant for the reader (or the writer, in the act of sd poem). [← !is not true, finally, but the other is—and is, the point.]

All that does come to matter, here, is what, precise, this palm tree is, in the poem's entity, what, there, it is, what there, its presence.

And that seems abt the end of it. Tho this much more, to make clear I have no argument against a mixture, of this biz of, recall, coupled with the other, of the instant. Well, this very wonderful example:

> "The blossoms of the apricot
>   blow from the east to the west,
> And I have tried to keep them from falling . . . "

That is, there, so hinged, held, the instant against the matter of all time, or of all action—& the care: a lifetime, & the loss: eternity.

(It is Pound & the words, Kung, & here, or in just this: the sum of all his work.)

Well, enough of it. Ok.

(But it seems I can't yet shut up, or, this much to show you where it cd get ridiculous:

> "How the bucket, this rust,
> the edge of it, that redness
>
>> being Mary who had left it out in the rain
>> that time we all went picking blue-berries
>> up on Foster's hill . . .
>
> Is present, is the
> color of
> present, has no time but
> now
>
>> tho it is almost 5 yrs old
>> & is pretty good even yet
>> under the circumstances."
>
>> (Creeley/ unpublished mss(hit)!)

Ok. Is enough.

Anyhow, a confusion, when it comes to exist, between where the 'presence' is to be [^ *emphasized*], either of past, or of present, can fuck you up, but good. But wd make it clear: this hasn't a damn thing to do with sd poem, & sd palm-tree, more than to make my logic for taking this palm tree, ONLY in the PRESENT the poem insists on. Ok.

On the new one: a hard thing for me to figure (if only because I had the lines of the other 2, in my ear, before I saw, in yr letter, it was made from them). Anyhow, one or two things (which, damn well let me insist, are only what comes, immediately into my head, being my, head, & so that limit, etc., etc., etc.)

One thing: certain things here & there, seem (in some sense) to break out of what 'pattern' of coherence the poem has. It's a hard thing to lay out, & perhaps best to make a copy here, marking by '( )', what bothers me (& following up same, with some more notes).

> [1](Precise
> as rain's first spitting
> words on the pavement)
> pick out
>   the core of violence
> give it back
>
> (aware of[2] (cool dawns) paused
> over strident avenues
> [3](come in simplicity unnoticed))
>
> iron satyrs stamping
> in desire
> jagged heads
> pushed up
>
> the city: inordinate!
> red honey on its towers
> smoking . . .
>
> spring evenings in sea light
> facades relax
> & always nightfall can impose
> a fantasy on the black air
> chips of light
> flashing scattered
>
> [4](but many fathoms down
> men are walking
> in clefts of hacked rock –
> are running
> jostled in dirty light from[5] (far above)

(reflected light) –
are dying
the derelict & the diamond-sharp)

speak to them!

words must beat
(iron heart of the unconscious street)
until a child might echo

[6](until a man looks up: angel)
under the unturned stone:

kick it away!

1/ a confusion of my own, i.e., is the rain spitting out words (as a figure, of speech), or are these words, there, like the rain is, on, literally, the pavement (as that impetus, to them, i.e., so available in that 'place'), or are the words in the 'men', implied as being there, because there are words? Anyhow: I confess to no clear pick-up, on the base sense of this section, & further, do not think a poem picks up quickly enough if its beginning is, as this is, a simile.

2/ a minor thing; mainly that 'cool dawns' comes to my senses, as a generalized specific, i.e., it implies an immediate sensing somewhat put out into generality— primarily that neither 'cool' nor 'dawns' are, in themselves, forceful enough to carry the image. The contrast, i.e., where it seems the words do carry such: strident avenues', tho, again, there's a little of the cliché in it, too.

3/ I get this ok, now; I didn't at first, that is, because of my own wondering of who it is, is the subject of these lines (i.e., who it is that is "aware"), I had wondered, at first, if this line was an address to a third person (which seems somewhat ridiculous now). But to make a comment on all of this section: are the avenues strident, when these dawns come?, at that time?, of day? Because there is no 'superior' context to enforce the image, against a 'literal' truth here, i.e., nothing that can twist the context out of a literal exposition of these dawns, in a literal place; hence, NYC, say, or any city similar, at 5am, & is such a city, then, strident?

4/ my only question abt this section, taken as a lump, is: IS this the central image, is it to be such? I.e., it's not a question of if it does the work, etc., being, it can as well as any other. The question: how many figurations can you work on this street, before its own actuality is muddled? As, say, image 1: street & the rain hitting it, that cleanness, etc., I mean, cleanness, of the hit (not that is washed, etc.); image 2: hot noisy streets (as opposed to, "cool dawns"); image 3: city, in its height, brute, iron, lust & power, etc.; image 4: a mixture of this sea-light, & an electric light (as of, flashes, perhaps, thunder storm, lights (tho only to suggest, the possible parallel), I mean, electric, flashes, precisely yr: "flashing scattered"; image 5: the sea city, under, pressure of water, light filtering down, reflected, the acts, in that light; image 6: hardness, streets, as of iron, metal, hard core, of the 'heart', under, streets, or more simply, that is, we are back to the literalities; image 7: almost the 'proverbial', or mythic, i.e., (DON'T leave a stone unturned, etc.), an 'air' of this mythic, of angels, & men, as those for whom angels can be, & the child, as the innocent, etc., & so on.

I do all this only to suggest the number of images, thru which a reader is compelled to move, & that further fact, he's given no central one, call it, on which to base his references, etc. Because the street is metamorphosed from the very 1st line, etc., & is never given time to be: "street", etc.

(at the end of these notes, want to take up a main head, which comes in, precisely, in this section.)

5/ my only question: is it too vague, this phrase? Perhaps the 'vagueness' serves a use, but anyhow, my question.

6/ two senses come to me, here, & I am wary, frankly, of both. Well, 1) that this man, with the stone off, becomes angel, or 2) finds angel [^ *under stone*]—& the thing, that the gain, of either, seems rather vague, or perhaps only that, angel, strikes little in me, unless substantiated (viz Blake, et al).

To get back, & wd again repeat, that these comments are only my own inexactness, i.e., only where the poem gets out of my reach, etc.

The thing: yr strongest image hits me, as being this sea-one, I mean, it is the one in which action & development takes place—it runs, then, not as an extension, as of, horizontal [^ *like this does* →]

> "the board like a line
> the head like a melon
> the sand like a sky"

but rather, is, base root: [^ *like this* →]

> "the sea, in its distance, marks
> the line of wonder, where rise, the several
> angels, or wonder, of
> these fish, marking a coastal range
> of, etc., etc., etc."

which is only to show, how angels & fish, et al, might assert a co-existent, a simultaneous, presence.

Which is the problem here, i.e., that this one sea-image, of these men, these lives, under it, takes on a central weight. Now, see what happens as the poem moves on, from this point.

You say, mark you: "speak to them!" That is, speak to them, these men (and where are they???), 'many fathoms down', & that's the damn rub, i.e., that they are, these whom you wd address, very much in the substance of this <u>prior</u> image, & no immediate way to get them out. So yr speech, involves men <u>still under the sea</u>, as far as yr reader is concerned, and so, frankly, all subsequent action is trying to shake off such, as no man cd reasonably kick off a stone, many fathoms down, etc.

You see the kick? Well, myself, I take it as <u>the result of a</u> [^ *developed*] <u>metaphor which has been treated as tho it were a simile</u>, that is, <u>as tho it did not, itself, assert a continuum, of action</u>, etc.

(To explain same: <u>a simile</u> has <u>no reality beyond that which it's the 'extension' of</u>: to wit—a head <u>like a melon</u>. The underlined has no existence, minus head. MORE, it can allow of any number of OTHER similes attached, as it is, to the SAME referent. As: a head like a melon, like a football, like a overripe peach. That is, each, in turn, in turn ride back, clearly, to <u>head</u>, & there's no fight, of any import, between them.

But, <u>metaphor</u>: is something else again. Take it so:

> "(Sun) The ball of fire falls & gashes against the substance of the land, burning there, its myriad fuels . . . "

I can't then say, with out trouble.

> "The place where all are warm, where
> there's no heating problem, where it's summer every day."

You just can't side, against a <u>developed metaphor</u> (as yrs is), any other action that doesn't admit of its own 'conditions'.

Well, metaphor can be so sided, <u>IF its referent runs clearly at the head</u>. Like this:

> "He was a brute, a lion, a beast, of courage, a veritable jungle of lust" (altho, even there, the shift to 'jungle', & that other 'basis' for action' is apt to disturb . . .)

Well, the rub, as I take it, here: that this metaphor, of the sea-land, sticks too good, its too damn fine, if such can be! What it does: fuck up all other similes, & actions in the poem, as it does fight with them, for the BASE reality. Ok. And that seems abt it.

(But note, anyhow, that in <u>the poem</u>, the "main action" (in literal terms of, he bought 7 apples, & then went to a movie & then, came home), occurs in this passage. Hence, the effect of such does impose its presence on all other 'actions', & most notably: that of the end.

Wd say, either 1) make of this sea-image, the full thrust of the poem, i.e., make it the center, & push it to the limit; or 2) break it back to simile as (as rain's first spitting, or even as other adjectives, etc.) such. Now, there are too many scatters, of adjective, of metaphor, of action, etc. And no prime, to which to refer same, but that implied, implicated in, such phrases as: "pick out the core of violence, etc." You don't have sufficient force, in these, to carry the relation of these other things to them, i.e., one slacks off.

To hell with it, for now—I say too much, anyhow, & expect it's: total confusion. Anyhow, do think that the problem is: 1) over-reach of this section noted (as developed metaphor, etc.); 2) under-play of base referent, action, for reader to string these metaphors, actions, on. Ok.

It's almost torture, to break these things out, at this distance. I see my own slackness, but how to get them back to 5 pages later without making it a morass of confusion (a veritable jungle! ha). Anyhow, it does seem finally, gain, to clear these things somehow, because I do insist: 1) an idea of what 'energy' is, in a poem, 2) What can break this 'energy' down, 3) all the related heads—all these things must be got to, not, finally & lord help us if they become so as dogma, as that rigidity, of attitude or practice, but altogether as the necessary clearing of a few possibly pertinent premises on which the act, final, of poetry might come to rest comfortably. And it's into this same collection, call it, the notes of metaphor, et al, can go. Only a few damn things, christ knows, that seem to re-occur in poetry & seem, as well, to make trouble each time they do. And so, the tentative observations. Ok.

Which ends me, for the moment. (I never thot I'd get thru it, damn frankly! I mean, my notes—& make same plain. I don't figure the poem can't be cleared. Myself, I wd be curious to see what this undersea biz might get to, pulled out whole, that is, let loose to run to whatever force it contains: that thrust, of same. Now, she's a poem, within, a poem, & it's a tough one, etc. Well, I don't want to take off all over again, so will drop her, just here.

Will bring the Olson bklet/ also, hope soon, or someday, to have the new one— Emerson has been damn near a yr on same, as it is. Someday. But will have stuff, anyhow, with me. Very much wish I cd bring recording of his reading—is the end! But, cannot at the moment see the use of lugging along such equipment as wd be necessary to hear it: to wit—recorder unit, simplifier, & speaker.

Also, a copy of ORIGIN off to you, with this mail.

So abt it. Figure Bereaved is a good one, & don't want to finger same further, i.e., you have all I cd think of, to object to, in same, & this can get ridiculous, if I set out to badger, etc.

I find I didn't mail that other letter, so will stick it in here. So / this for now. Will get back to it soon.

Yrs/ in chaos:
Bob

[note above salutation] *Have not read any Ford—will be borrowing some from you when we get in.*

. . .

LETTER TO PAUL BLACKBURN

[Fontrousse, France]
May 23/ 51

Will check with Gerhardt on the Levy directly; also, will keep my eyes open for Sordello edition. Also, postcards, et al. Ok.

(Saw part of G/s 1st issue in print, & substance of same, pretty fair. But, lacks Cid's flexibility at this point.)
Dear Paul,

An incredible number of hitches & delays to getting here, but with all possible anti-climax, we made it. A very beautiful place—& the rooms (3) very wonderful, i.e., a winding stair up, to these 2 bedrooms: high weirdly angled ceilings, & all a fine flat white (&/or : whitewash), & the kitchen, below, very fine as well. These rent for $5 per month, which is somewhat high for the locale, but we can hardly kick with a conscience.

Well, very hard, at the moment, to give you very much more of this place. The land is fantastic, & a fantastic ease to it all—we look out of our bedroom, to the south, & a very odd mountain, something like a boat, beyond which, or at the foot, is the place where, so they say, the Romans had put an end to the invasion of the barbarians, & all such things.

And, as there wd be, acres of grape vines, which, it turns out, are not high or on trellises, but are closely cropped little "trees" which stand abt 2 ft high, & all very neat & fine.

Really, a wonder, this place, & tho both kids are, now, screaming in my ears, & both of us, beat with the travel, which is the worst possible (to mean: the most hopelessly miserable & confused biz imaginable)—is real cool, even so. In fact : the end. Ok.

(Font Rousse, is a very small town, of some 6 families, & our place, at the end of the street, stucco, joined, as they all are, to the ones before it, etc. We have a small plot of ground, to ourselves, & our kitchen door opens out to the road, where, for example, someone's loading hay from the place next to ours. Sort of a 'dutch oven' like arrangement, where our gas stove sits, a small 2 burner one, & tile all over & the room, itself, very cool & pleasant tho it's hot as hell outside now. Roman ruins all over hell.)

I wd advise, immediately, that you put in for a Fulbright fellowship, which, on the strength of yr translations (1) & yr poetry (2) you can certainly get, & come to hell over because it is very great.

So, this for the moment, to thank you again for all yr kindness in NYC—& my own very certain pleasure at having had that time with you. It holds.

Will write soon again. I find mail is an expensive biz, so will hold off eloquence till we have more loot.

Write soon, &, if it's not too expensive, wd very much like to see what comes from now on. Was very much taken by what you showed me, & the 3 copied, & here—very fine. (The SUMMER one: very cool. Which is abt it—being, my head somewhere back in le Havre, & very glad to be rid of same.

All our love to you, & thanks again.

Write soon/
Bob

c/o GOODMAN, LES CAMUS, PUYRICARD, BOUCHES DU RHONE, FR/

. . .

LETTER TO WILLIAM CARLOS WILLIAMS

Fontrousse,
par Aix en Provence,
Bouches du Rhone,
FRANCE
June 29, 1951

Dear Bill,

I'd heard from Paquette and Olson that you'd not been feeling so well these past months. Very, very sorry to learn of it and very much hope it's done with by the time this letter gets to you. There damn well seems enough on your shoulders without that too.

A difficult thing to put, but anyhow—on the boat, coming over, jammed as we were with the kids and a cabin about the size of a public john, I was going through, again, your IN THE AMERICAN GRAIN. Damn well cannot tell you, or tell you enough, how it hit me. Well, sitting out on the deck, and neither here nor there, just that passage between—it all stuck, cut in with a fantastic strength. So, thanks. Which is the point.

Here, we make out. Cheap living and very damn fine surroundings. We're in a small village of some 6 or so families , and very decent people. I was even offered a job on one of the farms near here, so if we go broke, have an out. But it's what we needed, at least for the time. Living in NH had got too tight, too cramped for all of us, and there was no damn rest in it, no chance to figure it. But I very much miss the openness, the kind of room one can't find here. Everything seems worked out, drained out—no room. And the kind domesticated landscape isn't going to keep us too long. But certainly no kicks for the time.

Had good news from Laughlin, though no hulk ever made port on fainter wind. Anyhow, he'll print the 5 stories I'd shown you last fall in the coming ANNUAL along with a preface by Chas Olson. The latter is damn fine—it notes the kind of commitment now possible, now damn well necessary, in prose, and why it hadn't got said before, I don't know. Anyhow, he says it, and that's what counts.

I'm damned if I can figure why Laughlin prints them, or listen:

"Frankly, I find them awfully dry and dull reading . . . " But his business. Ok.

Hope all goes well with you, and that you're better. Anytime you have time, let me hear from you. But know that you're rushed, so only when you can.

All my best,
Bob

• • •

LETTER TO WILLIAM CARLOS WILLIAMS

August 1/51

Dear Bill,

A copy of PATERSON IV, sent on here, finally got in this noon, and I had been waiting for it, certainly, because of the fineness of the first three.

In any event, I was sitting down, having read it, too quickly, and my wife getting supper ready, etc., began to read it to her, trying to figure, frankly, if it was you, or it was me, was off.

How can I put it—but as, straight, did read it, the works, sitting there, to her, and damn well <u>heard</u> it, myself, got the whole thing hard, and how it damn well came in.

It is dif-
ficult to say it, because, for one thing, I revere you. I take you as something I can
take, very much in my own hand, and very exactly there. The difficulty is that
one supposes a thing, a man a thing, like yourself to be complete, to be a fix, as
Olson would say it, beyond inessential intrusions.

But here, this distance from what comes to sit hard in my own
guts, anyhow—here, I have to make it anyhow, or say it—the fineness of this
writing.

The sea part, the opening
of 'III' & many many other 'places' are as beautiful, as firm as the ground that
makes them. Damn simply—it is an organism, a continual growing in the head
of whoever can listen.

Very damn wonderful to know you are there.
All my very best to you,
Bob

. . .

LETTER TO WILLIAM CARLOS WILLIAMS

Sept/27, 1951
Dear Bill,
Yours in, and many thanks for the permission. Gerhardt will be equally
grateful.

France: beat, dead place at this point, and the people are simply without any
energy. What can one expect, I damn well suppose. But depressing—a very mild
word for the present sensation. I think we can stay on, mainly, because it is a
cheap living for us, and, too, I can use the perspective, although it is a deeply bit-
ter experience. We don't see, frankly, very many, i.e., we have kept more or less
in this town (small, farming, etc.) but going out, now & again, it strikes in as the
same thing. No one can be moved very much; no one has that part of him left.

What it does do: make the US a
damn clear thing, unavoidable. Americans here, or those I've met up with, don't
really know quite what to say to each other.

But cheap, certainly that, by any US standard. We
do very well on some $30 a wk, the 4 of us (2 kids), and that covers everything.
The present place we have rents for $6 (a little under) a month, and serves fair
enough.

I don't know where one can go; I really don't trust place, anyhow. I am certainly
young, but have never felt it did anything more than catch me up, trip me, into
assumptions, etc. It is hard to keep clear, in any case.

Otherwise, I wish I could see India again, as it was the 1st time, a damn war, etc. They were fine, fine people; they were on to something, it seemed to me then.

What about any of the other places, although I wonder what they come to, now. But I can't see Europe, not with this death on it. They say, Italy, and oddly, Spain, are better, i.e. the people, though deadened by simple hunger & lack of clothing, do rise even so. A friend just now in Italy writes with a great deal of excitement, about the movement in architecture, how he feels they have struck on to something that can hold them. But France—jesus, you are well away from it, or it doesn't offer a place.

(Again, we hang on, because it makes a gauge, for us; but you know it anyhow, and what is new, to us, would not be so, for you.)

Should make very clear that I say any of this from a very limited knowledge; we are very isolate. We see, really, very few people. What we would know about—small farming town. Useless to generalize about the 'country', France, even though I suspect parallels.

Very kind of you to make the comments on the work in ORIGIN; it means considerable to me. Have never forgot your kindness, all of it. Thanks again.

Will look for the AUTOBIOGRAPHY with all possible excitement; I damn well need something just like that to lift me out of this for awhile. Very grateful.

So, this for now; and will write soon again. You make a damn fine place to put these things. Glad that the novel does come. And all best luck on it.

All best to you,
Bob

Have you seen Olson's APPOLONIUS OF TYANA*—I think he has damn well rung the bell again. Very exciting thing, and prose,—really he hasn't handled it this firmly since CALL ME ISHMAEL. I know you'll like it, and hope you can get hold of a copy, there.

Cid told me abt your letter to him, re ORIGIN; very damn kind thing. That magazine means a good deal to me, to any of us, finally, like Blackburn, Olson, and the rest. The sheer wonder of having a sympathetic outlet—what that damn well does do.

The damn ones like KENYON, the big-wigs, they trap you, but quick; they took another story, of mine, and when, getting here, etc., I felt it was finally a little easy, and asked for it back, I take it they felt themselves insulted, or I have never had a damn word in answer, from them.

In other words, the younger one is, the more they assume the favor they do, in printing, etc. And the more they assume one should damn well have NO feelings, about his OWN work. Fuck them all. Good that Cid gives us just that chance.

[note in left margin] *issued there at Black Mt/College; book. He is staying on there for the time; they expect their baby anytime now, I think—theoretically, October. He also got out, LETTER FOR MELVILLE: protest against the recent Melville Society business, which seemed a rather cheap commercialization— "birthday party", etc. The usual.

· · ·

LETTER TO DENISE LEVERTOV

October 3, 1951

Dear Denny,

Your other letter just here, & do think it a very good idea to do just what you say, i.e., to write Williams. Finally, all one ever gets out of it: those readers who can get it. Ok, and the address: Dr. W. C. Williams, 9 Ridge Road, Rutherford, N.J.

I felt nervous, frankly, writing about the poem, and particularly, because I am as apt to generalize as anyone, and get off into certain backwaters (so they are, usually, in the face of the poem) that are not much more than my own; in this case, the whole problem of description, and what it relates to in my own things, etc. In short, did not feel I did very much, in that reading, or that much of what was said, after, could be of help.

But more abruptly, or at least now: the fact that I have a stronger sense, of the content, from the little note you put on the back of the poem, i.e., read it for yourself, and tell me which of the two 'instances' (the poem, or this) come to the actual substance you are after.

> "The point is supposed to be, but I'm pretty sure I haven't shown it, that the wonderful crammed future we leaned into for a moment, almost believing in it ("Let's go round the world together when the war's over"): our "Youth" in fact—was right there to hand just then in that very idea, in our eagerness, in the unspokeness at that time of love. Does it seem to say that at all? or have I left it all out in trying not to stuff it? I don't want any feelings of nostalgia in it—just to pin it. ~~for a moment.~~"

Difficult to say much more, than just to put that there, i.e. how else. The one thing, "art", and of what use to pretend it is anything if it cannot give this same exactness, even in the loopings, or the passage of, a feeling.

Id est: why worry about 'art', or anything, if one can make a clarity on any occasion, on any way,—really, if there only be something that does say it, that does get it over, poem or whatever? If the note seems to me more exact, more a <u>thing</u> than the poem finally does, perhaps I do read in, too easily, knowing you, etc. But I doubt it. I would want the poem to be better, etc., I have that hope for such things.

Well, enough, I figure; any one time doesn't really matter, or if it does, it is not that 'every time' be a success, etc. All of which, saying it this way—sounds too much, much too much, like leaning on this poem, too hard, and trying to damn it, etc. Not that—many things in it I like very much, but against the note : it can't quite hold, I think.

I always keep talking; I damn well never know exactly when to stop.

Etc., etc.

No sign of Aldington, and can't figure what happened; i.e., no letter, or any sign that he doesn't still mean to come. In short, still wait for him, though I begin to wonder if he will show, etc. A matter of vanity, at this point; can't still think of what, finally, to say to him. The feeling of Lawrence, all of it, gets very much in the way.

Well, no matter. Otherwise, not much excitement. Ashley [Bryan] will be in Spain until November, or thereabouts, I think; I've had two letters from him and his own excitement, at being there, sounds very much like the release you felt, getting out of here & into Italy. I sometimes think we'd be smart to follow suit; but I hate to move Dave again, or any of us, for that matter, having this foothold now here. D/ makes out very well with the language, and the change might be too dirty a trick to play on him. As well, do get in a little, feel somewhat more settled, and so suppose it wiser to hang on, hoping we can get around to some extent once we have the car.

(A/ sd: people very, very poor—& unmistakable horror of their position, etc.—but tremendously warm & kind, and that means a great deal to him, after the flavor here. He says the children all flock after him, come to the place where he stays to get him out; trying to buy something (just your own experience) he has it given to him, nine times out of ten.)

Nothing more re a house; a few more leads, but nothing substantial. We have heard there might be a place vacant by that chateau opposite the farm where we get milk, i.e., that one sits up on the hill there, to the left, and has all the fine trees in front of it—1st place on yr left, in fact, after the shrine. Would be ok, if we can't find anything in Aix; am anxious, in some ways, to get into Aix, i.e., could see more people, and move a little faster, etc. Now & again, the isolation here gets a little rough, though I can't say I really kick about it. Altogether used to it, after NH. It has its advantages.

Now gets cooler, and we've all been having colds, what with the dampness; kids especially, and see we can't hang on here too much longer. Upstairs rooms, with those high ceilings, couldn't be heated by any means I can now figure; would all go up, etc. Otherwise, we can heat the kitchen ok, with the little stove, and not much work picking up wood for it back on the ridge—burns a little easier than coal, & is, of course, no expense, etc.

Emerson wrote, he could put out a small booklet of my poems, come spring or thereabts. Don't finally trust him too much, i.e., he did screw up Olson incredibly, and I think O/ now wants out altogether (something like almost a year over-due on the book in question). But I don't really care how 'fast' they come out, etc. No hurry that I can see, and he does print decently (viz. Williams' PINK CHURCH) & wd make a good book, etc. Not much matter; prose interests me much more, etc.

Which is abt it : the news. What with the other letters. Will write again soon, and you do the same. Certainly will try to get down, to see you all, whenever it's possible. Damn delay on car (all the mess of papers) makes it now difficult to say when exactly. However. And will keep you in touch.

All our love to you all,

Bob

POEM:

This feeling about it, mainly, granting you anyhow its fineness, of content, and wish to see it all held. That it could move a little faster, through the details, i.e., the adjectives, perhaps, and certain nouns that strike me as a little abstract. Will copy it out, anyhow, and then can say more abt. it:

Perched on bristly grass, a shaved steep slope:
"Africa" . . . "islands" . . . Forcing <u>belief</u>
      almost <u>belief</u> . . .

          What succession!   *[possible place for this emphasis?]*
Of continents, migrations . . .
          dark-faced cities in another
    sunlight—and details!
    Awaking to the shrill voices, the shadows leaving
    a certain street.

Even perhaps
    partings: again, again   *[perhaps: again <u>and</u> again. No matter.]*
Even that far for anything, and all of it.

And after night, one quiet
Morning

The sun meanwhile raised odours—tar & cinders—from   [circle around
                                          "meanwhile"—*Necessary?*]
the track, the glittering rails now gripping   [*Don't feel altogether easy about this one.*]
the east & the west. [*Keep "fierce tensions"—Ann goes for that—and I do myself.*]

And something we made from   [circle around "And"—*Don't finally need that.*]
what lay to hand: the unspoken
and love.

Which is the usual problem, of me intruding, etc. But several things anyhow.
First verse: I wish that the belief could be brought down from the abstract (i.e.,
this noun) to an action which would give the particular instance or anyhow,
grab 'belief' more tightly. I thought perhaps, "Forcing belief to
            almost belief . . . "   or something, perhaps, more action, there.

The whole problem, or what it usually is: to wrap in details so that they don't jut
out as a horizontal, call it, from the poem's main line. Viz., for one thing, the
possible problem of "awaking to shrill voices" which define further, the line pre-
ceding, or that last of it, but don't move the action of the poem too much, even
so. I felt the same way about the, "renewed, a rhythm . . . " since the rhythm at
least is so clear in the two words, "again, again . . . " I.e., some doubt in my mind
about repeating, or stating their overt 'meaning' in the line subsequent. Also,
would, perhaps, avoid overt definitions, like: "Future: . . . " It is a little out of the
main line, i.e., juts out, and seems to say: I can only say it, not contain it, which
may be, I know, true, but I think it takes, even so, saying in the actual language
of that block, and not this sudden plunge out into, the general, as this word
must always be. Looking back, see no real reason for that last "and", i.e., just
to get those two possible senses, and the line break gives them to you anyhow,
without hammering it in, like that. I.e., unspoken / love.

Main headaches, as I feel them: 1st verse,—perhaps to redo all of same, to get it
off, a little smoother, and not so much lean on the descriptive, which is always,
a little static. Perhaps the 2nd verse, where you bring in, "awaking . . . ", tho I
don't really kick much at that, but only feel it, against, or after, the 1st verse; i.e.,
it juts out, now, because it has that first verse with much the same thing in it,
i.e., the same kind of description.

                        3rd verse—very important, or I feel
it so, and so, very important to have it moving as quietly & as deeply as possible.
I.e., it is, in some sense, the poem's crux? I feel it that way.

                  Let-off of 4th verse—ok, with me. I.e., I get that and
feel the necessity.

5th verse: again the suggestion that 'future' be not overtly given; that you do it, more simply, and perhaps only by, the bare statement of, the feeling, i.e., what was done.

> something we made
> out of what lay to hand: unspoken love.

Or perhaps quick, say, as in this copy:

> and something we made from
> what lay to hand: the unspoken
> love.

Always the job, tho pardon the damn tone, of : keeping description IN. Not letting it EXTEND beyond the main line. Description most usually supplementary, i.e., most usually a question of one or two minor details, necessary to a complete grip of the action, i.e., of the feeling coming over.

Figure the thing as the novelist has to (ask yr husband!): he knows that John Jones will come clearer, to any reader, by picking up the ax and letting his mother have it, than by any talk about the rather sinister cast of his face, when his mother happened to be present, etc. I know one can't always 'anticipate', but wherever the action can do this work of description, without going into it directly, then there is considerable gain. Description means, sadly, putting down the action to describe; action keeps the reader on, i.e., never lets up its hold. Action can be any thing, i.e., can be the tweaking of the thumb, or raising of an eye-brow, etc., but has to move, something has to, move. Same headache in poetry, I think, as in prose. Figure how the damn prose writer can bore you stiff by talking ABOUT his characters rather than letting them come thru by their actions. It comes to much the same thing. One action: worth a million descriptions. It simply says more, quicker, more hard.

Very damn hard to say much, without getting you into my own headaches, but that you know. So, this much, anyhow, and hope it doesn't ride too far off it.

(Check Olson's comments on description, in PNY piece, i.e., he gets it all very clear there; the way it can slack attention, the way it is apt to run loose.)

. . .

LETTER TO MITCH GOODMAN

October 3, 1951

Dear Mitch,

Getting the letter off to Denny, etc., wandered about this room, banging my head; miss you all very much, as must be apparent from these frequent communications, like they say. But doubt if I could get thru, very well, to anyone at the moment; get blurred, not so much in the divers intentions, as in the feeling, under, that I am not up to much.

But sane, but always, sane. Even so, putting aside the more basic considerations (food, clothing, heat, & the modicum of love, call it)— something well under, and much deeper than anything. Would you feel that? I think it is, finally, what I try to reach thru to in the stories, a kind of sensing, if one can say it without pretension, etc., of the separation that comes, even, of any two together. I think, and forgive me, that perhaps in coitus two people do get as far away from one another as is ever possible; Lawrence used to harp on it, always the 'dark river' which he made, at last, into 'gods.'

But it is love; I mean, one doesn't sentimentalize that, or queer it by any such statement. No one can know very much about it, who depends on a glowing sympathy, etc. I really give the novel up, now, because I take myself as too much in passage, too much on the way. If ever I feel, or say, that you can likewise afford to give up your own, it will be that same sense of it. No use whatever in making a tyrant for oneself; that is, too much that obliterates & dulls us as there is. But it is great (& I do, by god, envy you) to hear it comes; this must sound pretty grey against it.

Right now so much rides in that I wish to christ we could talk about: I miss you very, very much in that way. Not simply a 'listener'—or not the simple ear, put it, but one who digs, who makes the basic communication. I damn well thank you for giving me that, for insisting on it, when you were here. I get, now, beginning to have it hurt a little, i.e., the way things can balk, can go dull, I get the way you must have felt the first months. It's a question of holding, I suppose; and there's little pleasure in such a static position. I can't see that one can ever enjoy it, or feel himself to be deriving profit, as some might insist, etc.

I keep wondering what Bob is doing; perhaps a way out for me, to think of his own hell. Too often delight in someone whom we take as being worse off than we are, etc. Our social standard, etc. Anyhow, I wish he would write, I keep thinking of him, feeling impotent, unable to get thru to him, or so it seems.

Buddy [Berlin] sounds a little careful; I know the sound, etc., know what pushes it. I do it myself, etc. Anyhow, one is more sensitive to any caution, to any kind of reserve, at this point of hanging on, or really, of slipping in spite of himself. (No matter, finally, and this is of course for yourself—Buddy is someone I never speak of very easily; he is very close to me & I have the confusion, sometimes, about thinking of him.)

What the hell I did want to say—keep on with that concision you came to, in that one comment on S/ Lawrence, and you'll never have a damn thing to worry about.

I wish to god you were close enough to be reading this Fenollosa, i.e., his base sense of <u>verb</u>. Very damn fine and rather than talk, etc., will attempt to wind up on it, and get it off to you. I've hesitated because I think I have another copy coming, and wait to see if it will.

This to whet your appetite:

"A true noun, an isolated thing, does not exist in nature. Things are only the terminal points, or rather the meeting points, of actions, cross-sections cut through actions, snap-shots. Neither can a pure verb, an abstract motion, be possible in nature. The eye sees noun and verb as one: things in motion, motion in things, and so the Chinese conception tends to represent them . . . "

Which is still in the beginning, i.e., still before that point where he really picks up speed, <u>and</u> weight. A very clean thing; a very helpful one for considering the base character of language. And like it or not, we have to. Well, enough here; will have it on to you as soon as I can.

Etc., etc.

Novel: all possible digression (I still feel that); all possible sequence from a to b to c. The whole problem of: sequence—is there ever any use in trying to deny anything that does happen in the actual writing, i.e., if one thing does ride in upon another, even though we have intended something else, what can we do by forcing, or what can we do but follow?   Which is the old song, etc.

The thing: to <u>hinge</u> oneself by a 'plan', an intention flexible enough to allow oneself growth in the act; i.e., the embarrassment of change, of how one does change, can't help it, etc.

And yet, can't write 'all out doors', etc. Have to begin, etc. The question seems to continue: how? But only to, begin—i.e., the 1st word, right or wrong, gets that out of the way?

Two problems: 1) to be able to follow the depth, the actual plunge of any per-
     ception (any <u>thing</u> coming to find its own character, in your-
     self), to be able to get down to that depth, somehow, to make
     it straight dive;
    2) to be able to move, with all swiftness, between the divers
     perceptions, to be able to change, to shift, to play it like any
     broken-field running—because nature abhors, among other
     things, that gap between perceptions, etc.

Ok, and I only repeat, Olson's Laws, etc. I used to have those 3 main dicta nailed
to the wall over that table back in Littleton; perhaps I should have taken that
part of the wall with me.

Write soon, or anyhow, when there's time. Great pleasure to hear; I look for
them.
       All love to you all, & will write again soon,
           Bob

       • • •

LETTER TO HORACE SCHWARTZ

[Published as "A Letter from Robert Creeley," *Goad* 2 (1951–52): 16–19]

                [late 1951]
Dear Schwartz,
 A few notes I'd wanted to get into the last but there wasn't time.
 Anyhow, it's about the Pound article. Certainly it's a more honest position
than any I've yet met with. All the usual blatting about this and that which has
attached itself to the "Pound controversy" hardly clears any of the necessary
ground—or makes the least sense.
 But here's what I'd like to put against the implied judgment—"How many
powerful, illuminating lines are found in the published work of Pound? If you,
like myself, have not found many, then you too may want to forget the whole
thing."
 1) very simply, 50 years work, and at what? Criticism. Translation. Hauling
over into the English of at least 3 major areas of thought, including American.
 2) a principle of verse (kinetic) which has made, literally, the basic condition
which now makes it possible for us to go on with it—Retrospect; How to Read;
The Serious Artist—this hardly begins it.
 3) a body of work, of verse, which I can mainly defend, or only, in terms of
my own respect for it—it is based, surely, on a man's actuality, and isn't that
what, precisely, poetry is supposed to be?
 There's no defense for the anti-semitism, not even your own. There's none

that I can, myself, admit. And so, perhaps, I have an even greater difficulty than yourself (if you stand back of your own statement) in adjusting to the concepts of certain of the Cantos; and honestly, I don't adjust—I go to that work to get what seems to me of <u>use</u>, and the rest I toss out, condemning it just by that act.

What else? If we forget the other insistences of that same book, forget the emphasis on the Confucian ethic, on the literal horror of the Usury we inhabit, of all of it, one man's hardness, his ability to hold to himself, what the hell ground do we have left, to stand on, to call him: traitor? Well, tell me, because I don't know.

There remains, in any case, books that you should have there, to be going at, to answer your own problem of 'powerful, illuminating lines . . . "

Take off on the criticism: POLITE ESSAYS; MAKE IT NEW; PAVANNES AND DIVISIONS; ABC OF READING; KULTUR; etc. I mean, go at these, and see if there isn't as hard and as direct a mind there as you've ever met with. "Damn your taste, I would like if possible to sharpen your perceptions, after which your taste can take care of itself . . . "

Have you read his things on Dolmetsch? Did you know that he picked up on composers like Antheil, et al., long before any public had thought of looking for them?

You should dig into these things; not be put off by a disgust with all the present palaver—it means nothing, and it will come to nothing. It's demonstrated exactly that capability already. So, to hell with it—go about your own business as you've absolute right to.

But don't lose any chance for additional clarity, which is to say, don't toss out this man's incredible sharpness. I damn well say it's there to be got—and any of the aforementioned books will give it to you straight. The CANTOS are, first of all, an incredible condensing, as speech is, no man is going to pick up easily or quickly. They take work.

I'd say: XXX, XIII, XLVII, XLV, and the section marked <u>libretto</u> on the end of LXXXI –all will give you a straight pick-up, quick, of what is here going on. Anyhow, please read them, or read them again, if you already have—tell me if I'm full of shit, and that's ok with me. Only try it. Ok.

But (lord/god) let's not suggest, even by murmur, that Housman, who (did he not, damn well right he did) sold out, and cheap at that? The pretty lyrics, the cheap little sentiments, of horror, of death, of all the tremendous LOSS, of death—that such is to be put against Pound, the implications to be: he is more?

Goddamn it, I had no sympathy there. I could not stomach that. And yet you <u>have to mean it</u>—you have no right to write what you do not mean, and do not mean exactly.

Anyhow, Housman? Christ, he is a cheap little prick; with two-bit rhymings, all the easy penance of a bankrupt man.

(Read Pound's HOUSMAN AT LITTLE BETHEL—I mean, that's a much kinder attack than I could myself make.)

> Listen: "There died a myriad
>   And of the best, among them,
>   For an old bitch gone in the teeth,
>   For a botched civilization,
>
>   Charm smiling at the good mouth,
>   Quick eyes gone under earth's lid,
>
>   For two gross of broken statues,
>   For a few thousand battered books."

Write when you can.

>   All best,
>   Creeley

· · ·

LETTER TO LARRY EIGNER

[undated, 1951]

The truth is: I smoke hashish & fuck a good many women other than my wife? The truth is: I read 24 hrs a day, sometimes more, & make extensive notes, exhaustive notes in what time's left me?

Dear Larry,

Yr notes very cool. Figure we cover that, at this point. One thing, tho,—comment of mine abt infinity of form relates, only, to this belief: form is the extension of content—content, I take to be, infinite. Content: each man's IN, inside. Here's where the "idiom" can exist, ONLY here. It has nothing to do with idiomatic language.

Neither understand nor see the point of: this comment. "I'd say, though, that you and Cid, for instance, handle more stuff than I seem able to . . . " What's your grounding, say, for that comment? What do you know abt (1) what I read and (2) what do I know abt what you read (you've noted abt, say, 4 bks, and I'm not certain I've noted even as many as that). Just to point to this, i.e., what you have that sentence lead into: "And it wd seem that the more stuff you read the higher your floor and perhaps the more types of experience you have no use for . . . " Well, shit, I certainly can't speak for Cid here, and wish to hell you wdn't bracket us, since WHY? I.e., let's deal (1) with what we KNOW and (2) with ONE at a time and (3) keep these to SPECIFICS. Anyhow, that statement. I'm no Horatio Alger, that is, I haven't a wish to refine myself out of existence, nor, say, does one experience cancel another cancel another, so on &

so on. What the hell are you on to, there? I.e., why not this, man as continuum, accumulation, powered by, say, pitch & intensity of that complex: self/emotion/ intellect. Just that.

Don't mean to bug you with this biz, abt yr sentences. But for what, eh? I mean, what you do here, it seems, is only duck out on something that relates, finally, to neither Cid or myself: and/or: what you figure you've read & what you figure you can get out of it. I mean, what's that to do with me, yr 'floors' and all, like flying carpets, yet. You can't measure this biz, on the wall, like I grew 2 inches this past 6 months. Or, say, to drunk sits next to you, I'm sorry: I'm no longer interested in the experience which you constitute. I just don't get it. I damn well assert, the FLOOR is the FLOOR, and if it is worth talking abt, at all: IT'S GROUND. Dirt. GROUND. That stays PUT. Well, like this very good example, for what, by yr standards, yr scales, am I writing to you? I.e., you wd suppose, I take it, since I am beyond you in point of reading (which is yr statement, brother, NOT mine), you wd be a type of experience I have no longer use for. Riddle me that. I mean, I am not that in love with my own platitudes, & I figure I'm getting as much out of this biz, certainly, as you are, & probably, & why not: a hell of a lot more. You've got to set up something else.

      Let me put it this way. As for writing poetry, reading it is the secondary thing. Very secondary, when you come to the act. I don't, by that, throw it out. But I assert : not, in any sense, at root of push.

A good many people read poetry, read books. Very damn few write ones worth their reading. Why.

      Who wants to be calm, analytic. Frozen. Sd Pound: lot o' eunuchs with tape-measures busily measuring the Venus de Milo . . . you see, the alternative to yr diagram, which comes to, I take it, a belief that 'experience' is mass, i.e., exists in same sense that block of iron might, & governed, also, by that law proposes: no 2 objects of equivalent mass & volume can exist in the same 'place'. Shit. It's REACH, we don't leave HOME, to extend so, to make that thing. Vide: "I have travelled much in Concord . . . " Thoreau didn't move on dogmas, didn't lay down one thing to pick up another, abcdefg. Experience is Extension, is the grip, or so one might hope, on RELATION. The reach of a man's experience comes to his apprehension of the RELATIONS (the what happens between himself, objects, himself AS object) posited by the 'happening' of experience.

Again, for what: try to figure editors, opinions of other, other people, UNLESS you figure their direction has its points of contact with your own. By 'direction': not ONLY, say, we're all going to heaven and/or: hell.

Am sending you a copy of POETRY NY. Because I want you to read Olson's article there. Nothing else in it.

Am not an editor of anything that I know of. Cid had asked me to go on as a contributing editor, on this new gig, but I cdn't take it on.

So it goes,

Best to you,

Bob

. . .

LETTER TO RENÉ LAUBIÈS

Sunday [May 25, 1952]

Dear Rene,

No time to say anything yesterday. As said, everything is ok—no damage that matters, or, only, one of the matts (the one on the larger pastel) got a little torn—that can be repaired in Freiburg, i.e., simple enough to give it another if it's ok with you. (Could keep the old one for customs' stamp, etc.)

Which is dull—the thing I damn well want to make clear: how very incredible these all seem to me. We put up the five drawings, on the wall back of me (big stretch—lets them all have room) and fantastic how they hold on.

Really, you teach me a very great deal. One thing: variation, how christly infinite its use can be. I thought of,—take a black square (or form of that kind) & there it sits, static, without 'time' or movement. Put one of these against it, that juxtaposition, and it's a christly WORLD—it has that dimension.

'Time', variation, the rhythms which effect it—your work has incredible hold here,—it is as dominant in this particular as any painting (or verse, or anything finally) that I've ever known. Hence, my own excitement,—to have them there, insisting on that,—that one know it, be forced to know it.

I hate to be too damn subjective about it, that is, it would be easy enough. No man ever gave me this before. It has that shock in it,—to know it is possible.

In any case—character of the one for 3rd part of 3 FATE TALES: it defines me, damnit, it allows me into my own content in a way I'd never had given before. (And how,—but by just such an act as this drawing is?)

No damn use saying one is 'nicer' than another, or any rot like that; 'IN THE SUMMER', 'THE PARTY',—christly GROUND they maintain, force out—just fantastic damnit, there isn't a way of repeating it here.

(Only regret that, in the note, I could not more insist on this character, now so present to me—that structure in these things is no damn simple matter of 'oppositions' (like black to white)—that black, say, in these has precisely that same 'infinite' as a sound (like, I had heard a record of Casals, a Bach sonata for unaccompanied cello, etc., and one note became an infinity under, literally, his hand.)

It's damn hard to say it all, all that I do get now. In that way, you do teach, you force conception to instance, to literal presence. The arbitrary, the conjectural, both damn well have FORM, have (what form is) presence in these things.

(Olson always saying,—those who don't know confusion,—how lucky perhaps, but how goddamn not ourselves. Not anything we can allow,— i.e., these two simple equations, like color for its redness, its singleness, and NOT engaged as FORM.

I do damn well remember the paintings (and very anxious to see them again),—how, there, color (the single character of any—all that rot that Kandinsky was gargling in those notes, etc.) became 'structure', and the headache is, for me, defining it actually, i.e., not letting it go as 'impression', etc. What I intend: that, in those, color was line, if that makes sense—that it was not to be separated, could not be, from its precise instance in the work.

Like, you can say, there goes a lady with a red dress, etc. And then, it's like the color of my coat, etc. And 'red' in such a place, has only itself—it is distinct from its occasion, or what, say, is carrying it.

But that is not at all the way in your work—you can't say that, then. Color, there, is not to be 'color' as these separate 'values' of the eye, etc. It is as much 'line', that position, that character of rhythm, as it is 'red' or 'blue' or whatever.

Well, what the hell TO say. You knock me out, no other way of putting it. The wall is damn well MOVING, wish you were damn well HERE.

(Sometime, would very much like to pull all this out, i.e., to do something allowing me more room, more space for a definition of these impressions, i.e., what now hits me.

It is very damn exciting; the fact of an authority (altogether beyond usual notions of 'power') is always that. What else.

Character of the paintings only more, I think, than what these drawings are, because more, literally, is present, is being used—but to suggest that there is any superiority, etc.,—can't do that. Like saying, man & horse, more interesting than man, etc. Just isn't true. Or isn't 'true' in a sense I can admit.

Anyhow, thanks, thanks, thanks—never will be able to say it right. But they are so very very good, so damn much their OWN fact.

Looking to seeing you,—am sure that we will now get to Paris, I'll keep you in touch about when, etc.

Will take all these with me, if that's ok with you (i.e., drawings along with pastels, etc.) Hope that we get there when it's being set up, etc. That is, to make sure they are set unequivocally. (In this respect—would it be ok to substitute fresh matts on the drawings, ie., something not white (since that wd throw off the lights in the work, etc.) but something of your own order—only that these matts are a little bent, etc.,—wish to have them set real hard, fresh, there in Freiberg. Ok; not, I expect, the major issue.)

Anyhow, all our very dearest love to you, you are incredible!

Bob

· · ·

LETTER TO PAUL BLACKBURN

[Lambesc, France]
June 22, 1952

Dear Paul,

Yours in, and that poem is real, real cool. Verbs and whole slide of it, too much. You make it altogether. In fact, let me put a bid in, if you haven't sent it out, etc., for this gig with our boy SS/—his magazine. But time enough, but if it is free you got yrself a deal. Ok.

That letter off to you at the old place yesterday. Hope to god you can see it. Reading here about the HUDSON biz,—makes more sense than ever. Whole damn context of such as that magazine isn't it,—the booklet would give you the whole room, and cut out that damn dribbling in the corner, etc. Well, what you think—it's there if you can use it.

On Lash, etc. Write him, I'll tell him to write you anyhow. He is apt to be slow,—I suppose there's some damn reason for it though wouldn't grant him it anyhow. But he's amiable, and you can count on it. He got John Husband for the poetry editor,—I was somewhat sad about that, or thought if one of us could get in, it would make sense—not just the outlet, etc. But I guess H/ is ok, or I don't really know a damn thing about him. I see Wms/ makes him the 'listener' in the end of the AUTO/BOG. O well.

I forgot to say G/ is still hunting down that Levy,—he's a tough one. It turns out the publisher is in East Germany, and that's not good—or takes a bit of doing to get the book out. Or so G/ reports. Anyhow we're on it,—never fear. I tell you what,—I got contact now with a bookseller, etc., in England, and prices are pretty cheap on the exchange—I'll give them the Sordello title, also the Levy, and also ask ole SS/ to see what he can dig up, since he's on it I guess himself. (I damn well thought he was, come to think of it, seeing that one poem I sent you,—it's part of it in any case.)

Things here ok, though I am not so cool as I might be. The baby coming, though that isn't it. What it is, is the damn wall on all four sides of this place,—I just noticed it yesterday. They have a whole field of flowers, planted for seed, etc., just the other side of it, and I can't see a thing.

Very nice last night though,—part of the garden space, almost all of it, we've given over to friends here, man is Spanish and wife French, and some nice kids too. He'd been out hoeing, and came in after, for some wine, etc., and was telling us about Lorca, who it seems he grew up with,—this time for real. Anyhow was saying how L/ at this Grand Concourse des Poetes, etc.,—guitar starting up, plunk etc., in the background, L/ was about 17, everyone saying, you go first Garcia, and Garcia blushing, and saying no, no, no, etc. But they keep pushing, and he reaches over & drains a bottle of cognac, and then starts off:

> The church is a bizness, and the rich
> are the bizness men.
>   When they pull on the bells, the
> poor come piling in and when a poor man dies he has a wooden
> cross, and they rush through the ceremony.
>
> But when a rich man dies, they
> drag out the Sacrament
> and a golden Cross, and go doucement, doucement
> to the cemetery.
>
> And the poor love it
> and think it's crazy.
> [*CP* I, 121]

Really too much,—gestures he was making, and always those sounds. I made this trip to Perpignan, about two months back, with two friends here, and all the way the man was reeling off Lorca,—and it was damn fine. And also G/, or his wife said, how he could look through any collection of Spanish poetry, and knowing none of it, could still pick out L/ by the sounds.

He also said, how L/ didn't write them down, etc. He made this movement with his hands, writing,—but had them in his mouth, whereupon he put his fingers close together, and made this movement toward his own mouth, just a little open. [note typed in left margin: Same man won't learn french, he don't like it, although he's also tried to translate all of Lorca into french, so his wife can hear it too.]

Well, what's new. Just see that the poem is slated for Cid, and that makes sense. I have had such a goddamn dull time with him, the past week,—I know what you mean by evasive, though I don't suppose he ever damn well means it. I'm damn sure there's something about this in the Analects,—not that it matters that much.

I don't get much done, I had that sort of push, I guess, just before we left Fontrousse. Going over there a few days back to see the people and give them some pictures, etc., Ann was saying, it was very, very lovely now. It always was, really—but the house, or the three rooms didn't give us any room, to make it. But the place is a damn fine one, hope I can show it to you sometime.

Mostly that I don't have much ground under me right now. And that's why, too, my place is so much on the paper, and not where it might, even ought, to be. I'm real portable these days, like the fucking typewriter. I argue against 'place', and that false sense of what it counts as, which is usually generator for an altogether dead memory, etc. But I don't even mean that,—or not that sense. I miss where we were very much,—isolate, it only makes sense where there can be a use, in it, and one likewise used. That was some of it in NH, though about the time I met you, in NY, I'd had too much, and was too damn close to screaming. Anyhow I guess we'll be coming back, sometime this winter—probably go to BMC, and hang on there for awhile. I've been reading some of these books from the middle 1800's, i.e., US—Dana, Crevecoeur, and had read Parkman one winter in NH; they had the whole string in the library there. It must have been wild, though god knows that's a sterile track.

I am beat in some ways, mainly the way of being too damn tired too much and no reason at all for it; and also tired of a lot of sterile and repetitive thinking. I know my hole pretty well at this point, anyhow I know some of it—what Olson calls, 'the shaft'. What blocks the kill, it is a damn kill at best, is having to parry so much, by way of my body, really, instead of my tongue, or hands. I can't talk here, and that is a kind of dullness. Too I stand on the damn ground of a 'tourist', and that is nothing at all; sometimes I can get through, one time, for example, I had gone in to look at some exhibition in Aix, and a young girl came up with some programs, sort of a sheepish smile, and offered them, and I started to take one, then said, how much are they, and she said, forty francs, and laughed. And I did too. It gets that simple at best.

Otherwise it is hell. You goddamn well can't picture, I think, utter dullness of almost every damn word I hear. Or what christly patter of idiots, etc. It makes me damn complacent, I think that is the damn horror of it,—can't even make an edge.

That lyric is too much, too—where I get gas, for the car, etc., man always saying,—c'est moi. I guess it is at that.

If I could load a thing, like this of yrs to hand, I mean make it right down to the damn letters, like that—phew. But anyhow. It's a real nice one.

The 'poetic' is, for yrs truly, a damn hard nut,—every now & then I get scared that I don't make enough of what, at least, I've heard of,—if I don't know. In prose, never this embarrassment; I believe, right or wrong, no one can show me a cadence I haven't, to some extent, been aware of. I mean of course in english.
                                (I'd thought to write it like these characters playing the piano these days, though that is perhaps idiotic to hope for. The way one pulls into chords,—changes,—so that sequence becomes the kind of quick 'siding' this gets. It's the ideogrammic method at that,—but even so a little otherwise. Olson quoted me something from a young Fr/ composer, Pierre Boulez, on 'series'—Fr/ have the phrase I think ordre seriel, to mean 12 tone scale, and, anyhow, B/ aiming against the vertical-horizontal positions of usual composition, and/or, more clearly, that most people depend on that order of up, & down, & along. There is another sense. I am sure of it, in prose, or sure that an 'order' need <u>not</u> be to the 'end', or that, say, a climax is a necessary structure for definition. Well, allons. Sometime or other.)

Here's something. Last night, too, when we'd got onto poetry, what it was then, I'd tried to say, music of Lorca, i.e., sounds, and he jumped me for making it that simple, i.e., went on to say, music of the actually sung (one kind of poetry), and then that chanted, (or the dramatic), and then that more simply spoken. Of course that is a familiar demarcation. Odd to get it from him, though I don't think so at that.

Wouldn't Ez' comment on all Gk/ art moving to: coitus,—be a comment on 'climax' generally. It is what we use to define it, or that relation. There is an impact of a somewhat different character—light suddenly on a leaf, or outside this window, now, just striking in—it comes to a thing something else. Climax is apt to destroy a poem. And what is it honestly that happens in Eliot's Sweeney—that poem has stuck in my head ever since you were talking about it, back then. It is an ironic extension,—but hardly that. Of course they would say, this sudden juxtaposition of two emphases, etc. But it is wilder than that?

Did you get to see that article by Elath? It's in INTRO, double number Vol/ I, #III & IV—1951. Very damn good prose. I wrote him c/o of the magazine, and got an answer—but don't yet know what to do with it. He is well into Korzybski,—also this Wm/ Hull,—see current issue of INTRO, who I don't make at all. I hate the goddamn leaning on irony to this effect,—I take it as damn well a cheat. Anyhow E/ is very cool in many of his statements, in sd article.

Here's a poem for you:

> THE DRUMS
>
> How are you harry the
> last time we met it was
> in heaven
> surely
> or so I remember.
> [CP I, 29]

C'est moi . . . .

Otherwise I don't know. Emerson is finally going to put out the pamphlet of poems, and is THAT premature. Got a real crazy drawing tho, i.e., E/ asked for a photograph, and fuck that, so I twisted my boy Ashley's arm till he did this THING. Phew. Scares hell out of me & will you likewise. Anyhow,—that's the poem. (I looked very hard in the mirror afterwards, but couldn't see it. However, I am still cheerful.)

> THE RHYME
>
> There is the sign of
> the flower -
> to borrow the theme.
>
> But what or where to recover
> what is not love
> too simply.
>
> I saw her
> and behind her there were
> flowers, and behind them
> nothing.
> [CP I, 117]

Maybe silly, but always wanted to write one poem like Thelonious Monk playing piano; second verse is it. But he is prettier. I guess.

Look, write soon, letters are letters,—it's all we've damn well got. I'll keep on anyhow,—things are cool enough. Once baby is here it will be more of a piece. Voila.

All our dearest love to you,
Bob

. . .

LETTER TO WILLIAM CARLOS WILLIAMS

Route de Caire
Lambesc, Bouches du R/
France
June 27, 1952

Dear Bill,

I'm sorry about the silence, i.e., that's our new address up above, etc. Finally got something and it's an improvement over the other place.

I heard from Rainer Gerhardt, they had another damn miserable stretch of luck; they lost that one damn room in Freiberg, kids had to go to the grand-parents, and not good for anyone. But they are going to get out the 2nd issue of FRAGMENTE, I think it should be done very soon—or he said about 2 weeks after this last letter.

Olson had written we could all go there, to Black Mountain, this winter; it makes a lot of sense to me. That would be Laubiès, the Gerhardts, and us. Perhaps it's too literal a 'vision', I don't know—but would be very great to be close to all of them, and to see what could happen. As it is, everyone dulled by the distance, and god knows more than that, current hell of money & all. Feel rotten with the G/s there, and no damn solution. Perhaps this BMC idea could be it.

My sister writes she heard you read at Brandeis, and how wonderful it was. "He sat to read, just turning the papers & looking at the people. Everybody I could hear near me responded in a way that staggered me.—Dead silence, tremendous applause—and the people who have money to go to these things don't read poetry. Common speech—and he really got to everyone. I was maudlin, with tears in my eyes—at the whole idea."

My mother was there too, I think it's the first time she ever went to anything like that. She used to worry about me in that way, i.e., 'I like to think Bob could work, if he had to.' Sometimes, in a kind of usual, I guess, desperation, because we couldn't get on the same place, there, I used to read her some of your stories, i.e., those from Life Along The Passaic River. My father was a doctor, and after he died, she went back to nursing, and still does.

Things come ok. We're waiting for the new baby to get here,—my wife very
distrustful, put it, of french medical procedure. Finally have the doctor here
in the town, very decent man,—first one we tried was a pretty damn common
type, i.e., lots of rich ladies,—he treats them cold & rough, etc. I guess they like
it. She'd told him about Rh factor, etc., perhaps to take the count, etc.,—but he
wasn't interested. It isn't, I guess, that one can, or could, do too much, in this
place, and also with no history of trouble, I suppose he thought, to hell with it.
But I damn well didn't like it, i.e., one visit prior to delivery, didn't even tell her
how to get hold of him should the baby start coming, etc. Not very cool.

As it is I've got a little piece of paper from the one here in town.—Villa
Pouget, accouchement, venire le docteur le plus vite possible. I hand that to
whoever answers.

I've been reading a book called Introduction to a Science of Mythology; by
Jung & Kerenyi—and very interesting, in part. K/ quotes something from
Malinowski, that Olson had:

> "The myth in a primitive society, i.e. in its original living form is not a mere tale
> told but a reality lived. It is not in the nature of an invention such as we read in
> our novels today, but living reality, believed to have occurred in primordial times
> and to be influencing ever afterwards the world and the destinies of men . . .
> These stories are not kept alive by vain curiosity, neither as tales that have been
> invented nor again as tales that are true. For the natives on the contrary they are
> the assertion of an original, greater, and more important reality through which
> the present life, fate, and work of mankind are governed, and the knowledge of
> which provides men on the one hand with motives for ritual and moral acts, on
> the other with directions for their performance."

Further on, Jung makes this comment:

> "Psychology therefore translates the archaic speech of myth into a modern
> mythologem—not yet, of course, recognized as such—which constitutes one
> element of the myth "science.""

It's an interesting emphasis,—or simply attitude; at least it clears for a moment
the pervasive sense of <u>end</u> with which such attitudes, i.e., 'scientific', more
damn usually present themselves. It is also a comment on writing, I think; or
could be.

It could hardly be 'conscious', or call it
<u>descriptive</u>—I don't think one could face the archaic like a ballgame, etc. But
it makes very clear that this centering on one's self, or just what to call it, is
neither egocentric nor necessarily isolate in effect.

Come to think of it,—it is a pointer for Hart Crane, too. I'd read an article by
M. Elath in an issue of INTRO, and was the first one that I'd seen giving any

recognition to this <u>particular</u> side of it. More often,—to say, Crane was 'reconciling' himself to 'science', etc., etc. This is a more pertinent sense, I think.

Anyhow, hot as hell here at this point. Sun is very damn strong these days, I guess that's what it's supposed to be. Everyone off to hear Casals, and wish I were with them. I got a card from a friend there,—" . . . during the past months I've felt it growing, a terrible lack of interest in dissatisfaction; which is perhaps just the pulling of myself together for the anything I will do . . . and that I am here." It must be fantastic,—I've heard records, I wish I could hear him there.

I hope it all goes well, it's ok here now.

All our best to you,
Bob

I wanted to note this, but may be only an imposition; am in touch with an Englishman who's doing a series of pamphlets, Brit/ & Am/ authors, for distribution in US, Canada, & England—I think between 16 & 32 pp/ in length, well printed. Would you have any material free, for such issue, in event it seems worth any time. He asked me to help with Am/ end, and thought to ask you in any case. His name is Martin Seymour-Smith,—lives in Mallorca. Material would be for this coming spring; am not now sure if he can pay anything. I'll try to get more details if it has any use in it for you. Ok.

. . .

LETTER TO CHARLES OLSON

[Fontrousse, France]
July 15, 1952

Dear Charles,

Poem is <u>very</u> cool, like it <u>very very</u> much. Last two lines are real <u>close</u>. All through,—<u>play</u> is working with great great care, and effect. Look, if this is free,—could you try [Raymond] Souster with i.e., he seems serious at least? I just got a letter from him, with your two, and he wants material,—he does keep straight enough to say the work is 'hard' for Canadian reader, but that of course is his business, and not at all ours. Anyhow, I'd try him—it's a fine damn poem,—see what he does. (I sent him THE QUESTION, but he hasn't yet made up his mind—I also sent a short note on 'poetry', but that is minimal, i.e., <u>poems</u> worth so goddamn much more, to anyone.)

Souster's address, in case you don't have it there now, etc., 28 Mayfield Avenue, Toronto 3, Ontario. (Again angered by Cid's deceit, i.e., this man reprinted, as you'd know anyhow; material from ORIGIN, and supposed Cid had got it straight with divers men printed. Bronk kicked, to Souster, and so made clear Cid had by no damn means cleared it with the people involved. WHY Cid can't simply forward addresses, and arrange direct contact, etc.,—I've yet to damn well know. I've damn well sworn off him many times now,—but god strike me dead, like they say, if he ever gets another word out of me. Fuck him utterly.)

No word yet from SS/—I wonder if he's damn well scared off. It could certainly happen. In any case,—now relevant to get some of these things together? I mean, if we can get in there this winter, a magazine, of the kind we clearly <u>don't</u> have, now, would be worth trying. I hope SS/ pulls out, i.e., comes thru. At least no news, good news, etc. Many damn thanks for the help.

Here's an item,—I'd sent, way back, your <u>the ring of</u> to Vince, and of course he's using the same in this anonymous gig. When he sent mss/ of the whole thing, looking thru it I found yr poem with this line at the end, like this:

> ". . . . . of like
> elements.
>   Very wild movement, very fine thing."

I.e., in writing it out, I'd put that on, to underline that <u>fact</u>—I didn't damn well trust him I guess. Anyhow, seeing it copied in there on copy for printer,— thought he might have done it in haste—certainly hard to figure otherwise, so wrote back saying I'd cut it off, this line (and I quoted it for him). (As matter of fact,—I didn't then feel as sure as Ann did, that it was an 'oversight', i.e., I fig- ured him capable of such idiocy,—it was a touchy point anyhow, and in 1st draft, call it, of letter then written him, I explained it all so laboriously Ann thought it would be insult to what intelligence he did have. So I made it a joke, i.e., what a compliment, ho, ho.) This is, anyhow, what I get back:

> "cant make out what the problem was with charley's <u>the ring of</u> ? did you both
> collaborate, and you strike out your lines, or what? anyway hope that the poem is
> coherent and entire unto itself."

What does one do now. Problem of Vince is exactly problem of a man, with very decent & kind intentions, literally incapable of that job or act to which he has committed himself. Man who cannot see the disparity of line in question, in body of poem, otherwise,—is not so much idiot as simply incapable of judge- ment, i.e., he just don't get it. He's printing the poem on no grounds relating to his own understanding of it. This is both goddamn well ridiculous & could be at least, embarrassing. Editor who prints what he does not understand with some thoroughness is up to something that doesn't interest me—and how can it, anyhow, interest anyone. Familiar enough. Cid never of this category, no matter other faults, i.e., he made a point of knowing what was up—his own tortured work, call it, some testament of that knowledge. Ferrini, of course, is utterly unaffected,—beyond a few superficial senses of 'spacing'—by any poetry. I think he is a genuine primitive to that extent. Primitives are hard to work with, and they should <u>never</u> edit anything. I like some of his poems, and that seems more importantly his business than anything like this to hand; the collection is not only tripe, but actively bad tripe—Cid has one of the worst poems I've ever read (SAGA) in it—it could kill an interest on the part of any reader, 'company' to that extent difficult. Says Vince: "I think we can all be proud of that brig! can you imagine the noise it will make!' Just sd 'noise' I know, and I don't like it. Damn late in the day to kick,—it's at the printers, by now, and yrs truly who 'arranged' that, etc. If I'd known, like they say, to what lengths Cid's ambitions were going to haul him,—I would have cut loose way back. As it is,—dubious damn pleasure of helping a man make a complete asshole of himself. That hardly helps anything.

What do you know about this 'ORIGIN' gig for Brit/ magazine, ARTISAN. V/ lists the 'nine young american poets': "Charley, you, levertov, blackburn, duncan, enslin, wilbur, cid and yrs t." I get sick of it, in fact I damn well won't play I think—I don't like it. Neither this 'group' sense, and its implications, nor in this case the actual components. Look at it,—levertov is, to begin with, British, she will hardly like that category here suggested; Wilbur is utterly separate from Origin, and does not need any such relation; blackburn & duncan are worth printing, I think, but I don't see that either fit into any such 'group'; enslin is I guess a nice man but his poetry, or one I saw, is not; cid & ferrini are holding on for what it's worth and all it's worth to anyone <u>is</u>, what it's worth to them. You are damn separate—I am claim that right, in any damn case,—no matter. This 'group' sense would <u>only</u> be possible in straight context of a specific & like commitment. I would knife Wilbur any day in the week; and also Cid & V/ himself, at least in this role. Well, fuck it—it is DULL.

[note typed in the margin: Maybe that 'autobiographical' notes biz, wd/ allow chance for dissociation, but messy biz in any case. Wd/ like to know more abt it, I'll write Cooper (who's editor) and see what comes. I suggested he print you Duncan & Blackburn, in bulk—also give you space for overt comment, if wanted. Leave all others out. That wd be 'American poetry' a hell of a lot more significantly. What do you think. Nine piddlers,—no good.]

One pleasure anyhow,—yesterday walking along the Cour Mirabeau, with Dave & the Hellmans, I was gawking as usual, and saw a man sitting with his family, i.e., wife & two kids,—table in front of one of the cafes. No one much around, they were only ones at the tables. I looked at him, and was so hit by his <u>eyes</u>, I kept looking, and must have stared at him all the way by, and he also, looking right back at me. It was very fine, i.e., sudden quickness of it, man so placed, there, and crazy intensity of his eyes beyond any embarrassment, or any sense of staring me down, and myself naïve enough, then, to look too without any nervousness,—I guess because he allowed it.

Getting past, feel that I 'knew' him came stronger, as he was by us, etc. And then woke to who he was, i.e., Picasso. Beautiful, beautiful thing,—absolutely. Going back, as we had to later, of course we looked, like they say, but then it was no pleasure, he had turned, and it was looking at any 'great' man, and dull to that extent. Otherwise, sheer sort of memory, of his face,—I had it straight at me for about a minute, it must have been that long. He sat with utter damn solidity, and at that point I knew him only as a man sitting there. His eyes are lovely damn things,—you would never forget them. Even in photographs, there is that quality—but faced, they are incredible, and his whole head is an intensity, and a fine kind of <u>humor</u> which I mean to mean balance, and presence, just there. Not big, Spanish in his body, or Catalan,—old suit, or usual French one, poorly cut always to my sense; wife, younger & pretty, and him so crazily separate, and yet them all in it too. Kids about Dave's age, sort of diminutive,—looking French which he can't much like. Well, fuck it,—it was pleasure, I wish you'd been there with me too.

It's worth as much to me as boatfare, etc., to have seen him precisely like that. What the hell should I ever say to him. That was the <u>one</u> damn way. It was damn well worth all the christly hell of the past year, etc. It was very great.

Ok. I hate to read of your own worries,—you make that distance honestly, and would be only man capable of knowing them. A christly kind of curse, to be at that point of knowledge. I don't know it and maybe I never will. You anyhow take yourself to that edge,—and cannot stop because you made everything to it, and it would seem, and I would insist, must be that that same pitch would throw you over, into content now bearing in.

Anyhow just now trying to shift myself, in the chair, found I was hooked on to it, by tear in the seat of my damn pants. It isn't simple. It is frightful at times.

Many, many thanks for notes on the Jung thing; also for this letter. I hope to god I can print it, I mean it in any case. Very damn good of you to haul it out for me,—and more than that god knows, to have given it to me in the first place. Ok.

Write soon, I'll do likewise. Take care of yourselves, I wish we were all there, & kick my ass when I think we could have been. Dull to have missed that.

All our dearest love to you all,

Bob

Skeats has, <u>irony</u>, at Gk/—this dissembler, but better, "<u>one who says less than he</u> <u>thinks or means</u>." Also Gk/ equivalent of straight noun irony, i.e., Gk/ noun for which this 'dissembler' is also a root—means, <u>dissimulation</u>, eipwveia.

[New page] Chas/ yr letter just in, with poem, and E/s and B/s letters, etc. Poem is very damn fine, I think up to the middle passage, i.e., to part which swells. Character of flat statement very damn firm, and gives reader full impression, or call it <u>mark</u> of the acts involved.

Problem of sd part, otherwise, i.e., that middle -"Why they are,"—thru there, is I think that it begins to say things <u>about</u> him, more than like 'the red-headed man' which is so damn clear, like that. But it isn't whole thing there, i.e., what does hit me, of like kind as the parts to there:

> Why they are . . . .
>   he,
> up to then, often in the glaring sun had sat
> . . . . , nor found
> tranquillity to ease his yearning, always
> sleepless cares within his soul wore him
> away, the while he looked

all thru to the end of sd stanza. Maybe relates to rhythms too? From there, to end, <u>time</u> it takes to go thru details relating to peach trees. Only kick there. From end of sd stanza, to end, very cool; particularly that beat on, would never forget/ their hateful deed/ of blood. Very damn fine. First four stanzas are what goof me, in any case—and this close. Middle part most of the problem, my own reading—and peach trees details—i.e., time of them,—in one following.

Content, no matter, <u>clear</u>. Very damn fine,—who else could write it.

[pasted in photograph of two hands shaping pottery on a wheel]

Just saw this photograph. Someday wd be very great to do book, i.e., not to 'do' book, but if it happened so, with just such things interspersed without comment.

So that text would have equivalent in visual, i.e., pictures. Both as 'rest' for the reader, and pulling out of his <u>sense</u> of content generally, i.e.,—so he gets it everywhere, is present in a multiplicity of things.

Not as 'illustration' but as like things. It could be good. I mean, real wide play,—of things like this, bits of cloth, anything that had relevance.
    ****

Wd go with you all the way on that biz of romanticism & realism, i.e., both are content-ual, and I think the same 'content' at root. Classic/ is method; emphasis on,—'cold doing' finally. Sense of, good enough to hold I guess. The ages & all . . .

This thing on irony,—re anger & all. One thing wd be I think the Poe essay noted,—and really not so much Williams there using that irony, but his emphasis on Poe's use of it. Note particularly Poe's reply to Lowell—and then, though apparently it did not actually then happen—how W/ says, "Poe might have added finally, etc." i.e., that then we get the straight statement, of what P/ thinks IS the way out,—and then irony-in-anger is component of a further position.

With irony-in-despair,—you have no 'further position'. That's it, and any act a man commits, in despair,—in that place, is peculiarly his act and he will have no other. Despair I think to mean without hope; and so an end, if the act be there negative. Or else, man is all act—and only that,—and so he is what the act is, purely.

It is here, again, that Hull becomes frightful, in his act—that it is irony,—and there cannot be any hiding. Irony then immense in its very smallness,—and so a human act, particularly, according to some definitions of the 'human'. At least one could have it so, be so—and have likeness to many others. [note typed in left margin: Irony: 'expression of one's meaning by language of opposite or different tendency'—so that H/ adopts the laughing, or what to call it, surface for a content of horror. He does not say as he thinks.]

Crane* tried to trust to act of poetry,—and feeling that go, his life was all that—all he otherwise had were friends who began to drop him with almost sole exception of Slater [Brown] and his wife, and homosexuality and his drinking— he could not go anywhere. Williams' sense of, man thinking

> *(Crane trying to use poetry for ALL objects of his emotion,—note range of 'subject'—huge difference from Pound—in this respect. It was all he had, all he meant to have—it was full content, all he could attempt.)

with his poem, and that to be the 'profundity', is here what happens; or the tragedy in Crane, that he took it to fail him. A man would not fail seeing himself, or so using himself, that in the base act of his breath he was already that substance from which a poem could, of an exact necessity, come.

Irony in despair is an end,—because all acts there have this finalness. They must carry back, or [^ not] back but to another, life. Irony has no such capacity of generation. Conjecture, and statement of such an act, could maintain a man in any place,—it is the very 'hope' that was supposed lost.

Irony in anger is small in another sense, i.e., not the major attitude. At
best, a weapon, or a means to dealing with some aspect of the surround-
ings,—but never the whole of them which despair would predicate. Williams
in AUTOBIOGRAPHY ironic often, i.e., in hitting at some minor detail, an
annoyance—like Poe angry at his own <u>misuse</u> by Lowell, who did not appreci-
ate what that <u>use</u> was—but neither without <u>further</u> statement,—as Williams
DREAM OF LOVE, or poems. Or Lawrence in something like essays on
Whitman, or on Melville. And the break-over, like, 'I have seen an albatross
too . . .'

Irony, in character you note, i.e., dissembling, is what it gets to; and if it means
the end act, the last,—hopeless in utter sense. And so beyond the human,
completely. Though human in that exit.

[note typed in left margin] Sarcasm wd be possible component, or instance, of
total, irony. A use. Irony is root process of a <u>sense</u> of expression; false. Also I
figure adjective, <u>ironic</u>, to shade word as it wd be read by general reader, i.e., the
noun.

· · ·

LETTER TO ROBERT DUNCAN

> Route de Caire
> Lambesc, Bouches du Rhone
> France
> July 19, 1952

Dear Mr. Duncan,

   I'm trying to find material for a series of pamphlets of British &
American authors; i.e., an Englishman is putting out the series and has asked
me to take on American component. The emphasis will be on poetry, I take it,
but some hope to get to related material as well. The length will be 16 pages,
well printed, decent format, etc. Would you have something we could use. To be
distributed in England, US, and Canada.

I know your work from one book, and also two, at least, of your later poems,
AFRICA REVISITED (very fine job) and SONG OF THE BORDERGUARD.
I like it, and hope that we can arrange something for this present series. The
probable date of issue, granted you have something free, would be sometime the
first of this coming year. Could you write me what you think.

> All best to you,
> *Robert Creeley*
> Robert Creeley

PART TWO

Black Mountain Review, 1953–1956

Mallorca, Black Mountain, San Francisco

[Mallorca]
January 9, 1953

Dear Paul,

We got your Xmas card ok, and very lovely it was! It made me feel somewhat bitter we didn't send any, although we never damn well make it, and haven't for the last five years. But next year, etc. Wait & see.

Laubiès wrote he had started on the cover for your book, and very happy about the dimensions—which will be, roughly, sort of tall, or that emphasis, and proportionately narrow. Anyhow don't get worried, I wanted to keep to the format in your mss/, and think this will do it most easily. I also want to use vellum for the paper, if what we lose on the size (i.e., on what paper may have to be wasted) doesn't make it too expensive. Once Olson's book is done for Cid, I'll start on yours.

Olson's book turns out a considerable headache at that, i.e., the mss/ runs to some 88 pp./, and had contracted for 64. I expect there is considerable discontent in Boston tonight, etc. Likewise in BMC. Anyhow it ought to be a very decent book, he has some very strong things in it—and wild to have THE KINGFISHERS, and like poems, in some place available. Otherwise, it gets loose toward the end, he has it in 4 sections, or parts, and for the last is: A PO-SY, FOR RAINER GERHARDT, and THE MORNING NEWS (another blague one, like PO-SY). The thing being, it makes G/ poem damn equivocal (and I've never liked the damn thing anyhow), and all seems tacked on—at least in point of general content which the rest of the book is making. But to hell with the sniping, KINGFISHERS is one of the greatest poems I know. It will be a very cool issue, if production goes like I want it to.

I finally heard from Rainer G/ yesterday, he'd been in the hospital for two months, and family without a house, etc. He has a hell of a life. Anyhow he's better set at this point, doing scripts for divers radio stations, some experimental 'drama', as he says, and also hour-long scripts on people like Williams, Artaud, etc. He wants to do one on Olson. The press is going again, and they have a series of pamphlets as well as FRAGMENTE: Confucius, The Great Digest (Pound); Wolfgang Weyrauth, Die Feüers Brünst (?); How to Read, Pound; Artaud, Brief über das Theater; Klaus Bremer, Poesie; and that thing Achilles Fang translated with Cid, and also a booklet of G/s poems, etc. I remembered you said you had a friend who was interested in German writing, perhaps G/ could send him the German material, etc. Or translated things as well, if he wanted to see them. FRAGMENTE #2 is out, he says, and #3 due in February. Very great he is back on.

I keep thinking of you, and this editing, etc. I do damn well want to submit something soon. Would you tell me what your deadline is. The reason I haven't sent poems, etc., is that I'm now damn well committed to this little booklet for late spring, and thought poems put in that might fuck up printing in ORIGIN. If they won't, tell me, and you can have whatever you want (i.e., edition will be very small, 300 copies, as against at least 500 on your PROENSA—maybe it wouldn't bother anything, though I don't like this damn printing over & over, etc. Like what's happened to most of the stories.)

Also, will you please tell me if you get the copy of LE FOU—I don't think Emerson has sent any of the copies I told him to. Christly bug at this distance, and whole thing has so much the air of a kindness in any case. I've heard from about three people, re the book—and get scared I've committed some frightful act, etc. If it <u>does</u> get to you, for god's sake tell me what you think of it. I would rather know the worst, like they say—but silence is horrible, I can't make it at all at the present. Such a fucking hell anyhow, trying to be 'serious' in this fashion. It seems a lonely and utterly rejected act.

I had started a story for you, but then O/s mss/ landed in my lap, and twelve or so hours later, I couldn't do anything. So that was that, etc. I don't like prose much at the moment, anyhow. I am very damn deep in some kind of 'morbidness', it's very much in rhythms, etc., and altogether poetry. I spend a hell of a lot of time fucking around with this & that, but when it finally does come, it's all a rush (usually I grab any pencil I can find, and do it on one of Dave's papers, etc., I have this sense of 'doing' it, like a shit!) This one I'd been sitting on ever since we left NH, i.e., was in that same spring, and how many damn things I killed like this I wouldn't like to remember.

> THE CROW
>
> The crow in the cage in the dining-room
> hates me because I will not feed him.
>
> And I have left nothing behind in leaving
> because I killed him.
>
> And because I hit him over the head with a stick
> there is nothing I laugh at.
>
> Sickness is the hatred of a repentance
> knowing there is nothing he wants.
> [*CP* I, 124]

Anyhow, all the rhythms are like that these days, which is the point. There was a crazy thing of conversation between Ann & [Robert] Graves when I was sick last month, and hellishly mean, etc. G/ was saying: "This is the first time we've seen Bob's dark side." "It's not his dark side, he's <u>suffering</u>."

That fucking Wm Merwin, whom I don't meet as yet, seems damn symbol of rot, I had seen his bk/, and then poems here & there, etc. He is somewhat afraid of you, as it happens, i.e., yr translation, etc. He is being crowded, tant pis, etc. Martin SS/ seems to have got very damn drunk Xmas, and told him I did not want to meet him, etc., and later seems to have either kicked or hit him—also chanting parodies of his grrrreat worrrrks, etc. Graves said, you shouldn't be so mean to Wm Merwin . . . Fuck 'em all. (Martin being violent little s.o.b., I love him very much.)

Write damn soon, shall do likewise. All our love to you,

Bob

. . .

LETTER TO CHARLES OLSON

[Mallorca]
April 8, 1953

[RC's hand-drawn musical notes, before salutation]
Dear Charles,

Feeling much your own impatience, about all the damn distance. And just now when all this comes up, and hopeless fact of how long it will take to get back to you. To hell with it. Leave us be stoic, etc. Voila.

Re the poem to hand—I get, and damn well respect, your premise. And think, in fact, this is precisely your method, either now or in the past. Or at least that is how the poems have read. The 'forms' you have effected in their own fact of the speed & apposition of all facts or detail, etc., have had to be just this 'form as present', or else they could never have made it. That is, junking the whole via of 'form' as an external discipline (sonnets, etc.), either one can effect the coherence just by means of a like tension between all substances dealt with—and/or, sufficient to keep all in play, etc.—or else they, the poem, fragment into the state they'd had prior to use of them.

I also see what you mean about 'music', i.e., can I take this to be the 'swelling' usual to that verse which maintains a 'rhythm' irregardless of the closer & more pertinent intervals called for—or one which does go, da/dum, da/dum, etc. And ignores the closer demand of any aspect of a sense just then occurring in the poem's going on.

Anyhow the battle against the iamb & all, seems to me dull primarily because it is a digression, both from the whole problem of rhythm and likewise from a sense that all things are relevant to the use which can be made of them. Which is too general, but no matter. But to fight the fact of iambic pentameter, etc., implies the search for an alternative means to form—and this, at least, doesn't worry me, and should hardly worry you—who gave me the solution. To think of the poem as a 'field' means, beyond anything else, that one think of the poem as a place proper to the act of conjecture—and to effect conjecture in form, can only come to—total assertion. If it is a poem. It would strike me that the only possible reason for this iambic pentameter line taking on the weight it seems to, is because, like they say, it might be felt as a general sign of the common rhythm of speaking, in English. I.e., that the stress pattern, generally, is weak/strong, etc., and that the breath, generally, can handle a five-stress line—more or less. The 'more or less' is the dullness, and the fact that it is all a 'general' practice, etc., the final one. Or, why the hell bother with it, beyond that. The practice, in any case, of any man either of us could read, would so alter this 'general' aspect of a rhythmic structure for poetry, etc., that it would be not at all 'iambic pentameter'—or here comes in, I'd guess, all the problem of caesura, and the like. In any case, it does not interest me. As for Williams—here, say, is one case where the iamb is probably at the root, no matter the 'five feet', etc., but also where the rhythms which then prove <u>particular</u> come to over-ride any such simplicity as this one:

	Liquor and love	[handwritten, upside down]
	when the mind is dull	*the throat*
	focus the wit	*of the bird*
	on a world of form	*day long + night-late*
What he does here	The eye awakes	*without fever, without*
→	perfumes are defined	*(the <u>rein</u> of)*
goofs	inflections	*art*
me! . . .	ride the quick ear	
	Liquor and love	
	rescue the cloudy sense	
	banish its despair	
	give it a home.	

Viz, it is somewhat ridiculous, for the man who wrote that, to worry about alternative 'forms', etc. Or the answer, in terms of rhythms, for the iambic pentameter line. In fact, when anyone can read that, and comprehend the rhythmic structure thereof,—and why it is so damn fine—then the whole thing is no longer a problem. But the problem of each poem, as it comes. Well, call it 'theme & variations', etc. [note in margin: *P(ound) or P(arker): constant + vari-*

ant] I have felt that if, say, in any poem I can manage the rhythms of one line, and feel their necessity, actually, then I have made the way altogether for all the lines subsequent. Anyhow—the above strictly in point of rhythms, i.e., that's what just now I would lean on, here—that such rhythm can be held in a poem. The second & third verses are all the 'proof' one needs.

Well, for christ sake, you might likewise examine the rhythmic structure of THE KINGFISHERS. Which is the wildest I know of. Can you tell me, for example, how else you could have got to that last part—and why, there, the rhythms are so christly exact. And why, also, you are allowed the whole swell (god knows this is another kind) of that, "With what violence . . . " If the steam is up—which is nothing other than, this hot world, etc.—then the rhythms come to declare it. And these rhythms must, of necessity, and their own, be particular to that content which they issue from. What else.

I only bug at the poem now here, because I think you run it too slow—or, isn't the damn mnemonic the headache, and doesn't it have the kind of rhythm pertinent to memory—"Without power, and only a poor oar . . . " I think that is the sound of memory, etc. The headache is, for me reading, that there exists a split, in force, between that which rides up as a detail out of memory, and that which is more properly now. I.e., I think the memory acts, here, do not exist on a like ground as the other things got to. Well, the lead-off: you're in hot water by line two I think—that once the 'depth' is declared, as what it is, etc., then how much longer can you continue with qualifications, even those which bear the sound of the act of memory—i.e., won't the reader bug, as I do, that he has to inhabit this revery finally proper to yourself. Viz, too much like sitting at a table with a man who has gone, if only slightly, to sleep. Which is no damn kick, but that I think it isn't properly in the poem. Likewise—I mean because of this same savoring—you get a problem beginning, "I had made the mast . . . " in the form. For example, think of this usage:

> And I twist,
> in the early morning, asking
> where
> does it stop

And then of that in this poem now to hand. I.e., does this pulling in, here, actually declare a tension in hand or is it 'formal'? It hits me, anyhow, as the latter.

It's a hard one to nail. My sense is, that the present, of the poem, is not of sufficient tension to involve the past actively—i.e., in a proper state of tensions. So it is, that the second mention of 'Cabbage' is lost in the first, etc. Or not enough, it seems, more. I have the sense, likewise, that the purest part of the poem is, finally, that section beginning, "that channel / would be bluer . . . ", to " . . . the years . . . "

That here is the least 'formal' usage. And that, otherwise, other acts of this same memory are too glossed with almost a feeling of 'symbolism'. Viz, [note in left margin: *And so, forward*] do not take on that straight throw, back. Likewise, that, in the opening, say, there is too much the tone of an 'explanation'—which, for example, differs entirely from either the kind of 'explanation' you get in the opening to AN ODE TO NATIVITY, or THE K/s.

Well, I think you are right, in short. That a poem must be this 'total assertion', and that same is possible only when there is sufficient cause, to provoke it. And what same cause can be sufficient, is so much a matter of just the present, and what there is, there, that how the hell can we ever damn well lay down 'general' rules of practice. At least we know what we want—which seems the gain necessary.

The 'technical equals obedience' is damn useful statement. Obedience to the nature of what is to hand, and it takes the 'technical', to deal with it. I had thought, last night, that just here came in that old thing of Bird & all, i.e., Charley Parker—and wonder if I have seemed too silly with all that. I.e., I am dead serious, and want sometime to do a gig on this whole area. (I had hoped to when Bud was here, to help me with notation, etc., likewise with examples, etc., but wasn't time or the place.)

Bird, and few others equal, are almost the only present relevance, in rhythmic structure, available. Viz, that only Williams is of this order. That, a poet can look to this usage for an analogy to his own—and, if he is not a literal goof, etc., can comprehend that Bird's premise for structure in terms of the musical (or harmonic) line, is or can be, his own.

The same thing is actual in flamenco, but this comes finally to another 'classicism', i.e., it is worn to that extent—and tho it can provoke me, it is not of the same use that Bird is, and was. For example, I am more influenced by Charley Parker, in my acts, than by any other man, living or dead. IF you will listen to five records, say, you will see how the whole biz ties in—i.e., how, say, the whole sense of a loop, for a story, came in, and how, too, these senses of rhythm in a poem (or a story too, for that matter) got in. Well, I am not at all joking, etc. Bird makes Ez look like a school-boy, in point of rhythms. And his sense, of how one rhythm can activate the premise for, another. Viz, how a can lead to b, in all that multiplicity of the possible. It is a fact, for one thing, that Bird, in his early records, damn rarely ever comes in on the so-called beat. And, as well, that what point he does come in on, is not at all 'gratuitous', but is, in fact, involved in a figure of rhythm which is as dominant in what it leaves out, as what it leaves in. This, is the point. Only one other man, up to this—viz: the Dr. Like this:

> If I
> could count the silence
> I could sleep, sleep.
>
> But it
> is one, one. No head even
> to gnaw. Spinning . . .

It's what they call <u>doubles</u>, in the other area, but here ok! I.e., that doubling on the, "sleep/sleep" and "one/one". That Williams hears this way, is the fact. And note where it falls, and rides off—to "even". Likewise the "Spinning . . . "

[at top of the page and over the following citation: RC's drawing of a sequence of musical notes; also a drawing of a cross with downward pointing arrow]

You are the only other, viz:

> And the too strong grasping of it,
> when it is pressed together and condensed,
> loses it
>
> This very thing you are.

Listen to Bird on, All the Things You Are. Too much! (Well, seriously, do sometime hear: Chasing The Bird, Buzzy, April In Paris, etc., etc. I wish to god I had my own with me, I miss them more, finally, than any other one thing—and sit here some evenings turning the damn dial on this damn radio up & down, just for even a fucking imitation, of what this is.)

I think we can afford the casual, to the extent, that for us there can't be any usage but that peculiarly of the moment, instant, or what to call it. Gratuitous equals fortuitous, etc. Tho not at all that simply. But rhythm is where the most work now comes in, that, if we can manage the declaration of rhythms more exact than those now in use—the iamb, etc.—we clean up. Likewise that rhythm is a means to 'going on' far more active than any 'thot', etc. And that sound is rhythm in another dimension.

Bach & Bird & Williams ought to be enough for any 'poet'—and he might do worse than not bothering to read anyone after Shakespeare, etc. Who I honestly, like they say, can't now read myself.

On this last—it is a constant damn embarrassment, that S/ at least in the books I can get, the forms of them, etc., is so slow on the page I get bugged, and don't make it. That, say, whereas Melville, Lawrence, Crane, Cervantes, Williams, yourself, Pound (in his prose), Parkman, Stendhal, and Homer—are all of particular relevance, immediately & unavoidably clear to me,—S/ is not. I'd be an idiot to say he was, etc. I cannot get into his content, or dig it, enough, to move me to a proper study.

I can't read, or won't, anymore, what doesn't damn well involve me. I don't go stiff, viz not try, etc., but will no longer read with that self-consciousness I had growing up, when the Great Books, etc., seemed damn far away from Acton, Massachusetts. And, of course, were. I have no damn wish to stay a provincial, etc., really the last two years have hoisted me out of that damn viciously. But there is nothing but what is—like you sd, all there is, is, etc. I have to see what there is for myself.

I don't think Rabelais is funny . . . I can't make Donne . . . I think James is a horrible old bore . . . I think N/ West's Day Of The Locust, in parts, is better than anything Faulkner or Valery ever wrote . . . I hate Beethoven, and get to hate Mozart . . . I think that Bird, Bach, and a few others are all the music one needs . . . Well, the sun is shining, it's a fine day, etc. Or leave us cry, etc.

> Liquor and love
> rescue the cloudy sense
> banish its despair
> give it a home.

Write soon, tell us how you all are. All our dearest love to you all.

Bob

. . .

LETTER TO CHARLES OLSON

[Mallorca]
July 19, 1953

Dear Charles,
    Your two damn beautiful letters in this afternoon, and saved my life, i.e., otherwise deluged with half-backbiting business from Cid & somewhat lukewarm reception of book from Paul B/. But, very happily, to hell with that. Ok.

It is very damn fine you were talking with those people about Bird and all. The more any of it comes clear, the more he does damn well seem the key—or one of the most substantial users of what time can do in any business. That thing of cutting an 1/8th off the quarter, etc., is it, and the precision of such rhythms so got is a) the necessary fine-ness of the intention and b) the greater potential of variation then possible. I.e., what bugs either one of us, in the old biz of closed verse, or any such partitioning of potential forms, etc., is the damn loss of variation effected. Not, to grant them the obvious, that infinite variation <u>within</u> the given isn't also possible, etc., etc., but that total set is pre-determined. Bird, in any case, first man importantly, call it, to stress the vertical potential of the melodic line, and by vertical I think I mean much of what you have always meant, i.e., that emphasis on the <u>single</u> & <u>total</u> content of any <u>one</u> word or note therein occurring without an overstress on projection-along-a-line, or what they loosely call 'sequence', or what you've called horizontalism. What I'm trying to say, in any case: that Bird manages <u>single</u> content of the note, call it, in conjunction with total content, and/or its place in the whole structure of the melody, etc., etc. Whereas, say, usual 'modern song' goes along, etc., i.e., moves from note to note (and gains our patience or impatience only in same), Bird clears notes one by fucking one, and reasserts a rhythmic structure with <u>each</u> note posited. Myself, I think you go back to Bach before you ever find it done quite so clearly.

Well, that is fuzzily put, etc. To hell with it. I know nothing about music more than I can hear, and that is enough for the moment. For example, we have a hell of a headache in just how much weight any one word can carry, either by virtue of its sound & rhythm, or by virtue of its implicated content, or finally by virtue of both these facts then conditioned by the context given, etc. At this point you might insist (I do, etc.) that most poets now writing have as much knowledge of sound weights & rhythmic structures, etc., as Guy Lombardo has of the equivalent in his own business. There are in both places the old devices, etc., and their use (ad nauseam) gets to the same end. Anyhow for one analogy is useful, Bird with his given line, what his rhythm section is doing, the base chords of the melody he is on, etc., and <u>then</u> what he does. I would claim that any poet worth the time, will come back to his own job more clear if he could, without feeling much one way or the other, hear four good choruses by Bird on the <u>same</u> base structure. People have the dull notion, all flows the same way, at the same time, and if we assert our own piddling 'individuality' against same, even so we die, die, die, etc. But poem or song is autonomous, or else nothing, so that is not really relevant. (It damn well pleased me to note in Ez' ABC OF READING, biz abt Provencal poets considering use of another man's forms the same kind of plagiary a steal of his content might mean for us now. I.e., When forms are given such emphasis and care as those apparently got, you don't really get an overfineness or mechanical procedure—but actually an insistence on each man

finding his own, which will best & most accurately serve him. The same condi-
tion obtains in the case of Bird & followers, etc. It would be a like sin. The extent
to which padding & like set device is condemned by same, gets evidence in the
contempt they feel for any man using what they call 'doubles', i.e., repetition
of a phrase (1,1). Same is stock in trade with any so-called swing band, etc., etc.
And very funny to hear Bird parodies of same, i.e., do de da do—etc., etc., like
yawning behind vaguely cupped hand, etc.

What I wd insist on, is that practice & conditions obtaining here have direct
parallel in present usage in poetry. When we call for a poetry the direct issue of
language in a given instant, i.e., when we say it is possible, and a gain, to make
a poem precisely in terms of <u>all</u> the words which can occur in it, their rhythms
& their sounds, & what each then figure as in terms of a total structure—we
argue the same premise that Bird uses when he hangs off the 1/8th of an instant.
Because there is another note to follow. And he knows it.

Well, fuck that perhaps. But that it is a useable stimulus. And hearing a line of
B/s music, one sees the possibilities for his own. If I write:

> . . . The unsure
>
> egoist is not
> good for himself . . .

same is my own extension of what sd Bird
has taught me is possible, more than any other man I can honestly think of,
offhand. Bird's effected relation between sound-weights & rhythms is the
greatest any man ever got to, or I don't see anyone as having done it any better.
This don't mean, sadly, that almost all of so-called BeBop is not dull, dull hash
of what B/ does. You should hear German bands (with their talent for precise
imitation sans feeling) play what they think they heard. It's what one finally <u>has</u>
to hear that's interesting.

Also, as Buddy pointed out to me, music played at the corridas is very much
Bird's way. And wild fact usual flamenco ends at that precise point you swore it
couldn't. It is too much, when it is good. (You should hear what they do with 1/4
& 1/8 tones, etc. How, I damn well don't know.)

So. I like yr poems, last one most of all. Ann suggests title of, THE TRAP—i.e.,
she knows what you mean, and I goddamn well do. Sayin 'you & me' is damn
well my arrogance. I think all that counts is not to care the way some do, i.e.,
to have it, I would try to, "we who have perhaps, nothing to lose, etc." I don't
finally see that I do. I.e., Cid climbing for a reputation, etc., is his business.
Luckily over here I am so much out I can get free of that most of the time. I

cannot bullshit so much, because there is no one to bullshit. I think kids & wife etc. are conditions of sanity. Fuck them all!

It wd be wild if you cd all come over. I damn well wish you would. Write soon. All our dearest love to you all,

   Bob

. . .

LETTER TO PAUL BLACKBURN

[Mallorca]
September 17, 1953

Dear Paul,
   Just back after horrible trip to yr beloved France. In fact we made that vicious jaunt from Marseille thru all the beloved places: Montpellier, Beziers, etc., etc. Only decent one is Perpignan—which is Catalan. Anyhow, if it were me . . . , I wd go live in P/, or any of that stretch back along the Pyrenees—which is real great, if no longer romantic, tho I did once see, there, a very damn lovely Shepherdess, guarding Flock of Sheep, in Leather Jerkin, with both Breasts most lovely & most hanging Free. Well, fuck that. We were dead broke, hungry, only making it for stamps on passports, etc., which will enable us to hang on here without becoming residentes, which wd entitle US gov't to take 30% of our already miserable 'income'.

In Barcelona we were so flat we ended up sleeping in a sort of 'bring yr own' whorehouse in little side street off the Rambla, which is a lovely street. Very odd making love to yr wife in a whorehouse. It seems very damn immoral, however familiar. Wow.

So what's new. Cid wrote of all of you making wild sortie to Cape. You should have brought bombs, tho it sounds as tho Carroll was adequate. That's another place I hate incidentally. Did you ever read what Thoreau sd of it, i.e., how they cut down all the fucking trees to boil salt water, etc., etc. Wouldn't they just, etc. Anyhow I spent some of the most miserable months of my life in sd place, so forgive me. What else.

Don't flip re book shipment, i.e., Cid is, so don't you too, etc. He should worry, he's only getting a handful, so there, etc. Anyhow I mailed them August 14th (of this year), and think you'll have them circa 5 to 6 weeks from sd date. Well, anytime before end of this month I wd guess. But they will get there. I hate C/s damn sour biz of, they aint coming, they aint coming—yaaaa/yaaaa. Fugg him. Don't you be like that. It is not attractive.

You never sd a damn word more re yr poems, i.e., one note re yr having enough for a book, and that was all. I think you know the ones I wd know, etc., so maybe make a list? Of what I know of, and maybe add copies of other stuff? I want to get a mailing list out with O/s [Olson's *Mayan Letters*] (which is due to be done late October at the latest), and want mss/ as set as I can get them. So if you still have eyes, let me know. (I think you sd something like 30 or more,—cd we work down from sd number to tightest selection possible? Not ominously, but what do you think? Let me know. I want the book very much, if it's free, etc.)

So that's abt it, at present. Cooler now. Life ok. Lonely sometimes, but that's usual. I hope you all make it here—but Aix . . . O well.

All our love to you both,

Bob

. . .

LETTER TO JONATHAN WILLIAMS

September 23, 1953

Dear Jonathan,

I had a note from Rainer, along with your last letter, and if this is any evidence, I think he thinks his wife is in love with you. At least that is the substance of his note: "big troubles with Jonathan for Renate. I think, our marriage is finished . . . " The rest of the note mainly a statement to the effect he does not want you to publish his book (which is understandable, assuming this idea on his part), and fact he is very mixed up, and a mess generally.

God knows what all that comes to. <u>Any</u> other man, like they say, is liable to have faced the same accusation, given the mess they have been in, and the fact you gave them the sympathy you did. However unreasonably, it's very likely (and apparently what did happen) that he should imagine you as so much better than himself (the monster, etc., etc.) It seems mainly a commentary on all the hell they have been facing. It is also quite possible that Renate is fed up (though she hardly sounded that from what you had said of her feelings for Rainer, i.e., that he was certain to be a great man, etc.), and did cast on yourself as at least imaginary alternative. I think that sort of problem is, or has been, faced by anyone who ever married.

In any case it seems the best thing might be not to see them at all for awhile. I.e., it sounds very deeply a family business—and subject to all the apparent unreality & lack of rationality such businesses can come to. In any case, I should not allow myself to be used, in any way, as a lever between them. That would leave you altogether the short end of the stick, and sooner or later you'd have them both after you. You can only convince Rainer, no matter what the facts may be, that his assumption is fact, etc., by allowing <u>any</u> basis of sympathy to continue between Renate & yourself, which does not include him. If you can force him back into it, that would be the answer—but even such a thing as his dependence on her for english words, etc. could become an irritation to him, and hence more of this sense of 'cause'. The point is, I think, that at this level of relation, you'll have to chuck out all notions of 'rational' behaviour, and take it as a mess involving two people—and more than that, a mess where a third will only lose his head perhaps too damn literally. Give them even a little time, and I think you'll find them as good friends as they had been—but the thing is, if Rainer keeps on with this notion, and if you even unwittingly provide him with the fuel for it, that can only make him hold still more bitterly than ever. Anyhow it calls for a hellish amount of 'Christian forbearance', it's rotten damn luck it comes when it does. Obviously it has, very damn ironically, almost nothing to do with yourself.

It may sound all so unreal you'll have a hell of a time either believing it, or else not laughing at the goddamn idiocy involved. But people damn well do act like this, in reaction to problems a hell of a lot more real than the ones assumed. Well, fuck that bullshit. But don't think too badly of Rainer's imaginary rivals, etc., etc.—they get to be like an army, when one thinks one is a rotten beast at best.

I'm very shamefaced not to have written about the photographs, we liked them very damn much. (And if you can put up with it, would very much like some more prints of same, for cost of which I'll send you a check, as soon as Ann has had time to decide which she looks best in, etc., etc. Ok.)

Also the type book—a hell of a big help. I've spent a good two days on it, looking it over & trying to get some kind of actual feel of the divers kinds of type & the actual uses to which they can be put. It's the first chance I've had to do this, and it is all very damn interesting.

Rene had mentioned the bookstore there, and very much hope it all works out. I wish to god I could be there. Well, to hell with that. As it is, I may see you a lot sooner than I'd thought, i.e., I may very well be back in the States this coming spring. Olson wrote of a possible shake-up at BMC (which will involve you, I think, as much as myself) & if it all falls the right way, and if there is any place for me, I'll be there for the new term in March. Ann & the kids will then be coming later, very damn sadly—but at least it will be a beginning. Finally, the sense of being foreign, here, is too much of a drag—or is after the first excitement wears off—as it has to after two years, etc., etc.

Anyhow there is that possibility, and have my fingers very damn tightly crossed. Olson said he would know pretty definitely what was to happen, in two weeks to a month. If it falls the wrong way, I guess he'll be without further interest, as much as anyone else. It's a question of funds, as usual—and whether or not the man providing them is sympathetic to the plans Olson has worked out. So damn well hoping. It could be the end.

Very great the books are going ok. (You should butcher an ox or something, and let the gentle reader get some conception as to what they all came out of.) Some damn thing to hang on to at least—though it must at times seem damn vague consolation. But this is temporary. I'm sure a hell of a lot will clear once you yourself are clear of the army & all. One can't make it, in same. There's simply no way to.

Sorry to hear abt money. Well, maybe something can be figured even here. If you should still be here until the 2nd week of December, then we could certainly have the money to you. Otherwise, any arrangement that seems feasible is damn kind of you to bother with. Ok.

This for now. Again, don't think me nosey, etc. I shouldn't have said a damn thing but for this note of Rainer's—and fact you were clearly entitled at least to have that information.

All our love to you,

Bob

. . .

LETTER TO PAUL BLACKBURN

[Mallorca]

October 15, 1953

Dear Paul,

Leave me try to muddle thru those 2 poems you note. Anyhow, I can't fool you—so maybe I can explain at least what I was after, or thot they should be, etc., etc. Ok. THE DRUMS [*CP* I, 29] (title of which pertains to droning kind of conversation I often hear, or heard—you're looking great, etc., etc.) is blague on 'old times'—rhythms of same, and particularly that first line (with internal rhyme rushing it on) to set tone. Perhaps there is whimsey in the 'in heaven', and jovial type wry humor in the 'surely'—last line mostly ironic. Really an echo of old times conversation—rhythm piece almost completely. I have a friend 'harry' or had one, who sells insurance & lives in Dobbs Ferry, etc. Perhaps it is too private—but I can read it with a fine sneer . . . (This is to get that, 'howarreya harreee, thee' hard—let the 'in heaven' and 'surely' stop it in a sense, then roll out on last line again—but it's a joke.)

THE PEDIGREE [*CP* I, 51]: title to serve as sense of 'breeding', claims to title
sense, with ambivalence of reference, i.e., dogs/people, etc. Whole sense of
conformance to an established system of 'proper' connection, etc.

The beginning 'Or' : to suggest sense of, if I will not get myself a normal
continuum 'pattern' (the Freudian, etc.), i.e., if I will not show the 'normal'
feelings—the lost man's wail (ironically)—"What will I do?" To snap it then,
to my own sense of how <u>any</u> of this occurs: What, of what occasion, is not
so/ <u>necessary</u> (i.e., doesn't ultimately seem so, etc., i.e., doesn't, because it has
happened, argue with that logic its 'rightness' qua 'natural occurrence'), we do
not/ "witless" (which is picked up from Wms/ vocabulary, but, as well, from a
further sense of the non-intellectual senses of action—Elizabethan, I suppose,
too) perform it. In short, statement of the self-evident—ironic, in part, but
also suggestion that the character of actual action has some aspects of a logic
not altogether shared by that theoretic 'action'. Well, the real, etc. Hence: Or
me. Who am of common stock: sharing these same patterns of actuality, etc.,
coming from the same sources, etc. As are we all. In other words, an alternative
'pedigree' to that suggested by a theoretic behaviour pattern—last lines citing
my claim to a common source, albeit I know, obliquely. Again, the first <u>Or</u> to
cite my antagonism to assumptional notions of how people are or work, etc., etc.

That's damn muzzy. To paraphrase it all, in brief: What <u>I</u> am (i.e., title). In any
case, not to be explained by a possible conformance with assumptional notions
of behaviour—viz, I <u>won't</u> rape my daughter, nor has any such 'longing' ever
plagued me, etc., etc. "What will I do?" I.e., that's the general cry—lacking
normal basis for behaviour patterns, etc. My own answer being, well what the
hell don't we do, because we 'have to', i.e., doesn't reality itself allow us both
such definition, of action, and one large part of the conditions for that definition
as well. And don't we 'do' it, etc. Well, then: me. I was 'made', I expect—just like
that—and continue as part of the same process. My pedigree. Finally, of course
that first 'condition' could be changed to almost any other of a like kind: OR if I
will NOT pay my income tax, OR if I will NOT take off my hat in the house—o
the shocked murmur: what WILL he do . . . I do what is 'necessary . . .' ho/ho.
As do 'we' all.

So much for that. I don't know if it ever makes much sense. These poems, like
the ones in this coming booklet with Laubiès, very much an attempt to <u>side</u>
'statements', i.e., 'ideogrammic' to that extent, tho I don't believe it finally
Pound's usage. Really more Stendhal's. Or Wms/. I want the barest possible
'frame'. When they break, or flop, etc., I think it is because either the refer-
ents are imperfectly stated or too personal, or else simply without sufficient
force, in themselves, to gain the kind of final 'welding' the form calls for. The

only 'classic' instance of same I've yet managed, for my own uses at least, is THE OPERATION [*CP* I, 128]—where literally each two line section is such a statement, the four together being the total 'thought'—and not at all that 'thought' in any one part, or combination of parts other than the one given. Earlier and perhaps most successful use of this same 'method' is THE RIDDLE [*CP* I, 115], with the shift in the middle, i.e., juxtaposition of those two base 'statements'—with the almost jingle-like & 'bitter' summary: give it form certainly/ the name & titles (which last has almost to be said the way a child might pronounce it., i.e., with that 'lilt'). I suppose there are several 'classics' of this method—certainly Stendhal is full of them. Wms/ 1st part of THE LION. Crane's ISLAND QUARRY—though more 'progressional'. But that is what had interested me. Where <u>tone</u> as well as content, is 'reasonably' variable. To make a total fusion. Well, it's my own headache. THE DRUMS is minimal at best. THE PEDIGREE perhaps a joke for my own sense of balance. It also interests me in prose, i.e., I finally did write a story in which two rhythms—god knows I did <u>not</u> manufacture them, but there they were—and characters of statement ran parallel throughout, coming to a final end when (just when) one of sd rhythms literally becomes dominant. (I think it's the best thing I've ever written, but listen to this, from PR, where I'd sent it, hoping for loot, etc., etc.: "I'm sorry we don't feel we can use this. It's very well done, I think, and I hope you can place it somewhere." It's Catherine Carver—and was 'grateful' for her 'opinion' in any case. I'm going to use it, in any case, for title of this book of stories—tho still don't know whether or not Trocchi will print it (he likes them, phew . . . , but says there is a 'board', etc.): THE GOLD DIGGERS. It's a frightening story, for me—i.e., the first one not at all me, but a man literally there, of himself. A damn incredible feeling. At the end, I felt utterly helpless—and so on. To hell with it.

Damn pain in my belly commencing—have to eat something. Wow.

I was in Aix this past week, with Ann. It was very nice, finally, i.e., we had to take the car back, permit here having run out—and drove up from Barcelona, to leave it there. Very lovely at this time of year—and perhaps I am too bitter. But it is damn expensive, almost the same now as the US. And I, at least, can think only of getting back, now. If this job at BMC comes thru, I'll be back in March—so will see you anyhow before you all go. It's a shame—to have you here wd be the end. But i have been here too damn long, and it's no longer any damn good. Write soon. Title for bk fair enough. Ok.

All our love to you both,

Bob

Will get photos
back this coming
week.

. . .

LETTER TO DENISE LEVERTOV

February 3, 1954 [Mallorca]

Dear D/

Writing you from my Bed of Pain etc. Goddamn cold now for 4 wks/ and
finally a fever—but Bizness As Usual in any case. Very gt/ you liked the bk/—I
do really, a lot of fun, and L/s (in Paris) inks goof me very much. He is a gt/
man. Anyhow calamares is octupuses, and canalones—kind of ravioli—I don't
know if either stimulate sexual prowess but may have been thinking of it. No
matter. 'Dull Movement': both sea thudding in, grind etc., as one hears it here
at nite, and also, allied I guess, sound I sometimes perhaps ridiculously think
of as re millions of people making love. Not important either—i.e., I think it wd
filter in sooner or later. The 'jagged encumbrance'—sexual relations, whole mess
of relations generally, sense of impending, restricting, even obscuring 'attach-
ment'. Not defined. But hung on etc. You may be right in any case. I like others
better too (Tho L/s ink is very gt/ for this one, very funny).

Mag// ok thank god. #1 now all in proof—I got so nervous I started feeding it in
abt 2 weeks ago & now have first proof on all 64 pp/ it will be—and well, by god,
on way to having most of the ms/ for #2 as well. It is, or will be, the same rush—
what with the move in the middle. Hopeless. #2 I think will be cool enough,
#1 is too really except it was very much a pick up. [note in left margin: *For #2
Also Ronald Mason on Melville's poems- do you know his book? SPIRIT ABOVE
THE DUST (English-the best I've found. Very very nice man.)*] Anyhow got
everything from very funny Japanese story to Artaud trans/ by none other than
K. Rexroth. How abt that. He also came in as a contributing Ed/, most politely,
along with [Irving] Layton, Paul [Blackburn] & Olson. I think it will be interest-
ing. Anyhow do damn well send what you can <u>soon</u>—I wd be very grateful for
something for #2 say, still room on po-ems. So.

Cid has been very gt/ all along. There is, in fact, no real reason even for compe-
tition, i.e., there's enough material—and my emphasis has to be a little more on
reviews etc. than his. It works out. (Very great actually—for one thing it turns
out I was the only one apparently who came thru for him on reviews for #12,
so we have wild honor of holding down sd position with 2 yet. O well . . .) Also
none of the people involved, Layton, Olson, Paul etc., etc., have shown him the
least sign of letting him down for this other. It will really be two fronts, which
I think can be used—granted we haven't simply been engaged in bullshit. I.e.,
here's another place to say what most of us thot, and think, necessary—fair
enough. (He was likewise one of the very damn few who came thru with
reviews for me on #1—so we know damn well who we can count on. Voila!)

One thing I have to mention, tho no pleasure—i.e., we'll be facing a like [^ *as you were then*] problem of money, for Ann's passage & the kids abt June—and can you get us any of that $100 back? I think you know I wdn't bring it up if I didn't have to—i.e., things will be very tight, because there won't be time for any money from the books to come in, and that backing we had will have run out by abt the next bk/—anyhow cd you please write me as soon as you can how it looks. If you cd get it to me by abt the first of May, then that wd be great. But write anyhow—ok/—I'm sorry it has to come up.

This for now. All our love to you all & all best luck on that issue—it sounds very good & I'd be damned if I'd worry. Who can.

Bob

[note in left margin] *Very good you liked the poem—many thanks for taking it.*

. . .

LETTER TO WILLIAM CARLOS WILLIAMS

June 6, 1954 [Black Mountain, NC]

Dear Bill,

I hardly have any excuse for taking this long to thank you for all your kindness that afternoon—both you and your wife. Which says it very damn dully & forgive me. I think I know your poems as well as any man living—which is obvious presumption—but anyhow now I know the man who wrote them too, & it means a very great deal to me.

Nothing is much simpler here, the place continues to founder on this headache of money—otherwise it's terrific & the past weeks, even if that's all it comes to, won't have been for nothing. I feel better in this thing than I've felt for a long, long time—& if you had wondered what I got out of it, then that's it. Some guts.

Anyhow, if it closes (and the test I guess will be very soon, i.e., no money & we can't get much beyond July, if that) for myself, I don't know what I'll do, I haven't really been able to think much about it. As well, I'm in a kind of break-thru or down depending on how you look at it, & don't even see anything but simply what's right in front of me. What a goddam pleasure it is.

I don't know whether or not my wife sent you a copy of the magazine, I'll send one from here soon in any case—also of what new books we've done. I'm just now waiting for copies to come from Mallorca. I think both of these things, i.e., magazine & books, can be kept going no matter. From what little I had time to find out in NY, I think they're our best bet for making some kind of front & holding it. At least it keeps us from being smothered completely. I was surprised that they get around as well as they do.

So to hell with this for the moment—I wish I could talk to you again, right now, but perhaps I'll be able to get up again sometime not too damn far away. I hope so. Could you let me know what happened on the play—it's very exciting & I hope to god they work it out. I asked around about Paige but got the same answers you had—I hope you've managed to get hold of him by now.

Well, thanks—& please bear with me for being so inarticulate about it, I hate that—not being able to say it the way I want to, how very damn much seeing you meant.

All my love to you both,
Bob

· · ·

LETTER TO KENNETH REXROTH

August 14, 1954 [Mallorca]

Dear Rexroth,

   This is not at all worth bothering you with but you are at least there. Ok. I had today a letter from Duncan calling me on the 1st issue, to wit, the review on Roethke plus the Patchen review which I of course wrote. The latter seems to have bugged everyone and god knows that was <u>not</u> the intention. I.e., I conceived the book or <u>much</u> better, I felt the book as written with pain, a fucking simple element these days. What I had hoped at least to say was that he cared to write, that it hurt, and that to write in this fucking world <u>does</u> hurt. And that if your back hurts, too, then it hurts. A fucking simple element, pain. All of which I seem to have misread. I can't believe it. Whereas the jacket says 'gayety' etc. I could hardly believe that either well, you know. Today we smile. Voila.

Also on Roethke—as again Duncan says Patchen is not 'rain' or is, as he says, Lewis Carroll 'pain' too? Jesus Christ—the review is 'cruel and attacking an 'insecure' man' etc. Here is a man who has profited by every fucking filthiness of literary practice in the US today and <u>Duncan</u> says, "cruel . . . " Is this man serious? Is he going to lay down and lick the fucking stick that's shoved up his ass? Well, again I am much too goddamn assumptive. But my god to praise this character of self-devotion is pathetic. I don't know what these people are thinking of. This <u>is</u> the end of the world, possibly—and <u>yet</u> we are to have these politenesses. Which he would hardly extend to another—at that.

Would you sometime write me an article on the West Coast, anonymous or whatever. I.e., I am if you will a lonely man living with a wife and three children. What else. I see no one here. Teaching, it was almost worse because at least I could hope. And I would rather live on the ground.

People cry, scream, yell—for what. So he can be kind, or generous, or polite. You know, anyone. Either way. A character of writing becomes the abstention from all care—do not be partial, goddamnit. I think I lost all respect for Patchen, because I know this man through his wife's family, I grew up there, where they came from and saw the pathetic picture to the great man they had over their fireplace. With care.

This idiot. This pathetic idiot. This is writing, for him. NOT to care, to be a great man. Fuck him.

So, you know, I guess it does mean sides. Of course I am lonely. How could 'I' be otherwise. I don't really care much anymore what people think, or even think of. Let Duncan worry as he will. I like your writing. I trusted you before, younger, and would again because at least I know what you care for, egocentric as it's become for me now to say so.

    All best to you,
       Creeley

• • •

LETTER TO KENNETH REXROTH

August 19, 1954

Dear Rexroth,
    That letter of yesterday can serve, I guess, as what I had to write but it is hardly what I wanted to. I can't yet believe it is all this simple, or that what I have taken in your work as care and a core of absolute seriousness can be so simply obverted. Perhaps even that is presumptuous, though I have to read you as I will. But that we should come to a difference on such a question as Roethke seems to me impossible.

I can't offer you any equivalence of experience, except to say, as what I am, that I do care, that writing, this process such as I have known it, gives me that relief. That is, it is, at best, what I am, it gives me that relief. At seventeen I used to hand out pamphlets at the Fore River shipyards, we were trying to break the company union and get the CIO in. My mother was a nurse, and my father died when I was two years old. I have one sister who is miserable. My mother, now almost seventy, will be up for retirement this year, whereupon she will go live with her sister. At eighteen I was in Burma, every morning I got up and to get out of the ambulance stepped over stretchers that had about an inch of blood in them. I saw people die, as many of my age did, in every conceivable posture. I have no longer, nor can I ever have, the least tolerance for any 'sickness' per se. I suffered too much from 'sick' minds and the purposes to which they commit themselves.

So what does that matter. I do not think it the least aggression to believe we can only say what we think, responsibly. I certainly accept all responsibility for the 'attack' on Roethke. I submit that other men have cared to keep clean, under equally difficult conditions. Artaud, of course, comes to mind and the description of him I had from a friend of the way he was after the war, of what he weighed, of how to speak even was difficult, of the people who then allowed him who had said, is this a poet . . . , earlier. I think, too, because you bring it up, of Hart Crane, and the one man who knew him, I think, as well as any other and better than most, Slater Brown. Rhetorically enough, this man was the first ever to care one good goddamn what I wrote, and hoped to. I learned a great deal from him, both of Crane—who certainly you misunderstand in your value of this [Yvor] Winters' attack—and of that kind of care poetry can be, as I also learn it, indirectly, from what even Robert Graves now has to say of Crane, from the meeting in London perhaps too long ago to matter. You see, you are much too solicitous of 'sickness' per se. We are all sick, if that matters. If we care, we are sick, because we are insane to care, now. You know that all your 'revolutionaries' are dead. How protest now, you think—except to rid yourself of the embarrassment of any attachment to people who cannot read Roethke, hopefully. That is nasty to say, i.e., I hardly mean to be. I would, if I were there, put you to a very simple test, to wit, ask you to prove it, what you say of me and of this man. And if you could not, of course I would deal with you as I have, and have to, with any man who assumes my 'unfairness', which is actually to say I am a liar. The point is that my generation doesn't give a good goddamn for any hope, or any pretension, or anything but what comes of actual care. How can we. You ask us to assume this man's seriousness? When every single word he writes is both self-indulgence and a distortion of those who do care. Even Crane, particularly Crane.

Well, fuck rhetoric. It hardly serves anyone. I wanted you on the magazine because, ingenuously, I thought here is a man who can spit, usefully, who writes poetry, a poem, who has cared for a long time. All much too simple I grant you, though you did write me, "Sure, I'd be glad to be on your editorial board. I do get a certain amount of stuff from young poets around the country, etc. etc." That's the last I ever heard from you but for that mimeographed note re the radio program, until this letter yesterday. I know you are busy, I only suggest that other men can be equally so, and with, I hope, equal purpose.

I don't know why you make it a case re Roethke, I have read that article many times since getting your letter. I read it after getting Duncan's. I think either I am completely mistaken as to the nature, call it, of what you had cared about, or else a fool, completely. In which case you would do both me and yourself a service by forgetting you ever read a single poem by me. I could not possibly be a 'good' poet by these criteria.

If I were there, I guess I wd have you by the lapels anyhow; jesus god to say only I don't understand. I want to, I don't. Because I will never forget this, one way or the other. I wrote five people to be on that fucking 'board', four of whom came, the other being Paul Goodman who never answered and that was honest of him. But you did. And you cannot answer me this way, now. If you're for Roethke, and if you're a man, say why. If you think the attack was dishonest, unfair, or any other thing, say it. I mean say it. With respect, absolute,—say it. You cannot go 'old' on me or claim a 'superior' bizness. This is the bizness, all it ever is.

Obviously I want you on, I won't take you off until you give me an answer. Not simply to be difficult, but I care to know. More than you tell me in this note. I want to know, poem by poem, what you see in this man. You are on the board by your own will. To deny that can't be simply a shrug of your shoulders. I think that is fair.

> Best to you,
> Creeley

I enclose a note I'd written earlier to follow your own, i.e., I had, as I said, to say something. It seems to me altogether inadequate, at least from what I know to be involved, but anyhow let it stand for now. I wish you would say it, what's on your mind—Roethke is the issue, not Thomas—who is hardly 'attacked' in your sense. Is there some question of a loyalty which I would certainly respect, however it came. At least I think it worth saying.

[Note appended to August 19, 1954, letter to Rexroth]

"Kenneth Rexroth wishes to state that he had nothing to do with the attacks on Dylan Thomas and Theodore Roethke in the first issue (Vol I, No 1) of the Black Mountain Review. He has never functioned as an editor, associate or otherwise,[1] and has requested that his name be removed from the masthead."

Kenneth Rexroth asked that the above notice be put into the Summer issue of this magazine, i.e., Vol I, No 2. But since that had already been printed and shipped by the time his letter arrived, it was impossible. A record of his wish, however, is due him, and should be noted by the reader.

Otherwise, and what should also be noted, is that the editor of this magazine does not withdraw one inch from the position asserted by the publication of the reviews in question. The reader can judge for himself whether or not these reviews were printed solely as attacks on persons, as opposed to the acts of those persons and their subsequent endorsement by a large portion of what passes for critical writing in America. Certainly it is not Roethke's fault that those very characteristics in his work which are most lamentable, eg., diffusion, generality, and a completely adolescent address to the world in which he finds himself, should be the ones on which his reputation is maintained. But it is to the point to attack such a maintenance, and this the editor believes was done in the review in question. Poems were given, were quoted, and discussed. And that fact alone allows the reader his own judgement. He has no obligation to agree, he has only to consider what lies in front of him. He can make up his own mind as to whether or not these poems constitute the possession of "enormous talent . . . " In the case of Thomas, he can also make up his own mind as to whether or not the question, "His work has imposed itself on contemporary readers as 'major', or, rather, it has been made 'major'. Why?", is a fair one.

Let him do this for himself. Who else can, or should. There is no possible defense for the editorial position of this magazine except that it believes in what it prints.

R.C.

[RC's note] [1]Mr. Rexroth accepted the post of 'contributing editor' in a letter of January 17, 1954.

. . .

LETTER TO WILLIAM CARLOS WILLIAMS

[Mallorca]
August 21, 1954

Dear Bill,

   Your letter just came but you'll have had my own by now about Rainer Gerhardt—which stays with me very much. Selfishly, I want to do something about it, it seems such an ugliness that he is dead so goddamn simply. As it is, I can only write 'notes', and they are hardly to the point. But I can't see letting what he did go unnoticed. Well, something at least god knows—it must be possible. He can't simply be shoveled under like that.

It's very kind of you to say what you do, of the stories. I've written a couple of others, one since coming here—perhaps I'm going too arch. I don't know, but anyhow something comes which is it I guess. Also I've written a few poems and that, too, is a relief. This process of sitting down again, more or less isolate, is difficult, or is against all the contact there was there at Black Mountain. Except I have it here too. It's simply in another character, which I have to manage as I can.

It's also very good to hear what you say of Olson's MAXIMUS POEMS—I like them very much. I think what you say, of their structure, is the point. He needs this size very much to declare himself, finally—he gets pulled almost too short otherwise. I hope that piece for Jonathan Williams comes ok, god knows Olson will be very happy. He cares what you think very much.

I'm glad I didn't jump you on that thing of 'women', but then I had to read the poems and trust to that. You know, I <u>was</u> scared meeting you. And felt utterly at home by the time I left. I.e., I'd hardly be so presumptuous as to say, I 'know' what you mean, but with that I've had chance to, you make absolute sense to me. As against those men very often, whose ways I can see & value, but whose content is simply too far from my own to make the tie. So I read the poems I guess caring more than it is very simple to say. And somehow, perhaps ridiculously enough, getting to Barcelona & seeing Ann, with that shyness, I ended up, or we did, sitting in a room we had in a pension, there, reading them to her as best I could. Well, they work, they say it—what the hell else can matter.

As it is, I'm fighting after a fashion, with both Rexroth and Robt Duncan on this article I'd printed on Roethke—and what a waste of time that is. To be separated from anyone on such an account. Rexroth thinks the attack was unfair, and he's right to, because R/ must be a friend. But the practice involved sticks, and I think it's filthy. I wish he did too, but he doesn't.

So, look, do come if you can. I don't even dare really think about it much—it would be terrific. I also think it would be on your route to Greece, and we're easily found, in fact we'll meet you & all, or anything that's simplest. Ok. I'll even see to it that Robt Graves pays you homage as you descend etc. Voila.

Write when you can, please. All love to you both,

Bob

• • •

LETTER TO LOUIS ZUKOFSKY

[letterhead]

The Black Mountain Review
Casa Martina

Black Mountain, North Carolina

Bonanova, Palma
Mallorca, Spain
November 10, 1954

Dear Mr Zukovsky:

Mr Edward Dahlberg has just come to Palma, and talking with him, he had mentioned you and your work. Also I had just seen your address in a recent issue of The Pound Newsletter. In any case I'm editing the above magazine for Black Mountain College, and should be very grateful to see anything you might be kind enough to send us. I have known your work from Pound's Active Anthology, also from your own very interesting 'anthology', so I very much hope that I can be of some use to you. It would please me very much.

Yours sincerely,
Robert Creeley
Robert Creeley

P.S. I'll send some copies of the magazine soon, so that you'll be able to see what I'm talking about—such as it is.

. . .

LETTER TO WILLIAM CARLOS WILLIAMS

Casa Martina
Bonanova, Palma
Mallorca, Spain
November 25, 1954

Dear Bill,

Many thanks for your letter about Kitasono's book—it's wonderful you found it that moving. You'll know, I guess, that it is not a very 'simple' book for the usual reader, i.e., I get some letters asking how we came to print it & so on, so many 'cliches'—o well. What they won't see is precisely this quality that you do see, so very clearly. This commonness—it moves me very much. My own favorites are the first (A Shadow) and one of the shorter (A Solitary Decoration). I love his tone—or what to call it—literally the movement of the words, the way they are in a sense always with the slightest of hesitancies, from the difficulties of his 'english' I guess—anyhow, it seems a very particular care. (In fact, just like this image, of the performer on the pole, the way the man does 'set' himself, for the consequent movement, etc.)

So that was pleasure, certainly. And again, I'm very pleased you liked it, and know he will be too.

I've just had a copy of your Selected Essays, which is not a simple book for me. Probably it's because I'm apt to hold your work with rather ridiculous fierceness, i.e., what I like & so forth. So it is that I miss things like that note on Women I had mentioned to you in Rutherford, also With Rude Fingers Forced (which always seemed to me very exact), the Letter To An Australian Editor (in which your references to Pound were stated very fairly and explicitly), and even something as brief but also as unequivocal as the National Book Award address. Well, how can you be expected to get it all in—except that I find myself perplexed, reading the note on Thomas, for one thing, or your being literally so charitable to Auden, when Crane (who cared I think so much more) is then put down elsewhere (in the piece called: Shapiro Is All Right—which I'm damned if he is!)

In any case the book puzzles me, sometimes I almost sense a gun at your back—which may be utter ridiculousness. But Charles Henri Ford! And as you say there: "To me the sonnet form is thoroughly banal because it is a word in itself whose meaning is definitely fascistic . . . But for Ford's sake I am willing to ignore the form as unimportant . . . " Put it, that at that point my understanding balks. I don't mean to argue a literal straightness of black & white, but rather that some kindnesses will be utterly misappropriated—as you had told me this one in fact was.

Well, this is no matter. I'll try to review the book as accurately as I can—tho that will also hardly matter to very many. I can't put it otherwise, than that I care for your work very deeply—and I'm damned if I can see it misused by what must have been a publisher's selection (?). Which is presumptuous—forgive me please. The American Background is what I value, completely; In A Mood Of Tragedy, for what?

Anyhow I had to say it. I hope things go all right for you, I wish very much I could see you. This distance is damn well impossible.

All our love to you all,
Bob

• • •

LETTER TO WILLIAM CARLOS WILLIAMS

December 6, 1954

Dear Bill,

   Many thanks for your letter—which is such a dull way of saying it, forgive me. I know, I think, what you mean, though god knows that is presumptuous. Anyhow—I did the review last week, and hope it makes some sense to you— also, now, I'll try to indicate more than I did (I can add a few footnotes to places where it comes in, etc.), what effect the omissions do have.

In any case, what I did want to ask you—very much at the time the book first came—was, would you have any use for, call it, a supplementary volume, i.e., something we could perhaps do here. I would have asked sooner, but thought perhaps this was your own final taking of these things—well, that was goddamn smug of me. Anyhow say what you think, it would be a readable job of print-ing, etc., and we could print maybe 1000 copies. Not to be grand about it—nor to trade on your name, etc. I'd simply like to see the rest of it said, or literally available. Because there is the impossibility of trying to find these things, now, in magazines out-of-print, scattered, and so on.

Well, the goddamn review—it was a messy (my messiness, that is), difficult job. So much of the book made its point, almost in spite of its subject—as many of your comments, for example, in the essays on Lowell (It is to assert love, not to win it that the poem exists), Thomas (What is more profound than song? The only thing to be asked is, whether or not a man is content with it)—and so on.

So I fumbled with that, in some sense. But, more particularly, I tried to take on this nightmare of measure—because I believe it is one. Again, the way the book is now 'presented', it's difficult to avoid mis-emphases. For example, I found that this thing makes three overt appearances, first re Pound's Cantos (Pound's 11 New Cantos), then in the piece on The Poem As A Field Of Action, and finally and at length in the piece at the end for Cid.

All thru it, I had the feeling I agreed with your sense of it all, but was damned if I'd grant you the word, not with the horror of its implications. Anyhow, some- one had been telling me about some elizabethan, Sam Putnam, who wrote it all: numbers & measure equals arhythmus; whereas that rhythm which we call 'poetic', is basically irregular, or rather is, that 'regularity just out of hearing'. For myself, when you say, a relatively stable foot, you're arguing 1) that a man trust his own ear, i.e., hear the weights of those words he's using; and 2) that a reader at least try some like care, etc. I don't see it as 'measure'. Nor do I believe a line must be measured, to be in measure. (Graves, for example, was telling me of some tests some idiots had made with a seismograph, yet, wherein poems were read & the patterns came out complete flux, i.e., no 'measure' at all. They couldn't even separate words, much less lines—and so on.)

But, if you'll forgive my presumption, again, this comes to me somehow from Pound (?)—or what is it—and also from god knows a reasonable wish to have some means wherewith to attack the 'typographical' poets, and also to argue the coherence of your own structure. But, for me, Marianne Moore is measure—there's the goddamn mathematics of it, I can't make it. Even as a 'relatively stable foot'. I think once this becomes the 'direction', call it, in which a poem is written, words drop their own weights, in an either/or battle with 'metric'. I mean, the coherence tends to become 'exterior'. Frankly, even this much discussion involves me in the weariest of generalities—I don't know, I don't think anyone ever did, does, or will. Like Campion and his own statement, that he wrote to no 'measure', etc.

> Kinde are her answeres,
> But her performance keeps no day;
> Breaks time, as dancers
> From their own Musicke when they stray:
> All her free favors and smooth words,

Wing my hopes in vaine.
O did ever voice so sweet but only fain?
   Can true love yeeld to such delay,
   Converting joy to pain?

   Lost is our freedome,
   When we submit to women so:
Why doe wee neede them,
   When in their best they worke our woe?
   There is no wisedome
Can alter ends, by Fate prefixt.
O why is the good of man with evill mixt?
   Never were days yet cal'd two,
   But one night went betwixt.

I don't think one could 'measure' it, to begin with—nor granted some 'flexible' system might allow that, for what purpose? The 'length' of anything is such a variable—and doesn't it, too, involve us in all this horror of time, literally? What is 'five minutes', etc. Or 'I thought you'd never come'. I think it's an impossible thing, to measure, in any sense. But that is willful, etc., I mean, not romantically, outside the window here there's a stone wall, sun, etc., and that, if one will, is measure enough. Because all the stones, tho of god knows a great variety, do 'fit'. And has an edge of sorts along the top which is 'rime' enough. And keeps the cows out, or in, depending. I don't think you should bother your head about me who have no ears—or they will not hear, I think, because of 'measure'. Writing, anyhow, this review, I remembered one of your Collected Later Poems, that had appeared in the London Times Literary Supplement, as follows:

> . . . But his forms are so irregular in outline that there is no way of measuring them. Any metrical ideas which the reader retains while reading him will be an interruption . . .

You know—how true! And at least you give us the <u>poem</u>. I just damn well don't see backtracking in any sense, from that very substantial victory. Like, even Ben Jonson—particularly Ben Jonson—was brought to write:

      Still may Syllabes jarred with time,
      Still may reason warre with rime,
         Resting never.

Poor devil, etc. Anyhow, again my own hatred of what the publisher involves you in—so much more to the point seems the kind of sense you made of Pound, i.e., one basically intuitive hit, where you point out his idea of mind generated by mind, a male process—head to head, sans body (female), etc. Graves was out here for supper a few nights ago, and that seemed to impress him, as much as it had me, when I read it. Well, like they say, that is so much more interesting than measure—if you'll forgive me that sense of it.

God knows it's all our battle—and the damn deep bitterness of it I sometimes feel, dispossessed, etc., tears & all,—ah well! You have done so much. That doesn't even imply a 'past', i.e., you do it. I wish, again and again, very selfishly, that there were not this great distance, etc.

I hope I don't tag to you (as I may have suggested, re Shapiro, etc.) any necessity of infallibility. I think your poems are often 'infallible'—god knows enough. I'm not very old, but I've read them for some 10 years now—and they've held me very kindly. I can remember doing one of those 'papers', at Harvard, on your work, at a time when all I really knew of it was the first Complete Collected Poems—and was stunned by the insight of, call it feebly (!), that Nantucket poem with its, "the immaculate white bed" or was it just, 'bed'. Anyhow. Granted loneliness, and often a feeling that no one else has possessed any of those dilemmas, with which oneself, etc., seems confronted, it helps to be contradicted. You've done that time and again for me. The most pleasure I got from that class at BMC was, after, one of the kids telling me, for once he got Williams—as opposed to 'Creeley', or whoever of course it could have been. That was damn good to hear.

So, anyhow, to hell with it, i.e., do tell me if we can be of any use, re the material that isn't in this Selected Essays—or anything else you may think of. I hope the review won't seem a complete waste to you, i.e., simply something presumptuous. I did attack the 'measure', because I don't see it—that may well be me, and granted the light ever comes, know that I'll acknowledge it. But that seemed to me anyhow one of the book's centers, as it was there given. As to the other things, The American Background, for one, argues so much your strength, seeing Ciardi (I think it was), singling out The Artist, in a review of The Desert Music, to quote, etc. But that comes to his and my taste, and has nothing to do with you—or often the poems, either.

I hope things go ok. Have you thought of coming here? Just now the weather holds fair enough, we get strong sun from roughly 11 to 3 or so—actually very good. And here it is December, etc. Nor does it come to that soporific bizness like in Fla, etc. Anyhow it's as good a place to be as we can now either think of, or manage. So.

Write when you can, please.

All our love to you both,
Bob

.   .   .

LETTER TO CID CORMAN

Merry Christmas & all
best for a good New Year!   December 24, 1954

Dear Cid,

This is a little close to the deadline, to make much sense—but I want to answer you, i.e., that way it's simpler to keep up & all. We just got a monkey—very lovely little thing, a lady, etc. I've always wanted one, it's the kind of thing one dreams abt—and last night in fact it seemed that I dreamed abt everything I ever have, at that—anyhow she is very nice. Now of course we worry abt her getting cold & so on—like having another kid. We gave her an old sweater of Tom's last night to sleep on, & she fooled around with it for awhile, then put it on! Too much. It's weird the way they parallel (and god knows equal in many cases) so-called human intelligence. So.

The pigeon book is by H. P. Macklin, who writes a series of articles in the Am/ Pigeon Journal (who is buying out the edition, for distribution etc) on divers odd & out-of-fashion breeds. Very nice man. Anyhow that's it—and I'll try to get you a copy. I hadn't really thought to send one, because it is, granted, a peculiarity of my own—and those likewise afflicted. Just now I'm trying to locate a good pair of Homers for Graves—who plans to use them for communication between Deya & Palma—very funny.

While I think of it—two Oxford students (both from Newfoundland, one [^ *Cyril Fox*] a Rhodes scholar, etc) came to visit this past week; I liked them very much, particularly Edward Flynn, whose whole character, to put it dully, seemed to me very damn decent. [note in left margin: It was a tremendous pleasure to watch Flynn <u>read</u> Irving.] Anyhow I took the liberty of giving him your address, in case he can get there—either going back now, or perhaps later. I think you'd like him, also both of them. The other's name is Cyril Fox (he had known Rainer & Renate, etc). Ed F/ is doing graduate work in English Lit/—very sensible and fine-humored man. I hope you have chance to see him.

As to the magazine—by all means, do send whatever you have, anytime. I know you don't want to waste time trying things you may think I'll have no use for. As to the Apollinaire specifically, I'm a little against using such as opposed to new work—but that's a 'general' feeling, i.e., I wouldn't use it for a club, etc. Well, you say. Prose is, god knows, hard to get—I have at the moment two stories in hand I hope to use this next issue (#5)—but that's not much of a backlog. As to doing 4 issues in advance, I haven't been able as yet to come anywhere near such a thing, i.e., it's always a pickup, or has been. At best I've asked people to do specific things, but that's invariably dependent upon their own time, etc. So it doesn't constitute a very deliberate 'plan', ever. I do hope to do an issue of 'parodies', to put it loosely, some time this summer—but that again depends on what material can be got together. I also hope to have some material on both dance & music, i.e., Katie Litz wrote she'll try at least; and has also asked David Tudor, for me, to see if he can't do something. She says the latter had just come back from a European tour—did you happen to hear him? Very fine pianist. (Of course both were at BMC, etc. I met Katie in NYC, very nice woman—and very damn good dancer I think.) But again, it all stays tentative which is perhaps best—at least it's the rule, at the moment.

I'll try to send some poems soon, I'm working ok thank god. Can you tell me what you have, from #13—is there anything of mine in #14? I haven't seen #13 as yet. I'm all confused as to what I did send & also what you accepted. Ok. To hell with it & I will try to send something soon.

All best,

Bob

[note in left margin] Thanks for asking about cars, etc. I hope we can get something.

. . .

LETTER TO WILLIAM CARLOS WILLIAMS

January 26, 1955

Dear Bill,

Olson just sent a letter to be added to all this discussion re 'measure'. It's an answer to that review of mine—such as that was. Anyhow, here are quotes of the main parts of his letter.

" . . . Would there be this use: that a line is at least all at the same time quantity, breath and accent. And that rhythm is something else again even though these three are its agents. That's so far as prosody goes. But the prosody is only itself one of three parts of the act of any given line simply that the line is also, word-wise, image and thought. And these are as much agents of the rhythm as the sound effects are: what you have in your mind and your soul is as much a matter of the rhythm as the words you get out of your mouth? I don't need to say, try and write without something to say. And see what you get.

"Foot, me eye. Or arthmus, me arse.

"What is patently true is that rhythm now is arhythmic—which certainly Campion wasn't, and that second stanza in the Williams' poem you quote is arhythmic. The Campion is straight lute music, and as different from the 'music' of Mr Bill as Boulez is not Bach. OK?

"All right. If what we got is arhythm—and that means that on one face of the line the image and thought too will be different from, say, the Elizabethans, it also means that on the other face the arhythm will be demanding other services of its agents quantity breath accent than what they were used for, either by the Elizabethans or the classical poets, then or now (Eliot Milton any of those Bill had it were, with forced fingers rude, diddling the nightingale)

"Thus a foot, like I say, is—my foot. At least we'd be best to throw some of these words out of the window, that they do go with a state and time of language and verse which ain't now, viz., meter, measure, foot, rhythm (if "rhythm" is still going to be what it became by a decay of its root meaning through mediaeval Latin: see definition of "Rime" in Shorter Oxford). And I suggest these be the words to go, because they describe a usage not a fact of language.

"There are these five facts of words in verse: (1) that they take an observable length of time to get out of the throat and mouth—quantity; (2) that there are certain terminals that require it, and anyhow the breath itself can't push 'em out forever, so there are stoppages or silences, for example caesuras, they used to call them, rests, they call them in music, here we call them—breath; (3) that words are pronounced with accents on definite syllables, according to the country you live in, but with general agreements which make the hearing of their meaning clear—accent;

and two too little noticed "facts", that (4), words have meaning as thought; and (5), that they have meaning as image, that they carry pictures, yet.

"Now beyond that—even syntax—you are into the confusion it will be how a man and a time uses these as to what rules of order you will be running up against. And because we are in a time when the American language is more and more self-isolating—and we are as good as we are, as good as we are—it behooves us, I should think, ... to get the words to preach what you practice.

"Rhythm itself, if understood as what it means, flatly, what damn well "flows", is what turns out to flow. And that's what a man makes, if he makes it. And it hasn't a damn thing to do with a foot. Or with the red-herring you drag over the question, "quantitative verse" either. Nor does it have to do with rhyme or no rhyme, even if rime (to get that word back to some cleanliness too)—I mean the agreement of terminal sounds—has a strong tendence to create backward along itself an order which is, in fact, meter. But meter is not rhythm: it is meter, measure, regularity of foot, something which may or may not satisfy as succeeding also to be rhythm.

"If you do without rime . . . , then whether you know it or not, the agents of . . . your powers over arhythm are the quantity, breath, accent of your words, and the image and thought you give them. And no more . . . "

I am impressed—to put it dully. At least, even in the letters to you, I felt first (and most particularly) that for my part, the attempt to 'state' the rationale for this character of verse I have felt you, in effect, have introduced and/or made the most complete evidence for was not damn well to be done with words like 'measure'. Perhaps I yank in Olson much too quickly for a shield—but what do you think? In many ways—some ways—the mechanics of the poem are both as absolute & as intimate as the act of love; which will not be stated, but which will be known—or else. At least no guides to complacent marriage will help; but the end is the marriage (literally in the sense of which you have spoken—a thing), no matter. Anyhow, I've felt that when you say, an order by which may be ordered not only our poems but our lives—that it was the poem as an absolute which you were asserting—as absolute as anything gets, which is in some cases, completely.

I am being more vague than ever. But — we don't need a "measure" so much as we <u>do</u> need, desperately, some sense of our materials, the elements if you will from which the poem forms, to be the form, that will dis-embarrass us. Isn't this the goddamn dilemma—otherwise why is Leonie Adams <u>such</u> an embarrassment. Aren't all 'irrational' forms an "embarrassment"*—sometimes as horribly as the man singing somewhere down by Houston street, who was kicked to death by some kids, for just that. I.e., they asked him why he was singing. They ask you—why this 'form'. Good christ, etc. Anyhow, let me get this off to you. Please write when you can—I will too.

All our love to you both,

Bob

[note in left margin] *to such as Leonie Adams—good guy or not? And yet there is no <u>possible</u> agreement, unless one go to the <u>poem</u>.

. . .

LETTER TO ALEXANDER TROCCHI

[Mallorca]

April 23, 1955

Wd you please also send what makes it for you, names or whatever, to me, i.e., anything you can think of for this BMR? Cd I snitch one of those Beckett stories—there I damn well envy you. He is good. Anyhow whatever you can as you can. New format etc now in press, goes ok.

Dear Alex,

It's goddamn kind of you to take such trouble—i.e., that's the softest rejection I ever got, and it matters, like they say. Certainly the 'style' is studied; I hope at least among confreres I don't pull over wig of divine inspiration for that 'manner', etc., etc. And I think I know what you mean re manner/matter, etc. It may simply be that the content of that one, doesn't seem worth the twitching (wherein I wd disagree with you), yet that's a point—and where my own gamble comes in, etc. At the moment I'm sitting here putting things down like:

> "Jason Edwards lived in a mansion. (stop) Jim Stuart lived in a shack. (stop) Jason Edwards lived in a shack. (stop) Jim Stuart lived in a mansion. (stop)"

And:

> "Can't keep his head. It's over his head. Pillow is under his head, it's over. Maid on her way. The head. The head is father to the mind? Mind is <u>inside</u>—the head. Dropped on his head, as a boy. Cats land on all fours."

Which is ridiculous, like that—literally, jawbreakers is all I'm after, things, anything, to break up set sense or sense patterns I fall into. (Viz, these are not 'from stories', etc., etc., etc.) Too, the syntactical seems my own crib, usually, so that too I want to examine with more care. I suppose it all begins with: "He over took—them. He took them—over." And so on. To hell with it. But will try to keep awake no matter.

So to hell with that, really. It's suddenly begun to rain, which—after the dryness here for months now—seems a much more relevant thing. Wow.

More to the point also—let me put down those few I myself respect, i.e., writers, and then you say, and don't feel that any show of interest obliges you to a damn thing. But I've been reluctant to ask people to send stuff to you, since I'd worried that might argue presumption on my part, and a possible embarrassment finally to you. Anyhow, like this: Robert Duncan; Charles Olson, Paul Blackburn, Irving Layton, Denise Levertov—and perhaps a few others, though I cannot at the moment think of them. And of those, Olson, and Duncan, seem to me the most able, i.e., all do interest me, often very much, for one reason or another,—anyhow that's enough goddamn rambling abt it. Too, as I wrote you in that last note, there are certainly people like Paul Goodman, I think would be interesting—also Louis Zukofsky? (He has a thing on Shakespeare, part of which was published in the last ND Annual, 'Bottom Dream'.) And there are other materials I hear of, that I would like to at least mention, eg., possible art notes by Harold Rosenberg, possible notes from John Cage, et al. Stuff like that. I cannot use all of it, nor do I mean to suggest here I'd be using you at all, for a watershed, etc. Nor for any 'community', and so forth. Thank god that is well dead . . .

I wish I could see you now, though at the moment it's not too hopeless here. I.e., a friend from NYC I'd met there last summer, a painter, John Altoon, is now here—and that's a pleasure. And also Duncan, who is very damn sharp, and good company. I wish you might meet him sometime, and will hope that you do. I think to try again sometime soon to get to Paris, yet you know how tedious said attempts usually prove—so leave me shut up till it's for real, beyond all question. Ok. Also—while I think of it—can you give me rough deadlines, i.e., before, say, next two or so issues, so I can send you several things at once, rather than one story (as this last time, etc). I'd rather do it like that—and think it would be better for you as well. And having a rough date, then I could make it, I think. I am a hell of a procrastinator, I believe.

So, wild. Hope it all goes well there, and will write shortly—and do tell me what I can do to be of use, ever. That's really what bugs me, as is—viz, my goddamn vague activity. Voila.

All our best,
Bob

Don't bother to send back copy (story) if you haven't. I have another here, etc.

. . .

LETTER TO JACK SPICER

Black Mountain College
Black Mountain, N.C.
September 5, 1955

Dear Spicer,

Thanks for your letter, and under any other circumstances but those which we now face, I'm certain that the college would be very interested in your qualifications as a possible addition to the faculty. But, sadly enough, we are at present in no position to hire you. I spoke to Olson, and his suggestion is that I keep you in mind; and bring the matter up as soon as things are a bit clearer–which I hope won't be too long from now. In any case, I will write you if any thing looks possible.

Both Jess Collins and Robert Duncan spoke of you very warmly, when I saw them in Mallorca. I also like both of them, very much. I hope sometime that I may meet you. If you have anything, or can think of anything, for the Black Mountain Review, I should be very interested to see it.

Yours sincerely,
Robert Creeley

. . .

LETTER TO ROBERT DUNCAN

Black Mountain College
Black Mountain, N.C.

Robert Duncan
Banalbufar
Mallorca
SPAIN
September 6, 1955

Dear Robert,

I'm very sorry not to have written, the past week or so has been excit-
ing to say the least, eg. last week I was a passenger in a car which found itself
being driven into a house at 40 miles an hour. The Asheville paper reported it,
under a picture of the car, as: Driver Hits Own Residence. Anyhow, the past
month has seen a pathetic variety of attempts to 'make it', one sleeping pills, one
wrists, and the car was the third. All of which, here, seems simple enough to
make a bit ridiculous, nor can I, I guess, not find it that in some sense, i.e., my
own dilemma never seems to take on that cast. I have at that a horror of being
'ridiculous' not by my own choice, so resolve on no such things as the above.
Anyhow I got a twisted shoulder, from the accident, and a bang on the nose—
and a never to be forgotten 'view' of a house rushing out to meet us. Somewhat
like a Triumph of the Home, at that. The car was completely demolished, and
the house was not even dented. Dan Rice and I were sitting in the back seat;
Tom Field was driving, such a mild young man usually, but of course with this
thing very much under it, and Jorge Fick, who was in position to be most hurt,
yet survived with very little to show for it, as I did. Dan fractured a vertebra, but
will be all right, praise god; Tom dislocated his hip, and will also be all right. It
was all unbelievable.

But, in such a milieu, which is nonetheless sane enough god knows, I am not
able to be broken by such things as Ann now sees fit to do, or John for that
matter. I mean I think, that I have such an intensity of human confusion, hope,
god knows what, present daily, I live with and in that. More to the point, the
last few weeks I have found myself more and more 'separated' from her. I don't
know how to 'qualify' this sensation, it is in any case organic, to the extent that
it 'grows' in me. You are kind, so very damn kind, to recognize this 'strength' in
me; at moments I would much rather flop down & cry, etc. But then, I am much
too involved, here, to manage that. Next week I am going up to New York for a
few days; and will, I hope, see Zukofsky, also [Philip] Guston, [Franz] Kline, and
what other people there I can. Certainly Dennie. But that will be a damn deep

pleasure. Too, we have just managed to sell some of the property, which by no means solves everything, but does help very much. For the past months we have had no salaries, and I have been living on what I could scrape up from Divers book sales, etc. Anyhow the sale helps that and also will probably mean that the magazine will continue for another number at least. (Do send me some poems for it; also either the Olson article, or the one on the imagination we had talked about? You say, but send them as soon as you can, please.)

Well, Robert—what the hell, really. I am ok, I hope soon to be writing some more prose, and have been possessed lately with almost painful sensations, senses, of space. My laziness proves a much more substantial difficulty now than my 'despair'. I can't manage the latter, i.e., I am eating, in fact, much better than I did there—thinking of those nightmare meals. A young lady all but proposed to me, if it's my future that's the problem. I find my head filled with all its old tricks, and so on. And the pleasure of Olson, Dan Rice, et al, has been as tangible as any I might hope for. Then I wrote to the girl in New York, whom I think I told you about, i.e., the 'witch', John was in love with her too at one time—and after not having written me since I last saw her in New York, this time she did, even with a (goddamnit) lovely poem, in Spanish, about riding a donkey through the corn, etc. Well, you know. I should finally like, enjoy, believe in, something very much like that. My loneliness is no thing I care to keep, but to betray its reality is something I cannot do. To have lived in a house with a woman as far from me as Ann was—that was and could be now no good. So I have taken the lead, like they say, and started to find out about a divorce myself. I think she will be willing to pay for it—we will all 'pay' for it. Wow. What I don't say here, is my fears for the children; yet I must trust to her, and what else she is, in that. And you as well, i.e., as you had reassured me, that they will know me, still. And, that for me to take hold will allow them a father they might otherwise not have had. So that is 'work' enough, and hope enough too.

Too—I saw Dan, in the hospital after the accident, still in much pain, being fed intravenously with his stomach being damn well pumped out at the same time,—I watched him hope, literally with his eyes, that Cynthia (now in New York) might send him some word, at least, even if she couldn't come. Not a goddamn sound. So I have been spared that death, at least for the time-being. I was not hit when I could not keep upright. Olson says, rightly enough, we can neither look for equity nor generosity, in a woman, i.e., they are not possessed by these things. The 'loveliness' of Ann, in those stories, was also another component, I guess. It would be very pompous to consider, now, even that something had gone 'wrong'. God, to learn how not to 'possess'; that possession is always, has to be, a seizure, an act we recognize by only that fact we are its end. I learn it a little, I hope to god I do.

So—let that all go for the moment. I have had several checks for your book, one from Ruth Witt-Diamant and another from a lady whose name I forget (I am writing this from Jonathan's, where I'm staying (very comfortably) for a few days), amounting to $20 which I have forwarded to Ann's account; and have also written her to ask her to give you a check or pesetas for the am't. Then a couple of days ago, more money ($24) from Ida Hodes, being a collection from several people (Moore, Carmody, Onslow-Ford, Helen Adam, Schaenman, Psaltis)—I'll send this to Ann's acc't too. And get you a note of the other woman's name, actually Ann will have it.

The announcement is a real lulu—very damn good. I tacked it up on the board, and everyone admired it hugely. If they only had some money . . . However. Once the shipment of these is in, will do my best to put them to good use; Jonathan can also be a help with them.

I'm sorry, only, that all this goddamn mess did separate us, i.e., did not allow us a summer I looked forward to so damn much. Yet that will yet be possible, as I know. Your place in my life is as certain as my face, if it comes to that. I am sorry you have both been so damn 'used' by it. But the 'good life', Robert, I do believe in—one night at the Olson's, we had all been drinking, etc., I had gone to the bathroom and overheard him saying to a somewhat puzzled listener, 'but you have to realize that Creeley always believes in the impossible, and has to try it, always . . . .' Etc. I know what he means, and so does he. Thank god.

Write soon. I hope things go well for you both. And that all the mess there escapes you. Gossip yet. Ah well . . . It's probably a preface to 'recognition' at that. Et pauvre John . . . Eh bien. 'Be me' & that's what happens. So—write.

All my love to you both,
Bob

ALL THAT IS LOVELY IN MEN is now in proof, and going ok—which defiance pleases me. I even wrote my own jacket-blurb, as you will see. Your sense of GOODBYE [*CP* I, 159] is a good one, but I don't dare 'touch' the book, I want to let it go. I think GOODBYE would be the end, also, to that ms/ I made up, before leaving, i.e., to have it follow, as an 'end', after THE DRESS; technically it has that place, I think, i.e., it's a relief that things that way continue to move, no matter. By the way, ask Ann for the ms/ if you see her—and I hope you do, simply re the kids now & again? I'd like you to hold it for me, if you would. I am anxious to 'vacate' that house as much as possible.

[Stefan] Wolpe also spoke to me a few days ago, about doing something together; he is a fine 'old bird', old world in a new way, etc. Anyhow I think he means poems, but I should like more to improvise. He is very clear, on how to do it at least. Perhaps I could spear him with my own impossibilities—and hence, the thing. He told me he had met & planned to do something with Charlie Parker, not too long before the latter's death this spring. He is a great admirer of Miles Davis, so we can begin with that—yet.

[note on envelope] *Everything finally that I say here of her is not even "true", i.e. it must be that only things present can be—and she of course isn't, which is what I survive at that. To hell with it all. Wow*

. . .

LETTER TO ROBERT DUNCAN

[Black Mountain, NC]
September 24, 1955

Dear Robert,

   I owe you so many letters I begin to blush, but let's get the goddamn business straight first, after which I can tell you of my journey to New York, etc. That check from Ida Hodes, together with the addresses of the people who had ordered, was received safely, and deposited in Ann's account. The only announcement for your book I've yet had, was one you had enclosed in a letter; but I should think the bulk of the shipment ought to get here shortly, and I'll then mail them out to your list, plus what Jonathan & I have, etc. Today I had another letter from Ida H/ enclosing a check for $6.00 (3 more orders) & addresses; and also an order from Harvard, for a <u>limited</u> edition. If you can mail them a copy there, enclosing invoice (i.e., Divers Press, 1 Caesars Gate @ $10.00, etc), I'll take care of the paper work from here, i.e., bill them and see that you get the money. Otherwise I have an order & check ($2.00) from Larry Eigner, which I'll also deposit in Ann's account. I think Jonathan has one or two orders independently, so that's a little more to count on—perhaps. Anyhow I checked with him, and try to keep the whole thing clear, i.e., $$$-wise. Ok. I'll send you a list of names & addresses of all people who have ordered, as soon as I have a minute here, i.e., am just back & class starting, and usual hellish confusion. But I won't forget it. As to your manuscripts—nothing to date, but I shouldn't worry. It takes 3 weeks to a month, sent straight mail. A package from Ann just arrived, which seems to be papers—and it may be Jess' ms/ is with them. In any case, I'll check all such things very soon.

So. New York was god knows a relief, if a very exhausting one. I had two very pleasant visits with Zukofsky. I like him very much, and found it possible to talk immediately. Also, his wife and son were a great pleasure. I looked over, like they say, quite a bit of 'A', and also 'Bottom', and will have about 25pp of this 2nd section for the coming issue—plus a poem sequence I had taken earlier,

'Songs of Degrees'. I also heard him read some of the poems, from 'A' and earlier collections, i.e., he had a record made when reading on the West Coast, and this was very interesting. I'm actually still engaged, very much, by that time you played Marianne Moore for me; and have since listened to, I hope carefully, her reading In District of Merits. That structure is extremely close I think, or is to what I sense (if I can't take hold of it) as my own concern. In terms of this, Zukofsky is also relevant—god, is he a <u>close</u> writer! For example, 'A'-9, if you read it. Anyhow all of it was a relief, after my harassments here—and/or to sit down to this character of conversation and concern. What else stays, at that. 'Devotion' I damn well suppose is it, as you say. Anyhow it gave me a friend.

I also went out to see Williams, along with Dennie and Mitch; and that was an equal pleasure. He seemed better, insofar as health goes, than he did a year ago. He has a book coming next month (the 'Of Asphodel' plus some shorter poems) and is working otherwise on a couple of stories & a play. He gave me the ms/ of that opera he mentions in the Autobiography; but it turns out witches & communism, and not too happy. He is a goddamn curious juxtaposition of qualities literal 'qualities' I think. He was in any case god knows generous; I like him, very much. There are literally instants when I feel myself speaking with him altogether; and then actually a vacuum. Dennie had persuaded me to bring out a record Charles & I made here, a year ago, to play for him; which we did, and clearly he was moved, by it, i.e., he got the poems as obviously the page had never given them to him. And spoke, then, of how it changed everything—and I thought of Kenneth Lawrence B/ of course. Yet, at one point following, he took my arm and said, you have a right to demand what is necessary to you for ful-fillment, it's not as though you have been 'static' . . . And after the hell of the past months, there and here—I cared to hear that, as you may suppose. Hearing of Ann's and my separation, I had to tell him at last else we could not speak clearly enough—Z/ said, might we write her a letter. I want not to hurt these people, over and over, Robert. Sometimes it seems I'm a solicitor simply for 'sympathy'. Z/ said something too about, perhaps the gentleness in your face will be hard enough, to show her. He walked with me to the subway till at last we were standing there, shaking hands, over the turnstile. Both said to bring her,—jesus, they don't know, poor devils, in their own right—there is nothing to 'bring' anymore anywhere. But I was very moved that they made that try to help. I am soon going to be beyond all this altogether, if anything at all is to happen.

Otherwise, I saw dozens of people it seems. The time with Dennie and Mitch was very good; her mother looks like aging & alert elf, etc. They say they are going to Mexico almost certainly in January. I saw Al Kresch briefly, who was just back from Europe. I had several very pleasant evenings drinking beer with Kline, who tells very damn good stories, eg., a lady and her lover are in bed together, when there is a sound of footsteps on the stairs, whereupon the lady answers, oh yes, here comes old Nosey, now everybody in town will know about it . . . Ah well. I stayed at Julie's for a few days, the same things happened, i.e., on way to see Cocteau's Blood of a Poet with her, we passed lady wheeling fat baby in large baby carriage, holding two cards in his hand—and when we passed, I looked back to see what they were, and could only see one: the 4 of hearts. So that was a happy introduction to that scene in the film, which I'd never seen before this. And so on. These things take on such a persistent quality in her company, I can never remember them all. I also saw Joel Oppenheimer, and others from that company—and even Vacuum Victor, who said to me: you're making it very hard for me to live . . . Gee whiz. He looked very ugly & heavy, like synthetic wood. I didn't talk with him, i.e., he actually doesn't really exist, in a funny way. Anyhow. I saw Cynthia the last night, and suddenly all that was back for me, again. And for her as well, I guess. Though what now comes of it, god knows. But at least for the one evening we had, I felt alive again, in a way I haven't since summer really. I was surprised to find how deeply all that had gone. She may come here, I don't know. I couldn't find energy then to persuade her, or in fact to ask 'questions' at all. I still stay 'out', in a sense. I am very distrustful about 'arranging' anything, hence could not 'arrange' for her coming. I hope she does anyhow, but wonder. To hell with it. It was a very clear evening no matter.

Things here are also now much better, we are getting salaries of some sort; and the place is secure through December at least. Charles will probably not be here, but he needs god knows to get away. The class so far has been much better than last term; and things generally much more possible. So. I'll write soon again, I'm still stuffed like a boa constrictor, hence must think about it etc., etc. Wow . . . Write soon. When will you be leaving there? I hope all goes well for you both.

All my love to you both,
Bob

.   .   .

LETTER TO WILLIAM CARLOS WILLIAMS

[Black Mountain, NC]
October 31, 1955

Dear Bill,

I'm sorry not to have written long before this—I've just had a few days in bed with flu, and before that a dragged out cold—and to write anyone in such circumstances is only to depress them. Anyhow, that much is done with. It's very kind of you to help me out with the Guggenheim business—and certainly it is impossibly hopeful. I don't hope, really. I thought to try it, anyhow, since it's there to try; well, even that isn't quite true I suppose. In any case, many, many thanks. That you'll put up with it is 'prize' enough.

Your new book came, and it was a great pleasure—actually, a thing to hold to. And now, it seems, more than ever. As the opening six lines of Book 3 of 'Asphodel'—I hold there. To all of it. I like 'Shadows' very much—literally what you say. At the moment I find myself so 'broken' in forms, more in manners, casts, of thought, or call it I guess what I had attempted to secure as 'values'. It seems, now,—well, it is, now, that everything is attacked, and thinking to come home, there is none, etc. That's my own dilemma, I hate to see it as 'common', I hate to suppose it is—yet it is, much of it. Anyhow I can't give an inch, in my own apprehension of what you stand for—as you once put it, in that address I heard that time back in N.H., 'knowing as you must, what I stand for . . . ' It's impossible to avoid, or mis-take, in such poems as these are. I don't go to them now, seeking 'relief'—though they are that, for me, very much—but to say at least, there, goddamnit, is the thing I care for. In no simple sense, I hope. What else is there but form—and (god bless the ladies) the energy wherewith to make it. I think you do it, over and over.

I have been writing little—trying to 'think', yet; but get something done, now and again. Here is one, an 'ayre' of a kind. I wish I could sing it, but suppose not—but I could.

> Cat bird singing
> makes music like sounds coming
>
> at night. The trees, goddamn them,
> are huge eyes. They
>
> watch, certainly, what
> else should they do? My love
>
> is a person of rare refinement,
> and when she speaks,
>
> there is another air,
> melody—what Campion spoke of
>
> with his
> follow thy fair sunne unhappie shadow . . .
>
> Catbird, catbird
> O lady hear me. I have no
>
> other
> voice left.
> [CP I, 165]

I finally got the ms. of the next issue of the magazine off to the printer's in Mallorca. I used your article as the 'kick-off' piece—I couldn't have had a better, and thanks again. Things with the college continue uncertain, but, for the moment, we are all eating. What else.

All my best to you,

Bob

Some of the students are still reading your opera, but I'll take good care of it. Don't worry what I think, etc., please. Tonight being Halloween, perhaps I'll be visited for my 'taste'. God knows the moon is very beautiful—and I, like they say, believe.

· · ·

LETTER TO CHARLES OLSON

[San Francisco, CA]

May 17, 1956

Dear Charles,

I'm out at Mill Valley trying to pull myself together like they say. Yours came just before I left. I'm sorry not to have written, but have had, almost literally, no mind nor face nor much of anything for a couple of weeks now. The city is all right, god knows very comfortable, a bit loose from an eastern sense—but easy—which has been a help to me. I have a small apt for $27.50, and have been doing odd jobs of typing, etc. People are very good to me, and I haven't really wanted for much of anything. But of course I leave little alone, and at present am up to my ears in a perhaps impossible relation with Marthe Rexroth, who is very great—and god willing, we may make it. But you can think of how Kenneth takes it—and so recently come from my own part in such a thing. Though I claim this is not the same—though that matters very little at best. Anyhow, I give a reading Sunday, and think to take off for LA the coming week sometime, and then from there to Mexico City, with Marthe at best—and without if that's what has to happen. I can't fight about it, and here already gets like that. I have that money from NH now—and it would hold me, or us, there for time enough to let something happen other than what now does. Well, to hell with it, for the moment—it's been on my mind so much it's not possible to say much more about it that would say anything. Ok.

I liked that long poem, very much—and brought your letter on weights & all out here with me the first time I came, so Philip Whalen, Gary Snyder, and Jack K/ who was also here saw it. As it happens, I'm out here with Jack now—he has just walked into town to get a fifth of port—and he has by this time read Mayan Letters, and I'm giving him Maximus, and other things of yours I have, when we go back to SF Saturday. You'll best get a sense of him as follows: 34,

Fr/Canadian (Breton), about 5'8", a little stocky, from <u>Lowell</u>, Mass. He writes <u>novels</u>, a lot of them actually. [note at top of the page: (very blue sharp eyes)] Anyhow he is god knows a pleasure. Talks very little, listens a lot—could have been a wino, but isn't—likes to be by himself. One of those slightly red-faced quiet men. He went to Columbia on a football scholarship, was star football player on Lowell team that used to play Salem, Worcester, etc. Ed is sending you a note Jack did—but the prose is really, often, much more interesting, i.e., a curious light skipping and merging of images, a real continuity of changing im-pressions. I'll copy out a bit to enclose here, to save time—ok. I like him very very much, i.e., like Dan, and yourself, and Robert, Franz—he has a beautiful will to endure whether or no he would think so. He manages.

It's very damn good to hear of Marshall's poems, I'll hope to damn well see them once I am again, or ever, settled enough. I've bought a sleeping bag and will get a rucksack the first of the week, and to hell with what can't go into it for the time-being. I guess I'm finally about to do that wandering I have really wanted so much to do for so long. Now that I've made it this far, I begin to trust it, and to not worry so goddamn much about what can, does, or will—happen. Voila. In the meantime I will not fuck up on the magazine and will try to keep you on re addresses, etc.

Take care of yourself. I hope things there are all right. I think of you very often, and wake mornings sometimes finding myself quoting the poems. So. I'll make it—it's just that I have this despair to break, and seize upon whatever means might conceivably manage it. That won't have to be it forever, or I can't see how—but anyhow I follow my nose as ever.

All my love,
Bob

You can get me: 1108 Montgomery, SF, because the fellow who is taking the place after me will forward mail all right.

• • •

LETTER TO JACK KEROUAC

P.S. Say goodbye to Locke + Valery and the kids for me, please. I'll hope to see them too, before too long. Say goodbye to Neal for me too—I'm sorry all the time was so short.

> If there is such a thing as fact
> it is possessed by happy Jack Kerouac—
>
> who sits in self-possession
> and climbs mountains to stop smoking.

He had a dream
that things were what they seem

and since that day or night has not broken his calm,
no matter who tries to harm him.

It is this wisdom which he has given to me,
that what is is not, and it is all one or two or three:

or many numbers, or none.
It is all one.

Thus blessed be the Diamond Sutra
which so allows men the wisdom of Buddha—

and blessed be Jack too,
because what he says, is true.

May 26, 1956

Dear Jack,

It doesn't now seem I'll get out there, for which I am, selfishly, sorry. Anyhow things here have not been impossible and god willing, we will make it. I leave for New Mexico probably Monday—or Tuesday at the latest. I'll write when I know where I'll be there. Take care of yourself. I'll hope to see you soon and thanks again for everything. My love to you,

Bob

. . .

LETTER TO CHARLES OLSON

[San Francisco, CA]
May 28, 1956

Dear Charles,

I was just going to write, like they say—and there was your letter in the box. It's a very great day, this aft/ I take off for New Mexico—it's the right direction, finally, as of any at least—and also it all comes clear, and around, with Marthe, with myself. I spent the weekend talking, drinking—then yesterday started writing, viz poems, feeling them as I haven't for months now—and making it, viz, ok, you sons of bitches, this I do. The occasion was both my own break-thru, and felt wonderful; and the fact a man here will do, or wants to, a small book, and had been bothered by one ms/ I gave him, because some of the poems had been printed before etc, so in trying to get 'substitutes', I got 8 more in one wild day—which, than which, nothing gets better. Then last night Marthe, at the end of her own rope—and all of us about to swing, thank god, to another—stayed, and I talked & talked, and what a deep clearing, just to lie in bed—and talk; that thing of Othello's, I only talked to her, always seemed to me my truth too. Anyhow she is coming Friday, with the kids—and it all begins again. I have to have it, Charles—as you certainly know. It's my so-called 'form'. It's awfully damn good to feel it there again, sans too much will—finally. So—you know. Ok.

Also very great yesterday—an ms/ from Winchendon, Mass, a page & half 'story', that has speed—wow. It's the goddamn NE renaissance I think we begin to be up to. Or who cares for labels, when it's happening. Anyhow very shrewd fast prose, like:

> 'Thighs, breasts, feet,' he thought. 'I love a sister. She is too thin for me. Not like Maggie Owens up at the farm.' He wrung his hands together desperately, gently, and thought of an old barn in wintertime . . .

Also, an ms/ of three very wild poems, very jagged, from that David Lyttle, friend of Jonathan's, who had been in Mallorca. No letter, and perhaps he does not know I am there, etc., or here, etc. Anyhow they are something too, viz:

> The sea
> Rocks on edge,
> And the minnows fly
> Like vultures in the foam.
>
> She slouches on the sand
> Between the sea and the forest-land,
> Under the sheets of rain,
> Encumbered by the rudiments of pain, etc., etc.

So—again you know. I got to pack my (mah) gear, like they say. Got a real out huge old ruck sack now. Hmm . . . Feel good. Like size, being (be) there. Very good. We had dinner with Ed & Helene [Dorn] last night; also a pleasure. They are very great to have there, thru such a scene as has just about concluded god willing. Ed talks. And we did.

I'll put in a few of the poems, another thing it was a breakthru, a bit, re 'form'. Let me know what you think when you can—and send me what you have, please, as you also can. There's only one bizness. Ok. Take care of yourself and know I damn well do, always. Voila.

All my love to you all,
Bob

[Enclosed with the following unpublished poems were "Just Friends," "The Picnic," and "Please," *CP* I, 163, 82, and 156.]

NEVER SEEK TO TELL THY LOVE

I know where they keep it.
I saw them put it there.

It was late. It was lonely.
But I know where.

I DON'T THINK SO

No one's going away
who wasn't here to begin with.
It doesn't matter what they say
who wasn't here to begin with.
I don't care what happens anymore.
It doesn't matter what they say
who wasn't here to begin with.

HOW ABOUT THAT

It must be horrible
when you are dead
to know you planned just a little
too far ahead.

PART THREE

For Love, 1956–1963

New Mexico, Guatemala, Vancouver

General Delivery
Ranchero de Taos, N.M.
July 18, 1956

Dear Mitch,

Your letter just got here—and was <u>good</u> to have. To catch you up: I finally couldn't make it in SF—I am too much a country-boy among other things—but there was and is Marthe as well; and though happily I think we can at last make it, it has been anything but simple—and often, impossibly hysterical. Anyhow I manage—which is always a pleasure, god knows.

As to SF for you all—thinking as you say if sometime someday—well, sure. It's physically the most interesting and simple city to be in I ever knew. The architecture alone is enough to keep me occupied for months; and the city is made for walking around in. Neither job nor housing is anything like the problem in NYC—because SF is still a "small town". And where in the east you will see people of a class dressing in that rigidity of fashion, in SF people try a variety of things, in hope. I suppose, they may be the ones to be right. They are immensely friendly—almost always. And some 20 minutes from the city one can be in complete country, even to deer sitting in fields a stone's throw distant. Otherwise—it was Ed I really leaned on there, for a friend; and Jack Kerouac (Lowell, Mass—French Canadian) and Allen Ginsberg (Paterson, N.J.)—in short, men who had edges, and the restlessness I find in myself perhaps too often. Ed—as you would both know—was at last very irritated by the <u>looseness</u>, and I knew very well what he meant. There is an image that stays in my head, perversely enough, re SF; and that is, the way in streets sometimes four to six lanes wide, with 5 o'clock traffic, even so a whole mass of cars would stop (!), so that I could cross. And that would seem immense courtesy—which certainly it was and is—but somehow it bred, in me, a feeling that there was a hellish almost <u>uncertainty</u> being declared as well. Well, that's a question of course.

I do think SF would make an excellent "1st place" to come back to, and that you would all find much there to excite you—so that way, I wouldn't have the least hesitation in saying: you would like it. I think. It's a sociologist's dream, really—it's sheer outcrop of New England in so many bizarre ways—the architecture to begin with—and, it's finally to be seen. As is LA, utterly different—for a shot at the entirety of the American <u>place</u>. Anyhow it would neither be waste of time nor difficult—so, voila.

But the <u>place</u> now most interesting to me, is here—i.e., this <u>American</u> south-west. Again physically, this is a wildly beautiful place—with the desert going down to the south—and the Rockies beginning about 5 miles distant. What mountains they are! I am living in a small 2 room house, back of (& owned by) a Sp-Am family's compound—and no touristas about, to bother—they are all in Taos proper. Next week I start work in a uranium mine no less—even look forward to that. Anyhow—I'll write at length, when I can get to a typewriter, about all these things.

The 7th issue of the mag is about put together & there is one story I think you'll like, as much as I do: Sherry Mangan, <u>Reminiscence From A Hilltop</u>—but time, enough. For "geography" of tone, this may be the most relevant I've yet managed, i.e., from Dahlberg to Williams, from Herbert Read to William Lee (author of a pocket book: JUNKY). So—I'm <u>together</u>, thank god. And Marthe is so <u>good</u> to have found—and the difficulties seem at last not the point.

All my love to you all,
Bob

. . .

LETTER TO WILLIAM CARLOS WILLIAMS

August 8, 1956
Ranchos de Taos, N.M.

Dear Bill,

I'm sorry not to have written, the past months have been a sort of poor man's odyssey, i.e., I have been pretty much all around the southwest, also San Francisco—where I am at the moment, about to go back to Taos—and then, if I can manage to earn enough, Mexico after that. I feel very open at least—and the impact of this place is considerable. Anyhow while out here, I met a number of younger writers, eg. Phillip Whalen, Allen Ginsberg, Gary Snyder et al. The next issue of the BMR will in fact make some use of what they are all doing; and, related to that, I should like to print a short preface you had written for a book of Allen G/s sometime ago (<u>Empty Mirror</u>), if that is all right with you? Also—if you have anything free, verse or prose, I'd be always very grateful to have it. As it will be—this issue is a kind of 'geography' of tones, all the way from Sherry Mangan, Dahlberg, Zukofsky—to Jack Kerouac, Allen G/ etc. Ed Corbett is doing the cover (I met him in Taos & like him, very much—very sol-idly 'American', and much interested in what you have done—literally, a Texas Irishman, now abt in his mid-thirties, with a real feel for where he is & can be—I hope he comes to see you, as I suggested he do, when he goes back east).

I hear that my ex-wife and children are settled in Conn., now, and much more happy I think. I talked to them all on the phone (which is a pretty hope-less means) about a week ago, and there was no bitterness, thank god. I guess whatever it is I have to do means 'by myself', and bitterly as I miss the place, of a home, it's no good not doing what it seems I have to. My so-called generation finds itself very isolate, actually split from all character of 'family', and it is <u>place</u> that gets to be more and more what the search concerns.

I hope you are all right, and your family too. Many times the past weeks I have used you as a kind of steadier, as that poem: The Mind's Games—and The Desert Music—and god knows others. I believe—like they say. I simply do not want to let the bitterness over-ride the images possible. Well, I'll make it—not simply to mutter to myself. Up at the Asian Institute yesterday, I had to laugh at myself, feeling that impossibly fine quiet of those Buddhists—I wish I could be one, but whatever it is, one is, one is etc. Voila.

Write as you can, please. It would be a great cheer to hear from you. It always is.

My love to you,
Bob

. . .

LETTER TO ALLEN GINSBERG

[Albuquerque, NM]
Wednesday aft/ [September 19, 1956]
Dear old dear friend Al,

Well, old friend. It was a pleasure, to have your letter—and much obliged at hearing. Always. Things here are making it, I have a vicious hangover from last night's activities, but it was kind of a test run, for the job, and found I got through the day very happily, albeit not able to speak very much. (I enclose paper of 1 student, very out kid—pretty crazy actually. Ha ha.)

I had the poems from Corso also today—as I wrote Phil, I like WAY OUT—and will write C/ soon now, telling him what I can figure re the magazine. I don't know exactly what I have left for space, since I've taken a woman's story, and want those 2 things by Wms in, too. Anyhow—I think something could be figured, and will try to—and write him soon. And thanks. (I met him very briefly there, with Bill Donlin (he was) and I was with Locke, and this woman Laverne (I think?—I was pretty far out myself I'm afraid.))

I haven't heard from Robert D. for a long time, I just in fact wrote him yester-day. Mike M/ was getting very much on my nerves—he does things so goddamn naively, in a way—like a man robbing you in broad daylight, who for some reason thinks you can't see him doing it. M/s desires are bitterly clear, almost always—and few coincide with mine. Well, he was ok, I guess D/ likes him and thinks he makes it—I like Joanne very much, also Price and so forth. Finally he seems simply pretty much of a kid to me—and that scene hardly could take much cognizance of same. I'm afraid it was only for grownups—or something different in any case. Fuck it.

Let's see now. I'd be very grateful for a copy of HOWL—and would certainly like to try a review of it. Maybe something some place could come of it. So let me try.

I'd like very much to see DeAngulo's poems—Robt D/ had told me of another ms (actually a book) on linguistics. Anyhow—sure. D/ is a good friend of theirs I think.

This translating gig is, to take a novel apart—a half-sense at least; the so-called discipline, the connection, and the money. I may not get very far with it, though I'd like to. I am writing a little otherwise, though it was a drear dry summer, in part—and otherwise, a fantastically lovely place, i.e. Taos is. I get up there weekends from here, which is good.

How is Jack? That is very great about Grove and I hope that works. Allen is a nice man, I met him in NYC once—he lived for a time in China, by the way. Well, of course.

So—things are ok, really. I'm a little dragged but also relieved to have this not impossible scene here, where-with I think to save a few $$$, against Mexico both at Xmas for a couple of weeks at least—and then some more continually into next summer. Anyhow, that would be very good to see you all there. Also, come here as & when you can. Ok. It will be a pleasure as there is not too much actually for company, but for Bud & his wife—who work so hard I rarely feel right about taking up their time. So.

All my poems are social crucifixions, Allen. You know that . . .

Also very great, what Phil told me abt NYTimes & all. That is very good. You all deserved it god knows. (I keep thinking of Rexroth's article . . . Ah well—what did I think, at that. And what a phoney he finally is—it is almost his talent; as Olson said, he may not write poems but he tells good stories & knows how to eat & drink.)

Take care of yourself, and let me hear, as you can. I'll do likewise, like they say. Voila. It was very good to get your letter.

All my love,

Bob

P.S. Here's a poem from last night while stoned, etc. It was one of a series so to speak, I was attempting thing called FOLK SONGS FOR PHIL—but he'll have to wait, for more than (2nd) fragment I'll put in here,—I did not make it enough.

FARE THEE WELL

Wandering around at the edge of the town
He was looking down, down there at me.
I couldn't see him.
His father was dead you see.

Twenty-five years later they came back
From the shack in the Sierras
With the grizzly-bear's hair,
There—in their hands.

She was smiling.
I couldn't look anymore.
I wanted, sickly, to go away.
I couldn't play with her.
. . . .

A FOLKSONG FOR PHIL

Hitch up honey for the
market race all
the way to the plaza.

If she don't run you
can push her like
hell. I know.
[CP I, 172]
. . . .

etc. I.e., I'll put one other short one (earlier) on the other side of this. I
haven't really paid much attention to any of these things in the past months—
but begin to come more awake, in some sense.

THE TUNNEL

Tonight, nothing is long enough—
time isn't.
Were there a fire,
It would burn now.

Were there a heaven,
I would have gone long ago.
I think that light
is the final image.

But time reoccurs,
love—and an echo.
A time passes
love in the dark.
[CP I, 177]

[handwritten student paper enclosed]
   Robert

   [illegible]   *[illegible]*
      poss.
      obj.
      nomin.

   1. *I caught the odor of George* <u>*Valiant's*</u> *smelly rump.*
                           poss.
      2. *The* <u>*girl*</u> *loves the* <u>*cottage*</u>
                  nom.   Acc.
   Diana is supposed to have lived <u>*in the sky*</u>
                        ABL.
         The boy gives roses <u>*to the girls.*</u>
                  DAT.
            Mts. <u>*Everest*</u> *and* <u>*Kilimanjaro*</u> *are the two highest points on earth.*
               nom.   nom.
   They're 30,000 ft high.

   I kicked Hilliard <u>*in the can.*</u>

   I saw many a <u>*horse's*</u> *dungheap in the [illegible] ship area. (I really did)*

                        • • •

                  LETTER TO JACK KEROUAC
Duncan wrote and liked   c/o Imported Motors
you. Never worry—   610 Central SE
though one does   Albuquerque, N.M.
                                            October 11, 1956
Dear Jack,
            I've tried to write a dozen times, but don't make it—but please
believe it's through no lack of will. God, I would like to—like they say. Anyhow
things here are fair enough, the teaching job asks nothing of me I can't do,
and it's $$$—which I can use for an eventual stake, and that's happy. In the
meantime this city as a place is ok—because it fits me, and/or how I feel—very
out of it. I think I'll be translating a novel for Ramon Sender, but have not as yet
begun; I am really pretty busy with the school, because it's all new to me—and
the kids are of course kids, and 8 hours a day is 8 hours a day etc. The magazine
is now 1/2 at the printer's in Spain—and the rest will be sent shortly. It is all
pretty much together, though I cannot say when it will be out (probably mid-
winter, now).

I haven't heard from Marthe for about 2 weeks. I don't know what happened precisely, but imagine she could not make it. We very nearly married—I wish we had—but then, she didn't want it to be a defiance of K/, and I am sick to death of him, utterly—and imagine he has a like feeling. Anyhow she is not here, and it would now be hopeful to think she will anymore be. That way—it's god knows lonely, and I hate the failure of it—but it was very great no matter. So.

It's good to hear of Grove, and all that—very damn good. Well, god knows you earn it all. I'll hope to see you sometime around Xmas, if you're still down there. Let me know. Tell me what you are doing. I enclose card re book will be out in Dec/, and that's about it for me—other than poems from the past months. At least I've done something. Please write.

My love to you, and take care
of yourself,
Bob

. . .

LETTER TO MITCH GOODMAN

P.S. Another joke: two Japanese shepherds out with their sheep
in a field; and they look up &there is a big atom bomb, coming
right straight down at them; and the one shepherd   November 4, 1956
says to the other—let's get the flock out of here!

Dear Mitch,

It was good to have your letter—though hardly happy to see that things are not very simple for you. I had thought of you waiting 14 weeks with no word, and thought of how that would have felt—and that was not good. A few weeks ago, at Sender's, he told me of a letter he had just got from Wm Faulkner, who had apparently been approached by the president of Random House, concerning a very large sum of money which the latter wished to make available to American writers, in one way or another. Faulkner enclosed a special delivery airmail self-addressed stamped envelope and asked what Sender thought the money should be used for. 'Do you think it should be used to collect all the writers & ship them to Siberia? To make registering personnel available? To catalog all American writers and make dossiers on them? To kill them? etc.' We do not have any status as 'writers' in this country. The most feeling or trying-to-feel men will ask you: who are the 10 greatest novelists of the last 50 years? 'You can't make a living writing poems.'

So what, etc. I don't see reason to lament—I don't god knows mean that word uglily—that you find yourself living where it is most cheap. One time in SF talking with Ed Dorn, we were suddenly able to see and to name the areas of economic activity—and it was a very strange knowledge, to see it in each thing. But it answers Pound—it was right he described a past area. Where money comes most hard it is least available; and many other things have more room. We can't despair that we have only ourselves. What 'hell' there has been for me, the past months, has mostly been lost arrows. I can't find where they've got to. Most of the time I am in a fairly lonely condition, and suffer a state of slight shock, due to discrepancies I in no way can control. For Marthe's part in it—she is a woman etc. I can't blame or think of her at times. I blame myself of course; I always do that. Though this time it has been a little foolish & weak. More, nothing has changed between us—it is as actual now as it was when it first happened, and that way, all I say about it is finally there. (I am very hungry for the sea, for room of a more deeply felt nature. But I did things with her, and much was informed and lovely, that never was so before. I saw things I never had: merry-go-rounds, parks, hands, eyes, children, growing up, love, and what's due.)

Dennie's sequence of poems, in ARK, were very beautiful. It was a deep pleasure to read them. Don't worry that I have changed, in my letters for example—I have to be what I am as I can be. I don't ever know what next. My loyalties as a poet are engaged completely by poems like those she has there. Perhaps it is even holding-on, hoping that my own nature will give me a like completeness, someday. I picked up a copy of a large group of Baudelaire's art criticism (The Mirror of Art), yesterday—he writes very well of Delacroix, the 19th century 'cartoonists' (British & French), & laughter (humor & wit). It's good that a man writes well, it makes order & peace—as James (whose essays I have also been reading, et al). My own order was more important to me, at the time we 'argued' about him; but he has held me very much this past summer—no matter how it sounds to say it. I'll send you a portfolio of mine that is just done, If You (about 8 poems)—a 'last-of-it' collection. Not too interesting, but some I do like, as Cat Bird, A Marriage, etc. The Dress will be more a book & also more interesting. Anyhow, I'll send this one, et celui-la . . . , when I can. All is well enough here, i.e., I haven't lost my job. I don't as yet know if I can come down, or will come down—but I will tell you as soon as I do—and am sorry that I don't as yet know. It is very good of you all, as ever, to let me come. Anyhow, that's true. I'm a little out of it just now, often very out of it—and that takes doing, like they say. It's a world like what's now happening in Egypt & Hungary. Who are you going to vote for? And—as a friend said on the telephone just now: I'm voting for Henry Wallace. Take good care of yourselves & with luck I will see you.

All my love,
Bob

. . .

c/o 610 Central SE
Albuquerque, N.M.
January 1, 1957

Dear Bill,

I've meant to write often, to thank you for your letter, as always—also to tell you how things had been. I got a job here teaching in September, which has had the use of giving me a means to eat for the moment—and also to pull myself together, for some more concerned attack. Perhaps it's the very formalism of how I acknowledge such things, that separates them so much at times from me—I don't know. For awhile I was certain I had fallen into a means of living, i.e., the teaching, which was both reasonable and sufficient, even to the hope of a family; but restlessness or not, that soon enough became untrue. I've been teaching french and english—caring nothing (per se) actually for the 1st, except for the delight that teaching a language I don't at all know sometimes gives qua improvisation (like they say), and caring too much for the 2nd. Tomorrow I start work again, there are 6 classes a day: English 7, French 8, English I, French I-A, French I-B, and English 8—all of which jargon means 12 to 14 year old boys, about 10 to 15 in a class, a finally lethally oriented group of eventual people. That is in fact very interesting, and (selfishly) makes the year no matter: the facts of a society which these 'children' at times provide. About 1/2 have no fathers, either widows or divorced, etc. There is no clear social 'referent' at all here, eg. Albuquerque is both new in the sense that it's the atomic city, from 50 thousand to over 150,000 in less than 10 years—and also is New Mexico, less than 50 years a state, and Mexican, Indian, and Anglo, etc. The kids give vivid occasion to see this, very often. Teaching them french (of all things) is often to see what 'artificiality' can effect—and leads to awareness (to call it that) of why clothes, this way of speaking, that hat & so forth—very much. But I can't clearly do it forever—and another year (because at the moment I have to tell the 'headmaster' whether or no I think to stay) would mean didacticism at best, and repetition, staleness, and—I don't really want any of it very much. It has or so I hope satisfied a fear that I couldn't manage, i.e. could not hope to earn enough either for myself or the family I can in my imagination sometimes find—I see that it's either easy, or hard, and not very much at all can be seen before the literal occasion. My salary, of 250 a month after taxes (!), has been adequate, has in fact allowed me to rent a comfortable house & to buy an old car—but again, I don't really want the literal size & bulk of either one attached to me. I was most content in a way, with the big knapsack I got in San Francisco, and also the sleeping-bag purchased in the same place. So—so much for salaries; and having the need for same, I think I can do it, eg. earn food & the like.

More to the point, I'm just back from Mexico, in which I rode endlessly on buses,—really delighted, and tongue-tied, but trying at least to speak spanish, sitting as straight in the seat as possible—god knows looking at all I could. I went from Juarez 2nd class to Durango, then to Mazatlan—by luck straight through the mountains, over 10,000 feet up, with drop-offs of 3 to 4000 feet on every other turn, and the driver (Indian) at one point putting the bus into neutral & letting it roll! It was good, i.e., the 'why not'—not caring, 'about such a thing'—the whole bus completely unconcerned. We went through towns I wouldn't have believed possible, labor towns so remote, hovels of rough cut lumber, all grey, kids running after us, everything in god's world getting on the bus, from 'conchitas' to one actual mad man (who cried so loudly at its being cold, he kept the whole bus awake, sullenly etc). In Mazatlan (too much like a deserted 'spa') I decided to keep moving, and went to Guadalajara—I spent Xmas eve in a cheap hotel, on the Calzado, 1st floor facing street—lying in bed tired out & reading Beckett's Malone Dies (and thinking it small, tired, and not enough). The next morning I took another bus to Barra de Navidad, on the west coast below Manzanillo—following Mitch & Dennie Goodman, who had left the city to spend the holiday there, Mitch having gone some time before to copy his novel & correct it I guess. The trip was another 12 hours, a dirt road—wonderful towns with huge cathedrals, always broken & falling apart (at one I watched a group of women with babies, waiting I guess to have them baptized, poinsettias & the like growing around the bars of the fence (iron) surrounding, two boys coming then to pull on a long rope, that came down from the (broken) bell tower, to make the clock (as it happened) strike three (in the afternoon)—then, at last, when the women had gone in (a high large wooden double door), I looked to see a big grey pig looking out through the gate, at the people going by.)

I got to Barra de Navidad about 9 it must have been, all dark—the town is a line of low thatched 'houses', on a strip of land between the sea (at the front) and a lagoon (at the back). There are 'hotels', for people from Guadalajara, etc. I was given a room, like a huge crypt, with no windows, dirt floor (I think), an army cot, and a candle & table,—and could hear the sea all night, hitting the beach about 50 feet from where I was sleeping. I found the hotel where Mitch and Dennie were staying, and found they had contrived to get the upper floor of an old building opposite, so went up through the dark, down a rickety corridor, toward the glow of a light & voices from behind a door—and knocked to find Mitch reading to their son, and at last could say Merry Christmas, to people I love, and hope to show care for, somehow. Dennie appeared, wonderfully, in a wrapper, from the next room—she had said to Mitch, what if I came etc—it was all very good. So we were able to spend two days talking, she showed me her new poems, written in an oblong copybook, with a picture of a tiger on the cover—beautifully dense thick poems, from a world that grows surer, on her, very much so. We lay on the beach all day, when hot went in, then back again, endless sand & water, a small bay stretching out, to the open sea—tropical, e.g. papayas, coconuts, strange birds, lots of pigs, also some beautiful young women I couldn't take my eyes off—and sat (we ate dinner all in a big room, i.e., the 'visitors') watching one girl's long hair, thick and heavy down her back, who also turned to look at me, often, in spite of herself, she was so curious, and had huge black eyes, very attentive & wide open with her curiosity. It was a relief, all of it—I have it seems so 'contained' myself, so intentionally, so long (although it's been 4 months only). At one point, on the beach one early afternoon, Dennie had not put her bathingsuit on but was wearing a summer dress—she wanted to swim with us, and suddenly ran in, laughing and it was very damn lovely to see—she was dripping, laughing, her hair wet, and the dress wet and hanging to her as she came stumbling (gracefully) out. Ah well. It was hard to leave. But I've come back (not 'at least' but) quietly enough—a test thereof was or is, that the 'headmaster' just came a minute ago, to wish me a 'happy new year', and I could reply decently enough, because he is a decent enough man, knowing I'll be telling him this week I'm leaving & so forth, i.e. I don't 'agree'.) Anyhow—to complete the so-called contract, to try to save a little money, wherewith to move again in June, I think to Oaxaca, where I can live cheaply and also, Mitch tells me, hope to earn a living teaching English to covetous Mexicans, who have the advantage of being adult, their own, to make what use they will of—hence not the sometimes pitifully undefended thing of being a child still caught in vindictiveness of a (failing) adult pattern.

I thought of your, 'I am a poet. I am. I am . . . ' I don't want any other 'excuse'. God knows a trade, of some sort—perhaps teaching can provide it, I like the improvisation that at least a new occasion each time gives room for—anyhow there are ways I find to eat & I had worried about it. My 'old' life gets far away, though at times painfully close too, in dreams, say—or the like. Anyhow, the image of what is left of the 'family' I lived in, we lived in, is hard to man-age—not the children, who must be happy there in New England, sliding now, snow, woods etc, that has to be good—but Ann, who wrote me a day ago: "It's pretty dull going. I'm learning to trade on the stock market on a pittance. Much reading of the Wall Street Journal and no profits. A neighbor is giving me lessons . . . " She was the first woman I ever made love to, which I don't know if I wear like a cross or a flower—though I hope. She was an orphan and I was a hick. It was pretty great, like they say. I was going to be a writer, and we lived on 215 a month she got from a trust fund no less,—like heavenly bird droppings. Embarrassed continually, that I did not 'support' her and the children—but equally endlessly covetous & anxious, of the time it gave me. I suppose. One time when she miscarried, I delivered what there was, of the baby; one time a baby born to us prematurely died in NH, and I & the undertaker buried it, in a plain white pine box, in a hole in a local cemetery (on the road to Littleton). It's hard to let go of it—the intention really, partly the man's part perhaps, at least of the hoping. Not being able to admit that the Wall St J/ is suitable reading for a woman as lovely as she often & must be. As this New Year's Day (no rhetoric) it would truly be a new world, again, were we able still to look for one another. But who is she, like they say—and likewise, who am I. There seems a lot to do; for my part, I'd like to find a wife this year & write a 'novel' at last. Thanks for the strength your own gives me—a hard thing to ever say, but true, continually. I hope all goes well for you. And—to end the rambling—I have your notes on Ford & Marsden Hartley safe, and the magazine itself ought to be out with luck early spring (it is now, partly, at the printer's in Mallorca).

   Happy New Year & my love to you
   & your family,
          Bob

· · ·

LETTER TO DENISE LEVERTOV

P.S. I've read Davis' poems—I like very much the 'big handedness' of them, i.e., farm-wise, rough & red & careful. That is a 'tenderness' I have great respect for, both as memory (of it) and as here. I used to see men handle things this way as a boy.   January 23, 1957

Dear Dennie,

          I have not written, god knows—but seem to have been 50,000 miles away (perhaps underground) since I left that day, so almost unable to etc. Your letter is a great cheer—the poems you enclose are very lovely. (I haven't as yet read the other poems, but will in a day or two, and will write you & return them—it will be an occasion like they say.) I would like to put 'Action' with the 'Everything that acts is actual', for this coming issue (now coming together)—is that all right? Write me as you can.

   I am bursting in part, albeit (at last) quietly—but met a few days ago only & by chance a girl here—which (myself included) changes everything, and I should die (beyond talking about it) if ever that should become impossible. I think I will marry her, eg—'just like that'. I am going somewhere it seems, and, beyond loneliness, want very much to be out of the (I suppose) old shell, husk, or whatever. Not however as contrary—as Marthe perhaps (?—she was very good to me) but as use of myself as a form, too, not to speak, of love, but to be where it is—hence, why talk.

   She's asleep now—or ought to be. We seem most together over tables & dishes, because she works nights as a lady disc-jockey, and I have not as yet lost my job teaching etc. She is Irish—which pleases me very much—I trust that— and has two daughters who cheer me up (one is 3½ and the other 6, and both are very literally beautiful)—and it's good not to prepare, argue, defend, etc—but to sleep—& to smile with a goodnature I thought had become sheer irony.

(That's a note for me!)

Anyhow, not to talk about it—please [arrow drawn from this sentence to parenthetical aside above]. You will see. I am sorry to hear of your having been sick, viz take care of yourself too. Tell Mitch I'll write him soon at Barra de Navidad—and not to think of Mexican ladies for me, they scared me as it was . . . Or perhaps not enough (I think).

It's all ok, thank god. To see you both again was very very good: What plans etc turn out I don't as yet know, but will see you no matter. Ok. And will write again soon. Please do as you can.

All my love to you all,
Bob

[note in left margin] Robt is as ever very good to be so concerned, but (as ever) it is that there isn't that need to—not as he does. We all live, like they say—and always would—and no one wanted to be careless. I think sometimes the 'world' a mind manages is almost too surrounded. Better we do shit etc.

[note in right margin] I haven't forgotten the bks and wrote Briggs (Books 'n Things) to send me some; and will also send the others (I have) soon. If you want anything, let me know—eg billboards, beer bottles. OR just plain desert.

. . .

LETTER TO ALLEN GINSBERG

1826 Griegos NW
Albuquerque, N.M.
February 6, 1957

Dear Allen,

I'm ashamed almost to say, nothing much at all has been the matter, i.e., I've wanted to & have thought to write often—and have had you & Jack & Peter much in mind if that is not pompous to say. Over the time I had off at Xmas, I went to Mexico, and caught up with Mitch & Dennie in Barra de Navidad (on the coast), and had at least some time with them; and so, as well, heard about your visit very happily. I wish somehow I might have been there as well (too).

Things had been (there is a past tense to it) pretty impossible, although the job makes it enough; it is never much work, and the kids, being kids, allow me space, like they say. But the continual & finally bleak loneliness of always going home to an empty house (no matter schmaltz) shut me up altogether. I had no actual complaints yet felt continually restless & misfitted—and so on, eg.

dull, out of it—and with no real thoughts as to what now. That way, though I've written, in my fashion, more or less continually since I saw you, it's been pretty hopeless, and there are about 5 poems that make it at all. I had hoped to try some prose, but haven't yet. Anyhow, that was that.

About two weeks ago, very stoned one night with my friend Max Feinstein, since left for SF, we ended up at a radio station, to see a girl he knew there who is a disc jockey, 12 to 6. I was tired, drunk—and wanted most of all to sit down, in a quiet place, so she spun discs & so forth; and soon enough, I guess, it was very quiet, and for once comfortable (no matter), so I stayed till she was through, then went with her to her place, where she fed us, then finally to school—where I got through a very far-out day, eg. kids asking me at last if I had been drinking (wow). Anyhow I married her last week (my way, not 'theirs'), and it's ok—which phrase, so to speak, has to seem I also suppose, also dull—but I am so sick with the élan (is it?) of whatever, the goddamned intention, so dead it has become, in so many ways. I am in short now living with someone, to put it socially—and beyond that, it is at moments very closely unspeakable, thank god.

It's good to know you saw Fee Dawson, Joel et al—I wish I might. I still don't much know what happens next, but that is a pleasure, too. But I think we won't stay here beyond the end of this time I have to teach, up at the end of May. BMR #7 will come at last, don't worry; part of it was trying to get it all together, and that is done (I took one of those poems Gary had marked—it is in the mess of my stuff at the moment, so the title I don't have—so that is straight.) I'll write to Phil and have missed him, as yourself & Jack & Peter [^ And _Locke_]. It is a very strange place here & someday will hope to tell you about it.

God knows—again, happily. Who else, etc. Thanks for the notes re places to try poems etc. I wish I had them to send, but ought to have something soon, viz I'd like to have, very much. You're welcome always to use whatever you want from past 'books', i.e., whatever you can & tell me what etc. But guess it is too late now, so no matter.

It's all ok, old friend. Wow. But I can see the humming bird in the window, and your faces. So—there. Take care of yourself, all of you. Please write as you can.

My love to you all,
Bob

I know O'Hara's work some, and knew Kenneth Koch at Harvard etc. But think both are lightweights, whatever that means—and/or finally dull. They don't seem to have much for blood. But I dig the line, at times.

. . .

LETTER TO ED DORN

April 27, 1957

Dear Ed,

Your letter was a great cheer yesterday morning, viz it was Saturday, and seemed that something should happen, I guess we both face that feeling of not many people around like they say. As to change of tone—for one thing it must be that so much else has changed. The conception of one's self as one self etc is finally an embarrassing one. Anyhow for myself it becomes so-called acts of feeling, etc. Wow. Ice cream for breakfast. Again.

I like your playing on rhyme, I think this poem just sent (Bowl of Flowers) is less to a center than others—but, re technic, is very interesting, eg.

> & I
>
> unwise self, will while
>
> it all, dwindle the hours
>
>   pick
> a bowl of floweres,
>   leave
>
> a water bowl of floweres
>
> disk of yellow, upon the shelf
>
> before I go . . .

Could you get it there, you might well be interested in reading H. D.'s war trilogy, viz a series of 3 books published during the 2nd world war—by Oxford University Press; I've forgotten all titles. (One is something like: Let The Walls Come Down.)

She uses couplets, and has, qua 'problem', the job of moving same through a variety of 'feelings', some for example so-called conjectural, reflective, and likewise simple narrative, also dramatic-narrative: the whole is very interesting, as rhyme. As is, always, Wms, with the same thing:

> Liquor and love
> when the mind is dull
> focus the wit
> on a world of form . . .

That series of three quatrains, the second verse of which breaks out—as I echo it in that poem for Dave, i.e., Juggler's Thot, etc. Campion is always a relief in this—Wyatt, et al. They seem about the last to allow apparent (at least) improvisation. By Donne it's a box for me. Until Blake etc. One thing I think is to be worried about: the tendency that rhyme has to slow, i.e., as any repetition, it 'brings in' (as sail) the so-called movement.

I'd also just got Joel's book, The Dutiful Son—and feeling far away from him at present, not having written in some time etc., it was very possible simply to read it. I think it is a very good book, that Approach To Le Bain is a beautiful thing, likewise: The Friend -

> whatever we have
> repeated it is
> too much to have said it once.
> this is obvious.
> each rose is different.
> if that is not too much
> to consider.
> serious i mean.
> i mean i was
> repeating myself.
> it will not change it.

I don't know that anything ever ends the work. Just now I feel as though everything had of necessity, to be begun again. Writing, the simplest sort of maneuver has to be managed as though I had never heard of it, etc. It is the difficulty with acquiring a 'way', it becomes almost directly a contrary force, and must be broken down & out of. Another very pleasant tempered book I just read (I don't manage to read much now): Ford Maddox Ford's Joseph Conrad—written very shortly after the latter's death, called 'a novel' in form, or so he does. There are some very interesting comments on structure, etc. It has, all of it, the grace of F/s intelligence, plus much of the airyness, but the emotion so to speak stays 'solid'. It is in part a competition; it must have been a strange arrangement, i.e., the collaboration between them. (Have you ever read any of those books they wrote? I haven't.)

Partly it's to believe, to continue to, that writing continues a levy upon the intensive actualities of this life. There was a time when it could be, itself, one of those most prime. Now I more or less hurry after—at moments with the feeling, it <u>could</u> be brought up to the front even; yet still passive to the extent I expect rather than put it forward, to see what, etc.

I know so damn little at the moment, and so damn much, at the same time. I know what won't do it, almost perfectly. I am summoning what guts I have I suppose, to think of a large form, physically big, finally, wherewith to get a 'field'. The stick by stick process of what's given to me as 'earlier work' is, now, too implicated with ideas of continuum I have rejected as I have been able to. I want a nearly frigid aloneness, or at least as much as I can take it: to have a completely white field etc. I want an ultimate humility of this 'I', in part: whereby he can attend, old style, upon events he is surprised to find himself included in. A witness involved by his own existence, etc. That has to be learned again, because I used to know it, at least. Bitterness always seems to me a sort of forsaken superiority; and most intolerably placed in one's self, etc.

My wife's name is Bobbie, i.e., I guess that is why I did not write it. Think of that. I suddenly hate information of any kind—in any case. But not at all 'really'. So much for that.

I liked Chan's picture very much—she is a crazily sweet child. Viz, if judges have to be, they should be like her. She is very good to me.

Phil Whalen wrote a few days ago: it seems that Jack sold rights to 'On the Road' to an English publisher, and is coming back to the States, and will try to bring his mother to Mill Valley, etc., as he used to speak of it. Allen, tho broke, wants to stay on there. Gary is going into seclusion etc. Phil is as ever—a great pleasure, i.e., very <u>sane</u>. The 2nd edition of Allen's Howl was suppressed by customs & presently a stink being raised etc., with Rexroth on same etc. The latter reading at The Cellar etc to accompaniment of that bad jazz. Layton got a Rockefeller grant, and Jonathan a Guggenheim. So that's good. J/ is due by sometime early June.

It's a lousy day here, dust storm—but Sunday. But then I should have waited, but then don't damn well write, putting it off—which I do mean to do. So—so. But it is a bad day to tell you what poems I would like for #8, Anyhow I think: *Peocek and Vaquero, from those you had sent earlier. But—for god's sake—please don't let that bug you etc. Please send whatever you have as you can, because there is no immediate scene re time, and I would like others, etc. Ok. There is no real need for me to hang myself etc. Ok. Write soon. I will do likewise. Tell me how you are making it there.

Our love to you all,
Bob

* This one I
like very much
in part but at times
back off the "I, . . . " Better to use "Hid
of Mr Mothers"—ok?
P.S. Can you get Zukofsky's <u>ANEW</u> in library there? That's a fine book for
'tones', and writing.

. . .

POSTCARD TO DONALD M. ALLEN

[undated, ca. 1958]

Dear Don,

I saw Frank O'Hara's book in the local shoppe, and I think I
could cut him. I have enough now for a fairly decent book, size that is, taking the
work from after The Whip. Doesn't anybody want to buy a book of poems. The
Whip sold 30 copies at the 8th St Bookshop. That's famous, no? Ah well again—
but someday it wd be very happy indeed to have a book it didn't it seemed came
out of my back pocket. Tho where else I suppose. If ever, please say.

Bob

I can write jazz poems? Wow!

. . .

LETTER TO JACK KEROUAC

General Delivery
Alameda, NM
January 31, 1958

Dear Jack,

I've got some start into the Subterraneans, and yesterday On The
Road came—so that's it. Your style is pretty incredible, old friend, i.e., how you
hold a thing, in a haze, then sharpen, then fade—I like it. To me—and it's no
simpleness—it means more than the content—or is the content, a disposition
in itself. Or 'all to be talked about'—a sharp, sliding web of consideration. So
that again is it. Beats is for supper, otherwise—but you pick and I'll read it, and
feel very honored in sd process. You are very damn good. Again, it's what you
can do, that makes me think about it all—the topic is already history, [^ but not
what you say to it] e.g., I see by the papers there is something new in the heavens
etc. I suppose I (not sickly) want to be handed the goddamn dream of it all, the
island just above the mist, landfall, and all the rest of it. Some things you don't
talk about, but you will.*

I wish I could get to NYC for the movie. It would be too much. And, self-
ishly, I should, viz it would again be too much. But then I equally wish you cd
come here, for the place—though you must know it. An hour ago I was getting
my hair, down over my ears, cut, with the radio on loud, Mi Corazon, and the
crazy vanity of the Mexican, two kids getting chopped as well, then waiting for
their father, to get the same, etc. The whole place, the Ideal, floats in the coming
downedness, of pot, and 'there'll be more . . . ' It's good—even to sit gringo, and
be NH, and Mass—awkward, but they are very polite, and ask how I am, etc.,
etc. Anyhow I dig very much the shyness of their formality, in the big white
city,—in the desert. Who doesn't want to go home.

I like you being famous. You make money, you hear—like they say. Voila. Your business is otherwise but it's good they pay you for it. Marshall just sent a gig, a letter, via Olson—off Dahlberg & Read, etc.,—wherein he cites you as the sound; which matters, I think. Likewise Selby digs you, etc. It's good, to be dug—it lets one take off, and figure the home remaining, etc. My sister arrived a few days ago with my bros in law, flying home, and was talking abt Keh/roo/ac—accent on the 2nd syllable—how abt that. It seems some yng man in the english dept at Colorado State was reading you to the ladies.

This is Saturday afternoon, and the heat's off for awhile; but I want to read the books, and write a decent letter. Take care of yourself. You are very good to me, so I have an interest. Bit by bit—which is the way—I get back together, and will shortly be with it, I think. It all feels good. I have kids to insist on it. You should know that. Ok. Write as you can.

All my love,

Bob

Duncan today wrote: "there is a sense in which Kerouac touches everything with his own life, so that this reader will go anywhere with him . . . "

[note at top of page] Later: *What made me say that god knows, but my own dilemma, not yours. I just finished On The Road, straight thru, and it's a beautiful solid & completely heart-open thing. I like it—which to say sounds glib, except that it has so much of the wet, half-struggling thing; viz, hope. So I'm the one that needs it. Ok.

[note in upper left margin] This was re The Subterraneans. The length of the other is a curious obtainment so to call it, viz all that movement, always about to stay—and then moving. By Mexico it was all 'must be . . . ' Too much.

[note in lower left margin] The fade off on Neal is very moving. He just stands there as one moves out—it hurts to read it.

• • •

LETTER TO PAUL BLACKBURN

I think you met Fee Dawson (?)—who can god
knows be impossible—but I like him +/or have known him
otherwise. Ah well. It could also have been Victor . . .

March 8, 1958

[New Mexico]

Dear Paul,

Your comments on those poems help very much—as always. It's very <u>good</u> to have your reading, i.e., you are very sure & sharp. Ok. I'd myself

finally either push that Tunnel harder (?—if I cd think how), or whatever; I
think it's that I don't think light is the final image, that has always hung me
up. Ah well. Equally the Friend poem: it is from the other side, like they say—I
expect I wanted well written & gracefully stated bugged-ness. Anyhow, that
you like The Ladies is pure joy, i.e., it's the last written (the end of New Year's
vacation)—and the first real swinger I've felt in some years now (except for Just
Friends, which equally bounced at the time, except it was on bottom/SF '56).

So. I'll take Myth, No Myth—with pleasure. Equally your Mexican bandit,
if free? And please send me anything else you can, as you can. Perhaps I collect
it all against nothing ($$$ being very scarce, though shortly I'm going to try
to figure angles, of which there must always be some, etc.) I like for a Cool
Departure, very much—the end is very good. I like your line, Paul—I always
did, god knows—but you hold it very quietly & I am held by it. Also, no one else
I know can take an angle of 'description', and move it as a 'counter' of percep-
tion. This gets very sure in your writing. At the Crossroad is a beautiful thing,
also. Ok. I think you work hard!

I'm sorry to hear about the Oxford dons, i.e., as the man just sd on the radio,
Jesus Christ . . . But then it's Sunday. Oh well. Wdn't you know it was to be the
old hassle,—wow! And for 180 years almost nothing. But I am certain there will
be someone to do it, i.e., porque no—because it's done.

I have been waiting for some copies of some poems to be in a book, The
Dress, to get a ms/ of some sort to Allen (it was my own idea); so don't be
concerned abt that, i.e., I have myself done nothing abt it as yet, but want to. The
catch just now is, and perhaps you can help me find out what's happening—this
friend of Larry B/s (I'm quite sure they are, i.e., Ian and Liz Robertson) under-
took to print a book for me, very damn decently, abt 2½ years ago now. The text
was done as of last May, and when I was in NYC last fall (August), Ian R/ told
me on the phone it was to be ready end of Sept/. And a letter last month sd it
wd be ready end of Feb/ etc. But nothing. I was also told by them I'd been part
of a hostage in argument they were having with J/ Wms. Hardly happy. The bk
(small edition, 100 copies, so that's why I am anxious to have the poems for this
ms for Allen) has a drawing by Philip Guston, and is they told me almost com-
pletely subscribed—so I am damn well in the middle all round. I don't have any
copies of the poems in it, which is why I am now anxious, since there are abt 12,
I cd add in effect to this new ms/ etc. Cd you ask Larry when you see him, if I
have it right he knows them & all, to check what is happening? This distance as
ever is the headache—usual but never much else.

I'm reading Wm Byrd's diaries for a gig in US hist/—only thing that begins
to keep me awake at the beanery etc. As exemplum: "March 10, 1712. I rogered
my wife this morning and rose about 7 o'clock but read nothing because Mr

Mumford was here . . . I neglected to say my prayers but had boiled milk for breakfast . . . " So it goes.

I hope Freddie is better soon. It's been a godamn miserable winter eg. Bobbie has been sick for nearly a month now, ear infection. Again, I thought that poem in Origin was very straight—so. And yr book was never part of my clouds etc. Poco a poco. Write as you can. I will do likewise.

All love,

Bob

Back at the Ranch etc.

P.S.

It's a little more possible to write here, i.e., that's done for the day—and once out of it, at least it's quiet and begins to all be more possible—each time more. What thing I was thinking of, re your poem, turns out a misprint on my part, i.e., both drafts you send are the same. Ah well! I think I was trying to play sd 'asshole' back on the line before (?):

> . . . the pistol. My asshole
>
> dropped out
>
> and crawled all the way back to El Paso.

Or perhaps by itself on that line where you have it. Or perhaps—because what I read is what I read, and what you wrote, and so I took it, in my so-called head at least, no matter. So it stands as the rhyme intended. And it's yr forte at that, and always was. So send me more poems. Ok.

Again, it's very good to hear the Provencal material is all together, and off to Oxford—and goddamn well good luck to you. I hope. Likewise it's good to hear you are reviewing in The Nation; as wrote, I had seen some of your things there. Where have you been publishing? How about the Black Mt Review, yet? Granted a beneficent god, #8 may yet make it. I've missed you. I'd likewise like you to see what I have as of about 1956 (?)—since then it's been mainly figuring, though now with abt 20 poems that shoot in 70 directions, but at least at moments make it. Anyhow do you have If You? It's only 8 poems, but I think you wd like some. Let me know. Viz, I'd like you to see these things if you haven't. I wrote Don Allen abt a book, taking that and what's in this The Dress, 'due anytime (but never as yet etc)' plus what I have since, about 50 odd all told. I never thought I'd weigh these things like hamburg. Eh bien . . .

So it makes it, vous avez. I have, that is—poco a poco. A crazy sort of endless openness.

• • •

LETTER TO DENISE LEVERTOV

April 22, 1958

Dear Dennie,

I'm sorry to hear about all the ugliness, and that you've had Kenneth on you in such fashion. I can remember it pretty damn well, eg the time he came up and harangued the Dorns in just the same style for six hours straight. And—the anonymous phone calls, and the threats, and viciousnesses, and god knows what all. Then of course it was hard to suggest what it was he was up to, at least apparently—but these 'psycho dramas' are I think even a pathetic necessity for him now, and god knows after two years unrelieved they must be as clear to others as they were to me then. Anyhow, I can relieve you about the supposed quote. If I'm right—and I think I am—the only thing you ever said to me on that subject, at all, was that you were very sorry Kenneth had to be hurt, because you knew how much he loved his daughters. You offered no sympathy to me, because you did not know what circumstances were present—nor the situation literally; and could not, as I am very sure now you did say, take sides against loyalties felt on both sides. In short, you were sorry to hear what was happening, and reasonably, could not be involved in judgements, etc—regretting that it had happened at all. So much for playing a large part in wrecking his marriage etc etc—which same he wrecked long long ago, helpless to act otherwise or not. Again, I am helpless as you to understand what occasion I'd have for quoting your letters to Marthe—if at all, it could have only been to show that my friends were by no means taking sides against him, but were in fact tending to assume his position god knows more tenable than mine, granting I was the aggressor. God damn him in any case. The irony is, well listen: (from Don Allen) [^ *17th April, '58*] "I'd like to see the 4 uncollected stories—to consider them along with <u>Gold Diggers</u>. No hurry about this. Rexroth has also been pushing this book with me—he's here reading at the Five Spot now." So in effect you are used, pretty obviously, to titillate an outraged & shot emotional system long after the effective causes (not even me enough) seem out of reach. I certainly did not see Marthe in SF, I would hardly even attempt it, knowing what it might provoke him to take out on her in retaliation. As for guns, he said that once to me on the telephone, and I answered, I'll be there in one hour— whereupon he said, I don't want any more trouble, etc. It's sick and impotent and dead. A utter patheticism. Anyhow how much of course he would like to involve you, wasn't this always the form.

If you can get out of range of the voice—let it all drop. I'm not a dope fiend and I'm not anyone's lover, and I know the old pattern so well, of involving others in his excesses—a big huge gooey sick mess of insane preoccupation with his own despair, not even faced or written out, but indulged and fed till it's nightmare for everyone who ever cared for him. To hell with it where it damn well belongs.

I'm sorry the whole letter is taken up with it—I wanted to tell you 1) at Robt's we heard a half hour of your reading, rebroadcast on KPFA—wow, wow, wow! It was so damn lovely I had tears in my eyes, looking out the window, hearing you move thru it all. Well, you know!! And 2) it was a great trip & visit & all, and I read—and that was good too, to be back in business, with Robt smiling—and so on. I needed it very much.

It's good here too. I figure to stay on, I got a raise to 4400, and it's easy—and the house very great, and Bobby & family much more than I ever thot wd happen. So. I'll write soon. Please do likewise. All love,

   Bob

[note at top of page] *P.S. I'll get that copy of the damn review* <u>*SOON!*</u> *Wow, again . . .*

[note in left margin] *P.S.* <u>*Nothing*</u> *very wild ever happened to me, i.e., an "orgy" wd scare me to death—not to mention "debauches." It's a New England limitation like they say. I've smoked marijuana* but that's not what he is saying either. Viz. that* <u>*world*</u> *I can't even imagine. So.*

[note in right margin] **never in any relation with or to Marthe—goddamn this DEFENSE!!! TO HELL WITH HIM!!*

. . .

LETTER TO DENISE LEVERTOV AND MITCH GOODMAN

         c/o Homire
         Juan Enriquez 66
         Veracruz, Ver.
         August 13, 1958

Dear Denny and Mitch,

     Our Odyssey made it this far, and this I guess will be it for the 12 days remaining. Oaxaca was good, that's where we first went—and stayed at Los Molinos, but it got expensive, the Americans suspected in the plaza were very damn much in force—and soon the almost blandness of the situation got impossible, I flipped after my fashion, and one morning we were gone like they say—so quickly I never got to see your mother as I had planned to once settled, or any of it. Our next stop was Las Casas—and precisely as you said of it, god knows fabulous. I went to see Blum, who was most kind—and again it was all very good except for weather, cold and wet, and also a yng

English professor who came wandering in the day we arrived with the kids, who had been playing in the park—much to his distaste I later found. So that same day we spent mostly at his place, he assured us we could find one very easily etc. But things soon got involved, he graciously gave me a sheet mimeographed, with 19 examples of enjambment, I got drunker—at 1 AM that morning I seem to have insulted him too finally, and he threw me out of his house (13 rooms, $20 a month like they say—"and at last the pretensions are ours!"). It was all so dreary it colored the whole situation and it was raining, and so forth. We made our way back, getting here finally about July 24th or 25th—and have a decent apartment for $20 a month (fuck him!) and with all of us, it is simpler to manage everything in a city like this, which same I like, very much—i.e., the openness, people, and ocean, and all. They are things we get little of in the desert, and the kids in particular are delighted.

But the damn summer seems pretty well lost, with 12 days now remaining before we start back. Yet that too is fair enough—I've banged myself about hard enough not to have to worry longer about that capacity etc. No 'vacation' could make it, in that sense. So it has to be figured otherwise, god knows quite how—but no terms can be managed with time limits. But to hell with it all here.

I've been reading Rousseau's Confessions, just finished. What a book—like they say—so painfully short a goddamn life, viz so aching and small and bewildered. It's a crazy image of what ideas are contained by, viz the can wherein, the beans. Wow. I kept thinking, this man drove how many years of hope, and/or romanticism, and like a kid, his note of masturbation, to make the dream that won't come true. All the sad sad smallness—with the largeness of self-actuality he keeps trying to drive to. Wow again. It took my head off like they say.

Otherwise I read Under The Volcano—liking mainly (and almost only) the sudden images of bars & conversations; but the 'plot' dreary & pretentious & finally childish, i.e., the end etc. He could certainly write as he surely gives sporadic detail in this book I was very struck by—but the goddamn groundwork seems like a drenched pomeranian to me. No good.

I hope things are making it for you. I wanted to write much sooner, and did in Las Casas, but then 'events' changed so quickly, it was no longer relevant (what I had said etc). Write as you can please, i.e., here (though there is not much time now but a letter would very much help get us back god knows) or anyhow to Alameda, where we'll be again about the 1st. Take care of yourselves.

All my love to you all,

Bob

. . .

LETTER TO ED DORN

General Delivery
Alameda, NM
November 16, 1958

Dear Ed,

      I was reading that long poem of yours re yr mother, I have had
for years etc: it's very like my mother in law,—and god willing will one day
appear. I.e., things have been impossible re $$$, and as yet there is not much
hope of getting out another issue. But Jonathan wrote last week about trying to
start another magazine, twice a year—it seems ER irritates him & that is good—
123 pp or abt that, and who knows: perhaps. Have you sent that poem around
elsewhere? It ought to damn well get printed before we are all old and dead and
bits & pieces etc. Ok.

    What are you doing? It's an impossible scene of bits & pieces already, with 3
courses (horses, forces, bourses, mabel etc) At Night:

> At night
> I see the light
> I am afright-
> ted, etc.

    English 5280b—the being b, depends you see, : how are you Eddie boy, howr
yer making It. Etc. Hearty handshake, harf harf: bull yer. Viz, go son: make
Aceodemic: ach, viz aches Only When I Sit Down, etcl: ecetlee, viz et-settle her,
Un-settled. Settee—it all comes back to yr point o' vision: I see/ a settee. In my
mind's eye, of course. I (doctor) am continually beset by image I am tired and
should (sewed, sued) set (beset, settled, suttee . . .) Down (dad) but that's what
I am tired from (fro, fru * go in & out the rainbow, go in & out the rainbarrel).
And pieces navel dripping from the sea. The blood you wore the last we 'twere
engaged . . .

    Anyhow we are making it, and how we are 'making it': Douglas Woolf told
me he had bilt himself a cardboard house within his house: viz illustrative of Yr
common function of Yr common metaphor, etc. Go dumborn dad, tell them's
that wastes yr time & me, etc.

    Ite, liber que no hablar: dige quibus, etc.

    I wanted 'Ed' to write. God & all the saints preserve me. I mean, I want to
write you—goddamnit. It is snowing, the desert, the place here, like they say,
is awash with same—Yr dust & damned small indeed particles of frozen water.
(9 odd chickens huddled out in the Gt/ Beyond: Our Responsibility). I am writ-
ing ok, ok.

    I never have excuse for silence, it droppeth as the gentle rain from heaven/
upon Yr leaking roof.

MY LOVE

It falleth like a stick.
　It lieth like air.
It is wonderment [^ *and*] bewilderment,
　to test true.

It is no thing, but of two,
　equal: as the mind turns to it,
it doubleth,
　as one alone.

Where it is, there is
　everywhere, separate,
yet few—as dew
　to night is.
　[*CP* I, 181]

　　We survive fair enuf. Life goes on, also enuf. Bit by bit I begin to construct
something of it all, not a goddamn self-improvement or damn self denial, etc.
Write, please. It's a favor I be asking. Ok.

All love to you all,
Bob

. . .

LETTER TO ROBERT DUNCAN

San Geronimo Miramar [Finca San Jerónimo Miramar]
Patalul, Such.
Guatemala, C.A.
August 20, 1959

Dear Robert,

　　We are still in the process of settling, but each day it all looks more possible.
The first somewhat chilling recognition like they say, was that the economy is
by no means Spanish, i.e., there are simply two classes, those with it and those
without which last group lives something roughly pre-Columbian, whereas the
other mocks the latest imports from America, thus Log Cabin Maple Syrup
and transistor radios from Japan in a store smaller than that one in Banalbufar,
etc. Ah well! Prices for such things (which our appetites happily lust after)
are incredible, e.g. a box of crackers selling for over $2.00, and a can of Crisco
for $2.10. The problem is that if one doesn't live on frijoles and mais, then the
alternative costs a good deal more than expected, since there is no in between.

　　More happily, the house is comfortable, and the countryside around us very
beautiful—old volcanoes, a sort of half-lush half-tropical vegetation but not

at all impossibly hot, etc., a very lovely lake some ten miles to the north, and a glimpse of the sea from the house of one of my two employers, etc. So that rests the soul. The people themselves likewise break into two halves, one (the finca we are on) very simple to get on with, a young couple from America, the husband of which grew up here (Italian) and a simple decent loneliness for other people that moves me. The others are more complicated, particularly by the husband—ex-Tennessean, who wants an 'image' of his power, and though their house and the grounds, like they say, are very lovely (sort of olde Connecticut), his personality is not. But I can stay away, and his wife is a sharp harassed woman who seems to feel a good deal more than she presently mentions. The kids as expected are all very uncomplicated, and the only problem being their poor English but that can be got around. The course materials are fabulously ordered, even to the hours of the day, etc. So that will work out.

Otherwise, we keep wobbling between diverse reactions, sometimes wishing we were anywhere else, and sometimes feeling it can prove what we hoped etc. To hope is the problem of course, yet how and/or why not. I think in part we remember how happy the visit with you was, and wish that we could be there now. I'm going to see if I can't get some kind of job there, against another year, or say after a year or two here—which will in any case be enough. In the meantime the ambitious employer has now two tape recorders (got since my arrival, to record, he says, meetings in which he is 'active' etc) so as soon as ours is going again (something gave out a week ago, and it's now being repaired), I'll make a tape of Charlie's, and also of the one I got of Ed (noisy because of the children but fair enough) and will do the rest myself, and mail it. Just now I am reading Jung's Psychology and Alchemy, which I've had for a couple of years, looking only at the pictures. Somethings are provocative, e.g. green is the feminine color, four is feminine, three masculine, men facing a unknown area project the terms of their unconscious into it, etc. It tends to be very damn 'enclosed' but I have time, etc. Otherwise reading Burckhardt on the Renaissance, too slow I think, diffuse, too much off the center of the materials—I don't know. Again the anecdotes, the few, and the illustrations are fine. But I get to dislike very much these inclusive/exclusive intelligences, which read however subtley the terms of their own reaction as necessarily more relevant than the objects from which they derive: fair play would make an equality at least. Hence this in Jung seems wiser: "there was no "either-or" for that age, but there did exist an intermediate realm between mind and matter, i.e., a psychic realm of subtle bodies whose characteristic it is to manifest themselves in a mental as well as a material form . . . when psychology has at the same time to admit that there are other forms of psychic life besides the acquisitions of personal consciousness—in other words, when psychology too touches on an impenetrable darkness—then the intermediate realm of subtle bodies comes to life again, and the physical and psychic are once more blended in an indissoluble union. We have come very near to this turning-point today . . . "

I read in places relevances to Charles' preoccupations, e.g. 'homo maximus'—but more exactly, like that 'new combinations of old personages' etc. It seems to me that his investment, or recognitions, take from Jung, as surely the premise of Maximus himself, a curiously 'alchemical' figure. Anyhow his idea of objects declaring their presence, their nature, seems to play back to this use of Jung's in part, albeit with much differentiation, but I can see why Jung consented to be on the Board of Black Mountain, and was so polite in sending me that piece for the magazine, etc.

So it all goes on. As yet we are in a sort of half chaos, but get to bed early, etc. Write please as you can, because this is beyond all else (or so it seems) a place wherein to answer. Wow. I had missed that feeling and/or ability in Albuquerque. If you see any books that look useful, and inexpensive, tell me and I'll get you money for them, since books coming in have no duty. That will be the only problem here (books to use) as it was in Spain, and since there will be time for reading, I'd like to make good use of it. Please send me Maddy's and Jimmy's and Jack's addresses, lost in getting here. Give my love to all when you see them. Ok.

All our dearest love to you both,
Bob

P.S. I am supposed to get proofs of the book any day, so assume that goes all right. They have turned down Louis' Test which is a shame, and seem to be interested in nothing else. J/ writes he is trying to get something of Charles' in, more acceptable to them. Also, a long letter from Donald Allen, contrite and humbled, and says he will try to make amends to you for past horrors. I'd be very grateful to see you in that anthology so-called, if only for my own security—but god knows appreciate the difficulties . . . Wow.

· · ·

LETTER TO ALLEN GINSBERG

> San Geronimo Miramar
> Patalul, Such.
> Guatemala, C.A.
> September 7, 1959

Dear Allen,

We made it like they say, and glad to hear you did likewise. So that's that. It was a very good ride back with you, and the chance to talk and all I'd been hoping to have. There is no one who makes more sense of the politics of the so-called scene than yourself, and likewise I think what you're making of the unresolved areas of communication & control, etc, comes in very usefully. I.e., when is a man a sandwich, if you ask him to, and so on. That stroboscope image still hangs in my head, like who controls rhythm controls, as Olson used to quote somebody or other. (Nirvana, the great mystic, etc.) Reading that part of KADDISH in BIG TABLE #2, hearing it again on the tape recorder (and I'll send shortly a tape of poems etc), it makes it, thicker, denser, more variable, than heretofore (HOWL), the 'message' Norbert Weiner style is registered in a wider range of 'frequency'—it anticipates, and leads, giving the reader less area to 'reject' in, etc., etc. Ah well! The 'feed back' of your own terms, as they occur, declared, in the poem, i.e., as you, say, get them, add to the interest likewise. That way I read Burroughs as coming to 'terms' in his writing, coming to not so much abstracts of the so-called experience, but patterns that amend and fix it. He uses his mind as a way out IBM machine, seeing what kind of charge the thing can take—because take it must, etc. Or else it can't matter. That humor of his is fatal (mortal) as is all same—only people who really want to live forever, or who don't get the joke, so to speak, never laugh. I am very damn taken by everything of his which I read.

I don't know that any goddamn ultimate (wow) solution is to be got here. It's jungle out of mind pretty much, very tiny in a strange way, you can look at it, it looks very crazy but to use it I haven't yet found the way. The whole scene is feudal, Burroughs' location without as yet the characters, Connecticut landscaping with volcanoes for a backdrop—and after the desert, my eye is very damn arid and calculating. So it ain't mecca yet. The people are tied up, strung with the whole scene, you know just where you can get hold of them—or the finceros do. There will always be someone to do the 'job' though it may take three weeks to accomplish, etc. So they are growing coffee on pretty little bushes, a red cranberry like bean, and they pick it by hand, each goddamn bean etc. At this occupation they make about $10 a fortnight—they wouldn't make anything otherwise, but it seems ridiculous, when costs are high, no exceptions, a wool sweater hawked for their benefit selling for $15, to Indians, etc. It can hardly last. So the next life maybe they'll pick me and I'll be drunk on Madison Avenue at high noon.

I saw Gregory's picture in TIME. It's curious the way they keep reporting. Well, it gives the picture, does it not. I can't yet get the fact of the 'audience', it's sentimentalism no doubt, I hope not a snobbism, but I would give much to be able to register what it is such people think they are hearing. Obviously there is a so-called current. Maybe we goddamn well inhabit an existence where anything happening is a miracle. Hit me again, etc. The age of majority. Getting here, one of the bosses said, first we got a homo, then we got a lesbian, and now we got a beatnik—oh no. He himself is deep in with political gig called Union

of Christian Agriculturalists. What would Jesus say. They drive madly about the landscape in Mercedes Benzes and drink (it's expensive), and bull shit each other, and the Prez when they can get hold of him. If you come across any old copies of the PAC political organization booklet in bookstores etc, that would be a good one for them. I sit and drink beer in guise of a literate employee etc.
    So:

NOT NOW

I can see you,
hairy, extended, vulnerable,
but how did you get up there.
Where were you going all alone,

why didn't you wait
for the others to come home
to go too, they would
have gone with you.
[CP I, 228]

    I sent that to Leslie (?) with one other, per request, and thanks for giving him the word, like they say. Write me when you can, what's happening there, who's on the cross these days, what regrets, and so forth: is Jack now in Florida, how does it look for India—and if you can, because we got a phonograph pickup (left in the 'school house') that record of Jack and yours when ready? Write anyhow and no matter. Take care of yourself, and likewise, Peter, and likewise, you. Ok.

Our love to you both,
Bob

"In this world one hand washes
    the other . . . "

(Verga)

[Unidentified newspaper clipping enclosed]

    Feb. 1 Tonight I learned something—how to keep squirrels from climbing up a pole and eating grain from the bird feeder at the top.
    Hurried from the office to the dinner meeting of our men's rose club. Most of us aim to get there early, so we can have a gabfest beforehand.
    The main topic of conversation tonight was squirrels. Seems these little pests worry the daylights out the brethren who feed birds. "I solved it," said Doc, the dentist. "I greased the pole. Now the squirrel just slips back. Can't make it to the top."

. . .

LETTER TO JACK KEROUAC

San Geronimo Miramar
Patalul, Such.
Guatemala, C.A.
September 28, 1959

Dear Jack,

Hola, como se dice, i.e., have been trying to make it across the wastes to you for months now. Faint silences, no less. I wangled a copy of DR SAX out of Don Allen and I like that book, like they say, very much. Allen had given me the plot on the way back from SF, so it was (plus my own growing up in Acton, where you get to eventually after Chelmsford, likewise in the Nashoba Fruit Belt) a gasser. I used to go to Lowell once a year to buy a suit. The big city, which it still is, to my mind. You were the kids I never saw! Wow! It's a lovely book, very straight and with everything but what comes later in it—i.e., you don't jam it with corrections which so many sick people do these days. (I met Herb Gold briefly after one of the readings in SF, it was strange to see what he wanted (?), and here was this dapper, sharp, shrewd, little commonplace cat, so to speak,—what in god's name did I have. Anyhow a cheap thrill was had by all. I can't read any of that anymore. I don't believe in their world, or, more accurately, in the 'objective' fingers with which they think to pick it up. There is always a sly chuckle somewhere back of it all, viz 'but you and I . . . ' Anyhow that's out.)

Allen said you might be coming to Mexico, Mexico City—and hopefully it would be very good somehow to see you, i.e., either if you could make it here (which if you climb the volcanoes high enough gets like a Japanese movie, with trees blasting in & out of the fog), or else see you there, somehow. Does it look likely? Guatemala, such as I can see, we are on a finca about 15 miles from the one main road in this country (fair enough), is like they used to say visually the end. People-wise, there are still witch doctors, so somebody still believes. But there is a GOLFO IMMENSO between Indians and owners, everything is hopelessly marked up, it's all a big plate glass window for those who can smash through and grab it. And curiously dull, also—because there is little edge to the politics (as with Mexicans) or anything else. But it god knows is lovely to look at, like a song yet. So. We can make it, just about, with our six heads, twelve feet, etc. Wow again. At this point we contain our own weather.

Anyhow please write as and when you can. What are you doing? I just 'marketed' a poem involving you, viz I like to involve my friends, anyhow for you, to POETRY, so I am respectable. I'll put it on the backside. I liked very very much the poem in YUGEN, Florida—every year my mother & her sister for a few months make a monolithic trip down in their old car, to live in a trailer, because my mother won't leave her, and can hardly blame her for that. In Florida. Write soon. Take care of yourself. Ok.

All love,
Bob

JACK'S BLUES

I'm going to roll up
a monkey and smoke it, put
an elephant in the pot. I'm going out
and never come back.

What's better than that.
Lying on your back, flat
on your back with your
eyes to the view.

Oh the view is blue, I saw that
too, yesterday and you,
red eyes and blue,
funked.

I'm going to roll up
a rug and smoke it, put
the car in the garage and I'm
gone, like a sad old candle.
[*CP* I, 219]

. . .

LETTER TO ROBERT DUNCAN

Everytime I hear the Webern I can't believe it!! He has a beautiful mind.

San Geronimo Miramar
Patalul, Such.
Guatemala, C.A.
[undated, ca. October 1959]

Dear Robert,
        There is a break in the day, i.e., noon—when I am back here to refuel, and then off for the older members of the school's community, which is, at that, increasingly the only one I find a place in here. I.e., the rest turns into an increasingly drunken rot of self indulgence. Hence I avoid it. We live here, in the house, and with what we can see out the windows. Curiously, fair enough—because Bobbie starts to paint, and I am writing, no matter what. Anyhow there is no fiber such as there was in Banalbufar, of people to be looked at, then

responded to, i.e., tangibilities of presence and warmth. It's a damn shame that there should be such visible beauty all about, and so goddam much a wear and tear of people. Well, the same is true of a cemetery, etc. Pues!

I have that tape on the gizzmo, of Antheil, and just now Stravinsky: my contribution to the racket of trucks passing et al. So I think of you both, and that's a pleasure. I try to keep the damn day opening, bit by goddamn bit. I hate to see it go closed and locked around me, i.e., all that anticipated displeasure it can turn into. Viz, 'didn't I tell you, etc.'

Also just now I'm looking for my book, to boot me out again, and to start a reformation of any kind at all. I'll put, backside, what I've done, some of it, since I last wrote. I've also been rereading PATERSON, and then all of MAXIMUS— which latter I curiously find more variation in, than in the apparent changes of Williams. I think it's because the counters are literally larger, like the turning over of huge fish, a real change of the dimension. Whereas Williams works closer to the signal detail, etc. A sort of scuttering too often, and the main line stays main line, etc. Though that's too quickly said.

I reapplied for a Guggenheim—this time asking all the professors I could think of, and leaving friends out of it. Viz I want a vacation with pay. Ha.

Please write as you can. Give everyone my love, and if you can send me Jimmy's and Maddie's address, I'd like to write them. So, none of it is impossible, but proves too often sterile—but either I am or am not, and what more there is is gravy. So, again.

All our love to you both,

Bob

P.S. I sent the tape off to you last Saturday (October 10th), and it should take roughly a month. It has the Olson, also some of Ed Dorn's, and at the very end (of Ed's), me: THE DOOR, THE HILL, and one or two newer ones, etc.

[Page 2 consists of the poems "The Wife" (*CP* I, 252), "The Joke" (*CP* I, 214), and "The Women" (*CP* I, 234). Also, the following note, handwritten at top right]

I also like the Cage
altered piano very much—
e.g. they make tangible
for me this headache of
rhythms, suspended +
otherwise. But does
the Reader even hear it -
I wonder.

· · ·

LETTER TO JACK KEROUAC

San Geronimo Miramar
Patalul, Such.
Guatemala, C.A.
October 20, 1959

Dear Jack,

It was very damn good to hear from you, i.e., the more so, grey day, not so happy place at all it gets to be, with the people on our necks, we are locked in with them, so all the wear & tear of that. Anyhow I'll put some poems in & use whatever you and Allen figure makes it. The hat one and the one re pride goeth are as of an hour ago—so they are for you particularly, like they say. Ok.

Thinking of Steve Allen, also like they say—and he seems straighter than many—could you get them to send me a copy of that record you made with him? Viz not to beg, but I want it, and we are broke—and so. I think the only damn thing I would ever want from any of this bizness is chance to get such things I want, and too often perhaps too stingily or stupidly don't have the money to get, i.e., just now we make it and nothing more. Ai-yi. We are rarely hungry in any case. Ok.

I'll ask Wilentz Bros, 8th St Bkshop, to send you book A Form Of Women, which ought to be done soon, i.e., take also from that what you want (as from anything else?), but clear with them please any things re copyrights, which they seem to have all wrapped round with huge ribbons, etc. Though good naturedly.

I was thinking of one thing, that 'greed for views' Gotama, i.e., what he said, like they say. That was a good shot was it not. I used to know rambling & amiably drunken painter who wrote poem went: too soon, too late, too late too late, too soon too soon too soon, too late too late too late, etc. But I am here, he used to say.

As & when you are in Hollywood, and me without the TV yet, if you have time to make it, John Altoon is there, an old friend, and very straight man. I like him. He is married now to Fay Spain, Allen & Peter & Bobbie & I almost made it there, but were impatient, and kept going. Hence, if you get time he is at: 4837 Agnes, Studio City, Calif. Has phone, etc.

Jack I sure wish you were around! I talk so much out of the side of my mouth these days it comes out the back of my head—at best. Always backing out of the room, smiling, etc. I should have been a butler. Anyhow we are cooling the fort, and it's ok. We saw W.R. Hearst's castle I think, there's an image for you. Setting sun, off she was there, over the gently rising hills yet. I have a quote like they say from Peter, at the Grand Canyon no less: viz he first stuck his head over & yells, anybody down there got a cookie? Then later, a sort of taking leave etc:

Anybody down there seen my dinosaur? But people are getting callous all over.
Perty soon won't be no place left to walk. A tall. Take care now you hear?
>   And youth replyed: Ah will.
Write soon.

>   All love,
>   *Bob*

*Ed was finally the only one there—but for Judson Crews, who is rock, rock,
rock. That sure stays put!*

>   . . .

LETTER TO GENEVIEVE CREELEY

>   San Geronimo Miramar
>   Patalul, Such.
>   Guatemala, C.A.
>   October 26, 1959

Dear Mother,
>   I've been concerned, like they say, not to have heard from you
since we got here, but Bobbie's mother had written that she had a letter from
you. Is everything all right? Have you sent any letters, i.e., it seems possible
enough that the mail just isn't reaching us. Anyhow, write me when you have
time to, and I as well will try to be a little more communicative.

We got here safely at least, and now, after three months more or less, know
our way around the limited area, finally, we have to do with. It is not very much
as we had hoped, sadly enough. It's not the look of the place or the climate—
both lovely enough for anyone. But the people are limited and depressing to be
dependent on, and there is little (in fact as we've found, no) way to find alterna-
tives to them. The whole country is sharply divided into two feudalistic classes,
i.e., the owners and the peons who work for them. The culture of the Indians is
about worn out, and hangs on a kind of ghastly pre-Columbian survival. Well,
maybe that's not true at all, but we of course see them only in the context of the
coffee finca, where they work for very little indeed and seem mired in a hope-
less life of dependence on the German, Italian, or American owner whose own
security depends on their extensive exploitation. The whole form of living seems
a bitter anachronism. I don't myself see any very expectable solution, since each
government in turn seems only to invest itself with what it can take, etc. Hence
the usual political formulas are not very applicable. Ah well!

Anyhow life takes on a defensive sort of form. My work is simple and I have
it pretty well ordered. Bobbie equally has the house running smoothly with the
one maid we are finally able to live with. The kids are over their initial sort of
exposure, to stomach upsets and the like. And the rainy season is about down,

which was the last of our worries in that sense. But we have only ourselves, I mean not even the pleasure of a common street nor store—every damn inch of human intercourse seems prescribed by the deadly feudalisms, e.g. the Indians of course do not expect to be looked at humanly by whites and a quick invitation to total confusion or contempt is any jump over that. It literally stands as a cultural pattern, and I've met as yet no valid exceptions. The 'bosses' are, both of them, pretty unhappy men. Neither is out to do us damage, yet they breed about them that desolation which any man or woman, basically unsure, unsatisfied, and hence aggressive, seems to, always. They are 'nice' to us, they are all contemporaries age-wise, but there isn't an inch of common ground between us (certainly not one I'd ultimately admit to, even to survival!)—and it takes a conscious sense of 'not rocking the boat' to make an evening with them pleasant. But we go, when asked, just to have that variety. We can't make our house do for it all, although it helps a lot simply to be a family, and to damn well believe in the values of this life as not finally commercial, sexual, or dogma. Wow. They are bored people as well—and that is catching.

So we again manage with what we can make of the house, and ourselves. In Spain, despite the unhappiness in just that area, there was always the place, and the people, just outside the door, and whenever it got too much, you went out to it, walked by the sea, talked to anyone, who always seemed to have a lucky sharpness of sympathy, people that were human likewise. The dead eyes here, or the live ones left to some Indians, reasonably have their own concerns. The roads are too poor to let us go anywhere without fear the car will be wrecked in the process. And the costs are high, to our surprise, e.g. a 3 lb can of Crisco sells for $2.10, and there is no local alternative to many, many things of this kind. It is not in any sense a cheap country, and is, in many ways, more expensive than the states. So, on the $3000 I took to come, we have the same old squeeze to survive—one of the main persuasions, that we wouldn't, that got us here to begin with.

Well, to hell with it. God willing we'll see a little of the countryside before going, because that is lovely, very much so—as from our porch there are three or four volcanoes, crazy green lushness of trees and flowers, and a beautiful climate. It's only unhappy that such a paradise, in so many ways, has to be a cultural swamp and burial ground. I guess the Mayans were the last men to see what a world it really made possible.

And the kids learn well—I sink myself in that sentimentalism, i.e., look to them for my pleasures o' the day. In the meantime I'm writing to divers colleges and universities, in hopes of a job for the coming year which seems likely. More than one here would probably break something permanently. Also I'm writing, which is a pleasure, and it seems to come well enough. Jack Kerouac wrote me from New York: "Everyone has the highest regard for you now, I guess you don't know, about your poetry, the secret magician . . . " That was very damn kind of him. So anyhow we all manage. And next letter I'll try to down my spleen and chagrin that it is not the idyll planned—and give you a better blow by blow description. I saw nothing but blurred or painted photographs, i.e., postcards, in Guatemala City (itself a blurred suburbia); hence have sent none. But we have a camera with us, and will try to get some of the surroundings and all.

Well, nothing is perfect. But, as Ed Dorn wrote, 'Cheerfulness is still a misleading humor . . . ' Only Sam Smiles himself could make of this place a 'happy time'. But endurance being an old New England character, I can at least try to live up to it. All the kids are at that thriving. So. Write as you can, please. I hope you are all well, and that the trip south went off all right. I'll write too, again, soon. It's just that I don't want to spill over on you this present disappointment, nor make it seem a day isn't no matter very often altogether otherwise. It's the 'long range plan' I'd thought to make of this move, that convinces me no plan is always the right one. Ok.

All our dearest love to you both,
Bob

· · ·

LETTER TO ED DORN

San Geronimo Miramar
Patalul, Such.
Guatemala, C.A.
October 26, 1959

Dear Ed,

I've been trying to write you, and get too goddamn sunk in the local pit, etc. But the rainy season has about lifted, so we'll soon have a rash of them ironically blue skies overhead at least. I.e., we stagger on with the white man's burden—and the Indians look more distant, out of it (good for them) daily. What a ridiculous life it turns into. When my head isn't splitting with, Oh look. See Dick, etc—and how can I blame ANYone for that, like they say—it's the patrones I have before my wavering eye. God they breed unhappiness, this pair. You get around people, too much, who have some goddamn sick self-indulgent wear to that old hunch and huddle, viz a drinkee, a quick one, a dog knows what next, etc—and the whole goddamn landscape exclaims TILT and off you damn well do slide. Having once been a carrier of substantial proportions, I can almost smell the rot long before anyone opens the so-called mouth. Sick. Sick. Sick. The hell being there is no one else to say good day to, but the mirror, the children, and my wife. Why I want more I don't know, and I'm fast learning not to. So—how are you all. I hope well, happy, cherished, good natured, blessed of god and mankind. Goddamnit, WHY NOT. Ok. What we don't damn well know we soon enough learn, and life, to be lived, don't take a bunch of ultimately if not immediately EVIL fuckers just a sucking and a squeezing the old dumb ones, for some mythical balance in the books of one million dollars, as and when they surely will drop dead. I.e., this is the hope of one of the two lads I play peon with. This—and a real hot time in bed, etc. Like the inner wall of some pimply adolescent's 'mind'.

I make it ok, despite. We all do, despite. I'm writing, viz back side, but whether coherently, or anything at all, I've long since lost track though it loads on all that paranoid bit of 'is it good'. Write please, i.e., help dad help. The shot heard round the world. I even wrote you a poem: (for Ed)

PRIDE

The end of the song is the end of the story,
I'm five feet high, huge and gory,
piddle pussed, scraped, lean, hard, and vainglorious
also.

There are like big creepers all over the wall here
and they have been growing for three thousand year,
and like when I think about it, you hear,
there is nothing I don't fear.

Jack writes you are a great writer, which you are, so write me a letter, ok. I.e., have you written since my last because I suspect everyone, i.e., of mails not delivered like they say. Anyhow this to resume contact, over & out:

All love to all,
Bob

I've been reading (finally) Jane Harrison's Prolegomena to Gk. Religion: *a beautiful damn book—and keeps me SANE—and HAPPY!*
START OVER!
["Kore" (*CP* I, 206), enclosed]

· · ·

LETTER TO ALLEN GINSBERG

San Geronimo Miramar
Patalul, Such.
Guatemala, C.A.
October 31, 1959

Dear Allen,

Your letter was very damn good to have, i.e., don't think my silence is ever anything other than the usual hang-ups. Y pues. We make it ok, it is dreary, often, but what the hell. The main headache is that it all costs more than figured, hence we are squeezed for money—but that too passeth away god willing. He usually is.

Jack wrote about the anthology you and he are editing. I sent him some poems, I don't now know if they are worth it—but most to the point, as I told him, please take whatever you care to, from anything, and let me know and I'll clear it if there's any hang-up. (I.e., the contract I have with Wilentz states I should clear all use of the poems from the book with him, i.e. subsequent use, but he has been very good, and I don't see any problem.) Also I'll put a couple of new ones here, like they say. Let me know what you figure to use as you can.

Too, that damn tape you gave me is sitting here, and that I want to do and get back to you. I tried it once, got all through, and then playing back a day later found it was recorded when the current was too low, so all went higher later. So I'll do it over, and thought as well to copy for you Duncan's ODE BEGINNING WITH A LINE BY PINDAR and THE OWL IS AN ONLY BIRD OF POETRY. And a little Olson, if I can get room. I.e., a clutch, since I'm scared by myself! Ok. (I asked Wilentz to send you a copy of the book when done, which it ought to be by now?)

I've been looking for Burroughs' book, and thanks—but that will take time to get here I would guess. That "IT is sending a message through Burroughs . . . " Wow, i.e., that says it. You know, that 'IT' is certainly an old time business. I begin to wonder what it does come to, to 'speak for yourself', and if all history, like they say, read as only a lot of little you-me thrusts, etc., wouldn't have just been a lot of dull, dreary, draggy old clothes. Though I've always liked them. But the 'speaking thru', in B/s case of such a curiously vacuum-like yet substantial 'thing',—it is eerie. He was never kidding, clearly. But you say it, of this world: " . . . even if it's only growing realization that the brain is mortal . . . " I.e., I guess is at that the only 'thing' by which we can, if we choose, keep track of such mortality, like they say: no one else would even notice. Meaning the 'voices'. Wow. But I listen too. But very little to my 'brain' except as via 'here they come again . . . '

So, that way, we are very happy. God knows prices are high, damn well impossibly so, for the most part. And our means of getting around, since the front of the car sounds like a bag of iron, are not good, and get worse. And time, that way, with kids, is short. But I wander all over hell here, in my head, in and out, and days, walking up divers roads close to the 'school house', fair enough. Crazy sky, look, lush greens, all the damn growing—really crazy, more and more. Theoretically there are no immediately active volcanoes, but who knows. It happens here very fast, all the whole goddamn world. No local intoxicants but for lush, that I can find record of, sign of: I can't even locate reasonable connection for myself & the known, like they say. So am growing what I can, though the deluge of rains & crazy sun, after, is almost too much for it apparently. Also caterpillies that eat so fast it looks like they're making disappear what they're walking on. I'd like to be able to do that.

So/so. I'll write soon. I want to get these poems down. Please write too. Take care of yourself. Am growing full beard, half-way, so I can turn my face around & look inward: BOO. No one will know where I've gone, and neither will I. Take cares! Four times daily. Ok. We make it, oh ho. I'll try to get on with some of the people you've sent me, thanks—by god you are kind, decent chap, you. Duncan: "Allen Ginsberg has carried news of and his enthusiasm for THE FIELD across country and sent it on to England . . . (I) find certain virtues in Part II of KADDISH appearing in YUGEN . . . " I.e., I don't think it's simply a bargain, i.e., D/ finds that world scary, and passes it, too quickly—he knows who you are. He's coming back, and he always will. So—write when you can.

All our love to you and Peter, *Bob*

[typed below: "Kore" (*CP* I, 206), and "Young Woman" (*CP* I, 238)]
P.S. Roi Jones sent Ron L/s book—which I thought was a very solid first shot, i.e., he had humors & ways of saying that brought me wide awake. Which is it, always.

· · ·

LETTER TO LEROI JONES (AMIRI BARAKA)

San Geronimo Miramar
Patalul, Such.
Guatemala, C.A.
November 8, 1959

Dear Roi,

Your letter came in yesterday, along with battered but substantially intact, like they say, copy of A FORM OF WOMEN. It both cheers and scares me, or now that the first wave of pleasure washes over, I get scared it doesn't make it, all those rhymes this time, god knows. It keeps changing and changing, never any of it done, at all, at all. I wonder what I think to do, etc. The problem of the 'public voice', no less, heared tuned to a personal wail, etc. Ah well. But it never will be done, will it? That's hard to learn, not until one is damn well dead—the final unreality. Wow! I feel as though I had blown myself out of my shell, like an uncooked egg, and sit here with all that necessary 'tentativeness',—which way to collapse?

Anyhow, also a fine wash of a decent sadness, like they say, listening just now to that Miles Davis blues album,—it fits. I think of Autumn in New York, for-getting of course the tedium of a day to day sound, but remembering the sharp air, colors, friends, etc. Ah well again. No, I am not impossibly fixed, at all, and bit by bit we manage to make a little more than make do. The house is at that the best we've ever had, with the most room for all of us. Resources, otherwise, always are personal—I take what I have for same with me, by virtue of a long apprenticeship, etc. I don't want the fight of living there, if it can somehow be avoided, so of course I am cheap to kick, and forget it so easily. Duncan's distinction between solitude and loneliness is a good one, i.e. in that recent poem in MIGRANT. The latter is I guess world ache for kin, but becomes destructive if indulged—should be, I guess, confined to remembering 'ole Bill' when with 'ole Harry', and sufficient liquor to add the right vagueness etc. Wow . . .

Otherwise it comes to so-called impeccable 'times' of crossing someone's path, like they say—as Ed Dorn and family getting off an early train in Albuquerque, New Mexico—Olson first standing in his door wrapped in a towel, at Black Mountain—Duncan reading from his notebooks, straight off, in a pension in Palma de Mallorca—Dahlberg followed down the hill there, to our house, by taxi driver & piles of luggage—and so on. I.e., the handholds that make the swing through the jungle possible. Well, you know.

I haven't got Mike M/s new book, and should much like it, if possible? I.e., can you spare a copy sans scene? I hate to freeload, but am, in present circumstances, i.e., the tightness of our so-called money (jingle jingle), brought to it, viz run to it. Ok!

Looking at the book, there is that SOMEWHERE, in it—so that is probably best not used, i.e., there is in the contract with Jonathan and Eli Wilentz clause to the effect no poems can be used without etc. Which would not be hard to get, but if it's there already, it probably serves no purpose. I don't have anything else on hand free, that makes it enough. So, this time at least, why don't you use if agreeable what you otherwise have, i.e., WHAT'S FOR DINNER (in form backside, I've made a few small changes) and THE JOKE—which latter you are very welcome to use with 'drawing' (!), i.e., it's pretentious, of me, but who cares. If you like it, do it. Likewise, if there is anything of use in that earlier letter, use that also—if Gil would not be too much bothered by it? I think use of things from letters is good, i.e., makes a usefully quick pick-up, so long as it does not describe a 'club' etc. Anyhow, let me know what roughly will be the deadline for the issue coming after this next one, and I'll promise enough to choose from to satisfy you, i.e., here it is November 8th, and five days for a letter to get there, and none that is too close to hope for anything more.

I wish I could hear some of those readings. And see Phil and Mike, and everyone. I wish home movies etc were simpler. But—it's a fine day here, now that the rainy season, like they say, subsides—crazy vistas, views, to all sides. Most to the point, I'll get there one of these days, no matter. In the meantime, I hope everything makes it for you. Ok. Take care of yourself. Give my best to everyone there. (I'm going to try to get the tape done for Allen this coming week, now having the book, etc., and that ought to get there someday. I'd be very happy to have you hear it, if that is possible, i.e., that's the hard part of this business, that distances make that difficult—except for tapes. I'm going to put some of Duncan on it as well, reading ODE ON A LINE FROM PINDAR, etc. Like Billy Goat Gruff ...)

All my best to you,
Bob

WHAT'S FOR DINNER

Only from the back
could I be seen clearly,
merely the fragment
into space hanging.

John jumped on Tuesday.
We had a date
but I was late, and he unduly
unruly.

Today my time come I
am hung from this 7th storey downtown window
to say hello
for the last time.
[*CP* I, 93]

P.S. Also I asked Eli Wilentz to send you "review" copy of the book. So save your money too!

· · ·

LETTER TO JEROME ROTHENBERG

San Geronimo Miramar
Patalul, Such.
Guatemala, C.A.
December 16, 1959

Dear Jerry,

Thanks for your good letter. God knows what to say of that poem (The Animal) finally, i.e., I'm inclined to say, if you like it well enough to use, by all means do. In any case, my own (pretty hasty) judgement was really that the rhythms seemed to 'hold' the poem longer than the statement (in your sense also) called for. I.e., at divers places in it, it got a little sparse in the latter character. And too, I feared the close struck too much as 'punch line', literally, i.e., the weight given to those last few words. But I'm not the reader, for this one—literally not as it happens, since I no longer have a copy. What I've been doing lately are poems following on those like THE WIND, in the book—domestic-social I suppose one could call them. Wow . . . But that area, pretty much as ever, stays central for me, albeit means and the sights thereof change thank god. Anyhow let me know what you think—not to put the onus of it on you, but if you like it enough to use, then do—because just now I'm a little badgered by divers 'possibilities' and obligations, and also—what with this Xmas to-do—dulled; and it may be a time before I can get you anything for another one or two, etc. (Whatever,—if you would please send a copy back when you next write; perhaps not having looked at it for awhile, I'll be able to see it better. I.e., often I in a sort of hopeful fit of judgement throw a hell of a lot away I later wish I hadn't, e.g. a story written years ago called UNGRATEFUL JOSIE & RICHARD THE LION, just because the copy I'd sent out got lost, and my own wiped out in above fashion, etc., etc, I'm sure was greatest ever, etc., etc. Y pues . . . Well, good luck!)

What you say of 'statement' strikes very close, and the more so since I, for the most part from Williams, believe in that character you describe, i.e., he somewhere says (in the AUTOBIOGRAPHY if I remember rightly), 'the poet thinks with his poem, in that lies his thought, and that is the profundity . . . ' or words to that effect. But I do not, as I read you to agree, consider the thought of a poem (taken either as content or attitude or hopeful surmise etc) to be extricable from its 'place' in the poem. Hence I remember at the time my own deep pleasure hearing that said by Williams, as he god knows says it otherwise in something like the preface to The Wedge: "When a man makes a poem," i.e., the revelation of the poem is this inherent statement which it bears, etc. Too, for myself, whether from early and then continued isolation from those who would have made it external, so to speak, anyhow I've used my own intelligence as a counter and/or term, in the poem, to find a purchase on what emotional charge, or fact, had first brought my attention, or intention, to rise. That's said badly, or you say it better: "almost intrinsically a statement beyond statement" since it is not extricable, but follows as a recognition within the very body of the poem itself. At best the intelligence devises the means, stands as witness to, and follows as it may, that which bears the poem more deeply, i.e., what for me is the otherwise inexplicable 'emotion'. Because "only emotion endures" seems true to me also. Certainly in a poem.

Anyhow you're right that, often, in my writing one finds a sort of monologic dialogue, so that even literally, writing, I wake up to find myself talking as I am writing, i.e., talking the poem to 'hear' it back upon my own mind—which, saying it, god knows clearly enough shows you what I conceive to be the function (or one of the functions) of intelligence, intelle-to (?), light o' mind, and so forth. Aperiens tibi animum, as Pound says; it is a complex. And it is curious, and perhaps even ironic, that Yin and Yang are in that way for me reversed, since the apparently amorphous, passive, pervasive 'emotion' sits as leader, always; and mind follows. Voila. So of course there is that 'dialogue' you mention, in that poem (it has to be there, even without a copy to read now), the subject so-called if roughly, partially, etc., etc., nonetheless is the above. I suppose I distrust the poem because I distrust an overt invitation to this occasion, i.e., don't like the mind's provocations to lead to such considerations, etc. Well, to hell with this. It's simply to say the "feeling of a conversation inside the head" is a constant pastime, if no mania, if not schizophrenia, if not something less interesting. Ok!

One thing: que es Sonia Raiziss, viz la bomba, etc. That is a strarange nambe [sic] for a magazine: The Chelsea, i.e., sounds like old hotel etc. Or back end of Boston, etc. Anyhow I got a carbon letter from her listing something approximating the Roll of Honor, etc., but no 'word' like they say, just huge shadowy suggestions etc. She says you suggested me (?)—but I can't make out for what (?). Anyhow thanks, and I wrote her back my gratitude, to get the letter you dig. Ok again. That's too bad Chester Gould is a schlemiel, viz too rich, too long, too often, etc. Anyhow write when you can, and will do likewise.

All best,
Bob

MERRY XMAS!
[RC's hand-drawn star and moon]

. . .

LETTER TO WILLIAM CARLOS WILLIAMS

San Geronimo Miramar
Patalul, Such.
Guatemala, C.A.
December 24, 1959

Dear Bill,

I heard last night from Renate Gerhardt, the wife of Rainer Gerhardt you may remember as the editor of that German magazine FRAGMENTE some years ago. Miserably enough, he died some years ago, the whole thing becoming too much for him (or for anyone faced as he was with so many impossibilities). I'd not heard from Renate since I left Spain, but in any case she writes me now that she has a good job with Rowohlt Verlag as their American and English 'reader', and wants me to start again where she and Rainer had left off, i.e., to publish a new magazine with the same cross-joinings of European and American writing. Also she wants me to act as her American editor—and god knows that is a pleasure, here with the jungle, the coffee beans, and los finceros etc.

So, briefly, may I use something of yours, nothing that will I hope prove a bother, or complication for you, but anything you either might want there, or else, if it's a problem now to be bothered with such things, might I use the poem which James Laughlin printed, <u>To Be Recited To Flossie On Her Birthday</u>, i.e., that's a very damn beautiful one. God knows it would be a pleasure to have it there—or anything you can think of. Ok. (I don't yet know just when she plans to get an issue out, but she is an old friend and will do it if she says so. Voila.)

Things here go well enough. It's a dull country, beautiful at times beyond almost the power to see it—and locked in people so goddamn familiar, the old exploiters, etc. So that prices on anything but beans or corn are sky-high. Y pues. It's an easy living for us, however, and proves time to write, and to be together—which same had been too long lacking in New Mexico. So, it's ok. I hope there things are all right. I think of you, very damned often—well, that's my hold. Ok. Enclosed is a belated Xmas card, like they say—and to correct the so-called blurb on the cover, call it 'privately offered in goddamn embarrassed homage to the one man I most revere, and love, in this so-called world of writing'. Ok.

All our love to you all,
Bob

. . .

LETTER TO CHARLES OLSON

San Geronimo Miramar
Patalul, Such.
Guatemala, C.A.
December 24, 1959

Dear Charles,

I've got a couple of days more or less clear, so had waited for that to write—and, happily, last night I got a letter from Renate Gerhardt, crazy, and she tells me she wants to start something again like Fragmente—and asks me to be American editor, etc. It hardly makes much room, or a time, but it's good no matter to be doing something of that kind again. Because one picture is always worth a goddamn million words, etc. That way I want to 'pose' and/or put Allen G/ for one in the context I read him, i.e., not in the popular image—though god knows that's a part also—but qua writing (which, for me, is of course the continual seepage, lost, of what now occurs; that the attitude starts too far back of the poem which is then meant to contain it. And yet Allen clearly, as Williams said, "thinks with his poem. In that lies his thought. And that is the profundity, etc." I.e., the poet, the poet, the poet, etc.) With Mike I read the poem too goddamn often as an extension of 'Mike', i.e., a personality stake, though that may be wrong, too simple—but what is stated, in the poem, say (as very much opposed to what Phil does, who, for me, from Williams buys the above, etc), plays back to Mike—and that's the wrong direction? Or something. The 'self' gets awfully goddam sticky, is not an occasion, place, another 'objective' finally material—but is rather, as Robt has it elsewhere in that piece: "McClure (who believes the self is an independent entity) . . . " Perhaps it's simply that I don't? But something bothers me there, some 'harping' quality—hardly permitted me to blame, since I equally 'depend', etc. Fuck it. But most to say, what I'd want to write of all these people, agreeing that Gary S/ is back, is 'substantive' in the old sense, the Rexroth/mistaken Pound way, etc, viz 'black dog bite house moon sink all gone, etc.' So that verbs, curiously, become only terms between master nouns, and though they is terms, that ain't quite true, they is only . . . I begin more to think all that happens is verbs, and nouns are more the what a verb throws off as by-product, than other way round. Well, goodbye Victoria, etc. Anyhow what to say is 1) technical—that here if anywhere is a continuum for the writing writing part of it, so goddamn much more than anything elsewise contemporary; 2) that also here is the fix from the structure of 'world' these people get, viz there Mike rings true, likewise Phil (with intelligence), that again finds only floppy mistakes elsewhere; and 3) that IF the cult of self begins to ride, what then IS the premise that will both extend it, and acknowledge it, i.e., how do we go from there. Well, that's an old fix, surely—as you had it in MAYAN LETTERS, re Bill W/s problem, of the self as, etc. That the shift is substantive—which Phil and Mike again, variously Phil by intellect, Mike by feeling, recognize—and Allen by society, I'd suppose. Make a manner these days, and the 'world' follows—not the other way round. The 'world' becomes a term of action, located by that occasion, etc. Because there seems to be generally (ah weh) a sense that no world is really there manana, or even was yesterday? But that's slippery. Anyhow, these several people bespeak a world, substantive insofar as it, substantially, provokes and carries their references thereto. That's something, and curious, in itself. But objects, i.e., who sees Phil, say—where is her, he, etc. Because in conversation with Allen, he was telling me of experi-ments he had made on him at Stanford, involving stroboscopic biz, wherein he 'learned' that a statically repeated light-flash duplicating the wave impulse of the vision becomes 'thought' in the mind, i.e., takes over beyond 'hypnosis', i.e., thinks you, as you, etc. And Mike moves too easily that way, for me.

Otherwise, myself I've been trying to break out, in several ways, i.e., where the poem is, for me, writing, has to be in the terms peculiar to it, and 'he who controls rhythm' (as with stroboscope) controls, or is controlled by, held together by, the structure then maintained. So that, rhythm, in the poem, again and again brings me back—how the hell to, for example, make it as close, to the mind/hand, as you in, 'and nakedness / is what one means'. And again I see you after the same thing in JABBERWOCK arrived also last night, Good News! from Canaan, etc. I am trying to find how to play the suggestion of rhythms, back and forth, throughout the goddamn line, breaking more easily 'terminals', and likewise, carrying it as closely as I can to what each word 'means'. It's only, all, fly by night, but repeated, maybe gets learned. I don't know. But I am sick of 'I', as only means, again and again, and want, 'to be taken away' too, etc. But I don't really want to come back, so to speak, to writing, to then tell all—but writing writing, make it there, somehow. God knows, i.e., I feel always about to fall out the backdoor, but I'm hardly a virgin anymore, etc. Anyhow as this (done a few nights ago):

> The love of a woman
> is the possibility which
> surrounds her as hair
> her head, as the love of her
>
> follows and describes
> her. But what if
> they die, then there is
> still the aura
>
> left, left sadly, but
> hovers in the air, surely,
> where this had taken place?
> Then sing, of her, of whom
>
> it will be said, he
> sang of her, it was the
> song he made which made her
> happy, so she lived.
> [CP I, 240]

I seem to be lucky in that anthology, i.e., he's got a good so-called group, and reads ok, i.e., from THE INNOCENCE to the last one for you, THE AWAKENING; and then prints some prose notes as well. That's fair, and useful, I think. But an anthology would be per se a particular headache for you, i.e., that's not so damn simple, to show scope, variation, all of it, in a relatively short space. But it will be useful, no matter—viz, don't worry! You'll be surprised. What do you think would be good for Renate, of yours? The goddamn german, i.e., that they won't know what's what, is a headache—so tell me? Also, she does not tell me what I can use for space. But I'll know soon and meantime, please see what you think looks good for it. I god knows depend on you, siempre. Y pues . . . i.e., Xmas, Xmas, Xmas—like a (happy but sticky) shroud about us all, and time, time, time. Fummmboooo. Write soon, and I will, i.e., what a goddamn pleasure to have your letters again. Ok. And a HAPPY NEW YEAR, that's for sure.

All our love to you all,
Bob

[circled] 2

Later

P.S. I.e., your letter just came, with those two goddamn crazy poems, i.e., how abt that—there IS a god. Ok. Anyhow what do you say to for certain taking that second one, the 'pah', (wow), for this gig of Renate's, and the first too, because I am goddamn grateful to make that company. Ok. Ok. Ok. That second is the <u>fastest</u> most lovely thing, it <u>happens</u> with such a crazy swiftness, like nature, yet. Well, I have not read anything so quick in years, and it makes a goddamn huge difference. So, as of first of letter, have you got any more at home like same. That's exactly what would make the USE of this space I expect she'll have for us—and what would rock those goddamn germans ich bin gewiss, like they say: aber gewiss ja! (Thank god we're not german, etc.) Anyhow, GO!!!

I don't know a damn thing about the KULCHUR magazine, i.e., no one ever told me nothing, but for you. That's the goddamn hangup of so-called communications, i.e., they are making it like a goddamn delicatessen (fressen), and reasonably enough I suppose like a little ketchup here, a little geschmaltz there, and a great big hunk of ice cream on top, etc. So if I don't make the menu, I don't make the scene. It gets, I think, despite letters from Jack K/, or personal assurance of Allen G/, and god knows friendly and devoted letters from a lot of the heads there NYC, hard to 'take' me, hard to goddamn well make my 'nice' manner, maybe. I don't know. I have had head & address for a long time, yet none of this—except from you, Robt, and old gang, so-called, and LeRoi thanx to Allen G/, ever gets to me. So anyhow I am not Kulchural. I <u>want</u> to be,—wow. It sounds good, i.e., where <u>does</u> one talk anymore. As Robt is making it in Jack Spicer's mimeographed bull-e-tin (and Jack hears); and I fiddle-faddle with something like Doc Turnbull's joye & travaile, etc.,—and where the hell is EVERYBODY. That's the damn loss, i.e., you know what would make it, just now, fast and hot, and UNconsidered, would be newspaper type gig, bi-monthly or more quick if possible, just shunt, shunt, shunt—and pack in all of the angles. I think. And would damn well do it, or would work my ass off for anyone who'd make it that clear—but no $$$. But 'love', but 'please send me zomesing', but 'oh how goood', etc. That doesn't move an inch. How abt a slow boat to China, dad, make the RAIL scene, the DECK bit, etc. Like LOOK . . . wow . . . Y pues. Nosotros vamanos manana por la manana y despues . . . The morning for the morning. Ah well. Nobody gets up anymore, that thinks to damn well call me, at least.

So, I don't know. Viz, Robt wrote me, re Credentials, like 'I had a prize from Poetry for poems I'd thrown away, and Rosenthal reviews me and Snodgrass . . . and WHAT will I say to them, etc.' Like—wow. And me, everytime I make that scene I 'tune' up, and blast like it was a clearing in a fucking jungle two feet square, and they was out there—oh please god SOMEwhere. (I hear Rexroth was to read in London with his All Stars, but the band didn't make the scene, so he just had to go ahead and read any-how, poor old fellow . . . Like.) Let's be PROFESSIONAL. I.e., if it has to be via Hamburg, via Hamburg it will be: a good three inches thick, etc. Wit dripping. Anyhow I think I'm being pulled out of the line-up, because like Corso sd, I'm intellectual gangster, at best. Y pues . . . How do you beat that. He's ok. I had a letter tonite from someone wants to start mag on basis of 'detachment', I don't even know what he's talking abt—i.e., ELEMENT, what burns out is a FILA-ment? Ai yi . . . We ARE in a fix, as G/ sd. Oh dear, oh dear—and here it is, Xmas eve!

I tell you what, i.e., I applied for the goddamn Gug/ again, gone again, gug again. Gug, gug, gug, etc. BUT let's just suppose, there, say, I made it, like. How wd it be to come up there, pues? Like, NEAR for a change. I think. I can't make it with the jungle drums or smoke signals anymore. God civilization ought to mean something. How's for rents thereabouts: there are 6 of us, etc. Ah well. But seriously.

Anyhow let me send something back, slow but sure, and write please whenever you can—and send more, i.e., you took ten yrs off my goddamn life with these too [^ + *too is four*.]. It will take that long to damn well catch up. Write! Ok.

All dearest love to all,
Bob

[enclosed in hand-drawn circle:]

Love comes quietly,
finally, drops
about me, on me,
in the old ways.

What did I know
thinking myself
able to go
alone all the way.
[*CP* I, 249]

[Also circled:]

THE HOUSE

Mud put
upon mud,
lifted
to make room,

> a house in
> form of cave,
> cool quiet
> and colder night.
>
> To sleep
> in, live in,
> to come in
> from heat,
>
> all form derived
> from need and kind,
> built hard
> with that in mind.
> [CP I, 237]

That 'least action . . .' really stands
me on my head, i.e., drives so close, so
finely. Well.
[handwritten, sideways on the page:]
    P.P.S.
    MARIMBA now wailing which will
    continue avec las bombas from
    time to time ("¡POW!") for three,
    SOLID fucking DAYS + NITES.
    Wow . . . . I mean . . . . Those Catholics are too much!

. . .

LETTER TO JONATHAN WILLIAMS

> San Geronimo Miramar
> Patalul, Such.
> Guatemala, C.A.
> January 5, 1960

Dear Dad,
        Mr Henry Rago suh of Po-et-ry is a-dunnin' me for proper
enclosures of yr olde self-address-ed stamp-ed envelope, etc. Wow. But the
poor devil probably has to account for every stamp to the Ladies, etc. Anyhow
can you please send me, for the enclosed dollar bill 6 15¢ air mail stamps. Wow
again—but it would be a great help, since he has 5 poems in hock there, and
want to keep him good-humored. He has taken 5 to date, for a new 'group' (the
one shot a year club, I guess). Anyhow I sent him another po-em and said help
was on the way. Ok.
        Sort of battered, Tuesday becomes the hump somehow, not Monday any-

more. That's a change at least. Bobbie's in on the bed reading the Saturday Evening Post (me next etc). Ain't we got culture . . . At least it's not Harpers.

I got copy of Allen G/s record I've been trying to hear since Sunday, i.e., came after lights had gone off with current—Monday Ruth washes her clothes in her automatic washer so there is none that day, likewise Tuesday (tho did get a brief part this morning before they cut us), and on, and on. Ai yi. Pretty crazy, no.

Do you know address (and cost of Burroughs' Naked Lunch) of Olympia Press? I want to get it. I.e., what I've seen I like a lot, for its own sound, etc.

So what's new in little old NY, etc. And do you remember the time we drove to NC via Brooklyn. I don't.

All love,
Bob

*"Keep the change . . .
—Old Saying—

. . .

LETTER TO ED DORN

Still trying to get the damn bk to you, don't know
what happened, i.e., my mother   January 9, 1960
likewise awaits & divers others.

Dear Ed,
                    Re the so-called magazine, let me get this straight & hence right away, etc. The poems you send I like less than A Country Song, a goddamn dull criterion I know. Anyhow, it doesn't matter how much they've been used this side of the Atlantic as long as their circulation in Deutschland has been minimal. Hence reprint is frequent in all the so-called selections. But (perhaps more to the point), to make your sound—or part of it, since the longer poems as those of the past summer make another place, etc—I want the compressed, flat, clear lyric you have in that set, i.e., in for the rest I suppose, to make a 'piece'. But let me show you what I'd thought of, all together, and perhaps it will come clear.

Duncan, that poem from THE NATION: 'Out of the Black'—do you
    remember it at all?

Williams: that poem for Flossie on her birthday, which ends: "you will
    believe me / a rose / to the end of time" (and perhaps another short
    one he's sent depending on Renate, i.e., not as good)

Zukofsky: 6 from Barely & Widely, that goes: "Send regards to Ida the
    bitch / whose hate's unforgiving . . . " and a stretch from "4 Other
    Countries" per:

..when their hymns
    and prayers

Brought no daily
    bread—and for fear no
other speech than
    out of their wild eyes.

Olson: a new one: "Least action love sat within the fire the spider / over the
    flame: 'pah' went the fingers (the spinnerets . . .)" (a wild one!)
Allen G/: Section II of <u>Kaddish</u>, with that:

"The key is in the window in the sunlight
at the bars the key is in the sunlight . . . "

Then you, i.e., that 2nd part, with the:

Thru the window
The man stood

Against a rake
He broods

By a burning bush
He thinks of the ground . . .

I love the <u>pace</u> of that poem, viz absolute, held so Christly sure, etc. Ah
well. Well I'm trying to twist yr arm of course—but most to the point,
send what else? There's time—though not much I'd guess since I want
to send the stuff off to let her get to work? Would it be ok to use above
to start? Then others, later? Because if anything happens it will be
continuous.

Agh/ etc. I'm sorry to be like a bull dog abt it, but what else.

We go to Gut City once a month, to stock up—a dreary city indeed, i.e., like
Mexico suburbia, with ugly modernistic mayan cartoons on public buildings,
etc. No thickness, no life—just commerciantes. Pretty damn sad at best. Though
anywhere—the drive in—is crazy, the mountains sticking up like Mother's
Milk, and everything growing, etc. Y pues . . .

That music sounds great and best I guess is to wait till we get there, and will
record it then. Viz will keep. And stuff coming in is apt to get hung up. As it is,
recorder now in getting repairs, condenser or something let go. We live in any
case.

Just now we is all getting over something, last night the Boss shot us full
of streptomycin, and take variety of capsules—look so good in brite plastic

wrappers—etc. Bobbie's stomack falling out, my head whirls . . . Otherwise fine. Certainly is warm, tho. Impossible to register sense of SNOW with sweat rolling off me in the late aft/ heat, etc. But I try/ till I die, etc.

Write. I read Rechy's gig re Los Lost Angeles, pretty funny. Like Juarez/EP bit better tho. Viz he knew the latter like he don't seem to (nor do I) former? Something. Ok. WRITE. I said that, and I will.

All love to all,
Bob

P.S. Viz later. (Alligator). Kirsten got a PARCHEESI set for Xmas, from a lady who felt sorry for her no doubt—so we've been PLAYING PARCHEESI, you dig? Howsa bout you turn the volume up on them records, maybe we could, hear them, down he/re? Pues. Anyhow Bobbie sends the en/closed.

He walked in the en clos ed night etc

Anyhow. What makes me out of those poems like you dig that sound you dig, is that, I think, the pitch is too much out of it, Ed. I am trying to say, you dig. Altogether seriously what bothers me always in such a poem (s) of yours is problem of you putting down your own pick-up,—somehow, i.e., the satire implied is goddamn painful, but of a kind of pain it doesn't let me off. Which is good? I goddamn well wonder. That way is in the longer poems too but placed among, so to say it, other ways, i.e., eyes, of looking & so forth. Anyhow the play of the so-called intelligence, it is something, in such a context, is I would guess even the curious shame-faced bewilderment of so-called intelligence, faced with definable minims of relevance which go crashing about like elephants etc. Like girls who shouldn't but do, etc. What about poems like the one ending 'I refused to go'. Or else—way in, viz deep as possible, as 'endurable' (?)—relevance seems to be the tension in them. The irrelevant is the edge of reality (?). Somewhere a voice is calling . . . Wow! To the tune of 3¢ in the foun-ting: THREE TRREEES IN THE FORRRESTTT . . . Anyhow. "We went thru the lumber mill together."

Because I think with very goddamn little extension, any of those would come home, viz like the way you IN-habit that terrifying woman in one of the longer, i.e., the one who 'digs' everything 'has a use', etc. In that context, there, she is given size by 'her' weight of interruption. Singly, viz as a single shot, I wonder cd she have, etc. But she sure does make it there. But by juxtaposition, reveals (call it weakly) the term of interruption, the waste, ludicrous, leaving one weak, ashamed, vicious, angry, laughing, sick, etc. That's good. And then on, etc.

The whole damn thing is a like emptiness here, bridged, broke, by not much—but family, solid, at best a crazy rapport, at worst a conglomerate lump of dissatisfaction, etc. So we live. After a time landscape becomes like could you fry an egg on it, with it, in it? Eh? How much em them cosas, cuanto questa, pues. You can never tell but you may go someday home with the wrong arms, etc. A common fate, like they say. One for all and all in one.

Wouldn't you? (I would propose it) [^ *DIG*] bing that thing? On the roof yet? Boy oh boy!!!! And that's a nice coat that guy is wearing. Dig the verticality of them fire escape pinnings, etc. I'm scared to death of HeighTs.

I wish I had a poem, something. Make the goddamn sign here, saturday night is the emptiest at the moment. Nothing but Saturday Eve-ning Posts, yet.

[Cut-out newspaper clippings/ads with RC's commentary follow:]

LIVE FLY BAIT: If you can't match a fly hatch, or even if you can and the trout won't take your artificial, try the real thing. Strip a small hook, say #14, and fasten a live fly to it with a drop of Duco cement.

Boy I'll bet that HURTS!!!

Trefflich's is the vision of an animal age,
and he goes gazelle-eyed contemplating   THE VISION . . .
the shapes of things to come:

If I had had . . . .
For the woman who
has everything . . .

[note in left margin] You know anything abt LANDSCAPE, edited there Santa Fe by JB Jackson etc? Looks pretty good.

. . .

LETTER TO WILLIAM CARLOS WILLIAMS

San Geronimo Miramar
Patalul, Such.
Guatemala, C.A.
January 10, 1960

Dear Bill,

Thank you, very very much, for those poems, and for all your kind words. God knows it is a blessing only you can give. I'll send them off to Renate Gerhardt, and I ought to hear shortly how all her plans are maturing, like they say. Then I will be able to tell you more exactly what is happening.

What you say of "structural elements" of course seems to me all the purpose. And I could, at that, make my own definition of the character of a poem, for me, from what you have written on this subject, e.g. the preface to THE WEDGE, the statement in the AUTOBIOGRAPHY that a poet thinks with his poem, "in that lies his thought," and god knows much much more, from the poems themselves and all the area they inhabit. Just now a new plague seems likely, or not really a 'plague', but a disposition toward the poem as though its character were given to declare a 'self-hood', actually a sort of re-investment of the old ego center, familiar enough from the worst of the Romantics. It must be that many of the younger writers, blasted as they are in their common living, secure themselves in the poem; or rather attempt to gain a presence less vulnerable there, i.e., from 'outside'. The very accomplishment of their techniques, at times, makes me wary of the outcome. I can't believe the poem can occur as a world partial to any nature, so to speak—or put it, I can't believe in an exclusive partiality, one that needs a ticket. But god knows we are blessed, any of us, younger, by having someone like Olson 'out there'—wow! He clears a lot, just as you do—the example is unforgettable, and forgives no embarrassment on any count whatsoever. Anyhow, I'd rather believe as he has it:

> . . . He left him naked
> the man said, and
> nakedness
> is what one means
>
> that all start up
> to the eye and soul
> as though it had never
> happened before . . .

For my own part—at times I feel the damn slippage, looseness, and become bewildered, lost in a kind of half-assed foray of what the hell next, etc. Sans the emotional tensions of the earlier marriage—which were always a spring-board for 'comment' no matter the vicious occasion, etc—I learn quiet again and more to the point perhaps a new term of endurance. At times the stakes seem high to me, the fact that we gamble daily (or not so dramatically, yet there they are) with a family of six people. Looking ahead is, at times, desperate, seeing myself so little equipped except by will to provide for us. Yet I begin to know how goddamn general is the usual ability which gets a job; and given opportunity (which is likely), I can make it.

But more to the point—it would be in the structure of the poem, long or short, that I would myself hope to see the 'world', not in the descriptive words which might otherwise attempt to state it. That accident and surprise, call it, revelation and violence have means to state themselves, there. Again and again the formal character of a poem becomes the crux—I don't mean that as inherited form, rather the nature of a poem in its own peculiar presence, etc. For me that would be where the <u>moral</u> takes hold, i.e., in the term of the building, not in the 'what'. I don't often know what I say, so to speak, or why I say it; but god willing am quite aware <u>how</u>. To think with my own mind in the vocabulary given me by my experience is work. It's such a temptation at times to grab the ready example, of a manner, and to let that carry me home. <u>Free verse</u> did make one very useful thing, i.e., a very particular self-consciousness about the use of any form—so that it would be, I think, very rare to find anyone now writing in a manner of which he was not aware. Perhaps this also breeds a lot of specious 'experiment', or loose imitation of the patterns of free verse, such as you have mentioned at times. But, thinking of Allen Ginsberg (god knows a conscientious man), it's curious to me that he speaks of HOWL (on the back of a record album far from any occasion that might ask the question) as "those poems are a series of experiments with the formal organization of the long line". He says other things too, but he says that. So we make a connection, he and I—we did anyhow, but I feel with him clearly, and it helps.

Anyhow just now I'm trying to keep moving, like they say—pursued by the things done and running like hell to catch up with what's to do, etc. An ideal state at that. God knows I can <u>afford</u> it, and what a pleasure that is. I.e., my boss here, fincero that he is—and he tries—comes over now and again and we find ourselves deep in a wish to get to common terms—and that's good. I.e., he wants <u>communication</u>, as he puts it, god knows as much as I do. That much is almost everywhere. A few days ago I went with him to give an intravenous to a sick Indian girl with a baby 7 months old, and the day before she'd been out washing clothes; this day she was it seemed in a coma, or so deep in resignation she hardly roused at all. The next morning she was dead. Here that is common, not quite daily but all so frequently it hardly is uncommon. What does one say to it, i.e., that life is not qualified by existence? I don't know. I see such a plethora of so-called riches in some places here, such a nothing in others—and yet no form not organic, a literal growth, could right the balance of it. All the more marked, it is, by the crazy growth of everything, all around us. Well, please take good care of yourself. Whenever you can write that would be wonderful, but I know you are busy—and I know you are there. Ok.

All my love to you all,

Bob

Here's one poem, like they say, y pues:
["The Rose" (*CP* I, 246)]

. . .

LETTER TO DONALD M. ALLEN

San Geronimo Miramar
Patulul, Such.
Guatemala, C.A.
January 16, 1960

Dear Don,

Your letter was good cheer, like they say, and I'll be starting on that review (using the books I have) over this weekend. That should be a pleasure. (It will be simple, even necessary, to refer to Charles' PRO/ VERSE, yet to include it specifically as a book being reviewed would tend to confuse it as major reference, and to sell it a little short by virtue of context. I.e., it ought to go into a general discussion on poetics per se, or else be given a single fix? I think.)

The BMR anthology idea is an interesting one, i.e. my wife had thought of it earlier and we had both been interested in what might be done; yet again I am loath to do that kind of work sans much hope of publication, etc. But what you suggest ought to be simple enough. (I don't have copies of the magazine here with me, but remember contents well—and most to the point could get some easily enough I think.) One thing in my own mind, though, is that the magazine stays an entity, a definition, and an activity—if allied to the college—still well distinct from it, and more a subsequence of ORIGIN's activity than of the college's, despite they paid for it. They paid for it because Olson talked them into paying for it, as a possible add for the place. Rightly or wrongly, at the time I think both he and I felt ORIGIN was getting diffuse—and/or Cid's intent to use so much foreign material meant necessarily less space for our own concerns— and would not run much longer; so that another magazine, taking over that area and extending it if possible would be of use to us all. That was what BMR began as, so to speak. The first issue was edited in Spain, with no referent to the college except title; and that was pretty much the case for all subsequent. I had complete freedom, from the college, and complete trust—two goddamn valuable things indeed. But I do not think BMR could be taken as a fair representation of the college itself—or if it could, it would only be the last two years of its existence. The college was apparently in constant process of change (one of its virtues, if one of its problems also), so that under Albers' administration, you would have found a totally different emphasis. You must remember that Black Mountain was, when I was there, never more than 20 odd students, and often less than a dozen. And of that number, Olson of course was my own center, and the magazine involved only Ed Dorn, Dan Rice, and one poem by Stefan Wolpe's wife, Hilda Morley, otherwise—as from the college directly (oh yes, Hellman, but he was an import, also). So descriptions or evaluations of the <u>college</u> per se in such an anthology would be misplaced I think. (The college was a support for the magazine, literally a backer. I forget above Mike R. [Michael Rumaker], Tom Field, and Duncan, who later taught there. I forget also perhaps the later associations the name qua <u>place</u> no doubt had, as instanced by the magazine, etc. But it was, or seems to me, an unreal predication. The magazine was a <u>term</u> of correspondences, among roughly a half dozen writers, who defined its center; and its value was that it had no geography or locus except in the work which they did. By that token it defined or related to a geography as variable and multiple as their attentions or situations might provide.)

Anyhow I wanted to suggest an alternative, granted it could be got, i.e., the divers letters on magazine editing—or sections from letters relating to that—from the letters I'd had earlier with Pound. They would make a very valuable statement I think. If he would allow their use, which is questionable. Anyhow that would be my own sense, plus a short note of introduction. The balance of material I would define a little more sharply, than did an actual issue of the magazine i.e., a greater weight of poems, prose, etc from the people I then thought central and continue to, e.g., Olson, Duncan, Layton, Rumaker, Zukofsky, and so on. Pound taught me one thing, for example, I never forgot, that granted a magazine must have a program—else it is all random chaos and uninteresting—that program must be felt as a core around which, not a box within which, every item. So that such an anthology could, usefully, make clear the core. Anyhow it's a fine idea, and I'd like to try it. Ok. This just to get back, and thanks for everything.
All my best,

> *Bob*

. . .

LETTER TO WILLIAM CARLOS WILLIAMS

> San Geronimo Miramar
> Patalul, Such.
> Guatemala, C.A.
> March 16, 1960

Dear Bill,

Your letter, and the two articles, were a great cheer and help, i.e., I think your own preoccupations are central for anyone now trying to make some sense. So the notes in SPECTRUM secure a lot for me, renewing older emphases of yours and citing the points of contact with the so-called tradition—and such a paragraph as that bottom of page 156, ought god knows to be clear to anyone. Ok! I suppose I read Mrs. Solt more cautiously, but then the <u>commonness</u> and <u>reasonableness</u> of her manner is, I think, very useful, granted she does grasp what you are doing—in general outline. So she makes a very useful and good-natured commentator. And god knows it seems to the point to have more of those, etc. I think she tends to 'talk it up' a little, with the philosophical implications—e.g. muddles 'behavioral', 'cultural', and esthetic (p. 23), and I think the <u>words</u> always 'beat time', albeit not to the exterior patterns to which they have been made to conform. (It seems to me Campion's singular quality, call it, that his ear could so 'nicely' place the variant of a minimally stressed extra beat, against the imposition of a pattern implying continuity, etc. Ah well. Anyhow what that was supposed to say was only: I don't think Mrs. Solt a poet, and I get very wary of comment of this kind—because the last 10 years, or simply those I for one grew up in, were so stifled with exterior regulations from people in no wise concerned, practically, with the issue.)

But most to the point, I think your own concerns find counterpart very widely now. For example, this from THE FIFTIES, re the iambic pattern, written by Robert Bly (who is no revolutionary, nor even a poet, himself, of a very inventive nature, etc—despite what this seems to imply): "(Re Donald Halls' work) The book was also praised and blamed for its use of traditional meters. But we can see the heavy use of 'traditional' meters in the fifties in a new light. The 'traditions' in question are not deeply American, but come from English poetry, and of course, for us the <u>cultural</u> 'father' is English. Iambic meter is used not only because it is the only well-developed meter in the language, but also it is used psychologically, so to speak, to avoid offending the English. Since within us, the English, the dominating middle class society, God, and the father, all mean the same, the iamb serves the purpose of avoiding offense to all these three." Earlier in the same article: "Poetry (at the beginning of the fifties, e.g. Ciardi) was writing itself in nice iambic lines, which the middle class in America has always loved, and with which it was long familiar . . ." To make that the issue of course tends to lead off into other dilemmas, social preoccupations, etc. But it's a sign, I think, of how widely the unrest, and suspicion, of such invested patterns, has gone, that this can be written by such an (ultimately) safe man as Bly. Curiously enough, I think now the danger may be that a 'pattern' may derive from free verse effects attempting to carry the same authorities that the iambic line has had, e.g. Mrs. Solt's poems in the issue of FOLIO after this one you'd sent.

But behind all that, the core of writing is very solid I think, in point of the men now available both for example and for help. I mean that ten years ago I used to think with dumbstruck awe of a <u>time</u> when Williams, Pound, H. D., Marianne Moore, and so on were <u>all</u> present, and available to one another. I've since learned that that sense of it may well carry its own distortions. But there is now such a 'school' to be gone to, in writing, I don't think anyone need feel cheated nor without available instruction, etc. I've been reading Zukofsky's work more and more closely, he takes time for me, but as in <u>4 Other Countries</u> (and too, the poems in Anew and Some Time, etc) I can find there certainly all the intensity of 'metrical' concern I could want. I.e., your work holds in my own ear as a kind of 'ground plan', i.e., my danger is, often, that (tired) I will write (or have done so) using the memory of your figures as a floor for what I do, etc. Equally Olson (almost Zukofsky's opposite, in his feel of the line, a horizontal thrust (in which last lies his 'vertical', i.e., the 'energy component, the <u>weight</u> he can push up into a word, or concept, in the line) in large patterns, but singularly close and fine many times in particulars). And too, Duncan, whose Poem Beginning With A Line From Pindar, in last Evergreen Review, razzledazzles the classic mode, for me, in <u>common</u> style, i.e., not a Wasteland of effects, etc.

These three, with yourself (and the Pound I know, I mean take to for myself and said uses), are my own disciplines, or sources of same, in writing. And there are others, god knows. But think of what Dennie has done—by reading and listening. I mean, the means wherewith to control the line, and to invent upon its nature 'fit occasion' like they say, I can't feel lacking to us. Talking last summer with Allen Ginsberg, I find the same concerns in him—and in opening sections of Kaddish, there seems a much more tangible (certainly closer, and more determined) sense of measure. What I do fear is that personal separations, and the size of the horrors surrounding, will break up useful coherences, i.e., too many of the letters I now get from New York, for example, are attacks on this or that man, arguing <u>personal</u> objection and the like. I am out of that here—though even here I get it, people who take that exception to me. Ah well again. But if the whole thing withdraws into 'teams', then I can only see trouble. (The 'beats' are the prime target at present and yet, and yet, i.e., Ginsberg is a very helpful friend, in many ways, and not least in the range of line he is attempting, no matter just now with what success, because the very width of the divergence attempted seems to me useful. In 1940 it seemed there were only five or six ways possible to write a poem—and now the 'security' is beginning to break. I hope!)

There is a sudden line in the introduction to Zukofsky's "All eyes!" (from BOTTOM, printed in this latest issue of FOLIO): " . . . the contest any poet has with his art: working toward a perception that is his mind's peace . . . " quoted from him. If it is one's nature, that the whole world must be subject to his desire, then I suppose only monstrosities can be the issue but I can't believe that would serve a 'measure', if only because words are common, eventually. I talked once to the painter Philip Guston, a wonderfully gentle and kind man, with wife and daughter, who told me, if he were painting, then even that his house were burning down and his family with it, he could not believe could distract him. That is 'amoral' but of such a kind that it seems only, to me, an issue of loyalties. Which same is endless, of course. Well,—thanks again, i.e., please write whenever you can, it's a great help to me, selfishly enough. I hope all goes well for you. Jonathan had told me of a new poem, The Italian Garden—and I certainly look forward to seeing that. I'll enclose a picture of us all, all six of us (by god!), and in this world that's probably amorality enough. Ok.

All love,

Bob

. . .

LETTER TO LOUIS ZUKOFSKY

San Geronimo Miramar

Patulul, Such.

Guatemala, C.A.

March 30, 1960

Dear Louis,

The book got here safely—and thank you very very much. I think it is a complete success, in all possible senses, i.e. most minimal perhaps (though not truly), the format is excellent, sturdy, quiet, and clear. The writing is of such order, to my mind, that there is nothing simple to say about it at all. Viz you are a great man. Ok! More specifically, I'm very caught by the image of 'time' in the book, and/or how it details a time, of the years of its writing, yet comes (as '12') to a round of itself, again and again, clear and solid. It's a very damn <u>beautiful</u> thing, I think. I don't damn well know how, very often, you manage such diversity of emphasis, and such a lightly graceful variation of line. Well, wow. And an image such as 'face of sky', as you play that, recurs to secure me, reading.

But look, like they say, rather than try to make clear, here, all I want to say about it (and to tell you all I hope to learn from it, selfishly enough), I want to wait a little till I'm not sitting here, waiting for lunch, and then through the afternoon, then the drive to Guatemala City to see about a stolen passport (mine, in a jacket that was taken out of a car there, window broken, etc.) I.e., <u>that</u> your book again gives me the ground whereby to use it. Ok! The essay for Paul is equally lovely, or if not 'equally', is lovely, well, <u>is</u>. That's it, isn't it. The note on you is a curious one, and I begin to realize, like they say, a curious thing about Dr. Williams, that the more he respects a man, the more worried he becomes about the statement of it. I.e., Z. plays a funny tune in his mind, and clearly one he listens to, of necessity. So that's good too. God, you have fine-ness. I really know of no one more exact than yourself.

A sort of footnote: since this edition is 200, I hope you will put aside one good clearly inked copy at least, because I must believe it one of the books of the century like they say. And I should think, soon, some publisher like Grove, or whoever, ought to do it. Offset from this format would be a simple and inexpensive means, e.g. Edwards Lithograph Co. in Ann Arbor, Michigan, could use this text, I'd think, and make a book in no way less than it is. Well, that's presumptuous and future: the two great sins I believe. Anyhow.

Is Spring there yet, i.e., I'm hoping. Unhappily we will not now be coming to New York (I couldn't get any readings, since it was a bad time of year for them—and I'm a 'bad time of year' anytime I think. So.) But we will, one of these days, no matter.

This is just a note, like they say—but I'd been concerned to tell you how much I do like the book, albeit I'd like to be more clear about it all, shortly. Ok. I hope all goes well there.

All our love to you all,
Bob

. . .

LETTER TO PAUL BLACKBURN

c/o Hall
520 San Lorenzo
Albuquerque, N.M.
[written in Guatemala]
April 24, 1960

Dear Paul,

We are trying to pull ourselves together como se dice for the hoist north—god knows many miles of pretty goddamn slow progress in the VW bus we have, but it is, most of it, crazy country, so will drive slowly and observe the view. It's good to hear that things there are making it. I had great hope of coming and am very hungry to talk, and all of it—yet the goddamn readings couldn't be worked out for the time I could come etc. So, that was no good. Ah well.

Re our multiple colleagues etc, I haven't seen much—or just now chance to read is pretty limited, and when I see magazines see them too fast, too etc. For me it is pretty much the same old biz, i.e., Zukofsky (have you read his "A"?), Olson, and Robt for the 'cosmos' and literal knowhow (the Venice Poem I think is so-called major, likewise Owl, likewise Ode (in ER lately), and so on, i.e., he knows I think), and Dennie many times, yrself. Then god knows also, Phil Whalen in much that he writes—I think the speed of his method makes sense, often. He is a very sharp man in person. Gary is deceptive, moving so quiet, Rexroth-like in earlier poems, now apparently much more relaxed and 'common', e.g., in Galley Sail Review poem called KYOTO SKETCH, viz 'easy'. He likewise is a very intelligent man. And a very nice one. I'm much impressed

by Ed Dorn also—e.g. THE AIR OF JUNE in last BIG TABLE: that line and
rhythm sense, very particular to him. He is from Olson, but more 'evasive',
wryer, lighter—more like Zukofsky in ways. Etc. Nobody very damn 'new',
nobody really very damn interested in the tecnics as I remember your copy
of Yeats et al. Does anybody talk like that anymore? I wonder . . . Jack Spicer
is an extraordinary man, one of the most perceptive I ever met. So is Allen
Ginsberg—and I think much that he does is missed in gas of the 'social effects'
etc. Viz I look (contrary to Dennie) to the terms of his area, that's where (no
matter how ludicrously my own relation to it must seem) I think the space
will come. The 'apposite' reality he's got hold of in any case fascinates me, very
much so in Burroughs' NAKED LUNCH, i.e., the only novel in years to tell a
story in 'apposition'. All the rest begin once upon a time etc. Too slow, I think.
Anyhow I both like and buy, so to speak, all that so-called area: from Kerouac's
MAGGIE CASSIDY etc to Burroughs, its apex, and the tension between is Allen
G/. Ah well again. I haven't seen <u>anything</u> come out of any university in years.
Okeydokey.

What is Pound's THRONES like? I want to get a copy once in States. (Re
above, I'd agree also on Corso, those shorter lyrics in particular, viz a natural. Y
pues—because that's it, always.)

Things go well enough re the children, but very damn far away, always. There
was no difficulty in seeing them that time I did manage to get there—she is
remarried (since) and that as well has eased things. But the distance is con-
stantly a problem, i.e., to manage to hold the relationship which I'm anxious to
do. The goddamn gossip etc was never very right, or interesting. I write to them
simply and that keeps a form at least.

So. We leave here roughly a week from today. I'll write a decent letter once
there, and relaxed again—but please write likewise, i.e., did Macmillan publish
your book? I'd like to see new poems anytime you can get way to type same.
Our tape recorder was stolen here but have hopes to get another in States.
Will get you a tape etc if I can. Things are going really goddamn well i.e. that
Scribner's stories break was a good one, and May issue of POETRY had got
ten poems yet. Wow . . . And/or that sure has changed some. Ok. Again please
write, and I will. I hope it all goes ok. Your life, the goddamn LIVE one, sounds
GOOD. And what else, viz creo que si.

All my love,
Bob

. . .

LETTER TO ED DORN

> San Geronimo Miramar
> Patalul, Such.
> Guatemala, C.A.
> September 14, 1960

Dear Ed,

Many thanks for the quick answer. Shortly after I wrote, I had a goddamn fistula, I never clearly heard of same, from a bruise on my knee, where I'd bumped the corner of the bed, viz nothing, but roughly two weeks later is horrible goddamn infection, all under minute scab, they say in horses goes through you dig. Wow . . . Anyhow that struck me down for a few days. Up and hobbling, lovely bad temper etc, today. Onward. Compresses every two hours, face squeezing the goddamn thing morning and night, gives the day a measure. Two shots of penicillin didn't make it, now on something else, three. Agh. I love it! I have my own little field hospital in bedroom, working with clocklike precision—myself etc. I hate the goddamn interruption, i.e., last so-called writing at nuvvel, was in bed, board over me, goddamn leg aching, and even then, there's nothing to say . . . What a life. So what's new.

I wrote 13 single-spaced pages of sd novel, really wailing, then dead full complete udder stop. I hated it, every goddamn sniveling word. Every thing seemed contrived, cooked up, cute, wise guy—partly it is, but partly is drag of not being able to do it all in an afternoon. I liked it, very much, as writing, i.e., as (3) so-called chapters started to make it etc. I think the death must be looking back in this bizness. Have you found that so, like they say. Viz HELP. Anyhow now a little cooler, and more desperate, think to go on, because it is there at least, what there is for beginning. I'm so hung with that squeeze it all up and throw, that it's hard to get another swing. This so far goes very anecdotal, really encouraged by reading that THE GINGER MAN, and partly tone of Douglas Woolf, [William] Eastlake, et al. Not near as fast as Burroughs, who is, nor as in and out, surreal—but I want to go with stories as they come. Hence in first few pages is a lot of digression, and little 'purpose'. Fair enough. It's third person, I suppose closer to THE BOAT and stories like that, than anything else. I don't know, i.e., it's doing what I thought it would at least, taking a whole goddamn new kick. I sent last section to Carroll, fool him into taking it and see what it looks like, if possible. Here I read it over and over, etc. Maybe it's funny? Oh dear.

So we are all alive. Settling more and more. I haven't started the school yet, due to leg. All the kids are restless. Vague hordes slide in and out of rooms, muttering. No sympathy etc. Bobbie has the house very damn comfortable and clear. Juana, who has as last year crazy way of putting books back in the bread cupboard etc, knives in the toilet, or the equivalent, but a good memory thank god, is likewise picking up. We eat well. Lots of oranges presently, avocadoes, and face the same damn social problem I guess it is, but more sturdily than last year, i.e., have always feeling of being on that limb etc. But we sawed it off last year, so no problem. Lonely at times, as last year. We miss you god knows very much, i.e., unequivocal friends like they say. In ten words or less.

That way it was crazy with John, so quickly getting through earlier hang-ups at Black Mountain, which had then seemed considerable to me at least, cutting into what was present. I like that, very damn much, with people. I.e., assuming someone is not carrying axe he'll drop when the right time comes etc, who can make it with the gang-angle of, we'll get yez yet etc. Or qualify the occasion with some goddamn memory that has not been reinvoked (as I felt Ribak did that last meeting, to excuse myself from that non-sequitur perhaps). Anyhow—I can appreciate it even if I can't always make it etc. But I think I can, or try to. Ah well. But it is dreary to be registered against a commitment so shallow as that I feel Max's must be, i.e., I don't know certainly, he don't say etc. Ah well again. John likewise talking of some young sculptor there he thinks might make it, apparently picked up on him, all but refuses drinks, any contact, takes anything J/ says now, as some involved irony etc. Perhaps Max suffers from that a little, because he's never once made any sign of using me at all, at all. Max will always make it but he needs angles, a straight scene would see him outside, all by himself, and sans occasion for the side-taking, the jolly conspirator, be it a night on the town, or the ultimate divorce, there is very little. He can't talk out, only off, the so-called sound. That's a painful limit, as I've had occasion to know like they say. But anyhow again here as last spring, when that scene was, it's hard to credit as a real bizness. They all stay local to themselves, and that's a hard union. The pleasure of Jack, for another, or completely Ray, is way they make it out to you, there, want to see for themselves the other term, viz human—not that bit of adding said presence to their own by weird process of osmosis a la Kerouac Serpent of the World. Anyhow I like to take rides.

Fuck Esquire. I don't think I was being nice etc. If you can control a <u>response</u> to an 'area' of speech, viz narrative, a sequence of speculation, terms of self-insight, problem of relationship, sudden 'objective' event, etc, that's better. It must be the idea of the controlled love making, the man in control, the man at the switch etc, that makes one think a novelist likewise has to 'control' his subject. Reminiscent of Kline saying, if I painted what I knew, it would be a bore only etc. You don't 'control' what you don't know, you make a way to it. What then happens, quien sabe. Morals exist in the term of response, complex of registration, or where else I can't quite think etc. I was reading again your piece on Maximus, <u>place</u>, e.g., "Place, you have to have a man bring it to you," likewise p/ 9, thinking of the story of Beauty, the novel's street, bar scene, woods and distance etc. I don't think you have to change a word, or any word that comes from that disposition. Y pues. I hate the so-called fight, it sickens me completely—I'm never fair! Presently I'm trying to con Herb Gold into being reference for me for Gug/, for bucks, oh city's stones, my fireplace etc . . . Wow what a cleaner . . . Anyhow I only con when it hurts. Yahooo! I got Hugh Kenner, I know people who know it, don't say it, to them committee, who can speak to nothing, an occasion yet. Viz they say it but into wood ears etc. So, bring on the Trojan horse etc, likewise wood. I just read that Lawrence book you gave me, lovely goddamn thing—and know more also. So. Things feel good. Write soon and I'll do likewise.

All our love to you all,

Bob

[Bobbie Creeley's note in left margin of p. 1] *Now it can be told—I <u>did</u> feel a strain the last two times we were there—partly the approaching departure—but was ashamed because I thought "Jealousy?" What night? etc—well not to get schmaltzy but your house feels like home & suddenly I realized all the beds were used up or some such thing—but Ed's letter describes it too—wanting to sit & talk without—oh I'm sorry was that <u>your</u> foot? . . . anyway_____*

[RC's note above salutation] P.S. It's very happy you met Buddy again, i.e., I think he is there always, and tries god knows, likewise always. So, that's good. I would very much like to have that picture as and when. Ok. Will hope to have some of this place to send before too long. Vamos a ver.

[note in left margin of p. 2] *P.P.S.* Later: 2 more pp/ on nuvvel, go go go etc. Five more & I can apply for a Saxton Award . . . Bobbie is writing at hers likewise. Read any new novels lately? Why doesn't Max start one.

[note in left margin of p. 2] I read Alex Trocchi's novel again here, much better 2nd time, because argument fades to events call them, also I lose my 'personal' investment bred of having known him etc. I'll send copy next time we get to city.

[Bobbie Creeley's note in left margin of p. 2] *"At least it's better than Parcheesi"—Bobbie*

[Bobbie Creeley's note in right margin] *Letters <u>do</u> make it out—I think people chose the wrong path somewhere way back when they started talking anyway— like if they hadn't we might all be mental telepathing now—save stamp money etc—also you could think back at 'em. love to all—Bobbie*

. . .

LETTER TO WILLIAM CARLOS WILLIAMS
San Geronimo Miramar
Patalul, Such.
Guatemala, C.A.
September 21, 1960

Dear Bill,

Yeah! I.e., I agree. As ever that's a concern, and I wish I could contrive for myself a way to hammer at least the <u>feel</u>, call it, of the argument home once and for all. At times I've been embarrassed by lack of a formal evidence, and/ or you must have heard that business of, well it's a common vocabulary by and large isn't it, and the syntax seems to be roughly the same, in fact very much the same, isn't it, and there are of course dialect variants I suppose one calls them, but aren't they minor ("isn't it") etc etc. I think that earlier statements of yours beginning "Therefore each speech having its own intrinsic character etc" is the best yet statement of the premise. It <u>must</u> be (as you keep it so insistent an attention) that the <u>context</u> of a language, the-place-where-used-and-by-whom, is the major aspect of its use in poems, not the generalized structure of tradition that may otherwise inform it.

That way, it isn't simply a question of slang, or small variants of like (dialect) order—but the whole sit of the words to their occasion (the <u>why</u> of speaking) that batters through to new distinctions. Such a poet as Ginsberg is utterly foreign to the English idiom, as are you, in another way quite separate. That way too, Whitman demonstrates the appetite for a new occasion for the poem, for speaking—a new content which the language must be brought to embody, carry, get there somehow. The English ... (but for Lawrence, possibly Lewis—though like him as I do, he shows still that analytic appetite peculiarly European, not the accumulative, 'creative' action of Whitman et al. Lowell, Emerson etc were the Englishmen, certainly were hot for that approval—as Whitman was debarred from being, just by his 'words'. Curiously Hopkins picked up on the <u>order</u> of Whitman's line apparently, but seems to have mistaken its purpose, thinking it to be an approximation (as Hopkins' own) of a nervous pattern, a tension of speech, etc. Hart Crane shows sadly enough a break-down between the two traditions, i.e., in his attempt to wed the impulses, energies, of the American term to that of the English sense of metric (Crane's weakest link god knows, except for the shorter poems wherein he feels the structure more immediately).) Well, the English—not the same.

Yet this summer, in company with a partly English friend, Gael Turnbull, I found this incomprehensible to him, i.e., he must have thought me a fractious colonial. He himself lives here, and had lived in Canada—but for him it harks all back to tradition, to 'colonialism'—and that of course ends that. I wish there were a simple means for registering, and/or demonstrating, for such argument the position of speaker in relation to words, and then in relation to intended hearer—i.e., I do think that's where the terms really separate. Gael for example supposes, English-wise, each poem to be a unit, complete, a finished 'work of art' [^ *necessarily "in the tradition"* . . .], and that 'work of art' is of course another divergence, for the American. 'Work of art' for him [^ *American*] is a pragmatic instance of use, of <u>fit</u> in terms of occasion. Does it <u>go</u>? (Olson echoes this appetite for <u>action</u>, as do all the goddamn painters now with hands and eyes etc.) The English want a misty sort of mystique, of beauty, formed from the world perhaps but ultimately out of it. Where else could Edith Sitwell be a major poet, or Dylan Thomas for that matter? American poets of that school seem almost embarrassed by a tangible reference to something that might really hurt, be not (Aristotle-wise) 'purged' (but what do they do with the evidence, viz do they flush that away down the traditional Toilet also?) etc. Well, it is that American poems are often such a close instance of the environment they spring from, are shots from the hip in that way. There's no time for English brooding etc.

But I'm getting vaguer and vaguer. I wanted to quote this for you, from a Harvard professor of linguistics, Whatmough, a pocket book called LANGUAGE:

> A 'new' poetry comes hand in hand with new departures in a language, its total resources. The most recent English and American poetry partakes of the great changes taking place in the English language, which are part and parcel of the contemporary environment; the same is true of political propaganda, or of advertising copy. The same 'emotive' and 'dynamic' components pervade all three, etc.

Not enough by any means, but tacitly a position which would allow for your argument, i.e., would better defend it than many. I.e., elsewhere: "poetic discourse is highly peculiar to <u>a language</u> etc."

This for the moment, rapidly becoming a digression! And aptly enough. But I would like to speak more of it, like they say—and god knows to say again I agree. Ok.

Just now starting to teach again, a distraction but not much. We'll be here another year I think and then something else, I don't yet know quite what. But time-wise, and family-wise, all feels very very happy. I've begun a novel, with hopes, but not enough yet to see much—but something to do and to pay attention to. I hear Laughlin is to do a collection of your plays and another book, i.e., I met Winfield T/ Scott in Santa Fe who had seen you not too long before, so that was a pleasure. Anyhow all goes well. And anytime you want to call out the militia, let me know! Ok.

All our love to you all,
Bob

P.S. As contrast to present applause for Durrell—old hat!- Wyndham Lewis'
TIME & WESTERN MAN shows English strength in language. Wm. Burroughs'
NAKED LUNCH—however "ugly"—is instance of American language structure
put to use with remarkable surety I think.

. . .

LETTER TO JEROME ROTHENBERG

San Geronimo Miramar
Patulul, Such.
Guatemala, C.A.
November 6, 1960

Dear Jerry,

Thank you so much for the copy of your book—which seems to
me very handsome and clear. Thanks too for the copy of Robert Kelly's notes.
As yourself I find them interesting. I think, however, that this concept of 'image'
becomes very general, i.e., generalizes, pretty quickly. E.g., "The clothed percept
is the image." This is too vague for me, since I feel that speaking, or writing,
itself becomes a "percept" and in this guise a deep influence on the "thing said."

More particularly, as a contrast, read Williams' notes on Zukofsky at the
back of A, i.e., Williams speaks of his own sometimes bewilderment at Z/s
intent, i.e., "The poems whatever else they are are grammatical units intent on
making a meaning unrelated to a mere pictorial image." I know that Kelly also
has more in mind than that, i.e., "pictorial image," and yet I feel he consciously
or not uses the 'picture' as a base term from which his sense of 'image' derives.
That is, I feel he means all to be shaped to the term of an 'image' (picture), the
"verbalized image" as he says. In my own sense, there is an 'image' in a mode,
in a way of statement as much 'image' as any reference to pictorial element,
e.g. the white night, the color of sorrow, etc. Pictorial image there relates of
course as any other element, but to my mind not as importantly as rhythm,
or structure in which rhythm may operate freely—as a 'poem' etc. Again, as a
parallel to these concerns, Zukofsky writes apropos some poems sent him: "(one
is best) when the analysis comes thru the lyrical; the danger of The Woman and
The Plan is that the analysis sometimes becomes melodramatic; on the other
hand, getting an image by something like the privation of it or transforma-
tion of it thru the physiology of the sound and cadence counteracts it—the
melodrama . . . " It is that Kelly describes all this question of mode too briefly,
i.e., "The image is the measure of the line. The line is cut to fit it . . . " Of course,
but in quite what sense? Isn't then the image as much that cut, of line, as it is
what that cut of line makes, of a reference, pictorial or otherwise? That's where I
myself tend to wander. I cannot agree to that which does not place great empha-

sis upon structure—in all possible reaches, certainly in Kelly's also—and so again feel the problem which something even as careful as this seems leads to.

For example, take the discussion of that line from your own poem, in which he drops the "No!", i.e., the first word in the line, in this case syllable, itself an exclamation, and so obviously of some inevitable weight in the whole term of said line? I at least wondered. I.e., what is a 'line' if you can drop such a word, and then calculate its measure. I don't follow that.

But I don't want to spend the whole letter with such apparent quibbling, i.e., you'll see simply enough wherein I am bothered—and why I can't quite agree.

The whole presence of this sense of image bothers me a little, in present work. I hope I understand what lacks, as Robert Bly might speak of them, are pointed out—but I don't honestly feel them as a lack, and/or believe poetry to encompass a great many manners and emphases, from 'epic' to 'lyric', and feel of course that in each a dominance will be aimed at for this or that aspect of the so-called whole. I think translation, dealt with too loosely, has not been able to surmount the problem of logopoeia, and this has made an accumulation of loosely structured poems exciting mainly for their 'content', their reference as 'pictures' of states of feeling etc. I'd hate to see that generalizing manner become dominant, no matter the great relief of having such information about what's being written in other countries etc. But I wouldn't back an inch off the need for as craftsmanlike poems as possible, not at all meaning 'tidy' etc. We are too far along, in many grounds so-called, now, to back off e.g., from Ginsberg in open- ing KADDISH sections, to Dorn's long line in THE AIR OF JUNE, to O'Hara's casual line, or Duncan's formal organization of 'canto' structure in POEM BEGINNING WITH A LINE BY PINDAR—Olson's <u>Maximus</u> and 'field,' Williams' late poems, etc. I.e., it seems a bad time to lose sight of those areas. It would make a poet like Corso if he might learn them. It makes Burroughs, in prose, singular in his ability. So . . .

In your book I like for example the first two verses of Invincible Flowers (then I feel it tends to wander out too much?). The first poem in the book, though the 'little boy' is a little hard, i.e., harks to almost a sentimentality for me. I like the one for "A Small Manufacturer"—and those of the 'president', i.e., where the poem comes clearly along, sans apparently concerned emphases etc, just says it very lightly. Less so, in that way, The Sorrowing Clown. I like "A Small Poem" in that sense, sudden and sure etc. You will know that I have to be at some distance from you on those poems depending on this sense of 'image' very strongly, i.e., The Taste of Joy, The Giant et al. I find the under-structure too let go there, i.e., not working as it might, and the line by that let to run out almost too simply. But that again is a preoccupation in which I may well be in error. I cannot so to speak agree to the error, but prove me wrong like they say and I'll hope to god I can see it. Ok!

It is anyhow a little goddamn specious to pick away like this. I am grateful to see the book, and very happy that you have it out—i.e., it's an interesting beginning in no sense 'polite' (for me to say so), and you will take it from there god knows. Anyhow figure my worry as follows: that the 'imagists' had in mind a sharp registration of an 'objective' substance, be it tree or woman's mouth, an avoidance of general words etc—and that proved dull once accomplished, i.e., the poems got awfully quick and then glib and finally banal in their laconic method—they left a lot out because they could only concentrate upon the 'quick picture' etc. Now 'image' becomes an involvement with the psychology of reference, what the preoccupation with structure tended to forget (and so became often dry in its lack of 'content', simply a machine of manner etc)—but I wonder if image can be isolated in this way, or if it will not tend to make sensational reference over-valued. This is the aspect of Surrealism to me least interesting for example—the scarey parts (however interesting on first contact etc). Anyhow that's what's on my mind.

All my best to you,

Bob

. . .

LETTER TO ED DORN

San Geronimo Miramar
Patalul, Such.
Guatemala, C.A.
November 20, 1960

Dear Ed,

That was a crazy letter, and thank you, very goddamn much, i.e., yourself at the controls that don't control like a goddamn nightmare: and that fence, and Uncle Billy Goat I did know who was, from time Chan wanted to go down thru there, but Helene thought it better not como se dice. The ogre, yet. Well, jesus christ. Ok. Likewise thank you for the pictures, I like them, fuck it—I can see. Ok. Paul keeps me completely sane with that crazy smile, so it works.

I figure you must have been (which is why no letter before) and may now be back from, NYC. Wow. Viz I am very anxious to hear what and where and who happened, there, i.e., are the streets really paved with gold etc. It seems an awfully long way away from here. Ok. How were the people? E.g., Dennie, Paul Blackburn, LeRoi, Allen, et al. I'm very curious. I hope to god it all went well, a fugging pleasure. Ok. That was very happy news about the new car, and maybe it's simple (tho it's not) but Buddy that way has always seemed to me god knows exceptional. Viz one cd say, well it's easy for him, but he does it, again and again. I like the clarity of his presence finally, the staying in, straight—no

matter the present hang-up or I hope to god not. Do you see him at all now. I.e.,
he's been a friend for me much as Ray for you in that that sense of him <u>there</u>
has always been true. It hasn't really meant I've had that much as so-called
years went by to do with him, being elsewhere all the time—but still <u>there</u>, viz
a man in a place I knew unequivocally with no changes or false faces etc. You'll
certainly know what that means.

So how's magnanimous Max, I really goddamn well hope well you dig. I've
got some hard news for him, viz Scribners took the goddamn poems lock stock
& barrel. I'm thru. Wow! Tell Max to think of the bright side no matter. It can
only get worse from here, so to speak. Y pues . . . But it is crazy, and unbeliev-
able—and presently a little hung up since must clear rights on A Form Of
Women, so as to be able to sign it all over to them etc. Well, wow again. The
goddamn sun must be shining somewhere. So if I can clear it with Jonathan,
and Eli W/, that's it. I've been scared to death, goddamn two letters stolen, no
word but a card beginning 'Dear Madam . . . We have received your ms/ etc.'
And finally last night it made it, I couldn't sleep the whole goddamn night, sat
staring up at so-called sky, so far, so long, so singular it felt. I've been saying the
past two weeks, to hell with them, they'll screw the book anyhow,—but it's very
different right now. Viz there's got to be a place for us if this can happen.

That aside, and finally it is, Olson's MAXIMUS just came in, looking too
much I thought, i.e., wild. How about that note following Burke poem, viz <u>that's</u>
it. You could knock anybody out with that one—and wow what metrics comes
in those later, read of a piece, he is really too fucking much. He wrote he had
finally got selected poems straight with Grove, and tho short, it has to get thru,
no matter. We need a damn magazine. Start pounding at Cid to let us back
in etc. This fugging standing around in alleys gets dreary. 'I'll see you in the
White Dove Review-who . . . ' Oh well, but that I think has got to come back, the
sooner the better.

I think this gig with Texas may make it, we'll all retire with Texas oil wells
and crazy wild blonde women be so respectable to our wives: like this is Mrs
Vast Oil Well of 1982, she blows, filthy bitch, but she likewise gushes. Oh well.
I have such dreams of place, all the ice cream I can eat, beer to drink—blow
up Winfield Townley Scott's who is really Edwin A/ Rob/—getting drunk here
Ed—with luck. Persistence.

I would love to talk, such an appetite this afternoon, to be with you all, if
wishes were horses then beggars cd ride—and we'd be there with you, pronto. I
wrote a story hey in which like a line you dig of English song, so nice like that,
England type light, etc., and the poor son o' bitch in same is wandering roughly
toward Sheridan Sq NYC to find Hudson St and has rapidly begrimingly be-
coming copy of book paperback song(s) he is trying to get to woman he (then)
loves, miles of intention, 4 pages only. He could never get it. I'll try to get that

to you soon, likewise shot one of even less 3 (?), 2 pages, of man who goes into church thinking it bar very stoned indeed that time, my Story you have to bear with me, carry me all the way home etc.

Did you see Burroughs in SIDEWALK 2, let me know: very good, the 'cut up' method, i.e., 'cut yr way <u>out</u>'—very fabulous in fact. He has the craziest sense of what goes on in socially hip housing developments. Wow . . .

So, no school today. Write soon, please. Again, I hope it's all ok there. Here is ok, sludge of nada for nothing, no people, whole universe dead here, far beyond Conrad's ambition <u>or</u> imagination. But uz is no matter. Send other pix soon of local locale, as ground under feet daily, and head sometimes stepped upon can get up after all. Ok. Let's go see that goddamn gen'l Winflap Brownpee Spot, make him read his whole goddamn poegtic worggs to tune of loud screaming as we fug his wifve and childrun, who hopelessly hang, from ropes (you dig). Ok. Take care. Do write. All is well.

All our love to all,
Bob

<u>P.S.</u> *Indians last nite as I was awake weird echo-box sounds as (outside the house) "who (who) ha (ha) huh (huh) hee (hee)" (an + on + on).*

· · ·

LETTER TO WILLIAM CARLOS WILLIAMS

*"To Be Recited To Flossie On Her Birthday"

San Geronimo Miramar
Patalul, Such.
Guatemala, C.A.
December 18, 1960

Dear Bill,

A small magazine in Albuquerque, for which I've been a contributing editor, needs a push, and I want to ask you if they may print (or rather re-print from James Laughlin's first publication of it last year) the birthday poem* for your wife. I had written you earlier about it, for a magazine that Renate Gerhardt was trying to begin in Germany—but I've never heard again from her nor know what may have happened. If it is still agreeable with you, this other magazine would be much honored to have it—and their printing is clean and clear, albeit their circulation is small. In any case I wrote them I would ask you about it; and will enclose an envelope addressed to them, i.e., if it's all right a note to them will make that clear, and if not, simply forget it and they'll understand it is not convenient. Ok. I'm embarrassed to ask the same favor twice.

Things here are ok, we just now have summer like weather. We do all the time we are here as it happens—and the climate is almost too idyllic if that is possible. But we are (always a but) too isolated finally, i.e., the romance of the place like they say breaks down seeing the poverty of the people, and the sluggish colonialism, forever and ever amen. I.e., how to like it, is of course not possible. I'm hoping for a job back in the States this coming year, in the southwest again, because our children get older and need company and more roots. This is often ok for us, but problematic in its tearing them up each time they get settled. So I think this is the last time.

Too, I had some good news, that Scribner's will publish a sort of collected poems of past ten years, i.e., all the pamphlets and small booklets at last in one 'whole' form god willing. I have yet to clear rights for last book with Jonathan, <u>A Form of Women</u>, but there seems little trouble. So—it feels very odd, after feeling so at odds. I don't know which 'world' has changed in that sense, but can't see that it's mine—since half the poems they take would not have been their 'poems' at all ten years ago. I think that's your victory more than any. Anyhow that will come out this next year it seems. I'm trying to write a novel otherwise, or simply to break out of habits, etc. But there is little time just now for it, that I seem to use at least. But it is no headache,—y pues.

I hope everything is well with you and your family. It must be real winter there now. I wish we might all be here talking like they say. I hope you have a good Christmas, and as ever send you all our love.

My thanks to you,
Bob

. . .

LETTER TO JEROME ROTHENBERG

San Geronimo Miramar
Patulul, Such.
Guatemala, C.A.
December 18, 1960

Dear Jerry,

I'm sorry not to have written, i.e., both your letters god knows were very good to have. I'd hate to think you were concerned about them in that sense. The past few weeks we have been much involved with getting papers straight for the car, and divers other horrors, which have cut me down to pretty goddamn minimal size like they say. So . . .

Don't think, please, that I make adamant distinctions between the use of image or any other 'thing' in a poem, i.e., I fear you feel me shutting doors on divers emphases that I really don't intend to close out. For myself, I had first to learn how to manage the very literal 'sound' elements in a poem before I felt much capability. It seemed that, first writing, I was constantly falling over my own feet trying to say what I wanted to. If, for example, I wanted to involve a sense of love, or pain, loss, whatever, I could not it seemed place it as clearly as I felt it. So I began, then, trying to articulate as carefully as possible areas of possible thought, call them—to the definition Williams gives in his Autobiography: The poet thinks with his poem, in that lies his thought, and that in itself is the profundity, i.e., you'll see very quickly the relation of that emphasis to what you've said of my own work. It was a very germinal attitude for me (as his has been more generally, god knows). I am finally a shy man, or was, when younger, painfully so—and began, I suppose, to use the poem as an articulation of all the 'unresolved' things I felt and found no other means to 'say'. It was also an exorcizing in some sense—the craft made exact, and partly absolute, fears or hopes, or literal experiences, that otherwise floated in an entirely personal term of threat, etc. I thought that if I made it possible, for myself as well as for others, to 'go through' these situations in a poem—where the formal unity provides a coherence and an objectivity of place—they might both better understand them and also find them at last related to tolerable entity—no longer ghost, etc.

Now coming from Pound as I also did, very much—i.e., for me his prose notes about writing continue to be the best rules of thumb I know, e.g., the notes in Make It New, as the Date Line and others re Daniel etc—I went, as he suggested, in fear of abstractions, though my very manner of thought soon became involved with that process. Yet I felt if I did it with 'tangibles' so to speak, at least I allowed for an understanding by the commonness of terms.

So all it comes to is, that, for me, the emphasis has been upon the prosody, i.e., again Pound's 'the total articulation of sound in a poem' or words to that effect. Which gets us to <u>mode</u> again—again for me one of the most determinant aspects of the poem, literally, the manner or way of its going (as 'mode' is the same word as 'mood' in grammar, etc.). There is, for example, an image immediately present in the subjunctive mood, or imperative—general but insistent, qualifying all that occurs within its term. Just so in a poem, the mode by setting the 'image' of address (again you write very closely to my own concerns, in that very generous review). So that mode, for me, becomes the primary arbiter of the poem's presence in its external (as well as internal) reference. It is in the mode of the poem that I would myself see its relation to the world in which it occurs, in, literally, the way it goes, the manner of its going, etc.

Why I have found it more difficult, then, to specify or make a general program for 'image', either for myself or (altogether) for others, is that that part of the writing remains for me very personal and occasional—a question of what proves to hand as I move in the poem, i.e., think by means of it, to a formal entity I qualify as poem. I go much more by feeling here—though it would be absurd to say that I do not go equally by that in other relations as well. Your quote of Suzuki is much to the purpose here—having practiced the 'effects' of this or that 'mode', and such practice rarely secures anything but a useful knowledge (it does not itself make poems in my own case), one is then able to follow the 'occasion' the poem otherwise proves,—inspired or whatnot, god alone knows. But see that this is not to either remove the importance of image, or to slight it in any sense—but only to show how warily I move with reference to it. Thinking again of that 'psychology of reference' that the image involves for me, the 'vision' by demanding its absoluteness makes such tracing secondary—Blake is a practical workman and hard thinker, who does (I suspect) use all means such as either poetry or prose as a means of statement, a larger thing for him. Coleridge, contrariwise, finds means to speak in the poem that are not otherwise at hand—the poem is more importantly his 'content' than are the thoughts one might abstract from his statement there. Not so with Blake, to my mind—nor with Whitman, despite (for me) the great technical skill (often) of the latter. (It is interesting that Hopkins, for example, felt Whitman closer to his means than anyone else, though he also thought him nuts etc—but he recognized the <u>technical</u> ability of Whitman beyond any doubt. He otherwise hated the 'philosophy' etc.

What the hell to say, finally. You are very right that in a poem like The Door I am much involved with 'image', as Olson also, very very much, in all the Maximus, and in something like The Librarian (that 'new combinations' etc). The topography of dream etc, seen as map-making—forms of relation outlined as their impact upon us, or their use in our hands. There is a certain clutter, however, most present in translations at present (not yours, certainly not in that 'Black milk of morning'—i.e., I agree with [David] Antin in Chelsea you enforce that one greatly), where the image has been translated, but rarely the mode—i.e., see the great variation in translations of Lorca, for example, and yet so few grasp the simplicity of the <u>mode</u>, the manner of the going in the poem. (Jack Spicer has done it best, perhaps.) Anyhow that's what I fear, that a vocabulary of image will be got too easily, without the mode that placed it in situ, to be a force established in words more than a mere collection, etc. Ah well! I don't answer you very well at all, nor speak of half I want to, here. Well, I will. Meantime do write as you can. I hope you have a good Christmas there, and that all goes well for you both. Again, my respect for image is probably as great as your own like they say, i.e., I remember that poem of Kitasono's The Shadow was why that little book got printed. So! Ok.

All best to you,
Bob

. . .

LETTER TO HUGH KENNER

> San Geronimo Miramar
> Patulul, Such.
> Guatemala, C.A.
> December 18, 1960

Dear Hugh,

Thanks very much for your good letter. What happened was that it came ordinary mail—and that's why it took so long, i.e., they seem to charge 15¢ for airmail letters to this remote location como se dice, or else an airletter for 10¢. Ah well. But it's good to know the crooks in the local postoffice hadn't got it— than whom none more, etc. (I hope that tape gets here ok, as and when—but just a few days ago the other people here got one safely, sent airmail, so again I think that ought to work—though, as said, perhaps register it also, to be completely sure etc. Wow . . .)

That's very happy THE NAME is usable. I'll put in two others, perhaps less so—I don't really know. I like the 'figures' one, simply for a kind of slow movement I find hard to hold, i.e., a completely quiet manner of statement, as it was about some small wooden figures made by Patrocinio Barela, of Taos, etc—a curious drunken wonder for the most part, poor goddamn man . . .) Anyhow. The other is familiar enough 'speculation'.

What you say of the limits of NR's audience is certainly reasonable. In some ways it's almost simpler than the more sophisticated, that tends to die very hard indeed. So.

Thinking of Zukofsky, there is one poem of his that makes the term of his 'range' (of address, and/or reference of 'world') quickly apparent to me, i.e., that one:

> Send regards to Ida, the bitch
> whose hate's unforgiving,
> why not send regards?
> There are trees' roots, branchtops
>   —as is
> one who can take his own life
>   and be quit
> except he might hurt—as he imagines
> here he's gone—
> a person, two; if not the sun.

Which is, very much, that constant shuttle he works between conjecture, and the application, back and forth, a check of his own mind, against his own mind, endlessly reiterated—i.e., suppositional tracking and testing of his own thought. Likewise in manner it is typical, in the syntax god knows—with the possibility of "There are . . . a person, two . . . " i.e., that sequence completed as a sentence, and also, more apparently, "he might hurt . . . a person"—but, not wildly I hope, the double term of personal and 'natural' common world, found in that former jump, etc. As also the way he puts himself 'beside', in the indentation, the 'natural' terms, almost as a parenthesis in a sense. I.e., to the bitch why not say hello, for what common world they both live in, as life is a root, to a 'top', a process not to be finally qualified by bitchiness, etc. As life can come to 'top' from 'root' in one who can be quit of it, except that he finds himself rooted beyond the personal, to the 'two', in a common form—again allowing for Ida in a world of roots and issues therefrom—ultimately objective, in "if not the sun", shines on all, etc. It's a wild one, I think, just for the crazy condensation of attitudes provided for in it, i.e., the 'arguments' posited within its statement. You can read the damn thing backwards and forwards, in that sense—with each phrase suggesting a 'conclusion' immediately qualified by that which follows. It also has his wild handling of vowels, and consonantal rhymes, etc. Well, he is very damn good, like they say. I suppose your difficulty, as often mine, or Williams' as you say, is that so much of the area is this intensely personal limit of the world, as thought, much more than felt, say, despite the clear history in his writing (certainly in "A"). But the lack of 'conclusions' finally, the sense what is, is always to be modified, again, again, again.

I.e., what he seems to fear is what he says of Shakespeare, "The risk his text takes when it sees and foresees at the same time is that at any moment creation may become like uncontrolled water . . . " So that in Zukofsky, more than any other I can think of, Williams' sense of the poet thinking with his poem, is true. I.e., it must occur within, so to speak, i.e., this will to the "Constantly seeking and ordering relative quantities and qualities of sight, sound, and intellection," that proves all his mind; hence no order more than thought, nor meaning more than in the thinking etc, not the 'what is thought' etc. Which is probably much too quick a sense, yet persistent in my own reading of him. The issue being, as he says, "the contest any poet has with his art: working towards a perception that is his mind's peace . . . " (i.e., this from notes in FOLIO Spring '60, apropos section of Bottom they print there, etc.)

Christmas very damn close at this point, the which with four daughters looms large, like they say, but pleasantly. I'll be glad, however, when the year here is at last done—it begins to be increasingly tedious, and the time I had free the first year (i.e., last) now is much less, as the work for the children increases etc. I'll hope to write again when things are a little more relaxed. I've heard now from the Guggenheim committee, asking for more material—so that much is o'erlept, etc. Wow . . . thanks again and again for the push with same. It does seem this year more possible. Ok. Write as you can, please, and I will also.

My best to you,
Bob

P.S. There is a younger poet I much like, and perhaps you would, i.e. Edward Dorn—whose poems you can see most simply in that collection, The New American Poetry (some very nice ones included, etc.) Anyhow his address is: 501 Camino Sin Nombre, Santa Fe, i.e., it's possible he would have something.

. . .

LETTER TO PAUL BLACKBURN

San Geronimo Miramar
Patulul, Such.
Guatemala, C.A.
January 11, 1961

Dear Paul,

I've missed hearing from you, and have wondered if you got my last letter ok, i.e., the damn mails here are often so poor such things happen frequently. In any case I hope you had a good Xmas like they say—it must have been busy there to put it mildly.

Just now I'm trying to clear my own head re 'deep image' and the like, i.e., both Kelly and Rothenberg have been writing to me about it, and I've seen that recent issue of TROBAR of course. I don't know quite what to answer—not pompously, but I'm reluctant to jump either way, since I have no base sympathy with such a concern as Kelly's note outlines, but I hardly refuse it to others. So. Anyhow so far I do not see a clear handle for its use and/or a means indicated that would bring one to anything but 'symbolic reference' or, finally, a psychology of reference—which interests me, very much, but which also seems to me a pretty large red herring in the context they intend. When Kelly suggests a balance between Olson's physiology of sound, i.e., the breath context, with all its reference, and his own 'deep image', I do balk because I don't believe them in this way equivalent counters in a general plan. I think Olson's notes have frozen in some minds, into an ultimatum of form, rather than a suggestion as to 'mode' and/or a calculus of possibility for the line, derived from the most available term we have in its management.

Well, that you know as well as I do, if not better. But with this 'deep image' I feel a demarche toward those 'dim lands of peace', i.e., a move toward generalization of the poem's terms which I for one greatly fear. It may well be that I am myself as guilty as any, in such areas—supposing often a content, so to speak, in my poems that does not practically exist. But I've felt that it was in the 'mode' of a poem (in the 'manner of its going') that that which was specific to its effect qua poem might best be controlled. Image for me moves equally between prose and poetry, for example, in the sense that a 'poetic' mode will not. Thinking that rhythm is an aspect of all language in sequence, of course it is specious to catalogue some rhythms as specifically poetic, and others as not etc. But thinking of Zukofsky's mean, of speech/music, with the poem's mode the term between, at least I can find there a figure, call it, for my own intention.

But in this discussion that they offer me 'image' is already a loaded word. It is not a 'verbal picture'—it is, better, derived from 'vision' which I know, say, like 'love', yet only so—I cannot specify its actual qualifications. Jerry finally seems to come to the 'preconscious' in that that becomes the point of issue for the 'vision' which in turn informs the image etc. Well—why not, except that it stays just so an observation on what has happened—more or less defensible as an opinion—but it does not provide a tool for working in the poem that I can see. It in fact takes away concern from that aspect of poetry I think we can profit- ably discuss, i.e., the structure of a poem as a unit of sound (in Pound's sense of prosody) and the ability of the man writing in that reference. This, of course, does not at all mean a 'good' poem in that aspect need not be a 'bad' poem in others. I try to say to them that for me the 'mode' of a poem, or more simply its structure proves itself an 'image' at times more influential than any other, by virtue of the fact that it informs all the words which it embodies. It is a way of saying something, and being so, has consequence in that sense.

In their poems to date I've found really little that impresses me; yet that too I have hesitated to say to them, because it is too simple to say to someone beginning as they both are, that they as yet show little technical competence as writers. Yet I hate to see them off up a garden path that only can lead them away from this need to learn which they patently have. Here I think 'transla- tion' has done them a disservice, in that it has given them—too often without an accompanying structure—a vocabulary of image they now use almost too glibly. Rothenberg is the most developed in his use of image, I feel; yet I find a tendency to generalize in almost every poem of his which I see. Perhaps I prove only a Pounder, after all this time, but I do continue to believe that 'Any ten- dency to abstract general statement is a greased slide.' Perhaps they feel me to be against 'image' per se, which would be among other things impossible. Ah well! It is this adamant choosing that I don't like, finally, but I suspect any absolutism of 'manner' in a program for poetry—and have really never read Olson's notes as embodying one. Yet others disagree with me it is clear.

Can you, in any case, give me your own thoughts here? You are there, and know the people—and will be much more able than I to understand the prem- ises that Kelly attempts to define in his note etc. I know you respect his work, so that also ought to help. I really am goddamn confused by them—wanting myself to be sympathetic, because they are certainly so to me, yet not basically believing much at all in what they tend, for me, to argue. Ok.

Things go very well, despite tedium of work here, also people—though we see almost no one. Well, it will be finally good to stop it, which we will about the end of April. I am hopeful for a Guggenheim, perhaps too goddamn much so, as ever—but that failing, I can I think get another job ok. In the meantime Scribner's have taken the 'collected' poems ms/, and have given me a good report on five chapters of novel I've done (a piece of which Paul C/ is printing in the next BIG TABLE etc), i.e., it's pretty certain they will take it if I can ever get it done etc. Too I'm pretty sure we will be east for a visit this summer—but that may be premature, but I think not. So, will see you again god willing. Please do write in the meantime as you can. And I will too.

All my love,
Bob

. . .

LETTER TO ED DORN

San Geronimo Miramar
Patalul, Such.
Guatemala, C.A.
January 19, 1961

Dear Ed,

I like that note you did, i.e., what you qualify as your relations to writing, and then that second paragraph, with culture as what men remember—that's very clear—and likewise the last, with its question. So that seems done, like they say. It's a goddamn curious question to begin with, in some ways—I think I, as you, would say what you do in that first sentence. The dullness is of course that for people who don't see it that way, it makes no sense to say 'there is that means which no other seems to provide for'; and for those who would, then I think it is the reassurance it is for me, hearing you say it. Voila.

Re desperation como se dice, I think we are beyond it in a weird way, i.e., this is simple 'misery' in Olson's sense of accumulated wear and tear. The time goes very goddamn quickly, and we have almost no sense of it, but as accumulation toward the end of, that's the end of it etc. Well, that's good—having an end. Yet the weather now is crazy, as ever—our physical senses at least ought to be satisfied, and yet a restlessness sticks in both of us. I suppose I use the pot much too goddamn much as a welcome euphoria, at the end of so-called day. I'd go a little nutty without some handy unreality in which to hide. I don't have the energy (or don't feel it) to take off into something more substantial. Anyhow the anti-social aspects of said panacea make the closedness we live in more tolerable. We don't go whooping around the house or anything, but it breaks the monotony a little, and is restful—makes—somehow with reliable continuity—a little difference to things felt and seen etc. I'm about out in any case and what I've grown this year is slow coming, and may not finally. I think that's just as well too, if it turns out so. It gets a habit in the dull sense of, over and over—no need but the familiarity and that it does, in the sense described, relieve much in the present locked scene. So to hell with it in any case.

Partly it is the curious hanging between what seems everything going my way, like they say, and fears re a job next year, e.g. I am waiting to hear now from Texas, it is pretty definite we could not do this again and keep sane, Bunker writes the job there looks now not too possible, the one I tried at UNM is out now, and so on, i.e., that's about it. We'll have, by saving here and perhaps from some advance on books of poems, enough to get us through the summer ok. Anyhow that way I fall back a little to previous fears like, partly, those in SF, what the hell to do etc. Not really—however. It would be a little goddamn faux naïf to claim trembling, etc. Much more, a kind of anger that always one gets hung with this impasse of <u>use</u>, no matter what else is going on. It's an irony that what we do in this world to 'make a living' has finally such a painfully corrosive relation to what we might otherwise be said to 'do'. But I god knows said that ad nauseam this summer. Ah well. Anyhow I can't at the moment see how to use such things as Scribner's acceptance of the poems, and now as well a favorable report on first five chapters of the novel—so that that will probably be ok also, as I can get it done etc—I mean that this is politics also, and I would like to use such 'gains' for what they seem to be usable for, beyond the work and results they are—already settled long ago in my own mind and with people as yourself I would take sight from etc. I feel like I've got a whole bunch of saving stamps and trying to find where to get my prizes etc. Perhaps there aren't any—that I can take at least. But I hope for example that I can lever myself into some teaching job with same, yet it seems that doesn't really make it, too fearsome or something to them—however respectful they seem to be. I just don't know at present. But things continue to break in that respect. I heard from Eberhart at Library of Congress they would like tape of a reading—god knows that seems new to me. What I really would hope was the use of such things is freedom from such as your boss, or mine for that matter—despite he is more human. I want less of that continual business of having to dance in the shadow of some problematic character, so as to hide my own 'personality'—i.e., moving in what area they leave hidden behind themselves, in the performance of my duties etc. As at that boys' school, shifting and turning with problematic Wilburn god knows, whose hang-up at times meant he had to twist a few screws to prove his own capabilities. Here I feel at times a slight tendency, or wish, to wipe one's arse with the 'poet', however politely, just to make clear you don't have to take that pansy shit etc etc. Or else it's like being put in an umbrella stand, for the look of the thing somehow. Anyhow to be out of that—just getting older making the earlier 'flexibility' and nod to authorities more a headache etc a pain in the ass too often. I find myself speaking up to people half my age, not quite, but clearly younger, simply out of that training of self-effacing anonymity that has let me work simply at all, at all. Well . . .

Anyhow I'm not writing anything at present. I've got some so-called jobs, as review of Olson for YUGEN which will be good, and note also on Burroughs, again good. I wrote Poetry to see if I can review your book when it is out—I'll let you know what they say. Nims is present editor there, and is so far good natured. They haven't as yet used that other, but I think he might agree. Otherwise will review it somewhere at least—i.e., I am very goddamn happy it is coming now, and would like to say why. Ok.

I don't see much goddamn else—as this 'deep image'. Wow. Dennie wrote first letter in months enclosing notes re her own putting down of same. It really seems a vague and softly sloppy red herring to me. Again your note cuts way past that sort of hopefulness to my mind. Thank you for that OUTBURST connection—I sent them a poem. I liked the look of their flyer. I still don't see any magazine of much goddamn coherence, but here and there makes it in the meantime I guess. LeRoi wrote he hopes to make 'critical' base now for YUGEN, if he can get money to continue. Have you been hearing anything from Olson? I haven't in some time now—well before Xmas. It must be a damn bitter season there now, weather-wise. Have you seen anything re his Maximus?

So, we'll get there. We are really counting the days at this point. It's not at least at all impossible. But sans friends as yourselves, the world (yet) is pretty goddamn flat after all. Write please anytime you can, send poems as you can too. I don't see anything I like here, i.e., very little in mags now I can see. Etc. Wow. Pues. WRITE!

All our love to you all,
Bob

P.S. *Have you seen Larry Eigner's book—On My Eyes—strange nervous business, with (finally) to my sense great clarity.*

[Bobbie Creeley's note in left margin] *I'm reading Spock re 6 & 7 year olds— Leslie fed one of the mice to the cat across the street—well not quite—but carried them both over (wasn't supposed to go without permission—etc) then, in the room with the cat put them on the windowsill having decided to return home by climbing through the window (!) Cried because the cat chose hers (fattest). One incident from a week of them—oh well, hell. I hope you are all well—Love Bobbie*

. . .

LETTER TO TOM RAWORTH

> San Geronimo Miramar
> Patulul, Such.
> Guatemala, C.A.
> January 23, 1961

Dear Tom,

That's very happy news about your new daughter, and I much liked the whole 'description' like they say. I never have got to travel in such fashion and much envy you. In any case, we have four (daughters), so are well acquainted with all the delights thereof. And conversely. Ok.

To begin with—I've enclosed some poems, and a note on Burroughs' NAKED LUNCH. Grove Press plans to publish the novel in the States this spring, and had asked me for a comment on its value etc. I'd just done it yesterday, and it may not be worth the time—but if so, you are welcome to it—perhaps adding a note that it was a comment written for Grove in response to their question etc. Ok. (I don't know that "Black Mountain Review" needs identification there, but would suppose so. Briefly, it was the publication of the 'avant garde' Black Mountain College, wherein appeared many of the Beat Generation writers as well as the so-called 'Black Mountain' group. Cf. Allen's The New American Poetry, 1945–1960, Grove Press—and the comments he makes about the logic for his divisions in the preface.) I don't have any story to send you unhappily. I will hope to by at least summer, but just now I have copies of nothing here—and anything new I have is at present tied up. But I will. Meantime, I will write Fielding Dawson (whose prose may well interest you) along with this, and ask him to send you something as soon as possible.

As to other people—here are names and addresses of some I myself think outstanding, and also sympathetic to such a magazine as you propose:

Charles Olson	Robert Duncan	Denise (Levertov) Goodman
28 Fort Square	P.O. Box 14	277 Greenwich
Gloucester, Mass.	Stinson Beach, Calif.	New York 7, N.Y.

I.e., those most interest me, and also, very much: Louis Zukofsky, 135 Willow Street, Brooklyn 1, N.Y. You have Ed Dorn's address of course—who is another. Thinking of prose:

Michael Rumaker	William Eastlake	Douglas Woolf
52 Main Street	Eastlake Ranch	Box 4231
Nanuet, N.Y.	Cuba, New Mexico	Spokane 31, Washington

Edward Dahlberg.→	He is presently writing a very interesting
88 Horation Street	autobiography—cf. sections in recent BIG
Apt 5B	TABLEs, and is an older man, very good I think.
New York 14, N.Y.	Anyhow I'd try him if I were you.

Ed Dorn also writes interesting prose, both 'fiction' and otherwise.

Then there are people like Hugh Kenner, 4680 La Espada Drive, Santa Barbara, California—who might be got if you asked them very nicely (or were interested to) for a short comment on American poetry as they now take it, etc. You ought to be in contact with Dr Gael Turnbull, 1199 Church St., Ventura, Calif. (who was old publisher of MIGRANT, and a very decent man generally I think). Also Irving Layton, the one Canadian poet I think exceptional—could reach him c/o Jack Hirschman, 14 North Park, Hanover, N.H.—and Hirschman, a young teacher now at Dartmouth College, is also an interesting translator and poet in his own right. Larry Eigner: 23 Bates Road, Swampscott, Mass. Paul Blackburn: 110 Thompson, New York 9, N.Y. LeRoi Jones: 324 East 14th St, New York 3, N.Y.—who is very sympathetic and helpful man, the editor also of YUGEN. Gary Snyder: Konoecho, Yase, Sakyo-ku, Kyoto, Japan. Mike McClure: 2324 Fillmore, San Francisco—through whom also could be reached Philip Whalen, a good writer.

It gets a little endless, so let me stop here, i.e., if you try any of these, I'm very sure A will quickly lead to B. You'll find most American writers very interested to be published there, and grateful for the opportunity—if a little shy of 'English manner' they suspect as a criticism of their own etc. But if you write them simply as you have me—god knows warmly and kindly—I'm sure you'll have no trouble. Do you happen to know where Martin Seymour-Smith is these days? I knew him when living in Mallorca, an old and very close friend then—and am anxious to locate him again. He as well might be a help to you.

As to outlets in this country: generally that gets to be a nightmare, if you attempt either wide coverage, or general coverage. What I'd suggest is this: ask specifically LeRoi Jones if he would mind acting as American agent for you, in New York area—with specific reference to 8th Street Bookshop and any like places he knows. I.e., put it to him, you'd like the magazine to circulate there, you know the problems of getting currency back and forth, so if shops would pay you in credit for books, say, only, that would be fine (I hope!). He will be able to tell you much more accurately than I what numbers he will be able to handle there for example: probably 30–50 of the first issue, simply circulating it as he can. I'd ask Paul Carroll, BIG TABLE, 1316 North Dearborn, Chicago 10, Ill., the same question for that area—though he may be more harassed, but then put it, can you simply tell me what bookstores etc. Then, last, Lawrence

Ferlinghetti's City Lights Bookstore, 261 Columbus Ave., San Francisco 11, Calif. would no doubt stock copies, if you write them, literally him etc. You are welcome to use my name in reference to any of the people here noted. Ok.

So, let me get this back quickly—and write again. Do write yourself, as you can. I like very much what you are trying to do, and again, would like to help in any way possible.

My best to you,

Bob

[note at top left of page]
Please don't
be swamped by } Re: 'NAMES'
this—I'm simply
giving you all I
can think of—to do with as
you see fit.

[note in left margin] If the magazine is available in NY, SF, and Chicago, it's enough—i.e., those, particularly the first two, are the centers for any such magazine and its effective circulation. It will go on from there perhaps, but no matter.

· · ·

LETTER TO CHARLES OLSON

San Geronimo Miramar

Patulul, Such.

Guatemala, C.A.

January 29, 1961

Dear Charles,

Winding up for a wail, como se dice. I hesitate like they say to write, thinking you have troubles enough—and don't want to make it, 'you know how difficult things are for us here, but with the help of god and good cheer, we continue in our little fashion, etc.' But we see the end of it now, more to the point—three months and/or 90 days I could do I think even in jail. There is, more hopeless, a constant vacuity to things, much in myself at present in any case, so that the landscape is like an ever smiling idiot—so bland and good etc. The recent political businesses underline only my (and as it happens, Indios equally) complete non-sense, or better, out-of-it pattern, of such things. I see it as local, and local, it stinks—e.g. the jets we now hear, one or two in a week— which obey a law as certain as daylight, for the powers involved.

I cannot write anything at present, sitting down again and again to get started, see it fall into patterns like finger exercises, and can feel no goddamn lift sufficient to break it out. That is very familiar god knows, and in one way, not even despairing—being so. But it is why I have not written. I cannot at the moment shake it—think of nothing else, if I 'think' etc. Bobbie is working, painting—this year has been for her much what last was for me, free time and space, despite she dislikes our situation here even more than I do. I am drinking a sort of perfumed local vodka, at $1.90 the bottle, also rum about the same— last year we didn't for some reason. Beer is 25¢ a bottle, more or less, as in the States. I get scared of an exposure, to you—so close to my own sense of myself at least as 'usable'—I don't write in that way either, fearing complete dissolve etc. And yet I seem to be in one piece, albeit complete subjectivism yet. Fuck the waste, anyhow. Destroying time is a vicious business. I am working now six days a week to finish by last of April—no job as yet for the coming year. With a little luck perhaps I can parlay the prose into an income for us, enough to make a free year of sorts. I would like to have it, very damn much. I have been in this fix, in divers guises now, for five years—i.e., since last seeing you, it has been a sort of self-discipline to keep 'attentive' etc.

The so-called novel is what I have on my mind finally—that seems the next place. I am very cheered that this time they like it, i.e., thinking of that earlier try with Wm Morrow that was so nowhere. I seem not to do it here, I wrote all I have of it in one week before I started working. But I think of it, like they say. BIG TABLE is printing a section, I'll ask him to send copy—I'm scared to death of it one way, yet has again 'conjecture' I've not remembered in years—the world that can be thought of like they say. Aie! Do damn well write. I miss you, very much, very selfishly. With a little luck will see you this summer, early—about June (first couple of weeks thereof), contriving ways at present—so. I hope it is making it there. Please take care of yourself. Write. I will—this is poor business, but it's what, always, five minutes conversation (we never have here) would completely take away. Ok.

All my love to you all,
Bob

Here's one poem if I hadn't sent it:

FIRE

Clear smoke,
a fire in the far off
haze of summer,
burning somewhere.

What is
a lonely heart for
if not
for itself alone.

Do the questions
answer themselves,
all wonder
brought to a reckoning?

When you are done,
I am done,
then it seems that
one by one

we can leave it all,
to go on.
[*CP* I, 254]

Hey! I'm still
  a hick!
        (I hope.)

P.S. LeRoi has asked me to review Maximus
for Yugen, which same I shortly will do.

[Bobbie Creeley's note along lower right margin next to a small drawing of a house and two flowers:]
Dear Betty and Charles,
  for the good things — we have poinsettias, bougainvillea, a hummingbird has a nest in an orange tree even with the window we sit by to eat, health, etc. also 2 rabbits and a closed yard below the same window so we see them down there white on green grass, the children are all getting great — leaving one set of horrible mannerisms behind doubtless enroute to bigger and better — But the people are bad. Believe the Ugly American's a great book and <u>art</u> of any sort is 'beautiful' or not at all and enforce their attitudes by making 100,000 a year — But we will leave all that in 3 months by the G of G and then never to return — It will be great to see you both and son also
            love Bobbie

· · ·

LETTER TO LOUIS ZUKOFSKY

<u>*After April 28th:*</u>
Our address in New Mexico   San Geronimo Miramar
is: c/o Hall, PO Box 34,   Patulul, Such.
Alameda, N.M.   Guatemala, C.A.
                                      March 17, 1961

Dear Louis,
    Your good letter, with the clippings from Paul's concert, were a great cheer, i.e., despite my silence in past months, god knows I've been anxious to know

how you all are—and really, you sound happy and active, like they say, and now I damn well fear to interrupt you with my own dullness. But that as well will soon be done with, once we leave here, which is not long now. With a little luck, i.e., no sickness for the children etc, I think we'll be on our way back to New Mexico at the end of April, and shortly after that we will be coming east (Bobbie and I), and should be able finally to see you all again toward the end of May. By god . . . Ok!

I'm pleased the use of yourself in that 'Quick Graph' did not prove a goddam presumption. It really did seem that 'quick' to me, I am more and more convinced your work has a very great use for those capable—and I think more and more become so, if only in restlessness and reaction to the deadness otherwise. Anyhow I should myself much like to see all the present excitement harnessed to a few useful attentions. In that sense, you can hardly be avoided. Ah well! I had a letter from Mary Ellen Solt, who mentioned seeing you (and who also seems good-natured? I am curious to know how she strikes you, in point of her critical work now.) She says perhaps Laughlin will do something, which would be about time.

Too, I'm trying to get that review of "A" and Barely and widely written, I seem to go into a revery (yet) each time I go to these books, i.e., I become so involved with my own interest in them I don't want to 'talk' like they say. But more to the point, I'll have that finally done (short unhappily as it must be, for their limits) this weekend, and will send you a copy as I do have it. That too I've felt badly about taking so long with.

I'm very interested to see your Catullus translations, e.g. the one in Anew always impressed me, as those also in Poetry not too long ago. I have by the way the December issue with the section of Bottom—it's a fabulous insight of juxtapositions and measures I think, i.e., '1 picture is worth 1000 words' and this way you prove, of so placing insight and apprehension—as also in that section earlier in Folio, i.e., the list of comparable evidences—is to myself very opening and useful.

Thinking of what you say of Whitman—I looked up that poem (or the one toward the beginning of that last section, then at the end the other)—I certainly would like to have written the first without question. No I don't think 'one' improves etc. So! Apropos EP, I have a tape of a recent series of interviews he has recorded for someone at the BBC (I'll bring them), in which he talks on and on in a completely interesting manner, and also does cite Whitman as the best critic of the writing of his period—and generally seems to approve of him in a way somewhat new. I suppose they were at that time scared to death of that apparently rolling, loose line—but the 'weights' in it, and the language, and the tenor of the thought, the risks of such curious tenderness and continuance, in the line be it said,—god knows that to me seems singularly 'great'. So.

The following is about all I've written in weeks now, it is not an open time for us, and that shows I'm afraid. Too, having the book taken by Scribner's has put a curious stop to things for the moment—but it is more the situation here, in its barrenness, that blocks things. Anyhow you will see your way in it, so to speak, which I am intent to understand. Too, I want to enclose the poem for you, published in <u>Trobar</u> (which I don't want to send entire, i.e., it depresses me, a luxury I guess . . .). So. Shortly I'll hope to write a decent letter, and to send the review. Ok. Again, it is very happy to know all goes well and please congratulate Paul for what must have been a very complete evening, to think of what he played. Well, <u>he</u> knew it like they say, before and after.

> All our love to you all,
> *Bob*

WATER

The sun's
sky in
form of
blue sky
that

water will
never make
even
in reflection.

Sing, song
mind's form
<u>feeling</u>
if
mistaken,

shaken,
broken water's
forms, love's
error
in water.
[*CP* I, 268]

I suppose I was most interested
to get that 'falling' sense of
words, without 'rest' through the
lines (as earlier in your 'Hear
her clear mirror / in her etc'),
to make the 'waver' of water partly,
though not consciously. I am not
finally interested in such parallels
except that they at times parallel
the thought that 'thinks to think
them'.
             (I suppose also this is
an echo of Catullus' "in wind and
quickly moving water"—here supposed
as relief to error, rather
than as problem of inconstancy etc.)

Aie . . .

[Enclosure: "The House" *for Louis Zukofsky* (*CP* I, 237) , from *Trobar* (1961)]

· · ·

LETTER TO ED DORN

> San Geronimo Miramar
> Patalul, Such.
> Guatemala, C.A.
> March 26, 1961

Dear Ed,

Your last letter got through safely—I think it's all now come ok, i.e., Bobbie's visit to the PO and questions seem to have done the so-called trick. But what a goddamn irritation to think of all that didn't get here, due to their malign finagling. Ah well.

You cheer me up, very much. I.e., I've been having shakes like that, who am I, what'll I do, will it ever end, etc., when it is hardly either that difficult (it is not) or that uncertain (which same Scribner's removes largely no matter now). And so on. I have a bitter goddamn fear of not 'earning' my way or rather support of us all, bred partly of the earlier situation with Ann—and continued in having fallen into the two jobs I've had as either stop-gaps or else apparent conveniences (as here) that proved otherwise. I.e., what I am afraid of apparently, is getting out on the goddamn limb, with all of us, and then having to lean on somebody (as Bobbie's parents—wow . . .) to survive. I can't develop the arrogance (which in such a case I think justified) that maintains a reasonable claim on help of others, since the work it does, i.e., the man does, cannot per se support him, and yet its eventual use, or use in wide terms, is nonetheless unquestioned. Ah well again. Well for christ's sake, it is clearer than that—to wit, I'm scared to death of taking a chance with all of us, who in turn define my responsibility, and I fear being caught out in a way that will only harass us more viciously than we now are. I have no stomach for the uncertainties of living that ten years ago would have been an excitement to me—you as I know, if not better, how viciously such worry makes impossible anything but thinking about it, over and over and over etc. Now the Eastlakes tell us that place will be available only till mid-July, though I think of course something equivalent can be found around there, at least for a low rent if not for none etc. So that isn't the problem. After the barrenness here I'd like more ease than we have had, perhaps that's gravy only—well, it is. But in one embarrassing sense I've nothing immediately to die for, except the novel which I hope to finish in one push this summer, it is that kind so to speak—and then I'd like to go to Paris like they say. Ah well . . . Or let's make it the moon etc. Simply some romantic nada land, beaches and all that shit etc. No—hardly, but what the hell will I write, Ed—something like that. I fear saying I'm risking whatever to do something I only do as I do it, and do no matter—so what's the excuse, I suppose. But to hell with it here. I think the whole so-called question which is impossible to speak of finally, will get settled as things are or are not open to me, job-wise like they say—so far none, so so far so good, really. This is one choice I'd feel better being backed into, like a horse etc. So.

I enclose sheet from Nat'l Review, partly the prettiness thereof, and 'new poems' from last winter now, and that 'name' one is finally ok to me—the other re figures, is of Barela's sculptures Bobbie lifted etc—and qua sign, to see if I can't mitigate the weird evil of that magazine. It underlines so clearly so many people, or enough to make this context, make $25000 a year and up etc. What do they care about who's feeling 'liberal', i.e., you fuck up the carpet out you go etc. That's what that money's for. So they come on like gentleman, not so gentle at all, amateurs who if they can't say it right can at least pay their way through it no matter. It's pretty ugly, and I am uneasy about being so a part of it, via Kenner—who himself has been helpful now to Olson and Zukofsky, say, and to me certainly, and wants to print what he can—and yet how clear can any of it be in this context. Greasily, I'd want to argue well the fucking poems have to 'speak for themselves', and if you can get into the enemy camp in such a way, so much the better. But if your terms argue a premise, vaguely put qua 'poems', etc, can't the people such as these very neatly vitiate your 'identification' and what use it might be, rightly situated among people you believe in—but then how would Dennie for example 'believe' in Mademoiselle, or me in the Nation (thinking of that little shit who edits poetry for them, MLR, or present Merwin, who is hardly liberal in any sense I understand at least, howbeit to me personally much more acceptable than MLR, who attacked me there almost sans reason, or none but to hear himself talk apparently—so that's a world, too) . . . The mess is I want to 'rationalize' everything, and feeling breaks in areas heretofore closed get shaky in how I should react to them. E.g. Donald Hall's recent approval in NY Times Bk Review makes me wonder if I'm turning into some kind of castrate fascist, or if we really have won our point. So—that we can talk about thank god. Ok.

I will get those dexedrine for you, that's simple. I want some myself. Do damn well watch out for them, i.e., Martin's wife Jan had a very unhappy habit with them—and they breed, used too continuously, a very problematic nervous-ness and 'withdrawal' which I don't feel pot to, for example. The latter, when you stop after some time, seems only to make a feeling of 'let down' for a week or so, not ever hard, and makes sleeping at first hard—but the dexedrine apparently gets a physiological scene going. Well, to hell with it . . . Confines of the civiliza-tion can be defined in terms of addiction, e.g. to food and friends. Ok . . .

We will be leaving here, as now planned, the 28th of April. This Tuesday we are going out to Mexico just for the day, to get our visas straight, i.e., by leaving the country we get an automatic thirty days more, etc. So that will do it. The school goes ok, and that I'm now sure can be finished in time, simply enough. So.

Again your book made it for me, altogether. I want to say more, god knows much more, than that quick note did. I haven't as yet located a place to, but I think I can. Anyhow, you've done your part like they say. Your letters make me feel you much happier now I think, and that comes over to me—to make myself feel self-indulgent and ashamed of needless worries, but much more to the point, equally hopeful. I.e., you make it. Ok. We'll see you all very soon so that's it.

All our love to you all,
Bob

. . .

LETTER TO LOUIS ZUKOFSKY

c/o Eastlake
Eastlake Ranch
Cuba, New Mexico
June 26, 1961

Dear Louis,

I'm very very pleased the review was all right, i.e., such a thing has a primary use for me at least in such reference like they say—and its shortness had seemed a problem; yet I did want to make clear my own respect and use of your work. So. That's very happy.

Donald Hutter is the editor at Scribner's—a younger man, about 30 or nearly that, and good-natured and enthusiastic in manner. He was I think interested. The one hitch seemed the 'mechanics' of the new series, and I suppose he wanted that more arranged before he committed himself to other material. I do know he took your name and address and the titles of <u>Barely and widely</u>, <u>Some Time</u>, et al; and I can keep at him in the meantime. He must know that the pseudo-academic people they have been printing prove nothing but an echo, and the very fact they've taken me on seems to show they're at least desperate. In that way I am hopeful. (Remember that John Hall Wheelock is the literal poetry editor there, you can see what a jump they must have made with respect to myself to take such a collection at all, at all.)

I've had tests now and an x-ray, and nothing seems very complicated, at least I've heard nothing, and the tb test seemed 'doubtful' or really negative (so the doctor thought). Too, the cold is finally gone and I suspect I was simply exhausted and took it hard in that way. Ah well. It got me to rest for a time in any case, and that was very welcome. I still sit here looking out at the space. It's fantastic. Anyhow we still simply unwind, which seems very necessary after the tensions of Guatemala, and the quick trip east with that confusion etc. If I pile necessities on my back, I'll write nothing of any pleasure, so I make that excuse, temporarily. There are thousands more but I will be working shortly, i.e., I can feel it coming in a way, and grow restless.

You both made very clear to us that we seemed 'reasonably' together like they say. God what a relief such a life is—I would never have known it by myself, or as that prior clutch of willful hopefulness—which I am reminded of, since it comes as a 'subject' in this novel, partly. Anyhow, feeling together as we do, it is possible then to go out from that, for my own part, sans the fear of separation or criticism etc. So you were 'expressive'—don't worry! I always feel 'at home' with you both, you make it so simple to be so; and knew in that way you felt as you do.

That's very good news that <u>Bottom</u> goes well, though Celia's part now must be god knows difficult and tedious. Well, it will be much a world of you all, 'in the best of all possible'—so that's <u>good</u>, qua definition.

I wanted to tell you how much Paul impressed us. I love his wit and intelligence, and I think he makes a fine man—or will shortly, i.e., not to rush him. That's good news about his own vacation. I hope this fall we can both come again, and too, that there will be more time to be with you all. I had wanted to ask him in particular about his sense of rhythmic 'weights' and what not in poems, as these relate to his apprehensions in music etc. Clearly, he knows what he is doing. Most to the point, I wish there had been more time to ask him about 'rhythm' and 'time' in either music or poetry, because we began to speak of that very briefly at the table; and I was quickly aware my own 'definition' was pretty much a 'working' one. There may not prove another, yet it would be interesting to have his sense of it, from his own use. So.

And really on and on, i.e., conversation with you is a great use and relief to me, and I have a hunger, always, for more. Tell me, please, what now seems possible for your Catullus translations, and too, how otherwise things go. I have written Cid to make my request for further issues of ORIGIN. And to compliment him, certainly, on the first one. I am wary at times of his 'use' of such things, yet can never forget his literal work and persistence. That's rare, and very useful to us all. Anyhow I shall be looking for the three other sections of "A"—and keep at these now in hand, both book and "A"-13. Which is a lot. Ok. I'll send a copy of that magazine with review once they have it done—it is, I'm afraid, a dreary one, full of Poetry Society people, but then, god willing, it will 'say' all the more in such context. I simply wish it could travel farther than such an instance, but that's time enough, or there will be.

Thanks again. Please do write as you can. It is very good that you have some relief from that shoulder. I hope more comes in all senses. I will write again soon. We are settling each day more, and I think it all comes together again.

All our love to you all,

Bob

. . .

LETTER TO ED AND HELENE DORN

1835 Dartmouth NE
Albuquerque, N.M.
October 9, 1961

Dear Helene and Ed,

I am very damn sorry not to have written. The poem is very good and I will like they say use it.

Anyhow I have to tell you of an impossibly tragic thing which happened. There was an accident involving Leslie, who had been out playing with Kirsten and some other children a week ago last Sunday on that mesa out toward Menaul. Apparently they were trying to build caves in that Embudo Arroyo bed, and the bank gave way and caught Leslie. We were able to get her out quickly but it was too late to revive her. I can't think it possible to say so quickly but there is no other way. Kirsten was trying to dig her out when I got there, and after that the firemen arrived with a respirator and all that but it was no use. I think it was mercifully quick, and it matters that it was, I can feel that all that possibly could be done was done.

I think we are holding together. Simply the continuity of work and some literal obligation to keep together makes a great difference to us all. Kirsten seems to show no permanent effects. I was very damn worried that she should but she went back to school two days later, and as a child will, went on with her own immediate life thank god.

Anyhow I do not want you worrying about us. We are really all right and by the time you have this, I can say very truthfully, even now, that the worst of it all will have been accepted. It is just that so much possibility did exist in her, and such a wild and honest mind. So that says it, please.

I am very happy that things there are working out. Finally they will here too, I think. The job is good and simple, and I have been given a so-called honors class as well, which means sharp kids and some extra money too. A week from Thursday I'll be going up to Toronto happily, and then to New York. That will be good. I'm hopeful of seeing Olson if a possible reading at Harvard works out, I don't as yet know. Bobbie's show is a great delight, it's on for this month, and all in one place like that makes a wild sight. So.

Do damn well take good care of yourselves and write as you can. We think of you very damned often.

Our love to you all,
Bob

P.S. *I'm pretty sure that the Hayworths are now in Taos*

[Enclosed is the news article reporting on Leslie Creeley's accident and death.]

· · ·

LETTER TO JACK KEROUAC

1835 Dartmouth NE
Albuquerque, NM
January 19, 1962

Dear Jack,

It was very very good to hear from you, i.e., I'd asked after you in New York both last summer and then this fall, but the time was always so short and people so vague, I could never locate just where you were. Anyhow I would give a great deal to see you—simply to talk, which same there seems increasingly less chance to do now, with the Dorns in Idaho, and another good friend, Ed Abbey left now as well—and so on. I have been teaching parttime at the local university since the fall, fair enough, i.e., I seem to be sufficiently unidentified for them to be polite and likewise to leave me to my own so-called devices. It takes off pressure of $$$, and involves me two days a week only. So that holds us for the time-being. The place, i.e., all this desert and space, I do love, and whenever I can make it beyond my own nose, there it is. So that's a pleasure.

I wish you could get here. Phil wrote earlier you had thought of going there, and perhaps might be able to stop en route like they say. Anyhow please do, as and when, for whatever time is possible—you are very goddamn welcome. Ok.

We faced a bitter time in the early fall, which I in one way would rather not tell you of, but you are a friend and so I can't not, in that sense. Our next to oldest daughter died in an impossibly sudden accident, no one could prevent, and yet it was such a damn deep shock and emptiness to get used to. I think we are now, at least the time passing helps no matter how much of an old saw to say it seems—well, it's true. I suppose such things do in no bitter sense make life as much as any others. How to live without it, always that exposure which used to seem to me almost an 'excitement'. I know a little better now and yet I cannot not feel that same exposure gives us all the possibility we have,—so. Again we are ok, I think the other children have not been painfully hurt by it—and our life does, I think, make it. That is a damn good thing.

Anyhow things continue. I have a book of poems coming out in April, and will get you a copy. I am trying likewise to get through a novel, old times in

Mallorca, long ago enough to be malleable, etc—and when writing, it's a plea-sure—and when not, as lately, it hangs on me like a stone etc. So god willing I'll have it done by summer. I was making home brew before I got too lazy, and that was wild, i.e., the luxury of having gallons of it around the house—great parties by the way. Ah well . . . I'll have to do that again like they say.

So don't be unhappy goddamnit. Ok. Viz get here and pull me out. That will keep you busy, and to see you again would be a real goddamn joy. Write as you can, and take care of yourself. I still vote wet.

All my love to you,
Bob

. . .

LETTER TO CHARLES OLSON

1835 Dartmouth NE
Albuquerque, N.M.
April 6, 1962

Dear Charles,

I am very pleased, and very grateful, for that review of the book, i.e. no matter what he thinks to do with it, it's <u>there</u>, like they say. I find the book itself continues to be somewhat unreal, I don't finally think of things that way—I am god knows pleased, completely, to have it a chunk like that—pues, como mi vida you dig—but I continue to see it piece by piece, looking ahead so-called. Ah well . . . I think you give me everything I ever wanted, the help with and recognition of the use of self, the instant to instant sense of form. Likewise the energy term—I have never got to anything that made more sense to me than that sense of the real you made clear in THE ESCAPED COCK, the risk as in the note to those MR BLUE stories in the ND Annual, and the means and terms of energy in the PV piece, and all that you then made follow. God, I can remember you saying, look out for the 'poeticisms'; and "And they shat in paper bags." Ok. Viz you told me. No one else ever did. So. There could be no measure more than yourself for me. I thank you very damn much for that care, as god knows here, and all the time. Wow!

I got the job by god, they were terrific, i.e., I was as ever vacillating like mad, caught by being here literally somehow. After so much moving the past two years, when they made a counter offer here, having money etc equivalent, I was very tempted to sit, but the Tallmans refused to let me—was <u>that</u> great! So as of July we move out there, and it feels like a real goddamn place to be. T/ himself is a lovely man, really too much, that shy quick careful care of mind—sans the least stir of any biz of assumption. He reads us like a new language, i.e., all the rest seem finally preoccupied with their own information etc etc. So really it feels like a place at last, and as of a summer from now he speaks of their plans to make some sort of 'writers conference', seven weeks, but free of the muck usually present, i.e., he much wants yourself, as a center. Those people are really pushing to <u>know</u> something, a very lovely sound. I haven't really met with such a push in people since the few at Black Mountain, as Mike, Ed, Dan, et al, back then. So that puts something ahead again, which is complete and solid pleasure. Here I've been ducking through doors, and hiding in men's rooms etc. Not the greatest, despite no one has bugged me particularly—but the sluggishness does, and the face of a student who is awake would break your heart—for my part, it becomes immediately a conspiracy. So it will be a relief to be out of it. So by god. Bobbie likewise is very happy. We have no friends here, despite the good house—and that gets wearing.

Anyhow all is ok. I've been trying to get on with the novel, no poems in a long time but I can't worry. It's taken a long time to let emotions work again, after Leslie's death, and I can't as yet take hold of things by means of them—but again the prose makes a way into that, letting it come as a conjecture one thing after another, lets me both into and out of where we've had to be in the past months. I think in that sense we are all right. Again, I cannot thank you for such reassurance as the note on the book, viz it is everything. I can't worry whether they use it or not, and/or I've got it. Ok. Write as you can please. If I can help with anything please let me know. We'll see you for sure in June, so that at least gets closer. Ok. And thanks again!

> *All our love to you all,*
> *Bob*

There's a little more time before taking this off to mail—I was thinking, perhaps it is the prose for me which makes the means again flexible, i.e., in poems a 'manner' many times tends to set, as against now, in the novel, the need to invent a form from what the 'subject' proves as written. Because the past year was a 'hell' of seen limits, I mean the accident in Guatemala, with the truck, killing the old Indian man by the side of the road, then on return here finding one of the boys I had taught with roughly two weeks to live, conscious of all as I talked to him, the will of that intelligence more persistent than any I have known and more innocent also, then the afternoon as we had to stand in the waste of the sand like a gravel pit in New England, watching Leslie's body be recovered, first her shoes, then herself, with a ring of people on the bluff of the arroyo above the diggers and ourselves, with a TV camera man and all that hell of that invasion—I found myself in each instance thrown back to pure 'seeing', it was such an instant reality—and in perhaps the perversity of my own nature, or literally what the 'I am' is in animal term, I watched with such an intensity, even as I myself 'did things' I was all that perverse act of recognition, so hungry for the exactness of 'sight', so unable to shed any of the consciousness, even seeing in the last reference Bobbie in the same way, again myself frozen in the term of a receptor. I note that only to make reference to the 'limit' it has left in me which I refuse as 'bitterness'—having at least come to have little interest in that—that is, I can only be alive is what I've come to know completely, and in others also, my own child or children now, too. I won't say I know what 'life' is, how should I being 'life' as much as I will know I suppose, ever. But I am beyond any 'reason' for living, any sense of 'plan' that is, want only to be with it, people as real as trees and water, and only as 'permanent' as these. The pain is the distortion only. What one's mind can acknowledge is perhaps even 'horrible' at times, but I cannot disavow it, and consider 'acceptance' almost as an arrogance, i.e., how can that be the point—if one lives at all. There can be no such 'argument' in what one is—but I will tell you, how very damn truly those words of yours were for me, just that afternoon, I mean a hand held that far to me, over that at times distracting distance of literal miles between us, of that, 'I left him naked/ the man said and/ nakedness/ is what one means . . . ' There is nothing that does not yield its beauty to that sight, not one human term that will not come true there. God knows thank you for all you have taught me to know—so never please think anyone could say more. Ok.

All love,
Bob

. . .

LETTER TO JACK KEROUAC

1835 Dartmouth NE
Albuquerque, N.M.
May 30, 1962

Dear Jack,

Goddamn huge confusions on us here, como se dice, as we get ready to take off for the east, then back again, then west north to Vancouver, where I'll be working the next year. It looks like wild country up there despite rain, and we haven't seen trees and green for some time now. So, it will be good. But the confusions of getting there, via New Hampshire etc,—ah well. Viz, On The Road With Wife and Kids—and why not . . .

I don't really damn well know finally what Don Allen wants—because I haven't heard from him now in some damn time, but he is off in Mallorca/Japan etc. So, good for him too. But if he says the anthology shot is off, viz the prose book, then off it no doubt is. He had said earlier he was seeing Barney Rosset in SF/LA and that's when I haven't heard from him since, pues. Anyhow who needs anthologies. I really think they muddle more than they help, or do at the moment. But then I was hoping a book such as planned might cut through the clichés of Herb Gold, Salinger, et al—that is the 'proper' 'style' sense of it, quite apart from what they write etc. Which I can't myself make (viz I was trying a few days ago to read Mailer's DEER PARK, and despite I think he does mean it, and does care, it was an awfully dreary thing to pay attention to, really . . . not that I mind tears either, but I hate the clichés etc etc.) Anyhow if I hear from him that anything is happening, I think those prose pieces you note would be very good to have in—so. Onward . . . And Don is a pleasure to drink with etc, so that I suppose is the point no matter.

This is late, but thinking of above, and fact I've been up to neck in people all year, viz students, you should know how they do hold on to you, as against Salinger for example, or simply the wise tone. In one thing, and they were sharp people*, they had been reading Huckleberry Finn, and I was trying to get them to say what they thought could stand with it, i.e., qua simply where things were, what, and why, and then how it felt to them—as it obviously did feel to them, for very damn real indeed etc. Anyhow that's just where you came ^ [*in. They could think of no one else who so thought of the world as such a "present" place.*] As it happens, happily, Warren Tallman, who did that note on your prose in EVERGREEN, is the one who really got me into university, now, in Vancouver. And I was thinking of what he does say in said piece, of prose as 'a sum of variations' etc. That is useful to me god knows, and/or makes clear that people can still read etc.

Thinking of moving now, again, I feel it is a good time to make clear as well what I value in you, that beautiful life you bring up out of things. I really love it very much. And I love the way you love people. So, if a truck hits us etc, I'd want you to know that, like they say. Ok! Selfishly I wish you were going to be around New York. (And if by luck you are, you can get me c/o of John Chamberlain, 74 Strawtown Rd, New City, NY—from a little after mid-June till about the 1st of July etc.)

Lawrence F/ came through briefly, and I liked his shyness, and straightness. He is a simple man finally to please, I mean in the old sense of make comfortable. So we had a good time. Here I've felt too often like the only odd ball, and do it, working, so quietly, etc, that is whatever difference etc, it's hard finally to find anyone to sit down with. So.

Anyhow god bless housewives, why not. Their laments make more sense than most things. They may even look out those kitchen windows etc.

Write as you can please. After mid-June, and trip east, you can reach me c/o Tallman, 2527 West 37th Street, Vancouver, B.C. Take good care of yourself.

All love,

Bob

[note in right margin] *It was actually an "honors" group reading Darwin, C. Wright Mills, "Ben Frank", etc.*

. . .

LETTER TO WILLIAM CARLOS WILLIAMS

1835 Dartmouth NE
Albuquerque, New Mexico
June 4, 1962

Dear Bill,

I feel guilty about my silence, but have hesitated to write, god knows why, except my own confusions of the past months have kept me tongue-tied, and likewise divers work, as the teaching. But Denny had written of seeing you, and if thinking of you has managed, then I've been there as well.

It's a miserably hot afternoon here, my wife is packing the house (Indian style!) while I'm 'grading papers'—wow! It is a little heart-breaking, and endless—but one I just had read brought things back, to wit a girl writing of your DESERT MUSIC, awkward with this place but working her way through in a good, hard headed fashion, reading it, in short—which is the pleasure. For example:

"The laws of the world give a corpse, which may be represented by the form which is on the bridge, dancing with the music of nature, but only the poem can give the music which makes the form come to life . . . "

Or better, this tight shot: "The whole of the world prevents an escape from any part of the world . . . " Apropos your saying 'I cannot vomit it up . . . '

Then, a little later: "If he cannot vomit up the ugliness he will compose a poem, which will turn the ugliness into beauty. But, as Williams says, inspiration is nothing; the writing of the poem, or the "made poem," produces a tangible idea . . . "

And then: "Now that the poem is almost made, the verb which has brought it into being detaches itself, and the poem is in existence; it is articulate. But before he had heard music in loneliness, and now he does not feel lonely when he hears it, for he is part of the music . . . "

Anyhow that's a freshman, with that happy decent awkwardness, and with that, so to speak, it's possible to work and/or to teach—or really to give something, if only my own confusions at times, that I can't feel the imposed critical hierarchy, hence go by a process of 'feeling' equal to that of the students. What else.

We are moving, shortly, to Vancouver, B.C., where I've got a job for the coming year, and I think it may well be where we settle. I like the distance, and I like, too, the still open freshness of things there, and that possibility of any not as yet 'settled' place, etc. I was there briefly in February, reading, and found people very good, i.e., open, wanting to see things, and so on. Teaching, the most tedious and finally degrading aspect is that authorities grow apart from all the literal life of things on which they both feed and depend. It's a vacuous, well, vicious, debasement of any use that otherwise might be there. Ah well!

Anyhow we do look to a life there, all of us. This past fall we lost our next to oldest daughter in a sudden accident, and that has left a residue of feelings hard at times to deal with—and the place tends to stimulate them, just now at least. Then too, there is a 'way of things' here that sometimes displaces me, it's what I'd first taken as an 'open' manner on the part of people—but too often it proves simply a slackness or an assumption not easily accepted. For example, down at a shopping center near here the other day, I was sitting in the car, having bought some envelopes for some letters, anyhow sitting writing addresses on them a man suddenly was looking in the car window, sort of quizzically, and asked if I remembered having insulted him, the day our daughter died, having been caught in a fall of earth in an arroyo near the house—and if I wanted now to apologize. I was dumbfounded—apparently I'd pushed him away, or said something, god knows caught in that moment. And now, eight months later, he thought of all things to remind me of it, having himself apparently kept the 'injury' fresh in his mind all that time. So I insulted him again, I couldn't think of any other fit response to him—I hardly understand what, even, he really wanted of me. So.

We are coming east for a brief visit, and I do want to call. I would love to see you again, but I wonder if that would prove an imposition—but I will call. I have thought of you again and again, the past months—very much so when my book came out, with your plug very generously to the jacket there. I hope you know what that meant to me. I can remember first writing to you, very scared, and then later meeting you for the first time, and your answer to my pretty shaky introduction of myself and comment that I was scared to death—'what, of me?' You've been very good to me indeed.

I think things strengthen, define themselves, or begin to. I feel they do among my generation and friends, and I hope things continue to work as they have these past few years. Lately I've been writing at a novel, trying to break through clichés of habit got in the poems—that is the book of poems even calls for a change, or so I've felt, and the prose gives me it just now. And all really does feel good.

I hope things are all right for you and your wife. It's impossible ever to thank you rightly, but at least I can say it, <u>thanks</u>. You've really made a whole world possible for many many people.

All my love to you both,
Bob

P.S. Just going on with "grading"—one kid turns up with a wild phrase: "He was a natural athlete, morally speaking . . . " And a little later: "Stanton went down heroically, trying to save a lady's maid larger than he . . . " They must really try!

. . .

The University of New Mexico
Albuquerque
English Language and Literature
June 12, 1962

Dear Warren,

            To recapitulate, i.e., I wrote you last night, and now in the debris can't remember clearly whether or not I got it mailed—I did mail a postcard, which is incomprehensible if you haven't got the letter. Anyhow, briefly:

I'd be pleased to accept the post described, for the summer session '63; and will do my best to persuade Olson to come also, when we see him shortly in Gloucester. (Please use that address for me, for any note you want to get to me quickly, about the 20th to 25th of June: Olson, 28 Fort Square, Gloucester, Mass.) I suggest otherwise these people, thinking of your own outline, and granting myself etc.

Myself	Olson	Tomlinson	(for the long period)
Duncan	Levertov/Zukofsky	Layton	(for the week etc).

I suggest Layton because I can think of no Canadian equal to him at present, for the purpose in hand; and too, he will get on with Olson and myself at least, from old associations on BMR etc. I suggest Tomlinson finally because he's the best poet technically now in England, certainly of the younger—and will be close, hence more likely to come. And Logue, though pleasant, would not be very much for the context. I suggest Zukofsky/Levertov like that, because I favor each of them equally. I would think in fact that Zukofsky would be the more articulate teacher, but Denny has a larger following at present—and represents very clearly an active element of younger writers etc. So, that's like that.

Or to take a chance: why not drop all English, shift Duncan to Tomlinson's position, put Zukofsky in Duncan's—and let it ride comme ca? Como no pues etc. Ah well.

Now apropos horrors of moving. Jesus Christ etc. I just found first registration given me, 'temporary' but legal, giving date of car registration as June 22, making it legal to bring our car in there sans duty then July 22nd, so that would be expected (give or take a day) time of arrival. Is that impossible? Please tell Eliott Gose I got and thank him for PRISM—and would be grateful for any help re settling once in. And also tell Frank D/ have his bk, much enjoy it, but too goddamn vague now to make sense—so will continue where left off on arrival. Then, could you call RR freight, in a week, or just before you leave, to say Creeleys will pick up or arrange for freight they have there on arrival as 'settlers' July 22nd or thereabts. So they won't sell it etc. That's abt it. I am really in fog, may forget all important bizness, but have feeling I've said this before, like, if I mailed that letter. I just mailed batch of huge xrays to Med/ Cent/ in Ottawa—like the Hall of Fame? So—crazy. And we'll be in touch.   All love to all,

Bob

. . .

LETTER TO ROSMARIE WALDROP

2527 West 35th Ave.
Vancouver, B.C.
Canada
August 17, 1962

Dear Mrs. Waldrop,
Thank you for your letter, and for the copies of your translations—which interest me very much, for example, how the rhythms seem held in the first verse of The Warning, or again, in the last of Heroes, etc. That's quickly put and/or actually read on my own part, because my German is pretty hopeless—but anyhow I'm grateful for the care on your part. Ok!

Apropos your questions: "for love" in The Warning has the sense of, 'for the sake of love' and is, in that sense, free even of the qualification of 'my love'. But certainly the association of 'for love of you' is also there, insofar as that is the specific relation etc.

Then, in The Hill, 'but that form' has for me the sense of, 'but that way of being,' 'but that structure of a way of feeling and acting,' etc. It implies a <u>manner</u> of acting and feeling, but one deriving from a whole way of thinking, as, earlier, I describe the 'head' as having been made into a 'cruel instrument' by this 'form' etc. Well, 'gestalt' may well translate it, I can't see why not, but then I am no judge of the associations involved. Its 'psychological' implications would be accurate enough. Yet there is no implication of a 'woman' finally since that would 'exteriorize' this 'form' and what I most wish to stress is that it is an interior or inner 'structure'—not one determined by outward terms, etc. Ah well! 'Weise' (still feminine?) might be more accurate, but again I'm only guessing.

I'd like to send something for Burning Deck—I enjoyed the last issue I saw, certainly. I'm embarrassed by not having written anything for some time now, distracted by being at work on a novel—and also the book tended to swamp me in a way. Anyhow I'll enclose the one I do have, but you'll find it pretty dense I'm afraid. What really concerns me now is to go back through all 'manners' or terms of my own thinking, as here the question of what existence things said have is god knows evident. Playing I guess upon that 'how is it far if you think it', to 'how is it real if you think it' etc. Sans, hopefully, dull assumptions. Well, it is clearly a way mainly of priming the goddamn pump etc. I hope you will feel very free to object, if it's of no use to you and your husband. I can't think, scrambled now as we are from just having moved here, who might usefully be sent or whatever notices of BURNING DECK. Really, I'd stick to those whom you yourselves feel close to—which is the point. Anyhow I'll try to write again as things settle, and to send other poems as I have them. Thank you again for the translations and for your very kind interest.

Yours sincerely,
Robert Creeley

. . .

POSTCARD TO JACK KEROUAC

Creeley
2527 West 35th
Vancouver 13, B.C.
Canada

Jack Kerouac
c/o Blake
PO Box 700
Orlando, Florida
USA

November 25, 62

Dear Jack,

This is quick—but I just read BIG SUR and though I can hardly congratulate you on the pain it brings so close, it is a completely articulate, human, and beautiful thing you make clear. I.e., if it's truth they want, that's it. So—you make it. Just now, here, it's like old New England weather I've been long out of, a misty evening, yet—fair enough, i.e., it makes one think, usefully. Things are ok. At times the teaching part gets dull—I do—but we stay centered—and/or here. Take care of yourself please. And thanks again for the risk of such truth. Ok.

All my love,
Bob

PART FOUR

Pieces, 1963–1973

New Mexico, Buffalo, Bolinas

May 7, 1963

Dear Warren,

Can you please find out as soon as possible <u>how quickly</u> a voucher for a ticket (<u>one way only</u>, if round trip can't be managed in advance) can be got for Allen Ginsberg—with place of departure <u>open</u> for New Delhi, Calcutta, or Benares. He is getting pretty worried about it (which is my fault) but I've written him along with this that he'll hear from you directly.— Otherwise all's well. Will write a decent letter shortly.

All love to all, Bob

· · ·

[Top of page: hand-drawn star, *Shine on!*]

Placitas, N.M.
August 30, 1963

Dear Paul,

It's good as ever to hear from you. Here we are just coming down after the wild business in Vancouver—which I thought, finally, one of the wildest things ever to happen, to me at least: viz, 1) Black Mountain 1955–56; 2) San Francisco 1956; 3) Vancouver 1963—with then the spaces of literal singular friendships, as yourself that first time we met, the two and a half days talking, Laubiès in France, Gerhardt coming back from Germany, times talking with Ed Dorn—und so weiter. But it was a great time—i.e., it opened everything up again for me, and, selfishly, that matters a lot like they say. Otherwise, I think it was a common feeling. You'll be getting reports there no doubt of varying kind, but I've never heard better readings of Charles and Robert, nor Dennie—who was really with it. And Allen was like a lovely damn open human being every moment of the way. Really, it was an extraordinary rapport for all concerned. Voila!

I'll try to make some sort of short tape, for you, and get it off within a week's time. Just now the Chamberlains are here with us, preparatory to moving out to Santa Monica at the first of the week, so things are swinging with that etc, and I don't know what I can manage to do immediately. But I'd like to do it, very much, and will. Ok. And god knows thanks for thinking of me. (Charles must be, by this time, back in Gloucester, so you'd best get in touch with him there.

265

Also Ed is of course in Pocatello—we had a good visit with him on the way back, likewise with Douglas Woolf—who is an exceptional man in all senses.)

Does 8th Street have the novel on sale, i.e., Scribners told me the publication date was September 13th, so I was surprised by your note of it etc. But don't buy it for christ's sake, i.e., I'd like to send you a copy—the more so, since it's of that place we both had a part in. Anyhow that at least seems now behind me, and I'm hoping shortly to get to work on another, of the time in Guatemala, just that it breaks any set locus of people, and makes the feeling of a kaleidoscopic 'reality' which I'm after this time. Too, I've got a contract to do a book now on Olson for that Twayne series [^ *US Authors Series*]—actually sort of a 'handbook' of 160–190 pp/ which is really best for me. I'm no good at the 'further explication' at all, at all. Anyhow that's also to do, and god willing I'll begin with poems soon likewise. That shot of Vancouver was what I needed very much.

So all's well, if a little chaotic from all the travelling etc. I go to work here sometime next month it is, god knows likewise when. But they'll tell me no doubt. I'm glad to hear things are going ahead with the Provencal book, and not disappointed, finally, that Macmillan won't do it—because I think you can damn well find better. Ok. Take care of yourselves.

All love as ever,
Bob

. . .

LETTER TO ED DORN

Placitas, New Mexico
September 13, 1963

Dear Ed,

I'm sitting here pues, in office, trying to kill time against same when I can go home—and the relief of that distance, despite drive to and from, is considerable, i.e., all the grey dusty tedium of having to be <u>anywhere</u> for no good reason is wiped off simply by that space opening up along that drive north, the mountains, viz just to get <u>out</u>. Ok. At least this year I'm given privacy, this room is in fact much like a cell, surrounded by empty bookcases—'a home away from home' I expect is the rationale etc—and a phone, which rings for two other people as well, elderly professors, and am tempted to leave it off the hook but lack the guts to, just to stop its ringing at times, and this huge office typewriter, which reminds me of that one we tried to get to you, i.e., big and solid, obviously my one friend here sans doubt. So. So, thinking of business, I have you now down to come sometime this fall, i.e., before Xmas say, and does that make sense for you? The assured payment is $100, and also, depending on what's possible, it might well be that one or two of the other local u/s would want you to read also, upping same. But the damn point is, I hope not selfishly and impossibly, to see you. When things get more straight, we can work out best time etc.

I am very damn grateful to you for your letter re the novel, just come this morning, just before I had to come down here—so that's on my mind, very much, and very happily. I have been sitting here also reading the Penguin RIMBAUD, which has a useful selection of letters etc, as the early one re 'seers' and that emphasis 'je suis un autre' which is part of that 'I' placement—or god knows one (I) never so 'place(s)' anything, or as R/ says also at that wildly early age: one is thought. The other lead for me, I think, must have been Stendhal, most in his journals, where the objectivity of himself is put as a 'thing' almost, and his sense thereof never somehow confused with his actual existence. Hence, cast in that way, 'I' finally sees the back of 'my(s)' head, etc. (I wonder if Dennie had that unconscious sense of person in that 'With Eyes at the Back of our Heads'—probably not, but present poem re the 'face' of the body, the fact that front of a woman's body makes: tits/eyes; bellybutton/ nose; cunt with hair/ a bearded mouth—and with that I make myself a cuntface no doubt. Etc. Well, I see said the blind man. Ok.)

Anyhow you let me think of the book as same, more and more—which is very useful right now, because I want to start another, before simply the habits of writing such a thing—for once in no ugly sense—I mean simply the sitting damn well down to—get faded out etc. I want to use that flux of Guatemala, beyond sociology god willing—beyond even committed sympathies of such an order—and/or to cast again, if possible. What I won't have—and what will be in that way the new thing to learn—will be the presence of an ingrained emotional context; hence invention and feeling, in the actual moment writing, will have to play an even greater part than they do in the present one etc. But as you told me, way back, i.e., that I might trust simply the act of writing to find its own way, it did damn well work for this one, to wit, I found thinking found its way, and I suppose that also is why Joan gets in there, as you say, beyond a 'criticism' of her such as I might carry in my own terms of that 'history'. Viz, in that sense, throughout the book, I never purposively understood what I was saying, and/ or was too pulled by saying anything, 'just now', 'here', etc, to let the intention of saying that 'one thing' ever get a warping hold etc. Ah well—but again, and again, and again: <u>thanks</u>.

I liked Dawn, I was very moved, uselessly, by the predicament she is in. I liked the other girl there less 'pitiably' simply that she is so much the nature of a woman, no matter what she 'thinks' etc. As you, I like that simple size and form. [^ *I mean more than such literal feeling.*] Anyhow there is not further point to any of it, thinking of the pillow I can't now remember clearly ever having slept on (?). Somehow & where no doubt. But that is very damn good of her, again woman-wise, Dawn, to think, so:

> Like murmurs
> the weeds grow
> faster—

Or something. And I really dig weeds, i.e., do, finally, associate my own nature with that term of growing. I was trying to think of the sun in any case.

> Pero otra Adan oscuro esta sonando
> neutra luna de piedra sin semilla
> donde el nino de luz se ira quemando.

> But another dark Adam sleeping there
> dreams neuter moon of seedless stone far off
> where the child of light will be kindling . . .

I.e., Lorca garbled between myself & Gili, again Penguin etc. That note of his on the duende is still there, certainly. But I was thinking of the hope and light sweetness of that name, for a girl, i.e., to give to one, Dawn—'child of light' against such 'neuter moon of seedless stone' etc. The darker thing, etc.

The goddamn office is killing me. Ah well. Hot. Dull. Sweat. And out the window a whole parking lot of dead cars etc. And some huge tinlike bldg which is making a constant roaring sound. A few cowed trees, and particularly a telephone pole with one of those cylindrical black things hanging from the crossbars, under the wires, like balls (?). Ok.

Last night Ken Irby came up—I do think he has had a breakthrough with that long poem he says you liked also—and I played him the tape of your Vancouver reading I hadn't myself heard since then, i.e., just now copied from Fred Wah who had had it etc. That _moves_—viz, that 'walker' of yours I damn well respect, and how it makes the back & forth of any being here. So—_that's_ true.

We have got another house, better in point of inside room, enough outside as always—'the whole _world_, boy . . .'—and still in Placitas, which was my worst fear, i.e., that we'd have to get sunk again back in this city etc. Anyhow all's well—except for dreary colds I'm just getting over and Bobbie is in the damn middle of. But we'll be in sd house by another week at the most and can begin to distribute ourselves therewith, etc. So—it makes it. And you equally sound too swing. That picnic is really where I'd want to be, ever & a day pues. Take good care of yourselves, and do write, and don't mind this rambling. Today is the day the novel comes out officially like they say: Friday the 13th -my sign.

All dearest love to you all,

Bob

. . .

LETTER TO DENISE LEVERTOV

Placitas, New Mexico
October 19, 1963

Dear Denny,

If I may say, I'd like to depend on your sense of those poems I sent—which much reassures me. I've come to a kind of locked sense of things that compels me to tear up almost everything I write, of the last year—except for the novel finally, where my ignorance of the 'formal' possibility gave me actually a relief when I saw that things were 'following,' so to speak. But with poems—and somehow that summary quality of the damned book, in that sense at least, and all the damn talking <u>about</u> poems my job has pushed me to—I am falling presently over my feet, viz confusions, constantly. That was the 'bankruptcy' sense that got so insistent at Vancouver this summer I think. I hate what I <u>know</u> in my own work, I mean what's there as a 'skill' and/or something I've accumulated almost as 'information'. I can't write a damn poem as an 'example' of ability etc etc. Well, you know.

So again—not to make you the goat pues, nor to be coy or whatever—I'll trust you to know more really than I can, right now. I write the damn things when an hour later feel jesus I hate it, see the trick, feel the goddamn slip of 'easiness' etc etc. It's not that I want it to be 'hard' but rather, want not to know so simply where the poem is, in that sense. I think it will get simpler shortly, as I get more relaxed about the whole business. The book again—with my New England nature—made the damn issue of, can you keep moving from what you have done etc. And there, you see, that ugly effort of 'intention' gets bitterly located at times. I think of Robert's 'be idiot awkward with it . . . ' and that sense I too often lose to my own (present) self-consciousness etc. But anyhow, just that my life, like they say, does not become itself in a way I hadn't really known before, is enough to trust to—and those 'orders' will come beyond all that my worrying can accumulate as resistance.

I think the two you take—as I remember, ridiculously in that I burned my copies etc—are best. The other was too damn simply a 'Creeley' poem. Damnit! Anyhow what you say of them shows me they <u>were</u> there—more than I 'thought'. Ok.

This is quick—but I want to write so, to say thanks for your very helpful hand with same—and also that happily this Texas offer of a reading will I hope settle the problems you note in your letter. That pleases me very much, and selfishly it will be so good to see you both. (I think it will be a better time of year also, not so cold and all.) So that's <u>good</u>. I saw a man from close to Presque Isle on television yet—a long way from home!—the other night, and got hopelessly nostalgic.

I think we'll contrive to get east for a year at least, as soon as we can manage it. I think it would be worth it for us all—because this space at times does get hard to fill with any human contact. Well.

Meanwhile all does go well, in that the job is simple—and fair enough people, and leaves much time free. And our house is comfortable, the children a real delight—and I feel clear in it all. So again I think things will come. Write as you can and I will.

All my love to you both,
Bob

Again re poems—I do want to touch things as fully and clearly as you are doing, from the given fact of your being a woman and then with your own nature equally—i.e., there is not other 'place' I respect from which to write. I have never intended to play tricks with such things, but whenever a way of saying something tends to habit, I get nervous—I mean, when my poems move in a manner I feel is the result of such habit, then I see no possibility being allowed. I suppose what I am now involved with is—curiously—learning to accept what I've come to, i.e., that I do write poems, and have to take that act as something less than amateur etc. But often it's like trying to find whatever can answer that question, <u>is it enough</u>. Just now I'm caught by all that wants to say no.

P.S. As postscript to that poem for Allen—which I'd sent him before the god-damn reaction came etc—:

> "B.C.
>
> I was waiting for Eternals
> superimposed on blue sky
> and apartment building walls
> I was in 15 years before
>
> come back through future doors.
> I can't wait forever,
> I didn't and came back here
> by myself feeling sure
>
> lost in this University
> with other males and females
> looking in Creeley's like eye,
> and we all told similar tales.

Oct 14, 63

Dear Bob:
    Battered that out last night, trying to approximate your style, the middle stanza almost makes it no?, but the last line sing-songs bad . . . "

I.e., Allen—who really I love very much, i.e., this side of him is so little recognized, all the way he tries, and studies, and thinks—and all the shyness therein. Anyhow that struck me, reading the above.

I read JUDE THE OBSCURE a few days ago—for a class that's a good one, just open talking sans 'program'—so-called 'Honors' etc. He is a wild writer—each time I read him, it hits—prose or poems. Just that reach of his emotions is so deep—it rides through all the 'style' of that 'period'. Anyhow that was a recent pleasure.

B.

Otherwise sitting here listening to twist music, e.g. "I got my job through the New York Times . . . "

. . .

LETTER TO LEROI JONES (AMIRI BARAKA)

Placitas, New Mexico

October 21, 1963

Dear Roi,

Your book takes on so much it's hard to speak of it very simply, like they say. I've meant to write for weeks now, but the damn confusions of moving again made me wait to see if some sort of time would come, to think of it free of all that distraction. Anyhow—and/or to hell with that—it really carries a lot, and I'm very goddamn impressed that you could keep it all together as you do.

The parts literally dealing with music, e.g. how this or that manner or form comes to develop, seem to me held on to clearly enough. Again, because of what the book covers, your way of doing it has to be quick, but the use of what you quote, or actually the social sense you keep emphasizing—i.e., what the distinctions were in that place, like 'dirty' blues as against the parodies etc that come of it—works for me very clearly. I am most interested finally—as I think you are—in that sense of it, and the music makes a sharp context for thinking of that history where it is, as apart from any generalizing sense of 'understanding' in a specious and god knows ugly sense. Again, all the details, such as the way your grandfather, moving north to Pennsylvania, met with a wall, keep one's own feelings in reading 'local'—and that, to me, is a great pain. Curiously enough, it is, again for me, only in those parts where you are obliged to cover quickly a lot of detail re the music per se, e.g. 'bebop', that things lose that particularity—just that the manner does there become of necessity 'objective' and reasonably enough 'cataloging' as opposed to those sections—as when you talk about the fear of the middle-class negro of that threat of the newcomers, etc, or of all those distinctions of feeling and position (those quotes re the twenties novelists, for example, say more in themselves than 'talking about' ever could)—where you are moving on the terms of your own feelings and involvement.

The last way seems akin to what gets such location in the 'Crow Jane' poems for example—which impressed me very much. Or in the Dante book, etc.

Anyhow, I think you make it altogether, in what must have been somewhat the confines of the 'text', call it. I mean, the set of such a book to begin with. I think in that way the book which they note you are at work on, the whole situation of the present negro intellectual—the ambivalence of where they can be, thinking of that middle class again, which you make so clear—will let you center more closely on your own concern. Which to say is presumption, but I could hear you all the way through this one with that very much in mind. Ok!

I just had word from Charles about you, Ed and Bob Kelly's scene at Buffalo next summer. That ought to be <u>wild</u>—i.e., that really seems the <u>place</u> to me, viz I don't mean 'Buffalo'—I mean you there as such a center. The one limit at Vancouver this summer was that we were working re people of what comes after you, and that skip at times displaced me, for one. What I mean is, without you, Ed, Bob et al as the 'sequence' literally there, it's very hard to 'place' anything. So again, it ought to be a <u>great</u> summer in Buffalo.

I am in slough of sorts, not hopelessly—but just that we have been moving about so damn much the past months. But the house here now is ok, and job is simple and fair enough etc. So, all's well. This is quick but I have already been too long about it, like they say. Write as you can please and let me know what's happening.

All best as ever,
Bob

. . .

LETTER TO CLARK COOLIDGE

October 26, 1963

Dear Clark,

Don't worry so much! Viz onward! The fact you write is all the reason that is—'sanity', 'cause', or otherwise. I thought you people were going to start something—not to bug you, but do keep moving—otherwise things begin to clog, and one is left stuck etc. Anyhow you make it, viz poems—so that's a blessing? How about counting them . . . Wow! But really, let's do laugh. Take care of yourselves and give my best to friends there.

All best to you both,
Bob

. . .

LETTER TO ALEXANDER TROCCHI

Placitas, New Mexico
November 1, 1963

Dear Alex,

Your letter just reached us, and what a damn deep pleasure it was, first, to know that all keeps moving and that you are all right, like they say, and then the very damn generous sense you give me of the novel.

Even more as much goddamn lovely was the way your letter and the outline of what you are planning came here, i.e., I'd just finished Whitehead's Science & Modern World for so-called class business*, Ed Dorn had just read two nights, and had been very centered on whole political fantasy, and all the sense of things got this summer in sudden concordium (as Olson called it) of people at Vancouver—and think of that re 'place': Allen G/, Olson, Duncan, Denise L/, myself, and the people who came drifting in from all over Canada and the States for gig on so-called poetry but what was much more: history as one telling the story, proprioception, cells,—or, to save time here, simply what you put as "What is to be seized . . . is ourselves." [note in left margin: *I'm teaching at UNM, which is simple enough for time-being and keeps us eating.]

It's no damn coincidence that all who were there were wailing right down that line, even to literally the issue of university as no 'place' or 'institution' but the literal instance of persons. Well, I hear you, like they say—and will be very pleased to give whatever help I can be.

Let me note people immediately who'd be I think interested, and some you'll know but may have lost track of for the moment, as Allen:

Allen Ginsberg, c/o City Lights, 261 Columbus Ave, SF 11 (and send him several of the off-prints, so he can pass them on to Ferlinghetti, McClure, etc— who will be equally interested. Also, Don Allen is starting new magazine, and might well be useful: 1815 Jones Ave, SF). [note in left margin, with arrow drawn to "Ginsberg": He's going to NYC for Xmas, so write him quickly.]

Charles Olson, Wyoming, New York—I'd think him a very useful root, simply that his thinking is primary in just this center you hope to actualise, and I hear that word in your thinking, as Whitehead, as Olson also insists on it, etc.

Edward Dorn, 10B Pocatello Heights, Pocatello, Idaho—the sharpest younger man on issue of politics, not as 'subject' but as defunct process you again note (and I had chance to give him the extra copy of the offset happily).

W. S. Merwin, Lacan de Loubressac, par Bretenoux, Lit, France—he's been much concerned with political maze lately, i.e., of last KULCHUR or earlier issues of THE NATION—and would usefully widen context simply he is outside the reference we usually make?

Stan Brakhage, c/o Nauman Films, Custer, South Dakota—a wild filmmaker, intelligent straight man, and again useful as further context—and I think he'd hear what you are saying.

John Chamberlain, 123 Oceanway, Santa Monica, Calif—very good man, great goddamn sculptor/painter, and old BMC friend—so he might come in, though he reasonably takes the whole political term as hopeless as we have it here—so might shy away from any apparent concern therewith, but still I think he'd get your point.

Then a group in Mexico City, which in turn could turn on rest of SA/CA groups: Margaret Randall, EL CORNO EMPLUMADO, Apartido Postal Num. 26546, Mexico 13, D.F. They are organizing, for example, "LA CASA DEL HOMBRE" which "plans a self-sufficient center on the outskirts of Mexico City, open to those who wish to come, etc . . . We direct this idea to the artist, feeling he is the social and spiritual conscience of our time, and realizing that the time for centers of nuclear investigation is at an end: the time for a new and living creativity has arrived . . . " Anyhow they get the point. Allen, again, will have much of this activity located from his own travels etc.

Anyhow—that much just to get started, and I'll pass on word to people as I write etc, and you tell me what, again, I can do. As so-called statement, beyond self-satisfaction etc:

"History is the act of each one of us. I cannot admit longer to forms which are not of that reality. I insist that we become ourselves." Well, fuck such abstractions no doubt—but anyhow, let's go!

Thanks for the warning re Calder. I'd heard (from Don A/) he was a pretty weird one, and got nowhere with him when he first wrote me directly etc. But Scribners' agent there, Curtis Brown, will at least be watching him for terms of contract, i.e., he's now signed to do three bks, novel, short stories, and poems, over next 2 yrs beginning spring—so when he goofs on that, I can at least get clear, if and as he does etc. He thot he had serial rights for pre-publication but they called him, so that's why he's being so bitchy re that no doubt. Ah well. Write as you can—take care of yourself. It's a damn deep pleasure to be back in touch.

    All love to you all,
     Bob

[note on envelope] *P.S. I very "innocently" sent your note re the novel back to Calder via Marion Lobbenberg—with note you were old, dear friend—and your generous comment might prove excellent for publicity, etc,—At least we can have that pleasure. ¡Onward! Bob*

. . .

LETTER TO ANDREW CROZIER

Placitas, New Mexico
November 15, 1963

Dear Mr. Crozier,

Thanks for your good letter. While I remember, The New Review I'd mentioned is one to be edited here by Donald Allen (who edited the New American Poetry anthology), 1815 Jones, San Francisco. From a note of its contents sent me by him, I think it will be very useful—particularly for reference to Olson's present work, etc. Kulchur is, as you say, often 'local'—and of course here that serves a purpose—and really what I thought should be of use to you is the material by Duncan, Dorn, Zukofsky, and a few others. But if you can see it there, even in bookstores, I think that should serve you well enough. As yet there is no definite publication date for Olson's new sequence of Maximus. You probably have the earlier book, published by Corinth/Jargon (Jonathan Williams). Do you know his Melville criticism, Call Me Ishmael? That was printed by Grove.

The people there I've been more or less in touch with are Tom Raworth—but not for a time now, Ian Finlay, Michael Shayer for a time when Migrant was still printing, and presently Charles Tomlinson, whom I much like and who is to edit an issue of an Oxford magazine on the so-called Black Mountain school, Alex Trocchi whom I'd known in Mallorca and Paris and whose present plans much interest me, and Martin Seymour-Smith, another old friend from Mallorca—and then odds and ends of people from time to time, as Jeremy Prynne, and divers editors there who write now and then. Of course Jonathan Williams spent the last year there and gave me a fairly wide sense of what was happening. I had met Robin Skelton while in British Columbia last year, and Carne-Ross, whom I didn't like, a while back in Texas etc, but only, happily, for a very fractured evening. And so on. I did have chance this summer to talk at some length with Charles Tomlinson, and got his sense at least of what was happening there. I like and trust him, and think he has certainly been sensitive to American practice far more accurately than others. Thom Gunn I met briefly in San Francisco last fall—there was no real sense of much happening, but then I only paid his class a brief visit, in company with Robert Duncan—and he politely enough let us do the so-called talking, etc. But this may, in any case, give you some sense of my relations there, etc.

Your mention of Burroughs suggests you might have interest in a new anthology of prose edited by LeRoi Jones, called The Moderns—and published by Corinth, which is literally the 8th Street Bookshop. It has work by a variety of people, i.e., Ed Dorn, Douglas Woolf, Burroughs, Kerouac, Rechy, Selby, Mike Rumaker, myself, etc. I think it's a good cross section of these writers—with some I would not have included, but then also with Fee Dawson, for example, whom I very much like. So it is useful, and the first of its kind, certainly. There's to be another brought out by Grove, edited by Don Allen, early next year I think, though the publication date hasn't been set. I helped with quite a bit of the editing, but then had to withdraw, not so much from any argument with him but for reason of not wanting to offend another friend whose work Don couldn't accept etc. Ah well! Anyhow that might prove interesting to you. I do like Burroughs, by the way,—I suppose I read him primarily as another writer, and find his ear, for one thing, extraordinarily accurate and close, and I like also his pacing, i.e., the collage effect he achieves. As social program perhaps it's something else again, but, again, I find his preoccupations god knows useful. What he isolates as volatile terms I respect, for example. I think Alex Trocchi has the more developed political sense (as Ed Dorn points out) but Burroughs also very much impresses me, very much as a writer. I don't want, otherwise, really to say more of William Stafford. I.e., he is a decent man, certainly, and your taste will prove as accurate as mine, and then, I read him as an American—and of course shy from the generalizing 'we' of his poems, and the personifications of 'nature', wind, mountains, et al, and question the overlay of his rhetoric. It is much more Frost's that Williams', by the way. In fact, I see no relation at all between him and Williams, because the sense of form, and especially line, is very different. Again the parallel seems to me Frost, with a heavy overtone of the Ransom-Tate school, certainly very familiar here, etc. Well, no matter, in any case. It's a pleasure that you are reading as widely as you are— which is the point. Anyhow, if you draw your conclusions from formal aspects, instead of contentual whatever, that really will give you sufficient ammunition to qualify the fellow studying Pound.* I'm surprised he, of all people, can't make those distinctions, i.e., what does he think Pound was making a point of, etc. So . . . I'm pleased to hear the poem was of use. I hope all goes well for you, and thanks again for your letter.

Yours sincerely,
Robert Creeley
Robert Creeley

Ask him about Zukofsky and Bunting—to whom Pound dedicated Kulchur, etc. Does he know their work?

[note on envelope] *Do you know Paul Bowles' work as a composer, novelist, e.g. The Sheltering Sky et al? He's not really so simply a disciple of B/s—much more a friend apparently.* [illegible] *is younger—and perhaps more as you suggest, but again, that does simplify. C.*

. . .

LETTER TO DENISE LEVEROV

Placitas, New Mexico

November 16, 1963

Dear Denny,

   I have mixed feelings about trying to review the Cantos (wow . . .), simply that I don't feel the background like they say called for. I would <u>like</u> to do it in a way—just to find out if only for myself what there has been in them for me, selfishly enough. But I had a lousy experience with Hatch the last time I tried to review—and I wanted to do as well as I could, i.e., it was Williams' Pictures from Breughel. But my first attempt he in effect rejected, on the grounds of 'difficult' style, and suggested changes of manner etc. So I tried it again, to my own mind much watering down the original by the attempt to make it 'clear' for I don't know whom at all, finally. But let me show you, since I still have both copies. Viz, for example:

  1st: There is no simple way to speak of this book. It is so singularly the work of a man, one man, that it moves thereby to involve all men, no matter what they assume to be their own preoccupations . . . (Then I quoted the opening few lines of The Yellow Flower.) The insistence in our lives has become a plethora of plans, of solutions, of, finally, a web of abstract commitments—which leave us only with confusion. Against these Dr. Williams has put the fact of his own life, and all that finds substance in it . . .

  2nd: There is no simple way to speak of this book. When a man makes something so much the fact of his own life, then we are all of us involved because each life is first of all that singular . . . (Now reading that, I don't clearly know what the hell it means! As against at least the snap, and feel, of the first draft—which was my way at least of putting it, etc. Then the quote again noted.) What we have been told too often to care for in our lives are the plans, tomorrow's solutions, what we can look forward to, and no one speaks of what is to be seen, right now. But that is what there is, to speak of. Against the confusions which come of a blindness to that fact, Dr. Williams puts the things he sees, feels, knows, in the life given him . . .

  I think the manner of 'spelling out' really did lose much of the whole point of the comment, and I hated it the more since this was my chance to make my own respect of his work completely unequivocal and declared—and as it was, the last chance—and I am bitter in that sense that Hatch had to put his damn finger in. In fact, when he came to print it he changed my title of The Fact—which I felt put it as straightly and flatly as Williams might himself, and I was no doubt even unconsciously punning on the title of a poem of his I've always loved, The Act—anyhow he changed the damn title even to The Fact of His Life—which is then pretentious, and somehow condescending to my own feeling, or rather to my sense of what I wanted to say. Ah well! But can you help me with this dilemma to this extent—ask Hatch if he will accept a manuscript you yourself find acceptable, since I am sure we can work out whatever obscurities etc come up without having such a completely different kind of mind and intention so inconsistently present, as Hatch's etc. That was the damn problem, i.e., he kept saying I had very interesting things to say, etc etc, but that my way of saying them was confusing. I wondered of course how he could find 'interesting things' if he then made the point he couldn't understand what I was talking about. Anyhow I would like to stay clear of him in all senses, supposing that can be possible. I would like in any case to do all I can, and I am flattered, very much, you think I could handle such a book—again wow. And I really would love to have again a sympathetic context in which to write such notes, i.e., to be so used. Well, I'm game, then, if you are—and there must be some way to get around Hatch. And I'll also try to keep my 'manner' as open as I can—pues. But I did want to mention that earlier difficulty with him, because he might now have that opinion of my way of saying something stuck in his head so that whatever I say becomes that occasion for his concern.

I hope I'm not reflecting simply a lousy mood here. I don't think so—but it has been a bleak week, first our dog getting hit by a car, breaking his hind leg, so he has to drag around with a pin in it, a hellish business—as you'll certainly know from the problem with your kitten. I hate animals caught in such businesses, especially this lovely damn patient one, with his huge embarrassed size. Well. Then we had got all excited about the possibility of getting finally some land north of here, cheaply, with chance then for putting a house on it etc—but find our credit extends only to the value of our car, and that for 12 months etc etc. Fuck it. But it was bitter to have it so close and then to have so firmly made clear that our sort is not the sort etc. Then, as a sort of endsville, I've somehow got entangled in a business with Cid re the novel, which he doesn't like, and says he feels 'something is missing'—and that of course is like waving a red flag in front of me, i.e., I scream you son of a bitch WHAT'S MISSING—and so here we are, locked in parallel moralisms no damn doubt. But he so much always tells me, 'next time . . . ' Well, you know—and I can never get through to him enough, or he to me, I guess—and I feel ten years old again, having tried but well perhaps the next time will show improvement. And—god! He can frustrate me more simply, and more completely, than any man I've ever damn well met—and make me feel guilty to boot! I suppose I should simply acknowledge him as a most personal saint, and have done with it. He also speaks of the tinge he feels in the book's look, etc, of 'business' and 'commerce'—and again I blanch redly . . . Today we didn't even have four goddamn dollars and ninety eight fucking cents to buy a fuse switch for the wiring here, and he tells me I've sold out—or he doesn't, just lets it drift in as it were with the breeze. So—all's well, actually, entirely—and I feel fine! Robert just did write, after the same long silence—and he keeps to that sense you note—so I assume all goes ahead in that way. Shortly I guess we ought to think of literal poems, in the way you note—I think that would be very good, and I agree Robt will be our most useful help with it. I can barely remember my name, most of the time—and my own suggestion to you both would be, read it all, it's goddamn lovely, I want it ALL. But we'll make it. Ok! This is quickly written pues, but I'm anxious to get back before Uncle Wiggly etc. All our love,

Bob

[notes in left margin of p. 1:]
P.S. I'll hand on that letter to Chris M/- she'll be <u>very</u> pleased to have it. No proof of those two poems as yet, but that's no problem. I'm a little curious now to see them again—and <u>thanks</u> again for saving them for me. Ok!

One wild thing—Robt and Scribners are apparently pretty settled now on what's to be the book for them- and they are very happy with it, and I think he equally is. ¡So!

[Bobbie Creeley's notes in margin of p. 1:]
Dear Dennie and Mitch—I'm enclosing 2 collages the size I'm working now—I hope you like them—love Bobbie-

Robt mentions in letter he heard from you about me sending poems etc—so it does go around. I'm so damn shy at the moment—but things do open. Thanks again.

[note in left margin, p. 2] *I'm very interested in these poems of yours now that center in such a close character of person—as body—I think they are moving something very deeply. As in Vancouver: Our Bodies: Hypocritic Women—and the one with the boat image bumping the pier. They are parallel in part to one I've always loved: THE FIVE DAY RAIN. I like too the grace of the shorter one—it's a lovely formal "set" it has I think. Please keep coming, like they say. Shortly I'll hope to as well. Again this "A Psalm Praising the Hair of Man's Body" is <u>very</u> lovely.*

[Enclosed are the poems "I" (*CP* I, 279) and "Something" (*CP* I, 281).]

[notes in margin near the poem "I":]
These are just two recent, the first from actually a clipping that came in a Belmont paper re the novel, which actually (actually) was the history of my grandfather who lived there plus a brief note on my father also. Viz the review had smaller heading: Grandfather Was Selectman, and refers to the outset as, grandson of onetime Belmont market gardener writes first novel, etc. It was a pleasure!

Among other things trying to "dislocate" "I" in some sense at least. I sent this to Don Allen for that new magazine of his, but I don't know as yet if he'll use it.

Some of these rhythms, curiously, seem to go back to poems I was writing in the late '40s.

[notes in margin near the poem "Something":]
I sent this to Ed Sanders – the nearest I seem to get to his context – ah well!

Later I thought of Williams "Turkey in the Straw"—again a lovely one! He really runs all through my head. But I am clearly the more tentative man—I suppose even intentionally.

. . .

LETTER TO TOM RAWORTH

[Placitas, NM]
February 7, 1964

Dear Tom,

Thanks for your good letter, and the copy of that translation, such as it was—that was the poem I'd remembered, particularly the last verse, and that reference in Olson's The Death of Europe is, I think, to the young man riding, i.e., his "I praise you/ who watched the riding/ on the horse's back . . ." Anyhow I made one or two small changes, just for the sound as follows:

A VOICE

Softness, and you dumb . . .
Bells from a mountain
want to come here . . .
I sing.

> My night is lonely,
> my voice sans guts,
> water spits on my rights,
> tongue twists . . .
> The air's warmth . . .
> a syringe.
> No metal, no dreams.

The water's red is a blood red,
and the seraphic beauty
a young man
on the roof tree
riding . . .

> The sun's march
> is by dogs escorted—
> the march of the earth
> by a rosy hurricane.

I remember there was an idiomatic use involved in that 'water spits on my rights' and 'tongue twists' but I can't find the original, nor Rainer's letter in comment on this translation—he had a diagram if I remember with hands cupped or 'fisted' over the 'I'—anyhow, blocked was the point there, and I liked the 'water' as a primary 'natural' blocking the personal order etc.

I'm glad to hear that your job and all go better. You certainly deserve, like they say, an easier time of it. And you sound god knows as active there as ever: wow! I will look forward particularly to Ed's and Fielding's work.

One thing before I forget, Renate Gerhardt is now active as a German editor and small publisher. I think you could reach her easily enough c/o Rowohlt. I don't know what she might feel about the memory of Rainer now—the last days of their marriage must have been very painful, but I'm sure she'd be interested to know of your issue on him—and might do a short note on their work together then, both translations and publishing. Then—there was a translation of Brief an Creeley und Olson in an issue of Origin, first series—I don't have the copy, but I'm sure the library here does, and I could get you one if that interests you?

Your new baby must be there now: wow again! It's our Kate's birthday today, five years old—I remember all the Dorns arrived that day five years ago now, i.e., time! Actually she was born the 6th, and we slid it to this Saturday (actually it's the 8th . . .). Ah well! But it's wild to watch them grow.

Things seem to be moving a little again here. I'm thinking of an issue of Northwest Review to come, with a great deal of Olson's work, both reprint and new—most usefully. The same magazine is now printing Ed regularly. Then there are an increasing number of small 'newsletters' that keep things open— and Kulchur plans an issue on Zukofsky's work shortly. So . . . Otherwise I'm still myself moving in crabwise fashion, somewhat obliquely, but at least writing poems again which is a relief. I've heard nothing further from Calder about anything—typical, i.e., he comes on, then fades—but contracts at least hold him to the publication of the various books etc. Anyhow if more works out re coming, I'll certainly see you there, which would be terrific. Do write anyhow as you can and let me know how things are, and if I can ever be of any help, you say.

All our love,

Bob

. . .

LETTER TO STAN BRAKHAGE

Placitas, New Mexico
March 28, 1964

Dear Stan,

I'm awfully sorry to hear of difficulties there. I enclose a check—like they say!—I hope as some sign at least. I'd just been reading, in the <u>Village Voice</u>, of what had happened, and it looks bleak indeed. It may well be it's Authority's way of getting back at the freedom presently in publishing, where it seems this influence is now almost completely embarrassed—e.g., <u>Poetry</u>, which is certainly conservative, will now take work with such reference, making no comment; to wit, from a recent poem I'd sent them and they've taken:

> . . . At night it
> is the complex
> as all things
>
> are themselves and
> their necessity,
> even sexual. So
>
> cunts and cocks
> as eyes, noses, mouths,
> have their objects:
>
> hermaphrodite, one
> sexed, bi-
> sected in that lust . . .
> [from "The Dream" (*CP* I, 300)]

I hope some such sense is equally soon allowed in films—well, it <u>has</u> been surely, well before its equivalent in writing in some instances. Again, were there larger film distributors to take on the issue also, the effects would balk this kind of power, etc. Grove, for example, as Robt points out, embarrassed this move by publishing so quickly so much of this material the moves to stop it could not keep up—and finally the whole ground of what's the qualification of 'obscenity' becomes embarrassed because it cannot qualify its intentions, even. Anyhow you probably know that there was a showing of <u>Flaming Creatures</u> in San Francisco, at a local, neighborhood 'foreign films' theater—in fact, two showings, at six and nine, sans any incident. It was there only one night, as part of a 'festival' program, but nonetheless, there were apparently no complaints.

I'm sorry not to have written in so long. That lovely abalone shell and 'magic mountain' came safely—thanks! We have had a good year, in fact all goes very well. I've got a Guggenheim for the coming year, which means that everything opens out ahead. We've also found a good house here we think to buy—on interminable 'time' but no matter. I've asked Betty Kray to send you tickets for that reading, and will certainly see you all there. It's been too damn long! So, this is quick, but do take care of yourselves and let us know what happens, and I'll see you in just about three weeks.

All our love to you all,
Bob

. . .

TELEGRAM TO CHARLES OLSON

WESTERN UNION TELEGRAM

AWSX BUE"025 NL PD = ALBUQUERQUE NMEX MAR 30 =
= CHARLES OLSON =
= WYOMING NY =
 = WE ARE VERY SORRY. PLEASE KNOW WE ARE WITH YOU.
ALL OUR DEAREST LOVE =
             BOB.

915A MAR 31

. . .

LETTER TO CHARLES OLSON

Placitas, New Mexico
April 1, 1964

Dear Charles,

I don't want to intrude with any sense of question, but must say to you how very very shocked and sorry we are at the news of Betty's death. I really cared for her and I very much hope she knew it.

But I love you so deeply, and necessarily for my sense of my own world, that I've got to insist that you not be hurt impossibly. Please tell me anything I can do—which is an impossible thing to ask, but as you will know, I'm here for whatever use or help I can be. That way, there is no need to write or anything else. I'll hope to see you very soon, but that too—if it isn't simple for you—is of no matter.

You are so much in the world of all that I know, please take care.

Our dearest love to you,
Bob

. . .

LETTER TO ALEXANDER TROCCHI

Placitas, New Mexico
July 16, 1964

Dear Alex,

Forgive the long silence—we moved the past month, and the usual chaos, like, followed. But in the meantime I've heard, as you must have, that Ferlinghetti plans to print one of your statements in the next issue of his Journal for the Protection etc, which circulates very well here. And I'd suggest also you get in touch with Lita Hornick, KULCHUR, 888 Park Ave, New York etc, since she would be interested, I think, to print such comments as you now want read—and again her distribution is active.

Otherwise, I'll be of what use I can. Having just seen, like they say, the Republican convention here, politics of that order seems to me to have become an instance of physics, i.e., screw & lever etc—not that it actually is much else in any case, with all respect. But I question staying within the conceptual frame of such thinking—I feel that CORE and like groups are limited imaginatively, in this sense, no matter how effective they may be in local protest. But such friends as LeRoi Jones, for example, want not the 'white man's burden' but an actively redefined sense of place in no way the complement or stereotype of white definitions, etc. I don't see that as yet they provide the terms except in negation—but nonetheless I feel them right as such reaction at least. 'Reform' is too simply an instance of recoil, before the next shot etc. Or so it does come to seem from this place. (In contrast—I much respect Allen Ginsberg's contemporary activity in politics—again very local, and making, at base, an active 'fantasy' of the content proposed by institutions as presidents etc. Likewise Olson in recent work.)

That book you note sounds very interesting. Will you tell me please when it's available? I.e., the anthology of writing on drugs. Ok.

I was very flattered and pleased to hear a photograph of one of your sculptures is used for the jacket of The Island. I.e., that's a pleasure, and useful sense of old times as well. Now I hope to god they manage to get the book itself out, at last—announced for March, and now mid-July etc etc. Onward . . .

I'm coming over in October, and will hope/plan to see you then. It's been a long time and as ever letters don't make it enough. But, selfishly, do keep writing as possible, and let me know what I can do. I like the poster idea—I think a form of that kind could be very sharp, even to jog with 'strangeness', as close to the generality [^ viz. The People . . .] as possible—well, why I dig Lenny Bruce etc.

So, take care of yourself and I'll see you. Voila.

All love as ever,
Bob

. . .

LETTER TO ED DORN

Placitas, New Mexico
July 26, 1964

Dear Ed,

I sent off the ms/ to Tom Raworth, and hope it's of use. Thinking of what he must be up against as fact of day to day life like they say makes me feel depressed and useless—but anyhow I hope something as this makes it.

Just now hearing reports of rioting in New York and Rochester—and also of possibility in Buffalo—what sense do you get? The Goldwater nomination was such a cold duck, the political distances seem absolute. TV at least gives some sense of the police in so-called action, and NBC report makes clear the officer was not in uniform and continued shooting after the boy had been hit, and that the knife was a pen knife—and is clearly hostile to Wagner among others. But that too becomes descriptive somehow, i.e., there seems little effective 'power' interested in doing more than try to 'return it to normal' etc. But again, I'd be very interested to get your sense of it there, thinking of, as you note, the reaction to Roi's living in that neighborhood (Buffalo) earlier.

The house we're in is up that dirt road that branches off from the highway past the church. It's a good one, i.e., roomy and sufficiently rambling to make enough privacy for us all. We are putting on one more bedroom in a kind of curve by the road, and that damn well done, I think it will be great. We ran out of money so it lacks final plastering, and finishing roof, but I think we'll make it ok.

There have been people through, Gary, Mike M/, Don Allen, etc—as I think I told you—so have not done much beyond odd jobs and/or I can't yet get with the novel pues. Then the work going on outside cuts off a sense of privacy I seem to need. But things feel ok and I'm not in that way worried, for once.

I'd love to have heard you all reading. Was a tape made and would there be any chance at all to get a copy? I have never heard John and have missed that a long time. I really dig very much his present work, all that I've seen. He really sticks.

Likewise, I liked sections of Gil's long poem in WILD DOG, the last one, very much—I liked it all in fact, and parts especially, i.e., the way it went, like they say, in the so-called form. He sounds steady again.

Most unhappily, Bobbie's father died suddenly the 15th, a repetition of the first heart attack while driving to Ruidoso with his brother. He was only 48— but not simply as rationalization, I think he would have hated the limitation of the continued heart trouble and clearly it wasn't going to stop. It shook the family—it hardly seemed possible, and he was a very decent and innocent sort of man.

Forgive the jumpiness of this letter but selfishly I want to keep in touch. Let us know how you all are and enjoy yourselves despite humidity etc. I really wish we were there, to talk and all—but ironically it's wiser that we are here.

Our love to you all,
Bob

. . .

LETTER TO LOUIS ZUKOFSKY

Placitas, New Mexico
December 29, 1964

Dear Louis,

Forgive my long silence—really the effect of all the confusion of moving about in October/November, and then, on return here, the kind of persistent restlessness that followed as the aftermath. I did get the copy of <u>After I's</u> you were kind enough to send, very gratefully—and love as ever the clarity, and the light (light) way it all makes—especially "The Translation", thinking too of your reading it to Robert and me that afternoon. Ok. (I'm fascinated by "The"—I should say so. Voila!)

Most happily, while in England I had a pleasant meeting with Basil Bunting, very unexpectedly, since I had no clear sense of where he might be. But I found him and vice versa in Newcastle, and spent that evening at his home in Wylam. Next morning we had a little chance to walk back of the town, and also across the river to the store there etc. I enjoyed him very much—really, that intelligence you are both possessed of shines through a very great dark indeed. In fact, I thought much of you as he told me his first sense of what he might himself do in poetry came from the awareness that sounds might lead the sense in a modulation of its own continuity. And too—speaking of Pound, he said, although he wanted obviously to be Chaucer, he is much more like Spenser in what he gives to the craft and those who then come after. Anyhow, I found all his company a very useful pleasure to me—in that pretty consistent chaos of bouncing about England, from London to Edinburgh and back again.

(Also happily—on return here, I read for two weeks in Michigan, by that point exhausted—but stayed for a couple of days with Donald Hall and his family, whom I did like. Hall is now advisor to Harpers for poetry et al, and is hopeful of getting Bunting's work collected and back in print. That would do wild things for 'British verse' come to think of it.)

I can't say I'm as yet able to do much more than chafe—it's a kind of habit of movement got from all that mumbly peg etc. But hopefully, I'll soon be rid of it, and at work in some sense. I had a good visit with Charles Tomlinson also, and was pleased to hear of his issue of AGENDA, of your work. They are really very interested there to be aware of more than Graves etc. And Charles is an intelligent and excellent friend.

So—all's well, and again forgive my silence. I came into New York about 8 in the evening, a Sunday, and was gone before noon of the next day—and fall to pieces on telephones, so that's what happened to that hope, unhappily. But we will or surely ought to have more time in June—a better season in all ways.

Our love to you all,
Bob

P.S. I'm very pleased to hear of your own work—and that "A" continues so well and all. I feel such an impatience just sitting here, that, clearly, something will come soon no doubt. Ah well . . .

• • •

LETTER TO ED DORN

Placitas, New Mexico
June 2, 1965

Dear Ed,

I'm sorry to have been so far off—somehow the past months have been pretty sluggish, i.e., distracted like endless Saturday afternoon sans much to do like they say. But that really has been the goddamn sum of it.

Thanks very much for that issue of Peace News, and that very sharp poem of yours. I do think England is going to offer terms for you, in a sharper more local focus, which despite whatever offers and so-called resistances, will be very happy and useful. To that end—I don't know if you're in touch with Alex Trocchi, but very clearly that might be of use to you both. Anyhow the enclosed 'portfolio' is what he'd recently done for me, and somehow I like it much better than the way it seemed to sit in recent issue of the Yale Literary etc. There is always a <u>form</u> to the way Alex sets something—as the way he makes the initial paragraph work here, etc. So if you could send him something, as notes of your own etc, I'm sure he'd both be grateful and put them to good use. The address is 6 Saint Stephen's Gardens, London W2.

I suppose what's really at so-called root of present balking, is like so-called 'lines' come walking for the mail—when I can get past the paranoia of being even that public etc. This town echoes so many for me, mainly from the times of living in Spain, and often I'm at a loss for a way to walk through it simply, no matter sitting out back and looking out at that wild space is to be somewhere in all senses. Anyhow said lines come as not so much random, but insistent wanting to strip something clear, get to a 'proposal' apart from the egocentric, yet make evident the actual appetites and feelings that seem present. Poems tend to be 'wrap-ups' otherwise, i.e., both data and manner too familiar to me. I was impressed, for example, by the way Gael Turnbull gets past that—thinking of the obvious containment of his nature—in that sequence in recent Poetry. I.e., it's only at a few points recently, and not so damn recently at all, now, I feel I've got like possibility actually in hand, and/or The Woman, Anger—and one or two others.

Not just to make her the goat etc, but in contrast I felt Denny's "Olga Poems" (and the title per se tended to stop me) had become too damn much the manipulation of her intention, and a literary manner all too damn decidedly. That's what I walk in fucking fear of—that what one knows how to do gets adamant—and at that point of course it's all over. Anyhow . . .

Otherwise it's great here, I can't really damn well deny it. One very happy thing. I got the tail of the Rockefeller scene at least enough to get us briefly to London next February—it's a goddamn odd business, i.e., I'd asked for a year there, but instead they are paying income equivalent to my salary here for spring semester, and flying Bobbie and me to Lake Como, where they have a villa, like, for month of February. But that is all that's come of them, i.e., Olson seems to have got nothing, and so on.

I very damn well much hope you get to SF. Otherwise we'll see you there or here as we can manage it. This is quick, but anyhow I'll be back. Ok.

All dearest love to you all,

Bob

[Enclosed, "To Bobbie" (*CP* I, 337)]

. . .

LETTER TO ALLEN GINSBERG

Placitas, New Mexico

June 2, 1965

Dear Allen,

We saw a note in NY Times about your being crowned King of the May, like they say, in Prague—which seems a lovely triumph. Bobbie made a collage of spritely cherubims dancing about it, so you are eternal. Ok.

Re the enclosed—you probably know about Alex Trocchi's Sigma and this was a note of mine he'd kindly printed. I like the form very much, and hopefully it gets around England a little. Anyhow he seems very much of our time and place, and if you had anything you think he might use, either poems re political terms or whatever, I know he'd be very grateful to get them and to distribute them in this fashion. Did you see him while there? I hope so.

Nothing much happening here, but nothing hopeless either. We look forward to seeing you in July—that ought to be happy, just in that way at least.

Too, very very happy you got the Guggenheim. That's progress for them clearly, and I hope it serves you to some use you've wanted. Ok. Write a card when you can please. Take care of yourself.

Our love to you and Peter,
Bob

Alex's address there is 6 Saint Stephen's Garden's, London W2.

I heard very indirectly here that Neal had been busted along with Ken Kesey in LA, and had jumped bail and gone to Mexico. What's happening, and could I be of any use. You say, please.

. . .

LETTER TO TOM AND VALARIE RAWORTH

Placitas, New Mexico
June 23, 1965

Dear Tom and Valerie,

I'm very sorry not to have written long before this. It's been a sluggish winter, and/or it was, and time went by sans much disposition of anything. But happily things begin to move, and at least I got through the editing of a Selected Writings of Olson for New Directions, lacking now the introduction only. I feel pleasure in that like they say, and hopefully the book can serve to put back in print some things that have been long unavailable—Mayan Letters, for one thing at least. They plan to publish it early next year, so it's not too hopelessly far off.

Thinking of that side of things, Penguin is doing I think a very active collection edited by Don Allen, to be called something like The New Writing in America, also to be published early next year. It has things like Olson's Human Universe essay, Ed's From Gloucester Out and his story, Beauty—and all of LeRoi's play Dutchman etc, and much other stuff besides. That note Alex published recently as a Sigma bulletin by me, will be the intro for it—then Don's done a preface etc. Anyhow that's action of a kind, clearly.

I still haven't seen a copy of The Gold Diggers from Calder, so god knows. I really had such a good time while there, and was so grateful to Calder for giving me bed and board etc, that I don't give much more of a damn at this point. Still, it would be pleasant to see. Scribners is publishing it here in the fall, and may well beat C/ to it at this point.

I just heard that LeRoi is to be there in London for the opening of Dutchman this summer, hence won't be at the Berkeley conference after all—so I'm given his teaching job, and Ed in turn gets the reading and lecture I'd had—which somehow is much happier, at least from my point of view. I think LeRoi is now so committed to cutting out all whites it could only have been a bitter mess.

So that's about it at the moment. Great weather—that clears a lot. And one damn day or another, perhaps will get to so-called work.

I do hope things settle for you now. That's a miserable problem with children, and it must have been a dreary time for you all indeed. Again, I'm sorry to have been out of touch. You were very good to me while there, and I hardly forget it—though then too I wish I hadn't been being dragged about so much, just that there would have been more time in all senses. One thing: please do thank Anselm [Hollo], very much, for his book. I've had too little mind even to write him to say so, but the point is, it was a pleasure. Ok.

> All love to you all,
> *Bob*

. . .

LETTER TO CHARLES OLSON

> Placitas, New Mexico
> October 16, 1965

Dear Charles,

      I'm just back from Oregon, 5 readings in 6 so-called days, but I can't think of simpler ways to make money or whatever it is. Your three letters were here on return and I'm very happy that damn introduction gets enough done to make sense to you. I didn't want to take on the poems directly—i.e., first it seems to me Projective Verse, and equally the one on Shakespeare, and the letter to Elaine Feinstein etc, must damn well give 'explanation' as is pertinent. But what I had wanted to do, writing it, and then got distracted from, was literally a footnote, first noting Robt's and Ed's and my own notes otherwise re the verse directly, with some tight 'unexplained' statement of the issue of structure in the verse with no tone of spelling it out etc. Anyhow what I now want to do is, following the bibliography material, which will be a listing of primary books, give a brief note of relevant critical material either followed or preceded by a short note re prosody. Like 'fine print' really, since I think the people who bother to read such are those also best served by it, i.e., such comment. The rest merely churn it into 'argument' etc, which I was very damn anxious to avoid—I wanted just to say things, then let the book follow as the very damned obvious fact of itself. Ah well!

One thing quickly: would you have any interest in coming out here for a reading either late this month or sometime next? I think I can get about $300, which would pay costs of coming at least. This house is a lovely one, and there is a comfortable bedroom and all. I'd welcome the damn chance to talk—the kitchen by the way is great too. It wouldn't be any demand on you more than that, and the people are decent. So, supposing that interests you, either call me or write quickly to let me know, and I'll get it set as I can manage it.

I can very much feel that sense of box the scene at Buffalo, or actually all such 'direction' of any order, beginning with the Historic Moment of Vancouver etc, i.e., yourself as such Focus etc, must have increasingly seemed. That really was what came so clear at Berkeley in that evening.

In that way, I didn't want to 'get to' the poems after the first Maximus book, first that no text as yet is there—second, that a whole new condition is there experienced, the outcome call it of the first, but so open that I don't see involving it in 'description' prior to its literal experience. And again, the terms are clear—that is, the proposals of all this prior material lead I'd feel to the conditions of the new work—e.g., persons gain an intensive location well beyond 'exempla' which they sometimes are in the first. e.g. Ferrini et al. In fact, it's the intensive, call it, which so declares itself in what I can now get from the tapes and the various texts of this sequence I have. Anyhow, supposing the Selected Writings to locate 'where' it's happening, then what's coming in the new book is the full condition of the act in so many senses it would take another such collection to document it in any sense—which sense I thought much better to let said text itself literally be. I mean, I hate the damn elbow of talking 'about' something at the literal moment of its own event, advent. Well. That poem, four lines, you read that afternoon on the grass, that was earlier in Fuck You etc, seems the statement of the advent, in sd way. I never saw that piece in the Tuftonian by the way. That's been the damned irritation the past couple of years—the fact that the texts were in this way scattered.

The point is, I can very easily understand you now, when you say, "I went to my own funeral there in Vancouver"—as 'I gave myself into the hands of others who were interested to sum up the fact of my own condition, albeit with great respect and so forth . . . ' Onward! I love that fact of JP Jones for example, and really wild that way it De-clares in Whitman, Song of Myself, i.e., just in like that, to the thought—what a lovely fact that is and was and will be, always. So anyhow, again I was leery of coming too far into present conditions, as of yourself and the present work, just that such 'set ups' run dangers of distorting, always, the first facts of any such condition, which reasonably enough do come first. I didn't want in short to be like sd British frigate etc etc. So, you know.

I'm presently in open condition of having thrown one far astern, sort of a great relief if a perverse one, to hear all the hounds of the sea barking off into the distance, with the GD/s etc. But also delight, as review in NY Herald Tribune, Book Week, for first time in such public place gets the point—11 years after. But it leaves me very free to make present terms, feeling that 'distance' still holds, or rather, that fact still manages its own connections.

Re the fucking money by the way: I do think that expense should rightly come from plant costs, i.e., of payment to me for the editing business. I really don't like the way he puts it between us, and I can't feel such costs can be other than 'plant' etc. But you say. Anyhow the damn book at least survives. Write as you can please. Do come if it makes sense—and let me know quickly if it does.

All our love to you,

Bob

P.S. Also, is it ok with you for me to get tapes of the first lecture you gave and also the reading right from Berkeley? They say they will send them if I have your permission, i.e. a note to me or them saying ok. If it is, just put a separate note, so I can forward to them sans further bizness etc.

. . .

LETTER TO STEPHEN RODEFER

Placitas, N.M.

January 11, 1966

Dear Mr. Rodefer,

The chairman here, Dudley Wynn, just showed me your note to him about the possibility of a position, and I was most flattered to see the subject of your dissertation. Re practicalities: Sylvia Bowman, of Indiana University, is general editor of Twayne's U.S. Authors Series—and had given a contract to Fred Weiss (of Pennsylvania Polytechnic at Troy, etc.- or how you spell it . . .) to do a book on my work, but he has, I understand from him, dropped it. You might well get in touch with her about the possibility supposing you'd be interested to publish it in this fashion—they pay no advances, but the distributor seems fair enough, etc., and you get a fair income in that scene.

I am of several minds about the situation here, but would certainly welcome a sympathetic face like they say. If I can be of any specific help, please tell me. I'll support your application in any case sans question—no doubt from vanity, but equally with respect. Ok—and best to friends there.

Yours sincerely,

Robert Creeley

. . .

LETTER TO CHARLES OLSON

Placitas, N.M.
Jan. 26, 1966

Dear Charles,

Al Cook wrote two days ago to make tentative offer of a job there, god knows a good one in comparison to what's become of the scene here etc. It's a so-called full professorship with two course load at $17,500—and for $9000 more per year than I'm making. Which isn't all that simply the point except things here have so deteriorated in the past semester that even the house and place can't make the difference. I don't want ever to face such useless frustrations again—like, Baker was nothing in comparison. And to make it duller, these people are "nice" and "like" me. I get to feel like the original horror.

Again I'd like very very much to see you there if you aren't simply so involved it's a poor time. I'd thought to take a train to Boston the 15th, and then to come out by bus from there. I could stay at The Tavern—like—in fact have always wanted to. What I really, selfishly want is a good bowl of clam chowder. hot. And equivalent conversation, so please do damn well indulge me.

It really is time to get back there somehow. I've run out the use of the past ten years here, and I'm not a "westerner" as some very properly are. I thought of the crazy wetness, dripping, in the woods, as spring, black water in the holes of the ice, sound of cracking, in the freeze—The quiet of the denseness of night, etc. Buffalo is hardly that, but it does seem one part of the way. Hopefully, we could get some place out enough to have sense of country. Anyhow that's on my mind—with much relief. Do write as you can, and I will shortly. All our love to you,

  Bob

. . .

LETTER TO ROBERT DUNCAN

April 8, 1966

Dear Robert,

I very much thank you for your letter. It focused, finally, all my own distrusts and confusions. I had, in effect, accepted. I was curious, flattered, interested to see the actual circumstance of such procedures—hopeful that I might talk to people in my own person, and equally hopeful to give some sense of a writing here we share respect for. But you are very right that the one inescapable fact is, the State Dept is the sponsor, and accepting the situation, I can hardly hope to absent my own position from that fact—in a country where I can't even speak the language, and in a situation where I'll be completely dependent upon their agency. Anyhow—the enclosed letter goes off with this one. I feel <u>much</u> relieved. I'm going to read—in Chicago April 16th—Bly again, and this time I accepted, or had, out of my own uneasiness with the Pakistan business. Anyhow—it feels a better context.—I leave here Sunday for Kansas. All's well. Bobbie then meets me in Chicago the 23rd and the next morning we're in London. It will be a <u>happy</u> time. The more so in Italy. Where hopefully I can unwind at last. I'll write once the smoke settles—and <u>thanks</u> again.

All love to you both, Bob

[The following letter to Bela Zempleny was enclosed. Duncan sent it on to Denise Levertov; it was found in her papers at Stanford.]

• • •

LETTER TO BELA ZEMPLENY, U.S. DEPARTMENT OF STATE

Mr. Bela Zempleny, Program Officer
Division for Americans Abroad
Bureau of Educational and Cultural Affairs
Department of State
Washington, D.C.

April 8, 1966

Dear Mr. Zempleny:

I am very sorry to have this sudden shift in plans, the more so after having given an initial acceptance—but I now find that I'll be unable to go to Pakistan this summer. Briefly, I am very disturbed by the growing dilemma in Viet-Nam, so that to go to a country as Pakistan at a time when an implicit political crisis is so evident, and to go as the guest of the State Department in apparent support of a President whom I deeply question, would seem a deep and inadmissible confusion of my own purposes and commitments.

I am very blessed to share a community with other men in the act of writing, and it is their respect and belief that I am also much aware of. I cannot outrage the community of my own identity. I have also a deep loyalty to the fact of this country and the persons in it, and in that sense also I cannot commit myself finally to any program which is involved with executive acts and attitudes so hostile to the nature of this country which, within the possibility of my own acts, I have tried to honor and make known to others.

I am very grateful to you for all your help and sympathy. I confess that my first acceptance was really a response to your conversations, but now—even if so inexcusably tardy—I must consider that my going will have a much larger content, both for myself and for those other writers whom I care for, than I had allowed myself to be aware of. I hope you will understand that, and that you will depend upon my interest in being of whatever service I can at any time when the executive branch of our government does not permit or create such invasion of national sovereignties as it now does.

Yours sincerely,
Robert Creeley

. . .

LETTER TO CHARLES OLSON

c/o Rockefeller Foundation
Villa Serbelloni
Bellagio (Como)
Italy
May 3, 1966

Dear Charles,

I'm sorry for the silence but things got heavy and useless while in Kansas, and I slogged through simply as a job—not that hopeless but very damn nearly. Then I met Bobbie in Chicago and we made it from there to London, where we saw Ed and Helene very happily, but without much time for actual conversation. He thinks now definitely to stay another year and it makes sense, i.e., he seems to have good company and they both look active and settled.

So after a few days there with much business, a reading etc, and many damn people including Jonathan who looks now a proper Englishman (he took us to a concert at the new Royal Concert Hall, thence to Rule's etc etc), we went to Paris for so-called lecture on Poe (!) which I almost didn't make it in time for, i.e., luggage got stuck in trunk of the cab taking us to London airport, hence missed plane, and had hopeless time trying to get on another—had been up all night, at one point met Ornette Coleman etc—but did finally in time to walk in on wild scene somehow of proper old fashioned lecture room with students in tiers all about plus Sorbonne professors. I could barely speak much less make sense. Ah well. Then the next day we walked around Paris with René Laubiès, who is a solid friend—Montparnasse, Notre Dame etc. Then here the next day where we are now settling in. It's an odd scene, e.g. also in residence a guy named Katz, international law from Harvard, Theodore White journalist who wrote The Making of a President, then lovely man Herbert Butterfield and his wife Vice Chancellor of Cambridge, historian—and a couple of others I haven't as yet focused on clearly. But it's still somehow a boyscout camp, with meals On Time—though can get lunch and breakfast privately at least, and the surroundings are a gas—viz 'where Leonardo stood looking across the lake:

× makes/marks the spot' and 'Flaubert liked this path . . . ,' 'Stendhal uses this
in the Charterhouse . . . ' Und so weiter. So, like, it's still me.

I feel some shake, at some damn depth—Bobbie equally withdrawn in to
herself, that time of life I guess one thinks deep. Yet I trust it. I look forward
to the fall, to conversation sans the need to be rushing off, at least not in the
same manner. I realize, like they say, how bitterly long it's been since I've had
a chance to let myself go open to anyone somehow—all a kind of hand on the
gun, too often—and days go by with a sort of float and emptiness. But hopefully
I can get something done here, it makes a 'view'—back to Mallorca, forward to
god knows what. So.

Before leaving Kansas I checked proofs of Selected Writings—and asked
Jerry to refer to you the few questions I had. I hope that got done ok. Do write—
a sign from you would help a lot just now. We'll be here till 1st of June, then I'll
go back to London till the 10th, then home. I'll write again soon. Ok.

All love to you,
Bob

. . .

POSTCARD TO ROBERT DUNCAN

BELLAGIO
Lago di Como—Villa Serbelloni
Lake of Como—Villa Serbelloni
Lac de Côme—Villa Serbelloni
Comersee—Villa Serbelloni

May 6, 1966

Dear Robert,

      We're settled in at this point and it's really a very happy rest and
time together. The villa is the large building well up the hill—and I have a place
further up in those woods for working. All goes well indeed. May 15th we go to
Venice to see Pound and Olga Rudge—she wrote he'd welcome the visit and that
his health was fair enough. So—will write decent letter shortly.

Our love to you both,
Bob

. . .

POSTCARD TO ALLEN GINSBERG

[Buffalo, NY]
Sept 10, 1966

Dear Bozo,

       Just to report position viz beachhead established sans bloodshed, and am now in bizness. I went up to Gloucester last Sunday and had word of you all from Charles and John. Will see you October if not before. I think it's going to work out here ok. Good people in so-called classes at least. The house is good. Kirsten decided to go to local highschool here which makes much sense. So—take good care of yourselves and keep in touch if possible.

All love to you both,
Bob

· · ·

LETTER TO CHARLES OLSON

256 Woodbridge Ave.
Buffalo, NY 14214
Sept. 24, 1966

Dear Charles,

       P.S. to that card, i.e., that so-called graduate seminar fell to pieces yesterday, after three turgid meetings. I'd begun with Eliot, just that I wanted the occasion of some literal cliché to see what terms might be got to, therewith to make evident what the work was to their own assumption of it, etc., etc. So anyhow at one point one of them says, the word's out you're "white-collaring" your classes, and you were hired to be "Robert Creeley" and that's why we're in the class, etc. It was a hopeless moment, and I felt the appetite of that "imagina-tion" so viciously and crudely present. Shee-it. I.e., a class is supposed to be a spectacle, and I thought I was going to get some active use of things. Thinking of the year ahead—I feel like I was back to cleaning hen houses. Hopefully I can make simply a stiffness of occasion by asking for <u>literal</u> information—but how dull to lose a human circumstance just because they have their fucking "ideas" as to who I'm supposed to be. I felt a very damn real <u>offense</u> in it—not just to protect myself as my so-called privacy—but that anyone could be so dumbly evident in such a fucking limit of fucking attention. So that's what it now means "to know."

Afterwards went to Onetta's with John and some of them, viz Mike Glover, Fred Wah, Steve Rodefer—you can see the "picture"—and a couple of others, and drank beer, and finally back here with John and Glover, who left after a time, smoking pot—then Kirsten home from visit with her English teacher and woman's husband, terrifyingly young. The "other way" viz Columbia—

Cornell—now here for Ph.D., a "critic"—scared and didactic. I don't know. Finally watching Italian horror vampire movie on late show, relieved to be looking at something. I'll have to figure another way. I will!

All our love to you,

Bob

. . .

LETTER TO ROBERT DUNCAN

256 Woodbridge Ave
Buffalo, NY 14214
March 6, 1967

Dear Robert,

I'm ashamed of the long silence—but happily it's that so much has been happening it seems each day is time to catch breath and start again, which perversely I very much like. Anyhow, I had a lovely two weeks in company with John Cage and Merce, and others I very much liked as Billy Kluver. Then last week Norman Brown was here, and he's a pleasure, then last night John lectured—a lovely statement of god knows real <u>condition</u>. Then Jim Dine and his wife were here—and on and on! Bobbie and I feel a very damn useful whirl, in it all, which recalls us to possibilities in ourselves somehow the quiet of NM sometimes lost us. So.

Congratulations on the new house and yourselves in it! Wow! I'm very very happy all has come to pass with such pleasure. It must be LIFE like they say, at that.

So apropos a reading here—I'll get hold of Irving Feldman, who is not the loveliest thing to have hold of—but I think I can get him to arrange a specific date, having your time-table in hand. I'll be back about that as soon as some definite business is clear.

You are so very kind—well, that's no damn word—but I mean that you are <u>there</u>, in what you say of WORDS. I am very happy to have it out, i.e., out of the house/head, or whatever it is, was, etc. That too opens things up.

I regret Don Hutter's leaving Scribners, just that he could be talked to, and heard. I don't know what our situation there now will be—I suppose ok, for the most part, but it somehow dulls the occasion for me I'd come very much to look to. But by this point there's only one so-called 'direction' no matter.

I get notes from Charles, and things sound ok—i.e., his energy is very evident, and I think he makes a company of people coming through, as now the Browns, and others there as Ed. God knows he is in a very comfortable house with enough money to open things. That should make some sense. I think he sees a doctor and keeps hold of that end.

Back to Hutter's letter: those sections of PASSAGES you'd know very much
I respect—eg. I read UPRISING at the recent Angry Arts bizness in NYC, and
I don't think any evidence of that fact and the feeling it confronts, could have
been more evident. Despite the fact you were not literally there to read it, it had
immediate and very evident response and respect of those present like they say.
Well, that's where editing ends—especially if it never really began—so I don't
see how there can be accommodation for such reaction from them. Which is the
limit of Scribners etc etc.

I wish we were here together talking, but we will be shortly—and now we
are returning to New Mexico this summer—we'll use that as home base—so
perhaps there'll be chance to get out there too. Again, I'll write as soon as I have
something straight about the reading here.

Our love to you both,
Bob

*P.S. Again—what you say of the poems is so much a <u>world</u> I love the <u>possibilities</u>
of. And thanks forever for making it. Just that, at moments, I tend to an almost
"agreeable" doubt, it's so familiar to me. –And <u>company</u> in only a few! So thanks
for being <u>there</u>.*

Love again,
Bob

. . .

LETTER TO GEORGE OPPEN

256 Woodbridge
Buffalo, N.Y. 14214
March 19, 1967

Dear George,

    I regret missing your reading, but at least I can get hold of the
tape—but anyhow I very much value the brief time we did have. You certainly
make sense to me. As it happened, I saw Ed Sanders not long after—I think that
whole business gets as vague for him as it must seem to any of us, and I think
(and hope finally) he'll not stay put in it. In any case, much does seem to be hap-
pening with and to this present generation like they say. If it can keep its eyes
open, who knows.

This is quick, but I wanted to say hello, and thanks again for coming. I'll look
for you at Basil B/s reading, and will hope to see you again before too long in
any case.

Our love to you,
Bob

. . .

LETTER TO ROBERT DUNCAN

9596 Knoll Road
Eden, N.Y. 14057
Oct. 26, 1967

Dear Robert,

Time has gone so quickly, I've been poised to write you like they say for months on end without managing to. Now in this house, much is relieved indeed. God—what an <u>opening</u> relief it is. I think my tenseness and irritability of the spring was that damn bleak house of Cook's, and all it stood for—otherwise urine tests etc don't show any diabetic problem, though it was very decent of you to be concerned in that way.

Enclosed the first poem of any <u>movement</u> in a long time—which is also such relief. This summer I took LSD on two occasions: once here before joining Bobbie and the girls in Gloucester (I was teaching a short summer session) and then once there, in her company. Although I've not now much impulse to "do it again," it <u>was</u> extraordinary, and <u>very</u> true to intuitive senses of the world I've long had. Most of all, it made absolutely vivid and explicit the center I have in her. So—that's that, like they say—and I don't know how many times one has to be shown it, which is why to "repeat" would be much as Lawrence's, "The repetition of a known sensation is sensationalism . . . " Voila!!

We saw a little of Charles this summer, at which point he was pretty down—but he's just been at Cortland, NY—and the people from here who went over (I had to be away—in Iowa!) said he's in fine spirits now and notes from him seem to indicate the same.

I wanted to tell you of a limited edition of "fugitive" poems Walter Hamady is doing for me—it really came out <u>very</u> handsome—which I've dedicated to you "by your leave . . . " While I'm at it, I'll put in here the text of the Berlin lecture that was reprinted in Harper's Bazaar, in case you hadn't seen it. Then, thanks to you, that possibility of The Black Sparrow Press doing something of Bobbie's and mine together goes well—in fact, the poem to be used will be this one enclosed. So really much seems "forward" in a usefully happy sense.

Your <u>Epilogus</u> is a real gift—and thank you so much for what you say of us—as with the handsome printing of the sequences from PASSAGES also. How you feel the occasion of love is always so close to my own way—well, you'll know.

I'll be out there in late March for a couple of weeks (for the KQED experimental businesses)—will you be around? Unhappily for the Arts Festival here, it contracted to being able to invite Charles, Lowell, and Allen—just that your having been here last spring made that choice seem best. But supposing Lowell doesn't make it, there would be then that chance. Write as you can. Our love to you both as ever,

Bob

. . .

LETTER TO WHOM IT MAY CONCERN

30 November 1967

To whom it may concern :

I cannot longer avoid commitment to the circumstance of those who, in respect of <u>conscience</u>, seek to avoid being drafted into service in the present war in Vietnam. I feel strongly that this war is an unjust one and that the United States involvement is deeply to be regretted.

Yours sincerely,
Robert Creeley
Professor of English

RC:gb

· · ·

LETTER TO PAUL BLACKBURN

9596 Knoll Road
Eden, New York 14057
January 15, 1968

Dear Paul,

A belated Happy New Year to you, old friend, and thank you very much for the copy of THE CITIES, sent us by Grove—and such a deep pleasure to have. And delight too to think of you now citting (sitting) in one of them citties—ok! I really think the whole book shows a crazy weave of your articulation, and the size of it makes a very useful room therefor.

We had heard of Sara and you having separated—which was not happy news, i.e., I think as you must, she was an extraordinary woman—but the difficulties you were facing can hardly be accepted. I.e., one goes where one loves, and is loved—and when that stops, there's damn little point in staying on.

Your remembering that wild evening in Banalbufar—wow. That really was 'women's work,' i.e., Ann was paranoid with sense Freddie was out to get her, no doubt partly right just from F/s habits of address—and I was being prodded to 'do something' and when whatever it was was said, I simply flipped—and remember at one point realizing that there I was fighting with a friend as yourself, for reasons god knows a little vague to me. Though happily not often involving close friends, that kind of situation did occur several times with Ann, e.g., one time on a boat back to Mallorca I flipped at a waiter with much the same sense of frustrated impotence, i.e., inability to 'deal' with whatever it was seemed to be the 'problem'. Ah well . . . I felt such a continual diminishment, really an inability to reassure her own sense of things and/or to provide for them—so that when someone as Freddie (this may have been our paranoia as well) started chipping, my response was very hysterical momently.

Well, there must be an easier way—which happily there does seem to be. I'm so pleased that Olson's book reads well for you. I sweated it out for months, trying to think of an 'appropriate' selection etc, then one morning simply went in and wrote down titles etc as fast as I could—and that was that. I saw Laughlin last Friday, briefly here to check Wms letters against the possibility of a book of his and Pound's correspondence which would be very interesting (and never, I think, very clearly given)—and he said the book is now in its 2nd printing, and he is now enthusiastic etc. At first I think he was doubtful about it all, though he's fond of Chas—so. His address by the way is 28 Fort Square, Gloucester— he's back again and we saw him briefly in December, at which time he seemed in excellent health and very good spirits as well.

We have decided to return to New Mexico come summer. I can get the job back with better terms, and anyhow will try it for a year as a visitor, while keeping this scene still possible. But Buffalo is a hard city to get with in all senses. Money alone just doesn't make a reason to stay etc. Too, I really feel New Mexico as home in a way no other place now is. Going back to various places in New England this summer, as expected they were hardly the same—though I was curious to see where parts of my so-called life had happened, and to experience the way people talk, act, etc, as I'd known it as a kid etc. I saw the monolithic river of my childhood, Teel's Brook, which is just that, and in midsummer, under the little bridge I'd cross over on my way home from school, was simply a bed of marsh grass—but nonetheless still somehow the same. The house was largely shifted, and most bitterly, the lovely barn is now just about to collapse. Woods the same for the most part—but suburbia is coming close, and all the sense of wildness that stretched out in back is pretty well obliterated. Scale was funny—what I thought was a walk of miles must be hardly one all told, and you can practically jump across the intervale I thought was like the plains of Siberia, coming home. But what it did all do, being back there, was rid me of that goddamn sense of having somehow not made it to that measure—which is so often such a tight-mouthed mealy pinch purse small minded crock of shit. Viz, to be even that briefly a Big Spender thereabouts rid me of that frustration forever—and to see the lovely Concord river again, and the sea off York Beach etc—that was what I'd hold on to.

I've got memories of Valencia too, my own dark night of the soul—and people there were somehow so decent and supporting, just the ones I'd meet sitting in the park. It's a lovely decent <u>human</u> habitation. So—give it my love.

All the same to you and take
care & send some postcards, and we'll see you.

Bob

. . .

LETTER TO LOUIS ZUKOFSKY

Box 567
Placitas, N.M. 87043
September 7, 1968

Dear Louis,
                I'm very sorry about the long silence, the more so after the
very happy time with you both in Buffalo. Things then went on, it seems, very
quickly—and then we had the move back here, and then summer like they
say—so, here we are. It's good, finally, to be back. This country is very relieving
and puts us back in ourselves in a happy, useful manner. Terms of people I find
a little bland and self-protecting, after the east, but the point I guess is we have
our own concerns and occupations, and it's a fine place to be thus at work. I'll
be teaching at the university here, which I don't particularly look forward to at
this point, but again, the house is great, one can stay absorbed by the place for a
long time indeed, and I don't think either Bobbie or I were aware how exhausted
we were by all the rushing about we'd been involved with.

    That was a lovely issue of poetry (Poetry!), and I was fascinated by Rudens
(and for an innocent, ignorant question: is that Plautus? It has the feel of it, or god
knows that was what I was trying to experience, like they say, in so-called Latin
B, like, at Harvard . . .) That Voice, and the tags of song, weaving in and out are
lovely. Anyhow—wow! It was a lovely and altogether honorific threesome to be a
part of, though I wish my own 'part' might have sounded more in voice, somehow.

    Apropos: I've finished or come to the 'to be continued' place of, a sort of
sequence I've called Pieces, and it's been a very useful opening for me. I'd got
awfully boxed in by senses of poems as 'A Poem'—which all too quickly argues
'The Poem'—and also had begun to dislike the enclosure of two or three lines
on a pristine page solely, etc. So anyhow—these simply 'run on' with minimal
typographical break, in a form that really lets them come and go, meld and/
or join, as occasion proves. There are some longer ones included, though I've
let them fall as they do in the continuity of the writing, e.g., "The Finger" and
another slightly longer one called "Numbers"—und so weiter. The point is, I'm
happy—and so would like to dedicate the book to you if that's not a presump-
tion, and to say no more than, "For Louis Zukofsky," i.e., no flourishes this time,
nor prefatory notes, but simply to begin as the first one does:

                        As real as thinking
                        wonders created
                        by the possibility—

                        forms. A period
                        at the end of a sentence
                        which

began <u>it was</u>
into a present,
a presence

saying
something
as it goes.
[*CP* I, 379]

Which ain't the greatest, like, but is so much the fact of so much you've made
clear to me, no matter I may well have learned the lesson badly. Ok. But please
don't hesitate to say no, if for any reason it would be an awkward occasion for
you. Happily, Scribners will publish it, just when I'm not as yet clear—but again,
I've wanted to say thank you in a non-leaning manner for a very long time, and
hopefully, possibly, this can be one way.

I had a note from Stuart Montgomery yesterday, mentioning among little
else indeed, that a second operation on Basil Bunting's eyes had been success-
ful—so his sight will be much improved I take it. Also, that he has another
year's employment at Newcastle, which also is good news for him.

Write please as there is time. I'm quite sure I'll be in the east at some point dur-
ing the coming months, and will get there to see you. For once I'll insist it not be
so hectic I end up vaguely in Times Square. Ok. Meantime I hope all's well indeed.

Our love to you both,

Bob

. . .

LETTER TO THE *ALBUQUERQUE JOURNAL*

Placitas, N.M. 87043
September 16, 1968

"The People's Corner"
Albuquerque Journal
Seventh Street and Silver Ave. S.W.
Albuquerque, New Mexico
Dear Sir:

I first came to Albuquerque in 1956 and was impressed by the friendliness
of the people here and the generally pleasant way of life one met with, a New
Mexico tradition as I was to learn. Another attraction was the number of artists,
writers, and musicians who claimed New Mexico as their home, no doubt due
in large part to the air of friendliness I have mentioned. Many of these men
wear beards—as I do also, and have for twenty years. Up until two years ago,
this fact constituted no problem in my personal life, nor did it during the last
years which I've spent teaching in Buffalo, New York.

We returned to our home in New Mexico in late July, and in the past month I have been stopped while driving three times, once by state police and twice by Albuquerque police, to be "checked out." No violation was involved—no charge was made. On asking why I was stopped the third time, one of the three policemen questioning me answered, "Because the car has a New York license plate." When I asked if all cars with out of state license plates were being stopped, he replied that I was stopped because I "certainly don't look like a tourist." I agree that this certainly makes me a suspicious person and that the police are right to stop me everytime I attempt to drive in Albuquerque. Of course tourists should look like tourists, if only to make things simpler for the police. Too, the policemen were right, I am not a tourist—I live here. I must drive weekly back and forth to the University of New Mexico where I am a visiting professor for the coming year.

What must I do, short of altering my personal appearance, to be allowed free access to Albuquerque streets? I am not a criminal, I am forty-two years old, the father of three daughters—one of whom is an entering freshman at U.N.M., the author of many books, published in many countries, the recipient of a Guggenheim Fellowship, a Rockefeller Foundation grantee, and a tenured full (!) professor at the State University of New York. I am also listed in Who's Who In America! Where did I go wrong?

Yours sincerely,
(Prof.) Robert Creeley

. . .

LETTER TO ROBERT DUNCAN

Box 567
Placitas, N.M. 87043
February 12, 1969

Dear Robert,

I've been sorry to be out of touch—but god knows you're familiar with the so-called problem. One thing I've been trying to get done, is to get sent to you both a 'portfolio' bound edition of NUMBERS, i.e., it's the same as the portfolio, but the sheets are bound—and it's very handsome. But it ain't the easiest thing in the world to wrap, like—so hence the delay as I ponder. It will get there never fear. (Too, did you get a copy of PIECES from John Martin? I was disappointed and so have tended to forget the book, but for friends and relatives passing through.)

All's well enough—but it's been a sluggish time here, possibly ourselves, but I really think it's the basic inertia of people here in contrast to that jazzed-up eastern manner. So, as of June 1st, we'll head back there, and spend the summer in that house outside Gloucester, happily available, then Eden in September etc.

Don't tell the young, please—who make me feel older and older—just that I'd dearly love some time with the birds and the bushes. And the beach.

I spent two weeks at a very pleasant small college outside Lake Forest—money, money, money, but somehow still agreeable, I suppose it really isn't hard to be, in that situation—but the people were active and decent, a very pleasant combination. It really is a better arrangement than leaping from the skies for an hour or so, then sh-zam etc. I think I was dazzled for awhile by just how far one could get in five minutes, but I'm beginning to get tired of it. I've taken on a lot for the spring, just to get out of here as possible—but I think another year I'll not be so egocentrically pleased to be asked etc.

One very happy thing: Tom came out over the Xmas holidays, i.e., just after Xmas, and we had a very happy six days with him. He's got a lovely sharp eye, and being in the middle, is usefully wary and singular—and not persuaded by quite the ambitions David seems to have got from Ann. So that was great and pleasant relief, and I'm now in touch pretty solidly with both him and Charlotte. March 10th/11th I'll be at Williams (in Mass) and that's where David is, so hopefully I can have chance to see and talk to him a little.

Kirsten also came home at Xmas, and I must say she sure looked good—like they say, and seemed very much about her own life. I confess to parental fears and whatever, but it is obviously hard to keep out of it when for some 16 years that's been almost the reflex response of 'how' she is, i.e., that unconsidered care for kids one learns unintentionally as a parent. Anyhow she seems to be making her way—and I daresay she doesn't really want us watching, at all. Otherwise the actual rapport between us does stay, i.e., the literal response. And—the world now is obviously what she hopes to enter.

Various other things go well enough, e.g., I've seen proofs now for the Scribners edition PIECES—and it looks ok, and much as I'd hoped it might (for once). They plan to publish it in the fall, but once I have copies, I'll send one on to you. It feels right, so am curious to see what you think. It is, in a way, really a response to a sense you'd put in my head long ago, i.e., 'take care by the throat and throttle it'—as that's said in that poem, and this book is the first letting go of some over-riding care about 'rightness' and so at moments anyhow a much more useful revelation, of a day's content, and days' continuity, than what I've got to before. I'm not getting anywhere thank god in any case—but this 'dabbling' has really been a pleasure.

So that's good. Then Don says proofs of the collected notes and so-called essays book are about ready, and that should be out before too long—and also his edition of THE CHARM, reset finally, with a few added poems as well. So one feels in movement of some order.

Finally, and most interesting at the moment, is A DAY BOOK, for Ron Kitaj, i.e. that business as you'll know that he has with Marlborough. Thirty pages, and am about on the home stretch. It makes a very curious texture—again a breaking up of some habits, so that the process is much like taking a design by 'rubbing'— the texture is curious, likewise the range of statement—and what I'm very curious to see is if an implicit 'continuity' occurs from the agency, i.e., myself writing it.

—Is there any chance you might be able to pay us a visit at some point, going to and fro, i.e., I see you're to be at Kansas in the spring. I don't now know if we will get to SF before leaving here. We'd like to but it may be we're short of money (getting the house straight to go) and also caught in that miserable business of getting stuff together, to be moved. Anyhow let us know what might be possible. I'd dearly love your company, while life remains. Ok.

Our love to you both,
Bob

If in debris I had not said how <u>lovely</u> NAMES OF PEOPLE is, in every sense possible, forgive me—i.e., it brings you both so much into this home, and has lovely 'echoes,' facts, of god knows very dear things indeed. So—thanks to you both, deeply, otra vez.

Ron called from LA a few days ago to tell us John Altoon had died, very unexpectedly, from a 'massive coronary.' I regret it deeply god knows, his life had come to such actual peace, I think, the past few years, and he was obviously now working in a new condition of that experience—yet, perhaps paradoxically, but I think I'd feel it with any friend, I was almost relieved that the death, which had to come and has to, was for him instant, not in any sense a preoccupation to be dealt with. You know what kind of measure he was for me—how much in fact I looked to him at times in my life for a reassurance and fact of manhood. No man possibly closer to me than him in senses of women. I really loved what he was.

. . .

POSTCARD TO GREGORY CORSO

[Buffalo, NY]

Oct. 21, 1969

Dear Gregory –

That was very happy time with you
all. The name of those cigars is
MARSH WHEELING-DELUXE
- 8¢ per. So onward!
The world awaits . . .

Gregory Corso
c/o Ginsberg
R.D. #2
Cherry Valley, NY
13320

Love to all,
Bob

. . .

LETTER TO CHARLES OLSON

9596 KNOLL ROAD, EDEN, N.Y. 14057
(716—992—3913)   Jan. 1 196 <u>70</u>

Dear Charles,

I was sorry to see you in the hospital—but such a <u>deep</u> and <u>abiding pleasure</u> to be with you, <u>always</u>. My head, like they say, comes away with a <u>very</u> useful stuffèd-ness. Ok! But more, you are so fully the center of so much the world makes clear.

That's all poorly said—like they say. I'll be back, hopefully about Jan. 10th— and will be in touch in the meantime. Any use I can be whatsoever, have Harvey let me know.

Meantime my dearest love,
Bob

P.S. I spent an hour or more reading CALL ME ISHMAEL at the airport—it made those jets seem like horse & buggies—AH WELL . . .

. . .

TELEGRAM TO HON. BYRON MCMILLAN

State University of New York at Buffalo

2/23/70

Department of English   Faculty of Arts and Letters
<u>Telegram</u>
Hon. Byron McMillan

c/o Geo. Chula, Atty.
522 S. Broadway
Santa Anna, Calif.
(856–5760)
Deeply question holding of Dr. Leary without bail. It is of great dismay to one's whole sense of legal act and responsibility.

Yours,
Robert Creeley
Prof of Eng.
SUNY AB

. . .

LETTER TO ALLEN GINSBERG

Gloucester
6/20/70

ECHO

I'm almost
done, the hour
echoes, what

are these words
I heard, was
it <u>flower</u>, <u>stream</u>,

Nashe's, as Allen's
saying it, "Brightness
falls from the air?"

Was I never here?
The hour, the day
I lived some

sense of it?
All wrong? What
was it then

got done? This
life a stepping
up or down

some progress?
<u>Here</u>, <u>here</u>,
the only form

I've known.

[*CP* I, 504]

Dear Allen,

That was a very happy and
useful time with you. It's now
very quiet here—crazy splatter
of light out kitchen window
midafternoon. Really thinking
and thinking of that "abstract"
activity I seem fact of. Any-
how—onward. I've read a
little over 100 pp. now of the
<u>*Indian Journals*</u>*: beautiful exact*
company to have, dense, various, thoughtful,
extensive—and very <u>human</u>. So—thanks.
Likewise listening to your Blake. You're
a deeply gifted man, old friend. A quatrain
like they say:

If you get sillier
as you get older.
as you get younger,
That's really abstract.

Dig, That's me.   With love,

Bob

[The note to Ginsberg is handwritten. The poem "Echo" is typed.]

· · ·

LETTER TO BOBBIE CREELEY (BOBBIE LOUISE HAWKINS)

Knokke, Belgium
September 3, 1970
9:45 PM

<u>Most adorable divinity</u>—viz. <u>you</u>, I'm here praise god, all but out of it with
lack of sleep (I'm trying to stay awake till 10 so as to make time change—ah
well . . .) in sort of creaky pension near promenade with sea then beyond that—
in company with many elder persons all watching tv in sitting room below at

the moment. I checked in with poetry scene—pretty awful—but had a pleasant day in Brussels with the stewards who met plane and much eased arrival. Also got a new "impenetrable" (raincoat) like a black box coat, short, after leaving old one in bus to get on plane, etc. I like it! I <u>love</u> you! I really feel entirely opened by actual intent to cut back teaching. Bless us all! Will see you in moments so that's the point. You are the works!

LOVE,
Bob

. . .

POSTCARD TO SARAH CREELEY

[September 4, 1970]

LATE AT
NIGHT—
[over the →   *FLYING!*
Atlantic
*   Ocean]*

Dear Sarah,
    The <u>WORLD</u> is terrific! The
    more <u>you</u> know—the more
    <u>you</u> know!

Love, Daddy

[RC's brackets around *"over the Atlantic Ocean"*]

. . .

LETTER TO BOBBIE CREELEY (BOBBIE LOUISE HAWKINS)

[ca. 1970]

    Monday afternoon (on the plane) / sunlight comes in window from left
Dear love,
    I feel almost woefully abstracted in this place, <u>nowhere</u> in curious fact. My thoughts have been filled—now at least two hours—with the prospect of seeing you, i.e., since I got on this plane, and into the static fact it obviously is, you, and me, like they say, have gone though my head endlessly. A very dear and wise confrere, Lars Gustafson, whom I left at the airport, was saying on our ride by train to Brussels this morning: marriage is a social invention, a construct in that sense, no less than a car. It's not, per se, a human experience as would be hunger, or happiness, or whatever is of that fact. The faintness and the distance, and the frustration these and their concomitants make, is of course intolerable. Somehow my life—marriage is, as you would most of all people known to me

insist, <u>two</u> people, not a <u>one</u> of melded condition ^ [*has turned a corner very
abruptly and insisted it's really me who's here*]. I don't feel we've "worn out" the
relation between us, <u>and</u> I feel, as you, that <u>my</u> life, as <u>your</u> life, has become a
bleakness in a way I don't know specifically how to define. I question that I'm
not "open" to you, as you to me: <u>openness</u> is a quality and I feel you are, almost
despite feelings, of that literal nature of fact. I'd feared losing you—I hadn't
thought of it—but your presence is so much a place of my life. The <u>habit</u> of that
perhaps overrode its actual occasion. So—what to say. I've talked so much, so
long. I feel very quiet. I can't "work" at anything, and again, love as an implicit
intention or measured event isn't for me possible to accomplish. <u>Wh</u>en we make
love, or <u>how</u>, are rooted in our feelings, not in our minds. We'll change, hope-
fully, so that we regain ourselves with each other—but no "purpose" will serve.
Whether you can find a life with me further or not—and don't assume, please,
it can be something you "want" to do, therefore will—at this moment I love you
entirely. Always you are measure of <u>generous</u> human <u>life</u>. My dearest love,

                                                                    Bob

                                    . . .

LETTER TO GENEVIEVE CREELEY

                                            Box 344
                                            Bolinas, Cal. 94924
                                            August 29, 1971
Dear Mother,
            I've finally got time and mind to tell you how very pleasant it was
to have that time with you there. All went well on return as well, and again, it
really was a very happy time indeed.
    We continue to be occupied with settling in here. The place is really so
beautiful at least when one stops with whatever chore and can look around, it's
an extraordinary pleasure. As of yesterday, it seems that fall has suddenly come,
i.e., the air is very clear and I think it must be the beginning of that lovely sunny
fall weather. So all is good.
    This shed I'm now sitting in, in fact, got all straight while I was away—new
roof, also joists on the backside, and the whole building reinforced, etc. It makes
an ideal place to work in and hopefully I'll be able to do just that. The house
itself is sound but needs a new roof which will be put on within the next two
weeks. We got a little of the tree work done, the so-called safety work, and will
now let that wait for awhile till we have a clearer sense of where the sun could
use more room. The garage-barn was finally too derelict to permit us to convert
it into a studio, but that too has been shored up, so it can be used for storage at
least for a few more years. We want to build a two room studio at the top of the

hill we're on the side of, for a studio quondam guest house, and hopefully that will get done in October. In the meantime Bobbie's been at work painting in the kitchen and much else, and I've been doing divers small jobs like making tables for this place, etc.

Our biggest news is a horse no less. I was finally so badgered by Sarah to get one, we went to see about a bay gelding over in Novato, and thanks to the very generous and bright young lady who owned him, we ended finding an ideal palomino mare about 14, who is perfect for them. She has pep enough and rides easily and surely, and at the same time won't run them into trees or off cliffs etc, which was really my sneaking fear all along. She's up in a pasture on the mesa and really occupies the girls most happily. It's an ideal place to have a horse and I'm pleased it's finally possible to have one for them. So they're much occupied with all the lore of horses, and that should keep them busy for quite awhile. Her name is Bonny by the way and I hope both you and Sarah can see her before too long.

Apropos, I do hope you can come any time it will be simple for you say toward the end of September and/or early October. If for any reason that time proves a poor one, just change it to whatever is more convenient. The point is we'd really love having you come. Ok!

Carlie came over about a week ago and seemed in good spirits. She was with a charming young man, so that seemed happy. She told me Lucy's present young man is one she's known previous to Lincoln, and that all seemed happy. I hope we'll see more of both them now that they have cars.

So, just to keep in touch—and I'll really write more frequently as things become more settled. Again, this house is all either of us ever really wanted—wow.

My dearest love,
Bob

[Bobbie Creeley's handwritten note follows signature.]
Dear Genevieve –

Bob had a good visit there—He's told me all about it—and now we're looking forward to your visiting us here –

Everything here takes longer than we had thought but there's nothing <u>unfunctional</u> it's just that it will be a relief when the basic things are finished—Each thing done is a real achievement—

Give my love to everyone there & come as it is simple for you –

love Bobbie

· · ·

POSTCARD TO ARMAND SCHWERNER

CREELEY, BOX 344, BOLINAS, CA. 94924

10/10/71

Dear Armand,

Paul's relation to me is really too complex to be
able to say anything more than how bleak and sad he
is gone. It all goes flat trying to say more. He was
a dear <u>useful</u> man.—I'd be pleased to write note re
Guggenheim, so that's fine.

> *Meantime love to all,*
>> *Bob*

· · ·

LETTER TO BOBBIE CREELEY (BOBBY LOUISE HAWKINS)

[Bolinas]
November 9, 1972

Dear Bobbie,

Before this plane gets there, and all the confusion and nostalgia of just being there comes in—what you're doing does make sense to me. However literally the fact—it feels as if we've been resenting one another's "reality" for some time. My drunkenness and ugly violence is one obvious fact in any case. For me there is a constant fear of being cut out or dropped—and that's inexorably difficult to live with. So time apart makes sense indeed, to know why we want to be together at all—granted a very literal love is also true. But as you said when I was leaving, you'd like to like me too—or have that left as a possibility if we can't make it further.

The phone calls really wipe me out—like instant changes of reality, as resonating as my drunken freaking out is obviously for you in much larger degree. Anyhow if a letter is possible, that would be great. I hate to think of you sans provision so any money you need let me know—it's yours as much as I'd feel it mine at this point. I've got specific reality to get used to and this seems as good a time as any. I love you. Do what you have to and want to, and that's it.

> *Your old friend believe it or not,*
>> *Bob*

PART FIVE

Echoes, 1973–1989

Buffalo, Maine, Helsinki

226 Linwood Ave.
Buffalo, N.Y. 14209
January 17, 1973

Dear love,

Finally down enough to write so-called proper letter. I get very
speedy with such movement as getting here, all the anticipation of what's to
happen, etc, etc. Again, it really feels simple, barring some ridiculous nose-dive
into gluggy glooms etc which I don't particularly feel like doing. A cat was
charmingly at the window here a few minutes ago, a big fluffy grey–with that
miaow of righteous insistence to be let in, but I held firm. Incredibly warm
for the season, near or into fifties today—even sun for an hour or so, breaking
through that wild grey yellow Buffalo haze. Ah well. I've been up to the U/ like
they say, and all that's simple enough. Saw numbers of my colleagues, even
Arthur Axlerod (now a student there) same as ever—though old enough now
to say 'I've g_ot to go' to without wiping him out. Helpful young couple prove
David Matlin and his wife Gail, I'd helped him get in here two years ago, met
at SF State though wasn't enrolled there—anyhow they are practical people,
good friends of Danny and Holly Zimmerman—so they'll know where I'm at,
without my having to spell it out, and also won't be leaning on me as desir-
able object etc. My neighbors upstairs, kind of charming young NYC Jewish
mother-about-to-be and local boy PR husband, fed me also last night, along
with the Matlins, and I sense we came to an unspoken agreement as to how
our interlocking lives might be discreetly placed. I wind up on energy and I am
n_ot working five days a week, which the husband is—no matter he can 'come
and go'—so it's really not a fair game. So I think I'll have more time to myself,
thankfully, without seeming to turn them off or down. Ah well. I dig there's a
whole protocol number I'll have to acquire, which life with you, my dear, has
fucking well spared me. I wish Don were here to give me the basic ritual.

Elsewise a copy of an article from PLAYBOY John Clellon Holmes wrote on
Jack Kerouac's death and funeral—strange sense of 'myself': "Suddenly, there
was Robert Creeley, too—wiry as a guitar string, and graceful, with the meticu-
lous small beard of a bravo or a cavalier, in a proper suit and short overcoat, his
one busy eye saying, "Yes. At last. Funny. Well. We all d_o exist, after all," as we
were introduced." Really funny the way people experience one—odd playback.
Curious article to come at this moment, being back here—thinking of going
there then—come from San Francisco—senses of time, and what came of it. As

being in the Albright-Knox, really strong echo of ourselves having been there, it seemed, only minutes before—or driving past Cole's, or seeing The Sample— Sammy's on Hertel, Bennet High—and again, Arthur Axlerod. Wow.

I've got the pictures up, took loads of John's junk down—like Al Cook's in that desperate attempt to make things add up to desired effect of 'I really am here'—and the place feels sparer, but simpler to move in. Your drawing is in cluster with Joe's piece, and postcards of Marisol and Jasper J/s—it's lovely! The print I have on the piano (I have a piano . . .) and your ^ [photo] incredibly lovely and erotically fascinating face dominates at least two rooms, viz living-room and kitchen—where the action is, you dig. Also found among stuff picked up in shed at last moment, lovely small photo of you in Eden house, sitting barefoot in front of fireplace on that bench, playing your guitar with crazy alert look to body and hands and head.

I figure the most evident problem with this separation, or what to call it, will be boredom, and restlessness that comes of it—which is where drinking gets in. Nights with people I have drunk since coming I've been able to 'get off' of, also—and go to bed and sleep sans some windup of frustration. Teaching itself will make a pace I think. I find, too, I can sit down and read a book, bless these glasses, and dig the movement of the day as a simple phasing of light changes and occasional people. I mean I don't have that scene as I did when younger, of restlessly pushing to get it on, and if nothing could be got hold of, the awful flood of vacant disappointment etc. I truly dig that I've got 'things to do' which I dig doing, and which make a form of 'time' as pleasantly actual as much else. Voila. Spring's also coming at some point, which will be a help. I'm sure glad it's pointed this way, rather than digging this feeble sunlight get less day after day—which would rot the head and affections like acid. I don't want to get into the paranoia you'll remember people here really do use as energy source (Duncan M/ like the classic of same) and so it means specific keeping to my own interior scene and work, not looking to the local people-scene as via for 'point' or 'occasion'. Again being this old is useful for knowing enough not to dash into that, etc.

Apparently local Buffalo paper had pictures of Bolinas' flooding, house falling down hill (?)—sounds like a wild time. I hope that creek kept the waters moving off our so-called property. Albuquerque, by the way, now has smog all through the valley from at least as far north as Alameda extending as far as you can see to the south. I was told by local garageman it was because it was winter and more people had furnaces etc going, but it looked to me like old-fashioned straight-on smog. Very fucking sad to have that lovely view of Sandias obscured as you come across the west mesa headed east, beautiful sun, by fucking sulphu-rish-grey haze of shit. Yuck . . . The whole city felt jumped into ultimate Princess Jean Park vision of 'success'—later saw 'The Brave Cowboy' on late-night TV, appropriately enough. Texas was COLD . . . panhandle frozen stiff, but in garage where I went to get push for frozen car by that point (morning), lovely conversations going on with 'good ole boys' and 'waal' and what you'd expect. Last thoughts of Albuquerque: local Buffalo radio/tv report of commissions' recommendation that LA would have to cut down on gasoline consumption, something like use 2 gal/s where previously consumption had been 10—reaction is, apparently, to lower the standards qualifying smog, since cutting down on cars is unthinkable. Too fucking much. Like the farmer's horse living on less and less till one day he just died. What a weird imagination of success!

One thing: could you give me a "recipe of the week," or month, or whatever—to get me out of rice & hamburg pattern, which I fear I'll fall into, like plummeting stone etc. Ok! You can even suggest the proper music, and what dress is required. Candles I have—John's delight were the dullestly fat thick red looking hunks of wax etc.

Tomorrow I meet first class, graduate—that'll begin the scene. I've already got in some sense cleared away for letters, the guy in England for example is going to print that poem for my mother sans problem and seems glad to have it, even mentions modest payment (right on!)—so it's moving. This typewriter works great. Even got a little table like in real writing scenes. I'll race you to the 85th chapter. God knows I love you dear sweet impecabbly (that's the way I spell it) unique person. So you all write, as possible—really lovely, again, to have word from you so soon on arrival.

My dearest love,
Bob

I get paid a week from this Friday, (the 19th so that's no problem.)

[Creeley's sketch on lower left of second page: floor plan of the apartment, including arrows drawn to "me" and "cat."]

[note on back of envelope] *"Keep those cards and letters coming in!"*

. . .

LETTER TO ALLEN GINSBERG

226 Linwood Ave
Buffalo, N.Y. 14209
January 28, 1973

Dear friend,

I saw Allen DeLoach on Friday briefly, and he said he'd heard you had slipped on some ice and broken your leg—which is sad to hear, and I hope not fucking impossible for you. I'm sure heaven must be getting ready some substantial eternal blisses and that present meat is only to whet your appetite. Or something like that, like.

Once things settle at all here, I hope to get over to see you, out of the traffic. I _did_ see you, by the way, in NYC—but there were so many angels floating all around you it was hard to keep a steady focus. What really entered my head that day was Gregory's sudden poem: The star is far as my eye can see. And the star is as near as my eye is to me. Or the eye—not _my_, etc. A lovely quick talisman to have in the head. He's a beauty. Anyhow that whole scene flowed on reaching peak pre-election night in the Record Plant off Times Square with Jimmy Roberts and Sea Train recording, energy vortex of absolutely satisfying dimensions like they say. I was clearing out a lot of gunk, clutter of various 'feel-ings'—like burning brush. Lovely conversation with John Wieners in closeby bar before the so-called reading. At that point, stoned tho I surely was, I felt feelings in that place had gotten painfully heavy and humorless. Ah well. Later heard via mutual friend of some dancer's take on 'My' 'Reading'—really dug the body state and what got 'said'. That was what I was doing certainly.

I've been here two weeks today I guess it is. I've sublet John Logan's apart-ment so have basic necessities, sheets, spoons, etc. People I otherwise have as company from the teaching scene are really much as remembered, very easy hopeful vibes, hardworking in keeping themselves together. The place is physical: so harsh people brought to recognize their own obvious need of one another. Always some tacit paranoia, but simple to relax it—as last night at party the people smoking dope were politely asked to go in backroom so as not to scare the non-dope smokers, later resolving as people drifted back and the differentiation got melted. Pleasant hands-holding and leaning on others—what I most miss from Bolinas etc. Diane di Prima saying she felt SF was very useful place to get body info located, so one don't go freaking out over 'middle age' etc. Not unlike the Middle Ages, come to think of it.

I came in used VW sedan which seems to hold together ok, though on getting here the valves were so shot had to get that straight. Let's see. Got shirts enuf, sweaters, warm shoes etc. Cooking is simple given what I eat with pleasure, rice etc. Likewise people closely by—one young couple, husband I'd met first in SF where he'd been working in heavy construction scenes and also iron or some metal foundry—so has very alert sense of how and what to do to keep physical states in one piece—also western sense of time and space, which is pleasant. She's from Kingston, N.Y., heavy middle-class money—a sculptor with good head. And Jack Clarke seems in good spirits—I just roll with him and that makes us both relax. No rules, etc. Just flashes of hopefully mutual insight, and affection.

Mark Robison whom I saw late fall gave me copy of Improvised Poetics— which is a very _useful_ clear text. I was very happy to see him get a specific piece of work done so well and so modestly. His wife really seems good news, inten-sive Italian body enthusiasm and mother wit—I really liked her. He is far more centered and also has lost some of the kid aggressiveness. Ed and Nancy Kissam are both here by the way, in good spirits—charming daughter. So.

I wanted to tell you and in that clutter at the church there was no chance to, that while my mother was dying in Marin General, just worn out at last physically, 85, I kept hearing in my head as I'd be there, watching the catch of her breathing, how the body was all going 'in'—anyhow those words of yours, "Relax and die"—also "Death's let you out." Obviously one wants to know if anything said can ever be of that measure, and what I'm trying now to say is that it, also obviously, can—and not just those specific phrases, but a whole experience of ways you have and do 'say things' that kept a measure of the reality clear and possible in myself. It's an incredibly <u>dear</u> human experience to realize others are with you in that place. Ok.

Copy of John Holmes piece was sent by magazine, I thought it was honest heart-felt piece of work, and must write him note to say so.

Miss my family, my people so to speak. Happily I don't have sexual restlessness I would have five or ten years ago. Can sit still more simply—let the day make a way etc. Also can 'go home' when tired more simply. So. The fall was a hard time, like they say. Bobbie and I came often very near to separating, some curious insistent itch of displacement between us—bugging one another in some habit not even knowing it. Finally we went to pleasant fellow in Berkeley, true contemporary and humanly warm person—and that helped far more than I had thought it would. So left to come here with a much more stable and open feel for each other, very thankfully. She's completing a fairy tale, a long one, she's been working on for some time, also has going lovely sequence of quick anecdotal narratives from life in Texas etc—really strong clear writing. Also doing pictures—so she's got it on, like they say, sans question. Sarah and Kate likewise moving happily—the highschool in Mill Valley is a very good place to 'come of age' in—Sarah now into inner 'community school' and teaching a day a week at the grade school back in Bolinas as 'project' in said scene etc. Kids there stay really good news—alert and open, and handle dope etc it seems with often a very canny wisdom. So to haul us all here for four months was patently ridiculous, given that action. I really like teaching here—i.e., find myself well used and people thus actively available in that scene. But the physical place is too wiped out to take much pleasure in otherwise—so stay with the people, like a campfire number. So far so good.

The phone here is 716-881-0288, if I can be of any use re whatever, and again, I'll get over at some point I'm sure. Meantime do take care of yourself—why not.

Love to Peter and other friends there.

All love to you,
Bob

. . .

LETTER TO BOBBIE CREELEY (BOBBIE LOUISE HAWKINS)

226 Linwood Ave
Buffalo, N.Y. 14209
January 29, 1973

Dear love,

Your letter just came—so will add note to mine mailed yesterday, just to say again like they say money scene should shortly get simpler—and also, John Martin just wrote to tell me he'll print that essay, so hopefully that means you'll get that $50 along with the $200 that's due about the 4th—and then on the 9th I can get another loan against salary for the two-week period; and that should be the corner. I was thinking, were I there, no doubt I'd be freaking with irritation and worries, a kind of sad way to hike up energy, but having no one to lay it on (aie . . .), it fades out with fact there is no hopeless problem involved and things can also be kept together in the meantime, it would seem. It's just the shift here, in any case, temporal, and getting so-called 'economy' together in the changed pattern. Or something like that.

Thinking of sanity/art—one definition of 'sanity' in decrepit dictionary John left here, "Sane moderation or reasonableness . . . " That's surely one of the hooks art gets caught on, if not the main one, in people's senses of the nutty artist. However 'reasonable' the execution, call it, rare indeed is its occasion as such. Robert's 'to exercise his faculties at large' presupposes there can be no 'reasonable' dictation of that event, i.e., it cannot be contained as that construct of purpose, it must move in its own initiation, 'reasonable' or not. As Olson's 'art is the only true twin life has . . . ' insofar as, like life, its 'purposes' cannot be determined apart from its experience of itself, and it seems to have no point other than that experience, however much those possessed by 'reason' work to make a context in which art is doing something, like they say, in accordance with an avowed purpose: for the greater glory of god, for money, for the people, etc etc. Whereas for me, it's really simply the fact: fire delights in its form—life likes living (feels pain as the negative thereof, the impedance of coercion, force, or otherwise factual limit). Williams' saying, why don't we say for once what pleasure we get writing, that we do it for the literal fun.

The sanity, the health, art gets to, sometimes clearly the only possibility thereof—as Kafka, or often John Wieners, not so dramatically to emphasize it—but even so-called 'sick' writing is paradoxically aspect of organism's health, to move to its relief, to realize itself thus. Anyhow that sanity/insanity trip re the arts is like old time western rationalist construct—and very hopeful. No doubt Sufis among must be countless others dug it wasn't getting them there—and mind failed in hope to get it all in, so had to let the 'irrational' have true place—and only in small areas of our own plotted consciousness (western) do we either value or permit that to happen, the arts being one and I gather mathematics, in some of its activity, another. I'd always questioned psychology previously because it seemed to have such rational intent—wanted a 'normative' that was too generalized and assumptive as far as I could see, e.g., Mike Rumaker's cure, almost like a lobotomy. Which I can hardly accept as a 'sane' or healthy state of being. Elsewise art realizes wholeness, in its activity—i.e., in its acts one feels all there, freely, specifically—which is the pleasure.

I remember Williams saying something in the 40s, in a piece, to the effect thank god for the arts, specifically writing, insofar as it gave a man a place he could go on living in his own head distinct from the insanity he met with around him. It wasn't some hole he crawled into, it was again Duncan's place to exercise the faculties at large in health.

Postman had to come through mucho snow to get to door this morning, VW a big fluffy heap of it outside kitchen window. Will get broom and sweep it off. Sun now shining—really great. Approacheth noon. Must get together, see to possible washing of clothes today—not yet disastrously necessary but time to explore that possibility, etc.

Just checking again: as sanity comes from sanus meaning healthy, healthy comes from old English, hælth, meaning whole—as heal is to make whole. And wholeness is all, like they say.

A lovely circle back to Robt, and with a lovely most simple obviousness. I really dig what's so simple, and so obvious—and also so curiously ignored. The nose on one's face, like they say—sniffing.

I wish Mickey were more 'healthy'—somehow a split in his experience, that would really feel most together practicing his faculties at large, Max's, not trying to make it a congruence of places and roles. No wonder he nags—he thinks sadly that's what you do in that category. Sharon, his first wife, dug he was entirely together only in the restaurant, and really turned on—and she in turn had to get to her own wholeness, viz be a doctor which was truly what she was drawn to. Whereas now Mickey gets splattered in all the agreed to 'intentions'—as when I got there (Great Barrington) last summer, was instantly witness to a crazy disjunct of 'things to be done'—like a mad shopping list of "plans." Ah well . . .

That's wild about the kerosene. Wow . . . Like the can was the 'idea'!

Haven't yet got the chowder together, will have it for midweek pleasure—or possibly tonight, if I get moving. Have to introduce student reading tonight, people who won so-called contest. At least woman who got 1st is one I helped get in there, sans any BA etc—and she's a sharp writer, momently going to Mexico with her two kids and charming painter she lives with. Again—real life.

I haven't (still) seen that NY Times review and don't think to, i.e., would have to go find it etc. For what. It's got to be beside the point, and that's that. Only quick sadness that should be the response to a book I have no doubts concern-

ing—but no doubt a take like that must seem in part it's still kicking. Fair
enough.

I'll be writing Sarah and Kate again shortly. I can hear that record player
etc. Will be looking forward to copy of fairy tale, very happy. And—you don't
have to do everything right now, or do, as you feel like it. Voila. Sun is so great
hitting in here, feel like lying on snow like a beach.

I love you,
Bob

. . .

LETTER TO KATE CREELEY

226 Linwood
Buffalo, N.Y. 14209
April 26, 1973

Dear Kate,

I've been trying to answer your lovely letter for weeks (months?)
now, and finally mind & time are clear enough to damn well DO it. Ok. Here
in Buffalo spring has almost truly arrived. All but the elm trees have leaves,
the iris, jonquils, tulips, etc., are pretty much all blooming and it sure is a great
relief indeed. Just before Bobbie came, it got very warm for a few days and
everybody thought that was going to be it—but no such luck. The trees had
budded but they stayed in a sort of weird 'frozen' state for weeks after. Well, it's
all but over now—and no doubt in a week it will be 102° in the shade.

I'm just back from Bard College—I mislaid my glasses* for reading, so got
myself a big magnifying glass to use instead, and must have looked like a mad
Sherlock Holmes tracking down an invisible murderer—or just like a nut more
probably. [^ *It made faces look very big when I looked out at the audience—and
no doubt made them see me that way too.*] Bard College is east, not far from
Albany—on the Hudson River where numbers of eccentric rich people used
to have great estates. Now most are abandoned, and so the whole place has the
feeling of decay somehow—sort of ghostly in fact. Timothy Leary used to have
his place, Milbrook, near there, but he didn't last all that long. I was told of one
sort of mad Polish millionaire, Zabriskie, who even had his own soldiers, some-
thing like the Zabriskie Light Brigade, in case the Germans might invade etc.
Apparently they never actually fought or shot anybody, but just drilled endlessly
all over his fields. In the town itself there was one great Charles Adams house,
looking very spookey with long narrow windows and towers etc. I was frankly
pleased to leave the place and get back home.

Then I was down at Kent State in Ohio last week, and very happily saw
Arthur. Really terrific to see a familiar face from home. That place was sad

in another way, i.e., it's where the students were shot and killed in 1970. Most strange was that the officials finally brought charges against them, despite the fact they were dead. As you walked around the place, you could literally feel where it had happened, i.e., the shooting—and I suspect it will be a long time before those ghosts are gone.

Less grimly, on the way back we left off a friend in Cleveland, a sports writer, who was going to cover a baseball game, and when he went out in the lobby of the hotel—we had all stopped in the hotel he was staying at to get a drink—he met Russell Means, the Oglala Sioux Indian leader, and brought him back to the table. Very handsome man—but very arrogant somehow. He had terrifically high energy, I will say, and made the people at other tables seem very small and faint. He has something like sixteen federal indictments against him at this point, but says he will fight his way back into Wounded Knee if necessary—ah well. He said he was in Cleveland raising money for arms etc., but what he expected to find in that hotel I don't know. He ordered a Bloody Mary, left to do something, and never came back to drink it. I guess we scared him.

So—life is exciting! But an awful bore, finally, without you all. So, I'll see you soon. I'm still going to locate those glasses—never fear. Meantime write as you can. It's not long now.

> My dearest love,
> *Bob, your dad*

*Happily I found them again

. . .

LETTER TO TED BERRIGAN

STATE UNIVERSITY OF NEW YORK AT BUFFALO
Faculty of Arts and Letters   Annex B
Department of English   Buffalo, N.Y. 14214

400 Fargo
Buffalo, N.Y. 14213
January 16, 1974
Dear Ted,

I'm very sorry to take so long to write. More to the point, I wrote the Guggenheim with pleasure, yea honor, how very much I respected your work and used it in fact as measure in my own. That at least I did do. Ok. I hope it works out.

Next is great pleasure of Alice's book! Which same I should address to Alice. HEY ALICE? You're terrific. Really a very particular and unique piece of statement—and/or <u>words</u>. Really <u>good</u>, as we say in this so-called country. I dug it throughout.

Just in here, as of Sunday—now Wednesday—feels ok. Typical Buffalo scene, overcast—but that's like Boston in the old days. I'm way over on the west side, paisano country, clears the head if I don't get it blown off. Anyhow left family and friends in reasonable state. The past year was a bitch—a bleak fucking drag too often, so that's well done with. Exceptions seem Bill and Lynn—they seem very happy. And Tom in new house looks baronial. And cool. Aram's in some back to nature scene and same feels a little late (what 'nature')—but anyhow they have as you must know new daughter named Cream—mother-in-law's insistence was the word (?)—but I saw very little of them. Great visit with John Giorno in fall. Diane diPrima is keeping it together but looks pretty tired. Eldest daughter Jeanie is really something. Ed Dorn rolling on, hoping for some place still around SF—may have teaching in fall at one of the local institutions, U of SF, etc.

Actually Bolinas has cooled off hyper community spirit with shrink of money, and thus demands in keeping it together getting heavier. Kirsten's still there, looking a lot more together—and Trane thus too. No next move as yet, but at least present seems ok to her.

I haven't done a damn thing of much interest but for poem or two since I saw you all. Hence have been many times hysterical—or just out of it by whatever device. But now feel it begins to get too centered again (like the ta hio spelled backwards)—or just I feel so fucking restless I can't longer avoid doing something, and am in benign good spirits paradoxically no matter. I read Wyndham Lewis' letters lately, selection by Bill Rose—and really impressed by that aspect of 'man of letters' and 'work'. Giving it 'your best shot' as you'd say. I think what I mean is I'd like to sit on the professionalism of my past 25 years and get on with it. Why not.

I may get over there toward middle of March but not at all certain as yet. If so, will certainly try to drop in pues. Meantime you all do maintain—and keep in touch as you can please.

My love to you,
Bob

Phil is in fine shape. He, Bobbie, and I read at The Dorn's—sort of a year's end trip—really a pleasure. In fact, he continues to teach me a lot.

[note on envelope] *P.S. Joanne up and down—she and Arthur were really closest friends there this past 8 mos.—I only saw Darrell once—he's in the city—but I think it's keeping together for him. Sadly his and Kirsten's splitting up means we see him rarely and/or either I can't locate him or he doesn't come around. So—.*

. . .

LETTER TO DIANE DI PRIMA

400 Fargo
Buffalo, N.Y. 14213
March 12, 1974

Dear Diane,

This is like selfishly writing a letter I want to (in short, it is writing a letter I want to) –despite the piles surrounding. Fuck them. Most recently one from young man Midwest lost job, loves a 'girl', has wife and kids—etc. Ain't love grand . . . I'll tell him all he needs is another girl. Voila.

I wanted to thank you for having that lovely substantial run of Floating Bears sent me, really impressive and terrific to have in hand like that. I got it just before going in to teach, so slapped it down on the table and said, don't ever no one ask me again 'how do I get published'—viz, LOOK. Ok. It was, again, so lovely to go through and witness again how much you literally get done.

Things here have been active and pleasant, and this apartment suits me altogether—it's sort of shipshape and just fits but has ample space and light, up over a small grocery store, in Italian neighborhood so lots of kids and talk. Anyhow that's been good, plus fact I'm starting to write again—what a relief! At present am working on text called MABEL: A STORY, sort of reverse side to LOBA in fact, trying to locate multiple projections of 'senses' of 'women' from diversity of random takes. Yesterday was the grim 'ownership' one, viz: "Fondling what he can unobtrusively reach, of it, he remembers the cut-away sections of the black gauzy nightgown, permitting the congested blood-red nipples to reveal themselves as just for him. Cozy. His own sex festers into a congealed erection. He gropes more particularly, one hand for the light switch, one for dearly enduring Mabel's meat . . . " Ugh! They's some happy parts, too.

Anyhow having that to work on has been a pleasure. There is a sort of loose plan for Jim Dine to work with it, in any way he wants to, once done—but writing it is the point for now. So.

I'll be back there March 16th–25th, to see the family and all, and to work with Kate's psychiatrists re her hang-ups and very probably our own. She's been in Langley Porter the past month, after really unrelievable depressions—just couldn't reach her with our own resources or understandings. At present, from what I hear from Bobbie and Sarah, she's markedly more responsive and at ease—which is a deep blessing. Anyhow that's very much on my mind, and getting there will be a very real help. I'll give you a call in any case.

Saw Carolee Schneemann not long ago, in very fine spirits. Hear John Giorno is now back in the city. I've been down only once—just wipes out energy and head, finally. Hope your life there is thriving, really think of you all often. Maintain!

My love,
Bob

. . .

POSTCARD TO BARRETT WATTEN

[depicting the cover of *Elsa's Housebook,* by Elsa Dorfman]

Creeley, 400 Fargo, Buffalo,
NY 14213
Friday-Dec. 13, 1974

Dear Barry, Just now	—THIS—
leaving here so can you	Barry Watten
come out (Bolinas) over	235 Missouri St.
Xmas holidays? Say the	San Francisco,
27th?* Like? Have prose.	CAL 94107

See you!
All best—love,
Bob

*Call (866-0147) and we
can get a clear time.

. . .

LETTER TO BOBBIE CREELEY (BOBBIE LOUISE HAWKINS)

400 Fargo
Buffalo, N.Y. 14213
September 29, 1975

Dear love,

Really good to hear from you—letter just in, and despite the damn sad problem I'm sure relieved that you're giving yourself space, and that friends as Shao and Susan, Sarah, and Diane are equally around. As you, I'd figure it's going to be a substantial time before Kirsten's out of it god willing, so whatever we can do to keep ourselves humanly together would seem obviously useful. Anyhow.

Allen called last night, and it seems that whole trip he's had with the palsy etc was caused by doctors giving him antibiotics which he proved allergic to, but somehow they didn't realize that until the treatment had been going on for some time. Hence the prolonged reaction I guess. He's now much better, is moving into a new place in NYC—and we'll see him down there assuming it works out for you to come. Elsewise we're invited to next year's Naropa Institute in the summer—and I said we could probably make it for about a week sometime late July/early August, coincident with being in Placitas. You'd get a reading for some pay, and I'd get that plus a brief 'workshop' I guess—and we could think of bringing Kate, who might well dig the younger people who show up. He said it was really a pleasure.

I've been taking it easy, reading a lot—just finished Richard Wollheim's book on Freud at the moment, which proves a clear, useful job. I'd written James Salter a fan letter re his novel, got a happy note in reply—he lives in Aspen, was getting his firewood in and all. He seems a pleasant man, which is a bonus.

And I put up another place to hang coats etc in the hall today. Got really hooked into cleaning some 'plates' around some door knobs last night, soaking them with alcohol etc—shades of your cleaning the floor in Vancouver! I was talking to Peter during call from Allen, he'd have been proud of me. Anyhow I backed off finally, when I found I was down to scraping the little grooves some had on the front with the end of a nail etc. Aie. This is certainly a <u>clean</u> apt.

Not drinking much at all. Friend George Tish passing through from Detroit on Friday, stayed the night—very pleasant man—I'd got a six pack, but turned out neither of us was into drinking it, nor smoking as it happens, either. I almost have to learn now to manage social patterns without liquor, and I can clearly do it most simply on my own ground. Drinking always dealt with either my boredom, or else restless uneasiness I might not find rapport with whom-ever, etc. Grass really makes me even more restless with general people than ever, so I don't have any difficulty missing that. Whereas at night here, circa nine, it's a pleasant way to let down from day's intensities. Anyhow. I'd like to get it, if truly it proves possible—if not, then fact would be to stop entirely— drinking, so I don't grab it for relief from tedium and/or nervousness, so have occasion less compulsive—as we do, say, in Placitas, wine with a meal, etc, and there isn't impulse at this point to drink on all night. Contrast with Bill Katz coming, certainly someone I care for and feel at ease with, but I felt apprehen-sive that specific night, so drank markedly as much as I could discreetly till he was gone. So if I can move to another means of confidence and/or directness of my own feeling in that kind of situation, again need to drink in that pattern will be less destructive. Part of it is being able to say "no" to persons, even dear ones, even in rather abstract manner I guess—because Bill was obviously not intend-ing that reaction in any way, nor was I at all wanting it. Ah well! It's like endless, when point is—it feels increasingly as though drinking as a major hangup is getting less. Ok!

Let's see what else is new . . . Sun's shining, which is terrific. Yesterday and today were incredibly balmy, shirt-sleeves weather, all the kids out etc. Bennie and his girl, Brownie—another B&B combination—were by Saturday, and we walked over to their place—they move in Wednesday, very pleased—it's terrific. Two story house in fact, back of one larger on the street, garden, weird charm-ing purple 'brush-like' flowers still blooming. It feels dear. So, that's a pleasure.

Enclosed, like they say, is check for October—I'll be paid Friday, at which time it is negotiable, i.e., I'll deposit my check here, and then things are back together pretty much. I've paid George & Jack $400 of what's owed them, and while I can now pay it all as the $1000 for the Stein piece comes in which should be, according to Bill, momently, I think I'll send them $400 in October, and again in November, and ask them what's then remaining, and pay that in December—so it will emphasize we're not ready for a whole new ball game etc.

So things are ok here—I miss you, and selfishly hope you can get here, but if not, there's a solid feeling now present which can hold in any case. So that's the point. Right now I'm figuring you'll be coming October 7th, if anything's stable for Kirsten—but I certainly realize all plans are very goddamn volatile. So just call or write if that's not possible as and when. I do think it's good indeed Trane's having time with you—I so hope she gets some relief of whatever nature very, very soon.

> I love you,
> *Bob*

P.S. Allen was calling about possibility of a reading here among other things with Mike McClure early Dec—so then Mike called—and heard charming news you're to read with Joanne early Nov. (11th)—great! They seem in fine spirits—also he told me Robt is much better now.

. . .

LETTER TO ALLEN GINSBERG

> Robert Creeley
> 400 Fargo
> Buffalo, NY 14213
> November 1, 1975

Dear Allen,

That was such a happy evening down there! Your apartment is charming! <u>And</u> your generous intro to myself was so sweet, truly. <u>Thanks</u>

Elsewise sad to miss meeting Bob Dylan (my hero!)—I thought Jim Brodey was putting me on! Apparently Bill Katz thought it was someone playing a record—etc. It's a hard life . . .

Apropos—the fucking student committee involved, at Buff State, is locked in internecine warfare, as we used to say; hence no invitation to you and Mike as I understand it. They're just fighting (as of yesterday anyhow). I'm damn sorry—maybe something will work out yet.

> *Meantime LOVE!*
> *Bob*

. . .

LETTER TO MR. AND MRS. HILTON POWER (HELEN CREELEY)

[on Fiji Mocambo Hotel letterhead]

Palmerston North, N.Z.
March 16, 1976

Dear Folks,

   I'm up here in the farm country for a couple of days—clouds rolling over
the fields now from the hills, great space, etc. We drove up yes—today from
Wellington along the coast. Then inland, etc. Day before that I was in cottage
hanging over sea at Taylor's Mistake near Christchurch—oysters just coming
into season, as are the dear cucumbers. Great Indian summer, after a very wet
and cold summer they tell me. And I spent about a week in Dunedin, which
I really liked, as a small comfortable city, with lovely sound, Port Chalmers,
etc. People are very great here, i.e., very easy direct manner, really helpful and
open. Only my colleagues, i.e. poets or professors, occasionally a drag with
some defensive maneuver. I love the scale of the place—the constant sense of
water, and the wild clouds (great sunsets, therefore). So! You sure came from
a nice place, Hilton! I heard from Russell Haley on arrival that both Stephanie
& Rachel had been in touch, so will have time with them for sure next week
when I go up to Auckland. Again. It really feels great being here—I only wish I
could pack in and stay awhile—and just might try to do it one of these years. Ah
well . . . Hope all's fine there! I'll be in touch.

My love to you all,
Bob

P.S. Write me please quick airmail card with everyone around Auckland's phone
numbers (e.g. Stephanie & Rachel's)—because I left them at home in last minute
chaos. Send to: Russell Haley, 27 Marlborough St., Mt. Eden 3, Auckland.

· · ·

LETTER TO BOBBIE CREELEY (BOBBIE LOUISE HAWKINS)

[on the Sebel Town House letterhead]

Singapore
April 4, 1976

Dear old friend—como se dice:

         Mid-day here in Singapore by god—and I sit wrapped in towel
after shower trying to get head together to hit the street. First one that's really
been intimidating since these people are really "different" you dig. Ah well . . .
Australia was a pleasure—Perth kind of sleepy and isolated, but saw charm-
ing black swans, as we sat by river bank of great old pub sloshing white wine
Bolinas style. It's one world!

Been writing a lot—the movement and being put thus into self seems to stimulate it—hence small book for charming Alan Loney in Christchurch, N.Z. was done sans problem. Elsewise my head's bugging with so-called impressions endlessly proliferating. Political, personal, visual—etc. Australia seems the new "affluent society"—as instance US $ worth about 75¢ their money, and prices ain't cheap. If you see Robt [Duncan], tell him Robert + Cheryl Adamson—the people who are getting him over—are really terrific— and he's an excellent poet as Robt will know. Voila.

Hope all's well there. I had just your one letter in N.Z. but assume no news is good news. Moving like this, time so expands that it seems almost years since I left, though it's only a little over a month now. Anyhow. One thing: write me* your sense of our meeting Hawaii c/o U.S.I.S., U.S. EMBASSY, TOKYO—I'll be getting in there April 21st—so's I can book flight through to S.F. if it doesn't look simple to you, etc. I'm truly pleased with either possibility—so that's it.

Ok! I must leave this room, else I never will! Off tomorrow morn at 8:00 for Manila. Wheeee!

> *I love you,*
> *Bob*

*Do it soon enough so I'll hear directly on arrival if you can.

[Variant of "Men" included with letter (*CP* II, 32).]

MEN

Here, on the wall
of this hotel in
Singapore, there's a

picture, of a woman,
big-breasted, walking,
blue-coated, with

smaller person—both
followed by a house men
are carrying. It's a day

in the life of the world.
It tells you, somehow,
what you ought to know

about it, e.g., if
a wife, a house, or
if a house, a wife.

. . .

POSTCARD TO BOBBIE CREELEY (BOBBIE LOUISE HAWKINS)

[depicting the Rado Flower Clock at Rizal Park, Manila]

CREELEY———————PHILLIPINES

4/10/76

Dear Bobbie,

Just back from set of APOCALYPSE NOW and seeing Tony Dingman in Coppola's* private plane no less—really a wild scene. So—sitting here waiting to get the plane back to Singapore—exhausted but god knows <u>happy</u>. Hope you're all the same & I'll write letter once things SLOW DOWN!

All my love,

Bob

I loved this "clock"!

*He did <u>The Godfather</u>, etc.

· · ·

LETTER TO BOBBIE CREELEY (BOBBIE LOUISE HAWKINS)

[on Hotel Okura letterhead, Tokyo]

STILL SCHEDULED TO ARRIVE
THERE MAY 3RD—AND <u>MEET YOU</u> 9:30 <u>IN TOWN</u>
TERMINAL "BABY"—A DEAL!

Call Rick & get name of place in Sausalito that has <u>great</u> breakfasts—como no . . . .

April 21, 1976

<u>6:00PM</u>

Dear Bobbie,

Just got in here—and happily good-natured people who picked me up at the airport had your letter in hand. Terrific! Hopefully you'll have had my letter from Singapore: to wit, fine for proofing—and thanks!; page size of AWAY same as THIRTY THINGS; and I've written Martin Booth re Cambridge Arts Festival. Voila! Cherry blossoms blooming out window in moon fading light—feel of the place elegant and clear, immediately. U.S.I.S. persons here really sharp, one a father [^ *met his wife later*] of young guy who was my host at U. of Wash. in Seattle last fall. Small world! Also, tomorrow morning before I go down south to Fukuoka for reading etc there, will do video tape with interviewer Father Mason from Sophia U.—smaller world! Elsewise there's a big transportation strike here—so tonight will probably be small scene (happily!) and as yet no word from Richard. I won't be in Tokyo again after tomorrow except for one night the 2nd, but will be in Kyoto for 3 days, 2 free over weekend—which sounds good. Also will go to Sapporo & Osaka—so get to see a little if like spaced whirlwind. To think, like they say, last night was sitting in house in Hong Kong with charming poets, including one older who chanted <u>lovely</u> Classic old Chinese poems—so <u>haunting</u> and <u>beautiful</u>. Wow! I read them ANGER, which got so fierce and <u>strong</u> in <u>sounds</u>, being in that company I guess. U. of Hong Kong gave me charming pennant—sweet! Continue writing a lot, squibs among them, viz:

AMERICAN LOVE   [OR]   HONG KONG: LAST WORDS

A big assed
beauty!

I want to get off
the fucking world and
sit down in a chair,
and be there.

<u>P.S.</u> Rock on radio—I sure <u>love</u> America!

11:30PM

Back! Really a <u>great</u> evening, with charming Japanese poets, including one inspired woman beauty, also young man playing sax (also flute) & bass—really terrific! And I was a hit, old buddy—<u>thank god</u>! So, now back in room in this incredibly splendiferous hotel—roses floating in absolute perfection of charmingly squared pools of water, etc—and plates selling for 70,000 yen—roughly 2000+ in interior shop windows, like ultimate subway scene. Ah well! I must say these people know how to get it on! So—on to Fukuoka late morn—and Japan looms most pleasingly. Ended reading with newly writ poem (on plane), dedicated to Ted Berrigan: "Things To Do in Tokyo"—charming dean of poets there told me it qualifies me as Zen master!—como no. They sure are <u>nice</u>, as we say in America . . . Anyhow, spirits high as body flips out in old spin of back-break exhaust-ion. WOW!   *LOVE,*

Bob

[note on envelope] *P.S. If persons there were interested, would be pleasure to give reading of new stuff, etc in church before splitting the 12th (recalling Berkeley reading is the 11th), since probably won't get chance to be back for some damn time—anyhow! Feel so high, want the whole world to—etc. Oh!*

. . .

LETTER TO PENELOPE HIGHTON (PENELOPE CREELEY)

400 Fargo
Buffalo, N.Y. 14213
May 24, 1976

Dear Pen,

Finally with mind together sufficient to write to you, like they say—certainly have been thinking of you. Also like they say. I came cross country in a sort of daze, just looking out the window at mile after mile of transforming so-called landscape. Stopped in Chicago, for reading with really pleasant British poet and old friend, Tom Raworth—city felt very handsome and specific, people outfront and quick in their energy. Then here, as of Tuesday night the 18th—and since then have been in zappy slowing process from all that traveling started, as I remember, February 23rd. Wow. . . . . So anyhow since then birthday, dancing in the dark, delightful dinner with teenage person hopes to be football scholarship fellow to Florida met on approach to entrance of great old restaurant-speakeasy here, and so on. Just letting it out as possible, smoking, drinking, and sleeping moments to leap up at 6 this morn, teach at 9—and it begins to feel like I'm here.

Brief report: Cambridge Poetry Festival invite for late April* next year pays to and from Europe, so that's together—plus report from Jim Dine and another mutual friend there tells me Kitaj expects me to use house in northern Mediterranean coastal Spain next spring, as I'd plotted—etc. All that feels together. So.

*would plan to go over mid-Jan—back here (USA) early May

I do hope things there are ok. Last letter from you (forwarded here) was painters in your house making movie, and very explicit kind careful words to me—and thanks, so much. You're a friend of mine likewise, to put it mildly. Ok.

Marisol book finally out, and will send copy very shortly airmail. Am sending softcover not to be cheap, but because it's the best physical fact of the book, and terrific. It really came through.

I've got to slow down! Writing now can feel words pounding like goddamn vein in temple. Probably momently to explode, but tonight will cook supper slowly, thoughtfully, and eat it in like manner—and see what's on tv—and let it relax.

Apartment feels easy and clear as ever. So good to walk in and find it feeling fresh, with old friends, pictures, on the wall, stuff where I remember having left it—and great yellow Korean bicycle Benny left for me down in the hall. Plants also in good shape, returned now by friends—likewise new ones, and feel like I'm living with something alive at least.

Elsewise it's been remarkably cold, for early summer, as it is now here. Snow squall first day I was back, weird! Re hat, before I forget, on one of those days recently now past walking down street here mid-afternoon, truck slows and guy leans out to shout, hey man, I like your hat! So it's a success, to put it mildly, and in fact is right in unexpected style, i.e., variations of same are seemingly all over the place. But none like mine, of course. Terrific . . . Meantime both Sarah and Kirsten are doing new knit ones, generously, so will be well equipped, plus to think to get something called a "Moose River Hat" which is your old "Silver Belly" in color with "Matching grosgrain band," you dig. Otherwise: "Makes an excellent outdoors hat for hiking, fishing, or shooting and its handsome appearance is suitable for street wear. Weight about 4 oz. And should last indefinitely . . . " That's it.

Sarah had this typewriter while I was gone, action feels good—loose and easy. Needs cleaning otherwise—feels like playing a piano to see if it needs tuning. It's an old Olympia, dating back to circa '56, and have written a hell of a lot on it, frankly—so good to have it here as well. Car still running, thankfully—had dire accident (Sarah did) caused by back tire blowing, car slewing around, off road to crunch on boulder drove motor and transmission considerably forward, and also shifted back of frame about 3/4s of an inch off center. But incredible mechanic got it all back together somehow, and it's now been 3000 miles plus, and is running well, so that's it.

So what are you doing? Hopefully at this point things are feeling easier for you. Write please as mind and time permit. List birds, people, dogs, cats, trees, et al you've seen in the last 24 hrs, for openers—then, continue. Any omens, etc. In movie yesterday aft, The Missouri Breaks, with friend, as Marlon Brando, the old killer, yanks the deceased upright from coffin in old Western setting, to make point to the aghast company, said to friend, I sure wish I could act like that sometimes, friend answered, you do! Well I never know at the time.

Meantime I'll quiet down, believe me—this scene is 5 days per week, from nine to 12:30, and that's going to keep me in place, believe me. Until July 9th. Actually first meetings with the two classes involved felt ok, bulky various group for early one, "a general approach to a very personal sense of 'American' 'poetry'"—and second is tender, much smaller, persons reading Williams— one's asked already if he can drop out of class early to go to Summer Solstice scene in New Mexico, roughly 2000 miles distant. Seems reasonable . . .

Dear most specific and personal and 'all the rest' friend—like, you—I'll be back shortly, and again please write as you can. Life's ok here, feel most simply put 'at one with myself' and in a place that likes me. So better than that it finally does not get.

All my love,
Bob

PS. Letter from Michael Volkersberg re money he does not *owe me—and sadly he really does not—mailed Wellington May 17th in today the 24th—not hopeless. Anyhow let me know how long this one takes—for a measure. Onward!*

. . .

LETTER TO PENELOPE HIGHTON (PENELOPE CREELEY)

> 400 Fargo
> Buffalo, N.Y. 14213
> May 27, 1976

Dear Pen,

So good to get your dear letter—really, right on time, like they say, just that fucking irritations of last night's company were producing ugly, insistent vibes you just shut off like a light. O wondrous one, etc. Anyhow, entirely terrific, and thank you.

What that was all about (e.g., card & above) was: Marisol is in town to repair two pieces of hers at the Albright-Knox (museum), that 'Baby Girl' you see at outset of enclosed (terrific) book (work of art), and latter one called 'The Generals' (I will let you discover for yourself, but listing anyhow is to be found at back of (terrific) book (work of art).) Ok. She called yesterday aft to ask if I would like to go to dinner with her, and to tell me George Segal (whom I'd not met, and who is very easy, bright, open, and good news altogether) is doing piece for the local Federal Bldg downtown—and it turns out we're to eat with Geo & his pleasant wife's hosts—real fucking culture-vultures, house stuffed with art, mags, the works—and conversation rotates on such realities as, do you remember when we bought our first Work of Art from Pace, dear . . . Incredible. Also, standing in line to get use of toilet because they're too wary to permit use of adjacent toilets one knows are damn well in the house. And they check me for trouble, though of course I'm given about 2 inches of tolerance because a) I'm with Marisol and b) am an Artist of one meager sort, if not The Real Thing. So whole fucking evening was wasted sadly—just tight with boredom and impatience, and no time at all to talk free of them. Anyhow, one true virtue in the writing biz is you do not have to make that scene, altho it has its own obvious conditions of social dullness (as you no doubt remember).

Well, god bless you. As Ezra Pound was wont to say, The right answer debunks all other. Voila.

Your letter was so wisely, dearly clear—in fact, you really should have it back some time, it's of that order of information, and it's the value of yourself truly that it makes so evident. Ok again.

Sitting here listening to tapes of reggae done last fall, happy echoes of time in a way. About two in the afternoon, a lovely fresh summer day, getting warmer by the moment. Despite headache from too much smoking last night etc, feel comfortably at ease and here—talking to you.

Your plans sound great, particularly if they lead you this way—which sounds to me like delight, both that trip cross country at this time of year would be lovely, and also, of course, there'd be a rainbow, and all that sort of thing. Why not.

Anyhow my scene is briefly as follows: teach here till July 9th, take a couple days to clean things up—had figured then to drift around locally, probably New England, till further employment in New Jersey the 31st till August 7th, that being bout 45 minutes out of New York City—and that concluded, head for house in New Mexico, then up to Boulder (near Denver) Colorado Aug. 16–20, then back to N.M., then back here, to Buffalo, circa the 1st of Sept. Now my youngest daughter, Kate, is to be, as far as all's been planned and I'm aware of it, at art school summer session till about July 30th, in Portland, Maine—so she may come with me to N.J., and/or so I'm hoping she does, so as to give her a chance to dig NYC a little, despite time of year, i.e., everyone tends to split if possible then.

Anyhow that gives you quick sense of that situation, i.e., where I so-called will be. It would be sadly ridiculous to have you literally in country sans means to meet you.

As to this room, where I'm sitting, table's adjacent to window, one of two, have half curtained with white, walls are white, it's the kitchen—where I always tend to hang out in any house. It is light, as matter of fact, especially in the early morning as sun's coming up, and at sunset, really slants through room, again this kitchen, and elsewise there are three other rooms, one not really used at all I plan to fix into viable workroom this summer, also for guest use with mattress cum couch on floor, long table against wall, shelves, etc. Then the livingroom, I can see it through door sitting here, where music is etc, and then bedroom, sort of charming blue walls, sun really comes in there in morning, wakes me up, and also moonlight (by god) comes in there, when moon is happily full. Pictures, postcards, etc—I was so attracted thus to your lovely bedroom, the same head, so to speak. The place is curiously simple, yet somehow expands to make a surprising room. Stuff in it (with exception of one old chair, wood for shelves, etc) all came with it, have shifted it about to improvise—'work with what is' etc. I've been here now, I realize, almost three years (as of fall). Neighbor, pleasant lady who owns store underneath me, now out sitting across the street with another neighbor—neighborhood is old Italian, single 'modest' houses side by side—easy walk past monolithic castle-like Armory to river and opening of Lake Erie, battered, pleasant old park there, etc. Can look across at so-called Canada, could walk over I suppose on Peace Bridge, as it's called. This is the West Side (not down as far as where that photo-card was taken, that's all below Hudson Street, as he told me, about eight or so blocks down. Crazy divers working, poor, scene.) I feel very secure here, not just because it's 'me' in it, alone etc, just that it really takes care of you, as a 'place'. I don't get lonely or freaked here, which is amazing, and useful. I keep it very sort of shipshape, neat—close to literal compulsive as friends tell me, but I like that clean specific edge to locate with. Always make bed in morning, hang up clothes, wash dishes—anal compulsive Puritan freak etc.

Present tuneful slip/slap song is "Branded by Love . . . " I've heard little of Patti Smith's work, I met her when she was primarily poet, time of McGovern campaign, she seemed really alert, quick person—she's really going great in this country. So I'll get off my ass and go listen. Ok. Will also write Bruce and Linley, which I haven't, this weekend—also other friends. Things just now do get together and settled, teaching going ok after bumpy start. So.

Again, so good to hear—and for the record, your letter, mailed the 20th, seemingly took the 7 days anticipated. That's by no means hopeless. Onward! Take care of your terrific self—like.

My love,
Bob

. . .

LETTER TO PENELOPE HIGHTON (PENELOPE CREELEY)

400 Fargo
Buffalo, N.Y. 14213

May 27, 1976

Dear Pen,

A 'ps' to letter just off with book to you—still a great day here, now after four etc—what I wanted to say was just after writing and all, on impulse I called Bobbie in California, feeling a sad shabby guilt apropos, insofar as so much had been left hanging, as though all were to be momently together again, really my own insistence for a long damn time. Anyhow we've decided to separate formally for a year, just stay literally away from one another with the presumed sense it leaves it thus open if and as and when. Mostly, it makes it simpler to do it at all because of a lot of accumulated habit and dependency and an affection and things known and gone through together make a very deep human bond. Hopefully we can at some point get to be friends again—past months, years now, it's as though we diminished each other's reality so painfully that I'd lose all self-confidence around her and she felt that I was continually criticizing her. Anyhow, that's hereby done with—and it's of true point to tell you, just that you are very specific and dear to me, and I want it straight on the so-called record. I'd love to see you, possible prospect of your being in this country really dazzling. Ok.

Lessee—got a whole page here to continue, right? Talking just now to

Marisol on phone, she'd called about possible dinner etc—hence first friend on line after previous call, tell her the news, like they say, she answers with, oh . . . I thought you <u>were</u> separated . . .

Sun dazzling in, Sonny Rollins on line playing To A Wild Rose—that's an old time beauty.

I felt so good with you, I felt I could make you happy—likewise, selfishly enough, you me, as day we took off for Christchurch in your car, so direct, so simple and clear with all that other stuff sort of buzzing around, e.g., Trevor etc.

Anyhow, let's resume, friend, viz

> <u>here comes the sun!</u>
> while we can,
> let's do it, let's
> have fun.

And to think some people would consider that frivolous—aie . . . Most of all, none of this is to lean on you, please, it's just like Part II of that letter written from Hong Kong, and at this moment I feel soared, but a great, great deal more clear. That's got to be life.

My love to you,
*Robert**

**just for you!*

. . .

LETTER TO ROBERT GRENIER

400 Fargo
Buffalo, N.Y. 14213
July 4, 1976

Dear Amigo,

Good to have your 'storm tossed' card 'there.' Haven't seen you around lately, etc, etc. I've been flat out with this 5 day a week teaching scene, like wrap-around echo box—and with fact I was already flat from trip when I got here, it's been <u>very</u> abstract. Plus now 'formal' separation like they say— hardly that 'new' just that that's where it's been pretty much the past three years anyhow. So no awful existential despairs apropos. I'm bored, often—again, factual constriction of present daily employment. But that's over end of the coming week, and have sub-let this place (tho may at last minute have to grab it back lacking another in which to be, like they say), and will head to NYC for a bit, friend's coming in from New Zealand the 11th, which is certainly 'on time', shortly after go up to see how Kate's doing and all—she finishes there on the 30th. Supposedly do workshop for a week in N.J. but they may cancel due to no takers, etc. Most anxious to go sit in house in New Mex/ for as long as possible. Have to be back here Sept 1st it looks like, but that will be a far more relaxed situation, thinking of present agonies. So!

I've been reading proof on the SELECTED, and its text is as ever a beautifully clear job—and thanks again & again. Elsewise it's a literal battle with them (and/or Scribners) to respect any of the fucking interests I have in how the 'running on' of the poems etc should be managed—just dumb-ass complacent stupidity. And it gets frustrating!! So frankly, I'll be deeply pleased if the book survives and does not look a total mess—they really are absolutely without eyes or ears. But our work, goddamn it, is still the point, and that's really it, for me. (I had asked them months ago, by the way, to send you copy of PRESENCES, when ready—two bits they didn't—anyhow please tell me. Their trip on that book has been equally bleak—no nothing, apparently—and it's lovely. Aie!)

So, brother—world actually feels both tangible and a pleasure. I get into curious scenes, like swimming with group of Lesbian Ladies (1st time in 2 yrs—but wait! I forget the Dine's Pool!) at Mendon Pond in Rochester. That was funny—one great lunky one on back, hair streaming forth, whilst she massaged toes o' my friend just 'above' her—like teen-agers somehow, wooly giggly sweaters etc. Ain't Art Grand??? Men in that scene feel like castrated oxes, just that spaced stricken look in the eyes, and very sweet, you dig. I fled that one I can tell you. Car's still going great, by the way—thank god.

People hereabouts in good spirits. Was in our local bar a few nights ago, and suddenly in company with an ex-bartender from Smiley's—weird! Like, mutual question: what was all that about???? Sure looks strange from this distance. So beautiful, and so faint, at the same time—or for me it was, i.e., I should truly speak for myself and stop the endless 'attack' etc. Really dull.

Jim Dine called yesterday, and that's all going well—great etcher/printer/head doing it, Crommelynck, getting proofs now, and apparently, as Jim says, going to the ultimate Class. Meantime collection of three prose texts (from ADB, P, and MABEL) coming out momently in England, which delights me. That way things keep moving. Small book of 'travel' writing coming out late in the year in N.Z. etc. I feel like I turned real corner on that trip, and with 50th birthday, suddenly decks were cleared, next decade looming etc. I must say ages 40–50 worst I ever experienced. Give you something to look forward to . . . Leslie Fiedler said same thing for him, incidentally. So take care of yourself. No kidding.

I don't know where I'll be but here Sept—Dec, then head for Spain (San Feliu de Guixols, north of Barcelona) early Jan till mid April, then England probably for a month, then back here. Have gig in Sun Valley for the summer, elsewise in N.M. I'm really drawn, like they say, to moving now as much as possible. It just feels so humanly good & interesting to me. Card with yours from Tony Dingman in Japan, as it happened—R&R—apparently Coppola's scene in the Philippines where I saw him will stretch on till Nov/Dec, whereupon he may head to Spain also. I guess it's just that long attempt to settle, get a house (houses), get it 'in place' etc—with this weird commuting, made it all finally a little ridiculous to say I wouldn't be moving every damn chance I get. I always have & I always apparently will.

Forgive insistent self-preoccupation here—it's been a singular time in past months, actually since I began teaching here again and Kate and Kirsten were then ill, and Bobbie and I farther and farther apart as two people, etc. As you'll well know, one wants just to say, let's go eat, or sleep, or fuck, or be happy—and that takes two, etc. So, I'm working on it I guess—I don't see any longer point in living as though I were waiting for the bus to come. There are things I can humanly do, and keep together, and I want that use of them—I'm tired of this fucking singular neatness, which you'll remember—so I'll get it on, be ye sure.

Well, sure think of you all. I see Benny from time to time, in good spirits. Also saw Rick Fields briefly in NYC, likewise. One damn day I'll be able to come back to that town & see friends sans the existential horrors. There was/ were day/days I wanted to tear the 'reality' off that beautiful sky & sea it was such a joke to me, given the human reality etc. So that was my 'problem' and here in this human complex weird density of old-time peoples, it really fades. Ok! Take care of yourself, bro, and write as you can.

Love to you and the gang,
Bob

. . .

LETTER TO DENISE LEVERTOV

400 Fargo
Buffalo, N.Y. 14213
November 17, 1976

Dear Denny,

Sitting here at dawn, it seems—feel like a farmer these days, and that's a pleasure. So much has happened since last we met, i.e., Bobbie and I finally decided to separate this past May, after I'd come back here to teach summer school. I'd been out of the country for a little over two months last spring, in New Zealand, Australia, etc. I really loved it, just walking around in the world, for whatever dumbass, irresponsible reason. Anyhow, that had been long coming, I guess—and the factual 'separation' of my being here so much of the time alone, the past three years, made the literal break humanly as simple as it could be. Meantime Kate finished high school, tried going to the Portland School of Art (in Maine) for a summer session, didn't really take to it, so came late July to live with me—and is now a charming neighbor, with apartment of her own in this same part of the city. Elsewise she has a morning job five days a week babysitting, works part time at a local food coop, has been taking non-credit courses at UB, and hopes to start at Buff State next fall. She's remarkably more comfortable with herself, much clearer in emotions, really in every way. So that's been a great relief and delight. Kirsten also seems much better, and Sarah, as ever, is the great maintainer, thank god.

Then I've of course fallen in love—why not—and have been living with a very dearly pleasant woman, met in New Zealand, of all places, last spring—family's all English, doctors, and she has a lovely simple way of living with other people, e.g., we (Kate, she and I) were all in this rather small apartment more or less from late July till the end of October sans great crises or screaming fits—and that is a true "first" believe me, and she was truly its possibility. I can't tell you what human wonder it is for me, insofar as my life seems to have been so committed to tensions and Dramas of the Self for so damn long. Well, she's an extraordinary friend and dear, dear pleasure to be with—and her name is Penelope Highton. Wouldn't you know it . . .

I was in Boston briefly in October, but so scatteredly and so ringed around with Stone Soup poets, I didn't try to get in touch with you. Most happy in that situation was time with Charlotte, who's living on the backside of Beacon Hill, and she actually put Pen and I up in her apartment, for our last night there. It was an extraordinary 'vote of confidence' on her part, and touched me very damn much. Meantime I've really been in touch with those children more than I have been in some time, and will have Thanksgiving with David and his wife Elizabeth (now a vigorous lawyer with her own office and sister partner (i.e., another young woman attorney) in Northampton) at my sister Helen's in Albany. Pen's presently in England seeing her family—brother and sister both doctors, and her mother, who's visiting, likewise doctor—psychiatrist, etc etc. (I hope I'm not providing for my old age???)

Anyhow I've got a reading in Cambridge on December 5th, which the fellow called to confirm last Friday while I was gone (Kate took the call etc), but it does seem for sure. I'll be coming in to Boston the 4th, Pen's coming in there the 5th—so presuming times all agree, could we have dinner together—I could claim need for hour or two of Quiet Meditation with Old Friends (namely you, Pen and me) prior to the Great Moment, and it would give us chance for some time together. In any case, write me a card apropos, and I'll be governed accordingly, like they say.

I hope things have gone well for you. Been thinking of you, both teaching your work, as it happens—and also just thinking of you.

My love,
Bob

. . .

LETTER TO PENELOPE HIGHTON (PENELOPE CREELEY)

400 Fargo
Buffalo, NY 14213
November 21, 1976

My dearest Pen,

Wherein I'd truly will to stay forever! Ah well . . . Back here last night sans 'problem', to find Kate watching tv in good spirits (she's really increasingly sturdy in her disposition, and factually 'good' to me, e.g., had thoughtfully put in milk, cheese, and crackers, had the mail neatly out on the table, etc etc)—and seems to me increasingly flexible and active. I'm so <u>pleased</u> that being here has proved such use to her.

Time in North Carolina was unexpectedly pleasant, not so much from the 'activities'—which were both drab and inept albeit no disaster—but James Dickey was really extraordinarily sweet and good-natured. He was also insistently complimentary, in the most lovely way, e.g., he asked me if I'd been an 'athelete' (which he was, a football player—he's about 6'3", close to 200 lbs), just that he thought I 'carried' myself in that habit—wow! He referred to me in his 'lecture' as 'one of the finest poets of our generation' (this man who's notorious for attacking all such company), asked me if I'd had any movie offers for THE ISLAND, since he thought it would make a fine movie, etc. It went on and on! He took my picture, like they say—gave me his address with note at top, 'At the beginning . . . ' Terrific! He told me his wife had been very touched by note I'd written after seeing her, years ago, and used to lament he was not more like me (aie . . .). He was pleased indeed to hear of our being together, just that he knew that I, like he, was a most domestic man.

Well, it's damn well a pleasure to have someone so specifically be so nice, like they say. I'd been anticipating a far more hedged and wary rapport with him. He's a real loner, and comes from a Georgia hard-times background, and lives now in a curious blend of high-powered wheeling & dealing, e.g., recently given 12 million dollars to do tv film (which he did, 'The Call of the Wild'), and apparent isolation, teaches at the University of South Carolina, lives, as he said, with company of red necks and army people. I <u>liked</u> him—not, I hope simply that he was so generous, but there's a wild diversity of <u>person</u> in him, and a very intense sensuous passion. That's very clear in his writing, which, when I was younger, had put me off because of its dense and, for me, seemingly over-emphasized rhetoric. But I'd now feel that the fact of two distinctly different habits of person, i.e., that north Georgia macho and the New England taciturn maintaining. Anyhow, it was a true pleasure to meet him. Voila!

Meantime my delight has been this book about Yeats, by Norman Jeffares (which you've got to come back and tell me how to pronounce!) It's really brought me back to reading Yeats in the most useful way—if I can find some simple edition <u>not</u> overshadowed by goddamn Rosenthal, who's done the SELECTED etc. I've been reading it just about everywhere, planes, motels, lobbies, classrooms, etc. I'll be sad to finish it, in fact. The writer's tone is so balanced and alert, a real <u>English</u> virtue in critics. His reading of the poems is especially agreeable—no awful sententiousness, simply makes his point, intelligently, and moves on. Lovely discreet report of Yeats' literal life otherwise, e.g., here's how Mrs. Yeats comes into the story: "In 1917 Yeats ignored her (Maud Gonne's daughter, Iseult) unsuitable horoscope and continually asked her to marry him; she 'still mentally fifteen', enjoyed flirting with her mother's famous admirer throughout the summer. Eventually he managed to get passports for the family to enter the United Kingdom; and he accompanied them to London in September. The authorities did not allow Maud to proceed to Ireland. On the boat Yeats had delivered an ultimatum to Iseult: that she must make up her mind one way or the other, that he found the whole business an immense strain, and that if she would not marry him he had a friend who would be very suitable, a girl strikingly beautiful in a barbaric manner. He must receive her answer within a week at a certain A.B.C. in London. Iseult refused him and he married Miss Hyde-Lees on 20th October."

Yeats was a hero of mine, starting out, college, etc. He was The Poet—for our imaginations then, just that his life seemed so specifically committed to its act. And he was Irish, of course. I recall taking his late poems to war with me, along with Pound's A DRAFT OF XXX CANTOS, and an anthology of War Poets, etc. He was the fact of poetry's power of imagination, and its transformational reality. So the return, of all that, now to my mind, call it, is most apt—just that my life, myself in that respect, is turning in my experience of it, after a long situation of almost willful stasis. And it's curious how literally this information comes now to hand—for one obvious fact, Yeats' late, first marriage, at fifty, and its relation with Maud Gonne—and the fact of his two children then, Ann and Michael. It's as if all that were being given me now to consider, as literal 'sign'.

I don't need it, of course. New Englanders don't <u>need</u> anything. They just <u>want</u> it all. So many mornings, these past days, I'll go back to the bedroom, for something, and be almost startled not to find you there, in the bed, hair all over the pillow, face scrunched down into same. Or, looking up, not to see you passing in the hall, in your dear red wrapper. I <u>love</u> you, Pen—so clear, so steady, to me, as what I do know. I haven't the least question now, if I ever did—it's something thus growing, of itself, like that wild piggy-back, you should see it!, goes on & on. So, it's Sunday morn—only two weeks more, and you'll be 'palpable to touch'—<u>praise</u> god.

I think simply let's get married in July, and let that be damn well that—i.e., it seems a 'discreet' 'period' 'of waiting'? Ah well . . . Can't wait for the world forever. Meantime come home, old buddy—mea domina, Life's Loveliest Lady—sings such wonder in my thumping heart. Help! Chuckling to myself just thinking of you—delicieuse, I guess one could say. I think the world can happen in our hands.

Hope to hell you get this fore you're off to France. I always loved that phrase, Shakespeare: "Fair stands the wind for France." Such a lift! So, have an extraordinarily good time—and I'll be back, and, I'll see you very soon!

My love, dearest P!

Robert

. . .

LETTER TO ROBERT GRENIER

400 Fargo
Buffalo, N.Y. 14213
November 24, 1976

Dear Bob,

Just to give you final word in this mess—Charles Scribner wrote yesterday, as follows, like they say:

"It has taken me a little time to answer your last letter only because I wished to make certain inquiries here within Scribners.

"All of us are distressed that you feel as you do about the handling of your recent book of poems. As is almost always the case there are two sides to some of your complaints, but in the matter of the order of the poems I believe we are absolutely at fault. Apparently our art department made some transpositions—possibly to meet design requirements—without approval of the editor.

"In any case I have the feeling that you basically wish to find a new home for your work and I cannot find a perfect argument to prevent that. We have virtually stopped publishing poetry and it would be consistent for us to accept your decision to leave."

Then there's a little more about procedure of reversion of rights to me as texts go out of print, etc etc. So that's that. I still don't know what they now propose to do with the errors of the SELECTED POEMS, if anything—but I've written to ask that they let it go out of print, i.e., let this 1st edition be the only one—and hopefully (indeed!) whoever takes me on can do an edition with some care as to getting it right parallel to your own in the first damn place. Onward! What a relief, in fact. I've had nothing but trouble & vagaries from those people ever since Donald Hutter left in the mid-sixties, so it's truly nothing new—and this is just the so-called final straw.

Meantime, back at the ranch, Peter Freeman (that magazine, 52 Dunster,

HU—as they put it) did apparently call when I was off reading in Oneonta November 12th—and told Kate the reading was on for the 5th. But I've heard nothing since, and it's getting damn close, Pen's arriving there same day—at 2:20 PM to be precise—so I'm getting a little nervous. If you can discover <u>anything</u> about what's going on, and write me pronto &/or call collect, it would be a lovely service indeed.

Thanks for that lovely piece of yours, sitting here waiting for action—but it will get it, be ye sure.* Just a fucking deluge of biznesses (Off to Albany this morn with Kate to have Thanksgiving with my sister & family, plus my son & wife—so). I'll be back! Hope all's ok there, and very much that I get to see you.

My love,
Bob

*Just did—really bright and various!

P.S. I'm asking <u>The Am. Poetry Review</u> to put note in to the effect that you are not acknowledged in edition of SELECTED, and that the <u>order</u> of the poems is solely the responsibility of the publisher—and has neither your nor my approval. Meager satisfaction—but at least it will make the situation in some sense public. Ok! Bob

• • •

LETTER TO ROBERT DUNCAN

Dia Libros
Sant Domenel 21
San Feliu de Guixols
(Gerona)
Spain
February 2, 1977

Dear Robert,

After endless peregrinations, we've now been here two weeks come Thursday, and have happily settled down to a less rushed & distracting 'life'. For the holidays, we went with Kate to New Mexico—and the house in Placitas is in such good spirits these days, complete with chickens and fresh paint—, saw Kirsten, Trane, and Sarah, who came from California—then went back to Buffalo, where Kate's now settled in her own apartment, and variously working parttime and beginning courses at Buffalo State (which she chose over UB in that it's in 'her neighborhood' and has active art program, etc). Then to New York, for five days—staying with Larry Poons, seeing old friends as Neil Williams and John Chamberlain and Marisol, and also, very happily, arranging the shift from Scribners to New Directions (!), and what a relief that proves.

Subsequently I learned that Burroughs Mitchell had also been summarily retired at 63, due, as he put it, to 'reorganization' and the other editor I'd had there, Patricia Cristol (useless as she was to me), has also left. So I'm well out of that mess—with New Directions planning to publish a first book, a collection of travel poems written last spring in that maze of countries called HELLO, next spring ('78). Voila!

Then to London, to find Kitaj and family in active spirits, as he works toward his show in April, for which he's generously asked me to do a note. He's centering more and more on <u>person</u>, parallel to 'characters in a possible novel', as he puts it. Preoccupations thus, as ever, seem very much those he notes in "The Human Clay," that introduction he wrote for his selection for the Arts Council of Great Britain last year. Also saw Sylvia, who says hello—and then Ron came down here with us, to open the house—which proves a sort of 19th century 3 storey 'town house' with 15 ft ceilings etc etc. We've managed to get three rooms of it usefully cozy, and heated—and so, hopefully, to work. Elsewise the city itself, about 7 or so thousand, is a typical Costa Brava resort (of actual use to my limited Spanish), with no one now here, thank god—and we walk out afternoons, either along the sea, which is as lovely as remembered from Mallorca days, or else back into the hills where one finds the same small farms I expect have been there for years and years. I've got money enough to keep everything together through April, and I'll do summer teaching then in Buffalo, from end of May till mid-July, etc. So, hopes are to be able to write some extensive prose now, free of the damn phone & casual dropper-in.

News of your trip, and the extraordinary poems, were so good to have. I do use you as my very own 'Rock of Gibraltar'—pardon the expression . . . But it's sure good to have you there, brother. Meantime—just finished reading Richard Holmes' SHELLEY, The Pursuit—very moving to me, because, early on, I'd decided Shelley was not for me, and this text makes clear his extraordinary interest, particularly the political thinking and 'ballads', and the later poems.

So I'll close, like they say, with a poem writ yesterday, having just finished the book, come from walk along the sea wall, musing on life & its meaning no less. Ok!

MYSELF

What, younger, felt
was possible, now knows
is not—but still
not changed enough—

Walked by the sea,
unchanged in memory—
evening, as clouds
on the far-off rim

of water float,
pictures of time,
smoke, faintness—
still the dream.

I want, if older,
still to know
why, human, men
and women are

so torn, so lost,
why hopes cannot
find better world
than this.

Shelley is dead and gone,
Who said,
"Taught them not this—
to know themselves;

their might Could not repress
the mutiny within,
And for the morn
of truth they feigned,

deep night
Caught them ere evening . . . "
[CP II, 95]

> My love to you and Jess,
> *Bob*

. . .

LETTER TO ROBERT GRENIER

> 400 Fargo
> Buffalo, N.Y. 14213
> May 17, 1977

Dear Bob,

Sent off the letter backside, like they say, to said person, and hope it's of use. Certainly small report of what I take to be your virtues. Meantime I'm off this aft for North Carolina, reading (thank god) at St Andrew's College, Laurinberg—Ron Bayes' place of employment. Anyhow we arrived back here pretty broke so it all helps. Things feel good—place clear & simple as ever, Kate surviving ok (though drifting without much apparent cutting edge. I don't see leaning on her as being much help to anyone, so am trying to keep as easy a rapport as we can.) After investigating ways to have Pen's visa etc extended, and finding none, thought to marry later in the year has now altered to momently, so going through weird procedures involved with getting 'permission'. Ah well . . . I loathe the bureaucratic thumb—which is only goddamn irritation in otherwise delight. Ok.

Your writing reads as sharp and specific to me as ever—that slide procedure would seem a good one, for getting it located for people. I.e., just to make it as 'apparent' as nose on their faces, etc. Or tree, barking dogs, etc. By god!

I've come back with divers collection of stuff written 'over there'—some I like, all sort of soft-edged, but it was that kind of time, reflective, otherwise isolate. We had a lovely visit with Basil Bunting whose wife had broken with him last winter in some dramatic fashion, took house etc. So he's at Jonathan Wms' house in Dentdale, Sedburgh, Cumbria—extraordinarily lovely country, close to Briggflats—walking distance. He goes to the Quaker Meeting House there, est. by Geo. Fox. Anyhow Basil is what I'd like to be, 'when I grow up'—so generous, uncomplaining, filled with explicit memories of people & places & acts. The conversation ranged over the whole literal world therefore. Last night listening to Correlli's 6 Concerti Grossi—as Basil put it, a lifetime's attention to 'getting it right'—no 'size' otherwise involved. Also talking of Byrd and Dowland, as clarity of music of that time—reminded me of your generous gift of the Dowland, 'back then'.

Anyhow all's well. We've come back just at the edge of summer—everything blooming now. I sure hope things move for you now, and any help I can be with whatever, please let me know. You're sure welcome here anytime. Voila.

Love,
Bob

. . .

LETTER TO CHARLES BERNSTEIN

Box 563
Placitas, N.M. 87043
February 6, 1979

Dear Charles,

Thanks very much for the copy of your book—which, happily, gave me an active sense of your range in all respects. One thing to me instantly attractive is the sturdy resource of your era, as Williams would say—which makes the resonance of the action a very coherent factor (e.g., "Soul Under" or any of parallel form with that one, using the shorter line pattern, etc) and then, as ever, the wit and brightness of so-called linguistic takes, like (like) "is like a"—a great pleasure indeed. So—thanks again.

I never got it together to note books of interest to me recently—but, briefly:

Illuminations and Reflections, the first of which I was introduced by R. B. Kitaj (wouldn't you know it . . .), just the political/morphological clarity, and his extraordinary powers as a literal reader. Charming to read with some one, in that old-time fashion.

Then—almost as personal memorial, now that he's sadly dead—Donald Sutherland, Gertrude Stein: A Biography of Her Works. Still for me the most provocative book on her particular genius, with equal range as to forms and specific cultural patterns in writing, e.g., Spanish/American takes on Surrealism.

Then—because I just did literally read it, though god knows why it took me so long to—still, seemingly, the best book to locate Williams (other than obviously all he himself got to say—which is it forever): Mike Weaver, William Carlos Williams, The American Background—such a lovely instance of legwork and so much said in such compact manner—as notes on jazz, rhythm, or surrealism will give instance.

Then Jackson MacLow called attention to November Scientific American ('78) article on children's language acquiring patterns—again much literal food for thought.

My best to you,
Bob

. . .

LETTER TO GEORGE BUTTERICK

Box 563
Placitas, N.M. 87043
April 12, 1979

Dear George,

Thanks indeed for your generous letters. God knows I hadn't meant to dump on you, but I really was displaced by the extraordinary emphasis on FOR LOVE, as against the selections from subsequent work. So, to that end, like they say, let me note some suggestions, not to kibitz (because I really don't want any part of the obvious responsibility you've got) but just to clarify my own senses of the problem. First, I'd cut down substantially on the present material from FOR LOVE, as follows: Le Fou, A Wicker Basket, Air: "Cat Bird Singing . . . ", The Traveller, A Marriage, Entre Nous, The Awakening, either The Rain or Kore (I question that both are needed—my own impulse would be to cut The Rain). That is, I think some of the poems are redundant in what they make clear as a 'style' of that time, e.g., The Traveller—and others I think are not that deathless, e.g., Entre Nous.

Then—I think the selection from WORDS is presently pretty weak, the one real absence being for me Anger. A Sight is one I like very much, but again, I do think Anger is significant indeed, in that collection. Pieces and The Invitation don't seem to me particularly useful—A Piece would be much more so, despite its briefness. Anyhow, I think selections here ought to be reconsidered more substantially.

PIECES is much the same problem. The Finger has a topical interest I guess—I continue to like it. But Numbers is far more significant, for me at least. Then—surely a classic antho piece: The Moon? And some excerpt from a sequence (like Mazatlan: Sea (to the end of the book), that shows what was then a decisive preoccupation. Or "Follow The Drinking Gourd . . . "

In the selection from A DAY BOOK, problem really comes clear. The selection seems to be following a domestic track and/or poems echoing that tone are getting favored clearly. Also the writing is 'familiar'. What about In London? Certainly more the center. Also poems like Rain (1 and 2)—or Massachusetts, or "Bolinas and Me"—or again, the moves of this text have to be more counted in? (Considering In Longing the most definite.) I'd choose something other than An Illness, in any case, and certainly more—as, too, with PIECES.

But what about HELLO??? I'd suggest So There, for one obvious. Etc. Again point seems to move <u>off</u> the understandably familiar center of FOR LOVE (really cut back on that material, as suggested?) and try to track subsequent activity as more than echo of that first disposition. "Twenty years have passed"—like they say. Not that I got better or worse, but did seemingly do something else?

Then I've enclosed text of the Hermes poem Charles mentioned (do give him my best!). Ok.

Well, as you note, there are 16 pages in your present selection from FOR LOVE, and 19 pages from the subsequent collections—but those are <u>four</u> collections, with <u>one</u> other (HELLO) not represented at all—so it does work out that one initial collection is getting 16 pages to itself, whereas the <u>five</u> subsequent (and there were more), more fugitive obviously) get average of <u>4</u> pages per. That aint democratic, Geo—and you an American . . . Anyhow, you'll see my much belabored point. In words of H. James, quoted by E. Pound, apropos prospective mate—in this case, 'selection'—I shd be married to a dissolving view???? Ah well.

Forgive insistence, but best get it out now—instead of passing final days in rancorous resentment as the Young bleat, I thot you were dead, like the anthology said (?). Ok.

As to decades incidentally, FOR LOVE is 1945 to 60, actually works out more as 50 to 60—as you say, the first decade. Then, by use of <u>my</u> fingers at least, we get two more effactually: 60 to 70/ 70 to present instant your eyes read these offensive letters, etc etc. Right? So how come first decade gets all the gravy? Don't you believe in me—uh?

So anyhow—I hope your life is very much otherwise than this kind of biz— where did we go wrong, George? We could have been bums.

All my best,
Bob

This might be interesting if there's chance to get there. Robert D's to be there et al.

[includes announcement for PEN American Center, Zukofsky Symposium, April 18 1979]

[attached poem, "Prayer to Hermes" (*CP* II, 183)]

. . .

LETTER TO JOHN TAGGART

Box 563
Placitas, NM 87043
June 12, 1979

Dear John,

Thanks for your very generous letter—a great reassurance. I felt very <u>small</u> facing that whole possibility, and was primarily anxious not to lean on Zukofsky in any glib fashion. Otherwise—to "review" over 800 pages and over forty years of work in "1000 words or less" . . . Ah well!

I've asked Bill Spanos to send you a copy of <u>Boundary 2</u> and hopefully he will. The issue on your own work—PAPER AIR—sounds a pleasure indeed, i.e., very bright people commenting. So that's good news. I did get DODEKA—and thank you. It's a fascinating construct—as ever active writing.

Hope all's well for you.

My best,
Bob

. . .

LETTER TO ROBERT DUNCAN

Robert Creeley
Box 563
Placitas, N.M. 87043
March 15, 1980

Dear Robert,

I just heard from Boston University that Mark Strand (!) got the goddamn job the day after his charming visit. Whereas three weeks after our time there, committee still hadn't met to talk it over. So—what did I really expect, I wonder. I <u>know</u> that snobbish disposition never quits—even in the wistful heads of initial poor girls like Helen Vendler. And clearly I wasn't going to get around her sad dumbness—viz. that Louise Gluck, Charles ~~Write~~ Wright, Dave Smith et al mean that "American poetry is in good hands . . . " She's pres of the MLA, incidentally. Ah well . . . Anyhow it was a stupidly battering business—and went on for four goddamn months of teasing invitation. Meantime there is possibility of being full time here, it seems—but that we'll consider more soberly. We <u>are</u> settled here, house sure stays a pleasure—but the social world, for us at least, is very faint. But it <u>is</u>—as you said back then when chaos with Bobbie was so adamant—time to be about one's own work, and here would make that possible I think. Anyhow—one way or t'other.

Just off for Buffalo for Mike's lecture—thinking of you there a year ago. So to hell with Helen Vendler and her "Part of Nature, Part of Us"—jesus! Who'd ever want that sad argument more than one literally <u>had</u> to have it.

Love to you both,
Bob

• • •

LETTER TO ALLEN GINSBERG

Box 563
Placitas, N.M. 87043
June 11, 1980

Dear Allen,

That was a charming poem re LATER, and thanks in all so-called respects. 'Who, me??' is really the question of our generation—like. Well, one day, etc etc. Meantime, as you may have heard, our lives have been really moved with respect of new person, i.e., Pen's pregnant, and it feels very humanly happy. I can remember Jack writing years ago, when Bobbie was pregnant with Sarah, to effect of how could one think to bring a person into such a then hopeless world—now more so, I guess, if that is the measure, viz, the mind's. But what otherwise to be human with or about, I wonder—so, onward.

Do call as you can when you're down here—phone is 867-5300. I probably won't otherwise get up there, for one thing Pen at this point gets queasy with car travel and that's some 80 miles all told—but I could certainly bring you down, for some time out, etc. So play it by ear and I will too.

Funny to be in this house now for the last time around. Feels good—but the human place otherwise is just too damn empty finally. I guess some things don't change at that.

Love to you and Peter,
Bob

Had a very happy old time visit with the McClures mid-May. I <u>do</u> love the old time affections and loyalties—e.g., "Be true to the dreams of thy youth . . . " Como no . . .

• • •

LETTER TO JOHN TAGGART

Box 563
Placitas, N.M. 87043
July 3, 1980

Dear John,

I had a note from Celia Zukofsky this morning apropos your sense that Louis had a decisive hand in the composition of "A"-24:

> "Now to answer your question re "A-24". "A"-24 is my work entirely! Louis' only contribution was "the gift/ she hears/ the work/ in its recurrences."
>
> "I don't know John Taggart. I never met him and I'd say he is presumptuous to assume that I could not do that work—"that whole complex thing." Louis not only accepted such a project, he was delighted with it. And that too, how does he know what Louis would or would not accept from Me?
>
> "Yes, you are correct about A-23's ending . . . "

That is, I'd felt Louis takes leave and/or melds as poet/presence with the materials and modes of the poem in A-23. So that's where his 'direction' ends, so to speak. In A-24 the words are entirely primary, including his presence or him as their artificer from a time previous—but he is no longer their 'control'.

In any case, you can now see another so-called 'plane' of the text, given this resolution now unequivocal—and the fact that Louis was delighted to have it be the 'ending'. Ok.

I guess I'd otherwise only caution against such large assumptions (that is, that Celia could not be the composer of A-24 despite the credits on the text itself, and also her statement in that transcription, etc etc. Unless you assume that she's not telling the truth, and I reject that possibility entirely, you must realize what a shimmy your presumption was making in the proposal of the poem itself—i.e., that you were mistaking the agency of the poem's ending (and/ or that the poet's ego [circled] was no longer a determinant).)

I know reading is its own delight, to put it mildly—but it would be bleak indeed to become an authority of misunderstanding. I.e., there's enough of them already—like they say.

All best,
Bob

[note on envelope:]
P.S. P. 806—Louis' note, which
Celia quotes—would be the final
point? I just can't see how one
would read it otherwise . . .
Bob

. . .

LETTER TO STAN AND JANE BRAKHAGE

> Back Cottage 2
> 388 Summer Street
> Buffalo, N.Y. 14213
> October 13, 1980

Dear Stan and Jane,

I'd hoped you guys might be just around the corner at this point, but gather the Cornell biz never jelled, to mix divers metaphors. We've been on the road, it seems, since about mid-June when we began to 'pack up' the house in Placitas, and just about a week ago now, we finally moved into this very pleasant house. It sits off the street, i.e., up a little sidewalk, on an 'interior' lot as it's called, a small brick cottage, 2 bedrooms upstairs, livingroom, kitchen, small 'study', and dining room down—and ample 'yards'. So it's very useful for us in all respects, thank god.

Anyhow here we are, and slowly things begin again to settle. As you must know, we're having a baby (!) in January—and that feels truly a happy prospect. We really thought it over, and obviously we both had various questions pertaining. But be that as it may, the prospect feels very happy and again this house is a very solid place to be therefor. Somehow things in Placitas increasingly fell apart for us, e.g., that little house is still not done and we have the sense of being persistently the victims of either ineptitude or else incompetence, etc etc, whether true or not—and just now the friend who was to drive our stuff east, for pay, has decided against it, etc etc—in short, all the information from there (with the sole exception of Kate's, which is amazingly steady and alert) is bleak, blurred, self-serving, and indifferent. So—you know. The classic suburban vibes that that particular part of the country is increasingly fact of, so we really congratulate ourselves on finally kicking the 'view'. Which reminds me, I finally have stopped smoking as well as all else. Onward!

I do hope all's well there and if you are to be east for any reason, that you'll be in touch if possible. I damn well don't want to lose touch with you, with this apparent distance, etc—but for all of us, 'tis but a whatever . . . Weather's just on the turn here, after lovely hot days—so it still keeps working no matter.

> Our love to you both,
> *Bob*

. . .

LETTER TO STAN AND JANE BRAKHAGE

Robert Creeley
Back Cottage 2
388 Summer Street
Buffalo, N.Y. 14213

January 29, 1981

Dear Folks,

Just to say all's well indeed—and I'm quite selfishly delighted. For one thing, I'm so grateful that finally I was able to 'be there' when he was born, and so to get past at last all the confusions and guilts that previous circumstance had, unwittingly, insisted upon. Too, I'm very reassured to recognize how comfortably 'at home' I am with babies and of course there will be crises etc, but anyhow that's not the point finally. He sure is an instant pleasure, all that incredibly alert attention, the information must be pouring into him like the Mississippi River. And accommodating, really—sympathetic to anything keeps a forward edge to so-called reality. Most of all I love the density it gives us, now, as three people. It cuts out a lot of restlessness (for me) on the instant.

Again, this is truly just to say hello. I'll keep in touch (with other than baby stories, as a genre as boring as any others I'd guess) and please do too.

My love,
Bob

. . .

POSTCARD TO CHARLES BERNSTEIN

[from Ledge Rock Motel, Wilmington, NY]

1/30/81
Buffalo, 14213

Dear Charles,

Thanks for the LANGUAGE # 13—Back Cottage 2, 388 Summer St. is it. I think I've got everything sent to 400 Fargo—particularly your book CONTROLLING INTERESTS—for which many THANKS! We have a son! WM. GABRIEL—born the 16th, so that's our preoccupation. Onward!

Our best,
Bob

. . .

LETTER TO CHARLES BERNSTEIN

ROBERT CREELEY
BACK COTTAGE 2
388 SUMMER STREET
BUFFALO, N.Y. 14213

January 5, 198t2!

Dear Charles,

Thanks for the Happy New Year, and the same to you all. I much
enjoyed the chance to talk with you also, and your response to the reading,
like they say, meant a great deal. I'm hopeful to get you up here at some point,
possibly late spring—but more likely some time in the fall, just that I don't now
have money until after March 30th, and then have a block of so-called previous
commitments. But I had not forgotten, and if it can be got together sooner, then
I'll certainly be in touch apropos.

In the meantime—Ron Sukenick of the American Book Review asked my
help (as he also did John Ashbery and Charles Simic) with getting their criti-
cism of poetry more active, i.e., more substantially based, less <u>sweetheart</u>, as
they say, more thoughtfully grounded. I'd particularly like to ask your help
therefore, with suggestions as to texts you'd like to see dealt with, either by
yourself or someone else—and possibilities for special issues. Anyhow, you'll see
the use, and if one doesn't simply swamp them with only the preoccupations of
immediate interests, then it could be very useful to all.

I just got a copy of L = A = N = G = U = A = G = E (that's a son of a bitch to
type!) 5th series, #4, and very much like it—the collaboration with Open Letter,
i.e., their doing it is very useful—and charmed that it was all 'set' by telephone.
I.e., I was talking to a friend of Frank Davey's, Chris Dewdney, who was telling
me about its production. Sadly I missed seeing Steve McCaffery, whom I
much like.

Thanks (!) for the copy of STIGMA, handsome as ever—very much like
manner of title poem, tone (always) of April, likewise May—almost like aspects
of Hart Crane aka Zukofsky, but <u>you</u> god knows specifically. Ok.

Again, it was very good seeing you in NYC, and hopefully there'll be chance
again sometime in the spring, either here or there—more probably fall for
Buffalo. Don't please mind the silences, we get tied into daily life, like they say,
and it goes by with sadly/happily <u>amazingly</u> literal time. Onward!

My best,
Bob

. . .

LETTER TO ALLEN GINSBERG

Robert Creeley
1908 Griegos Road, NW
Albuquerque, NM 87107

November 14, 1982

Dear Allen,

Many thanks for Sam Charters' address, also for that weird article(s) by jr fascist Dinesh D'Souza in the Policy Review. I'll be curious to see his interview with you, like they say.

Depending on students [^ _Re OLSON_], i.e., how intent, advanced (whatever that means), particular, read, they be, I'd use his Selected Writings (New Directions) I did some years ago, really prior to the great writing of subsequent two volumes of Maximus but very much the groundwork of place and person, 'history', crucial Human Universe essay and Pro/ Verse, etc etc. That is, that book would serve you/them well as a sense of what he's about, and they could then continue, take it deeper, as they chose. There's enough to engage him but it wouldn't serve the more determined student because it's too (still) leaning on the social/political, and hasn't as yet got solidly into that mythopoeia of what we then first heard at Vancouver '63. For that, there is no digest finally—so again, for teaching, I'd take particular poems, say, the sequence of the various Max's from Dogtown (including the Gravelly Hill one, tho not called so)—or something like the Hotel Steinplatz poem in last vol. I'd also get them reading particular essays like Poetry and Truth, Causal Mythology (actually both lectures as you'll know)—stuff collected in Muthologos, vols I & 2. But again, it's really going to depend on how intensively they want to get into it. If Don Allen still has editions of Poetry and Truth (Beloit lectures), I think that's an excellent center for their getting hold of his preoccupations. Then you might get them to doing reading and reports singly on particular texts, just to get the range clear to them. Good Luck!! Great we'll see you in Maine, and love to you both as ever,

Bob

. . .

LETTER TO ROBERT DUNCAN

Robert Creeley
1908 Griegos Road NW
Albuquerque, N.M. 87043

January 18, 1983

Dear Robert,

I got the first copy of my Collected Poems last Thursday, and have been musing upon it, like they say, ever since—very shyly, in fact, viz taking it with me to the bathroom, pondering it after waking up at 4 AM. I am delighted! Not only do I like every damn poem in this great work but it makes me feel so specifically that it was all worth it and did make sense no matter I often damn well wondered. I love its continuity, and the echoes of humor, the emotional patterns I can see in it now sans the dues. Anyhow the way it all goes together and the way the set of it all (thanks to a bright woman who was responsible for the overall design, Marilyn Perry) lets the divers typographical patterns balance are so happy for me. You'll know how I've always felt 'slight' in a way, that I could not formally find a means for 'longer' patterns. This book lets me off that hook thankfully, just that it keeps going to the end.

So thank you for the generous plug—the back cover reads like an ultimate testimonial dinner & why not—and shortly you should be getting a copy also. It will have card enclosed saying Compliments of the restaurant, not the chef—but you and I will know its true disposition. Ok.

Meantime, back at the ranch, Willy had his 2nd birthday this past Sunday. Truly like they say, it hardly seems possible. He is a great pleasant witty solid kid. At this point his language comes on like gang-busters. Not just 'cute say-ings' but the under-shift of conceptual recognitions is great. Also the syntax as it moves to accommodate and/or make his information. It is a very good time here, free of usual businesses, and with much familiarity, usefully. I'm sitting circa a hefty stone's throw from field in which Betty, Charles and I walked when they stopped here in '57 it must have been enroute back to the east after their time in San Francisco (when, Chas told me, Ruth W/D/ used to turn the heat down on leaving the apartment etc etc).

At the moment I've no labors in hand, but hope to get something moving in collaboration with pleasant French photographer now here (in Santa Fe), Bernard Plossu (friend of Denis Roche's et al), I think of short prose pieces, something that will allow me a range of easy tone, anecdote, all that wandering and also verse as it comes: an antithetical 'travel' book using (his somewhat classic) pictures of NM landscape. Anyhow we'll see.

I keep hoping to get out there but am damned if I'll read for meager fees (and

I don't get offered even those), so for the time-being that's that. Anyhow this is really a good time for us and there's a year to go before drear Bflo teaching recurs. By that time I'll probably even welcome it. (But I doubt it!)

Our love to you both,

Bob

. . .

LETTER TO ALICE NOTLEY

c/o Wilde
Upper Round Pound Road
Bristol, Me. 14539
July 5, 1983

Dear Alice,

Debby Daley just called with the very sad news of Ted—and rather than now try to say anything more, please use the enclosed for whatever meager use it can be. If there's anything specific I can help with otherwise, call collect: 207-563-5072. We'll be here till September 15th.

Our love to you and the boys,

Bob

. . .

POSTCARD TO ED AND JENNIFER DORN

[image of *Ossip Brik* (1924), Alexander Rodtschenko]

CREELEY STORKWINKEL 12
1000 BERLIN 31, W GERMANY
10/9/83

Dear Folks,

Curious place to be hanging out in—like return of the old days with pumped in action endlessly. Great subway—buses. Parks with naked formal persons still bursting faint NORDIC sun. Oh well. Maybe we'll learn some German tho I doubt it. Ted Joans lives upstairs, proving useful. Onward! Love to all,

Bob

. . .

LETTER TO DENISE LEVERTOV

38 Linwood Avenue
Buffalo, N.Y. 14209
February 1, 1984

Dear Denny,
It was all a very curious business, happily with a happy ending.
Anyhow when we got to Berlin (on a DAAD grant) first of October, we began
to check out possibilities first of doctors, then of midwives, for Pen's delivery.
About the middle of the month Pen finally got hold of one (they are in great
demand and English-speaking ones are especially so), and on checking Pen
out the woman (whom Pen much liked) thought the fetus was significantly too
small, for the proposed age, due date, etc. So she proposed Pen be checked out
at the Woman's Clinic, and the doctor there confirmed her suspicions, and said
the placenta seemed to be malfunctioning, that hormonal levels were danger-
ously low, etc etc. So we had two weeks, he figured, in which we had to resolve
whether to stay put or return to the States. Our dilemma was that we had to
have money in hand for Willy and Pen's airfares back to the States, no mean
figure. I was depending on readings etc to provide for the necessary money by
the end of December, which was the time we'd planned to stay. So anyhow we
resolved to split (<u>flee</u>, would be the word), [^ *Berlin was <u>SO</u> depressing!*] utterly
shaken and depressed by it all, compounded by the fact I had to go out for five
days* of labor, previously committed, just to have the damn $$$ in hand, etc. So
we got back here sans house, and crashed with blessed friends from November
8th till 21st, when we got this place (very comfortable), and all that time Pen
was having every imaginable business from scans, to stress tests ('mild induced
labor'), blood tests for hormonal levels, so the whole feel of things got to be
like watching some insistently abstract measuring system, that's telling you
whether the baby is to 1) live, 2) be severely retarded in ways that aren't at all
clear, or 3) none of the above but with all the likelihood of a need for incuba-
tion. Then, of course, there was the hovering prospect of a Caesarean which the
Germans especially were interested in. I forgot two attempts to induce labor for
real, both of which didn't work thankfully. So anyhow, the due date December
15th passed—and that felt good, that the baby was going full term—and on
December 21st, labor began in earnest—Pen went in just about one in the
afternoon, and Hannah appeared like a blessed Kore about five, a little after,
without the least problem, although we'd been told not very long ago at all she
barely weighed four pounds—in fact, she was 7 lbs 4½ oz. Since Pen's calcula-
tions of her last period and all were all correct, no one will ever know quite what
threw off, so dramatically, all the calculation and prognosis, not only of the

Germans, but of all the people here as well, in a very sophisticated facility, like they say. Ah well—and thank god! Presently she's almost 11 lbs, and lovely clear kid, so—here we thankfully <u>all</u> are.

Just as we were to move in here, and Pen was in hospital for the first attempt at inducing labor, a decision that was made while I was briefly in Maine to pick up our car there, left late summer when we went to Germany, etc., there was a bleakly sad family loss, literally I was told of on my way there at the airport, that is, my sister's youngest child Sarah was killed in automobile accident while driving back to her dormitory in Orono from the crisis center she was working at in Bangor. So awfully and harshly <u>sad</u> for my sister—just one moment all so solid and good, the next simply empty silent horror. Thankfully I could be at the hospital—she must have fallen to sleep, lost control, was thrown from car and suffered massive head injuries, though nothing else. Her kidneys and corneas were therefore used for transplant. Finally, at the funeral, Helen asked that people give whatever, rather than flowers, just to make some modest fund for kids from the depressed town (South Waldoboro) to help with getting to the University of Maine—and there's presently something over $1500. I am trying to think of various ways to add to it, and one possibility would be some modest 'benefit' reading, by friends, in the summer—not this one, but say a year from now—or like that. I'd like to ask your interest and help as things come together and your own time permits. I'd thought of Allen, Donald Hall who lives within an easy distance—say, ask one person a year for the next three or four summers, beginning '85. There is no ambition at all to have the fund be more than a few thousand dollars, but one hopes it can provide something like $500 to $800 a year for the recipient, so for that it will have to be larger than it now is, etc. Anyhow, I thought to tell you.

I'm just returning to teaching after a year and a half free of it—I can't say it's a pleasure, but at least the habits return simply enough. But I do wish, now especially, there weren't the often dragging distraction of it, having nothing really to do with students, etc. My colleagues, by and large, are as unrelated to my life as ever. Pen starts graduate work in Landscape Architecture next fall at Cornell, a three year program—so I'll commute from there, etc. Our house in Maine, so lovely, should be straight by early summer. I'm ready!

Otherwise I fear I'm having increasing dilemmas with ND—just the 'out to lunch' feel of it, and I thought much would 'get better' after Fred left, but it really doesn't, i.e., the girl who handles publicity managed to forget my recent book Mirrors in their winter list, and Griselda continues to feel hardcovers of it aren't really necessary, so neither Later nor Mirrors has had them—etc. I don't know. I've rehearsed all with J/ ad nauseam, but it still feels vague to me. Thankfully UC Press stays solid, they've done very well with the CP, and we're presently working out a volume of criticism. Marion Boyars has just published my Collected Prose—so it's time to write something more! Onward . . .

Our love to you,

Bob

*Muenster, Heidelberg, Mannheim, Göttingen, and Cologne—more of which I'd much like to spend time in—ah well. I'm afraid the echoes of my youth in this case are very spooky.

. . .

LETTER TO ROBERT DUNCAN

38 Linwood Avenue
Buffalo, N.Y. 14209
March 22, 1984

Dear Robert,

We are just back here from a quick visit with my sister in Maine, and there was a letter from Don Allen which spoke of your kidneys giving problems—and then moments ago Bob Bertholf called to tell us more explicitly what was up. Momently one wants to say, i.e., I want to say, do get damn well damn fast—or whatever gets you better pronto. You were looking so well, paradoxically enough I realize, in September. I'm selfishly wanting you Better and Better and Better. Ok.

Meantime I've written that preface, so-called, for B/s bibliography, a copy of which I've asked John Martin to send you since what I have here is illegible to all but me (like 'darkness'). So hopefully he will. I'd also like one sent to Griselda, if ok with you. It's fulsome. But heart-felt. And true.

I'm off momently to Birmingham, Alabama—a place I never in fact either wanted to or thought to 'see'. Once back, I'll be in touch less hysterically. So here's all possible dearest wishes for your very prompt recovery. Onward!!

Our love to you and Jess,

Bob

. . .

LETTER TO JOHN TAGGART

204 Cayuga Heights Road
Ithaca, N.Y. 14850
November 3, 1984

Dear John,

That time with you was a delight—and the reading with verbal 'notes' a very deep pleasure. (The household presently chants intriguing echo I'd

brought back, 'ma/ ma/ mooove . . . ,' especially Willy who otherwise got from
Williams: 'ai/yuh . . . ' Voila, like they say.)

Before I forget in usual rush, Bruce Jackson and Diane Christian were our
charming hosts for dinner, and their address is 96 Rumsey Road, Buffalo, N.Y.
14209.

As backside of this notes, I'd pleasure of meeting just by happy accident
Steve Lacy about three summers ago in Paris, thanks to Pierre Joris (ed as you'll
remember of Blackburn Sixpack etc issue)—it was a Radio France interview
and they connected me with Steve so as to talk about jazz, etc. I liked him on
the instant, and had known his work from years ago, late 50s—but not at all
after that. Anyhow it's all like dream become this extraordinary business. I've
got the scores for the settings of the 20 poems, but sadly have never really heard
any of them as yet. If and as I get a tape, I'll make copy. Which also reminds
me, do you have great record of him playing Monk (with Mal Waldron, Buell
Neidlinger, and Elvin Jones), Reflections, a happily cheap reissue on Fantasy,
'Original Jazz Classics' (OJC-063). Onward! *Could/can make copy!*

Also apropos, did you ever hear settings of 10 poems Steve Sparrow (bassist)
did on ECM, Home—with Steve Kuhn, Sheila Jordan, et al? I can make you
copy of that very simply. Keep those cards and letters coming in!

Also do keep me on/informed of any jazz you like, that list was/is very
helpful. I sent xerox of your Monk poem (lovely!) in Hambone to Steve Lacy
incidentally. It's a happily small world.

Best as ever,
Bob

P.S. Very moved you've now got the puppy (so lovely!) and do think it will be
happy for all.

• • •

POSTCARD TO BARRETT WATTEN

November 23, 1984

Dear Barry,

*God your book is <u>solid</u>! In all respects—like they say. Just working.
I'm very impressed by how solidly you take hold and how densely the "context"
offers. Wow! Very happily reminiscent of conversations with you there. So—please
let me know when [^ WILL!]* you arrive—all else is together. See you soon! Love
to all,*

Bob

*[Small drawing of a hand points to inserted word.]

· · ·

LETTER TO TOM CLARK

Box 384
Waldoboro, Me. 04572
January 9, 1985

Dear Tom,

A belated happy New Year, and herewith what you'll dig is book I've been trying to mail you since last October. Ah well. We've been up here, thankfully, since mid-December, and it is as great in winter as it was last summer. So, one damn day. We head back to Ithaca on Friday but at least know this is here and stays put.

Pen's labors this fall were incredible, just round the clock it seemed, like european tales of study in the xteenth century. My commuting in contrast felt almost frivolous, certainly light-hearted. The kids thankfully (that's a frequent word these days for whatever reason) have been very well provided for by girl now living with us, north of England—solid good nature and steadiness. All the virtues!

Re Barry Watten and his book—I just liked the shift in take he manages on Olson, for example, or Clark [Coolidge]—just that he keeps explicit and takes it in terms of literal language construct. I liked him on Smithson also. In my so-called line of work, the endless vagary and disjunct of thinking frankly makes him read <u>very</u> clear, not to mention that he's talking of action the academic won't touch with ten foot pole—like Olson or even Williams. For instance, nor Zukofsky, Oppen nor Reznikoff are in Norton Antho of English Verse, some title like that, the 'ages', tho I am, and persons yea younger I never even heard of. Not to be diffident, you hear, but Barry's 'subject' is already a lot. One tires of Alan Williamson who I haven't read at that. Otherwise I think Wesling is usefully easy reading, The Rhyme of Chance, actually the Chances of Rhyme—because again and again I'm trying to make ground, at all, for any comprehension of what the so-called structure of usual verse is, so any of this stuff is useful, anything I don't have to assert 'personally'. Onward!

I'm trying to do some sort of note on Brautigan's sad death. That's so bleak about the 'uses' it's instantly put to. I also couldn't accept fact that no one, either Montana or Bolinas, had apparently asked where he was, i.e., no one to say goodbye, no one certainly to say hello.

You'll have word now you got NEA remarkably deserved, old bro. Let's hope it's the first of several, e.g., the Guggenheim. I'd dearly love to see that book on Celine. Would people like Milton Hindus or David Hayman be of any use to you, as possible source for grant? The former I've known a long time, and the latter by report and just met him—seems pleasant, i.e., accessible for that request. Anyhow keep in touch!!!

Love to you all,
Bob

. . .

LETTER TO CHARLES BERNSTEIN

129 Burleigh Drive
Ithaca, NY 14580
Sept. 17, 1985

Dear Charles,

Here's the bibliography form of the seminar provided. It's hardly "strict" or extensive, but it got things started. So far there's been general talking (specifically of your preface to L<small>ANGUAGE</small> 4 and the selection in The Paris Review; various texts there of Michael Davidson's, Susan's Howe's, Michael Palmer's, and Leslie Scalapino's); and the SF State American Poetry Archive videotapes of Palmer, Howe, Davidson, Scalapino, et al reading. So it's really just beginning. M<small>IKE</small> B<small>OUGHN</small> ("B<small>ONN</small>") the grad. ass't's number is 716-883-6401. He'll be in touch also.

Love to you all and <u>thanks</u>,
Bob

P.S. Just to say again I can come up with $400 inclusive—and hopefully some "response," like they say.

. . .

LETTER TO CARL RAKOSI

12 Mayfair Lane
Buffalo, N.Y. 14201
February 16, 1987

Dear Carl,

Belated but heart-felt thanks for your generous book, in every way. It's such old time <u>good sense</u> (my mother would say!)—a lovely and unremitting clarity throughout, and the verse so holds the movement sans any self-consciousness. You are a veritable master!

The way you've put it all together is very useful—it "centers" each poem as it comes and breaks the simple logic of "time passing". Poems like "A Journey Away" are so uniquely your authority they stay a long time after. I really love that pace you can so hold—would that all the world, etc—!

Here time goes by like those old movies with calendar pages blowing in the wind. The house is a very solid comfort, and with the winter weather, becomes even more so—it heats easily and remarkably cheaply, and the fireplace is there for communal pleasure. Meantime Willy and Hannah keep on growing. They keep us all in good spirits.

Your visit here was very dear—again your reading brings such quiet sense and relation to things, makes them immensely human. I hope things there feel possible for you both. Selfishly I wish we were much closer. But "how is it far if you think of it"—ok!

Our love to you both,
Bob

. . .

LETTER TO TOM CLARK

P.S. Your advice re UC/ Press proved very wise, i.e., they have taken the Collected Essays, and also have clearance to do paper edition of the Collected Prose. So THANKS again! I was just about to pull out as you'll remember. Also I got elected to Am/ Academy etc, thanks I'm sure to Allen, Kitaj, etc. Politically it saves time—and also feels like some vindication.

12 Mayfair Lane
Buffalo, NY 14201
February 23, 1987

Dear Tom,

To get to your several questions and with fact of my own life was then so chaotic much will no doubt be confused—but anyhow: my memory is that I came back to BMC in summer '55 after Ann and I had really determined to call it quits (though I wanted it all to come right again, given the kids, my habit of living with her and depending on her, truly, etc.) I was probably teaching the writing class—I doubt if there was more than one, given the small enrollment at this point. As you, I'm sure the two letters you note are '55. Ann was to come over then from Mallorca to deal with her inheritance (she would then be 30 that December). I know Olson saw her—he serves as witness to the divorce papers (!). My memory of where I saw them was at Peter Stander's, as I'd said—which I recall as being close to Tompkins Square, Avenue B, 9th Street? That's where memory is vague—though Avenue B feels right, as does T/ Sq/. I recall we walked over midday to a Russian bar on up side of T/ Sq/ and old woman there, on Chas' insistence, gives me something [^ *(soup!)*] to eat "though they have no food," etc.

So. As I recall they lived in divers places, Stander's among them—"the Bronx" would be Betty's territory. She's now pregnant, etc. "Robt" must be Robert Hellman. The woman Ann is staying with is Elga Lippman, friend of the Hellmans we'd known briefly in France and that Ann gets to know much better than I. Possibly Ann is the connection? You might check for her NYC—she's somehow related to William Morrow Inc (I think!). Elga, that is. I wish to god

Ann would talk but I fear that's impossible. Still, you might try her c/o Tom Creeley, Box 87, Hudson, Me. 04449. Ah well . . .

As said, I would have come up to New York to see her re our situation, it must be winter, probably early December—though the actual situation except for seeing her and Charles and Betty etc at Peter's place is very vague now. I just can't be sure, but I presume, since she's getting her affairs together on inheriting the trust fund, or just about to, that time must be thereabouts. It's certainly crisis time for all concerned.

Charles' question, "tell me how long you think you are good for there . . . ," I'd take to mean, how long before you'll take off—because as marriage and all falls apart, I <u>want</u> to take off—"The Ballad of the Despairing Husband" is writ around this time—the bright side! I was gone that January, so that second quote also helps date it—winter 55 for sure.

Talking to Warren, he recalls Charles suddenly o'er him at time of Vancouver festival and saying apropos nothing, "keep you eye on the executive and the paternal . . . " But you have his quote of it directly—he plans to talk it, send you tape, etc/. I do think your reading it all as paternal/authority etc is absolutely on center. Onward! Just to keep in some sort of TOUCH!

Love to all,
Bob

Re Fee's sense of 54' [Fielding Dawson] *I don't see how that's possible I came first to BMC March '54—left June; returned about a year later Summer '55—left at turn of year early '56—as I remember. It's got to be that from all evidence. Fee wasn't there incidentally even when I was—I mean as student! He did visit possibly tho I don't remember. Wasn't he in the army by then?*

. . .

POSTCARD TO LESLIE SCALAPINO

12 Mayfair LN.*
Buffalo, NY 14201
3/6/88

Dear Leslie,

Many thanks for the handsome books by Ted Pearson and Rick London. They are lovely, inside and out—and usefully specific in each case. Tom Raworth is here now, in good spirits—read from new work felt very solid (crazy, shifting, dense RHETORIC, a mile a minute as ever). So—onward! All's well thank god!

Love as ever,
Bob

*We leave here end of May and will go to Finland for a year [inserted above the word "year" is "Real" with an arrow pointing to "year"] after Summer in Maine: Box 384, Waldoboro, ME. 04572. Como no . . .

. . .

UNIVERSITY OF HELSINKI
DEPARTMENT OF ENGLISH
HALLITUSKATU 11–13
00100 HELSINKI 10

> Tunturikatu 16, B28
> 00100 Helsinki
> September 25, 1988

Dear Susan,

Just looking at a letter on the table of Willy's beginning, "How are you? I'm miserable"—and continuing, like they say. The disjunct of languages, loss of friends, scale of apartment, have been a harsh drag for him, and despite the school he's in isn't at all hopeless (a seemingly good teacher, for instance) he's miserable, just as he says—but the three weeks we have been here can hardly be it. So, onward.

Perversely the rest of us are making out pretty well, e.g., Pen's located various action and friends with her generous way of coming on (really, "in"), I'm comfortable in the teaching (it feels very local and I can walk to work!), and Hannah just is indomitably happy (and in a kindergarten close by that works so/so at least). Willy's letter above refers to her as "—a certain Hannah," having said he has to share bedroom with this awful other. Ah well . . .

It feels expensive after Buffalo, or just the States—Finns tell us they find everything there cheap if and as they get there. This apartment, by the way, is ample really, and is also an easy distance from just about everything that interests us—downtown, etc. Also there are excellent trams, buses, trains, subway. The city itself is about the scale of Buffalo and weather, thank god, has done nothing hopeless so far. (Today we changed clocks back an hour, which feels far more ominous here.)

First couple of weeks I was writing a poem a minute, much like dog in new surroundings. They all felt deathless at the time but I must say most fade substantially. Still it is a very easy place to work, or feels so thus far—and the language isolation is paradoxically good news, not being forever. This past week we all went through recognition, we are here—help! Anyhow we are alive and well, like they say.

Pen's mother came and went very good naturedly—she was here about a week after we came, and it made a sort of place for us, and occasion to show her around a little. When she went, I felt as though we were being diminished—

which was surprising and useful. So onward. I hope you are all ok—simply said but I sure wish we were all closer. I was very moved by your Olson piece in <u>Writing 19</u>—very clear. There's an English grad student here teaching, doing his dissertation on Olson's "mythology," so it's particularly useful to have. Anything else? Your "procedure" by statement is very effective. Ok!

Our love to you all,
Bob

[handwritten postscript by Pen Creeley]

I'm glad Robert's written, because I was thinking of you very much today—I do hope all's well with you both. People tell us this apt. is HUGE for Finland—one person I met sleeps in 1 bedroom, not only with husband but 3 children as well. Even houses on market for up to U.S. $1,000,000 are small, or R would say, modest. Market hall nearby sells great bread & smoked fish—come for lunch!

All love, Pen

. . .

LETTER TO ROBERT GRENIER

Tunturikatu 16, B28
00100 Helsinki
December 18, 1988

Dear Bob,

Lovely to have that copy of <u>A.BACUS</u>—I remember that confusion of mine back last time I stayed with you, the phone call etc in which "Bob" was "Bob" forever in all possible dimensions and applications. Como no . . . So it's great to have your solid evidence of "BUSH TITS"—like. Onward!

Not at all happy is news of Kathy's having moved. I wish that situation you were all in had more give to it, but god knows the limits are adamant and if you're to live in it, that's that. I hope there's some resolution sans the simple split.

Our life here is a little unspeakable, as unlike things Anselm [Hollo] as one could possibly imagine—or they "look like" him but there it all stops. What a drab, depressed bunch they are, finally—more to be pitied than censured, etc. I haven't a clue as to what my "teaching" amounts to, they speak almost not at all—but we've contrived a means to "sit there" for the time it takes—almost none per month—and make do with the awkward "confrontation." That exaggerates expectably, but not a hell of a lot. It's really boredom here—far more than cold or little light—one has to manage. Thankfully I've been backed up with various work, and also writing a lot—and now that it's literally half over, it would seem to keep moving despite the sluggish company.

Meantime I've been in and out with other labors, a great quick trip to

Leningrad where despite poverty and political depression they really get it on—and Warsaw, Krakow and Poznan—equally moving. Then up north in Sweden—where they are as confused by the Finns as I am. Most interesting is the possibility of a new job in Worcester, Mass—Worcester Polytechnic Institute, some 3000 souls with impressive humanities adjunct—but best is the remarkable pay for teaching 2 courses a year on quarter system, which means I could wind down a lot and still keep a hand in till I drop. So we are thinking about it very seriously, like they say. The scene with Temple has faded a bit, i.e., there was an offer there in the works still forthcoming (like they say) but they don't like my need to teach as long as possible so as to keep income for Hannah and Willy's needs, etc. (Another virtue of Worcester apropos is that there are three universities with landscape architecture programs within easy distance: Harvard, U/Mass, and U/Conn, so Pen can finally complete said studies.)

The last months have otherwise been such a sad fact of friends dying, beginning with Robert, then Neil Williams, then George, then Joel—and now another very old friend in Albuquerque dying of cancer, Harvey Hoshour. And others as well it seems. It's like any memento mori makes me recognize no solution is possible, and far better to keep moving with the daily than to figure any rigging of stasis. Or really, now, to head for New England like the veritable hills I've longed for all the time. I was there last week for interview and realized it (weather and all) was all so familiar, an easy distance, in fact, from where I grew up. Fair enough! Onward! Merry Xmas! Happy New Year!

Love,

Bob

. . .

LETTER TO HELEN (CREELEY) AND WAYNE POWER

Tunturikatu 16, B28
00100 Helsinki
March 12, 1989

Dear Helen and Wayne,

A Sunday morning here after a wild week of travel and celebration—I was in Albany on Wednesday, being touted along with E. L. Doctorow (who proved a very sweet and whimsical man) by the State of NY and Governor Cuomo, who really is all that TV makes him look like, just taller. So that was a first. It took place, like they say, in an auditorium in one of those curious towers ("legislative offices") with banks of flowers, lots of pols, the works. Anyhow I think I was longer coming and going, than being there—but it was well worth going. Later!

While there, I saw people from SUNY/Buffalo and also from Worcester, and determined "verbally" to go to Worcester, so I'll now start retirement procedures from Buffalo, which blessedly means we will have health insurance provided by my 23 plus years there and accumulated sick leave days, etc etc, and will start teaching at Worcester end of August. Buffalo kept proposing higher and higher salary and less and less course load—sort of dazzling but unreal finally—but couldn't really change the basic dilemma, which is impossibility of Pen's getting final LA qualification without large family shift again, or dealing with all the accumulated "responsibility" there, or fact no matter how it's "structured" it still means the usual 8 plus months a year with whatever course load, as against Worcester's three and a half for almost equal salary. Then there's the fact we'll be so much nearer to Maine—and all the echoes, for me, of home. Fair enough.

Pen's just off last night with friend Linda (pleasant Canadian whose kids are close friends of ours) to pick up car in Sweden and then head south for some time out, through Copenhagen, Prague, Vienna, Salzburg, to end in Venice where blessed friends await with charming apartment o'er the canal. Sounds like heaven. Anyhow she has been so incredibly goodnatured about my endless comings and going I felt here was my big moment for some reciprocal action. The NYS poet scene pretty much covers the car, and since VW had collapsed, it seemed an optimum time to get one here (a 900 Saab four door, looks good). I also did suite of 12 poems to go with pastels of Francesco Clemente, who thankfully likes them and pays a lot, so we'll have as final scene here a rendezvous at the opening in Paris May 20th. Voila . . .

No matter the drear scene here, it's been idyllic for work—and just now walking the kids over to Linda's (her mother-in-law is minding that store and they had all been here earlier in the day), I realized I (as we all) will have made much specific personal connection here no matter we can't stand the general vibes. I've perversely (but characteristically) enjoyed being where I can't quite be held accountable for total ignorance to all's being said, and can be out of synch with rather grim social rhythms of this flat society—hence laugh without seeming reason, or just ignore. I also talk to myself incidentally—thinking of latter days of great Beethoven, roaming the streets whilst singing along. Shades of our grandfather's bedroom slippers . . .

Our love to you both,
Bob

. . .

LETTER TO SUSAN HOWE

Tunturikatu 16, B28
00100 Helsinki
March 24, 1989

Dear Susan,

Well, here it is good Friday again, and Hannah and I had a pleasant walk through local cemetery—on way to the sea. Pen's due home tomorrow morning, and Willy's off with friend Jack in the suburbs. All feels domestic and in place.

It looks like we're headed back to Buffalo. They offered such a deal it would have been perverse to say no, certainly after 23 years of accommodation and much use, actually. Both president and provost were calling both Pen and me (we didn't know they cared!) and the upshot of it all is I'll be a University Professor independent of department or faculty, will "negotiate" labors with provost directly, which he states will be in a range from "0 to minimal," they are paying such money I'm ashamed to tell you, and to that they add a new chair for backup. It's really incredible. For example, they'll work out with Cornell a "program" for Pen to let her get her landscape arthitecture degree with the least travail, even to "child care" for times she'll have to be in Ithaca. Anyhow I do hope you'll be there?

Pen herself is due back tomorrow after what seems a very useful time out. They had a good visit with friends in Venice, and otherwise all sounded happy. I felt righteously capable and enjoyed being with the kids in solid fashion, after so much time on the road—as walk this morning with Hannah, or just talking with Willy. They are a great pleasure.

Now we begin to feel end of time here approaching. Already that eases a lot, and one begins to feel these people aren't all that bad. There is a curious physical ripple that goes through them all, much like trees budding or flowers pushing up—the whole tone emotionally has very clearly shifted the past month, so that people touch a lot more, hug, kiss, look at each other, after all the winter (which was mild) of seemingly no outward person at all. Like bears coming out of hibernation, very physically "natural" and not at all simple sex—and probably they should have been holed up in caves all winter at that. Very curious people.

I am very glad to hear things with Jack and all get more open. That was such a sad impasse. I must say I'm glad to be out of the department in that respect, to be as much as one can be not a counter in the game. I will really be glad not any longer to be agency for visitors, much as I enjoyed people coming obviously— but the political side of it was finally awful. Now, of course, there's the same action with respect to Bob Bertholf's help, which seems to have been substantial in getting me this new situation, i.e., Greiner asked him what would persuade us to stay and Bob told him, accurately as it proved. But finally what I say is thanks, and that's that. It's Bob's pleasure to wheel and deal, and I can't say I begrudge him this instance. Thankfully what we hear at this distance isn't much at all. By the time we're back there'll be another preoccupation for sure.

Our love,
Bob

· · ·

LETTER TO ALLEN GINSBERG

Tunturikatu 16, B28
00100 Helsinki
April 23, 1989

Dear Allen,

It's very good news you are feeling back together after the gall bladder surgery—god knows never a pleasure. So, onward—by god. That notice for the action at Brooklyn College sure argues your persistent incredible action!

Here I've been traveling pretty much constantly, ducking in and out to cover teaching obligations, even to read with the locals (Klaes Andersson et al) who will now have continuing series for seemingly first time in Finnish History so something's worked but it was <u>not</u> easy. Anyhow I had very pleasant visit with Nanda in Milan, and also spent weekend out with Massimo B/ et al in Rapallo (whose card you will get/have got?), and otherwise went to Rome, Bologna, Turin, Messina, and Salerno—great food! Met pleasant new translator of Whitman, Marko Carona in Sicily—he'd sat in on Duncan's lectures back in New College in SF (!). Momently go to Uppsala and Stockholm, then the 27th to 4th to Israel, then Riga, Latvia, then Oslo, then Brussels, and finally Paris for FC/s opening, and connection with him and Raymond—and then home. I figured I've lectured/read more out of Finland these past months than in, including five other cities I've visited. Ah well . . . It truly is a weird place.

Meantime, sans intention, have had terrific requalification of job in Buffalo, which is now sans any faculty or dept attachment, called "University Prof and Artist in Residence," with duties qualified as being from zero to minimal, and a new chair for backup with travel, equipment and the like, so Gray Chair goes back to dept for their reassignment. I was just getting flattened with the logistics of keeping it moving and all, so I am <u>very</u> relieved to pass it on to whomever. They'd like to bring someone in, which would seem a good idea. Anyhow I got a six figure salary yet, with said chair as well—and have resolved coming year's work as one seminar on Wms next spring, so have fall free for my own preoccupations. They are also working it out with Cornell for Pen to finish her work in landscape architecture. It all seems to have happened because I was about to leave for that job in Worcester, quite seriously, and had also got the NYS poet's award, so I suppose my leaving momently would have had more than usual echo. Anyhow it sure serves our so-called needs. I could even manage this one from beyond the grave . . .

Otherwise working a lot—as poems for Francesco, which were a pleasure to do. Also bunch centering on window here to my left, my constant companion like they say. Plus odds and ends. Anyhow being here has been good instruction as to what a heavy shot of boredom can provoke. Onward!

Love as ever,
Bob

P.S. We'll be back in Maine May 25th, and aside from quick trip to Buffalo to locate house June 4th to 10th, will stick there through the summer.

P.S. I'll send in a second nomination for Carl Rakosi—referring to you for his vita, etc.

PART SIX

If I Were Writing This, 1989–2005

Maine, Buffalo, Providence

LETTER TO ROBERT GRENIER
Robert Creeley
Box 384
Waldoboro, ME. 04572

64 Amherst Street
Buffalo, NY 14207[1]
August 10, 1989

Dear Bob,

   "Mi tocayo" translates as "my name/sharer," in Guatemala (where I first heard it from fellow we met in San Lucas on Lake Atitlan, who could only give us directions by means of left turns because he'd forgotten the word for right: The Cocksman of San Lucas (was his nickname)) sign of affectionate acknowledgement and relation—like brother, brother. So there you have it. I also realize I'm fifteen years older than you, so can testify that same anos son possible a vivir, come se dice. Ganz gut.

  Y ahora—why not take up Finnish, with its terrific non-Indo-European-bog-banter and its 15 to (for finer shadings) 26 (?) noun endings? "The moon which [Robert Grenier has seen skeletal faces in recently?] is still your planet as it was Venus' before you . . . " And you, and you, etc. Marchons.

  Hey Bob—or as Hannah just now says, Hey Jude. How's Amy doing? What's happening in Bay Area presumably still existing? Tom Terrific Clark? Read any Good Books lately? You wrote one certainly.

  As long time paranoid and distinct depressive "it's" obviously a way of life but that's all—whatever "that" is. Back to Heidigger! Hei / digger / digger // I just pulled the trigger / and blew away face in the moon . . . " "This is what humans are like when they just come in from a rainy day . . . " "It jumps up on the chair." "It does this." "It jumps down." Drinks Pepsi. Remember "An ice cold Pepsi / that hurts your teeth"—like have an ice day. "That is so gross (says Willy) putting your fingers in your Pepsi . . . " "God . . . " says Hannah, "I put my finger in my coke and now it stings . . . Let's see if it does it . . . "

        Your tocayo,
        Bob
       Bob Spelled Backwards

[RC's footnote] [1]As of September 1, 1989 this will be it. We just heard yesterday mortgage was approved!

     . . .

LETTER TO PAUL AUSTER

August 17, 1989

Dear Paul,

I feel badly not to have thanked you long ago for your generous gift of your books. They are extremely impressive—and dear! I've been reading *The Invention of Solitude* and so much echoes my own questions of a father, just that mine died when I was four. In any case, the range and perception of your writing is altogether singular. Voila!

The summer's gone by in a flash and momently we move back to Buffalo, where our new address will be:

64 Amherst Street
Buffalo, New York 14207

That says it over-emphatically, but I'm getting used to it—the first place I've ever owned there, as it happens, despite 23 years on said job. Incidentally— would anything at SUNY/Buffalo ever interest you? Since John Barth left years ago now, the department has been looking for someone (present company is Raymond Federman) and I'm sure the job could be both attractive and much to your own needs, etc., so you could commute, etc. Anyhow! Meantime we've happily seen the Corbetts and so had word of you also. Thinking of mutual friends, I knew Michael Palmer way back when he was George—1963, en route to that Vancouver Poetry Festival. Only yesterday . . .

Thanks again!

My best,
Bob

. . .

LETTER TO SUSAN HOWE

64 Amherst Street
Buffalo, NY 14207
February 15, 1990

Dear Susan,

David's [David von Schlegell's] opening sounded great and only wish as ever we might have been there. There are times one feels like a veritable shut-in, but, egocentrically, I'll be so soon on the road being here the past two months sans action has been a very large blessing.

As you will know, I think, the chair went to Charles [Bernstein] with sufficiently solid backing to make the appointment quite sure. The two appoint- ments now most attractive for the bulk of the people are you and Nate Mackey.

Nate can be argued as the black academic/editor/poet the department has never had despite Carlene Polite's appointment years ago. You have the absolute interest of all the feminists obviously, all the graduate students who knew you as a teacher or simply knew of you as a teacher, and a wide range of people as Myles Slatin who are impressed by your articulate intensity as a scholar as well as by your poetry. Thus Jim Bunn (ex Dean) at the last meeting before the vote argued strongly on your behalf having really just read your work. So too (perversely!) Irving Feldman who has become a great advocate, having just now read your work as well. [Penelope Creeley's note in margin: *He has apparently been in twice to Rita's office, just to tell her how brilliant he thinks you are, a great genius, a major talent, he says . . .*]

Since the vote for the chair specifically is now so shortly past, politicking had best take a public rest at least, to let that part fade so as to renew the interest in a senior appointment for you as a fresh start come fall. Meantime Bill Warner and others will be keeping the possibility active in the so-called back rooms. To that end, and because the time now is so crowded till May, and the specific dates in March you note are the spring break here as well, it makes most sense to invite you up in the fall, when Charles is here as further support, for a substantial visit of a couple of weeks or whatever is simple for all, i.e., some time sufficient to renew contacts in every sense. There is really a very solid ground in your exceptional genius as a poet, your equally singular brilliance as a scholar, and the fact you'd be literally the only woman poet the department has ever had, thus a determining model in many senses indeed, which the women, both faculty and students, emphatically recognize. Well, you hear me rehearsing—but I do think it's a very possible business, as do a number, Clare Kahane, Bob Bertholf, Diane Christian, Bill Fischer et al. So.

I am off for a week in Israel (an international conference of poets in Jerusalem which lets me see old friends both in that company (as Holub and Tomlinson) and also in the city)—and from there to England, where I end up in Durham, so get see Peter Quartermain et al. A curious and exhausting busman's holiday but I brought it on myself and will no doubt enjoy it—but miss being home no matter. Ah well.

Love from us all!

Bob

[Penelope Creeley's note:]
   I'll call shortly—thanks <u>so much</u> for your letter—I was moved & relieved—so glad you understand. Love & thoughts, Pen.

. . .

LETTER TO SUSAN HOWE

64 Amherst Street
Buffalo, NY 14207
March 17, 1990

Dear Susan,

I think that Talisman interview is immensely useful in every way, clarity, intelligence, all the question of gender and marginalizing—and the particular sense of that Harvard perspect of the time (my time, incidentally, recalling that Matthiessen was the one professor I could speak to comfortably, and that I never recognized Emily Dickinson's not being in American Renaissance—but I remember asking his permission to discuss Hart Crane in the course on Modern Poetry or his saying in answer to my question that he did not include Pound because he found his politics reprehensible and did not understand his prosody, etc. One of the first communications from Pound was emphasis on fact that he'd got Eliot to override Matthiessen's advising Reynal Hitchcock not to publish Call Me Ishmael. Anyhow small world indeed.)

What to say of all that zapping about in Israel. One thing was that, confronted with Mount of the Beatitudes and where "He" "walked on water" and having hopeless cold on bus with wall to wall poets of languages too numerous to mention, I began to think Xtianity and its hero hopelessly late and tacky, so that "follow me and I will make you fishers of men . . . " in place he seems to have said same, seemed like all too familiar con, like, follow me and I'll help you hook the ones eat those fish. Ah well. In that place now somehow all religions get to be cacophony.

Time in England was therefore restoring, especially with horrendous storms and freak weather sweeping the isle—snow in Durham—and return to English, etc. Peter was very good—just utterly clear, usefully dramatic, very well grounded in detail—and really fascinating in the way he located Bunting as instance of a marginalized language against historic particulars as Elizabeth's slaughter of the north. One felt he could at the end have led the company into battle. Anyhow he made a great and very useful impression on the academic and administrative company, the ones crucial to the Bunting Collection's prospects.

Here we keep active, like they say, in your beatific behalf—Bob B/, Bill W/, Charles now as well, and the bulk of the dept I do feel. So I think it's no means over yet in any respect. I think you'll see for yourself come fall, though I hope there's chance to see you in Maine again? I am off tomorrow, like a yoyo, proving something of opaque kind. Onward!

Love from us all,
Bob

. . .

LETTER TO CHARLES BERNSTEIN

64 Amherst Street
Buffalo, NY 14207
March 31, 1990

Dear Charles,

Things are so fast at the moment a phone would make more sense, but frustrates attempts to say more solidly how great all you have in hand seems to me. Anyhow! As you will know, plans for getting the eastern European visitors over this fall had to slow down to manage the appropriate backup from administration, so now it will be scheduled for spring (with loose-leaf seminar of my responsibility attached). Thanks for the help with Arkadii [Dragomoshchenko], whom I'll write directly, etc. Meantime I've talked by phone with Mark Wallace and all that feels good. I'll hope to meet him when you come up to introduce Nate Mackey April 23rd. (I'm off again on Monday and not really home for more than two days between then and April 21. Thankfully all the family will go the 13th to LA and SF, so that's a break.)

I have not thought of anyone specific for the fall myself, but for Susan Howe and possibly Tomaz Salamun, who is to be in the States in the fall. All's flexible, in short. Also I've got a substantial budget from carry-over from this past fiscal year.

Susan's now in a "clutter" of five candidates for senior appointment (among them Joan Copjec) which purportedly is being offered to the administration for a block appointment(s)—that is, five "lines" at one go. The department is just now voting on "preferences" and is asked to "rank" the five, etc etc. Is that ever familiar. Anyhow I don't like Susan being again in such a defined competition. I don't really trust Bill Warner's support or interest at all—JC is clearly his choice. So during your brief stay, like they say, you might let go a few innuendoes apropos. At least keep him/them honest.

So I'll look to see you April 23rd. All I'd say re your provisions is use the local Best Western or whatever, because with settling and Emma you will need room and refuge—and people too, I do believe, like to get off the scene. In other words, don't sign up for all the labors of that order. If someone were, for example, to stay at that Best Western on Delaware, or the Lenox, it would be about $60 a night, and otherwise you could, or they could, come and go from your place easily in some ten minutes—cab or other. Onward!

Love to all,

Bob

P.S. I saw Ron Silliman and also Rae Armantrout in Tucson last week—a jovial time. [^ *Also Daphne Marlatt—old friend indeed.*] Edward Kamau Brathwaite was also there, and is classically sweet (we'd met years ago when he was still very much a colonial "British" poet). He was on his way to visiting chair at Santa Cruz, thanks to Nate M.

P.P.S. Dates and all have to be your decision, like they say. I'll be in and out— only substantial absence now in mind is Oct. 1–14 in NM, but not yet confirmed.

· · ·

FAX TO CHARLES BERNSTEIN

Creeley, PO Box 384, Waldoboro, Me. 04572
PLEASE DELIVER TO: *CHARLES BERNSTEIN* IMMEDIATELY
FROM: ROBERT CREELEY
    COMMENTS:
        ¡ONWARD!

August 21, 1990

Dear Charles,

        Many thanks for all the stuff! I think the promo materials for the "Wednesdays" etc is very clear and effective. Likewise the intensity of all the people who will be coming. After a year of pretty explicit quiet, it should get an active and particular company, which is really all one ever wants. Onward!

I talked to Bob yesterday but no mention of the Eastern Europeans possibility, so I gather he has his hands full with other matters and/or nothing's got through the various administrative holds. In any case, I will bring it up when back and get it all more clear, as well as a present budget status. That ought to make possible some support for the lean sprint months so as to keep the action. That is very happy news about Nate Mackey and my fingers are crossed. If Susan in turn can be included, then that's truly that.

I hope your settling in is proving simple. Pen was in touch with one of your neighbors as you'll know about babysitters, and it sounds like Jackie [McGuire] gave you all a royal provision and welcome. Here we are winding down with the various chores of getting things together for return and otherwise provided. We got an ultimate used boat (16 feet) a couple of weeks ago, whose motor works but barely. I had hopes of taking to the high seas but not in this one—at least not yet. I am hoping to persuade a neighbor to overhaul it for us during the winter. There are so many coves and inlets along the immediate coast, it's a shame not to have simple means to check them out by water. We do have canoe for paddling around, finally the most simple and pleasant of all, as you'll one day all see we hope. Yesterday we went to proverbial Union Fair, all the midway numbers— wild to see Hannah zapping by in some incredibly G/ torque on "ride" would freak me entirely. Ah youth . . .

Once again, if Mark [Wallace] feels competent to overhaul the computer program, that would be useful indeed. I don't see need for more than simple situation of the Word Perfect program, filing therein, and clear connection with printer. Then if he can install the modems both in that computer and the one back at our place, I'd think that would be that, although some kind of effective "windows" program for editing would also be very useful.

So we'll see you shortly. Was that "The drowning woman . . . " really on Page G-8 of the Buffalo News? "She treaded in her underwear." What next . . .

Our love to you all,
Bob

Hi Jackie! <u>Thanks</u> as ever!

. . .

LETTER TO ROBERT GRENIER

64 Amherst Street
Buffalo, NY 14207
June 4, 1991

Dear Bob,

Rumors of my etc have been greatly etc etc. Quantamatum est . . . I'm always impressed at how quickly the news flies, on wings of the great speckled Bromige in this case (?). Well, we all knew he didn't mean to kill me, so I ain't gonna die!!!

What a scene that all became, like umpteen kibitzers all crowding for their moment of serious regard. When I'd finished the so-called selection, I had that pleasant waver of question, which I must say these composite opinions have driven from my fading mind entirely. Like, if someone, namely ole B/, proposes to remove 17 count 'em big ones from one's heart's coffers and to substitute and/ or add therefore not one, not two, not three, not four but <u>thirty-five</u>, friend, you know he ain't just whistlin' dixie . . . Well, I hear ole B/ is aheadin north some point soon, in fact, right to this very place. I am sure we can think of a way to greet him will make him feel right at home, since we share such close concerns, as they say. I think we put him up last time he was here, come to think of it. That's probably why he took such pains to set me right on Olson.

Ah well . . . Another book "that will please no one" and I care less and less. Meantime those poem/s—I love it I can get two for one page!—are a pleasure, "sees/seeming" sighs! I'd love to have chorus, "Going own/going own, eyes a going own . . . " Meantime I'll dream on . . .

Love,
Bob

P.S. I'm ok, just postlude pneumonia doldrums, lungs looking like spider web-bies—so doctor says I got to ease off the usual manic enterprises. I am therefore safe in the bosom of ma famille whilst all else huffs and puffs.

. . .

Robert Creeley
64 Amherst Street
Buffalo, N.Y. 14207
Tel 716/875-2108—Fax 716/636-3408

January 1, 1992

Dear Allen,

A very Happy New Year, or else we speak to God personally, like they say. I just saw the enclosed in our local paper last night and since the date you are noted as taking ill is December 21, the solstice no less (and Hannah's birthday), I've got to presume the information of you recuperating in Cooperstown etc is accurate. Remember you up past two hustling cash for Steve Lacy's company in Boulder, and then up at five to say goodbye to me so generously, I must think it's time to be simply easier on yourself and/or more thoughtful as to what you need. Well, that you know, but (as like smoking which I seem finally to have managed to stop after getting pneumonia this summer about a week after seeing you) I guess it has to be work to in fact do it. Since you are truly that company most dear to my own ears and heart, do be provident and not simply providence itself. I wish I could see you much more often, but you are certainly always in mind no matter. Onward!

Love as ever,
Bob

. . .

Robert Creeley PRIVATE
64 Amherst Street
Buffalo, NY 14207
Tel 716/875-2108
Fax 716/636-3408

March 12, 1992

Barbara Jellow
University of California Press

Dear Barbara,

I wish there might have been chance to see you when I was out there, but it was such a whirlwind visit that nothing seemed possible. Now, as you'll know, the introduction is done and the text otherwise resolved. So the element most crucial now remaining is the format. Bill told me of conversations there apropos, and of his own wish to keep with the format used in my Selected.

I see the obvious virtues of doing that but, as I told him, I am very wary finally of any format that means either a severe reduction of point size (which would make reading difficult and the whole text seemingly pinched (as in Army Bibles etc etc)) or the need for even one instance of broken or run-over lines. Olson loathed the latter, and given I'm here the most specific one to argue for his interests, I must make his objection emphatic and my own completely the same. If you look in the Selected Writings of Charles Olson which I edited in the mid-60s for New Directions, you'll find the note he provided apropos such lines (which he utterly protested!) after we ran out of all alternatives. Thankfully they were very few. Anyhow, please do keep these two factors much in mind when your own resolution of the format is the measure. I feel so far from things here, in this one respect at least, that I worry the whole business will now prove vulnerable to this one factor and thus the book itself will be hurt. (I've already resisted suggestions of 1) a map insert and 2) a page of his handwriting, so I don't think my fears are ill-founded.) This book has been thus far remarkably distracted by "passing comments," call them, from those so marginally involved with Olson's poetry we might as well be using a ouija board for our instruction. Ah well.

When we last corresponded, the best type seemed the Aldus? That was back late October as I recall. I'd be curious now to know what seems most possible to you, i.e., does that 5X7 trim seem best still? This end of things I feel I've been too removed from, and yet, particularly for Olson's work, it's the absolute sine qua non of it all. If you can give me some present sense of things, I'd be very grateful.

My best as ever,
Bob

Xc. Bill McClung

. . .

FAX TO BARBARA JELLOW, UNIVERSITY OF CALIFORNIA PRESS

Robert Creeley PRIVATE
64 Amherst Street
Buffalo, NY 14207
Tel 716/875–2108
Fax 716/636–3408

March 16, 1992

Barbara Jellow, Design
University of California Press

Dear Barbara,

Thanks for your prompt and very helpful letter. I can now see, like they say, the various possibilities very clearly. Given the three options you note #1: keep the same even to typeface; #2: make it different as each poet's style qualifies; #3: make it the same but different, i.e., change the size and shape, for example, but keep the jacket and binding. Specifically thinking of the Olson Selected, I can see no possibility of an effective use of #1 insofar as neither typeface nor page dimensions can really accommodate his work, whose lines and rhetorical mode are so different than mine, for example. I can't see how one would avoid a pinchedness right from the beginning.

Option #2 is very attractive to me because it so clearly uses the text itself as the qualifying term instead of fitting the text to a preestablished form. (I am interested to know what other poets are in mind for this series. Zukofsky seems to be moving away, sadly, given the commitment now to Johns Hopkins and the lack of response concerning the possibility of a Selected Writings, etc. Robert Duncan's Selected is committed to New Directions as far as I know. So what particular authors are in mind? Possibilities such as Milosz or Deguy would only argue that the series per se has no coherence, or simply lumps "poets" as category, hardly an emphasis to the publisher's interests.) I especially like the format's being 5–3/4" by 8" in that it would set Olson's poems very handsomely in all respects, and still stay a comfortably small book. Option #3 would also be acceptable, I think, with the reservations noted (to wit, what is to be the nature of this proposed series of Selected Poems). I think one must know the proposal for the series in general, in short. If Olson and myself are "the series," then I don't think we need similar formats to make that evident, being so like the Bobbsey Twins as it's been. Far better to make distinctions. If there is a present range of poets now in mind so to include, then who are they and what's the relation of their work one to another? If there is no decisive link, then making the format the only link seems a bit bleak. (I recall from college days a Random House edition that had substantial works of Blake and John Donne in big book, to everyone's complete consternation. So much for "genre" printing.) So anyhow—Aster continues to seem best and that's very good news that the "shaped" poems aren't a big problem. Onward!

My best as ever,
Bob

. . .

FAX TO TOM THOMPSON, THE NATIONAL POETRY SERIES

Robert Creeley PRIVATE
64 Amherst Street
Buffalo, NY 14207
Tel 716/875–2108
Fax 716/636–3408
PLEASE DELIVER TO: Tom Thompson
The National Poetry Series

FROM: Robert Creeley
DATE: May 18, 1992

Dear Tom,
      I've now had chance to look through all the manuscripts sent, and then to review my initial choices. By and large I found an active competence but an insistent sameness in the rhetorical manner and, equally, in the various "subjects" addressed. Reflection, i.e., "a backward glance," seemed the common preoccupation. So finally I chose a manuscript altogether exceptional for its prosodic skill and its almost encyclopaedic density of detailing—what an incredible particularist this poet is! I went back to it again and again just for the wildly droll range of its information. Anyhow it's Gerald Burns, Shorter Poems—hardly an easy manuscript in its typography, the number of poems, or in its characteristic demands on a reader. But in this company, or any, it speaks with an exceptional clarity of means and with a drollness of wit I found emphatically singular.

                  Sincerely,
                      Bob

· · ·

LETTER TO WARREN TALLMAN

                      September 25, 1992

Dear Warren,
      Many thanks for your lovely book! Not only do I delight as ever in your terrific use of whatever it is I do, but the particular form of this one, its intimate address, so to speak, is lovely. Adeena generously brought it along to the first of the Wednesdays at 4 gatherings. So. My one bleak piece of news is that Jack Clarke died mid-July and Cass is only now beginning to get some purchase on things. They were such old cronies that life without him must be almost unthinkable for her. God knows one had to recognize he was dying, but he was so sweet about it truly no one finally had to deal with it until he was dead. Cass told us his last words were, with a lift in voice and attention,—Hi Ma—,

very early morning, a Sunday. There was a solid oldtime funeral and gathering afterwards at the house, so he is still here, god knows, in the common world.

The Poetics Program has started off with a bang, very attractive newcomers indeed. I've decided to go back to teaching a course a semester not wanting to be left out. Anyhow they are really attractive, so something's working for sure. Charles seems a little stretched but why not—he comes in a Tuesday eve and is gone again about the same time Thursday. Felix, incidentally, is an altogether benign baby, exceptionally in this case.

David is staying in Connecticut and Susan seems at times very forlorn, not just that he's not here, just that the world is isolating and untrustworthy—and men get it all. Ah well! Life, like they say, continues and we all thrive.

Love as ever,

Bob

. . .

FAX TO ALLEN GINSBERG

Robert Creeley

P.O. Box 384

Waldoboro, ME 04572

Tel 207/832–6301

PLEASE DELIVER TO: Allen Ginsberg

FROM: Robert Creeley

DATE: June 16, 1993

Dear Allen,

I *think* you just called apropos the American Academy nominations, but the phone here was fouled up so I didn't get a clear message, como se dice. Anyhow, I am here, and more or less together—trying, in fact, to write some prefatory note for Robin Blaser's pending magnum opus to be published by Coachhouse: *The Holy Forest*. I feel incredibly dumb! Meantime since I've got the computer, I'm holding the fort for Willy's fantasy baseball team and I *think* he also just called to tell me a player had broken a leg . . . What do I do now??? It's a lovely day despite. Great to get out of the hassle. Send me if you will what you think makes sense for those nominations—just now my head is empty to put it mildly. Tonight I go read with local company in church in Rockland. Small world! Thank god George managed to sell my so-called papers! Viz, that secures the children's education, like they say, not to mention my aging back. Onward!

Love as ever,

Bob

. . .

Robert Creeley
P.O. Box 384
Waldoboro, ME 04572
Tel 207/832–6301
PLEASE DELIVER TO: Allen Ginsberg
FROM: Robert Creeley
DATE: June 18, 1993

Dear Allen,

Sorry to miss your call last night, and also not have called back. I couldn't locate Terry's number sadly. Anyhow your suggestions for nominations seem fine to me, with these emphasized in this order: Roi, just that he's the sole person of that authority either I know or can think of; Carl R/, given his age and significance (It was moving to see how much it meant to Esteban Vicente, who was an elder back at Black Mountain . . .); Kenneth K/, who would be delighted and is again singular and our generation—and then to Ed Sanders etc, certainly deserving—and I'd also like to start thinking about Susan Howe, who is in her fifties now.—George Minkoff is a book dealer Bertholf suggested back when Peter Howard had done an initial valuation of my papers for Washington U/, St. Louis, and B/ suggested a "second opinion" would be to the point. George's appraisal doubled the amount and that's the figure that stuck and which, but for a reduction by a small amount to prove good faith in negotiations, I've just got from Stanford. They also have first option on material which accumulates, instead of flat rights to everything—so that will certainly be useful and seems fair. George sold Milosz's archive among others. He lives near Great Barrington and is in and out of NYC a lot. Severely crippled, which doesn't seem to hang him up. He's been trying to sell the stuff since '91, and given the market, did very damn well I think. I certainly recommend him. Onward!

Love,
Bob

· · ·

E-MAIL TO PETER GIZZI

12-Oct-1993 16:34:09.42

From: UBVMS::CREELEY
To: IN%"pgizzi@brownum.brown.edu" CREELEY
CC: CREELEY
Subj: Correction!!!

Dear Peter,

Cancel previous advice insofar as I have error in identify-
ing my own "userid"—such is AGE!!! Well, let's start again, using "our" previous
IN%" up to which all was well, and even "creeley" was on the mark, but shortly
thereafter "we" "fucked up," as follows: creeley@vbums SHOULD read creeley@
ubvms.cc.buffalo.edu—which I think you knew anyhow, looking at this page of
report re inability of your dearly anticipated letter's failure to ARRIVE. Help,
viz, "Will help arrive IN TIME . . . . ? Tune in next week, etc etc."

Your humble idiot savage,

Bob

. . .

E-MAIL TO CHARLES BERNSTEIN

Date: Tue, 01 Mar 1994 09:03:28 -0500 (EST)

From: CREELEY@ubvms.cc.buffalo.edu
Subject: GG/s
Cc: CREELEY@ubvms.cc.buffalo.edu

Dear Charles,

I hope to get to the reading but can't make the meal.

Bob

. . .

LETTER TO ERIC MOTTRAM

64 Amherst Street
Buffalo, NY 14207–2748
March 5, 1994

Dear Eric,

It's good to hear from you and to know all's well. Odd to think the fellow in
Helsinki has finally managed to complete that thesis! I recall he was a student of
yours? You're a nice man indeed.

All's well here, just hectic. I was three times to the Old World this fall and
winter, and it finally got to be simply work, e.g., a four day trip to Germany

with one day in Frankfurt, one in Munich, and the other two in the air. I got the so-called Beineke Prize from the Bavarian Academy of Fine Arts, which thankfully included money. More happy was a week's stay in Paris for action at the Pompidou Center and various other places, and despite the drear time of year I had happy company with a range of friends there, and unexpectedly the Waldrops also. But travelling is not the excitement it had been. The endless need to keep track of stuff, the isolation from family—I see its point less and less.

The enclosure is the latest remarkable production from the graduate students. What a wild range of publications they are turning out! Meantime Charles is seemingly surviving his endless commuting. Susan is much missed. Dennis is in and out. Ray stays as jovial as ever. Bob I don't now see at all. I fear we parted company absolutely last spring and the sale of my stuff to Stanford not long after put a finish to that business as well. God knows what he wants but I have no longer any interest in his scheming. Sad that he should so attach the Duncan material to his own sad ambitions. Yuk! Forgive me for my own obsession, and best wishes for all your undertakings—and to Marion and Arthur! Onward . . .

All best,
Bob

. . .

FAX TO STEVE LACY AND IRENE AEBI

Robert Creeley
64 Amherst Street
Buffalo, NY 14207-2748
Tel 716/875-2108
Fax 716/645-6276

PLEASE DELIVER TO: Steve Lacy/Irene Aebi
FROM: Robert Creeley
DATE: November 13, 1994

Dear Steve and Irene,

I've now talked with Monique Goldstein and we've set up a date for Buffalo as follows: April 19th at the Calumet Arts Cafe, 54 West Chippewa, Buffalo, N.Y. 14202 (prop. Mark Goldman), a small sort of lounge club with tables and a small raised stand, so it should be simple enough to work in. As and when, phone there is 716-855-2220. I've got $1500 for your flat fee (from the university scene) and Mark G/ will take care of the hotel (I said, a suite). The place has jazz in and out, and other music, so it's again I think fair enough. Not much else simply available for one night I fear. So a Buffalo first! Terrific!!

I'll try to get a check in advance if I can, but since it would only be a few days before you're here, I'll need US pickup address for you to cover period April 5 to 18 or thereabouts. Anyhow I am delighted it can work out. Hope it sounds ok at your end.

>Love to you both,
>   *Bob*

Also just now saw the space again and it looks fine for your needs—and the prop. is delighted. So there you have it. Onward!

. . .

LETTER TO JIM DINE

>64 Amherst Street
>Buffalo, NY 14207
>December 12, 1994

Dear Jim,

Thanks for that generous idea! Like Xmas already. Anyhow I'd be delighted to try to figure something with you, and have some fun, like they say. Just now I'm down here in this curious "Atlantic Center for the Arts" which proves remarkably comfortable, though having family here would be terrific (but kids are finishing up fall school semester—they'll all be here Friday.)

Do you have any ideas about what we could focus on—viz, do? I could either move from your images, else I suppose the other way (as with Mabel)—or we could try for a focus we could both start with, and then put together what comes of it in any way makes sense.

Otherwise length (of this charming instance) is intimidating, i.e., that's a lot in there—do you think we have to make that long, i.e., the text? Blank pages are always useful! "Give the reader some room . . . " But time enough to resolve same. I'll be down here till December 23, then back to Buffalo for the Xmas chaos, then in and out for most of the spring till mid-May, when I (and all of us then together once school's out mid-June) will go to Auckland (their winter!) for a Fulbright (about three months). That would be an excellent time for me to get something done.

Is one of your sons in active music ensemble??? I was taking Will up for guitar lesson (at university) and checking out the stuff on a bulletin board, was quite sure I saw a Dine!

>Love to you all as ever,
>   *Bob*

. . .

Robert Creeley PRIVATE
64 Amherst Street
Buffalo, NY 14207-2748
Tel 716/875-2108
Fax 716/645-6276

PLEASE DELIVER TO: Peggy Fox, Managing Editor [New Directions]
FROM: Robert Creeley
DATE: January 26, 1995
SUBJECT: Translator for Pound's Work into Chinese

Dear Peggy,

There is presently a fellow here I much respect the energy and intelligence of, specifically in our Poetics Program—but finally, and far more to the point, an active person on the world. His name is Yunte Huang and he tells me he has the request of a Chinese publisher in Beijing to translate texts of Pound's for publication there. Best you check with him for specifics, but I want here to emphasize my sense that he is capable and would do a good job. He says he can supply good references from Chinese scholars, both there as well as here. Please let me know as you can what seems the best way for him now to proceed. Thanks as ever for your help—and a very Happy New Year (or else)!

All my best,
Bob

. . .

[February 24, 1995]

Dear Peter,

Following is a note to Peter Glassgold, who's been anxious to get up here for some time, particularly with respect to his recent take on Boethius published by SUN & MOON etc. I've been musing on the fact of your questions ever since I got them, for which many heartfelt thanks. Because your address there is inquiry, not invective or recrimination, I think one might proceed in some manner of good faith to attempt to face the implications more directly. The atmosphere has become intolerable with respect to the holdings in the Poetry Room, just that "access" becomes a paranoid preoccupation of the graduate students. When Richard Fyffe was here from Connecticut, he was altogether bemused by fact the seminar people asked him not once but three times if, should they be able to get there, would he allow them to see Olson's papers. Anyhow . . .

My sense would be to have some across the board discussion of what such editing questions/problems are, presuming Bob's [Robert Bertholf's] acting in good faith whatever the fact, and therefore certainly including him (though I much wonder if he'd show)—and so forth. I'd undertake to pay your expenses in coming, and we could certainly give you some occasion beyond this necessarily dreary prospect. Though, goddamnit, it's legitimate defense of a dead dear friend's writing and the demand that its transmission and representation be fairly and openly arbitrated. Ah well . . .

So anyhow that's what's in mind, and here's the note/fax to Peter Glassgold:

PLEASE DELIVER TO: Peter Glassgold
FROM: Robert Creeley
DATE: February 24, 1995
SUBJECT: Visit to Buffalo

Dear Peter,

Fanny and Susan Howe were here last evening for dinner, and Susan told me of your recent call. I apologize for what must have seemed my ignoring of your interest in coming, but, as she will have told you, the meeting at which I thought to resolve the possibility proved one in which we discussed the dilemmas of delayed matching funds from the administration—and now we've learned that the $15,000 in question has been cut entirely. So you see our dilemma.

However, I'd like to invite you for some time in the coming year, using resources from my chair funds, if $500 will suffice. It's a small sum but at least I can commit it without problem at this time. If agreeable, I'd then refer you to Charles Bernstein for appropriate working out of schedule.

There is another matter which much concerns me, and which might be discussed as a part of the occasion for your visit as well. That is Peter Quartermain's disturbing review of copy-editing questions in the first forty pages of New Directions' edition of Robert Duncan's Selected Poems. What he makes clear was tacitly evident from the University of California Press reports of textual errors and questions in the pages of Bob's copy for the first volume of their Duncan Collected. Now, however, simply that Quartermain's material has been distributed on the Net through Buffalo's Poetics Program Listserve, and because it's far more publicly evident than other questioning has been, the whole issue of what is responsible textual editing and what particularly qualifies the editor's and the publisher's role in an edition such as Duncan's Selected constitutes a very present concern, both for graduate students and faculty, and for all others relating. I recall you had offered your own capabilities in reviewing such copy to UC/Press, sadly without response. But clearly you have thought about it all, and, since you are ND's editor for the publication in question, your own stake in the matter is very clear. Therefore I'd like to suggest a public discussion of some sort, as informal or seminar-like as seems comfortable, with Bob (I would certainly think to ask him and I presume it would be in his interest to clarify his procedures and resolutions) and Peter Quartermain, and someone from UC/Press, i.e., Doris or whoever she thinks to the point. I just can't believe, for anyone's interest or integrity, it can all be let slide any longer. (J. [James Laughlin], for example, must be up the wall to recognize he's publishing such a questionable text, presuming he knows about it.) Anyhow, enough said. If you can give me some prompt answer as to your own willingness to participate, then I'll continue with the invitations aforesaid. In the meantime, do rest assured I'll get you here whatever the particulars, and always with your own effective book the primary focus and occasion. Ok. . . .

So there you have it. I'll let you know what he answers. It's a long shot at best, but I can't see the use in doing nothing. Or of simply trying to "fight" Bertholf, for that matter. There's got to be a way of identifying his behaviour sufficiently to persuade him alternatives do exist. Onward!

    All best to you both as ever,
     Bob

• • •

E-MAIL TO BENJAMIN FRIEDLANDER

To: Benjamin Friedlander
Date: Mon, 10 Apr 1995 19:31:38 -0400 (EDT)
From: CREELEY@ubvms.cc.buffalo.edu
Subject: Olson

Dear Ben,

    Don Allen called today to talk about the Olson Collected. He's found a solid piece by George Butterick he thinks will make an appropriate intro, so that's happy news. He also asked about your interest, so I told him you had been looking over the mis etc etc. (Forgive typos! I am just anxious to keep in touch what with all else—and thanks to you both from Hannah & the gang for the great card! She is just home today thankfully.) Anyhow Don wants to talk to you and has only your old phone number—will that work? Otherwise let me know how to call you and I'll get that info to him. He wants to suggest you be co-editors, rather than have simple editorial fee—as co-editors I'd expect you'd split the royalties from the book which I get, incidentally, from the Selected.

    My elders' advice wd be to opt for co—so much more the point than small $$$ you'd otherwise get. Time enough. We are all dizzy from stress, like they say. Dig it . . .

    Love to you both,
    Bob

• • •

E-MAIL TO PETER GIZZI AND ELIZABETH WILLIS

Date: 2/15/96 3:49 AM
From: CREELEY@ubvms.cc.buffalo.edu

Dear Peter and Liz,

Belated but heartfelt Happy New Year to you both, and my apologies for being so long silent. Days have gone by in a veritable flash, and it's only now things begin to regain some usable pace. Nothing at all hopeless or depressed, just classic "things to do today," so that at one point last fall I was ten days in England, from Newcastle to Exeter to London and back again, and reading on eight of them. Help. When I would be at last home, then it was time to deal with family needs and chores of various plugs, notes and articles. So that's what's been up. This spring, thankfully, I am much less on the road and intend to keep it that way. For example, I was trying to get out to SF to see my new granddaughter (Miranda Rose!) born late August, and it wasn't until November that there was literally a weekend free to do it. Then when I was there, I had a day with her and my terrific daughter, and spent the other in meetings with UC Press etc etc. So that's why I wasn't in touch with you or any other friends there.

Anyhow, you dig it, like they say. Days now we just sit and take a walk in the park with newly acquired Sophie, a bouvier de flandres, cow dog, terrific—now a year after Maggie's sad death. Hannah and Will are both thriving, Will now at City Honors which he very much likes—and Hannah in characteristic good spirits at Nichols. Again thinking of our life: we had Gustaf Sobin as guest, here about ten (I had just written intro for his reading), then lunch with Susan and him, back to firehouse for more conversation, then out to u/ for reading, back then here for family (he'd gone off with Kristin and company) Valentine's Day and then to Hannah's musical evening at Nichols, and now it's dawn again. Fair enough.

Incidentally I'm doing a so-called project at City Honors thanks to a Lila Wallace/Reader's Digest Writers Award—to put them on line with a journal for the writers. Ken Sherwood is my ally and person for Just Buffalo's interests in it all—so I'll let you know when it's up and running.

Meantime I did a long poem (and/or thirteen stanzas for the thirteen etchings) for a collaboration with Alex Katz—images of branches, flower heads—very sweet. Otherwise bits and pieces as time permits. Like annual Valentine poem! I always admired Louis Zukofsky's great poems apropos.

How did Mills work out for Liz? We miss your news too, god knows. It would be lovely to amble along the beach with you both. Ah well . . . We saw Nate and Lew in the bookstore a few days ago. I sense their life is really demanding. Then Nate is such a sweet kid. Anyhow things keep going, and now we're gearing up for the Duncan fest. So there you have it.

This year going by has really been one I've had to recognize I could not keep doing scenes like that biz in England, nor could I manage all the usual mail or demand as I had. It's literally age—not a tottering, or failure, just increasing inability to run up hills, stay up talking all night, or hear clearly in a crowded restaurant. There is also the to be expected death of friends so sadly insistent, as Larry's [Larry Eigner], as another friend from the time in San Francisco years ago, and earlier another, my closest friend from days in college, and Franco B/, and on and on. So one turns to the obituaries almost without thinking, or other (surviving!) friends call to report a person's death one knew only casually, like last night, a call to say Caroline Lowell had died—etc. Anyhow we are here despite, really, and I look forward indeed to seeing you and your dissertation as and when. I do hope life there for you both proves solid and simply GOOD. Ok!

    Our love,
    Bob

. . .

LETTER TO KURT VONNEGUT

64 Amherst Street
Buffalo, NY 14207

May 23, 1996

Dear Kurt Vonnegut,

    A few years ago when your opera was being put on in Buffalo, Allen Ginsberg brought you over to our place for a curious breakfast of somewhat burnt toast and black coffee—with my dear daughter Hannah then about eight in attendance. It was a good-natured meeting which neither of us forgot. So, when a school friend said her favorite writer was you, Hannah said she had met you here in Buffalo which the friend wouldn't believe. Would you therefore do me this very particular favor, i.e., write a couple of sentences to say that Hannah had mentioned her respect for your work and that you have whatever reaction, like they say. They are twelve, hopeless time for girls in classic day school lacking alternative—and it simply matters to be believed when what one says is true.

    Otherwise I wish that academy would somehow one day get a real life. I have nominated Amiri Baraka over and over but as Jeannie Kim told me after she'd left the scene, they will never agree. Anyhow onward! Viz., let's start our own club.

    My best,
    Robert Creeley

P.S. Hannah's friend's name is Kerry Docherty, and I've enclosed the proverbial stamped addressed envelope to save bother.

. . .

LETTER TO KURT VONNEGUT

June 17, 1996

Dear Kurt Vonnegut,

That was such a sweet and generous reply in support of dear Hannah, and it did the job, like they say, with absolute effect. As it happens, it came on the friend's birthday, so it was all usefully converted into a genial extra "suitable for framing". So anyhow everyone was delighted and grateful—and thanks for coming through with such promptness and consummate wit. You are not a terrific writer for nothing! Anytime I can do anything of use in return, you got it.

Love from Hannah and me,
Robert Creeley

. . .

E-MAIL TO SIMON PETTET

Date: Fri, 11 Oct 1996 11:26:09 -0700
From: Robert Creeley <creeley@acsu.buffalo.edu>
Organization: University at Buffalo, SUNY
To: simonp@pipeline.com
Subject: Re: Hi Bob!

simonp@pipeline.com wrote:
>Hi Bob!—just thought to drop you this swift e note to raise a glass to
>your big seven oh etc (what again?) but being as you are currently being
>feted . . . "if I my add my two cents worth" . . . —fond regards—love -
>blessings etc—as ever Simon
>love to all dear friends. . . .

Dear Simon,

Actually my birthday was back in May but this is the institutional version, which proves very good natured thank god. Only glitch has been Roi's no show and then asking from LA (for christ's sake) should he still come. So yesterday I got to read twice so as not to leave patient Gil S/ in proverbial 2 hour hole. Cosas de la vida no doubt—but it was frankly much like a spoiled kid's leaning on the company's good nature and he obviously disappointed a lot of black kids who turned out hoping to hear them. I guess the honkies win in spite of themselves. Onward!

Anyhow it's been great. Almost worth being 70!

Love as ever,
Bob

—

Robert Creeley, 64 Amherst Street, Buffalo, NY 14207
Tel 716 875 2108 * Fax 716 875 0751

. . .

E-MAIL TO TOM RAWORTH

[October 1996]

Dear Tom,

Thinking I had your address ready to "paste," I got this from previous undertaking:

> Wislawa Szymborska, a self-effacing
> 73-year-old Polish poet who collects trashy postcards because
> she says trash has no pretensions . . .

Enough of that! It is very good to hear from you in the midst of all else. I've been on the road again, just back from curious two day visit with Georg Baselitz with whom I'll do modest collaboration, now possible even in Deutschland. So onward. We keep walking around that wee pond by the Albright Knox with our dog going ape over the foraging squirrels—days are much as there, sharper, colder, great detailing light. All feels well—just rushed, which is fair enough. When the winter comes, it will all slow down of necessity. Meantime both Will and Hannah are in good spirits in their respective schools though the new headmaster at Hannah's seems a complete idiot. I suppose that will keep him uselessly out of it for a time.

My birthday is in May, as you thought. This is simply an institutional after-shock—strictly for the public. Pen wanted Bobbie to come to be the wife, but there wasn't anyone for me. I saw Bobbie a couple of weeks ago very happily, and Kate—looking a lot better and certainly having a much more real life with a job and simply being out with daily people. Anselm as always a pleasure. I didn't see Ed or Jenny, being there just two days, one for work, the other for Kate, and then home.—I'll say hello to Jim for you. He's just coming in for that night after being in India (?). Will those drums never cease.

A friend from NZ, Murray Edmond, is presently staying with Lyn H/ I think, and will be here in a couple of weeks, so he will be able to say how things seem—he's a very dear man.

Do write as you can. I savor your clarity. Ok!

Love to you all three from all of us,
Bob

. . .

LETTER TO MARJORIE PERLOFF

[Sunday, November 10, 1996]

Dear Marjorie,

I feel badly about not having written you about your very impressive book, and the generous reading you give me in it. The whole address is a pleasure, and you make Wittgenstein the presence and influence I've always felt him to be. Curiously he in some sense "grew on" me—from Louis' quotations and also from that slim memoir of Norman Malcolm's—and rumors I'd hear that he'd been a gardener for a time in Cornell (!). He was so usefully antithetical to all the usual propositions of "meaning" and it's his own I'd finally most value in every so-called sense: If you give it a meaning, it has a meaning. I also dig what comes out as the English of his "last words"—tell them it's been wonderful. About a year or so ago I had happy company with Bruce Duffy at a writers' business at Bennington, and love the "fiction" he makes of W/s life, so that the fiction and the fact begin to meld: The World as I Found it. Most pleasant is fact he had never been to Europe nor did he speak German. Only the imagination is real!

Anyhow you do me proud, likewise "away"—up, up & away—or really that dour avoidance of my childhood I'd occasionally hear: he is not dead, he is just away. Oh yeah . . .

Take care! I must say being seventy gets to feel like an institution in itself, and it was GREAT to have Gil's company. Onward!

    Love,
    Bob

· · ·

E-MAIL TO BENJAMIN FRIEDLANDER

[April 7, 1997]

To: bef@ACSU.Buffalo.EDU
From: Robert Creeley <creeley@acsu.buffalo.edu>
Subject: Allen

Dear Ben,

Both sides of that exchange are so charming I do think you should post it if it won't simply offend—it's just so sweet and simple! I went down to the memorial this morning, like watching the Buddhists once again coopt—but one can hardly blame them. But it sure gets tedious sitting in those tacky places as they pin up the decor and the bells start in and the whining, muttering chants go on and on. Poor old Allen was stashed in a box up front meanwhile—and it all did get a bit tendentious and pious, till Roi really changed the communal mind by saying Allen had called him last week to say he was dying, then asked if Roi needed any money. Anyhow I am very glad I got there. He was terrific and will be forever. Onward!

Pen and Michele will hope to get to your reading tomorrow night but I am committed to Daemon College visit that evening, so cannot. But will hope to see you here Wednesday, and to deliver the Boldereff/Olson letters into your hands at last!

      Love to you both,

      Bob

• • •

E-MAIL TO BENJAMIN FRIEDLANDER

[April 19, 1997]

To: bef@ACSU.Buffalo.EDU
From: Robert Creeley <creeley@acsu.buffalo.edu>
Subject: Zukofsky

Dear Ben,

Thanks for your generous note. So much is swirling in mind at this point, much compacted by Allen Ginsberg's sad death—and therefore question as to what any of it means, not bitterly at all—just what. I take it all work on whatever with the particular purchase and appetite each are given—like Pound's Kung Canto 13: They have all answered correctly, that is, each according to his nature—or however it goes. I was so much part of a company whose habits, really from Paul Blackburn to Louis and including Olson and Duncan—were so founded on reference and its delights, that I contrived my own "echoes" and had also to recognize what intelligence I had was not of this kind (which is very much why Williams was so important for me, since he was "like" me etc.) It was always both mysterious and terrific that each of these dear people both respected and looked to me for response—and took me seriously far beyond the call of friendship or of duty. I was just now looking at what Louis, of all people, had to say of me (of all people), in an altogether unlikely review of THE WHIP (which was small book published on a pittance by Gael Turnbull's Migrant Press in California, with our daughter Kirsten's drawing on the cover) in Poetry May 1958. Reviewing was not his habit, believe me. He does it by terrific sequence of quotes, so characteristic—and what he says is really the point we're both making:

[Last paragraph] "The poems are to be praised for not counting up to the "conceit" of rhetoric which a generation or so ago misnamed "metaphysical," whose thought presumed more hope than the voice of a limited body."

But you'll need also the first! (He uses a quote as the title: "What I come to do is partial . . . ")

"As he says in his preface, Robert Creeley's honest metaphysical intention is: "—there is no use in counting. Nor more, say, to live than what there is, to live. I want the poem as close to this fact as I can bring it; or it, me." It is like Spinoza's definition of honesty—"I call that honest which men who live under the guidance of reason praise and which is not opposed to the making of friendship." With some disposition like that in mind Creeley can happily say: "I write poems because it pleases me, very much—I think that is true."

The T-shirts will be ready by Wednesday!
    Love to you both,
    Bob

· · ·

E-MAIL TO CHARLES BERNSTEIN

To: Charles Bernstein <bernstei@bway.net>
From: Robert Creeley <creeley@acsu.buffalo.edu>
Subject: Re: LZ@UB

At 12:25 PM 4/24/97 -0400, you wrote:
>Spent the morning with Ira Nadel, so very much thinking of all you are
>doing: truly great work this week and I want to say, even though you know
>it, how grateful I am that you have undertaken to do this LZ semester.

>Please leave a t-shirt for me!

>Love,
>Charles

Dear Charles,

Thanks for the well wishes! Just before the battle, brother . . . I haven't finally a clue as to what to expect or who will show up. Well, we'll see. Meantime I'm off to introduce Charles Simic. I am getting very versatile in your absence. Onward!

    Love to all,
    Bob

I'll get Marilyn to send you one of the terrific t-shirts. Here's hoping same brings them in if all else fails . . .

· · ·

LETTER TO DENNY MOERS

64 Amherst Street
Buffalo, NY 14207-2748
May 31, 1997

Dear Denny,

  I am way behind as usual, but at least I do have a new manuscript, now duly with Peggy Fox at ND and we spoke of you doing a cover if agreeable—so that's a very happy prospect. Thinking of those great images you enclosed in your February letter, that one of the lone house is a knockout. The book's title is *Life & Death* —so you get the point, like they say. There'd be no need for irony at all. Viz, I said "Life & Death," I mean etc etc etc. "It's about time . . . " So think of what you'd figure appropriate.

  All's well here, just as ever hectic. At this moment Pen is out with neighborhood crew planting some 40 trees (!) on newly opened up traffic islands close by that she persuaded persons first to get the concrete off, then to add fill and topsoil to, and finally to provide trees for (London plane and crab apple). Finally they'll paint the fronts of the ConRail bridges that front on same with underpass coming into our neck of the proverbial (and possibly now more actual) "woods." This neighborhood is not unlike where I was on Fargo, just if anything a bit more poor—so what she's managed is heroic indeed. Too, our neighbors are by no means tree enthusiasts, one suggesting that they all be painted white up to height of eight feet so as to prevent people from hiding back of them to jump out—and another saying they were worse than dogs, what with all the mess they made—and a branch could drop down and kill you. Ah well. I'll be in Maine from late June on pretty much, with Pen back here for Will to do internship at local radio station—but back and forth too. Be great to see you. Onward!

         Our love,
          Bob

· · ·

LETTER TO WILLIAM WADSWORTH, EXECUTIVE DIRECTOR,
ACADEMY OF AMERICAN POETS

64 Amherst Street
Buffalo, NY 14207

February 21, 1999

Dear Bill Wadsworth,

  Thanks for your thoughtful letter. At this age I have no battle with the Academy nor would I in any sense welcome one. The distance I feel from its conduct is a fact of years and habit for us both, and while I wish you well indeed, I would not anticipate that we'd now find much company with one another, even wanting it.

Particularly with respect to the book club, I see it as yet another threat to the independent bookseller, already battered by chains like Barnes and Noble and online distributors as Amazon. I would not think that the Academy itself undertakes to stock and distribute the books determined by the club. But even in such a circumstance, it would constitute yet another threat to the local bookstore. If it applies to a usual commercial distributor to supply the books ordered through the club, then it acts simply as a feeder for that hostile interest. Far better to help identify and link such regional and local centers though a program of publicizing and networking than to add to their competition. Here in Buffalo, for example, Talking Leaves is a great asset for all poets and readers alike. Much of what I say here comes from a conversation with its owner, and I am sure his sentiments and mine agree with other such centers across the country, whether Woodland Pattern in Milwaukee or Groliers in Cambridge. I fear that the Academy proposes to enter the bookselling business in all too ingenuous a manner—hence my demur with respect to becoming a nominator.

Again thank you for your care in this matter. I wish you good luck.

Sincerely,
Robert Creeley

. . .

E-MAIL TO BARRETT WATTEN

Date: Thu, 20 Jan 2000 14:17:03 -0500
From: creeley <creeley@acsu.buffalo.edu>
Subject: Impressive!

Dear Barry,

As ever your impressively patient and clear take on that fact of words is very moving—especially as relates (like they say) to LZ. My own relation to Basic English came at the boarding school I went to in NH, Holderness, where an English teacher, Mr. Abbey, set us to work translating sections of Joyce's The Dubliners into basic English—it must have been the late 30s or very early 40s. I know I much hoped to connect with I. A. Richards at Harvard (where I went the summer of 1943) but never even got to see him, as I recall—his was the active class for Celtic and such. Anyhow the process (BE) fascinated me—the way it made so evident what words per se were doing, and could do. When I first wrote Pound (then in St. Elizabeth's), his first reply was, "What hv yu read?"—to which I answered, Ogden et al. To that he answered "Ogden rather dead," and said further, he was the kind of person who expects one to translate "Basic

English" for every foreigner one meets, and why wasn't "seem" a legitimate
passive form for "see"—etc etc. Anyhow Basic English (as well as Korzybski) had
more action in my so-called generation than many now recall. Onward!

    Love t yu all,

    Bob

—

64 Amherst Street, Buffalo, N.Y. 14207
Tel 716 875 2108 * Fax 716 875 0751

. . .

LETTER TO SARAH CREELEY

PO Box 384
Waldoboro, ME 04572
August 2, 2000

Dear Sarah,

    Here's an AOL installation disc that may prove helpful. I am determined to
get you guys back online! So anyhow all's well here if pining for your email . . .
Pen came up for a little over a week and we had happy chance to relax together.
Helen is in good spirits and she's got her scene back together, so that's a useful
support. I've just taken it as easy as possible, enjoying the pleasures of the place
which stays very dearly substantial. We have had a lot of rain which has been
good news for all the new trees and shrubs. Onward!

    I've looked at your video many times now—what a delight! It keeps all that
incredible time very actual. So thanks again and again. I realize Miranda's
birthday is fast approaching so we'll be zapping something out there in her
honor shortly. Meantime I hope all's well indeed—it's great to know you are in
such a good news place. Ok!

Love from us all to you both,

Dad

. . .

LETTER TO FRANCESCO CLEMENTE

64 Amherst Street
Buffalo, NY 14207
January 31, 2001

Dear Francesco,

    What a generous and perceptive gift! It has the lovely resonance of Olson's
drawing way back then, trying to make clear to me what he was finding in the
Mayan materials while living in Campeche, etc. That you did it in Oaxaca (I

remember spending time there in a lovely ramshackle inn on the edges of town with a great old swimming pool geese had totally befouled) makes it all the more precious! So thanks again and again.

It was lovely seeing you there at that reading—as ever I wish there were not the rush but one day. You mentioned a portrait, which I'd forever be honored to sit for—I'll be coming briefly to NYC May 16—then again for work at NYU June 10–21 (though home for Hannah's graduation (!) the 12th). In any case, I'll hope something proves simple—and we get to talk while you work!

Love,
Bob

P.S. I wrote this poem for Gregory just after Raymond told me he had died. Better late than never. He was something, like they say.

FOR GREGORY CORSO

I'll miss you,
who did better than I did
at keeping the faith of poets,
staying true.

It's as if you couldn't
do otherwise,
had always an appetite
waiting to lead.

You kept to the high road
of canny vision,
let the rest of us
find our own provision.

Ruthless, friends felt,
you might take everything.
Nothing was safe from you.
You did what you wanted.

Yet, safe in your words, your poems,
their humor could hold me.
The wit, the articulate
gathering rhythms,

all made a common sense
of the archaic wonders.
You pulled from nowhere the kingly chair.
You sat alone there.
[CP II, 589]

. . .

64 Amherst Street
Buffalo, NY 14207
February 13, 2001

Dear Joel,

I've been dragging since I was last in touch and hopes to look through stuff have faded in classic winter doldrums here plus more than usually distracting departmental business. Anyhow here is a dub of the tape I'd mentioned—the Helsinki reading which begins with Anselm Hollo's taped intro (sound seems to shift between right and left at outset but soon enough steadies—and is fine. Later on side B there is some usual babble from the genial bar scene, but I can certainly live with that (and did for years), so see what you think.) Anyhow I do like it—and it covers a range rare in any other reading I can quickly think of. Once things ease, I'll take a look for other stuff. I know there is a great early tape at the Buffalo Public Library with Gwendolyn Brooks introducing. That would be great to have up. So Happy (post) Valentine's Day! Again, you got a great thing going.

Love,
Bob

. . .

October 1, 2001

Henry Reath, President
Board of Directors
Academy of American Poets
588 Broadway, Suite 1203
New York, N.Y. 10012–3210

Dear Henry,

As you will know, the situation of the Chancellors is at best ill defined. On the one hand, they seem barely included in the significant determinations of the Academy. On the other, they are that group within the Academy most identified by public interest and report. They have the responsibility of representing the Academy's particular presence in the public arena, not only among the general company of poets but also in the membership of the Academy at large and in the far less definable community of those who read and otherwise engage in the contemporary activities of poetry. Put bluntly, they take the heat—and when such an event as that involving William Wadsworth occurs, it is they who have to front the response from that same public sector.

I will not rehearse here the various petitions and communications I have received because I think you are well aware of them. You will recall that my first response was to write both you and Bill so as to ascertain what had happened, thus to be able to answer those who felt the Board of Directors' action had been tantamount to a palace coup. As the situation grew more demanding of my own time and attention, I had to recognize that all the Chancellors seemed as ignorant of the facts as did I. In short, none apparently had been given any warning of what was to happen and none, to my own knowledge, had been applied to for advice or for judgment.

In that unpleasant way, then, the Chancellors were forced to recognize that they counted not at all in the real life of the Academy, that, like children, they were subject to the determinations of the Board without being able to take part in those judgments or to offer even an opinion. I cannot emphasize sufficiently how offensive and unacceptable such a situation is for me and for others in the same circumstance. To be asked by the Board of Directors to represent its commitment to poetry and then to be deemed not even significant enough to be told clearly what is happening at the time specific creates an impression very hard to ignore. The Executive Director is that person in the Academy's structure most particular to the Chancellors' function. To keep the Chancellors so uninformed and unaware of the removal of that person argues a tacit contempt on the part of the Board for those poets it has otherwise proposed as its public representatives.

Sincerely,
Robert Creeley

. . .

E-MAIL TO SARAH CREELEY

Date: Sun, 18 Aug 2002 21:18:21 -0400
From: Robert Creeley <creeley@acsu.buffalo.edu>
To: Sarah Creeley <SarahCreeley@aol.com>
Subject: Happy Birthday for Miranda

Dear Sarah,

Just a quick note to say we mailed off birthday cheer for Miranda yesterday priority mail, so it should show up there (we hope) more or less on time. One thing: there's a sort of feathery business in a little backpack in said booty, and it needs not to be pulled out too vigorously (we also hope). So onward—ourselves back to Buffalo on Tuesday, hard to believe the summer's gone so fast. You must be getting ready to teach—and Miranda to learn!

All our love,
Dad

. . .

E-MAIL TO WILL CREELEY

Date: Wed, 21 Aug 2002 20:54:02 -0400
From: Robert Creeley <creeley@acsu.buffalo.edu>
To: Cappio16@aol.com
Subject: Onward!

Dear Will,
    That sounds to have been a very happy scene with you and Ceci, so that's a
pleasure for sure. Meantime I just got this:

> "I found a copy of my drivers license on this web site, they have a copy of every
> driver license in the USA in their database.
>   http://www.DriversLicenseSearch.net"

Looks familiar!
    Love,
    Dad

. . .

E-MAIL TO UB ENGLISH DEPARTMENT LISTSERV

Subject: Re: Office Hours for fall 2002
Date: Thu, 19 Sep 2002 12:31:21 -0400
From: Robert Creeley <creeley@acsu.buffalo.edu>
To: UB English Department List <ENGLISH@LISTSERV.ACSU.BUFFALO.EDU>

Dear Bill,
    Just for nostalgia's sake, please tell Marilyn (and anyone else trying to locate
me) that I am most simply reached by email:
    creeley@acsu.buffalo.edu
Or at the Poetry Collection:
    University at Buffalo, 420 Capen Hall, Box 602200, Buffalo, NY 14260–2200
Thanks!
    Best as ever,
    Bob

—
Poetry Collection/Rare Books
University at Buffalo
420 Capen Hall, Box 602200
Buffalo, NY 14260–2200

. . .

Subject: Re: Fwd: All's well!
Date: Tue, 08 Oct 2002 09:09:08 -0400
From: Robert Creeley <creeley@acsu.buffalo.edu>
To: PenHC@aol.com

Dear love,

This setup has been cranky but I got your second message and will contrive
to open the first by going to your sent mail on AOL etc. All went well last eve-
ning albeit I was really tired at that point. But I had good visits with everyone
from Anne to Jane and Anselm—so that was a pleasure. Today we see Kate and
then this evening Anselm and Jane again for dinner. Then Steve gets me to the
airport tomorrow morning—and that's it.

Meantime I forwarded to you a note I got from Colin Still to the effect they'll
arrive in Waldoboro the evening of the 10th—and will be ready to go the morn-
ing of the 11th etc. I still want not to start up on the 9th—I'll need that day to
get back together plus check to make sure I have what I need for Maine and all.
Anyhow!

I'll call Stan Brakhage today—they are apparently leaving for Vancouver
on the 10th. His health is not at all good but they think that will be the simpler
place now to be. So.

All my love,
Robert

PenHC@aol.com wrote:
>I guess I just sent this back to myself last night.
>Lovely morn again here, off to get Sophie pee sample to vet, etc
>Hope yr day is good, seeing Kate and all
    >XXXXXXP

. . .

Date: Wed, 09 Jul 2003 14:15:39 -0400
From: Robert Creeley <creeley@acsu.buffalo.edu>
Subject: Re: Memories—and thanks!

Dear Barry,

Thanks for all your useful news. Connecticut College ought to do well by
Asa. Best information I have had is from bright son of an old New Mexico
friend, who really had a solid time there. I also very much like Charles
Hartman—so there must be company. We'll hope to see you in Providence as

proves simple for you. Meantime here's the quote as Will had it in the valediction (at the Gallatin Commencement at Avery Fisher Hall, May 12 '03):

> " . . . Finally, leaving this company that has been so terrifically sustaining and empowering for me, I am reminded of a quote given to me in one of the first Gallatin classes I took, the poet Barrett Watten's immaculately precise observation that "the train is ceaselessly reinventing the station."
>
> "I don't remember the class, or even the context, but I have thought often of the implications of those words, and because I am not sure if I am the train, the station, the passenger, the conductor, or all of it, I have measured my progress against myself with that simple, clean illumination. "The train is ceaselessly reinventing the station." My fellow classmates, there's no way to go but to go, nowhere to be but where you are."

All aboard!
Best to you
Bob

. . .

E-MAIL TO ROD SMITH

Subject: Selected Letters
File: OppenIntroedit.DOC   36K
Thu July 17, 2003 7:42 AM

Dear Rod,

Thanks for the quick reassurance. Thinking of the Selected Letters, it would seem some general 'map' or sense of focus or parameter would be the first need. The book will certainly 'tell a story,' perhaps the most useful that can be told, thinking of UCP's selection of Olson's letters—or Gregory's, just out from ND. Here's a link from Stanford (in the unlikely event you've not seen it), which lists the names of correspondents collected in the three series of correspondences they have:

http://dynaweb.oac.cdlib.org/dynaweb/ead/stanford/mss/m0662/

I am not sure what Stanford has for carbons etc. Best to get in touch with Bill McPheron, the curator specific:

William McPheron <mcpheron@leland.Stanford.EDU>

There will be family (letters from Burma to my sister and mother in the 40s) and then continuing friends, Donald Berlin, Jake Leed et al—and the range of those specific to my so-called life as a writer, with its defining periods and persons, e.g., living abroad, New Mexico, etc. So again some sort of overall 'map' in mind would be useful, serving as center for the whole. Since May of this year, I've got something like 1100 emails and written almost 800. In the correspondence with Olson in the early 50s, we managed to fill ten volumes in something just over two years.

So obviously your selection will have to make a selective pattern out of all the bulk, not preempt its concerns but rather make evident the diversity and also the insistent continuities—simply what matters (and to whom) over fifty years.

For a means of getting some overall 'picture,' there's the drear Faas biography—which is in no way my pleasure—but he did determined legwork in getting to basic materials (letters, etc.) and to persons relating. It's his 'reading' of it all which I necessarily abhor, but nonetheless his 'parameters' may be helpful. Then there are takes like Tom Clark's 'American Common Place'—my own favorite just that it cuts to the chase so usefully.

So anyhow please depend on me to be of whatever help I can. We are just now moving to Providence but one hopes, once there, that the proverbial "things" will soon come together. I am very grateful to you (all) for taking on this responsibility and, again, any use I can be, please tell me.

Best to all,
Bob

P.S. I'll attach the introduction I did for the Oppen Selected—somehow the hardest part!

· · ·

LETTER TO CARL RAKOSI

P.O. Box 2584
Providence, RI 02906
September 22, 2003

Dear Carl,

Thanks so much for your generous note. I had worried that mine for your birthday might have been both too hasty and too meager—and so your saying you were struck by its insight is terrific. It's hardly an "essay" as you'll see—I enclose my email to Steve Dickison and the note itself, both written in a B&B in Berkeley. I had to go to Stanford, having signed up for the celebration there of Robert D/s and Denise L/s correspondence.

Anyhow you flatter me by suggesting said "piece" might be of use as an introduction to a collection of your new and selected poems. I'd question that it can carry that responsibility but, if deadlines permit, I could perhaps tinker with it and come up with a page and a half or so that might. See what you think. In any case, you are welcome to whatever works.

I've been teaching here at Brown since September. It feels very good-natured and a welcome shift from what had become the all too familiar habits of Buffalo. There I felt as if I were hanging around just for the paycheck, which of course I was. Here I am new in town, usefully, and have just enough to do to keep significant company with colleagues, who are excellent—C. D. Wright, Forrest Gander, Rosmarie and Keith Waldrop, etc. I also like being back in an active city—and close indeed to where I came from in Massachusetts. So all's in fine spirits accordingly.

Again, I am sorry I missed your great celebration. Onward!

Love,
Bob

. . .

E-MAIL TO AMMIEL ALCALAY

Dec. 1, 2003

Dear Ammiel,

This is Olson speaking of Parker in retrospect, like they say—about twenty years after—and after Charlie Parker had been dead for thirteen years. If the question is, did Olson either listen to or pick up on Charlie Parker during his (Parker's) lifetime, the answer, as far as I know, is still no. I never recall him listening to any of the records at BMC—there was a pleasant shedlike provision for same where I listened to them a lot, particularly those Miles D/ "Dear Old Stockholm," "When Lights Are Low," etc etc. (I'd been listening to Parker since the mid-40s, for example.) By the late sixties Parker is both public legend (like Pollock) and also primary example of "improvisation," and Olson would have been well aware of that from me and a tacit host of others. Too, you see the context of the questions is whether or no there was an active "poetics" being worked out at BMC to which Duncan and I still obtained, and the Parker reference is making clear that no, it was a practice, the event, which was the action and center—as it was with Dylan in the 60s. Ok!

Best as ever,
Bob

>Ammiel Alcalay wrote:
>
>thanks for thinking but i actually (!) found the olson quote i had asked
>you guys about—it appears in MAPS #4:
>
>Voice: Right. Well, in a sense it's not even relevant to discuss as
>poetry. Are you—in other words, the question I have is, are you and

>Creeley and Duncan—I mean is this a new movement? Are you creating,
>are you at all together?
>
>Olson: No, I think that whole "Black Mountain poet" thing is a lot of
>bullshit. I mean, actually, it was created by the editor, the famous
>editor of that anthology for Grove Press, Mr. Allen, where he divided—
>he did a very—but it was a terrible mistake made. He created those
>sections—Black Mountain, San Francisco, Beat, New York, New, Young,
>huh? Oh, I mean, imagine, just for the hear of it, "Young." Hear the
>insult, if you're young. You're suddenly classified into a thing—by
>one of the great editors, the founder of Evergreen Review. And the first
>issues of Evergreen, the first four issues of Evergreen were, really,
>first rate. But he made a big mistake; he made a topological error. I
>mean he had the wrong topology. And he created something which is very
>unhappy. For example, poets who just can't get us straight because they
>think we form a sort of club or a claque or a gang or something. And
>that there was a poetics? Ha ha. Boy, there was no poetic. It was
>Charlie Parker. Literally, it was Charlie Parker. he was the Bob Dylan
>of the fifties.
>
>this is from a transcription of a talk given by olson at beloit college,
>march 26, 1968
>
—
P.O. Box 2584, Providence, RI 02906
Phone: 401 383 0740; Email: Robert_Creeley@brown.edu

· · ·

E-MAIL TO ANGELICA CLARK

Subject: Re: precious breath
From: Robert Creeley
Date: Mon, 17 May 2004:12:46 –0400
To: Angelica Clark <eclark@mindspring.com>

Dear Hearts,
                    All's well blessedly and we did get Tom's NIGHT
SKY which seemed only moments ago, but I realize it's almost weeks. Just the
time here has gone by in the veritable flash, very good-naturedly, be it said.
Anyhow thanks very much for the wry and securing truth of said poems. It's a
horrible time except for the proverbial happy few I guess as ever. Meaning us,

incidentally. I spend 40 hours a day on the computer checking the latest news, all obviously to no avail—like trying to scratch itch I can't reach. Maybe we should all go to NZ.

As to breath, when finally I got catscan and checkup from doctor here, first eyeing of same led to stern statement that he thought I must have lung cancer, but blessedly comparison with older catscans hastily obtained from Buffalo giving a five year evidence showed him naught had really changed, thank god. Leaving, I ventured comment that I could now look forward to dying of old age, but he said, no, everybody dies of something. You can see I've finally come home.

    Love to you both,
    Bob

—

POBox 2584, Providence, RI 02906
Phone: 401 383 0740 * Email: Robert_Creeley@brown.edu

. . .

E-MAIL TO ANSELM BERRIGAN

From: Robert Creeley <creeley@acsu.buffalo.edu>
Date: Thu, 17 Jun 2004 09:21:22 -0400
To: Anselm Berrigan <ab@poetryproject.com>
Subject: Steve Lacy Memorial

Dear Anselm,

    Might there be some chance for a Steve Lacy respect in the fall there—he was so good to poets! Anyhow I am sure Anne Waldman would be in, and me—and we could take it from there. Perhaps Cecil Taylor would show up, just that Steve played with him those many years ago. We are just now back from busman's holiday in France where I happily saw your mother as 'twere in dream passing through Paris—she is sure something, forever!

    Love to you and yours, friend,
    Bob

—

PO Box 384, Waldoboro, ME 04572
Tel: 207 832 6301 * Email: Robert_Creeley@brown.edu

. . .

E-MAIL TO DONALD REVELL

Subj: Re: from Don Revell
Date: 11/6/2004 3:32:33 PM Pacific Standard Time
From: creeley@acsu.buffalo.edu
To: Utopical@aol.com
Sent from the Internet (Details)

Dear Don,

Thanks for the great story! Just back from visit to not one but two family cemeteries. Small world! Anyhow it seemed appropriate and thanks for advice of terrific Rev. K/.

Love to you all,
Bob

OLD STORY

from The Diary of Francis Kilvert

One bell wouldn't ring loud enough.
So they beat the bell to hell, Max,
with an axe, show it who's boss,
boss. Me, I dreamt I dwelt in
someplace one could relax
but I was wrong, wrong, *wrong.*
You got a song, man, sing it.
You got a bell, man, ring it.
[*CP* II, 631]

> Utopical@aol.com wrote:
> dear Bob,

Reading at the bottom of the garden in my post-election funk, I came to this passage in the tender *Diary* of Francis Kilvert—

"One bell did not ring loud enough to satisfy the people so they took an axe up to the bell and beat the bell with the axe till they beat it all to pieces."

I could not resist the urge to share such crazy apt occasion!
love,
Don

—

POBox 2584, Providence, RI 02906
Phone: 401 383 0740 * Email: Robert_Creeley@brown.edu

. . .

From: Robert Creeley <creeley@acsu.buffalo.edu>
Date: Tue, 04 Jan 2005 16:09:09 -0500
To: Anselm Berrigan <ab@poetryproject.com>
Subject: St Michael's

Dear Anselm,
  Just about there—lacking one email address for JOHN GIORNO, somehow lost in the chaos. Do you know it? I've asked other friends if not, so should have things together by tomorrow in any case. Meantime, Pen had been talking to pleasant mail guy at local post office about Ted, and it seems he went to the same school, St Michael's, and particularly knew Ted's younger brother Rickey. Pen was saying they should have a plaque on the house and he was saying, Ted was their most famous person ever. Anyhow today he loaned me his copy of ST MICHAEL'S, 1859–1959, wherein there is a picture of group with your grandmother included and also pleasant reference to "the Berrigan brothers" (second of the two pdf files, last paragraph; the first pdf is the beginning of the article)—see files attached. So you are part of a noble tradition as all always knew. Onward!
  Love to you both,
  Bob
—

PO Box 2584, Providence, RI 02906
Phone: 401 383 0740 * Email: Robert_Creeley@brown.edu

. . .

From: Robert Creeley <creeley@acsu.buffalo.edu>
Date: Wed, 05 Jan 2005 15:15:14 -0500
To: Anselm Berrigan <ab@poetryproject.com>
Subject: Re: St Michael's

Dear Anselm,
  To start with last things first, IF something can be made of the file I'd sent, so much the better—really let them make it material and/or grist for their mill, rather than only dogged repro, etc. It also saves me labor of de-framing said image—which I can still do if needed (and get off as pdf file etc etc).
  Meantime Irene emails to say (what she'd said earlier but not confirmed) that GEORGE LEWIS will be one of the gang that evening, anywhere in that second half, i.e., she writes:

"Is the Program already printed ? Its sounds very nice. There is only one important omission & that is George Lewis, who lives in New-York & teaches at Columbia, got a Mc-Arthur last year & has been very active in Steve's music for many years. So I invited him & he has no problem with Roswell, they are actually good friends & equally giants! Maybe I mentioned this to you, I want to do a few short tunes with him & Depending on Jeremy's disposition (he forgot his music here) something together with George. Also I had the idea that Douglas Dunn could dance with the two trombones. I left a message at his answering machine. So please include George if its not too late. I am also staying at his place: [address and telephone redacted]. I'll be there the 18th."

So now you know everything. As to "program," I had not thought there'd be one specific other than possible 'scoresheet' for list of people, etc. Anyhow you're the boss for whatever.

As to piano, now that Dan Tepfer cannot be there, I don't know if anyone thinks to use it—viz it looks like trombones are it, plus bass and soprano sax. I'll check again with Irene just to make sure she doesn't have someone popping up to play same.

One day you are again in Providence, you should meet the genial fellow in the post office for sense of St Michael's and all. He was particular friend of Ted's younger brother, his classmate. Anyhow he's a bright good-natured man and characteristically has some great jazz cd playing on a boombox he keeps just beside him back of the counter.

Then today happily I got proofs of the terrific COLLECTED from UC/Press, so as to write blurb for same—which will be my honor. It really is wonderful to see it all of a piece.

Love to you both,
Bob

P.S. Thanks very much for John G/s email address. That's it.

—

PO Box 2584, Providence, RI 02906
Phone: 401 383 0740 * Email: Robert_Creeley@brown.edu

. . .

E-MAIL TO ANSELM BERRIGAN

From: Robert Creeley <creeley@acsu.buffalo.edu>
Date: Thu, 06 Jan 2005 19:47:42 -0500
To: Anselm Berrigan <ab@poetryproject.com>
Subject: Re: We're good

Dear Anselm,

God bless you, as one says in Providence—and Gary, the fellow in the post-office, was pleased you had seen the photo of Ted's mother and all and says he'd like to show you around when you are able to visit and all. Ted's Collected is just glorious—and the work you all put in on it makes it absolutely shine. Wow!

Late breaking news is that Irene has brought a sculptor into the action on the 19th (who is also putting her up there)—I'll hope to get spelling of his name etc shortly, but this can identify him for the moment. Thanks!!

Love to you both,

Bob

—

PO Box 2584, Providence, RI 02906
Phone: 401 383 0740 * Email: Robert_Creeley@brown.edu

. . .

E-MAIL TO LISA JARNOT

Date: January 16, 2005 3:59:53 PM EST (CA)
To: lisajarnot <jarnot@earthlink.net>
Subject: Re: greetings

Dear Lisa,

I'm obsessed with Whittier's "Snowbound" at the moment, up here in aerie attic looking out small window to edge of harbor over Foxpoint roofs—feels much like Gloucester, Mass. There's a storm headed this way, so terrific memories of West Acton childhood come back—Whittier's Haverhill cannot be more than a short distance east (35.6 miles I see from useful Yahoo)—anyhow for the season:

http://www.darsie.net/library/whittier_snowbound.html

Ah nostalgia . . . I see Hamburg is staying consistent:

Tonight Tomorrow Tomorrow night
14°F
Precip: 80%

Snow likely. Low 14F. Winds NNW at 15 to 25 mph. Chance of snow 80%. 2 to 4 inches of snow expected . . .

St Agnes Eve time. Lovely to think of you in the British Museum. As you can, let me know what you think of Kitaj's wall-hanging:

"Visually dominating Wilson's vast lobby is a tapestry woven from one of R. B. Kitaj's seminal images, the 1970s landscape If Not, Not. This strange picture, at once jumbled and ethereal, was inspired by both T. S. Eliot's The Wasteland and the Holocaust, a typical Kitaj-conflation. "These fragments have I shored against my ruin," Eliot wrote in his poem. As we all know, the shoring up of fragments of literary and historical reference in fact proved Kitaj's ruin at the hand of London's inhospitable press. In anger and bitterness, longtime London-based expatriate Kitaj has since decamped to Los Angeles.

"Kitaj's wall hanging is the largest single loom tapestry to be woven this century, and required 7,000 hours of work. Enormous fan that I am of the artist and this particular painting (which hangs in the Scottish National Gallery of Modern Art in Edinburgh, where the tapestry was made), I have to say that it sorely loses in translation—mainly because the tonal gradations are jagged— although I stand by it as the perfect image for a magnificent setting."

Kitaj in the British Library
It's lovely to think of you there—and happy!
Love to you both,
Bob

—

PO Box 2584, Providence, RI 02906
Phone: 401 383 0740 * Email: Robert_Creeley@brown.edu

. . .

E-MAIL TO MICHAEL KELLEHER

From: "Creeley, Robert" <Robert_Creeley@brown.edu>
Date: March 7, 2005 11:44:29 AM EST
To: "Michael Kelleher" <michaelkelleher@adelphia.net>
Subject: RE: Hello &

Dear Mike,
    While doing a workshop in Wilmington, NC mid-February, I collapsed for want of oxygen getting into my blood, fact of pulmonary fibrosis, a longtime condition, together with secondary bacterial infection that was too much to handle—anyhow I am now on permanent oxygen feed and am getting used to the logistics. So far, simple enough—though travel by plane with the necessary provision gets more complicated, etc. Thankfully this place is ideal for sorting

it all out—very easy house and no pressure to do more than enjoy the very glorious physical scene. A couple of days ago we drove down to the border (the Rio Grande) with Mexico, some sixty miles distant—would that the world were all so specific!

    Best as ever,
    Bob

—

PO Box 816, Marfa, TX 79843–0816
Cell: 716 435 1460 * Email Robert_Creeley@brown.edu

The notes that follow are not exhaustive. They are designed to clarify some of the count-less obscurities that arise across these six decades of correspondence. We tend to privi-lege allusions that cannot be readily identified with an Internet search engine: small press ephemera (the print archive that remains undigitized because of post-1923 copyright laws), proper names (occasionally, the crowding of Jacks and Bobs can be difficult to keep straight), and Creeley's idiosyncratic shorthand (e.g., "Chas" refers to Charles Olson).

For works by Creeley, we generally cite the first periodical or book publication, except when he circulates a draft that remains unpublished at the time of the letter. Bracketed citations refer to later collected editions or archived papers according to the abbrevia-tions below.

The compilation of these notes was aided by Mary Novik's *Robert Creeley: An Inven-tory, 1945–1970* (Kent State University Press/McGill-Queen's University Press, 1973) and *In Company: Robert Creeley's Collaborations,* ed. Amy Cappellazzo and Elizabeth Licata (Castellani Art Museum/Weatherspoon Art Gallery, 1999).

CP I	*The Collected Poems of Robert Creeley, 1945–1975* (University of California Press, 1982)
CP II	*The Collected Poems of Robert Creeley, 1975–2005* (University of California Press, 2006)
CE	*The Collected Essays of Robert Creeley* (University of California Press, 1989)
Stanford M0662	Department of Special Collections, Stanford University Libraries, Stanford, California. Refers to the Robert Creeley Papers (M0662), unless otherwise indicated.
GB	*Charles Olson and Robert Creeley: The Complete Correspondence,* ed. George F. Butterick (vols. 1–8) and Richard Blevins (vols. 9–10) (Black Sparrow Press, 1980–96)

LETTER TO GENEVIEVE AND HELEN CREELEY 5/10/45: "Furioso": Poetry magazine from New Haven (1939–43 and 1946–53). Genevieve is RC's mother, and Helen, his sister.

LETTER TO BOB LEED 6/21/48: "the last letter before I see you": Jacob "Bob" Leed, college friend and collaborator on RC's planned little magazine the *Lititz Review*. See Jacob Leed, "Robert Creeley and *The Lititz Review*: A Recollection with Letters," *Journal of Modern Literature* 5, no. 2 (April 1976): 243–59.

"I can't tell you how many fights (actual) I've had with Ann": RC's first wife, Ann MacKinnon.

"reading several other books at the same time": Books cited include Susanne K. Langer's *Philosophy in a New Key* (Harvard University Press, 1942), Jean-Paul Sartre's *The Psychology of the Imagination* (Philosophical Library, 1948), William Carlos Williams's *Paterson, Book Two* (New Directions, 1948), Richard Wilbur's *The Beautiful Changes and Other Poems* (Harcourt, Brace, 1947), *T. S. Eliot: A Selected Critique*, ed. Leonard Unger (Rinehart, 1948), and André Gide, *Journals of André Gide*, vol. 2: *1914–1927* (Knopf, 1948).

LETTER TO BOB LEED [CA. AUGUST 1948]: "a brief, subversive member of the Advocate": Campus literary magazine the *Harvard Advocate*. RC also served on the editorial staff of the *Wake* (also known as the *Harvard Wake*) for a special issue on e. e. cummings; see *Wake* 5 (Spring 1946).

"that New Directions selection": Herman Melville, *Selected Poems*, ed. F. O. Matthiessen (New Directions, 1944).

"I would strongly suggest that you read this article": Hannah Arendt, "The Concentration Camps," *Partisan Review* 15, no. 6 (July 1948): 743–63.

"if you'll read Sorokin": Pitirim Sorokin, the Russian-American founder of Harvard's Sociology Department.

LETTER TO WILLIAM CARLOS WILLIAMS 2/11/50: "I'd like to ask you for your help with respect to a magazine": the *Lititz Review*, to be edited by RC and printed by Jacob Leed.

LETTER TO WILLIAM CARLOS WILLIAMS 2/27/50: "Very, very glad to have your letter": In response to a letter from Williams, dated 2/23/50, that ends, "I'm pretty well sunk with work, medical and literary, but I hope I'll never be so sunk that I can't help a guy with a piece of some sort if I think he's got the stuff. But I'm absolutely washed up for time right now." [Stanford M0662].

"Prof. Levin's progress": Harry Levin, Harvard professor and literary critic.

"PR": *Partisan Review*, dismissed by Williams in his letter, "has chronic constipation and no direction other than rearward view."

LETTER TO LARRY EIGNER [CA. FEBRUARY 1950]: "Horace Gregory": Poet, translator, and critic.

"One had a lovely face": W. B. Yeats, "Memory," *The Wild Swans at Coole*, 1919.

"About Basic": Basic English, a simplified system of writing with an English vocabulary of 850 words, based on various rules governing word order. Two main proponents of Basic English were C. K. Ogden (1889–1957) and I. A. Richards (1893–1979). Cf. Richards's *Basic English and Its Uses* (W. W. Norton, 1943). RC and Leed discussed asking contributors of prose essays to the *Lititz Review* to write them in Basic English.

"When I read on Cid's program": Cid Corman's radio show *This Is Poetry*, on WMEX in Boston.

"letter from William Carlos Williams": Williams's letter to RC, 2/23/50.

LETTER TO EZRA POUND 4/14/50: "a letter from Mr. Horton": T. D. Horton letter dated "28 Marck [sic] 1950" [Stanford M0662].

"a confusion about Del Mar": Alexander del Mar, late nineteenth-century monetary historian. Horton suggests in a letter, 5/2/50, that RC change the name of the *Lititz Review* to the *Del Mar Quarterly*.

"his note on Eliot": Williams, "With Forced Fingers Rude," *Four Pages* 2 (February 1948): 1–4.

"Simpson": Dallam Simpson, Pound affiliate, editor of *Four Pages,* and founder of Cleaners Press. See Alexander Del Mar, *A History of Monetary Crimes* (Cleaners Press, 1951).

LETTER TO WILLIAM CARLOS WILLIAMS 4/15/50: "your letter": letter from Williams, dated 4/13/50.

"what makes false history": See Pound's letter to RC, dated 4/24/50: "It is really quite simple. 2 questions : 1. Do you resent the falsification of history? 2. Do you want any contributors who do NOT resent the falsification of history?" [Stanford M0662].

"your own comment": Williams, "Letter to an Australian Editor," *Briarcliff Quarterly* 3, no. 2 (October 1946): 204–9.

LETTER TO CID CORMAN [4/23/50]: "CRISIS & GRYPHON": *Gryphon* magazine, edited by Richard Rubenstein from San Francisco and later St. Louis. See RC, "Poem for Bob Leed," *Gryphon* 2 (Fall 1950): 18. *The Crisis,* the political and literary journal of the NAACP founded by W. E. B. Du Bois in 1910. Du Bois was replaced by Roy Wilkins in 1934.

"[William] Phillips & [Philip] Rahv": editors of the *Partisan Review.*

"Ransom's method": Refers to the *Kenyon Review* 7, no. 1 (Winter 1945): John Crowe Ransom, "The Severity of Mr. Savage" (114–17); and D. S. Savage, "The Aestheticism of W. B. Yeats" (118–34).

"Emerson": Richard W. Emerson, editor of *Golden Goose* magazine (Columbus, OH, 1948–49, 1951–54).

LETTER TO WILLIAM CARLOS WILLIAMS 4/24/50: "Thanks for the push with Olson": Williams had recommended that Olson contact RC.

"what I find in the copy of X&Y": Charles Olson, *Y&X* (Black Sun Press, 1949).

"T. D. Horton . . . Donald Paquette": Poets recommended to RC by Pound.

LETTER TO CHARLES OLSON 4/24/50: "Olsen": In this first extant letter by RC to Olson, he misspells Olson's last name.

"So will print": RC refers to Olson's poems submitted for the *Lititz Review,* including "The Morning News," *Origin* 10 (Summer 1953): 122–28; and "Move Over," *Golden Goose* 3, no. 1 (1951): 41.

LETTER TO CHARLES OLSON 4/28/50: "Crews": Judson Crews, poet and owner of Motive Bookshop (Texas).

"For the note": Olson, "La Préface," "The Green Man," and "The Moebius Strip," from Charles Olson, *Y&X,* drawings by Carrado Cagli (Black Sun Press, 1948).

"Thinking of Stevens": Wallace Stevens, "The State of American Writing, 1948: A Symposium," *Partisan Review* 15, no. 8 (August 1948): 885. Stevens's response is to a question that begins, "It is the general opinion that, unlike the twenties, this is not a period of experiment in language and form. If that is true, what significance can be attached to that fact?"

LETTER TO CHARLES OLSON 6/5/50: "Blood from a stone": Likely refers to payment for publication of RC's story "The Unsuccessful Husband," *Kenyon Review* 13, no. 1 (Winter 1951): 64–71.

"*I see I misread you*": According to George Butterick, the allusion is to a lost letter from Olson. [GB, vol. 1, n81].

"that form is never more than an <u>extension</u> of content": This is the first occurrence of the now famous formulation that Olson makes use of in his "Projective Verse" essay.

"I had read once with delight": Likely refers to Remy de Gourmont, *The Natural Philosophy of Love*, trans. with postscript by Ezra Pound (Boni and Liveright, 1922).

"Opener in PG's": Paul Goodman, *The Dead of Spring* (Libertarian Press, 1950), 11.

"Vol. 2—Del Mar": See letter to Ezra Pound 4/14/50.

"Was thinking if, perhaps": According to George Butterick, the allusion is to Australian novelist Jakob Wasserman's *The World's Illusion* (1920). [GB, vol. 1, n86].

"to what the Dr. called": William Carlos Williams, *Paterson, Book One* (New Directions, 1946), n.p.

"Bud had written": RC's college friend Buddy (Donald) Berlin. He served with RC on the editorial board for the e. e. cummings issue of *Wake* 5 (Spring 1946). See also letter to Bob Leed [ca. August 1948] and letter to Charles Olson 10/18/50.

"comment abt the possible 'reason'": Ezra Pound, "Papyrus," from *Personae: The Collected Poems of Ezra Pound* (New Directions, 1926), 112.

"yes: abt Francis Thompson": Francis J. Thompson, "Courageous, Not Outrageous," review of *New Directions in Prose and Poetry* 11 (1949), in *Hopkins Review* 3, no. 4 (Summer 1950): 42–44.

LETTER TO DOROTHY POUND 6/15/50: "Dear Mrs. Pound": A condition of Pound's confinement at St. Elizabeth's Hospital (DC) was that he was not to engage in outside correspondence. See RC, "A Note followed by a Selection of Letters from Ezra Pound," *Agenda* 4, no. 2 (October–November, 1965): 11–21.

"one Uncle Dudley": Long-time editorial pseudonym at the *Boston Globe*.

LETTER TO CHARLES OLSON 6/21/50: "Never a man worked more deliberately": See André Gide, *The Counterfeiters* (Knopf, 1927); and the "Isabel" section of André Gide, *Two Symphonies* (Knopf, 1931).

"about conte & possible: novel": *Conte,* from the Old French *conter,* to relate, recount. Modern usage generally refers to a short story or novella.

LETTER TO CHARLES OLSON [10/18/50]: "Yr letters here": Butterick reports that Olson's letters to RC from 7/31/50 until the end of the year were lost in RC's move to France. [GB, vol. 1, xii].

"Or 1/ we are editors with him": RC and Olson are thanked for "advice" in a prefatory note to *Origin* 1 (Spring 1951), but Cid Corman is identified as the sole editor.

"tells me Kitasono is old hash": Katue (Katsue) Kitasono edited *Vou* magazine (Japan). RC publications in the magazine include "Divisions" (poem), *Vou* 37 (1953): 12; "The Trap" (poem), *Vou* 40 (March 1954): 22; and "Note on Poetry" (prose), *Vou* 44 (November 1954): 16. Kitasono designed the covers of *Black Mountain Review* 1–4.

"Now the thing I wd figure, to, say, let GATE & CENTER stand as prose": Charles Olson, "The Gate & The Center," *Origin* 1 (Spring 1951): 35–41.

"I think such a section, the letters": Charles Olson, "Letters to Vincent Ferrini," *Origin* 1 (Spring 1951): 5–6, 42, 53–54, 61.

"Emerson, he'd sent on the book": Richard Emerson, *The Greengrocer's Son* (Alan Swallow, 1950).

"What I flopped trying to write": RC's short story "Mr. Blue" was published the following year. See letter to Denise Levertov and Mitch Goodman 4/18/51 and letter to William Carlos Williams 9/27/51.

LETTER TO CHARLES OLSON [11/9/50]: "Lieber Herr Olson: zuerst mochte ich … ": George Butterick appends RC's translation of letter by German poet and editor Rainer Gerhardt, the beginning of which reads, "First I'd like to thank you for yr fine letter, which we were glad to get." [GB, vol. 4, 13].

"he takes it back wall is Perse/front Pound": Saint-John Perse (1887–1975), winner of Nobel Prize in 1960.

"On Kitasono": Katue Kitasono. See letter to Charles Olson 10/18/50.

LETTER TO PAUL BLACKBURN [11/29/50]: "Very good to have yr letter": There are no extant letters from Paul Blackburn before June 17, 1951.

"G. S. Fraser in opening": G. S. Fraser, "Mannerist Poem," *Nine* 2, no. 2 (January 1950): 30–32.

"The Olson poem": Charles Olson, "In Cold Hell, In Thicket," *Golden Goose* 3, no. 1 (1951): 34–40. In a letter dated 9/25/50, RC had written, "Dear Blackburn, Hate to have rushed you, or whatever. Just got a letter from Olson, that Emerson lost revised copy of the IN COLD HELL, etc. and O/ has none, so you, as it happens have the only one, which was mine. Anyhow, wd be very grateful if you'd rush it to: Emerson, the address given on the telegram. … "

LETTER TO CHARLES OLSON [12/7/50]: "a note he had written on Ez": William Carlos Williams, "Letter to an Australian Editor," *Briarcliffe Quarterly* 11 (October 1946): 205–8.

"Bill/ in Rasles gig": William Carlos Williams, "Père Sebastian Rasles," from *In the American Grain* (Albert & Charles Boni, 1925): 105–29.

"that biz in the Plumed Serpent": D. H. Lawrence, *The Plumed Serpent (Quetzalcoatl)* (Martin Secker, 1926).

LETTER TO MITCH GOODMAN [1951]: "To say a bit abt the Olson biz": See Olson, "Introduction to Robert Creeley," *New Directions Annual* 13 (1951): 92–93.

"PR": *Partisan Review.*

"I don't have a copy of": Refers to William Carlos Williams's *White Mule* (New Directions, 1937); *In the American Grain* (Albert & Charles Boni, 1925); and *A Dream of Love* (New Directions, 1948).

"A drab America, with or without": Uncollected poem by Larry Eigner.

LETTER TO DENISE LEVERTOV AND MITCH GOODMAN 4/18/51: "Perched on a bristly grass": Uncollected Levertov poem. [Denise Levertov Papers, Stanford M0601, series 2, box 1, folder 65].

"one with the door, & fire": Unidentified poem.

"another issue of that there WINDOW": London poetry magazine (1950–56), edited by John Sankey. Published RC and Olson in the third issue (poems that had previously appeared in U.S. magazines) and Martin Seymour-Smith's "La Foradada" and "All Devils Fading" in *The Window* 4 (February 1952): 2–4.

"2nd issue of GOAD": See letter to Horace Schwartz [1951] below.

"Rexroth's damn long thing": Kenneth Rexroth, "The Dragon and the Unicorn, part II," *New Directions Annual* 13 (1951): 370–453. Olson's "Introduction to Robert Creeley" and RC's "Mr. Blue and Other Stories" appear in the same issue (92–93, 94–116).

"Read Kenner's damn bk/": Hugh Kenner, *The Poetry of Ezra Pound* (New Directions, 1951).

"Henry Green": British-born writer who wrote his many novels in French.

LETTER TO DENISE LEVERTOV 4/22/51: "Then see it! in distressing": "The Last Turn," from William Carlos Williams, *The Collected Later Poems of William Carlos Williams* (New Directions, 1950), 44.

"The blossoms of the apricot": Ezra Pound, "Canto XIII," from *The Cantos of Ezra Pound* (New Directions, 1948), 60.

"Will bring the Olson bklet": Charles Olson, *Y&X*, drawings by Carrado Cagli (Black Sun, 1948).

"Also, a copy of ORIGIN": Cid Corman's magazine *Origin* 1 (Spring 1951), featuring poems by Olson and including RC's "Hart Crane" (57).

"Figure Bereaved": Levertov, "The Bereaved," first published in *Origin* 2 (Summer 1951): 83.

LETTER TO PAUL BLACKBURN 5/23/51: "the Levy": Standard reference work, *Dictionnaire de Provençal*. Blackburn was already well into his lifelong project of translating the Old Provençal poets.

"the Sordello edition": Thirteenth-century Provençal poet.

"G/s 1st issue": Rainer M. Gerhardt's magazine *Fragmente* no. 1 (1951).

"The SUMMER one: very cool": Blackburn's poem, "Death and the Summer Woman" was published in the RC issue of *Origin* 2 (Summer 1951): 81. It was later collected in Blackburn's *The Dissolving Fabric* (Divers Press, 1953), n.p.

LETTER TO WILLIAM CARLOS WILLIAMS 6/29/51: "news from Laughlin": James Laughlin, publisher of New Directions books and the New Directions Annual. See also note for Letter to Denise Levertov and Mitch Goodman 4/18/51.

LETTER TO WILLIAM CARLOS WILLIAMS 8/1/51: "A copy of PATERSON IV": William Carlos Williams, *Paterson, Book Four* (New Directions, 1951).

"The sea part, the opening of 'III'": The first section of *Paterson* (Book Four) is titled "The Run to the Sea." The third section begins, "Haven't you forgot your virgin purpose,/ the language?"

LETTER TO WILLIAM CARLOS WILLIAMS 9/27/51: "comments on the work in ORIGIN": Williams in his letter of 9/8/51 had written, "I see—saw—your stuff in Kirgo's—no—ORIGIN, Summer issue and liked it, especially the prose. Keep up the good work." [Stanford M0662]. See the special issue on RC in *Origin* 2 (Summer 1951); RC's "prose" includes stories ("In the Summer," "3 Fate Tales," and "Mr. Blue"), an essay ("Notes for a New Prose"), and excerpts from four letters to Cid Corman.

LETTER TO DENISE LEVERTOV 10/3/51: "Aldington": Richard Aldington (1892–1962), modernist poet affiliated with Imagism.

"Ashley": Ashley Bryan, painter. Designed cover of *Origin* 5 (Spring 1952).

"hate to move Dave again": RC's son David Creeley (b. 1947).

"Emerson writes he could put out a small booklet of my poems": Emerson published RC's *Le Fou* (Golden Goose Press, 1952).

"Perched on bristly grass, a shaved steep slope": Unpublished Levertov poem. [Denise Levertov Papers, Stanford M0601, series 2, box 1, folder 65.]

"Check Olson's comments on description in PNY piece": Charles Olson's manifesto "Projective Verse," published originally as "Projective Verse vs. The Non-Projective," *Poetry New York* 3 (1950): 13–22.

LETTER TO MITCH GOODMAN 10/3/51: "Getting the letter off to Denny": See letter to Levertov 10/3/51.

"Buddy": Buddy (Donald) Berlin. See letter to Olson 6/5/50.

"Olson's laws, etc. . . . those three main dicta . . . ": This likely refers to section I of Olson's "Projective Verse." The "laws" would be "(1) *kinetics* . . . A poem is energy trans-ferred from where the poet got it (he will have some several causations), by way of the poem itself to, all the way over to, the reader." "(2) is the *principle*, i.e. . . . the reason why a projective poem can come into being. It is this: FORM IS NEVER MORE THAN AN EXTENSION OF CONTENT. (Or so it got phrased by one, R. Creeley. . . .)" "(3) the *process* of the thing . . . ONE PERCEPTION MUST IMMEDIATELY AND DIRECTLY LEAD TO A FURTHER PERCEPTION."

LETTER TO HORACE SCHWARTZ [LATE 1951]: "Dear Schwartz": First published as "Letter from Robert Creeley," *Goad* 2 (Winter 1951–52): 16–19. Republished as "A Letter to the Editor of *Goad*," in RC, *A Quick Graph*, ed. Donald Allen (Four Seasons, 1970), 92–94. RC responds to comments on Pound in Horace Schwartz, "A Note on the Famous Con-troversy," *Goad* 1 (Summer 1951): 16. See also the follow-up response to RC by Leslie Woolf Hedley, "Letter to the Editor," *Goad* 3 (Summer 1952): 7–9.

"There died a myriad . . . ": Ezra Pound, from *Hugh Selwyn Mauberly* (Ovid Press, 1920).

LETTER TO LARRY EIGNER [UNDATED, 1951]: "I have travelled much in Concord": Thoreau, *Walden*. The original line reads, "I have travelled a good deal in Concord."

"copy of POETRY NY": See Olson, "Projective Verse."

LETTER TO RENÉ LAUBIÈS [5/25/1952]: "in the note": RC's note on Laubiès, "Divers Sentiments," for the Galerie Fachetti in 1953 or 1954. [*CE*, 377–78].

"character of the one for 3rd part": Refers to RC stories published in *The Gold Diggers* (Divers Press, 1954), including "3 Fate Tales" (39–52). "In the Summer" (77–88) and "The Party" (53–62) are two other stories from the same collection.

"record of Casals": Refers to Catalonian cellist Pablo Casals (1876–1973).

LETTER TO PAUL BLACKBURN 6/22/52: "Yours in, and that poem is real, real cool": Blackburn's letter to RC, dated 6/17/52, no longer includes the poem.

"our boy SS/": Martin Seymour-Smith, English writer living on Majorca.

"HUDSON biz": See C.R. Busby and Paul Blackburn, "Communications," *Hudson Review* 5, no. 2 (Summer 1952): 317–20. Busby criticizes Blackburn's Provençal transla-tions in the prior issue as "none too accurate and dubiously felicitous." In a long response, Blackburn defends his choices for "bringing these over into a modern English poem."

"Lash": Kenneth Lash, editor of the *New Mexico Quarterly*.

"I forgot to say G/ is still hunting down that Levy": Rainer Gerhardt; see letter to Paul Blackburn 5/23/51.

"The church is a bizness, and the rich . . . ": Published in RC, "After Lorca," *Goad* 3 (Summer 1952): 22. Republished in RC, *The Kind of Act Of* (Divers Press, 1953): n.p. [*CP* I, 121].

"Pierre Boulez, on 'series'": Quoted in Olson letter to Creeley, dated 6/15/1952. [GB, vol. 10, 153].

"article by Elath?": M. Elath, "In Another Direction: Commentary and Review of Three Anthologies," *Intro* 1, nos. 3–4 (1951): 112–36. A selection of William Hull's poems appears in the next issue.

"THE DRUMS": RC, "The Drums," *Golden Goose* 4, no. 5 (October 1952): 23. Published also in *Le Fou*. [*CP* I, 29].

"E/ asked for a photograph, and fuck that, so I twisted my boy Ashley's arm": Refers to Emerson's plan to publish RC's *Le Fou*. Ashley Bryan's ink portrait of RC appears on the title page. See letter to Denise Levertov 10/3/51.

"THE RHYME": RC, "The Rhyme," *Golden Goose* 4, no. 5 (October 1952): 25. Published also in *Le Fou*. [*CP* I, 117].

LETTER TO WILLIAM CARLOS WILLIAMS 6/27/52: "the 2nd issue of FRAGMENTE": RC appears in *Fragmente* 2 (1952) with two prose selections translated by Gerhardt: "Die Geisterrunde" (40–41) and "Der Liebhaber" (54–60). The issue also includes Williams's "Die Rote Kirche" (trans. Gerhardt, 60–64).

"an article by M. Elath": See letter to Paul Blackburn, 6/22/52.

LETTER TO CHARLES OLSON 7/15/52: "Poem is very cool": Olson's "Idle Idyll," unpublished at the time. Collected in *A Nation of Nothing But Poetry: Supplementary Poems*, ed. George Butterick (Black Sparrow, 1989): 91–92.

"yesterday walking along the Cour Mirabeau": Main avenue of Aix-en-Provence.

LETTER TO ROBERT DUNCAN 7/19/52: "an Englishman": Martin Seymour-Smith, writer and editor. He and RC became friends when they both lived on Majorca.

"I know your work from . . . ": *Origin* 6 (summer 1952) is a special issue on Duncan and Williams. Duncan poems include "Africa Revisited" (80–86) and "Song of the Border-guard" (122–23).

LETTER TO PAUL BLACKBURN 1/9/53: "We got your Xmas card ok": Card postmarked 12/22/52.

"the cover for your book": Blackburn, *Proensa: From the Provençal of Guillem de Peitau, Arnaut de Marueill, Raimbautz de Vaqueiras, Sordello, Bernart de Ventadorn, Peire Vidal, Bertran de Born* (Divers Press, 1953).

"Olson's book": Designed by RC's *Divers Press*, published as *In Cold Hell, In Thicket* (Origin, 1953).

"A-POSY, FOR RAINER GERHARDT, [etc.]": Neither of these poems appears in the book.

"THE CROW": RC, "The Crow," *Origin* 9 (Spring 1953): 33. Republished in RC, *The Kind of Act Of.* [*CP* I, 124].

LETTER TO CHARLES OLSON 4/8/53: "Re the poem to hand": Charles Olson, "The

Mast." First published in Olson, *The Collected Poems of Charles Olson,* ed. George Butterick (University of California Press, 1987): 286–89.

"Liquor and love": William Carlos Williams, "The World Narrowed to a Point," *The Wedge* (Cummington Press, 1944), 37.

"If I / could count the silence": Williams, "Song," *The Pink Church* (Golden Goose Press, 1949), n.p.

"And the too strong grasping of it": From Charles Olson, "The Kingfishers," *In Cold Hell, In Thicket* (Origin, 1953), which RC designed earlier in the year.

LETTER TO CHARLES OLSON 7/19/53: "Your two damn beautiful letters": Two very long Olson letters to RC dated 7/14/53 and 7/17/53.

" . . . The unsure // egoist is not": Published in RC, "The Immoral Proposition," *Origin* 10 (Summer 1953): 80. Republished in RC, *The Immoral Proposition* (Jonathan Williams/ Jargon, 1953). [*CP* I, 125]. See also letter to Paul Blackburn 10/15/53.

LETTER TO PAUL BLACKBURN 9/17/53: "Don't flip re book shipment": RC published Blackburn's *Proensa* in June 1953.

"re yr having enough for a book": Likely refers to Blackburn's *The Dissolving Fabric* (Divers Press, 1955).

LETTER TO JONATHAN WILLIAMS 9/23/53: "about the photographs": Likely the photographs taken in Majorca by Jonathan Williams; see the cover of this collection, as well as the *Collected Poems of Robert Creeley: 1945–1975* (University of California Press, 2006).

LETTER TO PAUL BLACKBURN 10/15/53: "those two poems you note": One poem is RC, "The Drums" (see letter to Paul Blackburn 6/22/52). The second is RC, "The Pedigree," *Golden Goose* 4, no. 6 (September 1953): 45. Republished in *The Kind of Act Of.* [*CP* I, 51].

"this coming booklet with Laubiès": RC, *The Immoral Proposition* (Jonathan Williams/ Jargon, 1953) with drawings by René Laubiès. Published in Karlsruhe-Durlach, Germany.

"THE OPERATION": RC, "The Operation," *Origin* 10 (Summer 1953): 79. Republished in *The Immoral Proposition.* [*CP* I, 128].

"THE RIDDLE": RC, "The Riddle," *Golden Goose* 4, no. 5 (October 1952): 27. Published also in *Le Fou.* [*CP* I, 115].

"whether or not Trocchi will print it": RC was on the editorial board for the final issue of Alexander Trocchi's magazine *Merlin* 2, no. 4 (Spring 1955). A note in the magazine announces plans to publish fiction by RC in a forthcoming issue.

LETTER TO DENISE LEVERTOV 2/3/54: "L/s (in Paris) inks goof me very much": René Laubiès collaborated with RC on *The Immoral Proposition* (Jonathan Williams/Jargon, 1953); Laubiès's "Eight Reproductions" appeared in *Black Mountain Review* 1, no. 1 (Spring 1954): 25–32.

"Mag// ok thank god. #1 is now in proof . . . ": *Black Mountain Review* 1, no. 1 (Spring 1954).

"Very good you liked the poem—thanks for taking it.": See RC's "The Warning" in *Origin* 13 (Summer 1954): 9. Levertov was guest editor for the issue.

LETTER TO WILLIAM CARLOS WILLIAMS 6/6/54: "copy of the magazine" : First issue of the *Black Mountain Review.*

LETTER TO KENNETH REXROTH 8/14/54: "the review on Roethke plus the Patchen review": Martin Seymour-Smith's "Where Is Mr. Roethke?" and RC's review of Kenneth

Patchen's *Fables and Other Little Tales* in *Black Mountain Review* 1, no. 1 (Spring 1954): 40–46, 63–64.

LETTER TO KENNETH REXROTH 8/19/54: "letter of yesterday can serve": In a letter to Rexroth dated 8/18/54, RC defended the Patchen and Roethke reviews against Rexroth's charge that they amounted to personal attacks: "I don't think the review is unfair. Its comment attacks Roethke and his reviews equally, and I think the responsibility is a joint one. Poems are given and commented on, no matter how 'truculently', and to attack the reviewer means to attack his comments on these poems—in short, either to defend the poems with specific criticism of one's own, or to abridge the readings offered or to do at least something of this kind. Because the review does deal with specific poems, and with various allegations concerning them and others, I don't see how one can avoid dealing with said poems. Which is the obvious point, at least. That Roethke is a 'sick' man does not seem to me a defense of these poems, nor a defense of the positions that they should not be so written about. Because how can it be? To say that is to say equally that Pound's Pisan Cantos are not to be so talked about, since they were written by a certified 'sick' man. In any case, much more interesting is the use to which this 'sickness' can be put, both by Roethke (who in this sense, personally, can certainly be excused as a man if not as a poet) and the criticism which sustains the reputation of his work. And that is what was, I believe, attacked, literally attacked."

LETTER TO WILLIAM CARLOS WILLIAMS 8/21/54: "about Gerhardt": Rainer Gerhardt's suicide.

"of the stories": RC, *The Gold Diggers* (Divers Press, 1954).

"also very good to hear what you say of Olson's": Charles Olson, *The Maximus Poems: 1–10* (Jonathan Williams, 1953). W. C. Williams received a copy of Olson's book from Jonathan Williams, along with a request to write a review of it, as he mentions in his letter of 8/9/54. He says of the book, "It's by far his best work" [Stanford Mo662].

"I'm fighting after a fashion": See letters to Rexroth, dated 8/14/54 and 8/19/54.

LETTER TO LOUIS ZUKOFSKY 11/10/54: "I had just seen your address": Zukofsky's name is spelled "Zukowsky" in the "Supplementary Distribution List" of *The Pound Newsletter* 4 (October 1954): 18. RC spells it "Zukovsky" in this letter.

"I have known your work from": See Zukofsky poems, including "Poem Beginning 'The'" and excerpts from *"A,"* in *Active Anthology,* ed. Ezra Pound (Faber and Faber, 1933): 111–53. *An "Objectivists" Anthology,* ed. Louis Zukofsky (To Publishers, 1932).

LETTER TO WILLIAM CARLOS WILLIAMS 11/25/54: "Many thanks for your letter about Kitasono's book": Katue Kitasono, *Black Rain: Poems & Drawings* (Divers Press, 1954). Williams had written RC a letter, 11/8/54, saying: "Of the three small books you have sent me recently the one by Katue Kitasono pleased me best. It came at a moment when I was low and lifted my despair as a light shining under clouds." [Stanford Mo662]. See also letter to Charles Olson 10/18/50.

"a copy of your Selected Essays": William Carlos Williams, *Selected Essays of William Carlos Williams* (Random House, 1954). RC wrote a review of this work, criticizing, as he does here, what he views as significant omissions. See *Black Mountain Review* 1, no. 4 (Winter 1954): 53–58.

LETTER TO WILLIAM CARLOS WILLIAMS 12/6/54: "Many thanks for your letter":

Williams had written RC a very humble letter, 12/6/54, that ends: "All I can ask of you is to dwell on what you find good in the book and to attack mercilessly its and my faults." [Stanford M0662].

LETTER TO CID CORMAN 12/24/54: "The pigeon book": H. P. Macklin, *A Handbook of Fancy Pigeons*, vol. 1 (Divers Press, 1954).

"As to the magazine": Page 2 of this letter is typed on *Black Mountain Review* stationery.

"I also hope to have some material on both dance & music": Katherine Litz (1912–78), dancer, teacher and choreographer. David Tudor (1926–96), pianist, and composer—longtime associate of John Cage. Tudor's was the first performance of Cage's *4'33"*.

LETTER TO WILLIAM CARLOS WILLIAMS 1/26/55: "Olson just sent a letter": This letter is unfortunately missing from the archive.

LETTER TO ALEXANDER TROCCHI 4/23/55: "the softest rejection I ever got": Trocchi edited a Paris-based literary magazine, *Merlin*.

"in the last ND Annual": Louis Zukofsky, "Bottom: Essay on Shakespeare," *New Directions in Prose & Poetry* 14 (1953): 288–307.

"snitch one of those Beckett stories": Trocchi published several Samuel Beckett pieces, including "The End" in *Merlin* 2, no. 3 (Summer–Autumn 1954): 144–58. Beckett's work never appeared in the *Black Mountain Review*.

LETTER TO JACK SPICER 9/5/55: "If you have anything, or can think of anything, for the Black Mountain Review": There is no evidence that Spicer ever sent poems to the *Black Mountain Review*.

LETTER TO ROBERT DUNCAN 9/6/55: "or John for that matter": John Altoon, painter then living in Majorca.

"You are kind, so very damn kind, to recognize this 'strength' in me": Refers to Duncan's letters to RC dated August 24 and 25, 1955. For more on Duncan's views of RC's family in Majorca ("the wreck of the house"), see his letter to Levertov dated 8/24/55, in *The Letters of Robert Duncan and Denise Levertov*, ed. Robert J. Bertholf and Albert Gelpi (Stanford University Press, 2004), 23–27.

"Do send me some poems for it; also either the Olson article, or the one on the imagination we had talked about": See Robert Duncan, "Notes on Poetics Regarding Olson's *Maximus*," *Black Mountain Review* 6 (Spring 1956): 201–11.

"Ida Hodes": Worked as secretary for the San Francisco Poetry Center. Close friend of Duncan and Jess.

"The announcement is a real lulu: very damn good": Refers to the limited edition of Duncan's *For Caesar's Gate: Poems 1945–1950* with seventeen collages by Jess Collins (Divers Press, 1955).

"ALL THAT IS LOVELY IN MEN is now in proof": RC, *All That Is Lovely In Men*, drawings by Dan Rice (Jonathan Williams/Jargon, 1955).

"Your sense of GOODBYE": In a letter to RC, dated 8/24/55, Duncan recommended using RC's "Goodbye" for the final poem in *All That Is Lovely In Men*, but RC went instead with the title poem, "All That Is Lovely in Men" [*CP* I, 147]. RC, "Goodbye," *Black Mountain Review* 6 (Spring 1956): 163. Republished in *A Form of Women* (Jargon/Corinth, 1959): n.p. [*CP* I, 159].

"that ms/ I made up, before leaving, i.e., to have it follow, as an 'end', after THE

DRESS": *The Dress* refers to a manuscript of RC's prose and poetry that was never published under that title.

"Wolpe": Stefan Wolpe, composer who taught at Black Mountain College from 1952 to 1956.

LETTER TO ROBERT DUNCAN 9/24/55: "will have about 25pp": Louis Zukofsky, "Songs of Degrees" and "Bottom: On Shakespeare—Part Two," *Black Mountain Review* 6 (Spring 1956): 15–25, 119–57.

"he had a record": Available as "Reading on KPFA Radio, Berkeley, August 6, 1954," available on the Zukofsky author page at PennSound, http://writing.upenn.edu/penn sound/.

"have since listened to, I hope carefully, her reading": Marianne Moore reads "In Distrust of Merits" on the LP recording *Pleasure Dome: An Audible Anthology of Modern Poetry Read by Its Creators,* ed. Lloyd Frankenberg (Columbia Masterworks, 1949).

"a record Charles & I made here a year ago": Available as "Studio Recording at Black Mountain College c. 1954," on the Charles Olson and RC author pages at PennSound, http://writing.upenn.edu/pennsound/.

"I stayed at Julie's": Julie Eastman.

LETTER TO WILLIAM CARLOS WILLIAMS 10/31/55: "Your new book came": William Carlos Williams, *Journey to Love* (Random House, 1955).

"Cat bird singing": RC, "Air: 'Cat Bird Singing,'" *Black Mountain Review* 6 (Spring 1956): 164. Republished in *A Form of Women.* [*CP* I, 165].

"I used your article as the 'kick-off' piece": William Carlos Williams, "Two Pieces," *Black Mountain Review* 7 (Autumn 1957): 164–68.

LETTER TO CHARLES OLSON 5/17/56: "impossible relation with Marthe Rexroth": See letter to Denise Levertov 4/22/58.

"I liked that long poem, very much": Charles Olson, "As the Dead Prey Upon Us," first published in *Ark II/Moby I* (1956–57): 12–19. The same issue features Jack Kerouac's "230th Chorus: From *Mexico City Blues*" (19–20) and RC's "Ballad of the Despairing Husband" (30–31).

"I'll copy out a bit to enclose here": RC enclosed his typescript of about a page, single-spaced, of a page of Kerouac's prose beginning: " . . . Mile post 46.9 is San Jose scene of a dozen interested bums lounging in the weeds along the track with their packs of junk," etc.

"It's very damn good to hear of Marshall's poems": Edward Marshall's poem "Leave the Word Along" appears in *Black Mountain Review* 7 (Autumn 1957): 38–51.

LETTER TO JACK KEROUAC 5/26/56: "Locke + Valery": Locke and Valery McCorkle, friends of Kerouac as well as Gary Snyder, Lew Welch, and others associated with the San Francisco scene.

"Neal": Neal Cassady. Close associate of Kerouac, Ginsberg, and Burroughs. Cassady was the famed "Dean Moriarty" of Kerouac's *On the Road.*

LETTER TO CHARLES OLSON 5/28/56: "and the fact a man here will do, or wants to, a small book": RC's *If You* (San Francisco: Porpoise Bookshop, 1956).

LETTER TO MITCH GOODMAN 7/18/56: "but there was and is Marthe as well": Refers to RC's relationship with Marthe Rexroth. See letter to Levertov 4/22/58.

"7th issue of the mag . . . Sherry Mangan, Reminiscence From A Hilltop.": Sherry Mangan, "Reminiscence from a Hilltop," *Black Mountain Review* 7 (Autumn 1957): 63–82.

"Herbert Read": English poet and critic. See Edward Dahlberg and Herbert Read, "Two Letters," *Black Mountain Review* 7 (Autumn 1957): 5–24.

"William Lee (author of a pocket book: JUNKY)": See William Burroughs, published as William Lee, "From *Naked Lunch, Book III*," *Black Mountain Review* 7 (Autumn 1957): 144–48.

LETTER TO WILLIAM CARLOS WILLIAMS 8/8/56: "Phillip Whalen, Allen Ginsberg, Gary Snyder et al. The next issue of the BMR": Poems published in *Black Mountain Review* 7 (Autumn 1957) include Ginsberg's "America" (25–29); Whalen's "3: Variations: All About Love" (134–39); and Snyder's "Changes: 3" (162–63).

"I should like to print a short preface you had written": William Carlos Williams, "Empty Mirror," composed in 1952 and printed in *Black Mountain Review* 7 (Autumn 1957): 238–40. Reprinted in Allen Ginsberg, *Empty Mirror: Early Poems* (Totem Press/Corinth Books, 1961), 5–6.

"Ed Corbett is doing the cover": Refers to *Black Mountain Review* 7 (Autumn 1957).

LETTER TO JACK KEROUAC 10/11/56: "It's good to hear of Grove": Likely refers to Kerouac's *The Subterraneans* (Grove Press, 1958).

LETTER TO MITCH GOODMAN 11/4/56: "things are not very simple for you": In a letter to RC (dated 10/13/56), Goodman described his publishing difficulties and sense of loneliness while living with his family in Guadalajara. [Stanford M0662].

"A few weeks ago, at Sender's": RC reviewed Sender's *The Sphere* (1950) and *The Affable Hangman* (1953) in "Ramon Sender: Two Novels," *Black Mountain Review* 5 (Summer 1955): 216–24.

"Dennie's sequence of poems, in ARK": See Levertov's poems "Central Park, Winter, After Sunset," "A Song," "The Springtime," "The Third Dimension," and "Laying the Dust" in *Ark II/Moby I* (1956–57): 1–4.

"I'll send you a portfolio of mine that is just done": RC, *If You,* illustrations by Fielding Dawson (Porpoise Bookshop, 1956). From the series *Poems & Portfolio* 8, edited by Henry Evans from San Francisco.

LETTER TO WILLIAM CARLOS WILLIAMS 1/1/57: "I thought of your, 'I am a poet. I am. I am . . .'": Lines from William Carlos Williams, "The Desert Music," *Origin* 6 (Summer 1952): 65–75, collected in William Carlos Williams, *The Desert Music and Other Poems* (Random House, 1954).

"I have your notes on Ford and Marsden Hartley": William Carlos Williams, "Beginnings: Marsden Hartley" and "Les Amis de Ford Madox Ford," *Black Mountain Review* 7 (Autumn 1957): 164–68.

LETTER TO DENISE LEVERTOV 1/23/57: "for this coming issue": See Levertov, "Action" and "Everything That Acts Is Actual" in *Black Mountain Review* 7 (Autumn 1957): 159–61.

"I've read Davis' poems": H.L. Davis's *Winds of Morning* (William Morrow, 1952). This from Levertov's letter to RC, dated 8/27/57: "An odd thing that HL Davis whose poems from the twenties I sent you (and did you read that pocket book called 'Winds of Morning'?) is sitting right here in Oaxaca. Expect to meet him in a couple days. Must be in the stars."

LETTER TO ALLEN GINSBERG 2/6/57: "you & Jack & Peter": Jack Kerouac and Peter Orlovsky.

"you saw Fee Dawson, Joel": Fielding Dawson and Joel Oppenheimer.

"BMR #7 will come at last, don't worry": *Black Mountain Review* 7 (Autumn 1957). See note for 8/8/56 to Williams.

"I'll write to Phil": Philip Whalen.

LETTER TO ED DORN 4/27/57: "Bowl of Flowers": Unpublished Dorn poem sent to RC in letter dated 4/24/57.

"H. D.'s war trilogy": Published by Oxford University Press as *The Walls Do Not Fall* (1944), *Tribute to Angels* (1945), and *The Flowering of the Rod* (1946).

"Liquor and love": William Carlos Williams, "The World Narrowed to a Point," *The Wedge* (Cummington Press, 1944), 37.

"Juggler's Thot": RC, "Juggler's Thought," *Measure* 2 (Winter 1958): 11. Republished in RC, *A Form of Women*. [*CP* I, 151].

"Joel's book, The Dutiful Son": Joel Oppenheimer, *The Dutiful Son: Poems* (J. Williams/Jargon, 1956).

"Chan's picture": Dorn's stepdaughter, Chansonette Buck.

"Peocek and Vaquero": Edward Dorn, "Vaquero," *The Collected Poems: 1956–1974* (Four Seasons, 1975), 4.

"Zukofsky's ANEW": Louis Zukofsky, *Anew: Poems* (Decker Press, 1946).

POSTCARD TO DONALD M. ALLEN [UNDATED, CA. 1958]: "I think I could cut him": RC is using the jazz lingo of the time to let Allen know he had a manuscript he considered superior to O'Hara's *Meditations in an Emergency* (Grove Press, 1957). It is worth noting that while editing his anthology *The New American Poetry: 1945–1960* (Grove Press, 1960), Allen sent RC a "tentative list" of poets that included O'Hara. Allen to RC, letter dated 10/6/58. [Stanford M0662].

LETTER TO JACK KEROUAC 1/31/58: "I wish I could get to NYC for the movie": Kerouac had written RC a letter, 1/13/58, praising two issues of the *Black Mountain Review*. He also writes, "We're going to make a movie in NY this May. Come on up, with beard, take the lead part. Be a painter in a movie. WE is just a photog and I, with foundation money." [Stanford M0662].

LETTER TO PAUL BLACKBURN 3/8/58: "Your comments": Blackburn had written RC, 3/2/58, offering detailed comments on RC's poems "The Invoice" [*CP* I, 183], "For a Friend" [*CP*, 188], "The Tunnel" [*CP* I, 176] and "The Three Ladies" [*CP* I, 157]. Published in *For Love: Poems 1950–1960* (Scribner's, 1962), 86, 91, 80, 61.

"So. I'll take Myth, No Myth": Refers to plans for the unrealized final issue of *Black Mountain Review*. Blackburn enclosed seven poems with his letter, indicating that "Myth, No Myth" was the only one not taken elsewhere. Published in *The Collected Poems of Paul Blackburn*, ed. by Edith Jarolim (Persea Books, 1985), 69.

"Equally your Mexican bandit, if free?": Blackburn, "The Encounter," from *The New American Poetry*, 76.

"I like your Cool Departure very much": Blackburn, "Song for a Cool Departure," *Evergreen Review* 1, no. 4 (1957): 143–44.

"At the Crossroad": Blackburn, "At the Crossroad," *The Nets* (Trobar Books, 1961), n.p.

"I'm sorry to hear about the Oxford dons": Blackburn wrote in his letter, "Oxford dons have farted all over my anthology . . . " [Stanford M0662]. Blackburn's lifetime effort of translating the Old Provençal poets, which started with his edition of *Proensa* (Divers Press, 1953), was published posthumously as *Proensa: An Anthology of Troubadour Poetry*, edited by George Economou (University of California Press, 1978).

"I hope Freddie": Blackburn had mentioned that his wife, Freddie, was ill.

" . . . the pistol. My asshole": From Blackburn's "The Encounter" (see above).

"I've missed you": RC and Blackburn had been estranged for nearly four years, following a violent physical confrontation when they were both living in Majorca in 1954. The only time they ever discussed the issue openly was in a letter by Blackburn, 12/9/67, with RC's response 1/15/68, included in this volume. For a sense of the lifelong regret RC felt over this incident, see the poem "Paul," published in his last book *On Earth: Last Poems and an Essay* (University of California Press, 2006), 10–11. [*CP* II, 609–10].

LETTER TO DENISE LEVERTOV 4/22/58: "I'm sorry to hear about all the ugliness": Levertov kept RC apprised of Kenneth Rexroth's reactions in the years after RC's affair (1956) with Marthe Rexroth. Levertov to RC, dated "Sunday" circa spring 1957: "KR is here & suspecting you saw Marthe in SF Easter wk. He's threatening again to kill you. He says he will go to Albuquerque & shoot you, & that he will not be punished as, in N.M., if a man kills his wife's lover it is OK." [Stanford M0662].

"I can relieve you about the supposed quote": In the same letter above, Levertov reports that Rexroth was spreading sexual and drug-related stories about RC, adding, "He says you quoted letters from me to you, in writing to Marthe, & that these quotations played some part in the affair."

LETTER TO DENISE LEVERTOV AND MITCH GOODMAN 8/13/58: "I went to see Blum": Franz Blum.

"Otherwise I read Under the Volcano": Malcolm Lowry, *Under the Volcano* (Reynal & Hitchcock, 1947).

LETTER TO ED DORN 11/16/58: "long poem of yours re yr mother": Dorn's poem "Hide of My Mother," in *New American Poetry*, 98–103.

"Douglas Woolf": Novelist. RC published Douglas Woolf, *Hypocrite Days* (Divers Press, 1955).

"My Love": RC, "My Love," *Poetry* (April 1959): 13. Republished in *A Form of Women*. [*CP* I, 181].

LETTER TO ROBERT DUNCAN 8/20/59: "Maddy's and Jimmy's and Jack's addresses, lost in getting here": Madeline Gleason, James Broughton, and Jack Spicer.

"a long letter from Donald Allen": Allen's letter to RC, dated 8/8/59, discussing editorial plans for the *New American Poetry* anthology. [Stanford M0662].

LETTER TO ALLEN GINSBERG 9/7/59: "KADDISH in BIG TABLE #2": Ginsberg, "Kaddish," *Big Table* 2 (Summer 1959): 19–23. The recording can be heard on the Ginsberg author page at PennSound under "Reading Recent Poems at Robert Creeley's Home, Likely 1959," http://writing.upenn.edu/pennsound.

"Gregory's picture": See Gregory Corso's picture in "Bang, Bong, Bing," *Time* 74, no. 10 (September 7, 1959): 80.

LETTER TO JACK KEROUAC 9/28/59: "I wangled a copy of DR SAX out of Don Allen": Jack Kerouac, *Doctor Sax* (Grove Press, 1959).

"I just 'marketed' a poem involving you": RC, "Jack's Blues," *Poetry* 96 (May 1960): 71.

"I liked very very much the poem in YUGEN": Jack Kerouac, "2 Blues and 4 Haikus," *Yugen* 4 (Spring 1959): 18–19.

LETTER TO JACK KEROUAC 10/20/59: "that record you made with him": Refers to album by Jack Kerouac (spoken word) and Steve Allen (piano), *Poetry for the Beat Generation* (Rosemeadow Music Publishing Corp/Hanover LP #5000, 1959).

"I'll ask Wilentz Bros": See letter to Allen Ginsberg 10/31/59.

"I have a quote like they say from Peter": Peter Orlovsky.

LETTER TO GENEVIEVE CREELEY 10/26/59: "Only Sam Smiles himself could make of this place a 'happy time.'": Refers to Samuel Smiles, Scottish author of the highly influential *Self Help* (1859).

LETTER TO ED DORN 10/26/59: "PRIDE": Unpublished RC poem.

"Jack writes you are a great writer": Jack Kerouac.

"Jane Harrison's Prolegomena": Jane Harrison, *Prolegomena to the Study of Greek Religion* (Cambridge University Press, 1903).

LETTER TO ALLEN GINSBERG 10/31/59: "Jack wrote about the anthology you and he are editing": Refers to unrealized project of a co-edited Beat anthology to be published by Avon. See the correspondence from 1959 in *Jack Kerouac and Allen Ginsberg: The Letters*, edited by Bill Morgan and David Stanford (Viking, 2010).

"the contract I have with Wilentz states I should clear all use of the poems from the book with him": Refers to RC, *A Form of Women*. Eli and Theodore Wilentz published Corinth books.

"I've been looking for Burroughs' book": Likely refers to William Burroughs, *Naked Lunch* (Grove Press, 1959).

"Ginsberg has carried news of and his enthusiasm": Refers to Robert Duncan, *The Opening of the Field* (Grove, 1960); and Allen Ginsberg, "from Kaddish," *Yugen* 5 (1959): 2–4.

"Roi Jones sent Ron L/s book": Ron Loewinsohn, *Watermelons* (Totem Press, 1959).

LETTER TO LEROI JONES (AMIRI BARAKA) 11/8/59: "Duncan's distinction between solitude and loneliness": See Robert Duncan's poem "Solitude" in "A Note and A Poem," *Migrant* 2 (September 1959): 22–23.

"I haven't got Mike M/s new book, and should much like it, if possible? I.e., can you spare a copy sans scene?": Jones had just published Michael McClure, *For Artaud* (Totem Press, 1959).

"there is in the contract with Jonathan and Eli Wilentz clause to the effect no poems can be used without etc.": Refers to RC's "Somewhere" from *A Form of Women*. [*CP* I, 184]. Jonathan is Jonathan Williams. See also letter to Allen Ginsberg 10/31/59.

"So, this time at least, why don't you use if agreeable what you otherwise have": RC, "The Joke" (with doodle drawing) and "What's for Dinner," *Yugen* 6 (1960): 29, 31.

"if Gil would not be too much bothered by it?": Refers to RC's letter to Jones discussing *Yugen* 5 (1959), in particular Gilbert Sorrentino's "Letter to the Editor: A Note on Gregory Corso's *To Black Mountain*." Jones and Hettie Jones published RC's "Letter" in *Yugen* 6 (1960): 30.

LETTER TO JEROME ROTHENBERG 12/16/59: "God knows what to say of that poem":

Rothenberg published RC's "The Animal" [*CP* I, 94] in his magazine *Poems from the Floating World* 2 (1960): 5–6.

"only emotion endures": Refers to Ezra Pound, "A Retrospect," *Literary Essays of Ezra Pound*, ed. T. S. Eliot (New Directions, 1935), 3–14.

"strarange nambe [*sic*] for a magazine": Sonia Raiziss was an editor for *Chelsea* magazine. RC published "The Hands," "Lady in Black," "After Mallarmé," and "The Eye" in *Chelsea* 7 (May 1960): 65–67.

LETTER TO WILLIAM CARLOS WILLIAMS 12/24/59: "might I use the poem which James Laughlin printed": William Carlos Williams, *To Be Recited to Flossie on Her Birthday*, folded sheet with 8 panels (New Directions, 1959).

LETTER TO CHARLES OLSON 12/24/59: "JABBERWOCK arrived also last night": Refers to *Jabberwock: Edinburgh University Review* (1959), a special issue on American poets (primarily Beat) assembled by outgoing editor Alex Neish. Hugh MacDiarmid introduces the issue, which includes Charles Olson's "Good News! Fr Canaan" (60–63) and RC's "The Warning" and "The Hill" (49).

"I seem to be lucky in that anthology, i.e., he's got a good so-called group": Refers to RC's poems in Donald Allen's *The New American Poetry*, among them "The Innocence" (77) [*CP* I, 118] and "The Awakening" (86) [*CP* I, 205].

"I don't know a damn thing about the KULCHUR magazine": NY-based *Kulchur* magazine (1960–65), for which LeRoi Jones was a contributing editor.

"Spicer's mimeographed bull-e-tin": Mimeograph magazine *"J"* (1959–61), edited by Jack Spicer.

LETTER TO ED DORN 1/9/60: "The poems you send I like less than A Country Song": Edward Dorn, "A Country Song" in *The Newly Fallen* (Totem Press, 1961).

"I read Rechy's gig re Los Lost Angeles": John Rechy, "The City of Lost Angels," *Evergreen Review* 3, no. 10 (November–December, 1959): 10–27.

LETTER TO WILLIAM CARLOS WILLIAMS 1/10/60: "Thank you . . . for those poems": RC was soliciting poems on behalf of Renate Gerhardt for a German literary magazine.

"nakedness / is what one means": Olson, "Maximus to Gloucester," *The Maximus Poems* (Jargon/Corinth, 1960), 107.

"those poems are a series of experiments": Allen Ginsberg, *Howl*, LP (Fantasy Records, 1959).

LETTER TO DON ALLEN 1/16/60: "starting on that review": Writing on behalf of *Evergreen Review* editor Barney Rosset, Allen commissioned RC to review several new books (by McClure, Snyder, Loewinsohn, and Whalen) and suggested incorporating Olson's "Projective Verse"; see Allen to RC, 1/12/60. RC turned in the review by March, but Rosset declined to use it, claiming that too much material was already accepted. It eventually appeared as "The New World," *Yugen* 7 (1961): 13–18.

"BMR anthology idea": Allen wrote to RC on 1/12/60: "Lately, I've wondered if a [*Black Mountain Review*] antho might not be a possible idea. Why don't you, if you take to the idea, come up with a proposed line up of contents for such a book, which could include other work as well, focusing on the BMC experience, etc.?"

LETTER TO WILLIAM CARLOS WILLIAMS 3/16/60: "Your letter, and the two articles": William Carlos Williams letter to RC, dated 1/18/60, includes sentence RC would use as jacket blurb on *For Love*: "You have the subtlest feeling for the measure that I encounter anywhere except in the verses of Ezra Pound whom I cannot equal." [Stanford M0662].

"the notes in SPECTRUM": William Carlos Williams, "Measure," *Spectrum* 3, no. 3 (Fall 1959): 131–57.

"I read Mrs. Solt more cautiously": See Mary Ellen Solt, "William Carlos Williams: Poems in the American Idiom," *FOLIO* 25, no. 1 (Winter 1960): 3–28.

"re the iambic pattern, written by Robert Bly": Robert Bly aka Crunk, "The Work of Donald Hall," *The Fifties* 3 (1959): 32–46. See also the prior issue containing Bly/Crunk, "The Work of Robert Creeley," *The Fifties* 3 (1959): 10–21.

"Mrs. Solt's poems in the issue of FOLIO after this one you'd sent": Mary Ellen Solt, "Three Poems," *FOLIO* 25, no. 2 (Spring 1960): 42–44.

"Duncan whose Poem": Robert Duncan, "Poem Beginning with a Line from Pindar," *Evergreen Review* 4, no. 11 (January–February 1960): 134–42.

"the introduction to Zukofsky's 'All eyes!'": Louis Zukofsky, "'All eyes!' from *Bottom: On Shakespeare*," *FOLIO* 25, no. 2 (Spring 1960): 7–13.

LETTER TO LOUIS ZUKOFSKY 3/30/60: "The book got here safely": Louis Zukofsky, *"A" 1–12* (Origin, 1959). Published from Kyoto in an edition of two hundred by Cid Corman. The appendices include Zukofsky's "Poetry / For My Son When He Can Read" and Williams's "Zukofsky."

LETTER TO PAUL BLACKBURN 4/24/60: "e.g., in Galley Sail Review": Gary Snyder, "Kyoto Sketch," *Galley Sail Review* 5 (Winter 1959–60): 19. The same issue includes RC's "The Dream" (4).

"Did Macmillan publish your book?": Blackburn tried Macmillan for his Provençal anthology after being turned down by Oxford. See letter to Blackburn 3/8/58.

"Scribner's stories break": RC's contract with Scribner's for *The Gold Diggers*.

"May issue": See RC poems in *Poetry* 96, no. 2 (May 1960): 71–82.

LETTER TO ED DORN 9/14/60: "I wrote 13 single-spaced pages of sd novel": RC, *The Island* (Scribner's, 1963).

"THE GINGER MAN": J. P. Donleavy, *The Ginger Man* (McDowell, Obolensky, 1958).

"THE BOAT": RC's early short story, "The Boat," *Kenyon Review* 15, no. 4 (Autumn 1953): 571–76. Republished in RC, *The Collected Prose of Robert Creeley* (Dalkey Archive, 2001), 69–73.

LETTER TO WILLIAM CARLOS WILLIAMS 9/21/60: "Yeah! I.e. I agree": Williams sent RC his two-page essay, "The American Idiom," 8/23/60, with the cover note, "AGREE OR NOT?" [Stanford M0662].

"Therefore each speech": RC quotes from William Carlos Williams, "Author's Introduction" in *The Wedge*.

"Whatmough . . . a pocket book called LANGUAGE": Joshua Whatmough, Harvard professor of linguistics, author of *Language: A Modern Synthesis* (Mentor Book/New American Library, 1957).

"poetic discourse is highly peculiar to a language": Same as preceding entry.

LETTER TO JEROME ROTHENBERG 11/6/60: "Thank you so much for the copy of your book": RC refers to poems from Jerome Rothenberg's *White Sun Black Sun* (Hawk's Well Press, 1960). Note that this letter, minus the penultimate paragraph, was previously published in "Jerome Rothenberg and Robert Creeley: An Exchange—Deep Image and Mode," *Kulchur* 6, no. 2 (1962): 25–42.

"Thanks too for the copy of Robert Kelly's notes": Robert Kelly, "Notes on the Poetry of Image," *Trobar* 2 (1961): 14–16.

LETTER TO ED DORN 11/20/60: "Scribners took the goddamn poems": RC, *For Love: Poems 1950–1960* (Scribner's, 1962).

"Burroughs in SIDEWALK 2": William Burroughs, "Have You Seen Slotless City?" in *Sidewalk* 2 (1960). Editor Alex Neish was formerly the editor of *Jabberwock*. See letter to Olson 12/24/59.

LETTER TO WILLIAM CARLOS WILLIAMS 12/18/60: "the birthday poem for your wife": See letter to William Carlos Williams 12/24/59.

"Scribners will publish a sort of collected poems of past ten years": RC, *For Love* (Scribner's, 1962).

LETTER TO JEROME ROTHENBERG 12/18/60: "not yours, certainly not in that 'Black milk of morning'": See Jerome Rothenberg's translation of Paul Celan's "Todesfuge," or "A Death Fugue," in *New Young German Poets,* ed. Jerome Rothenberg (City Lights Pocket Poets Series, 1959), 16.

"Kitasono's The Shadow": Poem by Katue Kitasono in *Black Rain: Poems & Drawings* (Divers Press, 1954).

LETTER TO HUGH KENNER 12/18/60: "NR's audience": *National Review* magazine. Kenner served as literary editor.

"Send regards to Ida": Louis Zukofsky, *Barely and Widely* (C.Z., 1958). This version of the poem contains slight variations to that which appears in *Anew: Complete Shorter Poetry* (New Directions, 2011).

"The risk his text takes when it comes and foresees": Louis Zukofsky, "'All eyes!' from *Bottom: On Shakespeare,*" *Folio* 25, no. 2 (Spring 1960): 7–13. Collected in Zukofsky, *Bottom: On Shakespeare* (Wesleyan University Press, 2002), 183.

"Constantly seeking and ordering relative quantities and qualities of sight, sound, and intellection": Also from *Bottom: On Shakespeare* (18).

LETTER TO PAUL BLACKBURN 1/11/61: "recent issue of TROBAR": Magazine of the "deep image" poets, edited (1960–64) by George Economou, Joan Kelly, and Robert Kelly. RC's poems "The House" and "Love Comes Quietly" appear in *Trobar* 2 (1961): 21.

"Kelly's note": Robert Kelly, "Notes on the Poetry of Image," *Trobar* 2 (1961): 14–16.

"Any tendency to abstract general statement is a greased slide": See Ezra Pound, "Go in fear of abstractions. Do not retell in mediocre verse what has already been done in good prose," from "A Retrospect," *Literary Essays of Ezra Pound* (New Directions, 1954), 5.

"Scribner's have taken the 'collected' poems ms/": RC, *For Love* (Scribner's, 1962).

"Paul C/ is printing in the next BIG TABLE": Poet and editor Paul Carroll cofounded *Big Table* after he and other editors of the *Chicago Review* were censored by the university administration for publishing an excerpt from William Burroughs's *Naked Lunch.*

LETTER TO ED DORN 1/19/61: "I like that note you did": Dorn's *Note for the Paterson Society* (Paterson Society, 12/6/1960).

"I heard from Eberhart at Library of Congress": Richard Eberhart, Library of Congress Consultant in Poetry from 1959 to 1961.

"Nims is present editor there": John Frederick Nims, Visiting Editor of *Poetry* magazine (Chicago) from October 1960 to September 1961.

"I don't see much goddamn else—as this 'deep image'": See Dorn's response to RC, dated 1/23/61: "Deep images, better, deep sounds, come mostly from the rectum."

"OUTBURST connection": Magazine edited by poet Tom Raworth from 1961 to 1963. The first issue features RC, "A New Testament: William Burroughs' *The Naked Lunch*," *Outburst* 1 (1961): n.p.

LETTER TO TOM RAWORTH 1/23/61: "note on Burroughs' NAKED LUNCH": See letter to Ed Dorn, 1/19/61.

"He is presently writing a very interesting autobiography": Sections from Edward Dahlberg's "Because I Was Flesh" appear in *Big Table* 2 (1959): 71–98, *Big Table* 3 (1959): 57–81, and *Big Table* 5 (1960): 23–30.

LETTER TO CHARLES OLSON 1/29/61: "The recent political businesses": The Guatemalan civil war began while the Creeleys were there, lasting from 1960 to 1996. The war pitted leftist groups supported by indigenous Mayans and poor peasants against an increasingly militarized and totalitarian government. According to the Report of the Commission for Historical Clarification, over two hundred thousand people were killed or disappeared over the course of the conflict.

"The so-called novel": RC, *The Island*.

"BIG TABLE is printing a section, I'll ask him to send copy": *Big Table* ceased publication (with the fifth issue in the fall of 1960) before it could publish a section of RC's *The Island*.

"Fire": RC, "Fire," *Between Worlds* 1, no. 2 (Spring–Summer 1961): 219. The same issue of this Colorado magazine contains poems by Bern Porter, Mina Loy, Barbara Guest, and others. Republished in *For Love*, 156. [*CP* I, 294].

"LeRoi has asked me to review Maximus for Yugen": RC, "Some Notes on Olson's *Maximus*," *Yugen* 8 (1962): 51–55.

LETTER TO LOUIS ZUKOFSKY 3/17/61: "I'm pleased the use of yourself": Refers to RC, "A Quick Graph," *Floating Bear* 2 (1961): 5–6.

"Mary Ellen Solt": Poet and editor. See especially *Concrete Poetry: A World View*, ed. Mary Ellen Solt (Indiana University Press, 1968).

"trying to get that review of 'A' and Barely and widely": RC reviews Zukofsky's *"A"* 1–12 and *Barely and widely* in *The Sparrow* 18 (November 1962): 9–11.

"your Catullus translations, e.g. the one in Anew always impressed me, as those also in Poetry not too long ago": "Catullus viii" appears in Louis Zukofsky, *Anew* (James A. Decker, 1946), 32–33. See also letter to Louis Zukofsky 6/26/61.

"with the section of Bottom": Zukofsky, "From *Bottom: On Shakespeare*," *Poetry* 97 (December 1960): 141

"Also that section earlier in Folio": See letter to Hugh Kenner 12/18/60.

"I want to enclose the poem for you, published in Trobar": RC, "The House (for L. Z.)," *Trobar* 2 (1961): 21.

LETTER TO ED DORN 3/26/61: "I enclose sheet from Nat'l Review": From Hugh Kenner, then serving as literary editor for the *National Review*.

"or me in the *Nation*": M. L. Rosenthal made slighting references to RC's work in a review in *The Nation*, 11/1/58.

LETTER TO LOUIS ZUKOFSKY 6/26/61: "I'm very very pleased the review was all right": See letter to Louis Zukofsky 3/17/61.

"Donald Hutter is the editor at Scribner's": There is no evidence that Scribner's sought to publish Zukofsky.

"I do know he took your name and address and the titles": Louis Zukofsky, *Barely and widely* (C.Z., 1958) and *Some Time* (Jonathan Williams, 1956).

"Tell me, please, what now seems possible for your Catullus translations": Sections from Celia and Louis Zukofsky's homophonic translations were published in *Origin: Second Series* 1 (April 1961) and appeared in each consecutive issue through *Origin: Second Series* 13 (April 1964). The translations were first collected in *Catullus (Gai Valeri Catulli Veronensis Liber),* translated by Celia and Louis Zukofsky (Cape Goliard/Grossman, 1969).

LETTER TO ED AND HELENE DORN 10/9/61: "very happy that things there are working out": Dorn's new job teaching English 101. See Dorn's letter to RC, 9/26/61. [Stanford M0662].

"The job is good and simple": RC was then a visiting lecturer at the University of New Mexico.

LETTER TO JACK KEROUAC 1/19/62: "It was very very good to hear from you": Kerouac's postcard to RC, dated 1/15/62, begins: "Your line, or phrase, in ND 17—'be wet'— reminds me of the time you were sleeping in my rosebush space & I woke you up in the morning yelling 'Be enlightened!'—You said: 'It's like asking water to be wet'—which I never forgot—which didn't go into *Dharma Bums* because including you in that story would've meant another novel" [Stanford M0662].

LETTER TO CHARLES OLSON 4/6/62: "I'm very pleased . . . for that review of the book": Olson's review of RC's *For Love,* from *Village Voice,* September 13, 1962, reprinted in Charles Olson, *Collected Prose,* ed. Donald Allen and Benjamin Friedlander (University of California Press, 1997), 285–87.

"a 'hell' of seen limits, I mean the accident in Guatemala, with the truck, killing the old Indian man by the side of the road": The editors consulted Bobbie Louise Hawkins on this passage. A truck in which RC was a passenger, driven by a worker on the *finca* they lived on, struck an elderly Indian man. The driver got out, established that he was in fact dead, got back in, and drove off. Bobbie Louise Hawkins added, "This is how they regarded the local Indians."

"I left him naked": Olson, "Maximus, to Gloucester," *The Maximus Poems* (Jargon/Corinth, 1960), 107.

LETTER TO JACK KEROUAC 5/30/62: "what Don Allen wants": Allen and RC edited *New American Story* (Grove Press, 1965).

"Warren Tallman, who did that note on your prose": Warren Tallman, "Kerouac's Sound," *Evergreen Review* 4, no. 11 (January–February 1960): 153–69.

"Lawrence F/": Lawrence Ferlinghetti, American poet and publisher.

LETTER TO WILLIAM CARLOS WILLIAMS 6/4/62: "your DESERT MUSIC": See letter to William Carlos Williams 1/1/57.

"your plug very generously to the jacket": See letter to William Carlos Williams 9/21/60: "Robert Creeley has the subtlest feeling for the measure that I encounter anywhere except in the verses of Ezra Pound."

LETTER TO ROSMARIE WALDROP 8/17/62: "Burning Deck": *Burning Deck* (1962–65), magazine edited by James Camp, D.C. Hope, and Keith (nee Bernard) Waldrop. RC's "The Lion and the Dog" appears in *Burning Deck* 1 (Fall 1962): 10–11.

POSTCARD TO JACK KEROUAC 11/25/62: "BIG SUR": Jack Kerouac, *Big Sur* (Farrar, Straus and Cudahy, 1962).

LETTER TO PAUL BLACKBURN 8/30/63: "after the wild business in Vancouver": Through their association with the University of British Columbia, RC and Warren Tallman organized the Vancouver Poetry Conference in August 1963, featuring readings and workshops by Duncan, Ginsberg, Levertov, and Olson.

"Does 8th Street have the novel on sale": NYC bookstore. RC's novel, *The Island*.

"a contract to do a book now on Olson for that Twayne series": A book that never materialized.

LETTER TO ED DORN 9/13/63: "I liked Dawn": Dawn Stram. Student recommended to the Vancouver scene by Dorn in letter to RC, dated 3/11/63. [Stanford M0662]

LETTER TO DENISE LEVERTOV 10/19/63: "except for the novel finally": RC, *The Island*.

"The book again—with my New England nature": RC, *For Love: Poems 1950–1960*.

"be idiot awkward with it": From Robert Duncan, "For A Muse Meant" (for Denise Levertov), in *Letters: Poems MCMLIII–MCMLVI* (Jonathan Williams/Jargon, 1958), n.p.

"I think the two you take": Levertov was poetry editor for *The Nation*. See *The Nation* 197 (December 14, 1963) for RC, "The Messengers" (404) and "For Leslie" (420). Republished in *RC, Words* (Scribner's, 1967), 31, 32. [*CP* I, 277, 278].

"that poem for Allen": RC's "The Messengers" is dedicated to Allen Ginsberg.

"B.C.": This Ginsberg poem appeared in the *Minnesota Review* (October–December 1965): 307–9. It was not included in any subsequent collection.

LETTER TO LEROI JONES (AMIRI BARAKA) 10/21/63: "your book": LeRoi Jones, *Blues People* (William Morrow, 1963).

"the Dante book": LeRoi Jones, *The System of Dante's Hell* (Grove Press, 1965).

LETTER TO CLARK COOLIDGE 10/26/63: "going to start something": See *Joglars* (1964–66), poetry magazine founded by Clark Coolidge and (George) Michael Palmer.

LETTER TO ALEXANDER TROCCHI 11/1/63: "people at Vancouver": Vancouver Poetry Conference, August 1963. See letter to Blackburn 8/30/63.

"Also, Don Allen is starting new magazine": Refers to *Writing* (1964–67), edited by Donald Allen from San Francisco.

"the warning re Calder": John Calder, founder of Calder Publishing in London. Published multiple RC books, including *The Island* (1964), *The Gold Diggers and Other Stories* (1965), *Poems 1950–1965* (1966), and *The Finger* (1970).

LETTER TO ANDREW CROZIER 11/15/63: "Migrant": Magazine edited by Gael Turnbull. RC published poems and notes on jazz and urban America ("From a Tape Recording") in *Migrant* 5 (March 1960): 14–19.

LETTER TO DENISE LEVERTOV 11/16/63: "lousy experience with Hatch the last time I tried to review": Robert Hatch, editor at *The Nation*.

"Williams' Pictures from Breughel": A version of RC's review was published as "The Fact of His Life," in *The Nation* 195, no. 11 (October 13, 1962): 224. The original draft appears as "The Fact" in RC's *Collected Essays*. [*CE*, 44–48].

"Then I quoted": William Carlos Williams, "The Yellow Flower," *Pictures from Brueghel and Other Poems* (New Directions, 1962), 89–91.

"and as it was, the last chance": Williams died March 4, 1963, at his home in Rutherford.

"with Cid re the novel": RC, *The Island*.

"Robert just did write": Robert Duncan, poet.

"Robt and Scribners are apparently pretty settled now": Robert Duncan, *Roots and Branches* (Scribner's, 1964).

"I'm very interested in these poems of yours": Refers to Levertov's "Hypocrite Women," "Our Bodies," "Losing Track," and "A Psalm Praising the Hair of Man's Body," in *O Taste and See* (New Directions, 1964), 70, 72, 74, 82; and "The Five-Day Rain," in *With Eyes at the Back of Our Heads* (New Directions, 1959), 13.

"These are just two recent": Two poems are enclosed with the letter. RC, "I," from *12 Poets & One Painter* (Four Seasons, 1964), 71. [*CP* I, 279]. RC, "Something," *Fuck You: A Magazine of the Arts* 5 (September 1964). [*CP* I, 281].

"Belmont paper re the novel . . . my grandfather who lived there plus a brief note on my father also": Belmont, MA. RC's father, Oscar Slade Creeley, and grandfather Thomas Laurie Creeley.

"Later I thought of": William Carlos Williams, "Turkey in the Straw," *The Collected Later Poems of William Carlos Williams* (New Directions, 1950), 204.

LETTER TO TOM RAWORTH 2/7/64: "Anyhow I made one or two small changes": Translation of poem by Rainer Gerhardt. A portion of this letter was previously published in the "Homage to Gerhardt" issue of *Work* 4 (1965), guest edited by Tom Raworth for the Detroit Artists Workshop Press.

"I'm thinking of an issue of Northwest Review": A forthcoming issue with Olson selections was the first casualty after the University of Oregon suspended the magazine as a result of the politically incendiary content of the prior year. See Olson's letter supporting the editor Edward Van Aelstyn, dated March 7, 1964, in Charles Olson, *Selected Letters*, ed. Ralph Maud (University of California Press, 2000), 308–10.

"Kulchur plans an issue on Zukofsky's work shortly": See *Kulchur* 4, no. 14 (Summer 1964), which includes RC's "A Note on Louis Zukofsky" (2–4).

LETTER TO STAN BRAKHAGE 3/28/64: "will now take work": RC, "The Dream," *Poetry* 104 (June 1964): 133. [*CP* I, 298–301].

"Flaming Creatures": 1963 film by Jack Smith.

LETTER TO ALEXANDER TROCCHI 7/16/64: "Ferlinghetti plans to print one of your statements in the next issue of his Journal for the Protection": See Trocchi, "A Revolutionary Proposal," *City Lights Journal* 2 (1964); Trocchi does not appear in *Journal for the Protection of All Beings*.

"Lita Hornick, KULCHUR": Trocchi was never published in Hornick's magazine *Kulchur*.

"I was very flattered and pleased to hear a photograph of one of your sculptures is used for the jacket of The Island": The photograph was not used in the end. Note that RC elsewhere identifies Trocchi with the character "Manus" in *The Island*. See RC, "Introduction," *Black Mountain Review* (AMS Press, 1969), vii. [*CE*, 509].

LETTER TO ED DORN 7/26/64: "Just now hearing reports of rioting in New York and Rochester": The Harlem riots of 1964 began on July 16 in response to the shooting by an off-duty police officer of fifteen-year-old James Powell. The Rochester riots began on July 24 in response to police brutality.

"I liked sections of Gil's long poem": Probably refers to Gilbert Sorrentino, "The Bullpen Is Up and Throwing," *Wild Dog* 9 (July 1964): 33–36.

LETTER TO LOUIS ZUKOFSKY 12/29/64: "I did get the copy": Zukofsky, *After I's* (Boxwood Press/Mother Press, 1964).

"Hall is now advisor to Harpers for poetry et al, and is hopeful of getting Bunting's work collected and back in print": Fulcrum Press of London published an edition of Bunting's *Collected Poems* in 1968, but Hall's involvement was unlikely.

"good visit with Charles Tomlinson also, and was pleased to hear of his issue of AGENDA, of your work": Tomlinson edited a Zukofsky special issue for *Agenda* 3, no. 6 (December 1964).

LETTER TO ED DORN 6/2/65: "the way Gael Turnbull gets past that thinking of the obvious containment of his nature in that sequence in recent Poetry": Gael Turnbull, "Twenty Words: Twenty Days: A Sketchbook & A Morula," *Poetry* 106 (April 1965): 136.

LETTER TO ALLEN GINSBERG 6/2/65: "note in NY Times about your being crowned King of the May": See "Czechs Oust Ginsberg, 'Village' Poet," *New York Times*, May 17, 1965. According to the article, Ginsberg was expelled from Czechoslovakia shortly after he was "elected king of the Czech youths' May Day festival."

"Alex Trocchi's <u>Sigma</u> and this was a note of mine he'd kindly printed": Trocchi published RC's essay "An American Sense" in his stapled 8.5" × 14" portfolio series *Sigma* 26 (1964).

LETTER TO TOM AND VALERIE RAWORTH 6/23/65: "Penguin is doing I think a very active collection": *The New Writing in the USA*, ed. Donald Allen and RC (Penguin, 1967).

LETTER TO CHARLES OLSON 10/16/65: "I'm very happy that damn introduction": RC's introduction to *Selected Writings of Charles Olson*, ed. Robert Creeley (New Directions, 1966).

"beginning with the Historic Moment of Vancouver etc": Vancouver Poetry Conference (1963) organized by RC and Warren Tallman.

"review in NY Herald Tribune, Book Week": See reviews of RC's *The Gold Diggers*, by Alan Pryce-Jones, *New York Herald Tribune*, October 7, 1965, and R.Z. Sheppard, *Book Week* 3, no. 5 (October 10, 1965): 16. Noted in Mary Novik, *Robert Creeley: An Inventory, 1945–1970* (Kent State University Press, 1973).

LETTER TO STEPHEN RODEFER 1/11/66: "subject of your dissertation": Rodefer's unfinished 1965 dissertation on RC.

LETTER TO CHARLES OLSON 1/26/66: "Al Cook wrote two days ago": Albert Cook (1925–98), poet and literary critic, chair of English Department at SUNY-Buffalo, 1963–66.

LETTER TO ROBERT DUNCAN 4/8/66: "the <u>one</u> inescapable fact is, the State Dept <u>is</u> the sponsor": Responds to Duncan's four-page letter to RC, dated 4/6/66. Duncan expressed misgivings that RC could "go in a non-political way" and encouraged him to withdraw from the trip.

LETTER TO CHARLES OLSON 5/3/66: "I checked proofs": Olson, *Selected Writings*, edited by RC (New Directions, 1966).

POSTCARD TO ALLEN GINSBERG 9/10/66: "Kirsten decided to go to local highschool here": Kirsten Creeley.

LETTER TO CHARLES OLSON 9/24/66: "Afterwards went to Onetta's": Poet John Clarke was on the faculty in the English Department. Poets Albert Glover, Fred Wah, and Steven Rodefer were students.

LETTER TO ROBERT DUNCAN 3/6/67: "I'll get hold of Irving Feldman": Poet and professor at SUNY-Buffalo.

"You are so very kind": Duncan responded to RC's *Words*.

"Back to Hutter's letter: those sections of PASSAGES you'd know very much I respect— eg. I read UPRISING": Donald Hutter, editor at Scribner's. Robert Duncan, "Up Rising," *The Nation* 201, no. 7 (September 13, 1965): 146–47. Republished as "Up Rising: Passages 25," in *Of the War: Passages 22–27* (Oyez, 1966), n.p.

LETTER TO GEORGE OPPEN 3/19/67: "I regret missing your reading": George Oppen read at the University at Buffalo on February 17, 1967.

"I'll look for you at Basil B/s reading": Basil Bunting.

LETTER TO ROBERT DUNCAN 10/26/67: "limited edition of 'fugitive' poems Walter Hamady is doing for me": RC, *The Charm: Early and Uncollected Poems* (Perishable Press, 1967). The book dedication reads, "For Robert Duncan who made me see that possibility is more interesting than perfect . . . "

"Berlin lecture that was reprinted in Harper's Bazaar": RC, "I'm given to write poems." Lecture delivered at the Literarisches Colloquium, Berlin, January 1967. Published in *Ein Gedicht und sein Autor: Lyrik und Essay,* ed. Walter Höllerer (Literarisches, 1967) and *Harper's Bazaar* (July 1967). [*CE,* 496–505].

"possibility of The Black Sparrow Press doing something of Bobbie's and mine together goes well": RC, *The Finger,* with collages by Bobbie Creeley (Black Sparrow Press, 1968).

"Your Epilogus is a real gift . . . the sequences from PASSAGES also": Robert Duncan, *Epilogos* (Black Sparrow Press, 1967). Robert Duncan, *Of the War: Passages 22–27* (Oyez, 1966).

"Unhappily for the Arts Festival here, it contracted to being able to invite Charles, Lowell, and Allen": Charles Olson, Robert Lowell, and Allen Ginsberg.

LETTER TO PAUL BLACKBURN 1/15/68: "copy of THE CITIES": Blackburn, *The Cities* (Grove, 1967).

"And delight too to think of you now citing (sitting) in one of them cities": RC's aerogram is addressed to Blackburn in Valencia, Spain.

"remembering that wild night in Banalbufar": See note to letter to Blackburn 3/8/58.

"Olson's book": Olson, *Selected Writings* (New Directions, 1966).

LETTER TO LOUIS ZUKOFSKY 9/7/68: "lovely issue of poetry (Poetry!)": *Poetry* 112 (August 1968) featured long selections by Zukofsky (297–322), Charles Tomlinson (323–30), and RC (331–36).

LETTER TO ROBERT DUNCAN 2/12/69: "get sent to you both a 'portfolio' bound edition of NUMBERS": RC and Robert Indiana collaborated on *Numbers* (Edition Domberger, 1968), published from Stuttgart in a slipcased book edition (2,500 copies) and a limited portfolio edition (160 copies).

"Too, did you get a copy of PIECES": John Martin, founder of Black Sparrow Press. Refers to limited edition of RC, *Pieces* (Black Sparrow Press, 1968).

"I've seen proofs now for the Scribners edition PIECES—and it looks ok, and much as I'd hoped it might (for once)": RC, *Pieces* (Scribner's, 1969).

"Don says proofs": RC, *A Quick Graph: Collected Notes & Essays,* ed. by Donald Allen (Four Seasons Foundation, 1970). RC, *The Charm: Early and Uncollected Poems* (Four Seasons Foundation, 1969).

"Finally, and most interesting at the moment": R. B. Kitaj's first solo exhibition, *Pictures with Commentary, Pictures without Commentary,* opened at the Marlborough Gallery in 1963, and today the gallery represents the artist's estate. See their collaboration on RC, *A Day Book,* with plates by Kitaj (Graphis, 1972).

"If in debris I had not said how lovely": Refers to limited edition of Robert Duncan, *Names of People,* illustrations by Jess (Black Sparrow Press, 1968).

"You know what kind of measure he was for me": See RC, *About Women,* with lithographs by John Altoon (Gemini Limited, 1966).

LETTER TO CHARLES OLSON 1/1/70: "I'll be back, hopefully about Jan. 10th": Olson died of cancer on January 10, 1970, in New York City.

LETTER TO ALLEN GINSBERG 6/20/70: "little over 100 pp. now": Allen Ginsberg, *Indian Journals: March 1962–May 1963, Notebooks, Diary, Blank Pages, Writings* (David Haselwood/City Lights, 1970).

LETTER TO BOBBIE CREELEY (BOBBIE LOUISE HAWKINS) 9/3/70: "Also got a new 'impenetrable' (raincoat)": The French for raincoat is *imperméable.*

POSTCARD TO SARAH CREELEY [9/4/70]: "Sarah": Daughter of RC and Bobbie Louise Hawkins born in 1957.

LETTER TO GENEVIEVE CREELEY 8/29/71: "Carlie came over about a week ago and seemed in good spirits. She was with a charming young man, so that seemed happy. She told me Lucy's present young man is one she's known previous to Lincoln, and that all seemed happy. I hope we'll see more of both them now that they have cars.": Lucie and Carly are Helen Creeley Power's daughters.

POSTCARD TO ARMAND SCHWERNER 10/10/71: "Paul's relation to me is really too complex": Paul Blackburn died September 13, 1971.

LETTER TO BOBBIE CREELEY (BOBBIE LOUISE HAWKINS) 1/17/73: "from PLAYBOY John Clellon Holmes wrote on Jack Kerouac's death and funeral": John Clellon Holmes, "Gone in October," *Playboy,* February 1973, 96–98, 140, 158–66.

"pictures of Bolinas' flooding": Bobbie wrote to RC on 1/12/73: "It's poured rain since you left—downtown & all the towns hereabouts flooding. I just came in from digging runnels to let some of the water pass down into the creek instead of settling on the bridge.—I looked out this morning & the bridge was a pond—I got scared at the thought of driving over it—but now I've got it draining the creek underneath is a rushing torrent—surprising—."

LETTER TO ALLEN GINSBERG 1/28/73: "Allen DeLoach": Buffalo-based poet and publisher of *Intrepid* magazine (1964–80).

"Gregory's sudden poem": "Proximity," in Gregory Corso, *Herald of the Autochthonic Spirit* (New Directions, 1981), 26.

"John Wieners": Famed Boston poet. Student at Black Mountain College.

"John Logan": Poet who taught at SUNY-Buffalo.

"Mark Robison whom I saw late fall": Allen Ginsberg, *Ginsberg's Improvised Poetics,* edited with an introduction by Mark Robison (Anonym Press, 1971).

LETTER TO BOBBIE CREELEY (BOBBIE LOUISE HAWKINS) 1/29/73: "That's wild about the kerosene": Bobbie wrote to RC, 1/26/73: "Running out of gas while with Yvonne and Mickey, a friend accidentally mistakenly puts a can of kerosene in the car."

LETTER TO KATE CREELEY 4/26/73: "very happily saw Arthur": Painter and Bolinas friend Arthur Okamura. RC and Okamura collaborated on *1234567890* (Shambhala, 1971).

LETTER TO DIANE DI PRIMA 3/12/74: "At present am working on text": RC, *Mabel: A Story and Other Prose* (Marion Boyars, 1976).

"sort of reverse side": *Loba* began appearing in Diane Di Prima, *Loba: Part 1* (Capra Press, 1973).

POSTCARD TO BARRETT WATTEN 12/13/74: "can you come out (Bolinas) over Xmas holidays?": Watten notes in correspondence with the editors: "The invite led to one of the most memorable evenings of my young writing career. At the table were Bob, Bobbie, and Richard Brautigan, who celebrated a publisher's advance by buying a shopping bag full of steaks. I was not eating much steak at the time. There was a ferocious conversation about the values of Kenneth Fearing as a writer, whom Brautigan liked and Creeley did not—leftism. But I remember Creeley waxing large about the Western subject—Hume and Locke. It was the like visiting the Grand Canyon."

LETTER TO ALLEN GINSBERG 11/1/75: "Elsewise sad to miss meeting Bob Dylan": See earlier, Donald Allen letter to RC, dated 1/19/66: "Did Bob Dylan stop by to see you? Spent a great evening with him and Allen and many other people and urged him to look you up on his way. What would you think of my adding him to the overhauled NAP I'm starting to work on?" [Stanford M0662]

LETTER TO MR. AND MRS. HILTON POWER (HELEN CREELEY) 3/16/76: "You sure came from a nice place, Hilton!": Hilton Power married Helen Creeley in the 1960s.

"I heard from Russell Haley": English novelist and poet who immigrated to New Zealand. Stephanie and Rachel are Hilton Power's daughters from his first marriage.

LETTER TO BOBBIE CREELEY (BOBBIE LOUISE HAWKINS) 4/21/76: "I've written Martin Booth": Organizer of the Cambridge Poetry Festival.

LETTER TO PENELOPE HIGHTON (PENELOPE CREELEY) 5/24/76: "great yellow Korean bicycle Benny left for me": Benny Nadel, student friend from Harvard who lived in Buffalo. See also RC's broadside, "For Benny and Sabina" (Samuel Charters/Portents, 1970). [*CP* I, 498].

"Letter from Michael Volkersberg re money": Refers to New Zealand Student Association that cosponsored RC's tour.

LETTER TO PENELOPE HIGHTON (PENELOPE CREELEY) 5/27/76: "Will also write Bruce and Linley": Student Council members who organized RC's reading tour.

LETTER TO PENELOPE HIGHTON (PENELOPE CREELEY) 5/27/76: "Trevor, etc.": Organizer of RC's reading tour in Welland.

LETTER TO ROBERT GRENIER 7/4/76: "Also saw Rick Fields briefly in NYC, likewise": Naropa-based writer and editor.

LETTER TO DENISE LEVERTOV 11/17/76: "Most happy in that situation": Charlotte Creeley, daughter of RC and his first wife, Ann MacKinnon.

LETTER TO PENELOPE HIGHTON (PENELOPE CREELEY) 11/21/76: "asked me if I'd had any movie offers for THE ISLAND": The film adaptation of Dickey's novel *Deliverance* (1970) came out in 1972.

"Norman Jeffares": Author of numerous books on William Butler Yeats.

LETTER TO ROBERT GRENIER 11/24/76: "final word in this mess": The publisher failed to credit Grenier as the editor of RC's *Selected Poems* (Scribner's, 1976).

"to put note in to the effect": See RC's letter to the editors in *The American Poetry Review* 6, no. 1 (1977): 47. The statement reads, "Robert Creeley wishes it known that the recent publication of his SELECTED POEMS by Charles Scribner's Sons does *not* acknowledge the editor of the selection, Robert Grenier, and also makes substantial changes in the *order* in which the poems appear in each of the five sections. The text, therefore, has neither the approval of Mr. Grenier nor Mr. Creeley—and is solely the responsibility of its publisher."

"Peter Freeman (that magazine": *Padan Aram,* the Harvard-Radcliffe poetry magazine.

LETTER TO ROBERT DUNCAN 2/2/77: "New Directions planning to publish a first book": RC, *Hello: A Journal, February 29–May 3, 1976* (New Directions, 1978).

"he's generously asked me to do a note": RC's introduction to R. B. Kitaj, *Pictures/ Bilder* (Marlborough Fine Art, 1977). [*CE,* 402–406].

"Preoccupations thus, as ever": See *Human Clay,* exhibition selected by R. B. Kitaj (Arts Council of Great Britain, 1976).

"just finished reading": Richard Holmes, *Shelley: The Pursuit* (Weidenfeld and Nicolson, 1974).

LETTER TO ROBERT GRENIER 5/17/77: "Also talking of Byrd and Dowland": Elizabethan composers William Byrd and John Dowland.

LETTER TO CHARLES BERNSTEIN 2/6/79: "Thanks very much for the copy of your book . . . e.g., 'Soul Under'": See "Soul Under," in Charles Bernstein, *Shade* (Sun & Moon, 1978).

"to note books of interest to me recently": Bruce Andrews and Charles Bernstein, editors of $L = A = N = G = U = A = G = E$ magazine, asked readers to list "5 non-poetry books you've read in the last few years that have had a significant influence on your thinking or writing, OR, send us a list of one or two non-poetry books, along with a brief (up to one or two hundred word) description of why they have been useful or important to you." Bernstein and Andrews letter to RC, dated 1/2/79. [Stanford M0662].

LETTER TO GEORGE BUTTERICK 4/12/79: "but I really was displaced by the extraordinary emphasis on FOR LOVE, as against the selections from subsequent work": Butterick edited, with Donald Allen, *The Postmoderns: The New American Poetry Revised* (Grove Press, 1982).

LETTER TO JOHN TAGGART 6/12/79: "'review' over 800 pages and over forty years of work": Likely refers to RC, "For L. Z.," in "Tributes to Louis Zukofsky" section of *New Directions* 39 (1979): 151–53.

"Bill Spanos to send you a copy of Boundary 2": Refers to the RC special issue of the journal *Boundary 2* (1978).

"The issue on your own work": Refers to the John Taggart special issue of *Paper Air* 2, no. 1 (1979).

"I did get DODEKA—and thank you": John Taggart, *Dodeka* (Membrane Press, 1979).

LETTER TO JOHN TAGGART 7/3/80: "your sense that Louis had a decisive hand in the composition": In a prior letter to Taggart, dated 6/25/80, RC cast doubt on Taggart's suppositions about *"A"-24:* "As I understand you, your proposal is that Louis [Zukofsky] made the selections of texts used in A 24, and then Celia then set/arranged them with the Handel material? I just don't see how that could have been the case, insofar as Louis would not be able to get the requisite 'fits' or congruences, since he was, by both Paul's and Celia's report, tone deaf and had no particular skill with such composition insofar as I know. So how would he have been able to get the five parts working together as you suggest? And could he choose them without a sense of how they would concur, etc etc." RC closes the letter by saying that he has written to Celia Zukofsky about the matter.

LETTER TO STAN AND JANE BRAKHAGE 10/13/80: "we finally moved into this very pleasant house": RC and family lived at Back Cottage 2, 388 Summer Street, Buffalo, NY, until May 1982.

LETTER TO STAN AND JANE BRAKHAGE 1/29/81: "I was able to 'be there' when he was born": William Gabriel Creeley, born January 16, 1981.

LETTER TO CHARLES BERNSTEIN 1/5/82: "with suggestions as to texts you'd like to see dealt with": *American Book Review* published several pieces by or about the Language poets during this time, including a multireview special feature called "Nonsyntactical Writing" in *ABR* 4, no. 6 (September–October 1982): 2–4.

"I just got a copy": Refers to *Open Letter,* 5th ser. (Winter 1982), the L = A = N = G = U = A = G = E issue, edited by Bruce Andrews and Charles Bernstein.

"Frank Davey": Editor of *Open Letter* in Toronto.

"Thanks (!) for the copy": Charles Bernstein, *Stigma* (Station Hill, 1981).

LETTER TO ALLEN GINSBERG 11/14/82: "Sam Charters": Historian of jazz and blues. Married to scholar Ann Charters.

"I'd use": Charles Olson, *Selected Writings,* edited by RC (New Directions, 1966).

"particular essays . . . stuff collected in": Charles Olson, *Muthologos: The Collected Lectures & Interviews,* two volumes, edited by George F. Butterick (Four Seasons Foundation, 1978–79).

"If Don Allen still has editions": Charles Olson, *Poetry and Truth: The Beloit Lectures and Poems,* edited by George F. Butterick (Four Seasons Foundation, 1971).

LETTER TO ROBERT DUNCAN 1/18/83: "the generous plug—the back cover reads like an ultimate testimonial dinner": *The Collected Poems of Robert Creeley: 1945–1975* (University of California Press, 1982) features blurbs by William Carlos Williams, Charles Olson, Edward Dorn, Allen Ginsberg, Denise Levertov, Robert Duncan, Michael McClure, and John Ashbery.

"Chas told me, Ruth W/D/": Ruth Witt-Diamant, founder of the San Francisco State Poetry Center.

"hope to get something moving in collaboration with pleasant French photographer now here (in Santa Fe), Bernard Plossu": See RC's memories of Plossu in "My New Mexico," catalog essay for *In Place* (Albuquerque Museum, 1982). [*CE,* 440–46].

LETTER TO ALICE NOTLEY 7/5/83: "very sad news": Poet Ted Berrigan, married to Notley, died on July 4, 1983.

LETTER TO ED AND JENNIFER DORN 10/9/83: "Curious place to be hanging out in": RC's artist residency in West Berlin sponsored by the Deutscher Akademischer Austausch Dienst.

"Ted Joans lives upstairs": Beat poet.

LETTER TO DENISE LEVERTOV 2/1/84: "modest fund for kids from the depressed town (South Waldoboro)": Resulted in the Sarah Creeley Prize for high school graduates to attend the University of Maine.

"Pen starts graduate work": RC and family lived in Ithaca during 1984–85.

"Griselda continues": Griselda Ohannessian, editor at New Directions.

LETTER TO JOHN TAGGART 11/3/84: "Bruce Jackson and Diane Christian were our charming hosts": English professors at the University at Buffalo.

POSTCARD TO BARRETT WATTEN 11/23/84: "God your book is solid! In all respects": Likely refers to Barrett Watten, *Total Syntax* (Southern Illinois University Press, 1984).

LETTER TO CARL RAKOSI 2/16/87: "heart-felt thanks for that generous book": Carl Rakosi, *The Collected Poems of Carl Rakosi* (National Poetry Foundation, 1986).

LETTER TO TOM CLARK 2/23/87: "To get to your several questions": Clark was then writing the biography *Charles Olson: The Allegory of a Poet's Life* (W. W. Norton, 1991). He also authored, with RC, *Robert Creeley and the Genius of the American Common Place: Together with the Poet's Own Autobiography* (New Directions, 1993).

POSTCARD TO LESLIE SCALAPINO 3/6/88: "Many thanks for the handsome books by Ted Pearson and Rick London": Scalapino had recently published Ted Pearson's *Catenary Odes* (O Books, 1987) and Rick London's *Abjections: A Suite* (O Books, 1988).

"to Finland for a year": Refers to Senior Fulbright Professorship (see letters from Helsinki below).

LETTER TO SUSAN HOWE 9/25/88: "First couple of weeks I was writing a poem a minute, much like dog in new surroundings": Likely refers to poems in the "Helsinki Window" section of *Windows* (New Directions, 1990).

"your Olson piece": Susan Howe, "Where Should the Commander Be," *Writing* 19 (November 1987): 3–20.

LETTER TO ROBERT GRENIER 12/18/88: "Another virtue of Worcester apropos": Worcester Polytechnic Institute offered RC a professorship that would have required teaching only six weeks per year.

"beginning with Robert, then Neil Williams, then George, then Joel": Refers to the then recent deaths of poet Robert Duncan, painter Neil Williams, poet-editor George Butterick, and poet Joel Oppenheimer.

LETTER TO HELEN (CREELEY) AND WAYNE POWER 3/12/89: "I was in Albany": RC later served as New York State Poet.

"suite of 12 poems to go with pastels": Francesco Clemente and RC collaborated on *It / 64 pastels / 12 Poems* (Bruno Bischofberger, 1989).

LETTER TO SUSAN HOWE 3/24/89: "It looks like we're headed back": Refers to communications with Provost (and later President) William Greiner that subsequently led to the formation of the Buffalo Poetics Program and RC's appointment to the Capen Chair.

LETTER TO ALLEN GINSBERG 4/23/89: "even to read with the locals (Klaes Andersson et al)": Claes Andersson, Finnish writer.

"spent weekend out with Massimo B/ et al": Italian Pound scholar Massimo Bacigalupo.

LETTER TO ROBERT GRENIER 8/10/89: "We just heard yesterday mortgage was approved!": Home at 64 Amherst Street (a former firehouse).

LETTER TO SUSAN HOWE 2/15/90: "chair went to": Refers to the newly formed Buffalo Poetics Program.

"week in Israel": Refers to writer's conference held at Mishkenot Sha'ananim in Jerusalem. Miroslav Holub was a Czech poet.

LETTER TO SUSAN HOWE 3/17/90: "immensely useful": "Talisman Interview, with Edward Foster," in Susan Howe, *The Birth-Mark: Unsettling the Wilderness in American Literary History* (Wesleyan University Press, 1993), 155–82.

"Peter was very good": Peter Quartermain, English literary critic and poet.

LETTER TO CHARLES BERNSTEIN 3/31/90: "Tomaz Salamun, who is to be in the States in the fall": Slovenian poet.

FAX TO CHARLES BERNSTEIN 8/21/90: "promo materials": The Poetics Program reading series Wednesdays at 4 Plus.

"very happy news": See letter to Susan Howe 2/15/90.

LETTER TO ROBERT GRENIER 6/4/91: "great speckled": Poet David Bromige (1933–2009).

"When I'd finished the so-called selection": Likely refers to Charles Olson, *Selected Poems,* edited by RC (University of California Press, 1993.)

"Like, if someone, namely ole B/": Likely also refers to David Bromige.

FAX TO TOM THOMPSON, THE NATIONAL POETRY SERIES 5/18/92: "hardly an easy manuscript": As the 1992 judge for the National Poetry Series, RC awarded the prize to Gerald Burns, *Shorter Poems* (Dalkey Archive, 1993).

LETTER TO WARREN TALLMAN 9/25/92: "your lovely book!": Warren Tallman, *In the Midst: Writings 1962–1992* (Talonbooks, 1992). Selections include "Statement on *The Island*" (21–22), "Haw: A Dream for Robert Creeley" (62–66), "Robert Creeley, LETTER" (198–201), and "Letter to Robert Creeley" (215).

"a little stretched": Charles Bernstein commuted between Buffalo and his home in New York City.

"altogether benign baby": Felix is the son of Charles Bernstein and Susan Bee.

"staying in Connecticut": Refers to Susan Howe and her husband, David von Schlegell.

LETTER TO ERIC MOTTRAM 3/5/94: "Meantime Charles is seemingly surviving": Charles Bernstein, Susan Howe, Dennis Tedlock, and Robert (Bob) Bertholf were colleagues in the Buffalo Poetics Program. Charles commuted to Buffalo once a week from his home in Manhattan. Bertholf was then the curator of the Poetry Collection, the University at Buffalo.

LETTER TO JIM DINE 12/12/94: "have some fun, like they say": Refers to their collaboration on RC, *Pictures: Poem,* with lithographs by Dine (Tamarind Institute, 2001).

"else I suppose the other way": They previously collaborated on RC, *Mabel, A Story: 1.2.3., 3.1.2., 2.3.1., 1.2.3., 3.1.2.,* with etchings by Dine (Éditions de l'Atelier Crommelynck, 1977).

FAX TO ELIZABETH FOX 1/26/95: "request of a Chinese publisher": See *The Pisan Cantos and Selected Essays of Ezra Pound,* translated and edited by Yunte Huang (Lijiang Publishing House, 1998).

E-MAIL TO BENJAMIN FRIEDLANDER 4/10/95: "Don Allen called today to talk about the Olson Collected": Friedlander co-edited, with Donald Allen, Olson's *Collected Prose* (University of California Press, 1997).

E-MAIL TO PETER GIZZI AND ELIZABETH WILLIS 2/15/96: "a collaboration with Alex Katz": *Edges* (Peter Blum Edition, 1999).

"gearing up for the Duncan fest": Refers to Robert Duncan Conference: The Opening of the Field, April 19–21, 1996, State University of New York at Buffalo.

"so sadly insistent": Franco Beltrametti died in August 1995. Larry Eigner and Lady Caroline (Lowell) Blackwood died in February 1996.

"your dissertation as and when": Gizzi's dissertation committee for the Buffalo Poetics Program consisted of RC, Charles Bernstein, and Susan Howe. It was published as Jack Spicer, *The House That Jack Built: The Collected Lectures of Jack Spicer*, ed. Peter Gizzi (Wesleyan University Press, 1998).

E-MAIL TO SIMON PETTET 10/11/96: "Only glitch": Roi is Amiri Baraka (LeRoi Jones). Gil is Gilbert Sorrentino.

E-MAIL TO TOM RAWORTH [OCTOBER 1996]: "who collects trashy postcards": Quoted from Jane Perlez, "Polish Poet, Observer of Daily Life, Wins Nobel," *New York Times*, October 4, 1996, www.nytimes.com.

"with Georg Baselitz with whom I'll do modest collaboration": RC, *Signs*, with etchings by Georg Baselitz (Graphicstudio, 2000).

"Murray Edmond": New Zealand poet.

LETTER TO MARJORIE PERLOFF [11/10/96]: "your very impressive book": Marjorie Perloff, *Wittgenstein's Ladder: Poetic Language and the Strangeness of the Ordinary* (University of Chicago Press, 1996).

"slim memoir": Norman Malcolm, *Ludwig Wittgenstein: A Memoir* (Oxford University Press, 1958).

"happy company with Bruce Duffy at a writers' business at Bennington": Bruce Duffy, author of *The World as I Found It* (Ticknor & Fields, 1987), a fictionalized account of Wittgenstein's life.

"GREAT to have Gil's company": Gilbert Sorrentino.

E-MAIL TO BENJAMIN FRIEDLANDER [4/7/97]: "Boldereff/Olson letters": *Charles Olson and Frances Boldereff: A Modern Correspondence*, ed. Ralph Maud and Sharon Thesen (Wesleyan University Press, 1999).

E-MAIL TO BENJAMIN FRIEDLANDER [4/19/97]: "unlikely review": Louis Zukofsky, "What I Come to Do Is Partial," *Poetry* 92 (May 1958): 110–12.

"T-shirts will be ready": Printed for Zukofsky in April conference, sponsored by Poetics Program, University at Buffalo in April 1997.

E-MAIL TO CHARLES BERNSTEIN [APRIL 1997]: ">Spent the morning with": Ira Nadel spoke on a panel with Mark Scroggins and Paul Zukofsky for the Zukofsky in April conference.

LETTER TO DENNY MOERS 5/31/97: "we spoke of you doing a cover": Denny Moers, photographer. His work appears on several RC books including *Mirrors, Echoes, Windows, Life & Death,* and *If I Were Writing This.*

"This neighborhood": Blackrock in Buffalo.

LETTER TO WILLIAM WADSWORTH, EXECUTIVE DIRECTOR, ACADEMY OF AMERICAN POETS 2/21/99: "the book club": Financially insolvent project that was discontinued a short time later.

E-MAIL TO BARRETT WATTEN 1/20/00: "impressively patient and clear take": See Barrett Watten, "New Meaning and Poetic Vocabulary: From Coleridge to Jackson Mac Low," *Poetics Today* 18 (Summer 1997): 147–86.

"My own relation to Basic English": See letter to Larry Eigner [ca. February 1950].

LETTER TO SARAH CREELEY 8/2/00: "I've looked at your video": Family home video.

LETTER TO FRANCESCO CLEMENTE 1/31/01: "I wrote this poem for Gregory . . . ": RC, "For Gregory Corso" [*CP* II, 589].

LETTER TO JOEL KUSZAI 2/13/01: "the Helsinki reading": RC reading at the University of Helsinki, February 14, 1989. Recording available via PennSound www.writing.upenn.edu/pennsound/x/Creeley.php.

LETTER TO HENRY REATH, PRESIDENT, BOARD OF DIRECTORS OF THE ACADEMY OF AMERICAN POETS 10/1/01: "situation of the Chancellors": RC was appointed chancellor of the Academy of American Poets in 1999. In the weeks leading up to this letter, the longtime executive director William Wadsworth was forced to resign under pressure by the organization's board. See David D. Kirkpatrick, "Poets' Group Ousts Chief, Igniting Ire of Members," *New York Times,* November 7, 2001.

E-MAIL TO PENELOPE CREELEY 10/8/02: "Anne to Jane and Anselm": Anne Waldman, Jane Hollo, and Anselm Hollo.

E-MAIL TO BARRETT WATTEN 7/9/03: "immaculately precise observation": Refers to the line, "Hollow blocks fill up in windowless rooms: the train ceaselessly reinvents the station," from Barrett Watten, "Real Estate," in *1–10* (This Press, 1980), 32.

E-MAIL TO ROD SMITH 7/17/03: "the drear Faas biography": Ekbert Faas, with Maria Trombacco, *Robert Creeley: A Biography* (University Press of New England, 2001).

LETTER TO CARL RAKOSI 9/22/03: "mine for your birthday": Carl Rakosi, poet affiliated with the Objectivists, born in 1903.

"said 'piece' might be of use": The poem, minus the note, appears in RC, "For Carl, Again & Again," *Jacket* 25 (February 2004), www.jacketmagazine.com/25/rak-cree.html.

E-MAIL TO AMMIEL ALCALAY 12/1/03: "If the question is, did Olson either listen to or pick up on Charlie Parker during his (Parker's) lifetime": Alcalay relates that the question he put to Creeley was a query he had received from his then grad student, the poet Karen Weiser.

"olson quote i had asked you guys about": Charles Olson, "On Black Mountain," *Maps* 4 (1971): 31.

E-MAIL TO ANGELICA CLARK 5/17/04: "and we did get Tom's NIGHT SKY": Tom Clark, *Night Sky* (Deep Forest, 2004).

E-MAIL TO ANSELM BERRIGAN 6/17/04: "just that Steve played with him those many years ago": Steve Lacy performed on Cecil Taylor's debut recording, *Jazz Advance* (Transition, 1956) and several other Taylor recordings.

E-MAIL TO ANSELM BERRIGAN 1/4/05: "Pen had been talking to pleasant mail guy at local post office about Ted": Ted Berrigan grew up in Providence, RI.

E-MAIL TO ANSELM BERRIGAN 1/5/05: "Meantime Irene emails to say": Cellist and vocalist Irene Aebi, married to Steve Lacy and frequent collaborator.

E-MAIL TO ANSELM BERRIGAN 1/6/05: "GEORGE LEWIS will be one of the gang that evening": George Lewis, composer, electronic performer, installation artist, trombone player, and scholar in the fields of improvisation and experimental music. Lewis has been a member of the Association for the Advancement of Creative Musicians (AACM) since 1971.

"he has no problem with Rosswell, they are actually good friends & equally giants!": Roswell Rudd, acclaimed jazz trombonist, longtime collaborator of Steve Lacy, Archie Shepp, and many others.

"the work you all put in on it makes it absolutely shine": Ted Berrigan, *Collected Poems,* edited by Alice Notley with Anselm Berrigan and Edmund Berrigan (University of California Press, 2005).

E-MAIL TO LISA JARNOT 1/16/05: "obsessed with Whittier's 'Snowbound'": John Greenleaf Whittier, "Snowbound: A Winter Idyl" (1865).

"Visually dominating Wilson's vast lobby": RC cites David Cohen, "Domes and Angles and a Palace of Projects," *Artnet* (April 21, 1998).

ACKNOWLEDGMENTS OF PERMISSIONS

The editors wish to thank the following publications in which some of these letters have appeared: Effluency, Jacket, Open Letter, *and* Poetry Magazine.

Grateful acknowlegment to the following is made for permission to print or reproduce material:

PHOTOGRAPHS

Frontispiece: Group photograph by Allen Ginsberg, Vancouver, 1963, used by permission of The Estate of Allen Ginsberg and Corbis Images.

Photographs of Robert Creeley by Jonathan Williams, from the Yale Collection of American Literature, Beinecke Rare Book and Manuscript Collection, and the Estate of Jonathan Williams.

TEXTS

Various excerpts from *The Collected Poems of Robert Creeley 1945–1975* and *The Collected Poems of Robert Creeley 1975–2005.* Reprinted by permission of the Estate of Robert Creeley.

Caption to group photograph and the poem "B.C." Copyright Allen Ginsberg Estate.

Various excerpts by Bobbie Louise Hawkins appear by the kind permission of the author.

"The World Narrowed to a Point" by William Carlos Williams, from *The Collected Poems,* Vol. 1, *1909–1939,* copyright ©1938 by New Directions Publishing Corp. Reprinted by permission of New Directions Publishing Corp. and Carcanet Press Ltd. (UK).

All Louis and Celia Zukofsky material copyright Paul Zukofsky. The material may not

Flaubert, Gustave, 53, 58, 296
Ford, Charles Henri, 132
Ford, Ford Maddox, 72, 168, 172
Fox, Peggy, 395, 405
Freeman, Peter, 346
Freud, Sigmund, 9, 10, 329
Friedlander, Benjamin (Ben), xxxv, 397, 402, 403
Fyffe, Richard, 395

Gander, Forrest, 415
Genet, Jean, 52
Gerhardt, Rainer, 49, 51, 52, 72, 75, 95, 107, 118–20, 129, 136, 200–201, 210, 229, 265, 282, 429n, 434n, 447n
Gerhardt, Renate, 118–19, 136, 200–201, 203–4, 207, 210, 229, 282
Gide, Andre, 10, 43
Ginsberg, Allen, xxxii, 157, 158, 159–60, 169, 173, 184, 194, 196, 201–2, 204–5, 207, 208, 212, 216, 219, 223, 226, 227, 265, 270–71, 273, 284, 288, 297, 300, 309, 319, 329–30, 354, 359, 363, 368, 375, 386, 390, 391, 399, 402–3, 437n, 439n, 448n; *Empty Mirror,* 158; *Howl,* 160, 185, 173, 212; *Kaddish,* 185, 196, 208, 226
Giorno, John, 326, 327, 419
Gizzi, Peter, 392, 398, 456n
Glassgold, Peter, 395–96
Glover, Alfred, 297
Gold, Herb, 187, 222, 256
Goldwater, Barry, 285
Goodman, Mitch, xxviii, 9, 37, 56, 61, 82, 128, 140, 147, 157, 163, 166–67, 169, 179, 240, 280, 437n
Graves, Robert, 109, 127, 130, 133–34, 136, 287
Green, Henry, 63
Greene, Graham, 63
Gregory, Horace, 22
Grenier, Robert (Bob), 340, 346, 349, 371, 379, 385, 452n
Gunn, Thom, 275
Guston, Philip, 142, 176, 216

Hall, Donald, 248, 286, 363
Hartley, Marsden, 168Hardy, Thomas: *Jude the Obscure,* 271
Hartman, Charles, 412
Hawkins, Bobbie Louise, xxxii, xxxiii, 173, 177, 179, 188, 190, 191, 207, 209, 220, 222, 239, 243–44, 245, 247–48, 251, 254–55, 268, 280, 288, 294, 295–96, 298, 300, 303, 309, 310, 312,

313, 317, 321, 322, 324, 326, 327, 328, 331, 333, 339, 342, 354, 401, 445n, 451n
H.D., 171, 215
Heidegger, Martin, 17
Hellman, Robert, 368
Hodes, Ida, 145, 146, 435n
Hollo, Anselm, 290, 371, 409
Holy Forest, The (Blaser), 390
Homer, 8, 9, 114
Homire, Cynthia, 144, 149
Hopkins, Gerard Manley, 223, 232
Horton, T. D., 25–26, 32, 33, 42, 427n
Hoshour, Harvey, 372
Housman, A. E., 85–86
Howe, Susan, 367, 370, 374, 380, 382, 383, 390, 391, 393, 396
Huang, Yunte, 395
Hutter, Donald, 249, 298–99, 346

Invention of Solitude, The (Auster), 380
Irby, Ken, 268

James, Henry, 13, 53, 58, 114, 164, 352
Jarnot, Lisa, 421
Jellow, Barbara, 386, 387
Jess (Collins), 141, 146, 349, 364
Jones, LeRoi (Amiri Baraka), 196, 204, 227, 239, 241, 244, 271, 275, 284, 285, 289, 391, 400, 403; *Dutchman,* 289
Jonson, Ben, 134
Joris, Pierre, 365
Joyce, James, 43, 53, 406
Joyce, Stanislaus, 20
Jude the Obscure (Hardy), 271
Jung, Carl Gustav, 96, 100, 183, 184

Kandinsky, Wassily, 89
Katz, Alex, 398
Katz, Bill, 329–30
Kelleher, Michael (Mike), 422
Kelly, Robert, 225–26, 235–36, 272
Kenner, Hugh, 63, 222, 233, 241, 248
Kerouac, Jack, xxxii, 151, 157, 160, 169–70, 173, 186, 190, 194, 195, 204, 221, 252, 255, 261, 276, 317, 354, 436n, 440n, 445n, 450n; *Big Sur,* 261; *Dr Sax,* 187; *On The Road,* 173, 174–75; *Subterraneans, The,* 174–75
Kitaj, 306, 335, 348, 351, 368, 422, 450n
Kitasono, Katue (Katsue) 45, 49, 131, 232, 428n, 434n
Kline, Franz, xxxii, 142, 148, 221

CPSIA information can be obtained
at www.ICGtesting.com
Printed in the USA
LVHW092305280120
645072LV00005B/668

9 780520 324831